The Maritime Silk Road between China and France

The Maritime Silk Road between China and France

Impulsions, intermediaries and industrial influences
of the long distance trade in the globalization
of 19th century

Zhao Chao and Lin Mao

The Maritime Silk Road between China and France

Zhao Chao and Lin Mao

First English Edition 2020
By Royal Collins Publishing Group Inc.
BKM ROYALCOLLINS PUBLISHERS PRIVATE LIMITED
www.royalcollins.com

Headquarters: 550-555 boul. René-Lévesque O Montréal (Québec) H2Z1B1 Canada
India office: 805 Hemkunt House, 8th Floor, Rajendra Place, New Delhi 110 008

ISBN: 978-1-987821-72-7

We are grateful B&R Book Program for the financial assistance in the publication of this book.

Contents

Introduction

Ⅰ Silk trade between France and China in the 19th century: the issues and problematics

This book focuses on the silk trade between China and France in the 19th century, with the aim of clarifying certain specific Euro-Asian trade in the course of globalization in the 19th century. We chose the Franco-Chinese silk trade as the objective of research, because, first, the use of historical records and documents, we find that the Franco-Chinese trade in the 19th century grew up mainly from the augmentation of the import of Chinese silk in France. The exchange of the silk is one of the most important and the most typical trade between the two countries in the 19th century. Secondly, the exchange of the Franco-Chinese silk plays a very important role in the trade in raw materials of the world in the 19th century. Because of the separation of production of weaving and the country of consumption, the raw silk is one of the raw materials whose international traffic are the most dynamic in the world of the 19th century. On the one hand, France, as the largest silk fabrics exporter to England, Europe and the United States for a long period of time, is also the largest importer of silk materials in the world during the second half of the 19th century. On the other hand, China, exporting substantial amounts of silk to major markets of the world, import the cotton and other goods from England, Europe and the United States. The route between the two countries is one of the most dynamic trade route during the second half of the 19th century, which is a perfect entry point to observe trade flows on a global scale during the 19th century.

Precisely, this book is intended to address the issues and further discuss on the Franco-Chinese silk trade itself and the Eurasian long-distance business, specifically on their evolutions, their impulses, their commercial intermediation and their industrial impacts.

In the first step, we will show the development of Franco-Chinese silk trade of the 19th century, and analyze the causes of its prosperity, at the level of supply and demand. On the demand side, we will examine the impacts of changes in the French industry on imports from China. In particular, it relates to the decrease and the limited increase of the French silk production. On the supply side, the question is to understand not only what makes it possible for the growth of the production of raw silk in China, but also the reasons for the limited development of domestic demand.

In a second step, we discuss the roles of the various silk trade corporations connecting the two sides of the Eurasian continent. First, the Great Britain is the most important country of distribution of raw materials and semi-finished products of the world during the period of the industrial revolution. We will observe the roles of the London market and English merchants in the indirect silk trade between France and China. Then, we show the roles of the French companies and foreign firms in the direct trade of silk between France and China, the prosperous of which starts from the 1850s and 1860s. In this part, we will discuss the influence of the growth of the direct import of Chinese silk in France to the installation and the development of French companies in China, and the relationship of these French companies with other intermediaries, especially the silk firms of England, Germany and Switzerland. Finally, we analyze the roles of different groups of Chinese merchants in the foreign trade of silk of China, the relationship between these groups and the relations between the Chinese traders and foreign firms.

In this book, we analyse also the roles of evolution in customs policies and the improvement of transport in the development of trade between the two countries. Firstly, by the research of the evolution of the customs duty on the silk in France and China and their level of protection, we will clarify the impact of tariff changes on the performance of silk trade between the two countries. Then, the question is to understand the influence of the improvement of the conditions of long-distance transport, consisting of the transport techniqueal evolution and the open of Suez Canal, in the development of Franco-Chinese silk trade. In addition, we will compare the importance of the impact of the two factors above: Between the two factors, which has better stimulated the Franco-Chinese silk trade and the integration of the world economy? At the same time, we will find if there are other important factors that lead to the emergence of the convergence of prices on the international market of silk, which is one of the most important symbols of the integration of the world economy of the 19th century.

In the end, this book will also discuss the impact of the silk trade to the silk industry in the two countries. In this part, we will select a new angle—interaction of the industrializations in the two countries— to analyze the relationship between foreign trade and industrialization in the 19th century. Firstly, there will be the discussions about the influence of the industrialization of western countries in the industrialization of the Asian countries. Secondly, we will also search for the effects of the dynamics of the silk trade between the two countries to their reactions of industrializations. In all these issues, we will try to link the eastern and western industrial revolutions to international trade together.

II State of the research in the history of the Franco-Chinese silk trade

Many issues of this thesis have already been widely discussed by the former historians. As we will also discuss precisely the bibliographies in the text of this book, we show here only the most important contributions from these historians to our problematic.

1. The importance of the exchange of the silk to the Franco-Chinese trade growth of the 19th century

The explanation of the performance of the French business in China focuses on two aspects: the competition of England, and the changes in the Franco-Chinese political relationship. The different performance of the foreign trade of France against England has been much discussed in the existing literature, including *l' histoire économique de la France du VIIIe siècle* of J – C. Asselain[1], *l' échelle du monde* of P. Verley[2] et *l' Économie française au XIXe siècle* of M. Levy-Leboyer and F. Bourguignon[3], etc. In order to explain the competition in the Chinese market, P. Verley presentes a list of the inferiorities of the French industrial products compared to those of England. He shows that it is the poor quality and high price of industrial products, the high price of transport, the complexity of the intermediates, the lack of local representatives, the lack of market

---

[1] J–C Asselain. Histoire économique de la France du XVIIIe siècle à nos jours. Paris. Editions du seuil. 1984.

[2] P.Verley. l' Echelle du monde. Paris. Editions Gallimard. 1997

[3] M.Levy–leboyer et F.Bourguignon. L' Economie Française au XIXe siècle. Paris. Economica. 1985.

information and the lack of companies of acceptance which led to the failure of the French industrial products on of the foreign market. We're going to check if all these deficiencies of French products really exist in the Chinese market, and then identify other factors leading to the weakness of French trade in China.

Many historians and economists have described the influence of the changes of the political relationship in the trade between the two countries. For example, historians such as J. K. Fairbank[1] and Yuan Jicheng[2] affirmed the importance of foreign concessions on the development of foreign trade in China. We will discuss the roles of political and commercial privileges obtained by the treaties in the growth of trade between the two countries. In this book, we argue that, even if the changes of political relations are a necessary condition for the growth of trade between the two countries, they are not the origin of that growth.

The most frequently cited in the Chinese historical works to describe the characteristics of the Franco-Chinese trade are *Modern History of Relations between China and France* of Xian Yuhao and Tian yongxiu[3], *Overview of Economic Influences of France in China* Tian Yongxiu[4] and *History of Relation between China and France* of Yang Yuanhua[5]. However, from the Chinese sources, they have not been able to clarify the complete quantitative evolution of the Franco-Chinese trade and its goods structure prior to the year 1905. With the help of the sources in France, we will attempt to clarify the structure, the quantity of trade and the characteristics of the Franco-Chinese trade in the 19th century.

2.Silk trade between France and China: quantity, supply and demand

For the development of the silk trade between France and China, we found some of the statistics in the existing literature, such as *the Chronicles of the East India company* of H.B. Morse, *Histoire de la concession française de Shanghai* of Ch.-B. Maybon and J. Fredet,[6] *France and the exploitation of China* 1885—1891 of R.Lee,[7] *Commerce de la*

---

① J.K Fairbank and Kwang-Ching Liu. The Cambridge Histoy of China. Cambridge. Cambridge University Press. Vol.11 Late Ch'ing 1800—1911. 1980.

② 袁继成.近代中国租界史稿.北京:中国财经出版社,1988 年.

③ 鲜于浩,田永秀.近代中法关系史稿.成都:西南交通大学出版社,2003 年.

④ 田永秀.法国在华经济势力之全貌.成都:西南交通大学出版社,2005 年.

⑤ 杨元华.中法关系史.上海:上海人民出版社,2006 年.

⑥ Ch.-B. Maybon, J.Fredet, Histoire de la concession française de Shanghai, Paris. Librairie Plon. 1929.

⑦ R.Lee: France and the exploitation of China 1885—1901. A study in Economic Imperialism. Hong-Kong: Oxford University press, 1989.

France avec la Chine of N.Rondot,[1] *les relations entre Lyons et la Chine au XIXe siècle* of E.Hamaide[2], *l' industrie de la soie en France et en Chine de la fin du XVIIIe au début du XXe siècle* of Mau Chuan-Hui,[3] *les relations de Lyons avec la Chine* of Tcheng Tse-sio[4] and *Lyons et le commerce de la soie* of L.Gueneauetc[5]. However, there is no work which has touched the full statistic of Franco-Chinese silk trade in the 19th century. We will show in the text with the help of our sources.

The growth of demand for silk in France is partly from the success of the production of silk textile fabrics. A lot of publications, *les industries de la soie en France* de A. de la Berge,[6] "l' industrie de la soie de France à Valée du Rhône" of P. Clerget, *l' Économie française au XIXe siècle* of M. Levy-Leboyer et F. Bourguignon[7], *la soie, art et histoire* of H.Algoud[8], *la relation entre Lyons et Chine au XIX siècle* of E.Hamaide[9], and *la Révolution industrielle* of P.Verley[10] had already described the scale of production of silk fabrics in France at the level of the number of looms, the quantity and value of production. Based on their data, we will describe quantitatively the growth of production of silk fabrics in France in the 19th century, which compose the foundation of the increasing demand of material of silk in France.

The inadequacy of French the local silk production is another factor leading to the increase of demand of silk of France in the international market. The works such as *la soie, c' est de l' or* of S.Lamb[11] often pointes out that it is the disease of silkworm which leads to the reduction of silk production in France. In this book, we will explain why the silk production in France is still very modest, even after Louis Pasteur had founded the

---

[1]　N.Rondot. Chambre de commerce de Lyon. Commerce de la France avec la Chine. Délibération prise sur le rapport de M.Rondot. Séance du 12 janvier 1860.

[2]　E.Hamaide. La relation entre Lyon et Chine au XIXe siècle, thèse pour obtenir le grade de docteur de l' université Lumière Lyon 2. 1999.

[3]　Mau Chuan-Hui. L' industrie de la soie en France et en Chine de la fin du XVIIIe au début du XXe siècle: échanges technologiques, stylistiques et commerciaux. Paris. EHESS. 2002. 2 Vol.

[4]　TCHENG Tse-sio. Les relations de Lyon avec la Chine. Thèse soutenue devant la Faculté des lettres de l' Université de Lyons. Paris. Librairie L. Rodstein. 1936.

[5]　L.Gueneau. Lyon et le commerce de la soie. Thèse soutenu devant la Faculté de droit de l' Université de Lyon. Lyon. Imprimerie L.Bascou. 1923.

[6]　A. De la Berge. Les industries de la soie en France. Revue des Deux Mondes. Tome 101. 1890.

[7]　M.Levy-Leboyer et F. Bourguignon. L' Economie Française au XIXe siècle, Analyse macro-économique. Paris. Economica. 1985.

[8]　H.Algoud. La soie, art et histoire. Paris. Payot. 1928.

[9]　E.Hamaide. La relation entre Lyon et Chine au XIXe siècle, thèse pour obtenir le grade de docteur de l' université Lumière Lyon 2. 1999.

[10]　P. Verley. La revolution industrielle. Paris. Gallimard. 2005

[11]　S.Lamb. La soie, c' est de l' or. Lyon. Bureaux du courrrier de Lyon. 1856.

precaution against disease.

There are already a lot of estimates of the quantities of silk production in China in the 19th century, which is a part of the explanation of the supply capacity of China in the global market of silk. Of these estimations, the most important are the investigations applied by N.Rondot, Jiberboman, Akeda Hirome et Uehara Shigemi in the end of the 19th century and at the beginning of the 20th century, as well as the contemporary researches on this subject, including *Une grande divergence: la Chine l' Europe et la construction de l' économie mondiale* of K. Pomeranz,[1] *The development of capitalism in China*, published in 1985 by Xu Dixin and Wu Chengming(吴成明),[2] *Evolution of the commerce in Jiannan region in the Ming and Qing dynasties* published in 1998 by Fan Jinmin[3] and *The amount of production of silk, and the influence of the growth of export of silk on the increase in parts of sericulture in China* published in 2008 by Zhang Li.[4] In fact, every of these means of calculation has its advantage and disadvantage. Based on these calculations, we try to recalculate the quantity of the Chinese silk production on considering more influencing factors. Concerning the raisons for the growth of China's production, G.Federico[5], in his book *An economic history of the silk industry*, indicates that the increase in the production of the world's silk is from lower the opportunity cost of the silk production than other agricultural activities. In this book, the opportunity cost of the Chinese silkworm will be studied so that we can find out if the case of China is also adapted to the theory of G. Federico. At the same time, we are going to discuss other factors which could drive the increase production of silk in China.

At the same time, the increase in the supply of Chinese silk to the international market can also be bought by the reduced demand at the Chinese domestic market. Wang Xiang, in his book *A comparison between the structure of the silk industry of China and Japan*[6], affirmed that the increase in the export of Chinese silk in the 19th century is at the cost of reduction of the local market. But the data that he has used are based on the researches of Xu Xinwu published in 1990[7], which is old and is not accurate. In the

---

① K.Pomeranz. The Great Divergence: China, Europe and the Making of the Modern World Economy. Princeton. Princeton University Press. 2000. p. 328—330.

② 许涤新,吴成明.中国资本主义发展史.北京:人民出版社,1985,第325—326页.

③ 范金民.明清江南商业的发展.南京:南京大学出版社,1996年.

④ 张丽.鸦片战争前的全国生丝产量和近代生丝出口增加对中国近代桑蚕业扩张的影响.中国农史. 2008年第4期,第48页.

⑤ G.Federico. An Economic History of the silk Industry, 1830—1930. Cambridge. Cambridge University press. 2003.

⑥ 王翔.中日丝绸业近代化比较研究.石家庄:河北人民出版社,2002年.

⑦ 徐新吾.中国近代缫丝工业史.上海:上海人民出版社,1990年.

text, we will compare the two variables again in consulting the recent studies on this subject, especcially the publication of Zhang Li. After the comparison, we could confirm whether the increase in the export of Chinese silk in the 19th century was indeed due to a decrease in the local market of silk in China or not.

3.Silk cooperation in the trade between France and China

P.Verley affirmed in his book *L'Echelle du monde* that the merchants play a very important role in long distance international trade in the modern history.[1] Showing the process of circulation of the silk from Chinese producers to the silk textile manufacturers in France, we will analyze the roles of all these traders in this Franco-Chinese trade.

According to the research of R.Findlay and K.H.O'Rourke, the proportion of the re-export is often very high in the total export of the United Kingdom from the late 18th century to the middle of the 19th century.[2] P. Cayez, in his book about the Lyons industry of the 19th century, has already mentioned the export of silk from London to Lyons.[3] But in his research, there is neither quantitative data, nor explanation for the existence of this business. This book will verify if the import of Chinese silk in France is often by the market of London. If so, we will try to explain it.

The researches, *Histoire de la concession française de Shanghai* of Ch.-B. Maybon and J.Fredet[4], *Les Français de Shanghai. 1849—1949* of G.Brossollet[5], *La relation entre Lyons et Chine au XIX siècle* of E. Hamaide[6], *the Movement of Foreign Firms in China before and after the Opium War* of Lin Rizhang[7], *History of Foreign Merchants at Shanghai 1843—1956* of Wang Chuifang[8] and *the Movements of the French Traders at shanghai during the last Period of the Qing Dynasty* (1847—1919) of Cao Shengmei[9] noted French firms and their situations in China. But they did not specify the number of French companies involved in the silk trade, and their role in the import of Chinese silk to France. We will try to supplement and develop the previous research, and anulyze the

---

① P.Verley. l'Echelle du monde. Paris. Editions Gallimard. 1997.

② R.Findlay and K.H.O'Rourke. Power and plenty. Trade, war, and the world economy in the second millennium. New Jersey. Princeton University Press. 2007.

③ P.Cayez. Crise et croissance de l'industrie lyonnaise 1850—1900. Paris. Editions du CNRS. 1980.

④ Ch.-B. Maybon, J.Fredet, Histoire de la concession française de Shanghai, Paris. Librairie Plon. 1929.

⑤ G.Brossollet. Les Français de Shanghai. 1849—1949. Editions Belin. 1999.

⑥ E. Hamaide. La relation entre Lyon et Chine au XIX siècle.

⑦ 林日杖.鸦片战争前后外国在华洋行经济活动初探.福建师范大学硕士学位论文,2001年.

⑧ 王垂芳.洋商史:上海1843—1856.上海:上海社会科学院出版社,2007年.

⑨ 曹胜梅.晚清时期法商在沪经营活动述略1847—1910.载于上海市档案馆编.上海档案史研究·第一辑.上海三联书店,2006年.

roles of foreign (mainly english) firms the direct import of Chinese silk in France.

There is already a lot of researches on the Chinese trade groups. *The Causes of the Decline of the Capitalist Nanxun* of Xu Faxiang[1] and *the Largest Group of the Modern Merchants* of Chen Yonghao and Tao Shuimu[2] have demonstrated the features of silk merchants in China. *History of the silk industry of china in the modern period* of Xu Xinwu[3] and *The Modern Chinese Industry and its export* of L.M.Li[4] indicated the important role of the Chinese entrepreneurs in the modernization of the Chinese silk reeling industry. *The Birth of the Class of Compradors China Denies* of Nie Baozhang[5], *Compradors during the 19th century—the Bridge Between the East and the West* of Lindsay Yong[6], *Comprador Class in ancient China* of Huang Yifeng and Jiang Duo[7] and the *Evolution of Comprador of in the System of Conghong* of Xiao Chuxiong[8] have studied the role of comprador in the foreign trade of China. With the help of these existing researches, we are going to describe the composition of Chinese silk traders, their inner relationship and their relationship with foreign firms.

4.Effects of the changes in customs policies and the improvement of the status of transport

The doctrine of P. Bairoch was considered as the conventional wisdom explicating the economic influence of the customs policy of France of 19th century to its foreign trade over a long period of time. According to his research, the period of liberalism in France began just after the signing of the *Treaty of Gobden-Chevalier* with England in 1860, and was completed after the application of the "tariff of Meline" in 1892.[9] France, as a typical continental Europe country, is pursuing a trade policy much more protectionist than that of England from 1840 to the end of the 19th century. However, the expansion of international trade and the economy of France was generally more rapid in the periods of protectionism than during the period of liberal trade, so the decline of the custom barriers has played a negative role to the increases of international trade and

① 许发祥.近代民族资本浔商衰落原因新探.中共中央党校硕士学位论文,2009 年.
② 陈永浩,陶水木.中国近代最大的丝商群体.杭州:浙江人民出版社,2001 年.
③ 徐新吾.中国近代缫丝工业史.上海:上海人民出版社,1990 年.
④ 李明珠.中国近代蚕丝业及外销(1842—1937),上海:上海社会科学院出版社.
⑤ 聂宝章.中国买办资产阶级的发生.中国社会科学院出版社,1978 年.
⑥ 郝延平.十九世纪买办——中西间桥梁.上海:上海社会科学院出版社,1988 年.
⑦ 黄逸峰、江铎.旧中国的买办阶级.上海:上海人民出版社,1982 年.
⑧ 肖楚熊.行商制度到买办制度变迁研究,广州大学硕士毕业论文,2009 年.
⑨ P.Bairoch. Mythes et paradoxes de l'histoire économique. Paris. La Découverte. 1994. pp.38—39.

the economy of France.[1] These conclusions are challenged by the researches of many other economic historians, of which the most representative is J.V.Nye Who reluted his theory in his thesis *War, Win, and Taxes: The political Economy of Anglo-French Trade 1689—1900*.[2] Examining the changes of the average tariff of customs of France and England, J.V.Nye discovers that the first was lower than the latter at the beginning of the 19th century until the end of the 1870s. This, according to the author, shows that the policy of the customs of France was freer than that of England during most of the 19th century, contrast to the case at the conclusion of P.bairoch. The theory of J.V.Nye isn't perfect, but it has begun a broader debate on the trade protectionism and liberalism in Europe. In France, the debate between P. Bairoch and J.V.Nye is developed by J-P. Dormois[3] and P. Verley[4], who seeked to clarify questions such as: Is the country in the Europe Continent are so protective that P. Bairoch described? How to measure the level of tariff protection of a country? How do we measure the impact of the custom tariff on the economy and trade growth? This debate on the role of protectionism has also taken place outside of France, among K.H.O'Rourke[5], A. Estevadeordal[6], A.T.Junguito,[7] D.A.Irwin[8], F.Capie,[9] A.Vamvakidis,[10] J.Foreman-Peck[11], and B.Dedinger[12] Compa-

---

[1]　P.Bairoch. Commerce extérieur et développement économique de l'Europe au XIXe siècle. Paris. Éditions Mouton. 1976. p .162.

[2]　J.V.Nye. War, Wine and Taxes: The Political Economy of Anglo-French Trade, 1689—1900. Princeton and Oxford. Princeton University Press. 2007

[3]　J-P.Dormois. " The I' impact of late-nineteenth-century tariffs on the productivity of European industries (1870—1930) ". In J-P. Dormois, P. Lains, eds. *Classical Trade Protectionism*, 1815—1914. London and New York Routledge. 2006.

[4]　P.Verley. l'Echelle du monde. Paris. Editions Gallimard. 1997

[5]　K.H.O'Rourke. "Measuring protection. À cautionary tale". Journal of Development Economics. N°53. 1997. pp. 169—183.

[6]　A.Estevadeordal. Measuring protection in the early twentieth century. European Economic History Review. N°1. 1997. pp. 89—125.

[7]　A.T.Junguito. "Assessing the protectionist intensity of tariffs in nineteenth century European trade policy." In J-P. Dormois, P. Lains, eds. Classical Trade Protectionism, 1815—1914. London and New York Routledge. 2006.

[8]　D.A.Irwin. "Free trade and protection in nineteenth-century Britain and France revisited : A comment on Nye ." Journal of Economic History. Vol. 53. N°1. pp. 146—152.

[9]　F.Capie. Tariffs and Growth : Some Illustrations from the World Economy Trade. Manchester. Manchester University Press.

[10]　A. Vamvakidis. "How robust is the growth-openness connections ? Historicall evidence," Journal of Economic Growth. Vol. 7. N°1. 2002. pp. 57—80.

[11]　J.Foreman-Peck. "A model of later-19th-century European economic development".Revista de Historia Economica. Vol.8. N°3. 1995. pp.441—471.

[12]　B.Dedinger. "From virtual free-trade to virtual protectionism: or, did protectionism have any part in Germany's rise to commercial power 1850—1913". In J-P. Dormois, P. Lains, eds. Classical Trade Protectionism, 1815—1914. London and New York Routledge. 2006. pp.219—241.

ring and calculating of rate of these authors, we attempt to measure and calculate the level, the trade and economy impact of entry custom silk tariff in France.

The evolution of foreign trade policy of China before and after the Opium War has already been mentioned, presented and discussed by many eastern and western scholars. For example, in the article "The Old Canton System of Foreign Trade" of R. Edwards, the author has described precisely the foreign policy of the Qing Empire, to find out the raisons for the closed door policy of the People's Republic of China in 1970s[1]. P. Bairoch, in order to approve the disaster that liberalism trade has given to the people in the third world, has discussed the evolution of "protectionism" to "liberalism" in China during the 18th and 19th century in his book *Mythes et aradoxe de l'histoire économique*;[2] stressing the essential role of ports to the development of foreign trade and the progress for the East-Asia and the South-Asia economy, F.Gipouloux has analyzed the effects of the forced opening ports of China by the treaties on Chinese external trade in his book *La méditerranée asiatique*;[3], in a very recent article, "Asian globalizations: market integration, trade and economic growth, 1880—1938", the authors D. Chilosi and G. Federico also mentioned the limitation and the opening of the foreign trade of China, in order to verify the effects of trade barriers to the east west economy integration.[4] In China, "the old trade system of Canton" and "the new Chinese customs system" are often involved in the research on the comparison between the economies of China and Japan, for example, in the book *Comparative History of the Economic Policies of China and that of Japan*, published by Gao Shujuan and Feng Bin[5], etc.

However, in most of the historical research on this issue, China is conventionally determined as a closed or half closed country before the Opium War, and as a country more and more open after that war. In the same time, the foreign trade of China is often considered to be constrained by "the regime of closure before 1842", and developed more and more fast with the opening of China. But actually, there is no research that has determined the level of protection of the Chinese customs tariff and that discussed the effect of the tariff on the trade from the measurement results. In this book, we will try to measure the level of openness of the Chinese customs for the silk trade, and to estimate

---

① R.Edwards. "The Old Canton System of Foreign Trade." in V.H.Li. Law and Politics in China's Foreign Trade. Seattle and London. University of Washington Press. pp. 360—378.

② P.Bairoch. Mythes et paradoxe de l'histoire économique. Paris. Éditions La Découverte. 1994. pp. 50-51.

③ F.Gipouloux. La Méditerranée asiatique. Paris. Éditions CNRS. 2007. pp. 173—185.

④ D.Chilosi and G.Federico. "Asian Globalisations: Market Integration, trade and economic growth". 1800—1938. Economic History Working Papers. No°123. 2013. p.21.

⑤ 高淑娟,冯斌.中日对外经济政策比较史纲.北京:清华大学出版社,2003 年.

its impact on trade. We will show that the abolition of the quota on the export of Chinese silk in 1843 offered the possibility of exporting Chinese silk in great quantities, which has eliminated a major obstacle to the later increase of silk trade between France and China. The reduction of tariffs on raw silk in the new system of customs has increased the price advantage of exported Chinese silk, which ensured the competitiveness of the Chinese silk in the French market during the second half of the 19th century, especially after the 1870s.

The economic impact of the revolution in maritime transport excited more and more attention of the economic historians during the last two decades. In 1995, P. Krugman published an article discussing the question "why the world trade has increased", and the author affirmed that, in theory, the growth of world trade is necessarily linked to technological innovation.[1] This conclusion was later questioned by S.L.Baier and J.H. Bergstand in 2001. According to their calculation, the contribution of the reduction of the cost of transport to economic growth is very limited.[2] K.H.O'rourke and J. Wlliamson began to study the relationship between the decrease of the cost of transport and the evolution of prices in different Atlantic markets, and they determined that it exists a correlation between the Atlantic prices convergences and reduction of the transportation cost.[3] In another book of K.H.O'rourke collaborated with R. Findlay, published in 2007, the authors find out that the reduction of transportation cost could lead not only to the growth of the volume of international trade, but also to the change of the nature of the goods transported.[4] In 2010, D.S.Jacks and Krishna Pendadur published an article to discuss the problem of correlation between the trade growth and transport costs. They compared the data of different period, and conclude that the cost of transportation play an important role in the growth of international trade only for a certain period of time, instead of a constant factor.[5] In a recent publication in 2013. D.Chilosi and G. Federico have analyzed again the problem of factors of the integration of the international market. Observing the integration of the Asian markets with the rest of the world during a long time (1800—1938), the authors have found that the lower cost has played a very important

---

① P.Krugman. "Growing World Trade: Causes and consequences". Brookings Papers on Economic Activity. 1995. No°1. 327—377

② S.L.Baier and J.H.Bergstrand. "The Growth of World Trade: Tariffs, Transport Costs, and Income Similarity". Journal of International Economics. Vol 53. No°1. 2001. pp.1—27.

③ K. H. O'Rourke and J Williamson Globalization and History. Cambrige et London. The MIT Press.1999.

④ R. Findlay and K.H.O'Rourke. Power and Plenty. Princeton and Oxford. Princeton University Press. 2007

⑤ D.S.Jacks and Krishna Pendadur. The Review of Economics and Statistics. Vol 92. No°4. 2010. pp. 745—755.

role during 1838—1870, instead of during all the periods.[1] We will revisit this issue in analyzing the effects of the evolution in the condition of transportation to the exchange of the Franco-Chinese silk. We will show that the introduction of the maritime express expanded the direct import of Chinese silk in France, while the opening of the Suez Canal offered definitely to France the advantage of the direct silk trade with China.

5.Modernization of the silk industry in France and in China and the silk trade

The relationship between the industrialization and the growth of trade is a very classic question which has already been discussed by many scholars and economists. On the influence of the relationship on the industrialization of western countries, P.Bairoch has discussed in article "Le commerce international et genèse de la révolution industrielle anglaise"[2], the contribution of foreign trade to the start of industrialization, in the case of Britain by five criteria, and concluded that the external trade played only a "marginal role" in the beginnings of industrialization. His point of view is only partly accepted by R. Findlay and K.H.O'rourke in their recent work *Power and Plenty*[3]. These two authors assert that foreign trade is not the origin of the English industrial revolution, but it would be one of the important factors in the expansion of industrialization in England. In the book *Histoire économique de la France du XVIII siècle à nos jours*[4], J–C. Asselain studied on the effects of the foreign trade to the industrializing of France and found that the trade had a significant industrializing impact. In terms of the impact on the industrialization of the western market in Asian countries (e.g. conventional wisdom, whited in the book of P. Bairoch) is that the exchange with the western countries has leaded to deindustrialization in the Asian countries after the period of the Industrial Revolution.[5] This view was questioned by other scholars. In a paper published in 1990, Sanjay Subrahmanyam argues that the decline of the cotton textile industry in India has already started prior to the influx of industrial products.[6] G.Riello pointed out at the end of the book

---

① D.Chilosi and G.Federico. "Asian Globalizations: Market Integration, trade and economic growth". 1800—1938. Economic History Working Papers. No°123. 2013.

② P.Bairoch. Commerce international et genèse de la révolution industrielle anglaise. Anales, Economies, Société, Civilisations, n°2, mars-avril 1973, p.541—571.

③ R.Findlay. H.O'ROURKE Kevin. Power and plenty. Trade, war, and the world economy in the second millennium. New Jersey. Princeton University Press. 2007.

④ J–C.Asselain. Histoire économique de la France du XVIIIe siècle à nos jours. Edition du Seuil. 1984.

⑤ P.Bairoch. Mythes et paradoxes de l'histoire économique. p.79.

⑥ Sanjay Subrahmanyam. Rural Industry and Commercial Agriculture in the Late Seventeenth-Century South-Eastern India. Past&Present. No°126. 1990. 107—108.

The Fabric that Made the Modern World that the commercial relationship lead also to an industrial convergence between the East and the West.[1] Mau Chuen-Hui has shown in his thesis and research[2] that the Sino-French knowledge communication and the mechanization of the textile industry of the silk in Europe have advanced the technology of the silk industry in China. In this book, we will show the positive role of the foreign trade of silk on the modernization of the silk industry in China, but with a different explication. As a result of the industrial revolution in the silk textile production, the buyers of raw silk in France and other western countries require import the mechanized silk. In order to adapt to the need of the customer, the silk producer in China, especially in shanghai and in Guangzhou have begun the modernization of reeling silk, the raising of silkworm and the control system of the quality of the silk. This reaction between the Western and Chinese industrial revolutions is just origin from the exchange Franco-Chinese silk trade.

Ⅲ Archives and sources

Our research work is historic, since it is based on the archives and other historical documents. There is, first of all, possibilities in the field of archives in France. These last archives are produced by different authorities. In the French National Archives, conservation funds concerning our subject are very rich, including records of imports of silk, the customs statistics, the customs tariffs and the trade treaties, etc. The Archives of the Ministry of Foreign Affairs of France has retained almost all the rapports of business delegates, French consulates in China, in which we have found very abundant the trade statistics and the descriptions of the political and economic events records.

We have also tried to couplet and verify the French archives with the documents conserved in the Archives in China. The National Archives of China (Beijing)(中国第一历史档案馆) collected all the correspondences submitted to the Qing court. We can find the original texts concerning the foreign trade policy, the trade agreements and the

---

[1] G.Riello. Cotton: The Fabric that Made the Modern World. New York. Cambridge University Press. pp. 292—294.

[2] Mau Chuan-Hui. L'industrie de la soie en France et en Chine de la fin du XVIIIe au début du XXe siècle: échanges technologiques, stylistiques et commerciaux. Paris. EHESS. 2002. 2 Vol. Mau Chuan-Hui. L'introduction en Chine des sciences et des techniques européennes concernant l'industrie de la soie après la guérre de l'Opium. Etudes chinoises. Vol. XX. No° 1—2. 2001. Mau Chuan-Hui. Les techniques séricicoles chinoises dans le développement de la sériciculture française de la fin du XVIIIe siècle au début du XIXe siècle.Cahier d'Histoire et de Philosophie des Sciences. No°52. Lyon. ENS Editions. 2004.毛传慧.清末民初的蚕桑改良——传统与现代之间.中国近现代行业文化研究——技艺和专业知识的传承与功能.北京:国家图书馆出版社,2010年.

customs tariff of Qing dynasty by this documents. The National Archives of China（the second）in Nanjing（中国第二历史档案馆）retained and published all the old customs record of China, including a lot of valuable copious notes and data for our research. The Shanghai Municipal Archives（上海市档案馆）conserved the notes concerning the activities of Chinese and foreign companies, as well as the evolution of the silk filatures in Shanghai, which is very important for the studies of the intermediaries and the evolution of modern silk factories in the region of Yangzi river. Apart from the above, many municipal or provincial Archives, such as the Municipal Archives of Shunde（顺德档案馆）,the Zhejiang Provincial Archives（浙江省档案馆）, have conserved a lot of local annals, which contained a considerable amount of information on the modernization evolution of industries of the local silk.

The greatest obstacle to consult the Chinese archives of the 19th century is the accessibility to the archives. Many of the records are in inventories of the archives, but they are often not available. The most common cause is that the Chinese archives of the 19th century were not ranged, because of lack of knowledge of the language whited within the archives. For example, a significant proportion of the archives at the National Archives of China（Beijing）are written by the Manchu language, and very few archivist and historian can read them. Another example, the archives of the French Consulate in Sichuan, which is one of the most important parts of the production and export of Chinese silk, is located in the Provincial Archives in Sichuan（Chengdu）. However, no records are available, because none of the archivists in the Archives can read the archives, which are written in French.

Apart of the archives, libraries in France and China have also conserved a lot of historical documents interesting to us. There is a lot of funds about the foreign silk trade of France in the French National Library, in which the most important are the *Les Annals* published by the Ministry of Agriculture and Trade of France, and the *Bulletin des soies et des soieries-Revue Hebdomadaire Lyonsnaise* during the 19th century. The library of Sorbonne retained as well a geat number of books about the silk industry in France published in the 19th century, gives us the views of the authors at the time. In China, the National Library of China（中国国家图书馆）in Beijing, the Shanghai Municipal library（上海市图书馆）, the Library of Zhongshan of Guangdong（广东中山图书馆）and the Library of Nanhai（南海图书馆）have conserved very abundant sources of reviews, newspapers and local annals. These documents, as the North China Herald（《北华捷报》）, Journal of Agriculture and Business（《农商公报》）and Newspaper of Shen

(《申报》), have noted a lot of information that is important for this book.

IV Structure of this book

This book consists of five chapters. The first chapter focuses on the history of trade between France and China in the 19th century. The aim is to explain the importance of trade in general trade between the two countries and the economic, political and diplomatic contexts of the trade. This chapter is divided into three chapters according to different historical periods, 1815—1859, 1860—1884, and 1885—1914. This choice is according to the possible driving forces for the Franco-Chinese trade of the 19th century.

In Chapter 2, we discuss the evolution of the exchange of the silk between France and China in the 19th century, and analyze the relationship of supply and demand in this trade. The first section presents the background of the world silk market during the 19th century and the position of the silk trade between France and China in the world market. The second section demonstrate the quantitative development of the French-Chinese silk exchange. The next section will explain the growth of the demand of silk in France by the prosperity of the silk and textile industry and silk crisis in France during the 19th century. In the last section, we will discuss the increase in the quantity of the production of silk and the decline in the production of fabrics of silk in China, which has led to a growth in the supply of the Chinese silk to the international market.

Chapter 3 analyzes the roles of the French silk companies, Chinese silk companies, the silk companies of other countries and their relations. The first section deals with the indirect exchange of Chinese silk between France and China by the London market, in which the foreign firms play a very important role. The second section discusses the evolution of the French companies and other foreign companies in the French-Chinese direct silk trade flourishing after the 1850s. The section 3 of this chapter will discuss the role of the Chinese merchants who participate in the export of Chinese silk to foreign countries.

Chapter 4 will discuss two factors relating to the possibility of the growth of the silk trade, the evolution of the foreign trade policy and the improvement of transport. The first two sections of the chapter analyze the level of customs tariff of silk in France and in China as well as their influences on the trade. The third section will analyze the influences of the implementation of the Far-Est line of la Compagnie des messageries Maritime and the opening of the Suez Canal to the silk trade between China and France. At the same time, another important issue, the impact of changes in trade policy and the reduction of the cost of transport on the convergence of prices of different markets of world, will be discussed at the end of the third section.

Chapter 5 will discuss the relationship between the silk trade and the modernization of the silk industry in the two countries. The first part of this chapter will introduce the traditional techniques of the production of silk in China. The second section focuses on the tension between the old techniques of production of the Chinese silk and the mechanization silk industry in France. The third section will relate that, China, in order to adapt to the demand of the market, has begun its modernization in the silk failure since the 1860s, and started the modernization of sericulture and the quality control system later.

Chapter I   Importance of the exchange of the silk in the French-Chinese trade increase during the 19th century

The growth of exports to France was remarkable during the 19th century. After the fall of Napoleon Empire, the export value (in francs) of the France grew at an average annual rate of 3.6% from 1825 to 1840, at 6.2% from 1840 to 1860, and at 10.8% per year between 1861 and 1865. In the rest of the 19th century, the volume of exports was marked by a slowdown in growth, but with a trend of 4.0% per year between 1867 and 1875, 0.7% per year from 1875 to 1894 and a further 3% per year from 1895 until the First World War.

However, it would be difficult to argue that the French have no difficulty to export their products throughout the world. During the 19th century, Asian countries import very few, only 1% of these French products (in francs) in 1890, and a little more than 2% between 1900 and 1910. On the other hand, at the same time, France relied more and more on the import of Asian products: the Continent of Asia accounts for 4% of French imports from 1830 to 1860, 10% to 12% in 1890 and 1910. Therefore we could conclude that the French-Asian trade is dominated by the French imports from Asia. The historian P. Bairoch identified the dynamics of free trade of French-Asian trade in the 19th century: Asia absorbs very few of French exports, but its export to the French is evidently increasing, and therefore, there is an increasing deficit in trade between the France and the Asian Continent.

China is one of the most important trade partners in Asia to France. We are going to demonstrate, in this chapter, the development of French-Chinese trade corresponds exactly to character of the French-Asian trade at the period. In particular, the import of Chinese silk has taken a large proportion in the total value of trade between the two countries.

In this chapter, we will describe, in a first step, the evolution and the importance of the exchange of the silk in the trade between the two countries. We will show the changes in the value and in the structure of the French-Chinese trade, as well as the role of the exchange of raw silk in that trade relationship. In a second step, we are going to observe the politic, economic, and the diplomatic context of that period, and analyze their influences on the development of trade between France and China, focusing on several issues: First, is the expansion of trade of France in the Chinese market have been affected by competition from England in the far east? If yes, why England, rather than France, has a dominant position in the Chinese market? Second, have the changes of political relationship and the treaties signed between the France and China had a impact on their trade relations?

I Take off of French-Chinese trade before the 1860s and the inferiority of the French business influence on the Chinese market

After the French Revolution and of the First Empire, which has tried, without success, to reserve to French industry a market of continental Europe by the blockade, the French foreign trade needs to be completely rebuilt.[1] The Great Britain has benefited from 30 years of absence of France on the distant markets to develop its trade relations with the United States, Latin America and Asia. It is difficult for French industry, which is a pioneering phase at that time, to compete directly with its English counterpart, the producer of tissue in series, especially the cotton tissues at much lower cost with high productivity. In order to protect its industries which were unable to compete in the domestic market with the English products, the French Restoration government has rebuilt protectionist barriers in 1816, by high tariffs on the iron and prohibitions to the tissue. The July monarchy inherited the protectionist policies of the Restoration government though it is more flexible, because the mitigation measures are made for certain products by the automatic effect of declining prices.[2] Under the protection of the state, the French industry accelerated its modernization after 1815, particularly in the fields of energy, metallurgy, chemistry, textile, etc. At the same time, the foreign trade of France

---

[1] J-C Asselain. Histoire économique de la France du XVIIIe siècle à nos jours. Paris. Editions du seuil. Vol. I. p.132.

[2] In fact, in the case of the "specific duties" of the July monarchy (set as an absolute amount per imported unit, as opposed to "ad valorem duties" fixed as a percentage) , if the price falls under the effect of technical progress, for example, the relative weight of the tariff will increase.

joint gradually its increase rate before the revolution: from 1825 to 1840, the annual growth rate archived 3.6%.[1]

The decades 1840—1860 hold an exceptional place in the French economic history: it is at the same time the apogee of agricultural prosperity, the large scale rise of industrial productivity, the birth of the modern banking system, the era of major urban renovation and the decisive phase of the railway revolution. Despite a reliable growth of the French economy before the 1860s, a notable disadvantage that sudden France is to have been outstripped in the export markets compared to the English economy. In such a case, the French administrations pursue a protectionist policy in their commercial interactions with foreign countries during this period: with the "specific duties" fixed in the form of an absolute amount per imported unit, the July Monarchy holds a customs tax fairly high during the last years of its domination[2]. The government of the Second Republic takes up almost all the external commercial policies of the July Monarchy[3]; at the request of the industrialists and economists of liberalism, the government of Napoleon III lowered various tariff rates during 1850—1860, but tariffs on the main industrial products at the time, notably textile products and iron products are still very high[4].

During the industrialization of England and France in the first decades of the 19th century, China, under the domination of the Qing Empire, is still in a period of preindustrialization. Under the prohibition policy of the Qing court, the foreign trade of the Empire is monopolized by the Co-hong (公行) in a single port to the south, Canton, while the natures and quantities of goods in the Foreign trade is strictly determined before the 1840s. Although English merchants, who are a dominant position in the Canton market, make every effort to expand the Chinese market, China remains a closed country until the Opium War.

The Chinese market has been expanded by England since 1842: four new ports are open to foreign trade, and tariff rates are lowered to 5% on average, and the Cong-Hong (公行) monopoly on trade Chinese exterior is eliminated. Despite an inferior position in the competition of foreign trade with the English, the French do not want to lose such an opportunity to open up again to the Eastern world, because they believe that "many arti-

---

① P. Pairoch. Commerce extérieur et développement économique de l'Europe au XIXe siècle. Paris. Editions Mouton et EHESS. 1876. pp.221.

② Idem. p.136.

③ P.Verley. Nouvelle histoire économique de France contemporaine. T.2. L'industrialisation. 1830—1914. Paris. Editions la decouverte.2003. p.60.

④ L.Ame. Etude sur les tarifs de douanes et les traités de commerce. Vol. I. Paris. Imprimerie Nationale. 1876. p.287.

cles of the French factories would find advantageous outlets in China and in the neighboring countries".[1] The administration of the July monarchy immediately sends their trade delegates to China and obtains the same privileges as his English rival.

In this section, we will observe and explain the performance of France in the market of Canton before the 1860s, in view of the competition of Great Britain to the oriental market and China's foreign political evolution. We shall try to explain why Franco-Chinese trade does not flourish immediately after the peace of 1815, when French foreign trade generally begins to resume its growth rate, and to analyze the effects of the opening of China and other elements on the evolution of Franco-Chinese trade.

1. An interrupted and stagnant trade relation between 1815—1844

The starting point of the Franco-Chinese relationship is the arrival of the commercialship "l'Amphitrite" of French Jourdan Company in Canton on 2 November 1698.[2] After this profitable trip, the Company of China[3], the result of a collaboration between the French Jourdan Company and the French East India Company, sent successively several commercial vessels to China, but unfortunately did not succeed in making these efforts profitable[4]. The Perpetual Company of India, which is a new company specializing in trade with China under the direction of the French East India Company, creates

---

[1]　Archives Nationales, F12.6498. 4, novembre 1839, la pétition de Chambre de Commerce de Bordeaux au Ministre de l'agriculture et du commerce.

[2]　赵尔巽.清史稿·一五五卷.北京:中华书局,1977, 第 4561 页."法兰西一名佛郎机,在欧罗巴之西。清顺治四年来广东互市,广东总督佟养甲疏言：'佛郎机国人寓居濠境澳门,与粤商互市,仍禁深入省会。'" Translation："France, which is also called Foulangi, is located in the west of Europe. The French come to Canton for trade from the fourth year of Shunzhi. The viceroy of Guangdong Department Tong Yangjia wrote to the monarch: the French, who are forbidden access to the capital of the department, live at Amoy to trade with the Cantonese merchants." The French merchants present themselves at Amoy for the first time in the fourth year of Shunzhi (the year 1647). Hosea Ballou Morse, an American who worked in the Imperial Customs Service of China, wrote in his book The International Relations of the Chinese Empire that "the trade relationship between China and France should have started after the 1660s." Henri Gordier, a well-known French sinologist, said that the Franco-Chinese trade began in 1698 when the ship "L'Amphitrite" left France to go to China. Most researchers consider the latter's opinion to be the origin of trade between the two countries, because the sources consulted by Henri Cordier are fairly reliable.

[3]　The Compagnie de Chine is a new joint venture between the Compagnie des Indes Orientales and Compagnie de Jourdan for develop business with China. She was appointed in 1705 as the "Royal Company of China" after by the Government Consult.张雁深.中法外交关系史考. 长沙:长沙史哲研究社,1950 年,第 13 页.田永秀.法国在华经济势力之全貌.成都:西南交通大学出版社,2005 年,第 294 页.

[4]　M. Arnoud. De la balance du commerce et des relations commerciales extérieures de la France. Paris : Librairie Puisson.1791. p. 275.

a "factory"[1] in Canton in 1728, which is the first French firm in China.[2] Since the creation of this factory, the Franco-Chinese trade entered its first period flourishing. Among the twelve Western ships arriving at Canton in 1736, five come from England, three from France, two from the Netherlands, one from Denmark and one from Sweden; in 1753, ten ships come from England, six from the Netherlands, five from France, three from Sweden and two from Denmark who arrived at Canton. Commercial profits rose from 4,220,000 livres in 1725 to 6,940,000 livres in 1736, and to 10,367,000 livres in 1743.[3] At the beginning of the second half of the 18th century, France became one of the principal countries of exchange with China.[4]

In order to expedite French commerce in Canton, the French East India Company created a French Commerce Association at Canton in 1772,[5] and the Royal Government installed a French consulate there in 1776.[6] However, the East India Company was suppressed by Louis XVI on 3 April 1790, and then reorganized as a private company.[7] During the Revolution and the Empire, commerce from France to Canton was almost interrupted. The Consulate of France exist no longer since 4 August 1801 after the return of the consul of Guignes in France. The French factory in Canton, then managed by Charles de Constant, a Swiss merchant, was sublet to an Englishman in 1804.[8]

It was only under the July monarchy that almost thirty years later, on December

---

① Theword "factory": During the period of the foreign trade of Canton, dwellings and commercial movements of foreign merchants are limited to a small area in the city of Canton. In this region, foreign administrative representatives or traders from each country have the right to rent a building such as their dwelling or office. This building is called "the factory". It should be noted that the factory is not to be confused with "industrial factory".

② H.B.Morse. The International Relations of the Chinese Empire. New York. Longmains, Green. 1910. p.64

③ A.Martneau. Dupleix et Inde française 1722—1741. Paris. Librairie Ancienne Honore Champion, 1920.p. 31.

④ L.Dermigny. La Chine et l'occident : le commerce à Canton au XVIIIe siècle, 1719—1833. Paris. S.E.V. P.E. 1964. Vol.I. p.394.

⑤ The Association was founded in Canton on September 7, 1772 under the suggestion of Pierre Etienne Bourgeois de Boynes, the Secretary of State of the Navy. For the détail, consult. 张雁深.中法外交关系史考.第18页.

⑥ Ministère de l'agriculture et du commerce, Document sur le commerce extérieur, Chine et Indochine, Fait commerciaux n°12, Paris : Imprimerie et Librairie administrative de Paul Dupont, 1852, p. 10. Selon les archives, le premier consul français en Chine est Pierre Charles François Vauquenlin. Il prend son poste le 20 août 1776. Après la mort de ce dernier, Philippe Vieillard reprend le poste à partir du 23 septembre 1782. Il faut savoir que les consulats étrangers à Canton n'ont jamais été reconnus par l'empire de Qing avant la Guerre d'opium, donc ils n'étaient pas des consulats au sens moderne. Ils n'avaient même pas le droit de communiquer avec les officiers locaux par correspondances. Leur principale occupation était de rassembler les renseignements commerciaux, d'aider les maisons de leur pays d'origine à développer leur commerce, et de servir d'interprètes à leurs compatriotes. De plus, les consuls eux-mêmes étaient souvent des commerçants à Canton.

⑦ 张雁深.中法外交关系史考.第20页.

⑧ 田永秀.法国在华经济势力之全貌.成都:西南交通大学出版社,2005年,第296页.

13, 1832, the tricolor flag floated again before the French factory in Canton. Benoît Gernaert is appointed as the new French consul in Canton by the King in 1828.[1] Nevertheless, as the first three decades of the nineteenth century, France's trade with China did not progress at all (consult Table I-2). In "the information that the Ministry of Agriculture and Commerce offered to the Delegates in charge of the mission in China in 1844", he wrote:

> The relations of foreign trade with China have been almost exclusively in the hands of England and the United States. We must add those of Russia, which take place chiefly on the land side; And if, through the intermediary of the British and American ships, as warehouses of the English, Dutch, and Spanish Indies, our merchandise has found some outlets in China, we must admit that our own direct commerce with the Celestial Empire, that is to say, that which we have been able to make by our ships, has hitherto been scarcely zero.[2]

Although we can't offer a list of the exchange values between France and China before the 1840s due to the lack of statistical sources for that period, we can still make some estimates by some particular cases. Indeed, in terms of exchange values, France is not only significantly lower than England, but also in relation to the United States and the Netherlands. From 1836 to 1837, two French ships arrived at Canton. Its export value in China is 116,456 dollars,[3] and it carries a value of 138,547 dollars of goods from China. During the same period, the United States carries 3,214,726 dollors worth of items in China, and return with 9,527,139 dollors of goods. For the Netherlands, the two figures are 526,032 dollors and 1,070,290 dollors.[4] The commerce of Canton in 1844 had a total value of 1,296,911 dollars (7,263,000 francs), of which France occupied only 70,933 dollars.[5]

In terms of the nature of goods traded between the two countries, raw materials ap-

---

[1] Archives Nationales. F12.6498. le 3 septembre 1829, la lettre du ministre des affaires étrangères au ministre du commerce.

[2] Ministère de l'agriculture et du commerce, Document sur le commerce extérieur, Chine et Indochine, Fait commerciaux n°5, Paris : Imprimerie et Librairie administrative de Paul Dupont, janvier 1852, pp.21—22

[3] 1 dollar Américain égale environ 5.6 francs à l'époque.

[4] H.B.Morse. The Gilds of China. London. New York; Longmans, Green, 2d, 1932. p. 220—221.

[5] Ministère de l'agriculture et du commerce, Document sur le commerce extérieur, Chine et Indochine, Fait commerciaux n°10, Paris : Imprimerie et Librairie administrative de Paul Dupont, janvier 1852, pp.22.

pear very rarely in the list of Franco-Chinese trade flows at that time. Goods exchanged between the two countries include both beverages (wine, brandy) , agricultural products (dry fruits from France and teas, sugar, rhubarb from China) as well as manufactured goods (porcelain, Nanking cloth and silk tissues of China and linen, wool and silk tissues of France).[1]

The structure of the Franco-Chinese trade is very different from that of the English-Chinese trade: in commerce between England and China cotton is already one of the two main commodities of exchange during the same period(another is opium). In 1841, the export of cotton from England to China had already reached 6,606,230 piasters, or 27.82% of the total import value of China. On the import side, England had already imported a large quantity of raw materials from China: 80%—90% of the exported silks are destined for England before the 1840s (we will show the details in another chapter). In other words, at the beginning of the nineteenth century, England had already exported a large quantity of industrial products to China, and imported a great quantity of raw materials from China. But Franco-Chinese trade is still at the stage of exchanges of exotic and luxury goods, a trade model remaining at a very primary level.

2. The long-term influence of the Franco-British Wars from the end of the 18th century to the beginning of the 19th century

The commercial relationship interrupted between France and China before the 1840s is explained often by the long-term influence of the Franco-English Wars during the Great French Revolution and the Napoleonic Empire.

A common explanation for the inferiority of France's foreign trade during the first decades of the 19th century is that the Franco-English conflicts of the early 18th century to the year 1815, notably the wars with England during the Revolutionary period and The Empire of Napoleon, have restrained the foreign trade of France. According to Jean-Charles Asselain's research in his *Histoire économique de la France du XVIIIe siècle à nos jours*, the importance of French foreign trade reached one of its peaks in international trade at the end of the old regime(before 1889) , remaining equal to that of England. "Between 1716—1720 and 1784—1788, the value of foreign trade increased five-fold... The comparison with Great Britain (which was by far the most important commercial

---

[1]　Ministère de l'agriculture et du commerce, Document sur le commerce extérieur, Chine et Indochine, Fait commerciaux n°4, Paris : Imprimerie et Librairie administrative de Paul Dupont, 1852, pp. 7; 姚贤镐.中国近代对外贸易史料,1840—1895.北京:中华书局,1982 年版,第 301 页.

power in the early eighteenth century and later in the nineteenth century) is particularly striking: French foreign trade accounted for scarcely more than half of British trade circa 1720, but almost the equivalent in about 1780.[1]

Table I-1 Share in the world trade (%)[2]

	1720	1750	1780
Great Britain	15	15	12
France	8	9	12

And then he says that the ravages of wars on French foreign trade are much heavier than those of England. "However, the historical significance of this comparison should not be exaggerated. In particular, French foreign trade remains much more vulnerable in times of war: it is experiencing a sharp fall, while Britain's trade (which has control of the seas) is suffering a mere slowdown in its growth ... The growth rate (of the volume of foreign trade in France) declined by about 3% per annum between 1720 and 1750 to just over 1% between 1750 and 1780." When he discussed the effect of the wars during the Revolution and the Empire, he said: "The contrast will be clearer than ever, during the wars of the Revolution and the Empire, between the collapse of French commercial positions and the decisive assertion of British supremacy."[3]

To sum up, Asselain determines that the French-English wars before the French Revolution interrupted the growth of French foreign trade, but did not change its tendency to expansion. On the other hand, the wars during the Revolution and the Empire destroyed the distant trade of France and definitively assumed the superiority of England in relation to France in the following epoch. Asselain's point of view is supported by most economic historians. "We will have to wait until the Second Empire to regain a dynamism of the French economy comparable to that of the time of Louis XVI," concludes J-P. Poussou in his article "'le dynamisme de l'économie française sous Louis XVI."[4] Patrick Verley writes in his book *l'échelle du monde* that "The British superiority that asserts itself on the seas will cut all relations between France and the West Indies,

---

[1] J-C.Asselain . Histoire économique de la France du XVIIIe siècle à nous jours. Edition du Seuil. 1984. pp. 55—56.

[2] Idem. p.55.

[3] Idem p.56.

[4] J-P.Poussou . le dynamisme de l'économie française sous Louis XVI. Revue économique. 1989, vol. 40. n°6. pp. 984.

24

destroying the essential French oceanic trade ... As early as 1793, Pitt seeks to weaken France by a blockade, which prompted him to send his navy to the Mediterranean to drive out French commerce and establish points of support."[1]

Since the historians asserts that the Franco-British wars before and after 1889 have different effects on the trend of the evolution of French foreign trade from 1700 to 1840, we shall also check whether the Franco-British wars have certain influences on French trade with China during these two periods:

Before the French Revolution, the main conflicts between France and England were the "War of the Austrian Succession" between 1740 and 1748, the "Seven Years' War" between 1756 and 1763, and the "American War" between 1775 and 1783. According to the research of Henri Cordier, the commercial line between France and China is greatly disturbed by these wars. For example, during the War of the Austrian Succession, three commercial ships for China, "Jason" "Dauphin" and "Hercules" were plundered by English military ships; In 1756, the first year of the Seven Years' War, English naval forces captured "Pondicherry" and "Penthievre", which are also on their way to China.[2] Moreover, if we compares the movements of navigations on the Chinese sea in Table I-2, we will found that the growth of the numbers of English ships is more marked than that of France. However, the supremacy of the navigation of England over the China Sea was not absolute before the French Revolution. The number of British ships arriving in China exceeded for the first time the 10 in 1851, the 20 in 1776, but still floated around 20 in the early 1780s. The number of French ships reached 5 in 1753, and then 7 in 1777. When England had 16 ships arrived in China in 1783, France had 8 ships. The wars limited indeed the expansion of French trade in China during that time, but the effect was not so great.

---

[1] P.Verley L'Echelle du monde. Paris. Editions Gallimard. 1997. pp.469—470.

[2]   H.Cordier. Histoire générale de la Chine et de ses relations avec les pays étrangers, Paris. Librairie Paul Geuthner, 1920. Vol III. p. 337

Table I-2 Comparison of number of vessels in the English-Chinese and Franco-Chinese trades[1]

Years	England	France	Years	England	France
1698	—	1	1786	53	1
1701	—	1	1787	62	3
1704	—	2	1788	50	1
1713	—	1	1789	58	1
1714	—	2	1790	46	2
1716	—	6	1791	23	4
1722	4	1	1792	39	2
1724	6	1	1802	38	1
1730	—	2	1803	43	1
1731	—	2	1825	61	1
1732	—	1	1826	85	2
1733	5	3	1828	73	3
1734	1	1	1829	72	2
1736	5	1	1830	72	5
1737	5	2	1831	93	1
1738	0	3	1832	90	3
1739—1740	7	3	1833	107	7
1741	5	2	1836—1937	2	

[1] The amount of 1698 from PELLIOT Paul. L'origine des relations de la France avec la Chine. Le premier voyage de l'Amphitrite en Chine. p.115. The amount of 1701 from YANG Yuanhua. L' histoire de la relation entre la Chine et la France. p.9. These amounts of 1704, of 1713 and of 1714 from ZHANG Yanshen. Les études sur l' histoire de la relation diplomatique entre la Chine et la France. p. 17. These amounts from1716 to 1833 from the table of comparison between the commercial ships of england and France from1716 to 1833, YAO Xiangao, les données du commerce extérieur de la Chine moderne 1840—1895, Beijing : Zhong Hua Shu Ju, novembre 1982 pp. 300. These amounts from 1837 to 1840 from the table of the Direct Navigation in England, America and France from 1837 to 1840, Ministère de l' agriculture et du commerce, Document sur le commerce extérieur, Chine et Indochine, Fait commerciaux n°1, Paris : Imprimerie et Librairie administrative de Paul Dupont, janvier 1852, pp. 82—83. These amounts from 1841 to 1842 from the table of the Direct Navigation In the seas of the East Indies and Indochina from 1839 to 1842, Ministère de l' agriculture et du commerce, Document sur le commerce extérieur, Chine et Indochine, Fait commerciaux n°4, Paris : Imprimerie et Librairie administrative de Paul Dupont, janvier 1852, p.2The amount of 1843 from Archives du Ministère des affaires étrangères Canton 1 1824—1844 67CCC 1.pp.111—114. lettre de C. Alex.ChallageThe amount of 1844 from Archives du Ministère des affaires étrangères, Canton 2 1845—1865 67CCC 2. pp. 1-2 : 1er Janvier 1845, lettre de Charles Lefevre de Bécourt.

（续表）

Years	England	France	Years	England	France
1750	7	4	1838	92	6
1751	10(?)	2	1839	68	2
1753	10	5	1840	47	6
1775	13	4	1841	43	3
1776	24	5	1842	54	2
1777	18	7	1843	100 plus	3
1778	17	4	1844	100 plus	5
1783	16	8			
1784	21	4			
1785	28	1			

Notes: the correspondence of the French diplomats in Canton helped us to verify the accuracy of the painting. For example, in the letter of the French Consul to the Minister of Foreign Affairs of December 10, 1831, it is mentioned that the only French ship to arrive at Canton in 1831 is the "Damar" de Bordeaux;[1] Another consul wrote in his report that there has been no French ship arrived in Canton in 1835.[2]

Are the wars during the Revolution and the Empire the turning point for the trade of the two western countries with China? The evolution of the English navigation movement in China is initially marked by a great leap in the late 1780s, and then a small decline during the French Revolution and the Empire of Napoleon, and finally resumed the growth rate after the year 1815. On the other hand, communication between France and China decreased again to 1—4 ships per year (the level before the 1750s) during the revolution. The communication of the French consul with France was completely cut off, and this fact continued until the 1830s, when the French consulate was once more established in Canton. After the 1830s, the number of French ships arrived in China increased slightly, but at the same time the gap with the number of England grew steadily larger. This information draws attention to the fact that Franco-Chinese commercial communication is almost interrupted during the period of the continental bloc, but English trade has only slightly decreased during this period of conflict. The effect of the Franco-

---

[1]　Archives du Ministère des affaires étrangères Canton 1 1824—1844 67CCC 1.pp.65—66.
[2]　Archives du Ministère des affaires étrangères Canton 1 1824—1844 67CCC 1. pp. 92—95

British conflict on Franco-Chinese trade continues after the 1815 peace. As more and more English ships arrive in China after the wars, Franco-Chinese trade remains at a very modest level in the 1840s. The wars during the Revolution and the Empire are therefore indeed the turning point in the commerce of the two western countries with China: the commercial influence of France is almost eliminated by England, but the trade of England with China is more and more prosperous.

In investigating the consequence of the wars during the Revolution and the Empire, and how those wars become the turning point of the commerce of France and England with China, we can see the disastrous influence of the blockade policy on French trade and the sharp fall of France's navigation capacity during the Revolution. The blockade was carried out for the first time by the French government in 1796, which went so far as to seize the neutral ships carrying British goods[1], and was reinforced several times by the Conventions, Directories and Decrees distributed by Napoleon I. A great number of books have discussed the effects of the bloc on the French economy, and the negative effect on the distant trade of France is already confirmed by most historians: France wants to control trade with European countries and eliminate the economic influence of Great Britain. At the same time, however, it is isolated from the rest of the world by British military ships. The maintenance of French inferiority may be explained by a sharp decline in the number of French commercial ships during the wars and by maintaining the inferiority of the French naval fleet after the peace. Let us look at Table I-3, the tonnage of French merchant marines was close to that of the United Kingdom in 1780, but much lower after 1815. Until 1840, the tonnage of French merchant marines did not recover to the level of 1780. Moreover, the inferiority of the Steam tonnage of France in 1840 decides her inferiority of the capacity of the long distance trade at that time.

Table I-3 Tonnage of European merchant marines (miller of British tons) [2]

	1780	1840		
Countries	Sail	Sail	Steam	Total
UK	882	2680	88	2768
France	729	653	10	663

---

[1]　G.Dejoint. la politique économique du Directoire, Paris. 1951. p.161—223.

[2]　S.P.Ville. Transport and the development of the European Euronomy. 1750—1918. Houndmills Basingstoke and London. Macmillan Press. 1990. pp.68—69.

（续表）

	1780			1840	
Netherlands	398				
Denmark et Norway	386				274
Italy	235				
Spain	150				
Prussia and					
hanseatic cities	123				352

3. The opening of China and the acquisition of commercial privileges

China maintains a policy of "closure" for its maritime security during most of the Qing Dynasty, especially during the era of the Canton Commerce (1757—1842).[1] At that time, China's foreign trade was limited to Canton, monopolized by several Chinese firms (公行 Cong-Hong), the only intermediaries between foreign merchants and Chinese buyers.[2]

The signing of the *Nanjing Treaty* (《南京条约》)[3] between China and Great Brittan expands significantly the Chinese market. The French no longer want to maintain the monopoly of this great market of the Far East of England. In order to enter into competition with England, the government of the July Monarchy sent its delegates to China in 1844 for a commercial treaty negotiation. Before the departure of Theodore de Lagrené, who was appointed by the French king as the plenipotentiary minister of the "mission in China", Foreign Minister Guizot entrusted him with several tasks[4]:

To sign a commercial treaty with China, which will assure France the same rights as those of England.

To negotiate with the Chinese Government problems of recognition of consuls, an-

---

[1]　Canton was the only commercial port opened from 1757 to 1842 in China. This time is called the time of 一口通商. 梁廷枏.粤海关志.广州：广东人民出版社,2002 年 2 月.

[2]　H.Cordier Henri. La Chine en France au XVIIIe siècle. In: Comptes-rendus des séances de l'Académie des Inscriptions et Belles-Lettres, 52e année, N.9 1908.pp. 762.

[3]　The "Nanking Treaty" is the agreement after the First Opium War, which ended in 1842 with a clear victory of the United Kingdom over China. It was signed in Nanking on 29 August aboard a British warship, HMS Cornwallis. The treaty opened up new trading possibilities for the British. It opens four new ports, Shanghai, Ningbo, Fuzhou and Xiamen to trade and proclaims the cession of the island of Hong Kong to the United Kingdom; The Chinese Government is obliged to negotiate with the English Legation when formulating the Customs Tariff; China is also obliged to pay compensation of $ 21 million over four years for the drug destroyed in 1839.

[4]　张雁深.中法外交关系史考.第 27—28 页.

choring of warships, opening of commercial ports, and relations between peoples of both countries. To study the Chinese market with the help of specialists from each industry branch.

To look for a port next to China as a stopover for French merchant ships by observing mainly the regions of Indochina, Anambas, Natunas and Singapore.

Lagrene leaves Brest, on the steepest corvette Archimedes, accompanied by representatives of the Chambers of Commerce of Marseilles, Paris and Mulhouse etc. Auguste Haussman for the conton industry, Natalis Rondot for the of wool, Isidore Hedde for that of the silks, and Edouard Renard for those of the articles of Paris. He is equal to Guizot's confidence: he signed the Treaty of Huangpu on 24 October 1844 with the governor of Guangdong.[1] In the Chinese archives, we found that the latter treaty not only offers France all the privileges formulated in the Sino-English treaty, which include the opening of five French ports (Canton, Fuzhou, Ningbo, Shanghai and Xiamen) , extraterritorial privileges for French citizens in China, fixed customs duties on Franco-Chinese trade, the right of France to set up consuls in China, but also the privilege of protecting Catholic missionaries with the French consul if a local Chinese authority judges them undesirable, and the absence of persecution for the Chinese Catholics to whom nothing else can be reproached. France thus becomes the fourth country which concludes trade treaty with China, after England, the United States and Italy.[2]

Among all the privileges that France obtains by the Huangpu Treaty, the right to access the port of Shanghai is particularly important for French merchants. Although the foreign trade monopoly of China's "Co-Hong (公行)" has been terminated by trade treaties between China and Western countries, there is still "a trend of revival from Co-Hong at Canton".[3] The English merchants, in collusion with the merchants of "Co-Hong", still control the commerce of Canton, which severely hinders the exchanges of other countries with China including France. On the other hand, there is no Chinese Co-Hong in Shanghai. The creation of the French concession in Shanghai in 1849 by Consul Charles de Montigny offers a more egalitarian commercial competition environment to French merchants. In this concession, the French merchants successively obtained the privileges of constructing the residences, having an independent justice, an independent administration, levying taxes on all the residents (including Chinese) , employing the

---

① Archives Nationales de France. F12.6498. 15 mars 1845, le traité 1844 et le tarif de douane.
② 中国第一历史档案馆.明清宫藏中西商贸档案 06.北京:中国档案出版社,2010 年,第 3876—3889 页.
③ Archives Nationale de France. F12.6341. rapport du consul de Canton. p.1

30

police force, Churches, hospitals, orphanages, schools and cemeteries, etc.[1] All these privileges ensure security and a quality of life for French merchants and facilitate their commercial.

4. The beginning of the growth of the exchange value since the 1840s and the continuation of the old structure of exchange

What is the effect of the French diplomatic efforts on Franco-Chinese trade? Let us look at the statistics of trade between France and China during 1844—1859.

Table I-4 Trade of France with China, Cochinchina and Oceania from 1844 to 1859 (special trade) [2]

Years	Export to China (fr)	Import in France (fr)	Total (fr)
1844	186,027	204,215	390,242
1845	145,479	511,555	656,304
1846	843,000	1,275,000	2,118,000
1847	580,000	1,762,000	2,342,000
1848	148,000	1,810,000	1,958,000
1849	610,000	2,468,000	3,078,000
1850	448,000	1,309,000	1,757,000
1851	138,000	1,302,000	1,440,000
1852	200,000	1,859,000	2,050,000
1853	3,459,000	1,426,000	4,885,000
1854	2,558,000	1,858,000	4,416,000
1855	1,625,000	2,376,000	4,001,000
1856	3,985,000	3,314,000	7,299,000
1857			4,544,000
1858	774,000	3,997,000	4,771,000

---

[1] Ch-B.Maybon. et J.Fredet. Histoire de la Concession française de Changhai. Paris. Librairie Pion. 1929. pp. 25—26.

[2] Ministère de l'agriculture et du commerce, Document sur le commerce extérieur, Chine et Indochine, Fait commerciaux n°7, n°9 et n°14, Paris : Imprimerie et Librairie administrative de Paul Dupont, 1852. Le Ministère de l'agriculture et du commerce, Document sur le commerce extérieur, Chine et Indochine, Fait commerciaux n°16, Paris : Imprimerie et Librairie administrative de Paul Dupont, 1852. le Ministère de l'agriculture et du commerce, Document sur le commerce extérieur, Chine et Indochine, Fait commerciaux n°24, n°26, n°27, n°31, Paris : Imprimerie et Librairie administrative de Paul Dupont, 1868.

（续表）

Years	Export to China(fr)	Import in France(fr)	Total(fr)
1859	2,268,000	2,647,000	4,915,000

Notes: (1) The figures for the first three years (1844—1846) are the trade statistics between France and China.

(2) Figures from 1847 to 1859 are the statistics on France's trade with China, Cochin china, and Oceania. However, the values of trade with China dealt more than 80% of the exchange value of France with all three regions.

(3) All these figures come from the official statistics of the Customs of France.

(4) Statistics on exchange values between France and China of Chinese Customs do not exist until 1905. Before this year, Chinese Customs only notes exchange values between China and Europe.

(5) Most continental countries in Europe categorize their foreign trade in two ways: general trade and special trade. The first includes all goods entering or leaving the country; the second includes goods for domestic use or produced domestically.

(6) For the graph that summarizes these statistics, see Chart I-14-A at the end of this chapter.

According to the table above, Franco-Chinese trade is growing significantly after the signing of the Treaty.[1] During the year 1846, the total value of trade between the two countries tripled comparing with the previous year. In particular, the export value of China in France multiplies by 2.5, and the export value of France to China by almost 6 times. Since this year the average value of trade between the two countries remained at the level of 2,000,000 francs until 1852. Another remarkable growth appeared in 1853. The value of trade between France and China rose at 4,885,000 francs, 2.4 times more than that of the preceding year. The total amount of Franco-Chinese trade remained stable between 4,000,000 and 5,000,000 francs until the end of the 1850s.

Table I-5 Main merchandises in the Franco-Chinese trade in 1858 and 1859[2]

Import in France	Values in 1858(fr)	Values in 1859(fr)
Tea	1,329,000	1,367,000

[1] We must be careful that growth does not occur in 1844, the year of the signing of the Huangpu Treaty, but in 1846. In fact, the Huangpu Treaty was not signed until the end of 1844 In addition, it is necessary to count at this time about 16 months for the return trip France-China. Thus, if French ships began their journey to China at the end of 1844 or at the beginning of 1845, French Customs would record their turnover at least during the first half of 1846.

[2] Ministère de l'agriculture et du commerce, Document sur le commerce extérieur, Chine et Indochine, Fait commerciaux n° 31, Paris : Imprimerie et Librairie administrative de Paul Dupont, 1868, pp. 11—12.

（续表）

Import in France	Values in 1858(fr)	Values in 1859(fr)
Raw Sugar	701,000	
Pepper	271,000	
Silk in cocons	267,000	
Raw silk	260,000	788,000
Wool	250,000	
Cinnamon	145,000	124,000
Total	3,223,000	2,279,000
Papers	110,000	33,000
Vines	104,000	996,000
Metal tools	62,000	47,000
Silk textiles	57,000	57,000
Potery, glass and Cristal	50,000	64,000
Manudacture Skins	48,000	64,000
Effets to use	39,000	122,000
Life Water and liquid	37,000	225,000
Meats	13,000	73,000
Total	520,000	1,681,000

According to the table above, the most popular French product in China is French wine. Moreover, goods exported from France to China consist mainly of exotic and luxury products, semi-luxury goods in the late 1850s. During this same period, the most imported Chinese product in France remained tea, while the goods most imported from France into China are always exotic or luxury goods.

However, a slight but significant change is to be noted in China's export list in France: raw silks and cocoons are beginning to appear regularly in the list of exchanges between the two countries. In fact, from 1852 France began to import silk materials directly and regularly from China, as a result of the increase in the productivity of the silk textile industry in France and the epidemic of silkworms in the middle of the 19th century (we will clarify the details in chapter II).

In summary, the Franco-Chinese trade take off during the years 1844—1859 for the first time. In terms of quantity, the value of trade between the two countries multiplies by 13; at the level of the structure, France begins to regularly import raw materials silk from China.

5. A position of inferiority in contrast to other countries

Nevertheless, the success of the expansion of Franco-Chinese trade over this period should not be overstated for the following reasons.

First, despite remarkable progress, the value of Franco-Chinese trade is still low compared with those of England and the United States, whose trade relations with China have developed very rapidly over the same period. In 1846 the total value of China's foreign trade was 278,633,000 francs, in which the Sino-English trade comprised 201,558,000 francs, and the Sino-American trade for 51,750,000 francs. In the same year, the value of trade with France, after a six fold increase in the value of 1844, was only 2,365,000 francs, or 1.17% of that of England and 4.56% of that of the United States. In 1855, only 37 French ships went to China, but 1,319 English ships and 457 American ships.[1] Indeed, during this period, the French position in China's foreign trade was not only inferior to that of England and the United States, but also lower than that of the Dutch, Portuguese and Germans. In terms of trade with China, France ranks sixth behind the countries mentioned above, just ahead of Sweden and Denmark and Belgium.[2]

Second, concerning the nature of exchange goods, the structure of the Franco-Chinese trade is underdeveloped in comparison with the Sino-English trade structure. Let's look at the tables below.

Table I−6−A Values of the most traded goods in canton by the English ships 1843—1850. (piasters)[3]

Export to Canton	1843—1844	1845	1846	1847	1848	1849	1850
Cotton textiles	4,039,182	2,450,482	2,755,223	1,470,296	1,214,344	1,475,644	1,616,900

---

① Ministère de l'agriculture et du commerce, Document sur le commerce extérieur, Chine et Indochine, Faits commerciaux n°24, Paris : Imprimerie et Librairie administrative de Paul Dupont, 1868, pp. 38—39.

② Ministère de l'agriculture et du commerce, Document sur le commerce extérieur, Chine et Indochine, Faits commerciaux n°14, Paris : Imprimerie et Librairie administrative de Paul Dupont, 1854, p. 4.

③ North China Herald. Le 27 septembre 1851. p.34. Fonds de la Bibliothèque municipale de Shanghai.

（续表）

Export to Canton	1843—1844	1845	1846	1847	1848	1849	1850
Woolen textiles	1,898,866	1,875,042	1,386,534	1,027,346	1,866,980	768,042	992,800
Cotton	683,654	313,835	792,876	830,756	2,791,615	4,769,641	3,432,000
Others	7,884,538	5,753,575	5,062,950	6,297,362	661,685	888,917	859,200
Total	15,506,240	10,392,934	9,997,583	9,625,760	6,534,597	7,902,244	5,900,900
Import from Canton							
Tea	13,432,958	15,825,954	11,112,627	11,844,232	7,382,449	9,335,700	7,672,771
Raw Silk	2,172,263	2,424,897	1,344,286	2,007,770	444,220	860,000	1,447,500
Others	2,320,139	2,483,167	2,921,647	1,869,938	826,364	1,290,235	798,540
Total	17,925,360	15,378,560	15,378,560	15,721,940	8,653,033	11,485,935	8,020,606

Table I-6-B Values of the most traded goods in Shanghai by the English ships 1843—1850(piasters)[1]

Export to Shanghai	1843—1844	1845	1846	1847	1848	1849	1850
Cotton textiles	1,670,672	4,254,864	3,080,054	3,311,385	1,836,031	3,051,625	2,617,191
Woolen Textiles	557,279	803,553	623,352	782,016	327,120	808,786	500,555

---

① North China Herald. Le 29 juillet 1854. p.206. Fonds de la Bibliothèque municipale de Shanghai.

（续表）

Export to Shanghai	1843—1844	1845	1846	1847	1848	1849	1850
Sugar	1,945	0	0	42,571	169,751	82,211	147,421
Others	291,610	136,176	185,534	175,522	200,007	470,213	642,989
Total	2,521,506	5,194,593	3,888,960	4,311,494	2,532,969	4,412,835	3,908,156
Import from Shanghai							
Tea	322,152	2,221,180	2,026,862	1,833,691	1,653,049	2,018,916	2,426,711
Raw Silk	2,002,602	3,803,947	4,430,318	4,819,483	3,330,720	4,416,670	5,529,267
Others	33,380	18,509	34,946	72,557	96,173	78,285	64,628
Total	2,360,134	6,043,636	6,492,144	6,725,731	5,079,942	6,513,871	8,020,606

The *North China Herald*[①]establishes statistics on the most traded types of goods in Canton and Shanghai transported by the Pavilion of England from 1842 to 1850: the cotton textiles, the woolen textiles, the cotton, the sugar (import to China), tea and raw silk (export from China). In fact, it lacks one type of commodity, opium, in import lists in China. In fact, the import of this commodity was still officially prohibited by the Chinese government before 1860, and therefore the value of smuggled opium cannot appear in the lists. Among the seven types of goods imported into or exported from China by the English, cotton, sugar and opium are transported from South Asia to China. So it remains only four commodities, cotton fabrics, woolen fabrics, tea and silk in direct trade between England and China. The two main commodities exported from England to

---

① The North China Herald, whose Chinese name "北华捷报" is the first English weekly in China. Created by Englishman Henry Shearman in Shanghai in 1850, this weekly newspaper often carries information on shipping and commerce, which offers a large amount of sources for this thesis.

36

China（cotton textiles and woolen textiles）are industrial products, and the two main goods imported from China to England are tea and raw materials. At that time, China became already an important market for English industrial products and a supplier of tea and raw materials to England. Over the same period, France has not yet been able to pour large quantities of its industrial products into China. Similarly, it imported only a small quantity of silk.

Why did the French trade with China situated in such a position of inferiority comparing with other countries before the 1860s, particularly in relation to England, even after the opening of China in the early 1840s? Certainly, its inferiority related to the high cost of transport and the small number of French company in the trade relationship with China comparing with that of other countries, which we will discuss and specify in other chapters. Here, we will point out other equally important factors that slowed the Franco-Chinese trade before 1860.

（1）To explain the underdevelopment of China's exchange with foreign countries before the 1840s, many historians, especially Chinese historians, emphasize China's prohibition policy and its negative impact on trade between China and the Western countries, as what is written in Yang Yuanhua's book *the History of the Relationship between China and France*[1] and Chen Dongyou in his book *Penetrate to Maritime Trade: the Activities of Chinese Merchants in the World Market*[2]. China maintains the policy of "closure" for its maritime security during most of the Qing Dynasty, especially during the "era of the Canton Trade"（广州贸易时代）[3]. At that time, China's foreign trade was monopolized by several Chinese Companies（Cong-Hong）at Canton, which are the only intermediaries between foreign merchants and Chinese buyers.[4] Foreign merchants even have not the right to walk alone or bring their families in the city of Canton[5]（details of China's maritime policies before the Opium War will be discussed in Chapter IV）. All these policies have limited the economic communication between France and China.

But the policies of prohibition alone are not enough to explain the inferiority

---

① 杨元华.中法关系史.上海:上海人民出版社,2006 年,第 9 页.

② 陈东有.走向海洋贸易带:近代世界市场互动中的中国东南商人行为.南昌:江西高校出版社,1998 年,第 239—273 页.

③ Canton was the only commercial port opened from 1757 to 1842 in China. This epoch is called the time of 一口通商. 梁廷枏.粤海关志.广州:广东人民出版社,2002 年.

④ CORDIER Henri. La Chine en France au XVIIIe siècle. In : Comptes-rendus des séances de l'Académie des Inscriptions et Belles-Lettres, 52e année, N.9 1908.pp. 762.

⑤ 中国第一历史档案馆:两广总督李鸿宝奏折,明清宫藏中西商贸档案 06,北京:中国档案出版社,2010 年 6 月,第 3212—3214 页.

France's trade with China, since England has confronted exactly the same problems encountered with the France. Without benefiting from any privileges under China's prohibition policy, their business deals are much better than those of France. So even if the policy of prohibiting foreign trade in China is a negative factor for Franco-Chinese trade, it does not explain the inferiority of the Franco-Chinese trade compared with that of England. This confirms a conclusion of P. Bairoch in his book *le Commerce extérieur et développement économique de l' Europe au XIXe siècle*: the dynamics of trade between countries is not necessarily linked to customs policy.[1]

(2) The monopoly of England on opium and cotton and the mismatch of exports between France and China to the markets of each other.

Since "the era of cloture of China", England's advantage in the trade with China comparing with that of France is its monopoly on two kinds of goods—opium and cotton. Moreover, these two kinds of goods are the most demanded commodities by the Chinese. Let us consult the statistics in 1841. The values of these two types of goods exported by England to China amount to 14,000,000 piasters and 6,606,230 piasters, which is 58. 95% and 27. 82% of the total import value of China.[2] The French colonies produce scarcely any opium.[3] The price of the French cotton is much higher than that of England. Thus the export rate[4] of the French cotton is very low compared to that of England. According to R. Davis' research, the proportion of the value of cotton goods exported from England to its total value of cotton production was only 6% during 1784—1786, rising to 15.6% during 1794—1796, to 42.3% during 1804—1806, and to 48.5% during 1834—1836.[5] According to P. Verley's estimation, this proportion of France was only 16% until the 1840s, which was much lower than that of England.[6]

Certainly, France has its own advantage industrial sectors of comparing to those of

---

[1] P. Pairoch. Commerce extérieur et développement économique de l' Europe au XIXe siècle. Paris. Editions Mouton et EHESS. 1876. p.311.

[2] Ministère de l' agriculture et du commerce, Document sur le commerce extérieur, Chine et Indochine, Fait commerciaux n°3, p.3.

[3] L' infériorité de l' industrie de coton de France est déjà bien expliquée dans P. Verley. l' Echelle du monde. p.544 ; M. Levy-Leboyer et F. Bourguignon. L' Economie Française au XIXe siècle, Analyse macro-économique. Paris. Economica. 1985. p.55.

[4] The degree of openness of the economy is the intensity of its participation in international trade, which can be measured by the relationship between the amount of exports and imports of the domestic industrial product.

[5] R. Davis. The Industrial Revolution and British Overseas Trade. London. Leicester University Press. 1979 p. 15.

[6] P. Verley. l' Echelle du monde. p.587.

England. In *Economic Growth in British and France: two paths towards the 20th Century*[1], P.O'Brien and C.Keyder argue that France and Great Britain followed two different but parallel paths until the 20th century. The authors indicate that French industry is characterized by focusing on high-quality products, which corresponds to the "comparative advantage" of the French economy. For example, 66% of silk Fabrics were destined for the foreign market during 1827—1834, and this proportion maintain at 52% during 1835—1844; the degree of openness of the perfumeries of France also reached 35% during the years 1827—1834, and then increased to 39% during 1835—1844.[2]

However, the strong point of the French industry (the luxury goods or high quality) does not also meet the demand of the Chinese market. On the one hand, the average purchasing power of the Chinese is so low at that time that they cannot afford the high prices of high-quality products from France. GDP per capita in China was 600 dollars Geary-Khamis[3]in 1820, still 600 in 1850, and down to 530 in 1870. They are a half, one third and a quarter of Europe's purchasing power during the same periods.[4] On the other hand, high-quality products from France may suffer from the fort competition from similar Chinese products. Let us take the example of silk fabrics. The silks from France sell very well in Europe, but it's very difficult for them to find buyers in the Canton market, because the Chinese produce also so elegant and high quality silks.

Equally, the goods exported from China do not adapt to the French demand. During that time, the two most exported products by China are tea and raw silk. France imports much less tea than England. Great Britain, from 1821 to 1840, import an average of 15, 000,000 kilograms of tea each year, most of which is consumed by the British. During the same period, the quantity of Chinese tea imported by France is only 140,000 kilograms per year. At the same time, France absorbs very little Chinese silk every year because of the growth of domestic sericulture production and the abundance of silk supply of the Mediterranean region. (For the details, see Section 3 of Chapter II).

After the opening of China, the fact that the structure of foreign trade in France does not adapt to the needs of the Chinese consumers prevents still the seal of French

---

① P.O'Bien et C.Keyde . Economic Growth in Britain and France: two paths towards the 20th Century. Londres. G. Allen and Unwin. 1978.

② P.Verley,l'Echelle du monde.p.587.

③ The Greary-Khamis dollar is a unit of account (a fictitious currency) that has the same purchasing power in a given country as the US dollar in the United States at one time. The year 1990 serves most often as a basis for comparisons over several years. It was invented in 1958 by Roy C. Greary, then developed by Salem. H. Khamis between 1970 and 1972.

④ A. Maddison. L'économie mondiale. Statistiques Historiques. Paris. OCDE. 2003. p.63—65 et p.90.

products in China. As indicated above, the years 1840—1860 there is a strong growth of the foreign trade of France. The French export rate rose from 5.1% in 1830s to 7.4% in 1850s, and to 10.8% in 1860s (those of England were 7.8%, 11.4% and 15.3%); The relative share of French exports relative to the European total rose from 15.9% in 1830 to 19.2% in 1860 (that of England were 27.5% and 29.8%).[1] However, the structure of French foreign trade hardly changed during these two decades. Industrial sectors with the highest rate of openness are still the luxury industries with high quality or traditional industry in France: the silk industry (76% opening rate during 1855—1864), the Perfumery (48% opening rate during 1855—1864) and the paper industry (49% opening rate during 1855—1864). But all these goods among the most exported by France have few consumers in China. The rate of openness of the recent industries in France, especially that of the sector producing the most popular industrial product in China— the cotton industry—is still very low, only 13 % during 1855—1860.[2] In contrast, the export share of the cotton industry reached more than 60% in England from 1840 to 1860. From 1854 to 1856, England exported 34,952,841 pounds of cotton, occupying 34.1% of the total export value, or 15 times of the export of the cotton textiles of France.[3]

During 1840—1860, the goods from China is also not adapted to the demand of the French market. During this period, the most exported commodity from China is tea. But even if the tea takes the largest place in contrast to other items imported from China to France during the 1850s, the French buy much less tea than the English. The quantity of tea imported into France often does not exceed 200,000 kilograms per year, which is little compared with that of England at the same time. An English consul in China wrote the following recommendation: "Franco-Chinese trade cannot develop unless the Chinese change their traditional habits or the French begin to drink tea."[4]

① P. Bairoch. Commerce extérieur et développement économique de l'Europe au XIXe sièle. 77—79.
② P. Verley. l'Echelle du monde.p.587.
③ J-C. Asselain. Histoire économique de la France du XVIIIe siècle à nous jours. pp. 137.
④ YAO Xiangao : les sources de l'histoire du commerce de Chine à l'époque moderne 1840-1895. pp.622—623.

Table I-7 Volumes and values of tea imported from China to France and to England from 1843 to 1860[1]

	France		England	France	England		
Years	Volume (kilogr)	Value(fr)	Volume (kilogr)	Years	Volume (kilogr)	Value(fr)	Volume (kilogr)
1843			7,977,488	1852	189,989	854,000	42,210,945
1844			31,714,425	1853	137,573	825,000	45,552,150
1845			36,087,300	1854	168,864	675,000	49,216,095
1846	220,000	1,289,000	37,807,200	1855	164,000	881,000	50,697,315
1847	143,000	838,000		1856	230,300	1,368,000	
1848	537,000	2,416,000	34,179,300	1857			41,595,795
1849	287,204	1,723,000	37,341,225	1858		1,329,000	46,603,980
1850	77,720	350,000		1859		1,367,000	
1851	110,058	495,000	44,635,700	1860			54,624,645

In summary, Franco-Chinese trade situate at a fairly primary level before the 1840s, both in terms of quantity and in terms of the structure of trade. Even during the first 15 years after the opening of China to France, the trade between the two countries is still negligible. The main cause for the inferiority of France's trade with China before the 1840s is the long-term influence of the conflicts between France and England since the Great Revolution. After the opening of China, the monopole of England on the cotton textiles and opium trade in China, and the mismatch of exports from France and China to the markets of each other as well, continues to prevent the Franco-Chinese trade growth.

---

[1] Ministère de l'agriculture et du commerce, Document sur le commerce extérieur, Chine et Indochine, Faits commerciaux n°16, Paris: Imprimerie et Librairie administrative de Paul Dupont, 1852, p.11; le Ministère de l'agriculture et du commerce, Document sur le commerce extérieur, Chine et Indochine, Faits commerciaux n°23, Paris: Imprimerie et Librairie administrative de Paul Dupont, 1868, p.9; le Ministère de l'agriculture et du commerce, Document sur le commerce extérieur, Chine et Indochine, Faits commerciaux n°24, Paris: Imprimerie et Librairie administrative de Paul Dupont, 1868, p.49; le Ministère de l'agriculture et du commerce, Document sur le commerce extérieur, Chine et Indochine, Faits commerciaux n°26, Paris: Imprimerie et Librairie administrative de Paul Dupont, 1868, p. 19. Data for the part of England come from Ministère de l'agriculture et du commerce, Document sur le commerce extérieur, Chine et Indochine, Fait commerciaux n°24, Paris: Imprimerie et Librairie administrative de Paul Dupont, 1868, p.45 ; 马士.中华帝国对外关系史 1.北京:商务印书馆,1963 年 6 月. H.B.Morse. l'histoire des relations de l'empire chinois avec les étrangers, Beijing : Editions de Shangwu. Vol 1, 1963. p. 143.

II A remarkable growth of exports between 1860—1884

France and England signed the Cobden-Chevalier Treaty in 1860, abolishing all French import prohibitions, replacing them with very moderate tariffs, lowering the tariff for the export of coal from England and that of wines to England and containing the most-favored-nation clause between the two countries. Most of the countries of Europe concluded a series of similar treaties during the following years, opening the era of liberal exchange in Europe during 1860—1890.

But this policy of liberal exchange does not accelerate the growth of European trade. On the contrary, according to P. Bairoch's estimate in the "Commerce extérieur et développement économique de l'Europe au XIXe siècle", the annual growth rate of Europe's export value drops from 4.6% during 1840—1860 to 3.6% during 1860—1880, and then to 1.2% from 1880—1890. France's foreign trade performance is lower than that of Europe: the annual rate of growth of the French export value is marked first by a slowdown of 5.2% during 1840—1860, at 2.3% during 1860–1880, and this slowdown turned into a stagnation, a growth rate of 0.7% per year during 1880—1890.[1] Moreover, France's foreign trade is affected by two facts: the first is the permanent trade deficit during the period of liberal exchange, which stabilized at 5% of the total value of French imports until the 1890s[2]; The second is the devastation of the silkworm epidemic on the export of silk textiles from the mid-1850s, the most exported French industrial products at that time.[3]

On the other side of the planet, the French still make a lot of efforts to expand the Chinese market. The Anglo-French army's attacks in Tianjin and Beijing in the late 1850s forced the Chinese government to sign several new trade treaties, by which French merchants obtained much more commercial privileges. Immediately, three historic events, the opening of the Suez Canal, the creation of the direct maritime line between France and China and the connection of the Euro-Asian telegraph, have greatly improved the means of transport and communication between China and France. In this section we will check whether all these changes during the 1860s accelerate or slow down Chinese trade.

---

[1]　P. Bairoch. Commerce extérieur et développement économique de l'Europe au XIXe siècle. Paris. Editions Mouton et EHESS. 1976. p.74.

[2]　J–C. Asselain. Histoire économique de la France du XVIIIe siècle à nous jours. p.158.

[3]　M. Levy-Leboyer et F. Bourguignon. l'Economie Française au XIXe siècle. pp. 65—67.

1. The evolution of the economic circumstance during the years 1860—1880

The years 1860—1884 brought great changes in the context of international trade. Among these changes, several influence directly the evolution of Franco-Chinese trade.

（1）First, the signing of the new treaties and new conventions between China and Western countries, including France. We have already shown that the Treaty of Nanjing, following the Opium War, had opened five ports available to the West for trade, eliminating the Co-hong's monopoly over China's foreign trade, and fixing the customs tariffs of China at an average level of 5%. Despite these agreements, the Western powers, including England, France and the United States, wanted to gain more trade privileges from China, including the possibility of extending their trade to the North and to the inland of China. In 1854, the ministers of England, France and the United States asked to the Viceroy of Canton for the revisions of the treaties signed after the Opium War in order to:

— Being able to penetrate without hostility in Canton.

— Being able to open new ports in northern China and along the Yangzi River.

— Legalize the trade in opium, which is still illegal.

— Deal directly with the court in Beijing.[1]

The Imperial Court of Qing refused the requests for revision of England, France and the United States. Since then, the Powers sought other means to make the Qing Empire to change its position. This event is the origin of the Second Opium War.

The war began on October 8, 1856, and ended on October 24, 1860. During the War, the Anglo-French Alliance brought the flames of war to Canton, Tianjin and finally, to the Empire Capital, Beijing. The Chinese central government is obliged to consent to the demands of the Powers to end the war. The *Treaty of Tianjin* (《天津条约》) in 1858 and the *Beijing Convention* (《北京条约》) in 1860 extended the privileges of the occidental countries in China. France, which was one of the main belligerent countries in the Second Opium War and who enjoyed "the treatment of the most favorable country"[2], obtained as much of the fruits of war as its ally and its English rival.[3] Among the

---

① P.Tain. L'expédition de Chine. Paris. Michel Lévis éditeurs. 1862. p.22.

② "The treatment of the most favorable country" first appears in the *Treaty of Humen* (《虎门条约》) as the annexes to the *Nanjing Treaty*. France also obtained this privilege by the *Treaty of Huangpu*.

③ In fact, although only France and England participated in the war, the United States and Russia also obtained the same privileges as "the most favorable country".

clauses of the two treaties[1], several strongly push the trade relations of the occidental countries with China :

① Eleven new ports are open to foreigners, which include Nanjing, Zhenjiang, Jiujiang, Hankou, Yingkou, Yantai, Shantou, Qiongzhou, Tainan, Danshui, Tianjin. This means that the Chinese coastline will be fully open to western countries, from the far north (the port of Yingkou) to the great south (the port of Qiongzhou). In addition, the openings of the ports of Hankou, Jiujian, Zhenjiang and Nanjing will bring foreign trade to the domestic territory of China.

② Foreigners are allowed to travel from the opening ports to inland of China. This offers the possibility to foreign traders to buy Chinese products or to sell foreign products directly to inland of China.

③ The twenty-eighth article of the Treaty of Tianjin stipulates that foreigners only pay the domestic customs duty once when they transport foreign goods into the interior of China or export products that they have bought inside the ground. This inland customs duty is called "under-port tax" (子口税), the amount of which is often half of the maritime customs tariff, or 2.5 teals per 100 tons of goods. Compared with the amounts claimed by Chinese merchants, the tariff of "under-port tax" is much lower. This will help to strengthen the competitiveness of foreign goods and reduce the prices of products from inland of China.

(2) Secondly, the improvement of transport and communication between China and Europe and the opening of the Suez Canal during this period (see Section 3 of Chapter IV).

(3) Thirdly, the production of European silk, following that of France, was destroyed by the silkworm epidemic after the 1860s. Since the 1860s, France, the largest producer of silk textile of world at that time, is obliged to look for the materials of raw silk outside of the European territory to ensure its production of silk fabrics (We will deal with details in the other chapter).

2. The prosperity of trade with China thanks to the growth of silk imports

Do all these changes have a real influence on the evolution of Franco-Chinese trade during 1860—1886? We will look at the evolution of the trade value between the two countries during that time.

---

[1]　Archives Nationales de France, F12.6499. Traité 1858 et Traité 1860.

Table I-8 Trade of France with China from 1860 to 1884 (special trade) [1]

Years	Export China(fr)	Import France(fr)	Total(fr)
1860	3,703,000	2,005,000	5,708,000
1861	1,880,000	2,106,000	3,691,000
1862	2,862,000	2,328,000	5,190,000
1863	6,987,000	7,142,000	14,139,000
1864	5,410,000	8,224,000	13,634,000
1865	1,625,000	22,216,000	23,841,000
1866	2,964,000	8,885,000	11,849,000
1867	2,037,000	22,150,000	24,187,000
1868	2,783,959	37,903,444	40,687,039
1869	2,854,995	28,087,744	30,942,739
1870	1,865,895	41,063,721	42,929,616
1871	976,075	24,832,129	25,808,204
1872	1,862,404	50,732,348	52,594,752
1873	3,120,103	52,162,105	55,282,208
1874	1,626,302	75,555,121	77,181,423
1875	3,149,677	88,605,745	91,455,431
1876	2,421,476	140,834,121	143,255,597
1877	3,051,086	36,619,550	39,670,636
1878	2,757,370	93,380,260	96,137,630
1879	3,509,475	95,366,492	98,875,967
1880	3,448,545	100,875,228	104,323,773
1881	3,415,498	96,340,523	99,755,751

---

[1] Ministère de l'agriculture et du commerce, Document sur le commerce extérieur, Chine et Indochine, Fait commerciaux n°33, n°36, n°38, n°40, Paris : Imprimerie et Librairie administrative de Paul Dupont, 1868, du Ministère de l'agriculture et du commerce, Document sur le commerce extérieur, Chine et Indochine, Fait commerciaux n°45, Paris : Imprimerie et Librairie administrative de Paul Dupont, 1870 du Ministère de l'agriculture et du commerce, Document sur le commerce extérieur, Chine et Indochine, Fait commerciaux n°50, Paris : Imprimerie et Librairie administrative de Paul Dupont, 1876 , du Ministère de l'agriculture et du commerce, Document sur le commerce extérieur, Chine et Indochine, Fait commerciaux n°51, Paris : Imprimerie et Librairie administrative de Paul Dupont, 1879, du Ministère de l'agriculture et du commerce, Document sur le commerce extérieur, Chine et Indochine, Fait commerciaux n°52, Paris : Imprimerie et Librairie administrative de Paul Dupont, 1884.

（续表）

Years	Export China (fr)	Import France (fr)	Total (fr)
1882	2,958,422	88,165,532	91,123,954
1883	2,523,100	84,884,999	87,408,099
1884	4,001,291	86,981,493	90,982,784

Notes: (1) The figures from 1860 to 1863 are the statistics for China, Cochin China and the Kingdom of Siam, the three regions together. The exchange values between France and China during these four years are therefore lower than those indicated in the table.

(2) The figures from 1864 to 1884 are the statistics of China alone.

(3) All these figures come from the official statistics of the Customs of France.

(4) Concerning the graphic that summarizes these statistics, see the Graph I-14-A at the end of this chapter.

The commercial exchange value between France and China increased sharply from 1863: it was multiplied by almost 8 times from 1862 to 1868; the growth slowed relatively between 1868 and 1884, but the exchange value increased still 2.5 times. Except for the years 1871—1872, during which the Franco-Prussian War took place, trade between the two countries progressed steadily. The Taiping rebellion, which threatened the port of Shanghai from 1857 to 1864, seemed to have little influence on the Franco-Chinese trade. Moreover, the first great growth has already taken place before the end of this last historical event.

This notable increase is clearly linked to the growth of the Chinese products export to France, which is multiplied by 40—50 from 1860 to 1884. Conversely, imports from France to China did not increase during this period. As a result, a growing deficit was formed in France's trade with China after the 1860s. The value of the deficit rose from 155,000 francs in 1863 to 82,980,202 francs in 1884, or an increase of 535 times.[1]

In fact, it is the rise of the import of raw silk which makes the importation in general jump. The quantity of exchange of this kind of commodity between the two countries began to increase rapidly from 1863, replacing tea as the most traded commodity be-

---

[1] In French economic history, the period 1860—1890 is marked by an unfavorable trade balance over the long term. In the research of J.C.Asselain, he finds that this is due to a slowdown in France's industrial export growth, a marked increase in industrial imports in France and, above all, a very serious agricultural deficit in France's trade relationship with France. The conclusion of J.A.Seladain deserves to be supplemented by explainning that the trade deficit with China is another element leading to the unfavorable balance of France's foreign trade during this period. For the details, J-C.Asselain. Histoire économique de la France du XVIIIe siècle à nous jours. pp. 157—159.

tween the two countries. According to the statistics below, the value of imports of Chinese raw silk into France jumped from 190,000 francs to 5,150,000 francs in 1863, an increase of 27 times; This last value is multiplied three more times from 1863 to 1864; From 1864 to 1867, the import value of Chinese silk increased by 350%, to a value of nearly 60,000,000 francs. Compared to the growth rate of silk, the growth of tea imported from France to China is very low: between 1862 and 1866, the value of the tea exchange between France and China increases only 1.7 times. From 1863, raw silk became the most exported commodity from China in France. The proportion of the value of silk in the total import value of China in France rises from 8.47% in 1862 to 95.88% in 1867; In contrast, the proportion of tea decreases from 62.58% in 1862 to 1.32% in five years (we shall return to the silk trade in the following chapter).

Table I-9 Imports of silk and tea of China in France from 1862 to 1867 (general trade)[1]

Years	Silk import(fr)	Tea import(fr)	Total import in France(fr)
1862	190,000	1,403,000	2,242,000
1863	5,150,000	1,310,000	20,140,000
1864	16,249,000	2,816,000	21,039,000
1865	38,400,000	1,920,000	44,635,000
1866	35,331,000	2,348,000	40,749,000
1867	59,706,000	819,000	62,270,000

3. Little importance of other goods in Franco-Chinese trade

According to the official reports of the French trade commissioners, apart from raw silk, other Chinese articles exported from China to France during 1860—1884 include tea, silkworm eggs, and cocoons silk, porcelain, musk, tin, furniture, haberdashery, unwrought hair, rhubarb, volatile oil or gasoline, rubber, gutta-percha crude or remelted in mass, fish glue, tabletterie, raw hides and skins, phormium, abaca and filamentous vegetables, crude, rough reeds and reeds, gall nuts, cinnamon of all species, etc. Each type of commodity represents very little value in total imports compared to silk. The

---

[1] Ministère de l'agriculture et du commerce, Document sur le commerce extérieur, Chine et Indochine, Fait commerciaux n°36, n°38, n°40, Paris : Imprimerie et Librairie administrative de Paul Dupont, 1868 et du Ministère de l'agriculture et du commerce, Document sur le commerce extérieur, Chine et Indochine, Fait commerciaux n°45, Paris : Imprimerie et Librairie administrative de Paul Dupont, 1870.

goods exported from France to China during 1860—1884 are wines, silk, wool and cotton fabrics, saffron, raw lead, watchmaking, apparel, leather or leather goods , jewelery, quinine sulphate, metalwork, potassium, furniture, medicines, and so on.[1] We find out that, apart from raw silk, most of the types of goods traded between the two countries after the 1860s are still exotic and luxury products, which are goods not produced in the buyer countries, or "no-competitive" products.

The goods exported by France still do not meet the needs of the Chinese. The most exported goods by France between 1860 and 1886 were silk textiles, woolen textiles, articles from Paris and so on.[2] All these articles are finally very little requested by China. The most imported commodity in China, the cotton textiles, accounts for only a small proportion of the total French exports, and only one-fifth of the export value of silk textile.[3]

In summary, Franco-Chinese trade has seen a remarkable growth since the 1860s. This growth is due only to the prosperity of the exchange of silk between the two countries. It must not be forgotten that, from that time, Franco-Chinese exchange began to become an important part of the multilateral exchanges of world, if we put the Franco-Chinese exchange into a wider context. France exports its silk textiles to England to pay for imports of silk material from China, England exports cotton goods to China to pay for silk textiles manufactured in France, and China exports its silk material to France to buy the products of England. The economies of the countries on different continents integrate into each other by international trade, and Franco-Chinese trade is a very important part of it.

---

[1] Ministère de l'agriculture et du commerce, Document sur le commerce extérieur, Chine et Indochine, Fait commerciaux n°33, n°36, n°38, n°40, Paris : Imprimerie et Librairie administrative de Paul Dupont, 1868, du Ministère de l'agriculture et du commerce, Document sur le commerce extérieur, Chine et Indochine, Fait commerciaux n°45, Paris : Imprimerie et Librairie administrative de Paul Dupont, 1870 du Ministère de l'agriculture et du commerce, Document sur le commerce extérieur, Chine et Indochine, Fait commerciaux n°50, Paris : Imprimerie et Librairie administrative de Paul Dupont, 1876 , du Ministère de l'agriculture et du commerce, Document sur le commerce extérieur, Chine et Indochine, Fait commerciaux n°51, Paris : Imprimerie et Librairie administrative de Paul Dupont, 1879, du Ministère de l'agriculture et du commerce, Document sur le commerce extérieur, Chine et Indochine, Fait commerciaux n°52, Paris : Imprimerie et Librairie administrative de Paul Dupont, 1884.

[2] M.Levy-Levoyer et F.Bourguignon. L'économie française au XIXe siècle. p.65.

[3] P.Verley. l'Echelle du monde. Paris. Editions Gallimard. 1997.p.587.

Ⅲ Trade summit in the 1890s and the decline in the early 20th century

The foreign trade policy of the Third Republic during the period 1880—1914 is marked by a gradual return of protectionism. The introduction of a new tariff in the early 1880s symbolizes the beginning of the return, raising the average import levy from 6.5% in 1880 to 7.1% in 1884. The "Méline" tariff implemented in 1892 innovated by distinguishing between a "general tariff" and a "minimum tariff"[1], resulting in a further increase in duties on industrial products of about one third and on agricultural products of 5%—20%. In 1897, the "padlock law" allowed the government to immediately increase tariffs on cereals and meat, a measure that took place on several occasions. The last increase in customs duties took place in 1910, especially the "general tariff".[2]

This restoration of protectionism is accompanied by a new growth in France's economy and foreign trade: the annual growth rate of the French economy rose from 1% per annum during 1860—1891 to 1.7% in 1892—1913 and that of the volume of exports rose from 0.7% during 1875—1893 to about 3% during 1894—1913.[3] We should pay attention that these new accelerations are not only linked to a "second wind" of the traditional industrial sectors after the 1890s (notably for the textile industry), but also to the development of new industrial (sectors chemical and automotive industries), reflecting a structural transformation of France's industry and foreign trade. Moreover, the export of French capital abroad grew very rapidly from the 1880s: from 1885—1895 to 1906—1913, the value of the export of capital multiplied by 270%.[4]

The occupation of Indochina after the Franco-Chinese War of 1884—1885 opened the border from south-west China to France. This event once again offers the French people the hope of extending the Franco-Chinese trade relationship beyond the silk trade. At the same time, France exports more and more capital to China from the 1880s. At the beginning of the 20th century, China is already the largest importer of French capital to the Far East. In this section, we will observe the changes in the value and structure of the Franco-Chinese trade during this period, and explain the effects of these changes on the

---

① The general tariff is applicable to countries with which there is no agreement, and the minimum tariff is likely to be granted in exchange for equivalent concessions from France's trading partners.

② J-C.Asselain. Histoire économique de la France du XVIIIe siècle à nos jours. pp. 179-180.

③ P.Bairoch. Commerce extérieur et développement economique de l'Europe au XIXe sièle. pp.221—225.

④ M.Levy-Leboyer et F. Bourguignon. L'économie française au XIXe siècle. Analyse macro-économique. p. 72.

French economy, the Chinese economy and Franco-Chinese trade relation.

1. The occupation of Indochina and the expansion of investment in China

As what we have mentioned in the introduction of this section, one of the most important changes in Franco-Chinese relations is the occupation of Indochina of France. France had long wished to have a colony next to China.[1] One of the most important tasks entrusted by Guizot to Lagrené was to find an island next to China for the supply of French vessels. In fact, Guizot's plan was only applied since the period of Napoleon III. The French began to take progressively the ownership of Vietnam from 1858 and established Cochin China[2] in 1864.[3] The occupation of the whole territory by Vietnam was only realized in 1885, when the Chinese transferred the right of protectorate of Tonkin to the French at the end of the Franco-Chinese War.

After the founding of a colony next to China, France is eager to acquire privileges that will help to achieve its goal. Thus, the Franco-Chinese Treaty of 1885 offers him the privilege of building a railway on the Sino-Vietnamese border; The import and export customs duty between Indochina and China is based on 4/5 and 2/3 of the normal tariffs by the treaty 1886; The ports of Longchou (龙州), Montez (蒙自) and Manhao (蛮耗) (changed to Hekou 河口 in 1895) were opened abroad in 1887; One more port, Simao (思茅) was opened in 1895, and French companies obtained the mining exploitation advantages of Yunnan, Guangdong and Guangxi in the same year.[4] Moreover, France successively created in Indochina a series of establishments and infrastructures which serve to develop the trade with China. The Bank of Indochina and the Haiphong Ship Company settled in Vietnam during the years 1870—1880;[5] The Compagnie Lyonsnaise Indo-chinoise was founded in 1898 and was responsible for all commercial transactions between Tonkin and Yunnan;[6] The railway line from Tonkin to Longzhou (龙州

---

① In fact, the occupation policy in Vietnam began from the time of Louis XVI. 田永秀.法国在华经济势力之全貌.第 37 页.

② In modern history, Vietnam is divided into three parts: Nam ky (南圻), Trung Ky (中圻), Tonkin (北圻). Nam ky is located in the south of Vietnam, comprising a small part of the territory of Cambodia. She is named as Cochin-China in 1864 from Napoleon III. Trung Ky is located in the middle of Vietnam. It becomes a country under French protectorate in 1874. It is also called An Nam. Tonkin is located in the north of Vietnam. It's occupied by France in 1885, named as Indochina.

③ 杨元华.中法关系史.第 37 页.

④ 田永秀.法国在华经济势力之全貌.第 38 页.

⑤ R.Lee: France and the exploitation of China 1885—1901. A study in Economic Imperialism. Hong-Kong: Oxford University press,1989, p.23.

⑥ LE Thanh Huyen : Les relations commerciales entre Lyon et l' Indochine(1858—1920). DESS RIDE. Rapport de recherche bibliographieque, 2002, p.27.

50

铁路）goes into operation in 1903; [1] Yunnanfu（昆明）and Haiphong are connected by the railway of Dianyue（滇越铁路）since 1910. [2]

If the occupation of Tonkin offered France a dirt road to penetrate to south-west China and thus the possibility of transporting its goods to China by rail, the second change, namely the growth of exports of French capital, would help it regain an important role in a new market—the investment market in China. France is one of the three countries dominating the world capital market at that time（the other two countries are England and Germany, see Table I-10-B）[3].

Table I-10-A Export of French capital 1878—1913（million francs）[4]

| | Export of | Saving of | Export rate | G.N.PP |
Periods	capitaux（million Francs）	G.N.P	of capitaux	（billion Francs）
1878—1884	70	3,155	2.2%	21.5
1885—1984	469	3,346	14.0%	22.4
1895—1905	973	4,478	21.7%	24.9
1906—1913	1,264	5,917	21.3%	34.5

Table I-10-B Share capitals of England, France and Germany（in billions of francs）[5]

Years	England	France	Germany
1862	3.6	—	—
1872	15	10（1869）	—
1882	22	15（1886）	—

---

① 田永秀.法国在华经济势力之全貌.第 199 页.

② 王彦成,王亮.清季外交史料.南京:书目文献出版社,1987 年 9 月,第四卷,第 17 页.

③ M.Levy-Leboyer. Capital Investment and Economic Growth in France. 1820—1930. dans The Cambridge Economic History of Europe. Vol. VII. part. I Cambrige. Cambrige University Press 1978. pp.230—295 ; POIDEVIN Raymond. Les relations économiques et financières entre la France et l'Allemagne de 1898 à 1914. Paris. Armand. Colin. 1969 ;GIRAULT Réné. Emprunts russes et investissement français en Russie, 1887—1914. Paris. Armand Colin. 1973 ;THOBIE Jacque , Intérêt et impérialisme français dans l'empire ottoman（1895—1914）. Paris. Publications de la Sorbonne. 1977 ;MARSEILLE Jacque. Empire colonial et capitalisme français. Histoire d'un divorce Paris. Albin Michel. 2005.

④ M.Levy-Leboyer et F. Bourguignon. L'économie française au XIXe siècle. Analyse macroi-économique. p.72.

⑤ N.Lenine. L'impérialisme dernier étape. Paris. Editions Librairie de l'Humanité. 1925. p.25

（续表）

Years	England	France	Germany
1893	42	20(1896)	—
1902	62	27—37	12.5
1914	75—100	60	44

The French, who did not want to remain behind their rivals in the Far East[1], actively engaged in investment movements in China. According to the research of the American economist C.F.Remer, the total investment of France in China reached 91,120,000 dollars in 1902, and this figure rose to 171,374,000 dollars in 1914.[2] The nature of the French capital invested in China is very diverse: from the bank loan to the constitution of railways, from the exploitation of mining to the creation of enterprises. Among all the types of investment from France to China, the export of French capital on Chinese railways is the most remarkable. The French then possessed two means of investing in the Chinese railway. The first was to seize directly the right of construction. As we mentioned above, France built two railway lines on the Sino-Vietnamese borders before the beginning of the Great War in 1914. A French company, Compagnie de Fives-Lille, took the right in order to cover the entirety of the business of the two lines: from geographical investigation to financing, from the construction of the road to personnel management. The Compagnie de Fives-Lille also took control of the two lines exploitation.[3] The second way was to lend money to the Chinese governments for the construction of the railways. The constructions of the Jinghan line (from Beijing to Hankou), the Zhengtai line (from Liulinbao to Taiyuan), and the Bianluo line (from Kaifeng to Luoyang) are completely or proportionally inverted by France.[4] Before the First World War, France directly or indirectly participated in the construction of 4,596 kilometers of Chinese railways, or 48.89% of the total length of China's railways at the time.[5]

---

[1] Pour les détailles, consulter Meuleau Marc. Des Pionners en Extrême-Orient. Paris. Fayard. 1990.

[2] C-F.Remer Foriegn investments in China. New York. H. Fertig. 1968. pp.465—468.

[3] R.Lee France and the exploitation of China 1885—1901. A study in Economic Imperialism. p.120;

[4] 田永秀.法国在华经济势力之全貌.第 205—212 页.

[5] Selon M. Zimmermann. Les Chemins de fer et le commerce extérieur de la Chine. In: Annales de Géographie. 1911, t. 20, n°114. p. 461.La Chine procède 9778 kilomètre de chemin de fer avant la première guère mondiale.

2. Sustainable growth of imports from China and the variety of export of industrial products

Are there any links between the above-mentioned elements and the evolution of the Franco-Chinese trade? We shall analyze the statistics of the value and types of goods exchanged between France and China during 1884—1913.

Table I-11 Trade of France with China from 1890 to 1914 (Chinese customs taëls and francs) [1]

Years	Import to France		Export to China		Total	
	taëls	francs	taëls	francs	taëls	francs
1884	15,532,409	86,981,493	714,516	4,001,291	16,246,925	90,982,784
1890	23,356,853	130,798,377	2,214,354	12,400,384	25,571,207	143,198,761
1891	24,212,345	135,589,134	1,847,310	10,344,940	26,059,655	145,923,620
1892	28,095,918	157,377,141	1,293,658	7,244,486	29,389,756	164,621,627
1894	21,604,302	120,984,089	3,566,350	19,971,562	25,170,652	140,995,651
1895	28,302,263	158,492,673	2,728,567	15,279,976	31,030,830	173,772,649
1896	18,949,735	106,118,517	4,167,086	23,335,679	23,116,821	129,454,196
1897	30,021,164	168,118,517	5,265,080	29,484,450	35,286,244	197,602,967
1898	26,717,857	149,620,000	3,580,893	20,053,000	30,298,750	169,673,000
1899	43,303,035	242,497,000	4,476,964	25,071,000	47,779,999	267,568,000
1903	54,276,964	303,951,000	5,081,429	28,456,000	59,358,393	332,407,000
1904	36,487,500	204,330,000	4,294,643	24,050,000	40,782,194	224,380,000
1905	18,872,233	105,684,505	3,811,634	21,345,150	22,683,867	127,029,655
1906	25,358,964	142,010,198	4,281,764	23,977,878	29,640,683	165,987,786
1907	30,658,585	171,688,076	4,158,626	23,288,306	33,817,211	185,848,382
1908	32,129,193	179,923,481	2,403,458	13,459,365	34,532,651	193,382,846
1909	38,598,327	216,150,631	2,181,627	12,217,111	40,779,954	228,367,742
1910	38,829,632	217,445,939	2,760,932	15,461,219	41,590,565	232,907,158

[1] The account from 1890 to 1899 is from des Archives du Ministère des Affaires Etrangères. NS563 pp 63—64. The account of 1903 from des Archives of Ministry of Foreign Affairs.148CPCOM564.pp.131—135. These accounts of 1905—1914 come from the archives.中国历史第二档案馆,中国海关总署办公厅.中国旧海关史料,41—66卷.北京:京华出版社,2001年10月.

Years	Import to France		Export to China		Total	
1911	39,102,325	218,973,020	3,018,343	16,902,720	42,120,668	235,875,740
1912	38,809,138	217,331,173	3,932,373	22,021,289	41,741,511	233,572,462
1913	40,749,782	228,198,779	5,299,517	29,677,295	46,049,299	257,876,074
1914	25,590,924	143,309,174	4,951,471	27,728,238	30,099,843	171,037,412

Notes: (1) The figures for the years 1890—1903 in the table are derived from French Customs statistics; The data for the years 1905—1914 in the table come from Chinese Customs statistics. In addition, statistics on data for the years 1886—1904 are different from those in the table in "Information from the Minister Plenipotentiary in Paris on the creation of the Universal Chamber of Commerce at the capital of France", *the Official Journal of Commercial Affairs. 1910. Vol 19, pp. 24—25* （驻法刘大臣为法京创设万国商会事谘商部文《商务官报》,1910,第 19 册第 24—25 页）, as well as statistics on data from the years 1905—1914 are different from those in the table in HUANG Peiyan, ZHANG Qi. China's foreign trade statistics over the past 45 years. *The last fifty-fiftieth anniversary of the Shen newspaper*（《最近五十年——申报馆五十周年几年》,《五十年来中国之对外贸易统计》,黄培炎,张琪著）. But French diplomats often use customs statistics in their reports, so it seems pertinent to cite them in this book.

(2) The French Customs often uses the franc as a unit of currency, while the Chinese Customs uses the customs taël. At the time, the customs duty was about 5.6 francs.

(3) For the graphic that summarizes these statistics, see Graph I–14–A at the end of this chapter.

The total exchange value on the eve of the First World War increased to more than 23,000,000 francs, or two and a half times of that of the early 1880s. This increase was mainly due to the increase in import values in France, by 2.3 over the period of thirty years from 1884 to 1914. French export values to China increased very rapidly during this period, which even increased more rapidly than exports from China to France. The figure in 1914 is almost 7 times that of 1884. However, at the level of the absolute value, the second is much lower than the first.

If we compare the commercial influence of France in China with those of other occidental countries during this period, we will discover that Franco-Chinese trade reached its peak in the mid-1890s. During 1880—1900, imports from China into France have exceeded all those of other countries, and it's much more reduced that the gap between the total Franco-Chinese exchange values and the Sino-English exchange values. In 1895, the total value of trade between France and China reached 78% of that between England and China, a figure never reached by France or any other country before. The monopoly of the English trade in China was for the first time challenged by another country.

However, this prosperity is fleeting. The trade values of other countries with China, especially those of the United States and Japan, are increasing more rapidly from the beginning of the 20th century.[1] After the year 1905, the exchange value between France and China was finally surpassed successively by those of the United States and Japan and descended to the fourth (sometimes even sixth) rank among the various countries.

Table I-12 Trade in China with France, England and Allemange (francs)[2] in 1895 and in 1905[3]

In 1895(francs)

	Export to China	Import from China	Total
England	137,161,000	85,512,000	222,673,000
France	15,280,000	158,493,000	173,773,000
Germany	44,288,000	24,514,000	68,802,000

In 1905(taëls)

	Export to China	Import from China	Total
England	86,472,343	18,064,270	104,536,613
USA	76,916,838	27,030,722	103,947,610
Japan	61,315,248	35,464,983	96,780,211
France	3,811,634	18,872,233	22,683,867
Germany	14,846,075	5,377,649	20,223,724

France took the second place during the 1890s by the expansion of its imports from China. Indeed, even during 1900—1914, the value of China's imports into France was not lower than that of England, the United States and Japan (the inferiority of China's imports into the Table I-14 originated in 1905 from a decline in the value of imports from China to France from the first decade of the 20th century). The real inferiority of

---

① The Table E1 External Trade: aggregate current values, B.R.Mitchell, International Historical Statistaics, Africa, Asia and Oceania 1750—1988 Second Revised Edition, First published in the Unitede Kingdom by Machillan Press Ltd, 1995, This version: Published in the United states and Canada by Stockton Press, 1995, New York, USA, p.521

② Archives du Ministère des Affaires Etrangères. NS563. pp.63—64.

③ These accounts of 1905—1914 come from.中国历史第二档案馆,中国海关总署办公厅.中国旧海关史料,41 卷.北京:京华出版社,2001 年 10 月,第 8 页.

France in trade with China compared to other powers lies in the exports of French products to China. The value of French exports to China is already very modest before 1900, and this disadvantage is much more evident after the beginning of the 20th century, because of the rise of the new industrial countries: the United States, Germany and Japan.

In term of the types of goods, raw silk is still the most traded commodity between France and China. The import of silk remains the main engine of the increase the Franco-Chinese trade. In 1897, the value of silk products was 207,820,910 francs, or 85.7% of imports in France and 77.62% of total trade between the two countries. The two percentages were 91.05% and 77.94% in 1903.[1] There were other Chinese goods, straw tresses, sesame, tea, silk textiles, pongee, raw beef and goat skins, silks pork, beans, musk, tanned hides, antimony, ramie and camphor, who are often exported to France at this time. Almost all of these items are agricultural products (except straw tresses and pongee), luxury goods, or exotic products. Apart from the raw silk, there is no other raw material in the list. Moreover, the exchange value of all these types of goods is very modest.[2]

Conversely, apart from the items usually exported from France to China (silk textiles, wines, watches, food products, etc.), some new items appear in the export list at the end from the 19th century to the beginning of the 20th century, such as railway equipment, building materials, machinery, cars and bicycles, etc.

The exchange value of silk textiles is the highest among all types of goods. That of the wine goes from the first to the second place. That of clocks is in third place. The values of the new goods are not higher than those three types of traditional goods exported from France to China. For example, from 1905 to 1908, China bought only 635,433 tons of railway equipment, 120,128 tons of building materials, 61,645 tons of cars and bicycles, but 4,108,334 tons of silk textiles (silk and cotton ribbons including), 1,163,747 taëls of wine and 1,114,707 taëls of clocks.[3] So the expansion of exports from France to China during this period is not due mainly to the appearance of new goods, but mainly to the increase in the consumption of traditional French products in China.

The strong growth in exports of French traditional goods to China is linked to the notable growth in the number of European and American residents from the 1880s in

---

[1]　Archives du Ministère des Affaires Etrangères. 148CPCOM564.p.132.
[2]　Archives du Ministère des Affaires Etrangères. 148CPCOM566.p.20.
[3]　Archives du Ministère des Affaires Etrangères. 148CPCOM566. p.19.

China. For example, according to WU Guilong's research, the number of foreigners in Shanghai stagnated around 2,500 during the years 1864—1880, to resume the pace of growth from the 1880s. From 1880 to 1890, the foreign population of the public concession increased by 74%, and that of the French concession by 45%. During the last decade of the 19th century, the number of foreign residents of the two concessions increased by 77% and 40% respectively. From 1900 to 1910, the foreign population in Shanghai is multiplied by 2 again.[1] This is the case of the port of Shanghai. With the opening of more and more Chinese ports to foreigners after the Franco-Chinese treaty in 1885 and the Sino-Japanese treaty in 1895, there is a notable increase in the foreign population throughout China. Most traditional French products are consumed by foreigners residing in China. It is therefore logical that the demographic growth of European and American residents leads to the export increase of French products in China.

3. The failure of France's strategies vis-à-vis the old and new competitors

Due to the increase in exports of the silk textiles, the clocks and the appearance of new goods, industrial products accounted for a considerable proportion of French exports to China during this period. However, their absolute exchange value is still quite modest. The proportion of the export value remains at 5%—10% of the total value of the exchange of France with China.

Why is the increase in the quantity of French exports in China so limited despite the increase in French investment in China and the occupation of Indochina?

First, if the failure of exports to China of French cotton goods is due to the competition of English cotton goods on this market, the greatest obstacle for the export of products from the new French industries to China is the same types of products not only from former competitor, such as England, but also from the new industrialization countries, especially from Germany.

The appearance of new goods (machinery, etc.) on the list of exports from France to China actually is the result of the increase in investments, especially the increase in French investments in Chinese railways. We have described that many Chinese railway lines are built or financed by France at that time. By financing or constructing these railway lines, France places her priority of exports to China on profiles, equipment, locomotives and trains, which lead to increasing the value of exports from France to China. With the increase of French investments and the acceleration of the modernization of

---

① 吴桂龙:论晚清上海外侨人口的变迁.史林.1998 年第 4 期,第 69—71 页.

China, China commands more and more machines and equipment from France. According to the data shown in Table I-13, in the late 1880s, France is already one of the countries that export the most industrial equipment to China, whose value is very close to that of England.

Table I-13 Orders of occitantal idustrial equipment at Tianjin, 1886—1890[1]

Countries	Values of total oders totales (francs)	Notes
France	15,334,196	6,394,560 francs for the base of the port of Arthur; Two loans offered by the Comptoir d'Escompte, one of 520,000 taëls (2,919,000 francs) for the government of Shandong, the other of 500,000 taëls (2,800,000 francs) for the Ministry of Imperial Finance; A lighthouse in Weihaiwei; Two dredges for the Yellow River; The purchases of the railway of Decauville, brass and various irons; Shells and various weapons.
Germany	9,931,900	Krupp cannons, rails and cement.
UK	1,713,040	Rails; Two locomotives and other equipment for the Kaiping Railway.
USA	644,000	A locomotive, gasoline for the Kaiping Railway.

However, since the 1890s, German industrial equipment and machinery began to threaten the place of the same natures of French products in the Chinese market. In 1894, the Chinese government declared a ban on importing foreign machinery into China, which interrupted the import of construction machinery in China.[2] After the suppression of the interdiction, Germany, bypassing England and France, became the main supplier of materials and construction machinery in China.[3] After 1900, the value of construction materials and machinery fell to less than 1% of total trade in the Franco-Chinese trade, which means that French machinery and equipment was almost completely erased from the Chinese market.

These results are not surprising, as the advancement of the new French industries is much slower compared to that of Germany. According to J-C. Asselain's research, "in 1913, France manufactures 8 times fewer locomotives than Germany, and exports 25

---

① Archives du Ministère des Affaires Etrangères. Affaires diverses commerciales 328. la lettre de Lefèbre à Lemaire, 20 mai 1890.

② Archives Nationales de France. F12. 6499. prohibition d'importer des machine en Chine. 29, avril 1894.

③ Archives Nationales de France. F12. 7223 Canton 1907—1914. lettre du consul français à Canton au Ministre du commerce, 19 november 1909.

times less—almost only to the protected colonial markets ... Other sectors—like the chemical industries—have even more serious deficiencies; The most characteristic example is that of dyes, for which France—like Great Britain—is almost totally dependent on German production ... The most striking imbalance concerns the products of the mechanical industries. France is little exporting, and on the contrary largely dependent on imports for many types of machinery and equipment—from textile machines to steam ships, including machine tools.[1]

Secondly, the occupation of Indochina over the Franco-Chinese trade does not make the Franco-Chinese trade much faster, because, firstly, the purchasing power of the three provinces of southwestern China (Guangxi, Yunnan and Guizhou) was very low. Although mining resources are important in these three provinces, as reported by the French delegates in China, these resources are located deep in the Yunnan-Guizhou Plateau (云贵高原) at an altitude of more than 2,000 meters. Operating and transportation costs are so high that there is little profit. Secondly, competition from the port of Hong Kong (香港) greatly limited the expansion of trade in Haiphong (海防, Indochina) with China. The possession of the port of Hong Kong facilitated the penetration by the English products of the market of South China. At the beginning of the occupation of Indochina, the port of Haiphong located in the north of Vietnam was considered by the French as the key to the prosperity of the exchanges of goods between China and France with a role similar to that of Hong-Kong. However, several years later, commercial communication between the latter port and China was not as prosperous as the French had anticipated, as the port of Hong Kong still concentrated most of the international trade on the China Sea from South. In reality, by the end of the 19th century, Hong Kong had already become one of the biggest commodity distribution centers in Asia, and even in the world.[2] This port is then a mandatory stopover for most goods coming in and out of

---

① J-C. Asselain. Histoire économique de la France du XVIIIe siècle à nous jours. p. 205—206.

② According to the Hong Kong Customs Office, the barrels of Hong Kong's entry and exit vessels reached 22,453,077 tons in 1906. Other major ports of the world at the same time:

    London (1907)　19,759,346 tons
    New York(1906)　20,390,953tons
    Hambourg(1906)　18,045,093 tons
    Anvers(1904)　18,663,023 tons
    Liverpool(1907)　15,425,288 tons
    Cardiff(1907)　14,746,435 tons
    Rotterdam(1906)　11,911,038 tons
    Marseille(1904)　10,523,922 tons
    Genova(1904)　10,436,600 tons
    Singapore(1904)　12,331,753 tons

southern China. The role of the ports of Indochina is much less important than that of Hong Kong in trade in Southeast Asia. In a report by a French consul, it can be seen that in 1890 most of the navigation movements in Pakhoi (北海, a Chinese port in Guangxi province and very close to Indochina) were ensured by the German and Danish ships. The French ships is only third among all countries, with 8 thousand tons in the 112,509 tons in total.[1] According to a trade report by Shantou (汕头, an important port of the Chinese Hainan island near Indochina), the exchange value between Shantou and Saigon (西贡) is far behind the value exchange between Shantou and Hong Kong.[2]

In summary, the growth of Franco-Chinese trade during 1884—1914 was still largely due to the prosperity of the silk trade. With the growth of imports of Chinese silk to France, the value of France's trade with China reached the second place of all countries who have the trade relationship with China in the mid-1890s, which is the summit of the French commercial influence in China. The development of new industrial sectors in France, the increase in French investment in China and the occupation of Indochina do not augment efficiently the export value from France to China because of the competitions of the old and new rivals on the Chinese market. With the disadvantage of the sale of French products in China, the commercial influence of France in China was successively surpassed by those of the United States, Japan and Germany, and declined rapidly at the beginning of the 20th century.

4. Franco-Chinese trade of the 19th century: prospered only by the exchange of silk

The quality of trade between France and China was very small before the first four decades of the 19th century, due to the policies of the limit of foreign trade in China and the long-term influence of the Franco-English confit since the Great French Revolution and the First Empire.

During the first 15 years of the opening of China, there was a jump in the abundance of French trade with China, but the commercial influence of France is still very low compared to other countries, England, because the export structure of France still did not adapt to the needs of the Chinese market and Chinese products also did not meet the demand of the French market.

---

① Archives Nationales de France: F12.7057. Rapport du commerce de Pakhoi. 25 mars 1891.
② Archives Nationales de France: F12. 7225. Rapport commercial de Swatow 1907—1908.

Even after the 1860s, according to data in Table I-14-A, the value of exports of French products in China was still very modest. This situation continued until the First World War, despite the priorities obtained by the occupation of India and the growth of French investment in China. The main cause is that England's export goods (cotton and opium) was better suited to the demand of the Chinese market (cotton and opium) and that France's offer (silk) was not quiet demanded in China.

Graph I-14-A Value of trade between France and China during 1844—1914[1]

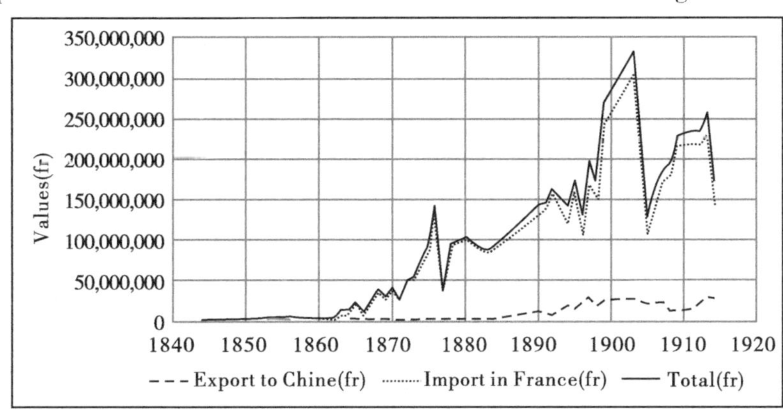

Graph I-14-B Percentages of silk import values in France on the total value of trade between the two countries 1853—1908 (percentage)[2]

[1] Due to the lack of sources on the values of trade during the period before the Huangpu Treaty, the year 1844 will be defined as the starting point.

[2] 1858: N.Rondot. Conseil supérieur de l'agriculture, des manufactures et du commerce. Rapport sur l'industrie des soies et des soieries. Paris. Imprimerie impériale. 1861. p.18.1862.1863,1864 : Ministère de l'agriculture et du commerce, Document sur le commerce extérieur, Chine et Indochine, Fait commerciaux n°36, Paris : Imprimerie et Librairie administrative de Paul Dupont, 1868, pp. 71—72.1865 : Ministère de l'agriculture et du commerce, Document sur le commerce extérieur, Chine et Indochine, Fait commerciaux n°40, Paris : Imprimerie et Librairie administrative de Paul Dupont, 1868, pp. 29—30.1866,1867 : Ministère de l'agriculture et du commerce, Document sur le commerce extérieur, Chine et Indochine, Fait commerciaux n°45, Paris : Imprimerie et Librairie administrative de Paul Dupont, 1870, pp. 115—118.1873,1874 : Ministère de l'agriculture et du commerce, Document sur le commerce extérieur, Chine et Indochine, Fait commerciaux n°50, Paris : Imprimerie et Librairie administrative de Paul Dupont, 1876, pp. 278—280.1876 : Ministère de l'agriculture et du commerce, Document sur le commerce extérieur, Chine et Indochine, Fait commerciaux n°51, Paris : Imprimerie et Librairie administrative de Paul Dupont, 1879, p. 29.1882 : Ministère de l'agriculture et du commerce, Document sur le commerce extérieur, Chine et Indochine, Fait commerciaux n°52, Paris : Imprimerie et Librairie administrative de Paul Dupont, 1884, p. 14.1883.1884 : Ministère de l'agriculture et du commerce, Document sur le commerce extérieur, Chine et Indochine, Fait commerciaux n°53, Paris : Imprimerie et Librairie administrative de Paul Dupont, 1886, p. 10.1897, 1903 : Archives du Ministère des Affaires Etrangères. 148CPCOM564.p.132.1905—1908 : Archives du Ministère des Affaires Etrangères. 148CPCOM566.p.20.

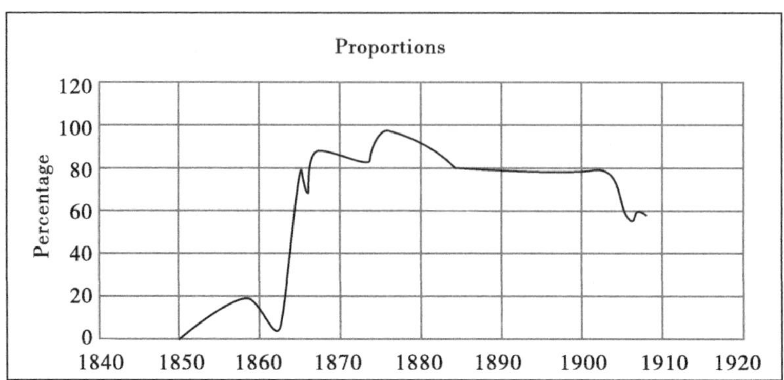

In contrast, the value of exports of Chinese products to France increased very rapidly after the 1860s. Let's look at Tables I‑14‑A, Franco-Chinese trade was growing at exactly the same pace as the growth of the importation of Chinese products into France. We can conclude that the growth of the Franco-Chinese trade of the 19th century comes almost entirely from the growth of imports of Chinese products, more precisely, the importation of Chinese silk to France. Table I‑14‑B shows us that in terms of proportion, the value of silk trade is composed of most of the value of Franco-Chinese trade from the 1860s to the early 20th century. We can affirm without exaggeration that silk plays a dominant role in the Franco-Chinese trade. This is why the silk trade is the essential subject of this book. In the following chapters, we will explain how and why the silk trade between the China and the France is so prosperous.

Chapter II　Silk trade between France and China: quantitative evolution, demand of silk manufacturers in France and supply of silk producers in China

In the previous chapter, we have demonstrated the specificity of the Franco-Chinese trade of the 19th century: it focuses on imports of raw silk from China to France.

Our research on the Franco-Chinese silk trade, which is the most dynamic element of Franco-Chinese trade of the 19th century, begins in this chapter. We will firstly show the evolution of the world silk market during the 19th century, which will help us to know the role of the exchange of silk between France and China in the world market. In the second section of the chapter, we will study precisely the quantitative evolution of the silk trade between France and China of the 19th century. The third and fourth sections of this chapter will focus on the effects of demand and supply of silk on the growth of international trade in the 19th century.

I Main exporters and importers in the world silk market of the 19th century

Places of silk production and silk textile production are well separated in the world of the 19th century. On the one hand, most of the production of raw silk is concentrated in only a few regions; On the other hand, the silk textile industry is located on other parts of the world. This is one of the most important causes that led to the dynamics of the silk trade in the international market during the 19th century. In this section, we will dismantle major exporters and importers in the world silk market at that period. We shall demonstrate, firstly, the historical and economic contexts of the silk trade between France and China in the 19th century; and secondly the importance of the roles of China and France in the silk trade of the 19th century world.

1. Producers and exporters of silk in the world of the 19th century

The sericulture production, which is a culture by its mulberry trees and a breeding by its worms, normally obeys two basic conditions: first of all, the climate of this region should be pleasant for the vegetation of the mulberry trees. Mulberry trees normally grow from 12 ℃ and grow between 20 ℃ and 35 ℃. Their vegetation will be faster if the temperature stabilizes between 30℃—32℃. Secondly, for the development of sericulture, a large number of cheap labor forces would also be required. We need to harvest a large quantity of mulberry leaves at the beginning of the season, and it will be necessary to work all day and even all night to occupy silkworm babies during the whole process of feeding, excavation, etc. Satisfying these two essential conditions, the sericulture has already appeared in many parts of the world during the 19th century.

In Europe, Africa and the Middle East, mulberry plantations are concentrated around the Mediterranean. Italy is one of the oldest European countries who produce silk. Imported in the regions of Sicily and Calabria in the 11th century[1], sericulture already extends to the entire peninsula at the beginning of the 19th century. Before the 1860s, the quantity of cocoons production in all the Italian states reached 53 million kilograms[2], which made them become the largest suppliers of silk in Europe at that time. Apart from the domestic market, their silk materials are absorbed by Lyons, London, the German States, Switzerland and Russia, who buy about 20%—25% of the total production of Italian silk at that time[3]. With the ravaging of the pebrine[4] in Italy during the years 1860 and 1870, the harvest of the Italian sericulture is reduced to one half of the figure on it. Thanks to the method of prophylaxis discovered by the French scientist Louis Pasteur in 1870 (we will specify in another section), the Italian v restore ery quickly their sericulture. Sericulture production in Italy rose from twenty million kilograms of cocoons at the beginning of 1880s to some fifty million kilograms of cocoons at the end that decade. The average production of Italy from 1904 to 1913 is 49,927,000 kilograms of cocoons, having supplied 4,272,000 kilograms of raw silk[5]. Thanks to the growth of the

---

[1]　H.Algoud. La soie, art et histoire. Paris. Payot. 1928. p.61.

[2]　A.Beaux. A Etat comparatif de l'industrie de la soie en France et en Italie. Paris. Charavay. 1886. p.22.

[3]　Archives Nationales de France. F12. 2552. le 8 mai 1832. Les soies expédiées de Milan et de Naples 1828—1832.

[4]　Pebrine is an epidemic of silkworms which first appeared in France during the 1820s. The ravage of this disease reached its peak in France during 1853–1875 and simultaneously spread to all European countries and devastated Sericulture of all Europe. We will touch on the details of this epidemic of silkworms when discussing its effects on French sericulture in another section.

[5]　G.Fédérico. An Economic History of the silk Industry, 1830–1930. Cambridge. Cambridge University Press. 1997. p. 201

harvest, Italian silk once again occupied the market of Germany, Switzerland.

The sericulture is widely available in other Mediterranean countries, although their production quantities are smaller. The sericulture production in Spain reached 12.5 million kilograms of cocoons before the epidemic, but fell to 1,100,000 kilograms (82,000 kilograms of raw silk) on average during 1860—1900, and then to 740,000 kilograms (73,000 kilograms of raw silk) in 1914[1]. The mulberry trees are also planted in Austria -Hungary. The average of its production of raw silk is 350,000 kilograms from 1865 to 1884, and this number has doubled since 1885. The cocoons harvest in Greece is 2 million kilograms (about 160,000 kilograms of raw silk) in 1855, but it began to decline since 1866, and decreased to 200,000 kilograms of cocoons (18,000 kilograms of raw silk) in 1890[2]. Asiatic Turkey was also influenced by pebrine, which only supplied an average of 142,000 kilograms of silk from 1875 to 1880. The restoration of silk production in this region began in 1900. From 1909 to 1913, it produced 1,128,000 kilograms of raw silk per year, three times more than the French production in the same period[3]. The Balkan countries, after the invasion of the disease of silk worms in 1868, produced on average only 400,000 kilograms of cocoons (32,000 kilograms of raw silk) per year. Sericulture also appeared in Africa in the 19th century. In Algeria, the amount of cocoon production reached its peak in 1881, or 21,000 kilograms[4]. All these countries (except Italy and France) around the Mediterranean produce cocoons, but there ware very few reeling factory or silk textile industry there. So the destination of their silk materials (raw silk or cocoons) are often the countries of Western Europe.

On the other side of the continent of Europe and Asia, China is increasingly supplying raw silk to the world market after its opening. We shall show precisely the proportion of exports of raw silk in another section, it's necessary to know here that from 1840 to 1894 the proportion of Chinese silk exports increased seven times, and the absolute silk exports quantity has grew 12 times. More and more Chinese silk is put in the international market in the second half of the 19th century, and therefore we consider this period is an "age Gold" of Chinese silk export. According to Table II−1, most Chinese silks were exported to Europe by London before the 1870s. After 1875, the import of

---

[1]　M.A. Carron. La production de la soie brute en France. Lyon. M.Audin. 1946. p.18.

[2]　V. Croffier. La production de la soie dans le monde. In : Annales de Géographie. 1900.t .9.n°44. p.111.

[3]　D. Quataert. The silk industry of Brussa 1880—1914. in Islamoglu and Inan. The Otomman empire and the world economy Cambridge. Cambridge University Press. pp.286—287.

[4]　M.Zimmermann. La production et la consommation de la soie. Annales de Géographie. 1916.t. 25. n°135. pp. 220—221.

Chinese silk from France exceeded that of England, and Lyons became then the largest importer of Chinese silk in the world. The import of the Chinese silk to the United States increase since the 1870s, and this country replaced the position of France on the eve of the First World War.

Table II-1 The quantity of raw silk exported from Shanghai to England, France and the United States (piculs) [1]

Years	Total	England		France		United States		Other countries	
		Quantité	Proportion	Quantité	Proportion	Quantité	Proportion	Quantité	Proportion
1870	30,482	22,145	72.60%	5,639	18.50%	1,081	3.50%	1,617	5.30%
1875	55,965	20,965	36.80%	25,625	45.80%	6,132	11.00%	3,243	5.79%
1880	69,685	17,620	25.30%	36,954	53.00%	8,093	11.60%	7,028	10.09%
1885	44,690	7,658	17.10%	25,938	58.00%	6,665	14.90%	4,429	9.91%
1890	51,808	9,288	17.90%	30,458	58.80%	4,714	9.10%	7,348	14.18%
1895	76,639	2,463	3.20%	41,521	54.20%	12,030	15.70%	20,625	26.91%
1900	60,432	2,188	3.60%	26,134	43.20%	10,193	16.90%	21,917	36.27%
1905	63,299	1,322	2.10%	23,581	37.30%	15,544	24.60%	22,852	36.10%
1910	87,540	1,148	1.30%	34,734	39.70%	21,858	25.00%	29,800	34.04%
1915	95,822	3,199	3.30%	32,821	34.30%	41,116	42.90%	18,686	19.50%

Because of the prohibition of Japan's foreign trade, the export of Japanese silk was almost zero before 1853. In 1859, six years after the opening, the export of Japanese silk was only 221,200 kilograms. The take-off of Japanese silk production began after the Meiji Restoration. In 1870, Japan supplied 411,800 kilograms of raw silk to foreign countries. This figure rose to 1,266,200 in 1890 and 2,778,500 in 1900. In 1910, the export of silk from Japan reached 8,907,700 kilograms, already exceeding that of China, 8,416,600 kilograms. This country at that time, replacing China, became the largest supplier of silk in the world[2]. Most Japanese silks are destined for the United

---

① 海关贸易年报.引自李明珠:中国近代蚕丝业及外销(1842—1937),上海:上海社会科学院出版社,第95页.

② L.M.Li. Silks by sea : trade.technology and enterprise in China and Japan. Business history review. 1982. Vol.56. No°2.p.199.

66

States. European countries also bought a considerable quantity of Japanese silks after the 1890s[1].

In the countries of South and South-East Asia, the peasants also take care of sericulture. India, having been one of the silk suppliers to the London market, was also attacked by pebrine in the 1880s. Its raw silk production reached 562,000 kilograms during the year 1871—1872[2], but decreased to 194,000 kilograms per year from 1909 to 1913[3]. Silk production in Indochina maintains 800,000—900,000 kilograms per year in the 19th century. The destination of these products is often China or Hong Kong[4]. Although the climate and soil conditions are less adoptable, the people there have attempted to plant mulberry trees in the Philippines and the Dutch East Indies during the second half of the 19th century. But the bad harvest facts made them give up this agricultural activity right away.

Sericulture has been brought to new continents as well. Plantations of the mulberry trees in North and South America do not develop very well because of lack of handswork. Even in Chile, the country with the best sericulture crop in these two continents, only about 6,000 to 8,000 kilograms of cocoons are obtained per year. In contrary, the situation is much better in Australia. It is estimated that the quantity of cocoa production in this continent already reaches 350,000 kilograms on the eve of the First World War, with which 25,000 kilograms of raw silk can be produced. Because of the absence of reeling, almost all Australian cocoon products are transported to foreign countries: 38% are transported to China, 31% to Japan, 16% to Italy, 3.8% to Turkey and 3.2% to France[5].

It's quite impressive that sericulture, as an activity offering the raw material for the production of a luxury item (silk), is already in the six continents during the 19th century. However, most of the world's silk exports at the time were concentrated in a few countries: according to the statistics in Table II−2, during most of the 19th century, silks from Italy, China and of Japan occupied about 80% of the silk traded on the world

---

[1]　J.−Oono.A. Amakawa. The Japanese raw silk in relation to the American and French silk industries. Kwansei Gakuin University Annual Stadies. 1985.No°34.p.137.

[2]　J. Goghegan. Somme accounts of silk in India. Especially of the various attempts to encourage and extend sericulture in taht country. Calcutta. Office of the Superintendent of Government Printing.1872 p.3.

[3]　H. Maxwell-Lefroy. H.Report on an inquiry into the silk industry in India. Vol. I. The Silk industry. CALCUTTA ; Superintendent of the Government Printing Office.1916.p.11

[4]　II. Herbette. La soie en Indochine. Annales de Géographie. 1932. Vol.41. No°230. p.171.

[5]　CROFFIER Valérien. La production de la soie dans le monde. In : Annales de Géographie. 1900.t .9.n°44. pp.116—117.

market. The quantity of exchange of Italian silk took the first rank during the first half of the century; Chinese silk replaced it after the 1850s and held its head until the beginning of the 20th century; Japanese silk won first place in the last decade before the First World War and maintained this superiority until the Second World War. From 1820 to 1914, these three countries took the crown of the world's largest silk exporter one after the other.

Table II-2 Silk export quantities in Italy, China and Japan, 1820—1915 (thousands of kilograms) ①

Years	World	Italy		China		Japan		Other countries	
		Quantity	Proportion	Quantity	Proportion	Quantity	Proportion	Quantity	Proportion
1820	2,350	1,545	65.74%	280	11.91%	0	0%	525	22.34%
1825	2,650	1,640	61.89%	310	11.70%	0	0%	675	25.47%
1831	2,940	1,975	67.18%	260	8.84%	0	0%	705	23.98%
1834	3,370	1,960	58.16%	600	17.80%	0	0%	810	27.04%
1838	3,545	2,310	35.45%	150	4.23%	0	0%	1,085	30.61%
1843	3,935	2,270	57.69%	570	14.49%	0	0%	1,095	27.83%
1848	4,470	2,495	55.82%	900	20.13%	0	0%	1,075	24.05%
1851	6,000	2,520	42.00%	2,210	36.83%	0	0%	1,270	21.17%
1856	6,970	2,040	29.27%	3,540	50.79%	0	0%	1,390	19.94%
1860	6,234	1,566	25.12%	2,778	44.56%	761	12.20%	1,129	18.11%
1865	5,668	1,362	24.03%	2,712	47.85%	575	10.14%	1,019	17.98%
1870	7,662	2,178	28.12%	2,972	38.79%	412	5.37%	2,100	27.41%
1875	9,550	3,444	36.06%	4,831	50.59%	708	7.42%	567	5.94%
1880	10,577	3,400	32.14%	4,969	46.98%	877	8.29%	1,331	12.58%
1885	9,043			3,505	38.76%	1,474	16.30%		
1890	11,411	1,720	15.07%	4,860	42.59%	1,266	11.10%	3,565	31.24%
1895	14,685	2,546	17.31%	6,687	45.54%	3,487	23.74%	1,965	13.38%

---

① These accounts from 1820 to 1859 come from FEDERICO Giovanni. An Economic History of the silk Industry, 1830-1930. Cambridge. Cambridge University Press. 1997. pp.196—197. These accounts from 1860 to 1915 come from a chinese research 顾国达,滨崎实,宇山满.近代(1842—1945 年)世界生丝市场的结构.浙江丝绸工学院学报.1993 年,第 10 卷,第 3 期,第 106 页.

（续表）

		Italy		China		Japan		Other countries	
1900	17,236	3,459	20.06%	5,876	34.09%	2,779	16.12%	5,122	29.72%
1905	19,051	5,519	28.97%	6,403	33.61%	4,345	22.81%	2,784	14.61%
1910	23,133	4,062	17.56%	8,417	36.38%	8,908	38.51%	1,746	7.55%
1915	23,587	3,604	15.28%	8,650	36.68%	10,688	45.32%	645	2.73%

2. Importers of silk in the world

At the same time, silk purchases from the world market of the 19th century are also concentrated in the hands of several countries: England, France and the United States are the three main importers of silk at the period. According to the statistics in Table Ⅱ-3, the three countries monopolized 70%—80% of silk purchases put into the world market during 1840—1915.

Table II-3 Raw silk imports quantities of England, France and the United States, 1840—1915 (thousands of kilograms) [1]

		England		France		United States		Other countries	
Years	World	Quantité	Proportion	Quantité	Proportion	Quantité	Proportion	Quantité	Proportion
1840	1,761.30			537					
1850		2,843.50				1,095.00			54.4
1860	3,673.90			2,290.00			135.1		
1870	7,662.30	1,613.40	21.06%	3,198.00	41.74%	264.7	3.45%	2,586.20	33.75%
1880	10,577.40	1,214.30	11.48%	3,852.00	36.42%	1,162.20	10.99%	4,348.90	41.11%
1890	11,411.00	1,034.20	9.06%	5,493.00	48.14%	2,695.90	23.63%	2,187.90	19.17%
1895	14,685.00	784.3	5.34%	6,206.70	42.27%	4,132.70	28.14%	3,561.30	24.25%
1900	17,236.40	785.2	4.56%	5,661.00	32.84%	3,723.90	21.60%	7,057.30	40.94%
1905	19,051.80	475.8	2.50%	5,936.30	31.16%	7,037.30	36.94%	5,899.40	30.97%
1910	23,133.10	463.1	2.00%	8,195.30	35.43%	9,781.10	42.28%	4,693.60	20.29%
1915	23,587.00	472.6	2.00%	4,762.90	20.19%	14,051.60	59.57%	4,299.90	18.23%

---

① 顾国达,滨崎实,宇山满.近代(1842—1945 年)世界生丝市场的结构.浙江丝绸工学院学报.1993 年,第 10 卷,第 3 期,第 105 页.

England was the largest buyer of raw silk in the world before the 1870s. At that time, London was the most prosperous silk market in the world. As shown by the table above, the quantity of the importation of the silk of England rose from 1,761,300 kilograms in 1840 to 3,673,900 kilograms in 1860, which is a durable growth during the 20 years; What is impressive is that during this period, the quantity of the importation of silk into England is even higher than the totality of those of France and the United States.

Table II-4 Proportions of silks of different countries on the London market. (percentage) [1]

Years	Italy	Europe(except Italie)	Japan	China	India	Middle East
1815—1819	42.3			12.6	45.1	
1820—1824	47			11.7	32.5	8.8
1825—1829	50.9			9.7	28.4	11
1830—1834	36.6			22.2	29.7	11.4
1835—1839	29.6			26.3	30	14
1840—1844	38.8			8.8	33.1	19.2
1845—1849	24.1			43.1	25.7	7.1
1850—1854	13.7			50.6	24.6	11.2
1855—1859	6.6			73.5	17.1	2.7
1860—1864	4.7		19.1	60	11.9	4.3
1865—1869	5		18.2	58.3	16.8	1.7
1870—1874	6.1		15.3	68.4	9.4	0.8
1875—1879	6.1		19.8	70	3.7	0.5
1880—1884	9.5		16.6	71.4	2.2	0.3
1885—1889	1.8	20.7	5.4	61.7	3.2	0.5
1890—1894	2.2	29.5	5.8	49	8.6	1
1895—1899	1.3	49.7	1.8	34.5	10	0.3
1900—1904	4.3	46.7	2.7	32.9	13	0.3
1905—1908	17	21.2	2	35.4	12.3	1.5
1909—1913	15.8	12.9	4.9	43.3	3	2.2

[1] G.Federico. An Economic History of the silk Industry, 1830—1930. Cambridge. Cambridge University Press. 1997. pp.214—215.

70

We could know the main countries of supply to the London silk market throughout the 19th century by Table II-4. Italian silk and Indian silk dominated the London market until the early 1840s, which account for 70%—90% of all silk imported into London at the time. After the opening of China, Chinese silk replaced them as the greatest provider of silk material in London, which shared 50%—70% of the London silk market. Although this proportion droped to 30%—50% after the 1890s, Chinese silk still retained an advantage in the London market compared to the silks of other countries, and this advantage continued until the First World War. Despite the prosperity of the export of Japanese silk to the world market at the end of the 19th century, it still occupied only a small proportion in the London market: 2%—6% after the 1890s.

Despite the prosperity of sericulture during the first half of the 19th century in France, the growth of silk production still did not satisfy the demand of the silk textile industry. The import of raw silk in France rose from 22,975 kilograms in 1815 to 198,636 kilograms in 1832[1], to 1,095,000 kilograms in 1850. The disease of silkworms in Europe since 1856 aggravated the deficiency of silk materials in France. French sericulture never recovered during the second half of the 19th century (we will explain in another section). The quantity of imports of raw silk in France is multiplied by 7.5 from 1850 to 1910, increasing from 1,095,000 kilograms to 8,195,300 kilograms[2]. With the strong growth, France, having replaced England, holds the lead among all silk importers on the international market during the second half of the 19th century. She often bought more than three tenths of the silks offered for sale in the world market at that period. In 1892, in the 12,550,000 kilograms of silk delivered to the global market, Lyons brought in 6,000,000 kilograms, or 47.81% of the total[3](We will discuss the details of the increase in demand and progression the production of silk textiles from France in another section).

Table II-5 shows the main suppliers of silk to the French market. According to this table, more than half of the silk materials used by the French textile industry are offered by the French local market before the explosion of the pebrine. The Italian states are also important suppliers for the French at the time, occupying about 25%—30% of the silk import of France[4]. A large quantity of the Chinese were transported to the silks of Ly-

---

① Archives Nationales de France. F12. 2552. Commerce spéciale de soie, résumé de 1815 à 1832.

② 顾国达,滨崎实,宇山满.近代(1842—1945 年)世界生丝市场的结构.浙江丝绸工学院学报.1993 年,第 10 卷,第 3 期,第 103 页.

③ N.Rondot. L'industrie de la soie en France. Lyon. Imprimerie Mougin-Rusand. 1894. pp. 14—15.

④ Archives Nationales de France. F12. 2552. Des soies importées en 1832.

onss by London from 1850 to 1875 (we will clarify the role of London in the exchange of silk between China and France in another chapter) and by the direct maritime line between Canton, Shanghai, Hongkong and Marseille since the 1860s. From the late 1850s to the First World War, China offered about 30%—40% of the silk used by the textile industry in France. Japanese silk also occupied a proportion of the French market, which rose from two percent in the 1860s to about ten percent on the eve of the First World War.

Table II-5 Proportions of silks of different countries on the French market (percentage) [1]

Years	Italy	Japan	China	Middle-East	India	England	France
1831—1840	34.8		0.1	4.0	0.2	2.1	57.5
1841—1845	26.6			8.7		2.8	59.9
1846—1852	25.3			9.0		5.3	60.6
1853—1855	30.2			9.4		16.4	50.7
1854—1858	30.0			10.8		33.8	25.8
1859—1863	20.0		0.8	10.6	0.1	42.1	23.0
1864—1868	19.4	2.5	4.6	8.1	1.8	25.4	29.3
1869—1873	27.3	4.3	11.1	5.8	1.8	20.6	23.4
1874—1878	27.4	5.3	23.7	4.8	2.1	9.9	19.8
1879—1883	27.3	8.3	27.7	4.4	1.5	4.7	20.1
1884—1888	24.1	10.0	30.0	7.1	1.4	2.3	19.9
1889—1893	12.3	17.7	36.5	9.0	1.2	1.1	17.9
1894—1898	11.5	16.1	37.6	9.9	1.5	0.1	20.5
1899—1903	9.5	9.1	46.0	9.9	3.0		18.9
1904—1908	11.9	8.3	39.3	10.6	9.6		18.4
1909—1913	10.0	15.5	41.0	9.0	5.5		16.3

The United States silk industry developed from the beginning of the second half of the 19th century, but its rise did not date until after the 1890s. In 1860, the value of A-

---

[1] G.Federico. An Economic History of the silk Industry, 1830—1930. Cambridge. Cambridge University Press. 1997.pp.214—215.

merican silks was only 6,600,000 dollars (33 million francs)[1]. To protect the local silk textile industry from the foreign competitor, the US government imposed a 50% duty on all foreign silks since the late 1880s[2]. In 1890, the United States was able to produce a value of 250 million francs of silk[3].

By producing 624 million francs of silk, the American silk industry exceeded the French manufacture in 1904, and this value rose to 904 million francs in 1914. The number of looms in the United States rose from 5,044 in 1890 to 73,504 in 1904 and to 87,215 in 1914[4]. The expansion of silk production led to the growth of imports of raw silk into the United States. The quantity of silks supplied by the foreigner rose from 135,100 kilograms in 1860 to 14,051,600 kilograms 1915, which means an increase of 104 times in 55 years. At the end of the eve of the war, silk imported to United States occupied almost 60% of the silk traded in the global market[5].

China was the largest supplier of silk to the United States until 1878. Due to the mismatch of Chinesemanual silk with mechanical weaving in the United States, Japanese silk took the place of Chinese silk and dominates the American market at the beginning of the years 1880. Italian silk also holds a small proportion in this country.

Table II-6 Proportion of silk consumed in the United States (percent)[6]

Years	Italy	Japan	China	France	Europe
1869—1873		2.9	89.9		7.3
1874—1878		12.1	79.4		8.5
1879—1883		34.5	47.7		17.5
1884—1888		44.8	26.2		28.2
1894—1898	16.7	50.0	27.2	4.0	
1899—1903	20.7	46.7	26.3	3.7	

① 张迪恩.外国洋行垄断生丝输出对上海地区丝厂业的影响 1894—1937.中国经济史研究.1986 年第 1 期,第 116 页.

② G.R.Hawke. The United States Tariff and protection in the late nineteenth century. Econominc history review. 1988.No°28. p.90.

③ A. De la Berge.Les industries de la soie en France. Revue des Deux Mondes. Tome 101. 1890. p.91.

④ F.R.Mason. The American silk industry and the tariff. Cambridge MA. American Economic Association. 1910. p.38.

⑤ S.Matsui. The history of the silk industry in the United States. New York. Howes. 1930. p.105.

⑥ C.Federico. An Economic History of the silk Industry, 1830—1930. Cambridge. Cambridge University Press. 1997.p.214.

（续表）

| 1904—1908 | 22.2 | 53.7 | 19.1 | 3.4 | |
| 1909—1913 | 12.5 | 63.4 | 21.6 | 1.4 | |

3. The exchange of silk between France and China: one of the most dynamic-business in the world silk market

During the 19th century, most of the silk trade of the world took place in the seven most important markets: Milan, Shanghai and Canton[1], Yokohama, London, Lyonss and New York. The biggest silk markets in the world are distributed to the six countries: Italy, China, Japan, England, France and the United States, the top three of which are the main suppliers, and the last three play the role of the major buyers.

Table II-7 Quantity of silk traded in the world's major markets (1,000 kilograms)[2]

Years	London	Lyons	New-York	Milan	Shanghai	Canton	Yokohama
1820	1,200	445					
1865	2,850	2,900	200	1,650		1950	700
1895	1,000	6,250	3,300	6,300	3,980	1,500	3050
1910	950	7,950	9,100	9,850	5,450	2,200	8,550

Among the three major suppliers of raw silk, the proportion of silk in Italy shows a declining trend in the world's major silk import markets (London, Lyonss and New York) throughout the 19th century ; On the other hand, the silk market occupancy rate of the Chinese silk increases permanently in the markets of the three importers, and finally dominates these three markets until the end of the 19th century; The Japanese silk replaces the role of Chinese silk only at the beginning of the 20th century. Therefore, it is no exaggeration to say that China plays the essential role for the supply of silky material to the world market during the 19th century. Among the three major importers of raw silk, England plays an intermediary role between largest buyers (France and the United States) and largest sellers (Italy and China), and its quantity of silk import dechines very markedly after the 1870s; France, as the world's largest exporter of silk fabrics,

---

[1]　Among these cities, Hongkong was not written because Hong Kong is only a stopover for Cantonese silk.

[2]　G.Federico. An Economic History of the silk Industry, 1830—1930. Cambridge. Cambridge University Press. 1997.p.153.

74

also becomes the world's largest importer of silk from the 1850s; its place is not surpassed by the United States until the beginning of the 20th century. So France is the most important importer of silk in the world of 19th century. What we will describe in this book is the history of the silk trade between the most important exporter (China) and the largest buyer (France) of silk in the world during the 19th century, making a very important part of the world silk trade of that period. In addition, raw silk is a product with the most dynamic circulation in the world of the 19th century. Its producers and consumers are well separated: a considerable quantity of silk is produced in one country to export to foreign markets instead of for local consumption; the buyer countries are obliged to import it instead of the product by itself. So the flow of silk between its largest exporter and its biggest importer is an impeccable entry point to observe the economic integration of the world at that period.

II Silk trade between France and China before 1914

In the last section, we have specified the important roles of France in the world silk market of the 19th century. In this section we will demonstrate the evolution of the silk trade of the two countries above, which play very important roles in the world silk market. We will discuss the beginning date of the exchange of silk between the two countries, confirm the era when this trade begins to flourish, and specify the quantities or values of trade until the eve of the First World War. Changes in the political or economic context in both countries will also be briefly presented, which will help us to identify the key elements shaping the development of trade.

At the level of the bibliography, the majority of the data to be cited will come from the National Archives, Commercial Annals and Commercial Bulletins in France and in China. We have also consulted some statistics in the books already published, such as "The Chronicles of the East India Company" by H.B. Morse[1], "Histoire de la concession française de Shanghai" by Maybon and J.Fredet[2], "France and the exploitation of China 1885—1891" by R.Lee[3], "Commerce de la France avec la Chine" of N.Ron-

---

[1] H.B.Morse. The chronicles of the East India Company. Guangzhou. Editions de l'Université de ZhongShan. 1991.

[2] Ch.-B. Maybon, J.Fredet, Histoire de la concession française de Shanghai, Paris. Librairie Plon. 1929.

[3] R.Lee: France and the exploitation of China 1885—1901. A study in Economic Imperialism. Hong-Kong: Oxford University press, 1989.

dot[1], "les relations entre Lyons et la Chine au XIXe siècle" by E.Hamaide, [2] "l' industrie de la soie en France et en Chine de la fin du XVIIIe au début du XXe siècle" by Mau Chuan-Hui[3], "les relations de Lyons avec la Chine" by TCHENG Tse-sio[4] and "Lyons et le commerce de la soie" by L.Gueneauetc[5].

1. Unstable business connection

When did the silk trade between France and China begin? E. Hamaide wrote in his thesis the relationship between Lyons and China in the nineteenth century that "Rémi would indeed have been the first to make a test of direct shipment of Chinese silk bullets to Marseille"[6]. The author asserts that "the first expedition" of Chinese silk in France was made by Pierre Dominique Rémi, a French merchant in Shanghai in 1852. In fact, the Chinese silk import to France existed already long before that date. According to HBMorse's *The Chronicles of the East India Company to China* 1635—1834, two French ships left Canton for France with 250 piculs of raw silk in 1741, which is the departure of the silk trade between France and China[7]. The sources of Morse come from the archives of the East India Company, so the date proposed by it is rather reliable. Since no transactions were found earlier than this one, we determinate that the first exchange of silk between the two countries took place in 1741. During the rest of the 18th century, the silk was transported intermittently from China in France, but the quantity of trade is scarcely increased.

---

① N.Rondot. Chambre de commerce de Lyon. Commerce de la France avec la Chine. Délibération prise sur le rapport de M.Rondot. Séance du 12 janvier 1860.

② E.Hamaide. La relation entre Lyon et Chine au XIXe siècle, thèse pour obtenir le grade de docteur de l'université Lumière Lyon 2. 1999.

③ Mau Chuan-Hui. L'industrie de la soie en France et en Chine de la fin du XVIIIe au début du XXe siècle: échanges technologiques, stylistiques et commerciaux. Paris. EHESS. 2002. 2 Vol.

④ Tcheng Tse-sio. Les relations de Lyon avec la Chine. Thèse soutenue devant la Faculté des lettres de l'Université de Lyons. Paris. Librairie L. Rodstein. 1936.

⑤ L.Gueneau. Lyon et le commerce de la soie. Thèse soutenu devant la Faculté de droit de l'Université de Lyon. Lyon. Imprimerie L.Bascou. 1923.

⑥ E.Hamaide. La relation entre Lyon et Chine au XIXe siècle, thèse pour obtenir le grade de docteur de l'université Lumière Lyon 2. 1999. 2.3. L'Arrivée des premiers négociants en Chine et les débuts du marché lyonnais des soies.

⑦ H.B.Morse. The chronicles of the East India Company. Guangzhou. Editions de l'Université de ZhongShan. 1991. p.283. 1 picul ≈ 60 kilogrammes.

76

Table II-8 Quantity of silk exported from China to France during the eighteenth century (piculs) [1]

Years	Quantity	Years	Quantity	Years	Quantity
1741	15,000	1779	9,240	1788	4,380
1750	12,000	1780	2,280	1789	7,080
1775	16,260	1782	12,660	1790	7,200
1776	34,560	1784	7,020	1791	5,050
1777	24,480	1785	25,380	1792	3,360
1778	23,400	1786	4,260		

There are no statistics on the exchange of silk between France and China after the year 1792, so it is estimated that the importation of Chinese silk into France is completely interrupted during the Great Revolution and the First Empire. According to the archives of the French Ministry of Commerce and Agriculture, the Franco-Chinese trade recovered only after the 1830s. Even after the 1830s, the quantity of trade is still rather limited. From 1830 to 1836, a total of 6,700 kilograms of Chinese silk was imported into France, or 957 kilograms per year. Of the seven years from 1830 to 1836, the quantity of the transaction of the year 1832 is the most remarkable: 3,016 kilograms of Chinese silk are transported to France. This quantity is negligible compared to that of English firms. In 1832, 399,060 kilograms of Chinese silk were imported into the United Kingdom, which is 130 times the quantity of silk transported in France[2].

The raw silk does not appear in the lists of articles exchanged between France and China until 1845, the year following the signing of Huangpu. According to the statistics of the French Agriculture and Trade Ministry, during the year 1845, there are 494 kilograms of Chinese raw silk which is transported by the French ships in France[3]. The silk trade between the two countries was suspended again in 1846, and was not recovered until the sending of 85 bales of Chinese silk from Shanghai to Lyons by Company of Rémi in 1852.

① H.B.Morse. The chronicles of the East India Company. Guangzhou. Editions de l'Université de ZhongShan. 1991. Les statistiques annuelles du commerce entre la Chine et l'étranger.

② Archives Nationales de France. F12. 2552. Des soies importées en 1832.

③ Ministère de l'agriculture et du commerce, Documents sur le commerce extérieur, Chine et Indochine, Fait commerciaux n°11, p. 15.

2. Expansion of Chinese silk in France

It was at the year 1852 that the French merchants began to import Chinese silk directly and regularly to France. In the work of Ch. Maybon and J.Fredet, we read that Pierre Dominique Rémi, French merchant in Shanghai (who is the son-in-law of Charles de Montigny, the first French consul in Shanghai and at the same time the adoptive father of Benedict Edan, Shanghai) sent 85 bales[1] of Chinese silk to Lyons with the help of the Consul De Montigny in 1852[2]. This is the beginning of the sustainable growth of the silk trade between France and China. However, there is a different opinion on the amount of these silks sent from Shanghai. According to the thesis of J.F.Laffey, the Lyons delegate in China, Lyons received only 52 bales of silk (instead of 85 bales) from China in 1852[3]. This point of view was adopted by Robert Lee in his book *France and the Exploitation of China* 1885—1901, "in 1852, Lyons bought 52 bales from China[4]." The reliability of two opinions cannot be judged by official statistics or correspondence or correspondence, because the information about this is very limited. We did not find the information of the Chinese silk expedition to France in 1852 neither in the statistics of the French Customs nor in that of the Chinese Customs. M. de Montigny has not mentioned it neither in his correspondence with the Ministry of Foreign Affairs. The different figures we have found today are from the memories or reports of other consuls or delegates. Nevertheless, we affirm that the "85" is more reliable than the other in this book, because: the figure of "85" offered by Ch. Maybon and J.Fredet is quoted from a report of March 31, 1881 made by Mr. Millot, who is formerly responsible for the municipal council of the concession of Shanghai. At that time, Millot is possible to access the archives in the city council, which are partly lost today. This means that the information he gives us in his report is possible to be more reliable. The reliability of the quantity offered by Millot is confirmed a report by Natalis Rondot. In the author's report to the Lyonss Commerce Chamber of January 12, 1860, he said that "in August 1852 I addressed my former colleague in the mission to China, M. de Montigny, Consul at Shanghai, and merchants that I had known during my stay in China, that M. de Montigny succeeded in deciding these merchants to send the consignment of the silks of China to Ly-

---

[1]　The 'bale' is not a weight unit, but a means of packing the bristles, so the weight of a ball is not certain. During the 19th century, a bale equals about 63 to 70 kilograms.

[2]　Ch.-B. Maybon, Jean Fredet, Histoire de la concession française de Shanghai, Paris. Librairie Plon. 1929. p. 215.

[3]　J.F.Laffey. French Imperialism and the Lyon Mission to China. Thèse soutenue à l'Université de Cornell. 1966.p.114.

[4]　R.Lee. France and the exploitation of China 1885—1891. p.21.

onss. These consignments were, in 1852, only eighty-five bales of silk from China[1]." As a former trade delegate of Mission Lagrené of 1844, a colleaguc and friend of the Montigny consul, Natalis Rondot is able to offer a more accurate statistic to the Lyons Commerce Chamber. Based on the reports of these two important French representatives in Shanghai, the quantity of "85 bales" is actually more accurate than the other.

Table II-9 Quantities and values of direct trade in silk between France and China (kilograms and francs)[2]

Years	Quantity	values	Years	Quanity	Values
1852	5,950				69,423,606
1855	192,000	527,000	1875	1,488,000	
1858	17,000		1876		132,735,905
1859	260,688		1877	1,236,576	83,687,972
1860	997	54,000	1878	1,602,912	
1862	3,452	19,000	1879	1,596,816	
1863	100,000	5,150,000	1880	2,073,024	93,193,000

---

[1]　N.Rondot. Chambre de commerce de Lyon. Commerce de la France avec la Chine. Délibération prise sur le rapport de M.Rondot. Séance du 12 janvier 1860. p.8.

[2]　5,950 kilogrammes in 1852 come from 85 bales of Silk dispatched by Rémi in 1852: 85 bales × 70 kilogrammes/bales = 5,950 kilogrammes. Datas in1855 come from Ministère de l'agriculture et du commerce, Document sur le commerce extérieur, Chine et Indochine, Fait commerciaux n°24. p. 21.Datas in 1858 come from N.Rondot. Conseil supérieur de l'agriculture, des manufactures et du commerce. Rapport sur l'industrie des soies et des soieries. Paris. Imprimerie impériale. 1861. p.18.Datas in 1859 come from Ministère de l'agriculture et du commerce, Document sur le commerce extérieur, Chine et Indochine, Fait commerciaux n°37. p. 28. Datas in 1860 come from Ministère de l'agriculture et du commerce, Document sur le commerce extérieur, Chine et Indochine, Fait commerciaux n°33. p. 19.Datas in 1862 and 1863 come from Ministère de l'agriculture et du commerce, Document sur le commerce extérieur, Chine et Indochine, Fait commerciaux n°36. p. 71—72.Datas in 1864 come from Ministère de l'agriculture et du commerce, Document sur le commerce extérieur, Chine et Indochine, Fait commerciaux n°36. p. 71.Datas in 1866,1867 et 1869 come from Ministère de l'agriculture et du commerce, Document sur le commerce extérieur, Chine et Indochine, Fait commerciaux n°45. pp. 115—118. Datas in1873 et 1874 come from Ministère de l'agriculture et du commerce, Document sur le commerce extérieur, Chine et Indochine, Fait commerciaux n°50. pp. 278—280. Datas in1875,1876 et 1877 come from Ministère de l'agriculture et du commerce, Document sur le commerce extérieur, Chine et Indochine, Fait commerciaux n°51. pp. 290—281, 314—317. Datas in 1882 come from Ministère de l'agriculture et du commerce, Document sur le commerce extérieur, Chine et Indochine, Fait commerciaux n°52. p. 14.Datas in1883,1884 come from Ministère de l'agriculture et du commerce, Document sur le commerce extérieur, Chine et Indochine, Fait commerciaux n°53. p. 10.Datas in1865,1880 et 1881 come from Archives Nationales. F12. 6498. Une comparaison des commerces Sino-Français et Sino-Anglais 1860—1882 .Datas in 1878, 1870 et 1885come from Archives Nationales. F12. 7058. Table of the comparation of Exportations of silk in China according to the statistiques of Chamber of Commerce in Shanghai.

（续表）

Years	Quantity	values	Years	Quanity	Values
1864	97,000	5,655,000	1881	1,352,688	89,906,000
1865		18,376,000	1882	2,636,993	79,217,942
1866	79,000	5,306,000	1883	2,735,108	73,208,263
1867	307,000	20,460,000	1884	2,452,108	72,960,897
1869		34,015,000	1885	1,609,176	
1873		45,586,086			

According to the data in Table II-9, it exists the regular silk trade between France and China since 1852. However, it should be noted that raw silk appeared only for three times in the French-Chinese trade lists from 1852 to 1859, which means that the importation of Chinese silk into France remains at the discovery stage throughout the 1850s. The export of Chinese silk to France began in the early 1860s. According to Table II-9, the silk exchange value between France and China increased from 54,000 francs to 34,015,000 francs from 1860 to 1869, multiplying by 630 times, which is a very impressive success.

Despite the absence of statistics on the exchange of silk between France and China from 1870 to 1872, it is estimated that the export of Chinese silk to France has decreased considerably during the War between France and Prussia. According to the description of E. Hamaide, "2/3 of the trades cease to function and stocks (silks) are moved to the South, to Switzerland or to London; the price of fabrics fell by 15% to 20%. After the explosion of the war, French exports of silk textiles fell by 77%, from 65 million francs to 15 million francs between the first and the third quarter of 1870. The exports to the English market fell 204 million francs in 1869 to 117 three years later".[1] However, with the restoration of the French silk industry after the war, the silk trade with China was resumed immediately in 1873, and the exchange value of this season (45,586,086 francs) is higher than that of every year before the war. The 1870s were completed by the prosperity of the silk trade between France and China. The value of the exchange of silk between the two countries is multiplied twice at the end of the period in comparison with that of 1873, which amounts to an average of 90,000,000 francs.

It's also remarkable that in 1875, having passed England, France became the lar-

---

[1] E.Hamaide. La relation entre Lyon et Chine au XIXe siècle. 4.2. une décennie de crises.

gest buyer of Chinese silk among the western countries. Among the 70,000 bales of silk exported from China in 1875, 31,000 bullets are sent directly to France, while England receives only 27,000 bales[1]. In Shanghai, in the 30,973 bales shipped from June 1 to September 18, 1875, 15,950 bales are for Marseille, 9,883 bales are for London, 2,625 bales are for Italy and Switzerland, 1,962 bales are for the United States, 476 Bales for Hongkong and 76 bales for Bombay[2]. In 1875, the quantity of Chinese silk imports into France has never been exceeded by other countries, and France has always kept the first rank by the buyers of Chinese silk until the beginning of the 20th century.

Table II-10 Export of Chinese silks from Shanghai to France and to England, 1873—1876 (bales)[3]

Years	England	France
1873	25,304	9,683
1874	26,337	22,497
1875	16,206	22,627
1876	31,000	33,000

The growth of the silk trade between France and China continued until the eve of the Franco-Chinese war (23 June 1884—13 May 1885). According to Table II-9, the quantity of silk imported from China to France rose from 1,488,000 kilograms to 2452,108 kilograms from 1875 to 1884. During the war, French commercial vessels were prohibited from entering or leaving Chinese ports[4]. The Franco-Chinese exchange is never interrupted because of this war, because there are foreign silk firms and shipping companies in Shanghai or Canton who import Chinese silks to Lyons. However the increase of the quantity of silk trade between the two countries was slowed down during the war: in 1885, their quantity of silk trade fell to 1,609,176 kilograms.

---

[1] Ministère de l'agriculture et du commerce, Document sur le commerce extérieur, Chine et Indochine, Fait commerciaux n°51. pp. 290—291.

[2] Ministère de l'agriculture et du commerce, Document sur le commerce extérieur, Chine et Indochine, Fait commerciaux n°50. p 259.

[3] Archives Nationales de France. F12. 7058. 31, janvier 1876, lettre du Ministère des Affaires Etrangère au Ministère du commerce. Exportation des soies chinoises.

[4] Archives Nationales de France. F12. 7058. la navigation française à Shanghai pendant le 4ème trimestre 1884.

3. Summit and stagnation

After the Franco-Chinese war, the amount of silk exchange quickly rose to the pre-war level. According to Table II−11, the quantity of imports of Chinese silk into France amounts to 35,083 bales (about 2,631,225 kilograms) in 1886, while this quantity continues to increase until the exchange of centuries. Having ascended from thirty thousand bales to a maximum of 45 miles of bales, the Chinese raw silk transported to France is multiplied by about 1.5 times from 1886 to 1903.

Table II−11 Chinese silk quantity imports to France, 1886—1903 (including Hong Kong)[1]

Years	Quantity	Years	Quantity	Years	Quantity
1886	2,631,225	1892	2,504,325	1898	3,402,075
1887	2,439,675	1893	2,902,650	1899	4,288,275
1888	2,409,075	1894	2,700,600	1900	3,343,275
1889	2,155,625	1895	2,818,500	1901	3,443,175
1890	2,071,800	1896	2,906,775	1902	3,778,650
1891	2,156,925	1897	2,477,075	1903	3,434,625

However, it's hardly related this growth in the quantity of silk trade between France and China to the occupation of Indochina. It has already been said in the preceding chapter that, one of the principal aims of conquering Indochina of the government of the Republic is to exploit resources of southwestern China and to develop trade with that region. In fact, they have also realized the possibility of exporting Chinese silk through the border between Indochina and southwest China, because Sichuan Province, which is also one of the main production regions of Chinese silk, situate just in this region. In the letter of June 25, 1886, the Minister of Foreign Affairs remarked to the Minister of Trade that Sichuan Province is "one of the richest in China, and its principal products are white silk and yellow silk", and at the same time proposes to him to open the trade of silk by Indochina[2]. J.F.Klein's research also asserts also that "at the heart of this imperial strategy of the Silkworms, the port of Hai Phong becomes a major stake, a

---

[1] 1890 à 1899 ﹕Archives du Ministère des Affaires Etrangères. NS563. pp.63—64. 1903 ﹕Archives du Ministère des Affaires Etrangères. 148CPCOM564.pp.131—135.

[2] Archives Nationales de France. F12. 7057. 25 juin 1886. lettre du ministre des affaires étrangères au ministre du commerce et de l'agriculture.

place where croiss the network of capital and the networks of business man, which knew nothing of the subtleties of the particular commercial trade of the Sea of China[1]. However, the data in the archives shows us that the business of silk in southwestern China does not developed so favorably as the expectations of the French government. On the statistics of the Customs of Longchamp, silk appeared in the list of articles only after the year 1900: the quantity of exports was only 119 piculs[2], A Sse-mao, the trade of Silk is also not very important. Only one picul was exported in 1899[3]and 12 piculs in 1901[4]. Three French companies moved to Mongtze in 1903. One serves as the agency of the Compagnie Lyonsnaise d'Indochine, but it does not occupy the silk trade, while the other two are for the railway works[5]. On the seaway, as highlighted in the previous chapter, the importance of Haiphong in the silk trade in Southeast Asia is very modest compared to Hong Kong, and very few French ships arrive in Haiphong after the French occupation.

With the support of boxers[6] who attacked foreign legations in Beijing, the Empress Cixi (慈禧太后) declared war on the eleven Western powers on 20 June 1900 (England, France, Germany, Italy, Japan, Russia, United States , Austria-Hungary, Spain, Belgium and the Netherlands), which led to the military attack of the alliance of powers against the Qing court in Beijing. The war lasted until the end of 1900. During this conflict, the Queen of Cixi fled from Beijing to Xian (西安) with Emperor Guangxu (光绪帝) and Chinese capital was occupied by the armies of alliance. This conflict ends with the victory of the alliance armies and the signing of the Treaty of Xinchou (《辛丑条约》)[7].

What is remarkable is that there is not decline in Franco-Chinese silk trade during the conflict. According to the data in Table II-11, the quantity of the silk trade floats securely 40—50 thousand bales in 1900 and 1901. In fact, the export of Chinese silk escapes from the ravages of the 1900—1901 war by the consciences of the "mercantil-

---

① J.F.Klein. Une histoire impériale connectée? Hai Phong : jalon d'une statégie lyonnaise en Asie orientale (1881—1886). Recherche en Sciences Sociales de l'Asie sur Sud-Est, N°13—14. 2009. p.55.

② Archives Nationales de France. F12. 7057. 12 janvier 1901. rapport de commerce de Long Tcéou en 1900.

③ Archives Nationales de France. F12. 7057. 20 avril 1899. rapport du commerce de Ssê-mao en 1898.

④ Archives Nationales de France. F12. 7057. 27 avril 1903. rapport du commerce de Ssê-mao en 1901 et 1902.

⑤ Archives Nationales de France. F12. 7057. 29 octobre 1903. maisons de commerce française établies à Mongtze.

⑥ L'organisation des paysans des provinces de Shandong(山东) et de Zhili(直隶) avec le but d'aider le gouvernement à résister l'invasion des étrangers.

⑦ About of the crisis in 1900, MABIRE Jean. L'Eté rouge de Pékin. La révolte des boxeurs récit. Paris. Editions du Rocher. 2006.

ism" of the Chinese mandarins of south—east China. At the beginning of the conflagration, the central administration of the Qing Empire ordered local governments to resist the foreigner's invasion at all costs with the help of boxers. Considering that this war with eleven powers can lead the ruin of the empire, or at least may lead to a severe declination of Chinese economy, trade and finance, the Vice-kings, governors of provinces in south-east China refused to obey the order of the Qing court. They signed a "Mutual Protection Rule of South East China" (《东南互保章程》) with consuls of the belligerent countries in Shanghai on 26 June 1900 (six days after the declaration of war). The Rule lays down the principle of peace between Chinese local governments and foreign armies in south-east China and specifies that they will protect together the security of Shanghai and the southeastern territories of China during the war[1]. The signing of this rule limits the war in northern China (mainly in Tianjin and Beijing), which ensures the silk trade between China and foreign countries. On the one hand, it protects the main production areas of Chinese silk (Jiangsu, Zhejiang and Guangdong) from the ravages of war; On the other hand, the exchange and transport of Chinese silk can also be continued thanks to the security of the ports of Shanghai and Canton.

Table II-12 Quantity of exports of Chinese silk to France, 1904—1914 (bullets, excluding Hong Kong)[2]

Years	Quantity	Years	Quantity
1904	34,607	1910	34,794
1905	23,282	1911	35,612
1906	29,945	1912	37,872
1907	31,409	1913	33,712
1908	37,173	1914	18,157
1909	35,964		

The growth of the silk trade between France and China stagnated in the last decade before the First World War. According to the data in Table II-12, the quantity of exchange (silks transferred by Hong Kong excluded) flew from 30,000 to 40,000 silk bales at the time.

---

[1] Pour les détails, consultez Li Xisheng. La crise de 1900. Shanghai. Librairie de Shanghai. 1982.
[2] 中国第二历史档案馆,中国海关总署办公厅.中国旧海关史料.第39—66卷.

Table II-13 Evolution of exports of Chinese silk to France (1844—1914, kilograms)

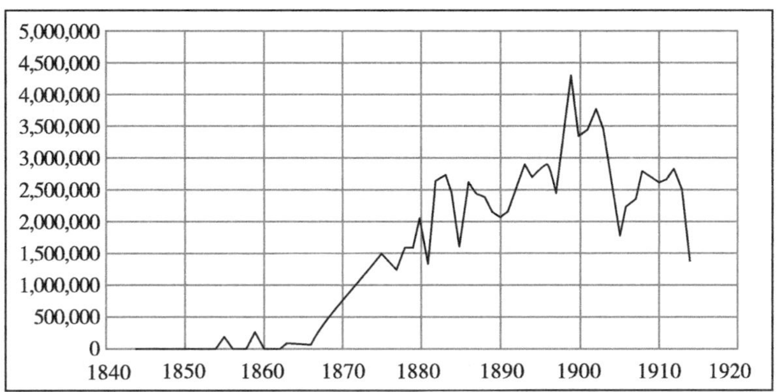

In conclusion, as shown in Table II-13, the volume of silk trade between France and China is very rare before the 1850s, becomes regular after 1852, and rapidly increased from 1860 to 1885, prospered from 1886 to 1903 and stagnated after 1904. How do we explain these dynamics? In *Globalization and History*, K.H.O'Rourke and J.G. Williamson argue that there are four basic factors that accelerated the integration of the Atlantic economy during the 19th century: Low transport costs, low tariff barriers, techniqueal progress and historical events[1]. The economic relationship between Europe and Asia is very different from that between Europe and North America, in terms of the type of goods traded, the transport distance, the techniqueal gap between the countries of exchange and the political relationship between the countries of exchange, etc. Is the thesis of the two authors capable of explaining the case of Euro-Asian trade? We will analyze this issue in the following sections and chapters.

III Growth in demand for silk manufacturers: the prosperity of the silk textile industry and the sericulture crisis in France

Europe's foreign trade shows a very strong growth trend during the 19th century. From 1815 to 1915, the average of the growth rate of the volume of exports of all the Eu-

---

[1]　K.H.O'Rourke et J.G.Williamson. Globalization and History. The Evolution of a Nineteenth-Century Athlantic Economy. Cambridge. Massachussetts. London. The MIT Press. 1999. p.29—30.

ropean countries reached 4.075% per year[1].

Among all European countries, the growth of foreign trade in France is quite remarkable, the average annual growth rate of which is even higher than the European average of 4.683%[2]. Thanks to the prosperity of foreign trade, the rate of openness of the French economy is becoming increasingly high. Exported goods made up only 6.2% of the national product of France in 1846, but this index reached 20.6% in 1875[3], an increase of more than 3 times for 30 years. In the 19th century foreign trade, the performance of the silk textile industry is the most remarkable. Until the 1870s, the value of silk exports still accounted for about 30% of France's total export value, while its export rate, which is the highest among all industrial the last decades of the 19th century.

In this section we will examine how changes of the demand of the French silk textile industry influence the evolution of the silk trade between France and China in the 19th century. Many publications, "les industries de la soie en France" of A. de la Berge[4], "l'industrie de la soie de France à Valée du Rhône" by P. Clerget[5], "l'Économie française au XIXe siècle" by M. Levy-Leboyer and F. Bourguignon[6], "la soie, art et histoire of H.Algoud et la relation entre Lyons et Chine au XIX siècle" of E.Hamaide[7], "la Révolution industrielle" by P.Verley[8] have already described the scale of silk production in France on the number of looms and the quantity (and value) of production.

In consulting their data, we will, firstly, describe quantitatively the growth of silk production in France in the 19th century, which is the foundation of the increase in the demand for silk materials in France.

Secondly, we will explain why the silk textile industry in France is capable to maintaining such a growth trend during the 19th century, especially before the 1870s. In the text, we will link the growth of production of French silks textiles to its export. In the end, we will analyze why the local sericulture cannot satisfy the demand of the silk tex-

---

① B.R.Mitchell. International Historical Statistics, Europe 1750—2000. London. Press Palgrave Macmillan. 2001. p.67.

② Idem. p. 221.

③ LEVY-LEBOYER Maurice. BOURGUIGNON François. L'Economie Française au XIX siècle. Analyse macro-économique. Paris. Economica. 1986. p.21.

④ A. De la Berge. Les industries de la soie en France. Revue des Deux Mondes. Tome 101. 1890.

⑤ P.Clerget. Les industries de la soie dans la vallée du Rhône. Les Etudes rhodaniennes. Vol 5. No°1. 1929.

⑥ M.Levy-Leboyer et F.Bourguignon. L'Economie Française au XIXe siècle, Analyse macro-économique. Paris. Economica. 1985.

⑦ E.Hamaide. La relation entre Lyon et Chine au XIXe siècle, thèse pour obtenir le grade de docteur de l'université Lumière Lyon 2. 1999.

⑧ P. Verley. La revolution industrielle. Paris. Gallimard. 2005

tile industry of France. The previous works on this subject, for example, la soie, c'est de l'or of S.Lamb[1], often underline the effects of diseases of silkworms, but why the sericulture production of France remains very modest even after Louis Pasteur find the precaution against diseases? We will specify in this section what the diseases really changed, and the cause for the prolongation of the crisis French sericulture after the years 1870.

1. Prosperity of the silk industry in France

"Our silk industries are not only one of the glories of our laborious France. They support a considerable part of our population, nearly six hundred thousand workers, farmers, manufacturers, traders and artists."[2]These are the comments of Albert de la Berge when he revises the textile industry of French silk of the 19th century. Indeed, his praise to the French silk industry is not exaggerated.

The silk industry in France, which is concentrated in departments in the region of Rhône-Alpes, especially in the city of Lyons[3], has already enjoyed prestige during the 18th century. On the scale of production, there were already 11,000 looms that worked in France in 1768 and 18,000 in 1787, but this prosperity was interrupted by the French Revolution. The quantity of looms in France fell to 2,500 in 1794 and never exceeded 5,000 before 1800. Thanks to the efforts of the commissionaires, bankers and merchants[4], the restoration of the silk textile industry of Lyons began already during the Empire era. The quantity of the trades was 13,000 in 1811 and 14,500 in 1815. In 1819, the silk production of the Lyons exceeded the pre-Revolutionary level with the operation of 20,000 trades. The number of trades reached 30,000 in 1825, then increased to 40,000 in 1834, to 50,000 in 1848, and to 60,000 in 1854[5]. This trend of growth did not slow down during the second half of the century. There are 100,000 in France in

---

[1] S.Lamb. La soie, c'est de l'or. Lyon. Bureaux du courrrier de Lyon. 1856.

[2] A. de la Berge. Les industries de la soie en France. Revue des Deux Mondes. Tome 101. 1890. p.1.

[3] The manufacture of silks in France is rather concentrated before the years during the 19th century. Above all, before the year 1870, the City of Lyon represented 40%−80% (varied according to periods) of the silk production in France. However, we will specify in the following text that the peripheral departments of the Rhone department play a very important role during the mechanization course of the silk textile industry in France. Lyon manufacturers choose to install most of their new mechanical factories in the départements around Lyon, including Ain, Ardèche, Drôme, Isère, Loire, Saône-et-Loire, Rhône and Savoie. Nevertheless, it should be noted that, despite this development, 95% of silk production in France still concentrates in departments of the Rhone valley. There is very little silk production in other parts of France.

[4] M. Saint-Olive, M.Pernon, P. Cayez. L. Gueneau et M.Dutillieu sont les industriels célèbres parmi eux.

[5] E.Hamaide. La relation entre Lyon et Chine au XIX siècle. p.9.

1860[1], 120,000 in 1871[2], and 230,000 in 1889[3]. At the end of the 19th century, there was a sharp drop in the number of looms in France due to the diffusion of the mechanical looms: the number of looms fell to 86,681 in 1900 and again to 58,036 in 1914[4]. However, the production of silk textile in France did not come down with this fall, because of the improvement of the efficiency of the production of silk textile in France (we will talk about it later).

Graph II-14 Evolution of the number of looms in France 1768—1914[5]

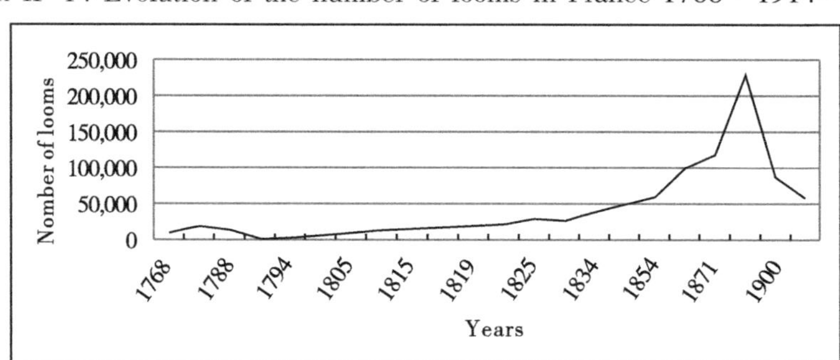

The value of French silk production showed a trend of growth until the year 1860. It rose from 100 million francs[6] to 144.5 million francs during 1825—1835[7], and then from 253.4 million francs to 640 million francs during 1840—1861[8]. Because of the fall of prices of silky products to the world market, a decrease of the production value of silk appears in France from the mid—1860s to the end of the 1880s. The average annual value fell to 461 million francs during 1867—1876[9] and then to 291 million francs during

---

<ol>
<li>H.Algoud. La soie, art et histoire. Paris. Payot. 1928. p.192.</li>
<li>N.Rondot. L'industrie de la soie en France. Lyon. Imprimerie Mougin-Rusand.1894. p.55.</li>
<li>A. de la Berge. Les industries de la soie en France. Revue des Deux Mondes. p. 11.</li>
<li>P.Clerget. L'industrie de la soie de France à Vallée du Rhône. Les Etudes rhodaniennes. Vol.5. N°1.1929. p.21.</li>
<li>Ce tableau est fait d'après les données cité dans le paragraphe au-dessus.</li>
<li>France implemented 'the gold franc' from 1803, whose value was defined at 0.33325 g of gold at 900/1000. This currency was used as a result by all French governments throughout the 19th century. The gold franc was not devalued until 1928, although it had been adopted as a common currency by several countries of the Latin Union from 1865 to 1927.</li>
<li>For the improvement and spread of the silk industry in France. Annale de la société séricicole. n°1. Paris. Imprimerie de Madame Huzard. 1837. p.48.</li>
<li>N.Rondot. Conseil supérieur de l'agriculture, des manufactures et du commerce. Rapport sur l'industrie des soies et des soieries.p.5.</li>
<li>M.Levy-levoyer et F. Bourguignon. L'Economie française au XIXe siècle. p.59.</li>
</ol>

1877—1886. The silk production in France dates back to the level of 600 million francs at the end of the 19th century, with a value of 660 million in 1890 and 620 million in 1894[1]. The strong changes in the value of silk production do not mean the decline of the textile industry of France during the second half of the 19th century. At the level of quantity, the production of silks in France reached 2,500,000 kilograms in 1853 (the year before the explosion of the pebrine). In 1900, the quantity of silks produced in France rose to 5,759,750 kilograms, which is 2.3 times the figure of 1853[2]. This growth implies that the silk textile industry in France is still in a phase of expansion during the second half of the year 19th century.

The success of the silk textile industry in France will be more evident if we compare the French production of silk with that of other countries. The Table II−15 show the production values of the major silk manufacturing countries in the world at the end of the 19th century. In 1890, France produced 42.22% of the silk textiles of the world's total production. What is more impressive is that this value of production is even higher than the total of those of the United States, Germany, England and Russia, which is the 2nd to 5th place in the production of silks textiles in the world. In 1894, the advantage of France was less obvious because of the rise of the silk textile industry in the United States, but its production value made up more than 30% of the production of silks in the world.

Table II − 15 Share of world silk production in 1890 and 1894 (millions of francs)[3]

Countries	1890	1894
France	660	620
United States	248	400
Germany	240	350
Swiss		132
England	65	90
Austria	60	75

---

① Archives Nationales de France. F12 6894 Chambre des députés cinquième législature session de 1891, n° 1354, le 21 mars 1891. Production des tissus de soie dans le monde 1890. p.16.

② R.Lee. France and the exploitation of China 1885—1901. p.23.

③ The account in 1890 come from Archives Nationales de France. F12 6894 Chambre des députés cinquième législature session de 1891, n°1354, le 21 mars 1891. Production des tissus de soie dans le monde 1890. p. 16.

（续表）

Countries	1890	1894
Russia	70	65
Italy	40	60
China		40.3
Japan		35.1
Spain et Portugal	30	20
India		6.4
Others	50	25
Total	1,563	1,918.80

2. Export market of French silk products

The spectacular performance of the silk textile industry in France stems largely from the prosperity of the export market for French silk fabrics. As a product with high quality and high price, French silk fabrics keep the highest opening rate among all products exported from France during most of the 19th century. According to the data in Table II-16, during 1827—1834, 66% of the silk textiles of France are produced for the foreign market. This proportion declined slightly in the middle of the century, and then rose to the level of 70%—80% after the 1860s.

Table II-16 French production sectors with opening rate exceeding 10% (percentage)[1]

Products	1827—1834	1834—1844	1845—1854	1855—1864	1865—1874	1875—1884
Silk products	66%	52%	40%	76%	81%	79%
Perfumery	35%	39%	41%	48%	43%	17%
Papers	27%	37%	43%	49%	39%	46%
ConttonProducts	15%	16%	16%	13%	11%	11%
Refined Sugar	8%	6%	9%	20%	30%	31%
Woolen products	7%	11%	16%	25%	35%	38%
Leathers	3%	2%	4%	6%	9%	11%

---

[1] P. Verley, l'Echelle du monde. p.587. Opening rate: the proportion of the export quantity of a product in its total production quantity in a country.

90

In term of absolute value, the export of silk fabrics kept often one of the top three places on the list of goods exported from France during most of the 19th century, just in front of or behind the wines or woolen textiles[1]. Its value of exportation increased from 115 million francs in 1827 to 138 million francs in 1847, to 460 million in 1856, and to 500 million in 1859[2], more than quadruple in thirty years. From 1860 to 1875 it varied between 400—500 million, and then went down to 200—300 million during the last two decades of the century because of the fall in prices. Before the First World War, exports of French silks returned to the level of the 1870s. Despite the devaluation, the quantity of French silk exports did not decline after the 1880s: it rose from 3,307,000 kilograms in 1879 to 4,169,000 kilograms in 1889, and then to 4,452,000 kilograms in 1890[3]. The export of the quantity of silks nevertheless maintained an annual rate of growth of 2%—5% during most of the second half of the 19th century.

Table II – 17 – A Importance of silks in French exports of manufactured goods, 1857—1913 (three-year average, millions of francs)[4]

Years	Textiles				Confec-tionff ashions, etc	Articles of Paris	Chimistry, drag, etc	Tool, Machine Automo-biles	Coal, Melting	Various	Total
	Silk	Wool	Cotton	Linen							
1858	438	179	69	17	92	131	38	64	3	310	1341
1873	444	365	80	45	134	244	112	145	41	522	2115
1886	225	392	113	20	114	169	90	120	17	518	1778
1899	262	272	164	30	216	223	151	170	58	736	2282
1912	347	289	386	45	382	386	413	484	120	1278	4130
Pourcentage											
1858	32.7	13.3	5.1	1.3	6.9	9.8	2.8	4.8	0.2	23.1	100.0
1873	21.0	16.8	3.8	2.1	6.3	11.5	5.3	6.9	1.9	24.4	100.0

[1] Archives Nationales de France. F12 6499. Bulletin de Statistique et de législation comparée. Paris. Imprimerie nationale. 1883. pp.384—385.

[2] N.Rondot. Conseil supérieur de l'agriculture, des manufactures et du commerce. Rapport sur l'industrie des soies et des soieries. Par MM. Natalis Rondot. Paris. Imprimerie Impérial. 1861. p. 5.

[3] Archives Nationales de France. F12 6894. Exportation des tissus de soie de France en 1890. p.70.

[4] M.Levy−Levoyer et F. Bourguignon. L'Economie française au XIXe siècle. Analyse macro-économique. p. 65.

（续表）

Years	Textiles				Confectionff ashions, etc	Articles of Paris	Chimistry, drag, etc	Tool, Machine Automobiles	Coal, Melting	Various	Total
	Silk	Wool	Cotton	Linen							
1912	8.4	7.0	9.4	1.1	9.3	9.3	10.0	11.7	2.9	31.0	100.0

Graph II-17-B The value of French exports of silks during the 19th century (millions of francs)

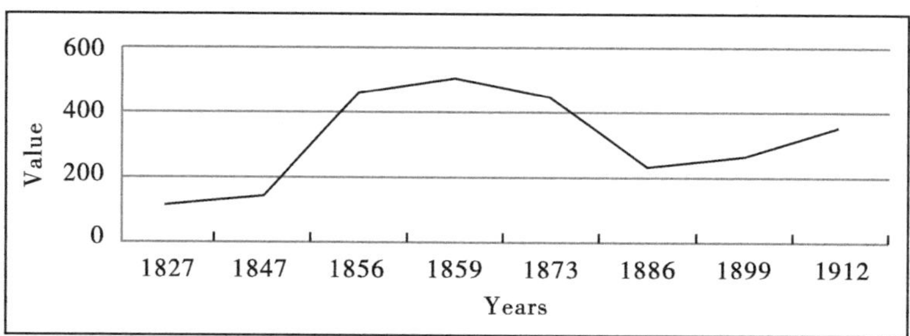

Table II-17-C Annual rate of growth of the export quantity of French silk

Périodes	Rate	Périodes	Rate
1851—1855	3.1%	1871—1875	2.3%
1856—1860	4.3%	1876—1880	3.7%
1861—1865	3.3%	1881—1885	2.4%
1866—1870	3.1%	1886—1890	1.0%

The silk textile industry in France is one of the industrial branches which, according to many historians, represents the perfect comparative advantage of France in the international competition of the 19th century economy. This point of view was first discussed in the debate at the end of the decade 1970, on different paths of industrialization of other countries with that of England[1]. Contesting the traditional historiography which emphasizes that the English model is the only way of industrialization, historians like R.Roehl, P. O'Brien, C.Keyder and L. Bergeon argue that France has followed its

[1] This traditional point of view is typically represented by W.W.Rostow In his book The Stages of Economic Growth: A Non-Communist Manifesto. Cambridge. Cambridge Université Press. 1960.

92

own path of "industrialization". Distinguished from the English model, which is based on coal, iron, cotton, and the factory, with a sharp increase in industries with a high capitalization ratio in a relatively short period of time, French industrialization is characterized by a specialization Based on their high-quality, elaborate products, which corresponds well to the "comparative advantage" of the French economy. According to their studies, the silk textile industry is one of the most typical industrial branches that manufacture high quality products with comparative advantage over those of England[1]. This idea of the comparative advantage of France on the branches of high qualities is extended by the more recent historical research on the specificity of the French economy of the modern period. For example, P. Verley writes in *la Révolution industrielle* that "French progress was by no means negligible. Of course, the strengths of French industry were not the same as those of British industry, less coal, non-ferrous metals, cotton textiles, but more woolen cloths and silk textiles"[2]. J.C.Asselin expresses the same opinion in *Histoire économique de la France du XVIIIe siècle à nos jours* : "France mainly imports from Great Britain elaborate products, coal, industrial semi-products, whereas in its exports to Great Britain, manufactured objects with high added value, silks, balanced almost agricultural products ... The delay of French industrialization is thus compensated, up to a certain bridge, by a favorable specialization, well directed by the comparative advantage of the French economy, and which allows it to benefit from a growing demand in the long term"[3]. More precisely, according to previous research, the comparative advantage of silk textile production in France is mainly reflected in the lower cost of labor, which is a very important determinant in H-O theory. P. Cayez made a comparison of the silk textile industries between France and England, and found that labor costs in Lyons were lower than those of England during the 19th century. In silk factories in England, labor costs often amount to 40%—50% on all production procedures (organsin, dyeing, warping, weaving, etc.), but only 20%—40% in Lyons[4]. Thanks to this advantage, the cost of production is lower in Lyons than in England.

Apart from comparative advantage, the specificity of high quality French silk is of-

---

① R.Roehl. French industrialisation: a reconsidération. Explorations in Economic History. No°3. 1976. P. O' Brien and C. Keyber. Economic Growth in Britain and France: two paths towards the 20th Century. London. G.Allen aud Unwin. 1978.L.Bergeon. L'Industrialisation de la France au XIXe siècle. Paris. Hatiers. 1979.

② P.Verley. La Révolution industrielle. Paris. Folio. 1997. p. 35.

③ J.C.Asselain. Histoire économique de la France du XVIIIe siècle à nos jours. Vol.1. De l'Ancien Régime à la première Guerre mondiale. p.156. p.207.

④ P.Cayez. Métiers Jacquard et hauts fourmeaux aux origines de l'industrie lyonnaise. Lyon. Presses Universitaires de Lyon. 1878. p.174.

ten considered by historians as another cause for the prosperity of their export. According to traditional theories of international trade (including comparative advantage), it is the different costs of commodities produced by different countries that lead to international trade flows. This idea is challenged by the new theories of international trade, which emphasizes the role of "product differentiation" on international trade. According to these new theories, the flows of international trade can also be brought about by the different qualities or different real characteristics of the products of different countries[1]. By using drawings made by qualified artists, the quality of French silk textiles, often defined as their artistic values, is considered higher than that of other countries. Having demonstrated an official report by an English delegate expressing an admiration for the superior quality of French silks, P. Cayez analyzes that "it is a qualitative aspect difficult to quantify which first struck the British inquiry: Art and industry since, at least in the field of fashion, textile work remained close to a craft industry. Technical training was provided by the Saint-Pierre School of Fine Arts. The courses were free and the manufacturers recruited the pupils on their way out, paying them 1,000 to 3,000 francs a year according to their talent. Drawers extinguished at the very source of fortune manufacturers. Maintaining the artisanal structure allowed the manufacturer a great deal of flexibility in the use of model designs."[2] P. Cayez's thesis is supported by more recent research. In the speech of Mayor of Lyons at the award ceremony of the school of drawing: "You give a new activity to our commerce by the taste, elegance, richness and variety of your drawings; You thus raise the celebrity, the brilliant brilliance of those fabrics which once made both worlds tributary to our industry", J. Rojon affirms that "The designers of the textiles thus occupy a central position in the artistic creation ... because their talent gives birth to the rich silk textiles that make the reputation of the Lyonsnais manufacturers."[3]

Certainly, as historians have shown, the relatively low cost of labor and the higher art value are two important factors that lead to the success of the French textile industry in international trade. Nevertheless, we must not neglect other elements that also favor the external export of French silk textiles, among which we will emphasize three other

---

[1] M. Rainelli. La nouvelle théorie du commerce international. Paris. La Découverte. 2003. pp.45—59.

[2] P. Cayez. Métiers Jacquard et hauts fourmeaux aux origines de l'industrie lyonnaise. Lyon. Presses Universitaires de Lyon. 1878.p.170.

[3] J. Rojon. Les soieries lyonnaises dans la seconde moitié du XIXe siècle et au début du XXe siècle : du produit artisanal de luxe au produit industriel de (demi-) luxe. in Pierre Lamard. Art & Industrie. Paris. Editions Picard. 2013. p. 123.

aspects.

First, it is possible that the general rise in purchasing power in all the countries of Europe and the United States during the 19th century allows the French silk industry to expand its international market.

During the 19th century, about 90% of the silk products exported by France were absorbed by the countries of Europe and the United States despite a change in the share between these countries. According to the data shown by P. Cayez, Germany buys about 60% of the exports of silk textiles from France on the eve of the Great Revolution, while the rest of such exports products are intended primarily for other European-continental countries. This situation began to change from the peace of 1815. With the rise of the Anglo-Saxon market, England and the United States gradually replaced the place of Germany during the first half of the 19th century. Until the middle of the 19th century, the latter two countries shared about 60% of exports of silk products. The proportion of absorption in the European-continental countries of the French silks reduced to 30% of the total. After 1860, the concentration of French silk consumption in the Anglo-Saxon countries was even higher than in the previous period. After the Cobden-Chevalier Treaty, England, which reduced 80% of the customs duty on French silk, is importing more and more silk products from France. Between 1874 and 1890, the English bought on average 45.29% of the export of French silks products, compared with 32.5% during the years 1850—1860[1]. On average 252,551,000 francs of French silks textiles were exported per annum between 1894 and 1898, and England bought 124,057,600 francs on average per year during these years, or 49.12% of French exports[2]. The United States, during this period, still occupies almost 30% of French silk exports during the last decades of the 19th century. Thus the distribution of European-continental countries, on the other hand, still drops to 10%—15% at the end of the 19th century.

Table II-18-A Import share of the French silk products in various countries[3]

	1789	1821	1838
Germany	59%	30%	8%
England	1.6%	3%	15%

① P.Cayez. Crise et croissance de l'idustrie lyonnaise 1850—1900. Paris. Editions du CNRS. 1980. pp.17—18.

② R.Lee. France and the exploitation of China 1885 —1901. p. 23.

③ P.Cayez. Métiers Jacquard et hauts fourmeaux aux origines de l'industrie lyonnaise. Lyon. Presses Universitaires de Lyon. 1878. p.37 and p.421.

（续表）

	1789	1821	1838
United States	8%	15%	25%
European continent (except Germany)	28.4%	37%	35%
Various	3%	15%	17%
Total	100%	100%	100%

Table II-18-B Values of exports of the French silk products in various countries in 1847 and 1859 (million francs)

Countries	1847		1859	
	Values	Proportions	values	Proportions
England	34	24.64%	163	32.60%
United States	48	34.78%	138	27.60%
Germany, Belgium and Russia	28	20.29%	89	17.80%
States of Italy	10	7.24%	21	4.20%
Spain	7	5.07%	21	4.20%
American States	11	7.97%	40	8.00%
Others	0	0%	28	5.60%
Total	138	100%	500	100%

The increase in the purchasing power of the peoples in the above countries during the 19th century promoted the export of the French silks to the foreign market. According to OECD statistics[1] (see Table and Graph below) , at the beginning of the 19th century, the per capita GDP of Europe and the United States were already much higher than other regions of the world: once more than in China during the same period. During the next century, Europe's GDP per capita rose from 1,245 dollars to 3,380 dollars, and that of the United States from 1,257 dollars to 4,964 dollars, a prospective growth of 3 times and 4 times. As a result of rising living standards in Europe and the United States, more and more people in these regions have higher purchasing power, hence have more possibility of consuming silk products, which can increase the French silks.

---

[1] Organisation for Economic Co-operation and Development.

Table II-19-A GDP per capita of Europe, the United States and China, 1820—1910 (in 1990 international Geary-Khamis dollars) [1]

Years	United Kingdom	Europe(12 contries)	United States	China
1820	1,706	1,245	1,257	600
1830	1,749	1,395	1,376	600
1840	1,990	1,520	1,588	600
1850	2,330	1,661	1,806	600
1860	2,830	1,890	2,178	600
1870	3,190	2,124	2,445	530
1880	3,477	2,298	2,880	530
1890	4,009	2,643	3,392	540
1900	4,492	3,077	4,091	545
1910	4,611	3,380	4,964	552

Graph II-19-B GDP per capita of Europe and the United States and China, 1820—1910 (in 1990 international Geary-Khamis dollars)

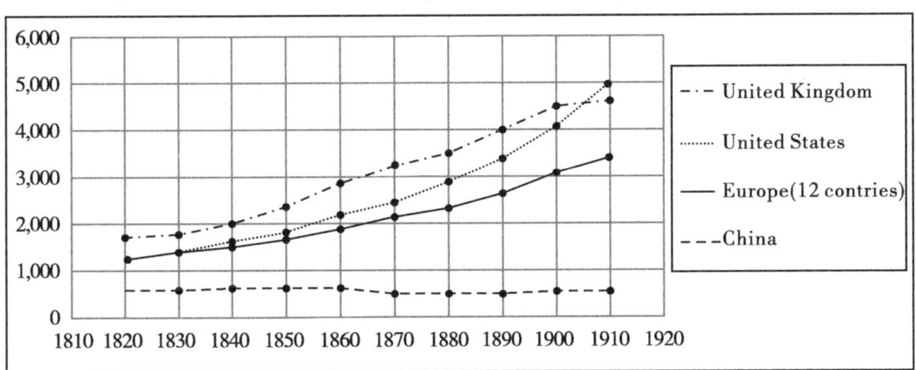

Second, the decline in the price of silk in Europe during the 19th century augment the consumption of silk in Europe and the United States. During the first half of the 19th century, the high price of silk limited its consumer group to nobles and wealthy classes. Because of the influx of Asian silks in Europe which has an absolute price advantage

---

[1] A. Maddison. L' économie mondiale. Statistiques Historiques. Paris. OCDE. 2003. p.63—65, p.93—94 and p.190. These 12 europe counties are : Autriche, Belgique, Danemark, Finlande, France, Allemagne, Italie, Pays-Bas, Norvège, Suède, Suisse and Royaume-Unis.

(we will compare prices later), a sharp drop in the price of silk material is happening in the European market from the 1870s, which widens the group of consumption of silk products to the lower classes.

Graph II-20-A Evolution of the real price of silk at the European market 1870—1915 (percentage, 1913 = 100%)

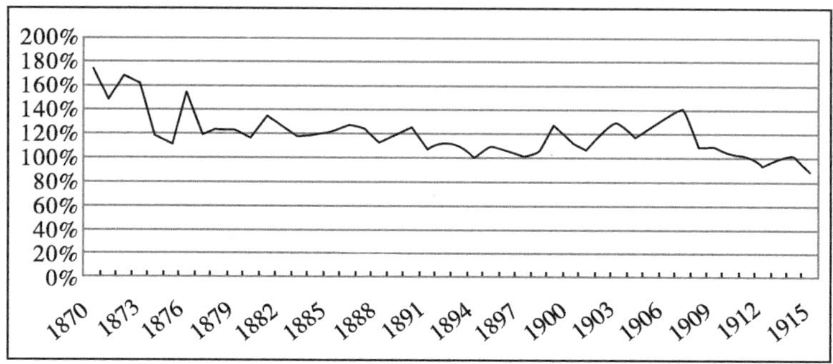

Table II-20-B Total silk consumption in Europe and the United States (thousand kilograms) ①

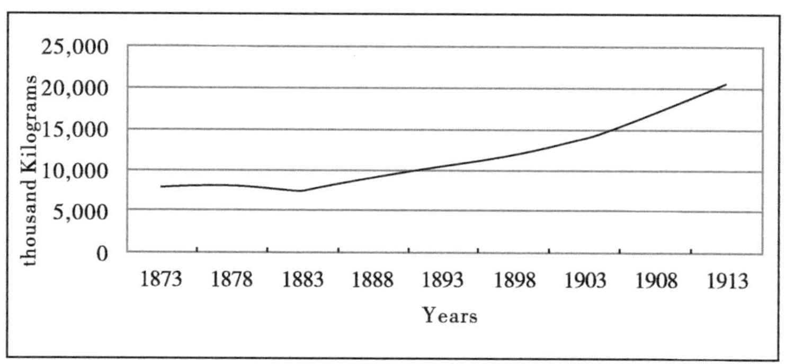

According to B.R.Mitchell statistics, the real price of silk to the European market fell from 180% in the early 1870s to 100% in 1913. In other words, there was a fall of about 2/5 of the price of silk to the world market during the 40 years before the World War. In fact, the price of silk products is decreasing at the same time as the cost of the raw material decreases. In 1859, one kilo of pure silk costs 146 francs Twenty years lat-

---

① Calculated by the data of F. Giovanni. An Economic History of the silk Industry, 1830—1930. p.213.

er, this price drops to 97 francs per kilogram, a decrease of 1/3[1]. According to the general equilibrium theory, the fall in price of an article will lead to an increase in demand and consumption. In fact, the quantity consumed by silk in Europe and the United States rose from 8,000 thousand kilograms in 1873 to more than 20,000 thousand kilograms on the eve of Great Wars, a growth of 2.5 times during the same period. This proves that the reduction in the price of silk actually led to an increase in the consumption of this product, which ensures the prosperity of the outlet for French silk.

Thirdly, the spread of mixed silk further expands the silk consumption group. With the innovation of weaving technique, mixed silk products appeared at the beginning of the 19th century. Blended with cotton or wool in the production, mixed silks cost less than pure silk. According to the Silk and Silk Bulletin of Lyons, in 1879, one kilogram of plain pure silk costs 97 francs, but only 72 francs for united mixed products, or only 50 centimes per meter[2], and such price may be assumed by consumers with ordinary incomes. Although it is not possible to show the exact evolution of the price of mixed silk because of the variation in the proportion of silk and the difference in the trades, we could say that this kind of product penetrates the lives of ordinary peoples immediately and succeeded in attracting this group into the market. The mixed silks gradually became, consequently, the main products of the French silk industry during the 19th century. In Lyons, out of a hundred looms, only 20 worked on pure silk[3]. And this is also true of Saint-Etienne, Saint-Chamond, Paris, Roubaix, and so on. In 1888, the production of mixed silks reached a value of 147 million. In the 3,991,000 kilograms of silk products exported in 1888 by the Lyonsnaise factory, only 1,313,000 kilograms of pure silk were imported[4]. In 1890, mixed silks constituted 40% of the total production of the Lyons products in value[5].

---

[1]　Bulletin des soie et des soieries de Lyon. N°146. 17 Janvier 1880. Silk fabrics is a product with very high added value. Their prices are varied not only by different qualities, but also by different arts and crafts, so one can not demonstrate the evaluation of the price here. For the same reason, there are very few sources on the exact quantity (kilograms) of silk consumption. So afterwards, we can only increase the amount of consumption of silk fabrics by the amount of the pure silk material.

[2]　Bulletin des soies et des soieries de Lyon. N°146. 17 Janvier 1880.

[3]　J. Rojon. Les soieries lyonnaises dans la seconde moitié du XIXe siècle et au début du XXe siècle : du produit artisanal de lux au produit industriel de (demi-) luxe. Art et Industrie. 2013. p.129.

[4]　A. de la Berge. Les industries de la soie en France. Revue des Deux Mondes. pp.14—15.

[5]　P. Cayew. Crises et croissance de l'industrie lyonnaise. 1850-1900. Paris. Editions du CNRS. 1980. p. 273.

3. The sericulture crisis in France: the silkworm disease and the influx of Chinese silk

The prosperity of silk products exports boosted the French silk textiles production of the 19th century. The great production determines a great need of raw material. During the second half of the 19th century, the silk industry of France consumed at least a third of the silks available in the world. Let us recall the contents of the first section of the chapter. In 1892, out of the 12,550,000 kilograms of material of the silks placed in the world market, the French merchant brought 6,000,000 kilograms to France. If the part for re-export is eliminated, there are still 3,640,000 kilograms for production for the French silk industry, three-tenths of the world's production[1]. So much consumption of the silk textile industry demands an adequate supply of raw material, but this often obsesses silk producers in France: the harvest of native silkworms can never satisfy the demand of the French silk industry.

The first sericulture activities in France took place in the Mediterranean regions. The mulberry tree was already cultivated in the vicinity of Venasque when in 1229, Raymond VII, count of Toulouse, but there is no reason to suppose that at that time the people have already knew the silkworm in that region. The sending to Queen Jeanne of Burgundy in 1345, by the Sénéchal de Beaucaire and Nîmes, of 12 books of silk from Provence bougnt in Montpellier 76 sols Tournois the books, is one of the first historical testimonies of a national production[2]. At the beginning of the 17th century, sericulture production already extended to the lower Rhone valley, the Mediterranean regions and the Cévennes[3]. The growth of sericulture production in France began in the early 19th century. Educational areas far exceed the regions of warm Mediterranean climate. A veritable sericulture fever seems to have taken possession of the whole country. In 1820, 13 departments in France took care of sericulture, 30 in 1834 and 64 in 1853: including the region around Paris, the plains of the Saône, Poitou, the departments of the southwest and even the Morbihan. The average cocoon crop in this country was only 10,000,000 kilograms during the 1820s, but it reached more than 14,000,000 kilograms during the 1830s, 17,000,000 during 1841—1845, and exceeded 20,000,000 kilograms during 1846—1852[4].

---

① N.Rondot. L'industrie de la soie en France. Lyon. Imprimerie Mougin-Rusand. 1894. pp. 14—15.

② E.Reynier. La soie en Vivarais. Etude d'histoire et de géographie économiques. Marseille. Laffitte Reprints. 1981. p.2.

③ H.Clouzot. Le métier de la soie en France. Paris. Devambez. 1910. p.10.

④ M.A.Carron. La production de la soie brute en France. Lyon. M.Audin. 1946. p.18.

However, even during the first half of the 19th century, which is the era that is considered the "golden age" of French sericulture, the production of cocoons from France does not satisfy the demand of its textile industry. According to the annual statistics of the sericulture society, raw silk of foreign origin accounts for 20% of the total silk used by the French silk industry from 1815 to 1830. Although French silk production jumped from 659,398 to 2,109,000 kilograms [1] (an increase of 320 percent) from 1825 to 1852, but demand for the French textile industry increased faster than the growth of French raw silk production. The proportion of silk of foreign origin increased by 20% in 1815—1830 to 32.5% in 1831—1840, and still 40% in 1841—1852[2].

Table II-21 Comparison of quantities of indignant raw silk and foreign raw silk in France 1815—1832 (kilograms)[3]

Years	Indignant Silk	Import Silk	Total	Import Proportion
1815	308,157	22,795	330,952	6.89%
1816	421,931	123,066	544,997	22.58%
1817	207,772	179,059	386,831	46.28%
1818	324,672	168,187	492,859	34.12%
1819	412,172	124,709	536,881	23.28%
1820	453,700	130,312	584,012	22.31%
1821	485,471	77,314	562,785	13.74%
1822	289,793	170,730	460,532	37.07%
1823	675,541	118,439	793,980	14.91%
1824	670,863	120,027	790,890	15.18%
1825	608,560	145,407	753,967	19.28%
1826	612,954	289,906	902,860	32.11%
1827	657,482	130,430	787,912	16.55%
1828	664,450	131,330	795,780	16.50%
1829	688,491	369,520	1,058,011	34.93%
1830	673,615	190,339	863,954	22.03%

---

[1] E.Hamaide. La relation entre Lyon et Chine au XIX siècle. p.9.

[2] G. Federico. An Economic History of the silk Industry, 1830—1930.pp.214—215.

[3] The accunt for the quantities of native silk originate from the improvement and spread of the silk industry in France. Annale de la société séricicole. n°1.p. 47; The accunt for the quantities of imported silk come from Archives Nationales de France. F12 7056. Commerce spécial des soies en 1832.

The production of cocoons from France reached its peak in 1853: 26 million kilograms (2,529,182 kilograms of raw silk). The city of Lyons is filled with an optimistic atmosphere on French sericulture at the moment. It is believed that "the future of the silk products production in Europe is there, because the production of material is abundant there, and because it will be there as soon as the Europeans want[1]." However, reality does not meet expectations: the silkworm disease broke out in France in 1854, and the harvests of cocoons in France fell sharply during the following years. Here are the statistics published by the Agriculture and Trade Ministry on the annual production of cocoons (kilograms)[2]:

```
1853 Summit of the century ·····················26,000,000
1854·············································21,500,000
1855·············································19,800,000
1856·············································7,500,000
1863·············································6,500,000
1864·············································6,000,000
1865·············································4,000,000
```

In order to ensure the harvest, the sericulturalists decided to buy new seeds from Italy, but this method did not proceed from the beginning of the 1860s: the epidemic quickly swept the whole territory of Europe from Italy to Italy. Turkish Epirus following France, and the seeds of all Europe no longer resemble usable. In 1865 the Senate was called upon to deliberate about the wishes of a petition signed by 3,574 owners of the sericulture departments, calling the attention of the Government to the disastrous effects of the silkworm disease and calling for taking the measures to cover it, "To reduce the burden of ownership by reducing taxes, to provide farmers with better seeds, and to study all the questions connecting with this persistent epizootic, both from the view of from pathology to that of hygiene"[3]. The government of Napoleon III organizes his scientists to find the method of prevention and medical care, but this is a rather difficult mission. It is thought to be "connected with a vegetable disease or animal disease, the double symptoms of which have already been manifested. Human science on such a sub-

---

① S.Lamb, c'est de l'or. Lyon. pp. 29—30.

② L.Pasteur. Etude sur la maladie des vers à soie: notes et documents. Paris. Imprimerie de Gauthier-Villar. 1879. p. 38.

③ Idem. p.9.

ject is impotent in its diagnosis and in its investigations."[1]

J.B.Dumas, senator of the Gard and former Agriculture and Chemist Minister, proposes to the Agriculture Ministry to entrust the mission to save the silk of France to his friend, Louis Pasteur. And then he tried to convince Pasteur to accept this mission: "I put an extreme price to see your attention fixed on the question that interests my poor country: misery exceeds all you can imagine."[2] After the hesitation, Pasteur decided to study the silkworm disease in the summer of 1965. On the recommendation of Dumas, he first moved to Sérignan du Combat to learn the knowledge about silkworms from Jean-Henri Fabre, a famous entomologist at the time, who explained to him that "for several years, sericulture manage were in disarray, ravaged by unknown plagues. The worms, without appreciable motives, fell into putrid deliquescence, and hardened into pralines of plaster. The astonished peasant saw the disappearance of one of the care and expense, it was necessary to throw the barracks into the manure". And at the same time teaches him the biology of the mulberry moth and the means of selecting the unharmed eggs[3].

Then Pasteur lives in Pont-Gisqiuet near Ales to seek a cure for the epidemic. Quickly, he developed a method of selection, called "cellular graining". Each couple is isolated in a wooden or cardboard cell and then, after laying, the females are crushed and examined under a microscope in order to detect diseased individuals (invaded with corpuscles) and thus to retain only groin eggs[4]. In the account of the Academy of Sciences of September 25, 1865, he wrote: "If these principles are true, if I have observed the facts on which they are based, to obtain a private seed absolutely from any original disease constitution, a precious result, industrially speaking, since healthy seeds always yield a harvest the first year, even in the most tried and tested localities. This means will consist in isolating, at the time of graining, each male and female pair. Harp the uncoupling, the female, set aside, lay its seeds, then it will be opened, as well as the male, in order to look for the corpuscles … " In 1867, he discovers that there are actually two independent epidemics, instead of only one, which communicate between the seeds of silkworms. Apart from "pebrine", "flacherie" is another disease leading to seed death. This is another contribution of Pastor, because the second is often overlooked by scientists before[5].

---

[1] S.Lamb. La soie, c'est de l'or. Lyon. Bureaux du courrrier de Lyon. 1856. p. 2.

[2] J. d'Aguilar. Pasteur et le ver à soie. Histoire des sciences. No°99. 1995.04. p.19.

[3] J.H.Fabre. Souvenirs entomologiques 9ème série. Paris. Delagrave. 1923. p.808.

[4] E. Kahane. Pasteur, pages choisies. Classique du peuple. Paris. Edition Sociales. 1957. p.117.

[5] P. Debré. Louis Pasteur. Paris. Editions Flammarion. 1995. pp.221—223.

However, it should be noted that Pasteur's method is not adopted at once. Already, during his experiments, there are hostile polemics in local newspapers published by scholars even by sericulturists. These criticisms are mainly due to Pasteur's proposals which are contrary to the habits of the moment. Moreover, the public authorities, in particular the Lyonss silk commission, are not yet convinced to adopt its method of reproduction. In the midst of these difficult struggles, Pasteur was struck on October 19, 1868 with cerebral haemorrhage and hemiplegia[1]. After a year and a half of hesitation, the Silk Commission of Lyonss finally decided to implement the method of prevention of Louis Pasteur in July of 1869. The cocoon harvest in France rose again immediately from 308,000 kilograms from 1869 to 1,096,000 kilograms (107,031 kilograms of silk) the following year[2].

Although Louis Pasteur found the precaution against silkworm disease, the quantity of French silkworm production still remains much lower than that before the outbreak of disease during the rest of the century. The production of raw silk in France, rising from 30,000 kilograms in 1866—1869 to 658,000 kilograms in 1871—1875, then no longer progressed since the 1870s. It even declined a little during the decades of the 19th century.

Table II-22 Raw silk productions in France and Italy 1871—1815 (thousand kilograms)

Years	French Productions	Italien Productions
1871—1875	658	3,171
1876—1880	510	1,922
1881—1885	631	2,766
1886—1895	747	3,686
1896—1900	650	4,868
1901—1905	591	5,262
1906—1910	583	5,654
1911—1915	358	4,561

In fact, the sericulture crisis in France lasted throughout the second half of the 19th

---

[1] J.M. Legay et G. Chavancy. La phase pastorienne de la sériciculture. La crise de la pébrine et ses conséquences. Natures Sciences Sociétés. Vol.12. 2004. No°4. p.414.

[2] E. Hamaide. La relation entre Lyon et Chine au XIX siècle. 3.1 Les conséquences des crises de la decennie sur la fabrique lyonnaise.

century (it was prolonged even in the 20th century). It was the disease that most seriously affected sericulture in the mid-19th century and opened up the crisis, but it was another factor, the lack of competitiveness of French silk vis-à-vis competition from foreign silks, which led to the prolongation of the crisis: as a result of the penetration of Asian silks, especially Chinese silks with a very low price, more and more farmers abandon the education of the silkworm.

After the explosion of the pebrine, large quantities of the silks of the Far East, especially Chinese silk, were imported to France directly from China or indirectly by the London market. Sericulture and silk reeling are labor-intensive production sectors. Thanks to the resources of the hands of much richer works and much lower labor costs (as will be explained in the next section), silk of Chinese origin sells at a very low price even when it is arrived in Europe. In 1855 the price of the French frame (second order) was 86 francs per kilogram, while that of Italy (2nd order) cost 78 francs and that of China (2nd order) costs only 55 francs in the Lyons market[1]. So it is very difficult for French silks to compete with them.

Table II-23 Comparative prices of silk prices in Lyons in 1869 and in 1876 (Franc / kg)[2]

Types			Price in 1868	Price in 1876
Warps	France	2nd order	155	74
	Italy	2nd order	142	70
	Belgimn	2nd order	115	59
	China	1st order	103	60
Frames	France	2nd order	141	72
	Italy	2nd order	127	66
	Bengal	2nd order	115	58
	China	2nd order	88	54
Raw Silk	France	2nd order	135	68
	Italy	2nd order	120	54
	China	Tsatlee	83	45

---

① S.Lamb. La soie, c'est de l'or. Lyon. p. 10.

② Bulletin des soies et des soieries de Lyon-Revue Hebdomadaire Lyonnaise. Lyon. Administration. 1886—1990. No°10. 9 juin 1877.

The improvement of transport between the Far East and Western Europe during the 1860s, especially the opening of the Suez Canal in 1869, brought the cheap silk materials closer to the French silk market (we will elaborate on this subject in Chapter IV). In such a situation, more and more Chinese silks are imported directly into France by foreign companies based in Shanghai and Canton (including both French and other Western countries) instead of the London market[1]. According to the data of the *Bulletin des soies et des soieries de Lyons*, the prices of each type of silks in France reached a fairly high level in 1868 (which is one of the most miserable years for sericulture French). In the same year, the Chinese silks prices are the lowest of all silks imported into France. The price of the Chinese warps of the first order is even lower than that of the warps of the second order of France, and of Italy and Bengal.

This means that silk textiles producers in Lyons can obtain silks with better quality by paying less if they choose Chinese products. In 1876, seven years after the opening of the Suez Canal, European silk producers were obliged to lower their prices as a result of the convergence of silk prices to the world market[2]. The prices of all kinds of silk at the Lyons market are generally reduced to one half of the prices of the 1860s. Chinese silks, especially the Chinese raw silk, always retain the advantage of the price: about 10—15 francs cheaper than French silk. In this case, French silk textiles producers continue to choose to import Chinese silk instead of buying the silk produced in France.

As a result, many French sericulturists abandon or no longer return to sericulture after the ravage of the silkworm disease. According to the survey of Mr. A. Carron, "From year to year, we see the number of sericulturists and the number of ounces being incubated. More than half of the silkworm farmers in 1874 had abandoned this occupation on the eve of the 1914—1918 war ... This could only bring a deeper disturbance in this area and aggravate even more brutally the fall of sericulture. On the eve of the war, only the Mediterranean and Rhone regions are still on the sericulture map. The less mountainous of the old sericulture departments lost much more than the others: the Ardèche accused only 32% of losses in 1914 Gard 30%; The Drôme, on the other hand accounted for 50% and the Vaucluse 53.5%."[3] Another author, VV.Germaine, described a scene

---

① These are questions about intermediaries in the silk trade between France and China. Another chapter of this thesis will specialize on these issues.

② The convergence of price is a subject already much discussed by economic historians, especially by K.H. O'Rourke and J.G.Willlamson when approaching economic globalization. We shall again discuss the convergence of the price of silk in the following chapter.

③ M.A.Carron. La production de la soie brute en France. Lyon. M.Audin.1946. p.21.

of decadence of sericulture in the French countryside: "In the Alpine Isère, the number of educators fell from 4,097 in 1858 to 2,120 in 1881, 1,870 in 1908 and 1,192 in 1914; In Savoie, where since 1860 everything related to silk now depends on Lyons, sericulture abandons its advanced posts of Basse-Maurienne and Basse-Tarentaise, rapidly decreasing elsewhere. In the Marches, between Montmelian and Chambéry, from 1875 to 1910, the number of silkworm educators dropped from 40 to 1."[1] Sericulture can no longer survive after the silk market of France has been occupied by Chinese silk from good price. The proportion of foreign silks occupied an average of 75% of the total silks of their consumption between 1854 and 1873, and rose to 82% between 1874 and 1914. In 1889 the silk industry consumed a total of 4,127,328 kilograms of silk, production of indigenous silk is only 595,000 kilograms, or only 12% of the total[2].

In conclusion, the production of French silk textile, which concentrates in the departments of the Rhone valley, maintained a trend of successive growth until the end of the 1870s at both value and quantity levels. Despite the obvious decline in the value of production during the crisis of 1876—1893, due to a fall in the price of silk, the quantity of production still continues to grow. At the end of the 1890s, its production value rose to the level of the 1870s, and the quantity continued to increase. This long-term sustainable growth of this French industrial branch is mainly due to the expansion of the market in Europe (especially in England) and the United States from the peace of 1815.

As a result, the silk textile industry in France needs a considerable amount of silk material for its growing tissue production, but French sericulture can never satisfy this demand. During the sericulture crisis in France, which began in the middle of the 19th century, the deficit between consumption and the supply of silk became more and more important. Under such circumstances, the importation of Chinese silk in large quantities becomes a necessity. However, the influx of Chinese silk, prolongs the sericulture crisis of France, which further expands the silk trade between France and China.

IV Supply growth: the increase in the quantity of Chinese silk production and the decline in the manufacture of silk fabrics in China

According to data in the world economy, OECD's historical statistics, GDP multi-

---

[1]　V-V. Germaine. L'industrie de la soie dans les Alpe du Nord. In. Revue de géographie alpine. p.140.

[2]　Archives Nationales de France. F12 6894 Chambre des députés cinquième législature session de 1891, n° 1354, le 21 mars 1891. p.9.

plies by 5 in the United Kingdom, by 3.5 in France, by 4 in the United States and by 3.5 in Japan during the period 1820—1900. In comparison with the countries above, the Chinese economy remains in a state of stagnation, even of decline during the 19th century. China's GDP fell from 228,600 million dollars[1] to 189,740 dollars from 1820 to 1870, and then rose slightly to 218,074 dollars in 1900, which is still lower than the level of the early 19th century[2]. The share of China's GDP in the world decreased from 33.88% in 1820 to 17.05% in 1870, and again to 8.83% in 1913[3].

However, the decline of the Chinese economy of the 19th century was accompanied by a strong growth in foreign trade, whose value rose from 10,896,480 in 1817 taëls to 15,406,930 taëls in 1833[4] to 61,826,000 taëls in 1868, and 403,306,000 in 1913, an increase of 37 during the 19th century. Among the main merchandise in Chinese foreign trade of the 19th century, the expansion of the silk trade is the most impressive. The value of the export of silk multiplied by 5 from 1817 to 1833, then by 11 from 1833 to 1868, and again by 2.3 from 1868 to 1913.[5]. From the 1860s, silk, having exceeded tea, becomes the most exported Chinese merchandise abroad, whose export value makes up almost 40% of the total value of Chinese exports. From the same period, France began importing more and more silk material into China.

Increasing the supply of Chinese silk to the international market is an important element in the growth of the silk trade between France and China. In this section we will discuss why the supply of Chinese silk to the foreign market is able to expand durably during the 19th century. Is it related to the growth of silk production in China, or it is linked to the reduction of silk consumption in China? Or both? To solve this problem, first, we will demonstrate the evolution of the quantity of silk production in China, consulting results of the 19th century sericulture surveys applied by N.Rondot, Jiberboman, Akeda Hirome (明石弘) and Uehara Shigemi (上原重美) as well as contemporary research on this subject, including "The Great Divergence. China, Europe and the Making" of the Modern World Economy of Kenneth Pomeranz[6], the "Development of Capi-

---

① Dollars internationaux Geary-Khamis de 1990. Equal for the following dollars in this paragraph.

② 郑友揆.中国的对外贸易和工业发展(1840—1948)——史实的综合分析.上海:上海社会科学院出版社,1984 年,第 23 页.

③ A.Maddison. L' économie mondiale. Statistiques historiques. Paris. Organisation de coopération et de développement économiques. 2003. p.50—52, p.90—91, p.183. and p.275.

④ 上海社会科学院经济研究所.上海对外贸易.上海:上海社会科学院出版社,1989 年,第 11 页.

⑤ Idem. p.23.

⑥ K.Pomeranz. The Great Divergence. China, Europe and the Making of the Modern World Economy. Princeton. Princeton University Press. 2000. pp.328—330.

talism in China" published in 1985 by Xu Dixin（许涤新）and Wu Chengming（吴成明）[1], the "Evolution of Jiangnan's Trade During the Ming and Qing Dynasties" published in 1998 by Fan Jinmin（范金民）[2] and the "Amount of Silk Production and the Influence of Growth Silk Export on the Increase of Sericulture Regions in China" published on the China Agriculture Review in 2008 by Zhang Li（张丽）[3].

Second, we will discuss the causes for the growth of sericultural production in China. G. Federico, in his book "An Economic History of the Silk Industry", indicates that the rise in sericulture production in the world is because its opportunity cost is lower than other agricultural activities. In this section, the opportunity cost of Chinese sericulture will be studied to check if the case of China also corresponds to the theory of G.Federico, and at the same time we will discuss other factors impelling the production of silk in China.

Thirdly, we will study the changes in the proportions and quantities of Chinese silk flocked to the foreign market and that remaining at the local market in all Chinese sericulture production. Wang Xiang（王翔）, in his book comparing the modernization of the silk industry in China and Japan[4], states that the increase in exports of Chinese silk from the 19th century is at the price of Reduction in the local market, but the data he used were derived from those of Xu Xinwu（徐新吾）published in 1990[5], which are old and not accurate. In the text, we will compare again the two variables by consulting recent studies on this subject, especially those of Zhangli（张丽）. After this comparison, we could confirm whether the increase in exports of Chinese silk from the 19th century is also due to the decline of the local silk market in China. If so, we will also find the causes for this decrease at the end of this section.

1. High quantity of silk production in China

"One day, Lei Zu（嫘祖）, the benevolent wife of the Yellow Emperor（黄帝）, is a train of drinking water in a mulberry forest. Suddenly, a cocoon of wild worm falls inside his bowl. The intelligent Lei Zu accidentally discovered that she can pull more and more silk when it lifts the cocoon, and that this kind of silk can be used to weave the

---

[1]　许涤新,吴成明.中国资本主义发展史.北京:人民出版社,1985,第325—326页.

[2]　范金民.明清江南商业的发展.南京:南京大学出版社.1996,第30—31页.

[3]　张丽.鸦片战争前的全国生丝产量和近代生丝出口增加对中国近代桑蚕业扩张的影响.中国农史.2008年第4期,第48页.

[4]　王翔.中日丝绸业近代化比较研究.石家庄:河北人民出版社,2002.第378—379页.

[5]　徐新吾.中国近代缫丝工业史.上海:上海人民出版社,1990.第110—111页.

textiles. To save peoples who suffer the cold, she decides to study this nature of wild worms, which is the origin of sericulture."[1]

This is one of the beautiful myths about the origin of Chinese sericulture. Many ancient Chinese historical or literary works, such as the *Historical Memory* (《史记》Shi Ji), *Sinogram* (《周易》Zhou Yi) and *Poems*(《诗经》), have noted this kind of folklores. Though, these myths (or folklores) are not reliable histories, they prove that China has a long history of sericulture, which often gains the exclamation of admiration of the Westerners. Following the commercial mission of 1844, the French silk industry delegate, Isidore Hedde wrote in his report to the French government: "It would be useless to insist on this fact, which has been recognized by the most the Chinese first understood the part which can be drawn from the production of silk. It was from China that Tire and Egypt received, through the caravans, those precious fabrics which the Romans paid for by the weight of gold. The West knew the silk thread a long time before possessing the insect that produced it"[2]. The French economist A. Beauquis asserts in his work *Histoire économ; qve de la soie* that "It is certainly in China that the silk industry has had its cradle, and it is in the Annals of that country that it is necessary to search for the proper documents to establish the history of the origin of silk. It was known there, from the earliest antiquity, and there is an uninterrupted mention of the silk stuffs in the history of the great Chinese nation, even going back more than twenty centuries before J.–C."[3]

Such a long history allows sericulture first to extend to most Chinese regions. We could estimate the date of the departure of Chinese sericulture by the archaeological pieces. In 1958, archaeologists discovered small silk thread boots, small pieces of ribbon and pieces of yellow lustrine without anthracolitization at Qian-Shanyang (钱山漾) in Wuxing (吴兴) in Zhejiang Province (浙江省). The silks and the silk fabrics in these ruins have been proved to have been produced at least four thousand seven hundred years before, which are the earliest fabrics of silk (which archaeologists have discovered) in China. Ancient times, the main regions of sericulture are concentrated in

---

① 黄为放.丝绸文化.长春:吉林文史出版社,2010.第4页.

② Ministère de l'agriculture et du commerce, Document sur le commerce extérieur, Chine et Indochine, Fait commerciaux n°12, Paris. Imprimerie Impériale. 1847 pp.89—90.

③ A. Beauquis. Histoire économique de la soie. Grenoble. Grands établissements de l'imprimerie générale. 1910. p. 2.

northern China. Because of the change in climate and widespread wars in the north, the sericulture center is moving gradually to the southeast from A.D. 300. Yet, according to the *Tong Dian* (《通典》)[1], the production of silk from the south-east is always less dynamic than that of the region to the north (around Fleure Jaune 黄河流域), even less dynamic than that from the Sichuan region (四川)[2] to the beginning of the Tang dynasty (唐代, 618—907). The wars at the end of the Tang dynasty still push the sericulture center to the southeast, and this displacement ends at the beginning of the Northern Song Dynasty (北宋朝, 960—1127). According to the *Song Hui Yao* Economic Party (《宋会要·货志》), among the silk fabrics received by the central government, the provinces of Zhejiang (浙江) and Jiangsu (江苏) deposited 1,251,991 rolls, which is 36.09% of the total[3]. This proportion increased enormously during the Yuan dynasties (元朝, 1271—1368), Ming (明朝 1368—1644) and the first part of Qing (前清, 1644—1840). It is estimated that silk products production in the two provinces can occupy 60%–70% of total production in China on the eve of the Opium War[4]. Moreover, sericulture already exists in almost all the provinces of the Chinese Empire at that time.

The long Chinese sericulture history also leads to an abundant accumulation of techniques on the production of silk, which reached its peak during the Ming and Qing era. During the 17th century, grain has already been obtained by hybridization and the silkworm diseases are prevented by the removal of infected grains for the education of silkworms[5]. For reeling, it is concluded that "dry fuels must be used for silk reeling so that silk does not discolor"[6], and that cocoons must be spun with clear water: Fountain is the best, the river water is inferior, and the rain water is more inferior"[7]. At the beginning of the 19th century, spinners already know the influences of temperature, moisture and water on silk reeling. During the second half of the 19th century, Chinese peasants produced under the direction of these trades and traditional knowledge, where new western trades were introduced in China (we will specify the traditional techniques of sericulture and reeling in China and its modern transformation in another chapter).

[1] Tong Dian(《通典》). One of the main official historical works written by the government during the Tang Dynasty. Being finished in 801 A.D., Tong Dian noted the evolution of the political and economic system of the previous dynasties.

[2] 王翔.中日丝绸业近代化比较研究.石家庄:河北人民出版社,2002 年,第 17 页.

[3] 徐松.宋会要辑稿·食货第六十四.北京:中华书局,1857 年.

[4] 许檀:明清时期区域经济的发展.中国经济史研究.1999 年第 2 期,第 20 页.

[5] 王翔.近代中国传统丝绸业转型研究.天津:南开大学出版社,2005 年,第 2 页.

[6] 宋应星.天工开物·乃服.上海:中华书局,1959 年.

[7] 卫杰.蚕桑汇编·卷四.北京:中华书局,1956 年 10 月,第 132 页.

Thanks to the expansion of the sericulture regions and the accumulation of silk production techniques in history, China[1] is already the world's largest silk producer in the early 19th century. Moreover, during the 19th century, the quantity of Chinese silk production showed a very strong growth trend.

Since the second half of the 19th century, some foreign trade commissioners or sinologists in charge of their government missions have done some surveys on the quantities of cocoons from China, and have left us some more accurate statistics.

Natalis Rondot attempt to estimate the total crop of cocoons from China from 1875 to 1880, and his survey was published in 1881[2], who instructed the delegate of the Lyons Chamber of Commerce in China at time. Another inquiry on the total production of Chinese silk took place in 1898 by a German sinologist called Jiberboman[3]. At the beginning of the 20th century, the Japanese government made great efforts to clarify their rivals in the Chinese market. Two other inquiries were made by a Japanese Akeda Hirome (明石弘) of 1915—1917 and in 1925. His mission of 1915—1917 was entrusted by the Minister of Agriculture and Trade of Japan, and that of 1925 was requested by the Shanghai International Examinations Chamber[4]. In 1926, Uehara Shigemi (上原重美), delegate of the Japanese silk industry in China, once again studied the production of silk in China[5]. This is the last inquiry before the year 1949 (the year of the creation of the People's Republic of China). Most of the data shown in Table II-24, especially those from the late 19th century to the beginning of the 20th century, come from the results of these surveys.

The data that will be adopted in this book on the quantity of production of Chinese

---

① China's silk production is concentrated in the few Chinese provinces, including Zhejiang (浙江), Jiangsu (江苏), Guangdong (广东), Sichuan (四川).

② Natalis Rondot has already been mentioned when discussing the sources that note the sending of silk from Cie and Rémi in 1852 in the preceding chapter. In fact, he has left us a considerable number of works on the silk industry of China, which are very valuable for our research. Having come to China as a former member of the Lagrené mission from 1843 to 1846, Natalis Rondot reloaded a mission to China from 1873 to 1875 to deepen his knowledge of Chinese sericulture and silk industry. To estimate the total quantity of cocoon and silk production in China, he asked the customs authorities of all Chinese commercial ports to collect information on the quantities of silk produced in each Chinese region during the 1879—1889 . By consulting the reports offered by these customs services, he publishes his estimate of the totality of cocoon and silk production in China in his work on silks. Historians present believe that these estimates of Natalis Rondot's harvest of each Chinese province are rather conservative, but these are the only statistics available today.

③ A.J.H.Latham et H. Kawakatsu. Intra-Asian Trade and industrialisation: Essays in Memory OF Yasukichi Yasuba. New York. Routledge. 2009. p. 198.

④ C.W.Howard and K.P.Buswell. A Survey of the Silk Industry in South China. Hongkong. The Commercial Press. 1925. P.27.

⑤ 蚕丝业同业组合中央会编纂.支那蚕业大观.东京:冈田日荣堂,1929,第429页.

112

silk on the eve of the Opium War are based on the estimates of contemporary economic historians. Although there are few direct sources of official statistics on the quantity of silk produced in China before the Opium War, some historians and economists have tried to estimate this quantity using indirect sources from the 1980s. With different calculation methods, they obtained quite different results.

In the Development of Capitalism in China published in 1985 by Xu Dixin（许涤新）and Wu Chengming（吴成明）, the authors tend to count the total quantity of silk consumed inside China in the year 1840 by multiplying number of the looms by the average consumption of a loom. Adding the export share（9,000 piculs）, they infer that the quantity of raw silk production in China on the eve of the Opium War is 64,000 piculs[1]. This number is often questioned by other historians because the number of looms in the Jiangnan region that they used is that in 1880 instead of the years before 1840. The former one should be much less than the last one, because the textile industry in the Jiangnan region was severely ravaged by the Chinese Civil War of 1851—1864[2]. In addition, they equal the quantity of production from Jiangnan（Zhejiang and Jiangsu）to that of all China. At that time, other Chinese regions, including Guangdong Province and Sichuan also produce a lot of silk. So the two authors have underestimated the amount of production of Chinese silk on the eve of the Opium War.

According to the evolution of the Jiangnan trade during the Ming and Qing dynasties written by Fan Jinmin（范金民）in 1998, 160,000 silk piculs were produced in the middle of the 1840s[3]. The author obtained this quantity by multiplying the surface area of Field of mulberry in the Jiangnan region by the average quantity of silk production per unit of field. He estimated that there were 1,640,000 Mu（亩）[4] of fields specializing on mulberry trees in the Jiangnan area in the mid-18th century. According to an overview of sericulture（《蚕桑指要》）written by an agronomist Zhu Bin（朱斌）at the period, "each Mu field produces an average 1,600 Jins（斤）[5] mulberry leaves, 10 Jins silk, 100 Jins of cocoons and 10 Jins of raw silk".[6]

So Fan Jinmin affirmed that about 160,000 piculs of silk were produced during the

---

[1] 许涤新,吴成明.中国资本主义发展史.北京:人民出版社,1985,第325—326页.

[2] Either the Taiping Rebellion, which was mentioned in the previous text and which will be discussed again in the following text.

[3] 范金民:明清江南商业的发展,南京:南京大学出版社,1996年.

[4] 1 Mu(亩)≈666.67 square meters.

[5] 1 Jin(斤)= 0.5 kilogramme.

[6] 郑斌.蚕桑指要.1725年首次刊印,1900年手抄本再次发行,第1卷,第25页,上海市图书馆馆藏资源.

18th century. There are also many debates about this number, because: firstly, the 18th century data from Sericulture Survey is not necessarily accurate to estimate the quantity of production of Chinese silks of the 19th century. Secondly, we are not sure if there is so much fields specializing in the planting of mulberry trees at that time. Third, it has the same problem with Xu Dixin and Wu Chengming: the production of the Jiangnan region is not equal to that of the whole of China.

K. Pomeranz is another historian who attempted to know the amount of silk production in China during the Qing dynasty, which claimed that 530,000 piculs of raw silk were produced annually from 1775 to 1820 in China in his Work *The Great Divergence: China, Europe and the Making of the Modern World Economy*[1]. His method of calculation was similar to that of Fan Jinmin. He assumed that 3/4 of the fields (except grain fields) in the Jiangnan area were used for mulberry planting (10,098,725 Mu of field), and that each field Mu produced 6.6 pounds (≈5 Jin, 2.5 kilograms) of silk. Then he multiplied the two digits and got the result that 60,000,000 pounds of silk are produced annually in the Jiangnan area. For the quantity of production of all China, Pomeranz obtained it by dividing the 60,000,000 by 85% (Obviously, assuming that the production of the region of Jiangnan occupies 85% of that of the whole empire). The result was that the annual quantity of silk production in China was 71,000,000 pounds (≈530,000 piculs) during the 18th century. The problem with the Pomernanz method is that it overestimated the area of mulberry fields and underestimated the amount of silk production by Mu of the time. The specialization level of mulberry plantation was not so high, but 3/4 of fields, except grain fields, were used for agricultural activity. Moreover, if each Mu of fields already produced 10 Jin of raw silk in 1725, as the agronomist noted at the time, the average quantity of silk production by Mu should not be lower than the quantity throughout the rest of the 18th century. Therefore, it is doubtful whether his conclusion is equally wrong.

By consulting all the previous methods, a Chinese economist Zhang Li (张丽) tried again to estimate this amount. She published in her thesis in 2008 that the figure should be 110,000 piculs before the opening of China. She used two methods to confirm this result. The first method was to count in the opposite direction. Having experienced the entire production of Jiangnan, Guangdong and Sichuan (three major productive areas) in 1926 by Uehara Shigemi's investigation, Zhang Li sought to know the scale of

---

① K.Pomeranz. The Great Divergence : China, Europe and the Making of the Modern World Economy. Princeton. Princeton University Press. 2000. pp. 328—330.

114

production in 1840 by comparing the surfaces of the mulberry fields of the three regions between the two dates. After this comparison, the author discovered that the areas of the mulberry fields in Jiangnan, Guangdong and Sichuan increased by 1/9, 20 or 25 times from the 1840s to the 1920s respectively. Costs of cocoons between the two periods, the author estimated that 5,000 piculs of silk were produced in Guangdong, 1,000—2,000 piculs of silk in Sichuan, and 102,600 piculs of silk in Jiangnan in 1840. Thus the production of the whole Empire Chinese people had about 110,000 silk piculs on the eve of the Opium War. The second method used by Zhang Li was to calculate the domestic consumption quantities of silk in the three regions (Jiangnan, Guangdong and Sichuan) in 1840 by transforming the silk textiles weights to the weights of silk material to be used, and then adding the quantity of the export. For example, it is already known that the textile industry manufactures 4,043,002 rolls of silk (including tulle, satin, crepe, etc.) per year during the 1840s in the Jiangnan area. According to the different weights per roll of each type of silk and their different costs of silk material, the author converted the weight of the silks used inside China to the weight of raw materials, which is 94,287 piculs. It made the same calculations for the regions of Guangdong and Sichuan, then added the amount of silk exports from China, and the result was that a total of 114,000 silk peaks were produced annually in China during the 1840s. With similar results using both methods, the author confirmed that China had produced about 110,000 piculs of silk per year on the eve of the Opium War.

The calculations of Zhang Li are not perfect neither. First, due to lack of data from the 1840s, it is assumed that the productivity of mulberry fields remained constant. Indeed, the modernization of sericulture (we will clarify in another chapter) of China raised sericulture productivity during both dates. Secondly, it equates the production of the three main producing regions with production in China.

In order to get closer to the true amount of production in all China, we assumed that the proportion of the production quantity of the three main regions in the total output of China in 1840 is similar to that of 1880 (88.76% of N.Rondot,). If the amount of silk production in the three regions is 110,000 piculs, then the whole of China will be about 123,930 piculs. In another chapter, the mechanization of silk reeling has not yet been popularized untill 1880, so the cost of cocoons remains constant from 1840 to 1880. The 123,930 piculs of silk should be spun from 1,611,573 piculs of cocoons. These figures, together with the results of the surveys of foreigners, help us to rebuilt the situation of the evolution of the quantities of the cocoons and silk produced from the mid-19th century to the beginning of the 20th century, presented in Table II-24 below (those of 1925 and 1926 are shown there so that we can see the trend more obviously).

Table II-24 Quantity of cocoon and silk production in China 1840—1926 (picul / year)[1]

	1840	1880	1898	1915—1917	1925	1926
	cocoons silks	cocoons silks	cocoons silks	cocoons silks	cocoons silks	cocoons silks
Zhejiang		825,500 63,500	1,017,000 78,231	876,766 67,444	1,000,000 76,923	1,140,000 87,692
Jiangsu		275,200 21,169	350,000 26,923	266,745 20,519	350,000 26,923	545,000 41,923
Guangdong		576,100 717,000	717,000 55,154	768,300 59,100	1,000,000 76,923	1,057,400 81,338
Sichuan		205,800 15,831	317,000 23,385	640,000 49,231	600,000 46,154	468,000 36,000
Hubei		70,100 6,085	7,846 100,000	100,000 7,692	100,000 7,672	122,900 9,454
Shandong		24,100 1,854	45,000 3,462	70,000 5,385	60,000 4,615	110,000 8,462
Anhui		10,800 831	30,000 2,308	30,000 2,308	30,000 2,308	97,000 7,462
Guangxi		—	—	12,000 923	65,520 5,040	55,600 4,277
Henan		100,800 7,754	142,000 10,923	121,000 9,308	100,000 7,692	42,900 3,300
Hunan		6,500 5,00	11,250 865	16,000 1,231	20,000 1,538	—
Shanxi		—	—	—	—	6,500 500
Fujian		—	—	—	—	3,900 300
Others		17,100 1,315	99,000 7,615	79,500 6,115	70,000 5,385	13,000 1,000
total	1,611,673 123,930	2,121,000 163,154	2,819,000 216,846	2,779,911 213,832	3,330,000 256,154	3,622,300 281,715

The production of cocoons already reached 1,611,573 piculs (96,694,380 kilograms) on the eve of the war of opium, and then increased to 2,131,000 picules (1,280,000 kilograms) in 1880, and 2,819,000 piculs (169,140,000 kilograms) at the end of the 19th century. Growth stagnated during the first two decades of the 19th century, then rebounded in 1920, rising to 3,622,300 piculs (217,338,000 kilograms) in 1926. The increase in silk production generally follows the trend of the co-

① 张丽:鸦片战争前的全国生丝产量和近代生丝出口增加对中国近代桑蚕业扩张的影响.中国农史. 2008 年第 4 期, 第 48 页.The account of 1880 comes from Natalis Rondot. L' art de la soie : les soies. Paris. Imprimeries nationales. 1885. pp.184—208.The account of 1898 comes from A.J.H.Latham et H. Kawakatsu. Intra-Asian Trade and industrialisation: Essays in Memory of Yasukichi Yasuba. New York. Routledge. 2009. p. 198,The account of 1915—1917 and 1895 1898 come from C.W.Howard and K.P.Buswell. A Survey of the Silk Industry in South China. Hongkong. The Commercial Press. 1925. p.27.The account of 1926 comes from 蚕丝业同业组合中央会编纂.支那蚕业大观.东京:冈田日荣堂,1929,第 429 页.Corporation de l' industrie de la soie du Japon. Aperçu de l' industrie de la soie de Chine. Tokyo. Editions d' Okada Nichiei. p.429.

coons. The total quantity of silk produced in China multiplies by 172% in 1840 on the eve of the Great War, and then increases again by 1.37 times until 1926. There is also a concentration of production 80%—90% of Chinese cocoons are produced in four provinces: Zhejiang（浙江）, Jiangsu（江苏）, Guangdong（广东）and Sichuan（四川）.

Graph II-25 Comparison of silk production with other major producers in the world 1840—1915（kilograms）[1]

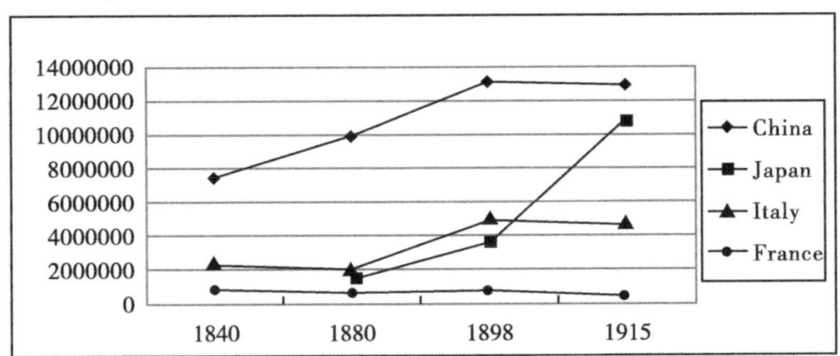

The advantage of Chinese silk production will be very evident if we compare it with those of other sericulture countries of the world during the same period. According to Graph II-25, the amount of silk production in China is much higher than the other major suppliers in the world during the 19th century. Until the end of the 19th century, China produced even more silk than the total production of second and third largest silk producers in the world（Italy and Japan). We have shown that the quantity of exports of silk from Japan exceeded that of China during the first decade of the 20th century. However, in terms of quantity of production, China remains the first in the world even after it has already lost the place of the world's leading silk exporter. The cause is that the rate of openness of the Chinese silk industry is lower than that of Japan at that time: a considerable amount of Chinese silk stay in China as the material for the silk textile industry.

2. Benefits and conditions for the performance of Chinese sericulture

Why can sericulture production increase in the 19th century? In this section we will underline the effects of several aspects on the prosperity of 19th century Chinese seri-

---

[1]　The figures for China's production come from table II-24; the figures of japan, of Italy and of France from 1880 to 1915 come from 石井宽治.日本蚕丝业史分析.东京：东京大学出版会社,1972 年,第 21 页）；The figures of Italy and the France in 1840 come from de Federico Giovanni. An Economic History of the Silk Industry, pp. 210—211.

culture production.

First, the abundance of workforce in sericulture regions is a necessary condition for the advantage of silk production and its growth in China. Many regions (like the United States) in the world possess a suitable climate for sericulture, but this agricultural activity hardly develops or develops very slowly in these regions, because the workforce are not sufficiently abundant. Silk production is really a labor-intensive industry. Each stage has its own workforce consumption requirement: for example, the education of silkworms requires constant care and nourishment, and sericulturalists are obliged to prevent the ravages of silkworm various epidemics; Another example, before the invention of modern methods of cocoa conservation, peasants or guerrillas must finish the reeling of all the cocoons in ten or fifteen days, for fear that cocoons be demolished by butterflies. Due to an obvious increase in the quantities of agricultural crops during the Qing dynasty, the Chinese population has grown during the last three centuries, which offers a large number of labor for the progress of sericulture.

From 1655 to 1700, the Chinese population rose from 50 million to 150 million. It exceeded 300 million in 1790, and eventually reached 440 million in 1900. The main Chinese sericulture regions, Zhejiang, Jiangsu, Guangdong and Sichuan, are also the regions with the highest densities of populations in China. In 1820, the population of these four provinces exceeded 20 million. It is difficult to find exact numbers of sericulturists in China in our sources, because sericulture production is often part-time agricultural work (We will present in another chapter that the peasants plant the mulberry trees in front of or near their houses, next door, or in the street instead of in the fields, spending about 45—60 days for the education of worms and reeling, which are only their additional agricultural activities). However, we could still try to estimate the minimum number of peasants involved in silk production activities in China during the 19th century. The total population of China's major sericulture provinces (Zhejiang, Jiangsu, Guangdong and Sichuan) was 108,634,000 at the beginning of the 19th century (1820). If one adopts the estimate of the demographer Guo Songmin, 90% of the populations of these four provinces are peasants, then there are about 97,700,600 peasants in these provinces. However, within these four provinces, the intensities of planting mulberry trees are not homogeneous. Thus, we suppose that the sericulture activity exists only in the prefectures that concentrate the most of the sericulture production of each province, where situate at least one fifth of the populations of each province①. Thus, we estimated that the sericulture population of these four provinces has a minimum of 19,540,120 people. In China, more than 15% of Chinese silk is produced.

The productivity of the sericulture production of these provinces is not higher than the first four provinces, so the number of sericulturists in other provinces occupies at least 15% of workforce of the total number of sericulture in China. At the beginning of the 19th century, the total number of Chinese sericuturists was at least 23,000,000. This is a very large number, which is even greater than the total number of inhabitants of Italy (20,400,000 in 1820)②, the second largest sericulture country at that time. Moreover, with the growth of the Chinese population, the number of Chinese silkworm growers continues to increase during the rest of the century. The enormous number of sericulturists is the foundation of the comparative advantage of this 19th century China's production sector.

Secondly, an extension of working hours in Chinese sericulture regions from the 17th century to the 19th century ensures the high quantity of Chinese sericulture production.

H.J.Voth affirmed that the annual working time in England increases from 2,700 hours to 3,500 hours per person per year with industrial evolution during the 18th century to the 19th century by the progressive abandon of rest on Monday and the decrease in the number of holidays③. His point of view is supported by Sugihara Kaoru in the analysis of the duration of the work of East Asia, especially in the case of Japan④. Is the great quantity of sericulture production in China in the 19th century related to an extension of working time in the sericulture regions? According to the research of a Chinese economic historian Li Bozhong (李伯重), the working hours of peasant households extend enormously in the Jiangnan region from the beginning of the Qing dynasty. According to the

---

① Sericulture is concentrated in several prefectures (县) of each province. For example, in Guangdong, the planting of mulberry trees is concentrated in Shunde (顺德), Panyu (番禺), Nanhai (南海), Foshan (佛山) in the 21 prefectures of Guangdong province at that time; The planting of mulberry trees are concentrated in Huzhou (湖州) and Jiaxing (嘉兴) in the 10 prefectures of Zhejiang province at that time. These prefectures comprise at least one-fifth of the population of each province. Indeed, in other prefectures of these four provinces there are also mulberry trees although their plantations are clearer. What is estimated here is the minimum number of sericulturists in China, some reserches neglect the sericultural propulsion of other prefectures in each province.

② Comité International de Coordination des recherches Nationales en Démographie. La population de l'Italie. Roma. Viminalgrafica. 1974. p.14.

③ H.J.Voth. Time and Work in England, 1750—1830. Oxford. Oxford University Press. 2000.

④ Pour les details, consulter Sugihara Kaoru. Japan, China, and the Growth of the Asian internatioanl Economy. 1850—1949. Oxford. Oxford University Press. 2005 ; Sugihara Kaoru. Labour-intensive Industrialisation in Global History. London. Routledge. 2013.

author, the agricultural pluriactivity of a peasant household in this region increases from 140% at the end of the 17th century to 170% at the beginning of the 19th century, leading to a 25% working time of the peasant in the household[1]. At the same time, the duration increases by another 75% because of the expansion of ancillary activities (such as the education of silkworms and cotton weaving)[2]. As a result, in the Yangzi region, the working hours of a peasant household with 10 Mu (亩)[3] of fields extend to 7,200 hours (12 hours/day×300 days/year×2) per year at the beginning of 19th century instead of 4,760 hours per year (12 hours/day×240+12 hours/day×150) at the end of the 17th century[4]. In this totality of working time, which proportion occupies sericulture activity? Another Chinese historian, Wang Xiang (王翔) wrote that the mulberry plantation counts 142 days of work (12 hours per day, or 1,704 hours) per 10 Mu in the early 19th century[5]. In order to calculate the sericulture working time in a given household at that time, it is necessary to add hours of work during the education of silkworms which often takes place in late spring, 24 hours a day for 40 days[6], which is 960 hours.

So a peasant household that worked on sericulture in the Yangzi region must devote a total of 2,664 hours to the sericulture production activity, or 37% of the total working time (if the total is 7,200 hours) of the home. This proportion must be as high in the Sichuan region, where a mulberry leaf season is also harvested, while in the Guangdong area, two to three times mulberry leaves per year are harvested. As an auxiliary agricultural activity, the working time of sericulture is quite long, while its proportion in all the activities of a peasant household is quite large. So the trend of extended working hours in some Chinese regions since the end of the 17th century has ensured the fine performance of sericulture production in the 19th century.

Third, in China of 19th century, the benefit of silk production is much higher than many other agricultural activities, which leads the peasants to take care of sericulture. As mentioned above, working time for sericulture production is quite long, and the intensity of the work of silk production is much higher than that of other cultural activities: first, the planting of mulberry trees increases the labor consumption of each Mu (亩) of land to 32.2 days of work. Then, sericulturists divide a cycle of silkworm education (40

---

[1]　The working time of a peasant is counted by totalizing the working time of a peasant musculine and feminine.

[2]　李伯重.江南农业的发展 1620—1850 年.上海:上海古籍出版社,2007 年,第 119,154,168 页.

[3]　1 Mu ＝666.7 square metre.

[4]　李伯重:"终岁勤动":夸张还是现实? 学术月刊,2008 年第 4 期,第 135—138 页.

[5]　王翔.近代中国传统丝绸业转型研究.天津:南开大学出版社,2005 年,第 34 页.

[6]　李超琼.石船居杂著剩稿·芙蓉行记, 作于 1895 年 8 月,转引自铃木智夫.洋务运动の研究.东京:汲古书院,1992 年,第 382 页.

days) into "five decortications," said five "Mians" (眠) in Chinese. During the last two Mians, each leaf of grain (about 25,000 grains included) needs to consume 100 kilograms of mulberry leaf per day. As a result, the entire peasant family must work constantly during the day and night at that time[1].

Why are the peasants always very passionate about this kind of work that requires a great work force? When G. Federico analyzed the origin of the growth of the sericulture of the main sericulture countries in the world (China, Japan, Italy), he asserted that, theoretically, there is a very important factor for sericulture growth during the modern period: the opportunity cost is lower than other agricultural activities[2], which means that producers can receive higher profits in a unit of time if it deals with sericulture instead of other farming activities. Indeed, this conclusion above can be very well attested by the case of Chinese sericulture. In China in the 19th century, the cycle of silk production is much shorter compared to other activities, while it can bring much larger benefits to the peasants. Li Chaoqiong (李超琼), in charge of the mayor of Wuxi (无锡, a town in Jiangsu province), wrote in the late 19th century that:

"If we ask how much profit we can get by planting mulberry trees, the answer is that it is more than three times that rice cultivation. In addition, education of silkworms lasts only 40 days in late spring, but rice cultivation requires three quarters from plowing to harvesting."[3]

According to the Japanese Yangshu survey (杨墅乡 a town in Wuxi) after the Sino-Japanese War of 1894—1895, the benefit of peasants who plant mulberry, rice, and wheat at the same time is about 3.45 times that of peasants who plant only rice and wheat. The details could be found in the table below.

Table II-26 Comparison of profits between rice, wheat and the mulberry sur one Mu of land (piculs, taëls) [4]

Years	Wheat			Rice			Total	Mulberry			Education o f Silkworms		
	Quantity	Prix	Valeurs	Quantity	Prix	Value		Quantity	Prix	Value	Quantity	Prix	Value
1897	1.2	2.5	3	2	7.02	14.04	17.04	15	1.5	22.5	1.25	35	43.75

① 王翔.近代中国传统丝绸业转型研究.天津:南开大学出版社,2005 年,第 34 页.

② F. Giovanni. An economic history of the silk industry, 1830—1930. p.83.

③ 李超琼.石船居杂著剩稿·芙蓉行记,作于 1895 年 8 月,转引自铃木智夫.洋务运动の研究.东京:汲古书院,1992 年,第 382 页.

④ 铃木智夫.清国洋务运动の研究.1992 年,第 384 页.

（续表）

Years	Wheat			Rice			Total	Mulberry			Education o f Silkworms		
	Quantity	Prix	Valeurs	Quantity	Prix	Value		Quantity	Prix	Value	Quantity	Prix	Value
1898	0.7	4.2	2.94	3	4	12	14.94	15	0.9	12	1.25	38.5	48.13
1899	1.2	2.5	3	2.5	2.8	7	10	15	0.8	12	1.25	36.5	45.65
1900	0.8	3	2.4	2.7	3.5	9.4	11.8	15	1	15	1.25	46	56.35
1901	1.3	2.5	3.25	2.7	3.8	10.26	13.51	15	3	30	1.25	37.5	46.85
Average	1.04	2.94	3.06	2.85	4.22	10.89	13.95	15	1.22	18.3	1.25	38.5	48.15

The reliability of these surveys is confirmed by research Li Bozhong（李伯重）on the economy of the Yangzi region. According to his calculation, the profit of rice cultivation counts 0.78 taël per Mu（亩）, but that of the sericulture counts 5.65 taëls by Mu. Considering the intensity of sericulture is stronger than that of rice cultivation, a man can take care of 4 Mu of mulberry or 8 Mu of rice. So a man could get 6.24 taëls of profit if he grows rice or 22.6 taëls of profit if he plants the mulberry trees. The benefit of planting mulberry trees is 3.6 times that of rice cultivation per person. This result is very close as the 3.45 times the result above[1].

The high profit makes more and more Chinese farmers engaged in sericulture production, which accelerates the growth of this agricultural sector in China. In comparison, the benefit of sericulture is becoming less and less attractive in Europe. On the one hand, there has been a sharp fall in the price of European cocoons and silk after the diseases of silkworms and the penetration of Asian silk since the mid-19th century, so the benefit of sericulture is much lower because of the fall in price. According to A. Beauquis's calculation, the profit for planting a Mu（亩）of mulberry trees in France drops to 26 francs (around 6.3 taëls) at the end of the 19th century, while a silkworm farmer who works with the family and his own leaves cannot obtain a profit of 85 francs (14.1 taëls) per Mu at that time. This benefit is not only much lower than the profit of sericulture in France half a century ago, but also much lower than this one in China at the end of the 19th century. On the other hand, thanks to the agricultural revolution, the output of other agricultural sectors was much higher during the 19th century[2]. According to P.Bairoch's research, some agriculture sections below have risen à 200% in

---

① 李伯重:明清江南农业资源的合理利用.农业考古.1985 年第 2 期,第 66—67 页.

② A. Beauquis. Histoire économique de la soie. Grenoble. Grands établissements de l' imprimerie générale. 1910. pp.60—62.

122

the early 20th century compared to the early 19th century. This mutation is especially dynamic after the middle of the 19th century, when mechanical agricultural and agricultural innovations are applicated.

Table II-27 Evolution of agricultural product yields in Europe excluding Russia (annual five-year averages) [1]

	1800	1850	1890	1910
Cereals(hectares)				
Wheat	8.6	9.4	10.9	12.6
Rye	7.8	8.6	11	14.9
Oat	7.2	8.9	12.6	14.9
Barley	7.9	9.8	11.9	14.9
Corn	9	10	12.2	14
Othersection				
Potato	50	60	88.1	114.5
SugarBeets		260	260	261.1
Wine	12.5	13	13.3	16.5
Animal products				
Milk	950	1100	1460	1800

Consequently, after the middle of the 19th century, the European peasants found elsewhere, in easier, more remunerative, less hazardous productions, and the additional resources they had demanded for silkworms. Especially in the Mediterranean region where sericulture was the most flourishing in Europe, the prosperity of the wine trade after the middle of the 19th century determined the European peasants to replace their beautiful plantations of mulberry trees by their vines[2]. The different opportunity costs of sericulture in China and Europe determine their evolving trends, which is a very important factor for the silk production advantage of China compared to Europe.

Fourth, the central government and local governments in China are pursuing a policy of encouraging sericulture. After the middle of the 19th century when the silk trade was more prosperous, the Chinese government took many measures to encourage the peasants to plant the mulberry or to produce silk. The measures are very diverse. First,

---

[1]　P. Bairoch. Les trois révolutions agricoles du monde développé: rendements et productivité de 1800 à 1985. Anales. Economies, Société, Civilisations. N°2. 1989. p. 322.

[2]　M.A. Carron. La production de la soie brute en France. Lyon. M.Audin. 1946. p.28.

local governments establish the "Sericulture Bureau" to encourage peasants to engage in sericulture production. The missions of this new office include: often offering free mulberry tree species during the planting season (usually early spring), lending money to farmers, buying the leaves regularly during the harvest season, purchasing overabundant cocoons produced by families who lack labor and sell them to the individual or to the reeling factories with enough workforce.

The first sericulture offices were established in the prefectures of Taicang (太仓), Changshu (常熟), Nanhui (南汇), Fengxian (奉贤) in Jiangsu Province (江苏), where the former cotton producing regions were. The sericulture offices in these prefectures distribute the mulberry tree species free of charge to the peasants, lend money for sericultural production, and buy mulberry leaves and surplus cocoons from the early 1870s. During the 1870s, each of these prefectures has planted more than 100,000 mulberry trees[1], which means they were already transformed from cotton to sericulture regions in the early 1880s. After the 1880s, those offices have already been settled in almost all provinces of the Empire. Even in provinces where was very little sericulture production, such as Henan (河南), Zhili (直隶), the Sericulture Bureau was established to encourage farmers to engage in sericulture production. In remote provinces, such as the Guangxi (广西) and Shanxi (陕西) provinces, the sericulture Bureau even buy, transport and sell silk produced by farmers to the ports of Shanghai and Canton[2].

In addition, local governments recruit sericulturists with abundant experiments and establish schools to learn recognition from novices so that new sericulture techniques can be popularized among all sericulturists. We will develop this point when we discuss the modernization of Chinese sericulture in the 19th century.

Finally, the taxes of the plantation of the mulberry trees, the sale of the cocoons and the silk are sometimes freed or reduced[3]. At the end of the 1860s, the government of Jiangyin Prefecture (江阴 of Jiangsu Province) freed taxes and rent from mulberry fields for the first two years of planting in government fields, and then peasants have only to pay part of the taxes and rent for a few years[4].The same policy is followed by the prefectures of Kunshan (昆山), Xinyang (新阳), Wuxi (无锡) of Jiangsu Province,

----

① 王祖畲:民国.太仓州志.卷三,1918 年,第 22 页,中国国家图书馆馆藏资源。庞鸿文:光绪.常昭合志稿.卷四十六,第 5 页,1904 年,上海市图书馆馆藏资源。民国.南汇县续志.卷二十,2009 年,第 9 页,上海市浦东新区地方志办公室影印.韩佩金.重修奉贤县志.卷十九,台北:成文出版社,1970 年,第 2 页.

② 郑起东:晚清政府劝农桑、兴水利的重农政策.广西社会科学.2006 年第 9 期,第 99—100 页.

③ 施敏雄.清代丝织工业的发展.第 7 页.

④ 陈思:民国.江阴县续志.卷十一,1921 年,第 4 页。江阴市史志办公室藏书.

and then by those of other provinces[1]. At the beginning of the 20th century, many new sericulture prefectures already possess more than 100,000 Mu of mulberry fields. The surfaces of the mulberry fields of certain prefectures, such as Wuxi, already exceed 300,000 Mu.[2]

Thanks to the abundance of workforces, the prolongation of working hours, the high comparative benefit of sericulture and the encouragement of the government, as has been demonstrated, the quantity of silk production in China is the highest in the world during the 19th century. So abundant silk production in China will interest the silk producers in western countries who need to import a lot of raw materials from abroad, including the manufacturers of the French silk textile industry.

3. The decline of the Chinese silktextile industry

The high quantity of silk production in China is an important condition for the prosperity of China's silk exports. But the former does not necessarily lead to the latter, because such a large quantity of silk produced in China can also be consumed by the manufacturers of domestic silk. It has been demonstrated that the total quantity of silk production in China was 123,930 piculs on the eve of the opium war, far higher than those of other countries in the world. However, in this totality of production, only 9,000 piculs of Chinese silk are destined for the foreign market at that time[3], which is 7.26% of the total production. At the beginning of the opening of China (in 1846), the quantity of Chinese silk exports rose to 18,600 piculs (see Table II-28), but it increased very slowly during the following years. Until the year 1852, 10 years after the opening of China, the export rate of Chinese silk always remains at a very low level. After two visits to rural areas of China, Robert Fortune, a famous Scottish botanist tells us in the early 1850s that:

"Foreign demand for silk is so easy to satisfy in China, because there is a large amount of silk in stock in the Chinese market. We must also know that, as in the case of the export of tea, the quantity of silk exports occupies only a very small proportion in proportion to that absorbed by the domestic market. The 17,000 silk bales exported per

---

① 汪垕.昆新两县续修合志.卷八,1880 年,第 10 页,昆山市图书馆馆藏资源.
② 满铁上海事务所.江苏省无锡县农村实态调查报告书.1941 年,第 9—10 页,上海市图书馆馆藏资源.
③ 徐新吾.中国近代缫丝工业史.上海:上海人民出版社,1990 年,第 110 页.

year have little influence on the price of silk or Chinese silk."[1]

However, what is remarkable is that there is a great leap in the export of Chinese silk in 1853. According to the data of Table II-28, China exports 25,571 piculs of silk abroad in 1852, but 61,934 piculs in 1853, a growth of 2.5 times all of a sudden. In addition, the amount of silk exports continues to increase after this year. In the early 1860s, the total quantity of Chinese silk exported already reached more than 80,000 piculs per year.

Table II-28 The China silk export quantity 1845—1864 (piculs)[2]

Years	Quantities	Years	Quantities
1845—1846	18,600	1855—1856	50,489
1846—1847	19,000	1856—1857	74,215
1847—1848	21,377	1857—1858	60,736
1848—1849	17,228	1858—1859	81,136
1849—1850	16,134	1859—1860	69,137
1850—1851	22,143	1860—1861	88,754
1851—1852	23,040	1861—1862	73,322
1852—1853	25,571	1862—1863	83,264
1853—1854	61,934	1863—1864	46,863
1854—1855	51,468	1864—1865	41,128

When the proportion of exports of Chinese silk was recalculated in 1880, the result is quite impressive: the proportion of silk exports rose to 50 percent in 1880. For 30 years, The Chinese silk industry multiplies by five, and the absolute quantity of the total export of silk multiplies by nine. The Chinese silk industry was not very dependent on the international market before the opium war, even in the early 1850s. But 30 years later it became one of the most open production sectors in China. Its rate of opening remained very high until 1815 by stabilizing 50%—60%. What happens after 1853? What are the factors leading to this transformation during these 30 years?

---

① R. Fortune. Two visits to the tea countries of China and the British tea plantations in the Himalaya : with a narrative of adventures and a full description of the culture of the tea plant, the agriculture, horticulture, and botany of China. London. Murray. 1853. Vol II. p. 12.

② A.F.Lindley. Ti Ping Tien Kwoh : The History of the Ti-Ping Revolution, including a Narrative of the Author's Personal Adventure. London. .Day & Son. 1866. pp. 696—698.

Table II-29-A Changes in the openness rate of the Chinese silk industry 1840—1915 (piculs) [1]

Years	1840	1880	1898	1915
Production	123,930	163,154	216,846	213,832
Export	9,000	82,201	108,821	130,389
Domestic Consumption	114,930	80,953	108,025	83,443
Opening Rate	7.26%	50.26%	50.18%	60.98%

Graph II-29-B Changes in the opening rate of the Chinese silk industry 1840—1915

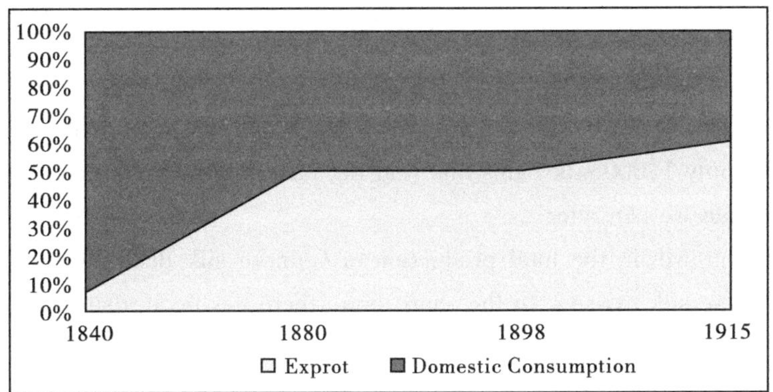

We have discussed in the first chapter that the new privileges obtained by the treaties and conventions between France and China during 1858—1860 hardly serve for the commercial expansion of France in China. As for the silk trade, the effect of the new privileges is also not clear: ten new trading ports are leading China to a wider opening, but the export of Chinese silk is still concentrated in Shanghai and Canton after the 1860s, which are already open since the first Opium War. The other ports export very little silk until the eve of the First World War. Moreover, although foreign traders have obtained the privileges of doing business in the provinces within China, they rarely buy direct silk by themselves. Chinese silk firms and compradors still act as intermediaries

---

① The quantities of total silk production in China are from Table II-29; The quantity of export of Chinese silk in 1840 come from 徐新吾.中国近代缫丝工业史.上海:上海人民出版社,1990 年,第 110 页 ; The export of Chinese silk in 1880, 1898 and 1915 come from 张丽:鸦片战争前的全国生丝产量和近代生丝出口增加对中国近代桑蚕业扩张的影响.中国农史.2008 年第 4 期,第 40 页.

between foreign firms and local firms until World War I. In other words, the privileges obtained by the second war of opium are very limited, if one does not say "zero", on the trade in silk.

Certainly, the expansion of European market demand will increase the export of Chinese silk. But it should be noted that in 1853 (the year in which the "big leap" of the quantity of Chinese silk exports took place), the cocoon harvest in Europe and France reached its peak, diseases of silkworms has not yet ravaged European sericulture, and the demand for silk in Europe is not so urgent. Besides, any foreign firms which make the exchange of silk in China are obliged to face a common and great rival: the Chinese silk textile industry. The silk manufacturers in China have already established a very stable trading relationship with silk suppliers, and they still master the price of silk. If the silk textile industry in China continues to prosper, it will be very difficult for foreign merchants to buy a considerable quantity of silk that they need. A representative of an American company (Augustine Heard and Co.)[1] at Shanghai noted in his report in the early 1850s that "the price of silk in the interior provinces is very high. We get to buy only 1,000 silk bales this year because the price charged by the sellers is much higher than we can offer".

Also, the growth in the total production of Chinese silk does not fully explain the growth of Chinese silk exports. In the short term, there has been a surge in Chinese silk exports since 1853, but there has been no change in the production of Chinese silk during the 1850s. In the long run, the increase of the foreign market demand has indeed stimulated silk production in China, but the growth of Chinese silk production can offer only a part of the export growth of Chinese silk. From 1840 to 1880, the quantity of silk production in China rose from 110,000 picules to 163,154 piculs, an increase of 53,154 piculs. But the export growth of Chinese silk during the same period reached 73,201 piculs. At the same time the quantity of Chinese silk destined for the domestic market of China decreased from 101,000 piculs to 80,953 piculs. We can conclude that a quiet part of the Chinese silk exports growth is at the price of the decline of the quantity of the domestic silk market of China.

Precisely, the decrease in the quantity of silk consumed by the Chinese silk textile industry is another very important cause which led to the surge in the export of Chinese silk after 1853. Although it is not possible to show a precise figure (it is not known how

---

[1]　Les archives d'Augustine Heard et Cie. Cité de LI M Lillain. L'industrie et l'exportation de la soie de Chine pendant l'époque moderne. p. 84.

much silk was produced in China in 1853 due to a lack of statistics), it is not difficult to estimate that the silk material used by the textile industry in China decreased very sharply (at least stagnated) from the year 1853. In the long run, according to the calculation in the preceding paragraph, the quantity of silk consumed by the silk textile industry in the first half of the year has decreased sharply (at least stagnated). The interior silk textiles production of China does not return to the pre-opium level until 1880. A quiet part of the Chinese silk that was selling to the domestic market have changed their destination to the foreign market.

It is easy to understand the fact that the quantity of Chinese silk exported increases with the stagnation of the textile industry of Chinese silk. But the real question to be settled here is: Who beat silk makers in China all of a sudden in 1853? Which led to the depression of the silk textile industry in the long term? In the first chapter, it has been shown that China has hardly imported any silk fabric of France or other foreign countries during the 19th century, so we could confirm that it is not the foreign competition that beat the China silk textile industry. In fact, the essential element that led to the decline in silk textile production in China from the 1850s was a civil war, the Taiping Rebellion, which ravaged almost all parts of southern China.

The Taiping Rebellion is a revolution of Chinese peasants against the court of the Qing Empire, whose army is composed mainly of Chinese peasants. This movement exploded in Guangxi Province (southwest China) in 1851, and its influence spread very rapidly to almost all the provinces of southern China. In 1853, the Rebellion Army conquered Nanjing (南京, the capital of Jiangsu province), and established there a Kingdom called Taiping Tianguo (太平天国, says the Kingdom of Peace Heaven). In June 1861, the leadership of the movement decided to continue advancing to the east. At the same time, the rebellions occupied the cities of Suzhou (苏州), Hangzhou (杭州), Huzhou (湖州), Jiaxing (嘉兴) and almost all of Lake Tai (太湖), where the center of silk production of China situated in. A considerable number of battles with alternating advance and recoil are taking place between the armies of the rebellion and the court of Qing in this region until the ruin of the Kingdom in 1864.

During this war, the production of silk has largely decreased because of the very frequent battles. According to a Shanghai Customs inspector, "a considerable number of mulberry trees were cut down, even from the rebellion, which led to a decline in silk production for a long time." [1] On the other hand, exports of Chinese silk increased very

----

[1]　N.Rondot. L'art de la soie: les soies. Paris. Imprimeries nationales. 1885. p. 71.

rapidly from 1853 when Nanjing was conquered by rebellion: from 25,571 bales in 1852—1853 to 61,934 bales in 1853—1854, and then rose to more than 80,000 bales in 1858—1859. The quantity of silk production in the Yangzi region has decreased, but the amount of export of this product has increased. This is paradoxical, but the explanation can easily be found by examining the situation of the silk textile industry in this region during this war.

In fact, during the Taiping rebellion, the cities in the provinces of Jiangsu and Zhejiang, where 80% of the silk manufacturers of China are concentrated, are ravaged severely by the war. Before the Nanjing (南京) rebellion attack, there are 35,000 looms in the city[1], and 15,000 in the suburbs[2]. But "it is the first city attacked, and most weavers flee from the city, leading to a major recession of the silk textile industry in Nanjing[3]. Only 14,000—15,000 remain when the attack on the Taiping army and this number continues to diminish during its occupation".[4]

The situation of Su Zhou (苏州), where there are 12,000 looms is even worse than that of Nanjing[5]. When the rebellion attacks this city, the Qing army burns most of the housing around the city under the pretext of defense necessity. "Suddenly, the suburbs outside the Wu and Jin gates of Suzhou, where many merchants once concentrated, became the sea of flame[6]." The order of society is very disturbed; armies and bandits plunder capriciously inside the city. Weavers and their employers have to flee to Shanghai[7]. The city of Hangzhou (杭州), capital of Zhejiang province, is also one of the most famous weaving centers in China in the past. "More than 10,000 weavers were working in Hangzhou. After the battles between the government army and the rebellion, most weavers have disappeared. There are only several left after the ruin of Taiping[8]. War wrecks not only the silk textile industry in the big cities, but also ruins it to small towns, even this one to small villages. In the towns of Changan City (长安), which are

---

① Nanjing (南京) is the largest center of China's textile industry at that time. One of three companies that manufactures fabrics for the court of Qing, the textile company of Jiangning (江宁织造局), is located in Nanjing. The other two companies in Suzhou and Hangzhou are also destroyed by the war.

② 王宏斌.太平天国时期生丝大量出口说明了什么.史学月刊.1987 年第 6 期,第 105 页.

③ 工商部技术厅.首都丝织业调查记.南京:工商部,1930 年,第 11 页.

④ N.Rondot. L'art de la soie: les soies. pp. 63—64.

⑤ 张丽:鸦片战争前的全国生丝产量和近代生丝出口增加对中国近代桑蚕业扩张的影响.中国农史. 2008 年第 4 期,第 46 页.

⑥ 李寿龄.鲍斋遗稿,姑苏衰.北京:五亩园,1906 年,卷三,第 6—7 页.

⑦ Archives Nationales de Chine(deuxième), Le bureau général de la douane de Chine. les archives de la douane ancienne de Chine. Special Series. Silk. No. 103.

⑧ 王宏斌.太平天国时期生丝大量出口说明了什么.史学月刊.1987 年第 6 期,第 105 页.

well known for their silk production, "70% of the buildings were burned; Of the wounded prolonged several kilometers on the street; A thousand inhabitants were plundered or killed".[1] Another example: the total population of the seven communes of Jiaxing City（嘉兴府）(they are: Jiaxing 嘉兴, Xiushui 秀水, Jiashan 嘉善, Haiyan 海盐, Pinghu 平湖, Shimen 石门 and Tonxiang 桐乡) counted 2,933,764 in 1838[2], but decreased to 958,053 in 1863. The silk production of the villages of Huangjiaxi（黄家溪）and Wangjiangjing（王江泾）, which lie next to each other, is well known before the Taiping rebellion. Because of a battle between the Qing army and the rebellion along a canal next to the two villages, Huangjiaxi was completely razed on April 24, 1861, and most Wangjiangjing houses were burned two days later[3].

The silk producers that sold silk to the weavers of Jiangsu and Zhejiang consequently lost most of their former customers. They are obliged to find new customers to sell their silks. The security of the port of Shanghai is assured by the Qing army and the foreign army since the year 1860[4], so the rebellion failed to conquer there until the ruin of the Kingdom of Taiping. These Chinese silk sellers in both provinces redirect their silk outlets and "manage to find a safe channel that leads to Shanghai"[5].

More and more silk is transported to Shanghai for foreign firms, which leads to the growth of the quantity of silk exported from China from 1853 to 1863 in Table II-28. This has also explained the evolution of the price of silk at the Shanghai market after the opening. During 1842—1852, the prices of Chinese silk, which showed a trend of growth, were decided by the domestic market. During the Taiping movement, Chinese silks are pushed to the international market because of the decline of the domestic market, and their prices are drastically reduced. The average price of silk on the Shanghai market fell immediately from 260 piasters per bale in the first half of 1853 to 192 piasters per bale in the second half of the year, and to 188 piasters per bale in 1854. The price rose a little after the first half of 1853, 1855, but it never exceeds 221 piasters per bale once again[6].

The production of sericulture in the Yangzi region was successfully restored after the

---

① 杨家骆.太平天国文献汇编.台北:鼎文书局,1973 年,第 6 卷,第 557 页.

② 罗婧:世界市场与苏嘉湖蚕桑丝织经济圈.上海师范大学学报.2010 年 5 月,第 100 页.

③ 王翔.中日丝绸近代化比较研究.石家庄:河北人民出版社,第 420—421 页.

④ Après la deuxième guerre d'opium 1856-1860, la cour de Qing et les puissances occidentaux retiennent leurs relations amicales.

⑤ LSHII Kanji. Le commerce de la soie à Nanxun pendant l'occupation de Taiping. 87—89. Cité de LI M Lillain. L'industrie et l'exportation de la soie de Chine pendant l'époque moderne. p. 120.

⑥ 姚贤镐.中国近代对外贸易史料 1840—1895.第 576 页.

ruin of the Taiping Kingdom in 1864. The local governments of Zhejiang, Jiangsu and Jiangxi have implemented many measures to restore the former sericulture regions and create the new sericulture regions. Investigations by Shanghai Customs also note that "many new mulberry trees have been planted since the restoration of peace. The quantity of silk production is at present considerable: it reaches, if not above, the level before the rebellion[1]". In fact, the average quantity of production in Zhejiang during 1864 - 1870 reached at least 50,000 piculs per year[2], which has already exceeded the level before the civil war. According to the statistics of Natalis Rondot, the total quantity of cocoon production in China is 163,154 picules in 1880, whose productions in Zhejiang occupy 63,500 piculs, even higher than the level of the 1860s[3].

On the other hand, the prosperity of the silk textile industry has disappeared forever in the towns and villages of the two provinces after this civil war. According to the data in Table II-30, in 1880, years after the end of the Taiping movement, the quantity of silk material consumed in this region is only 23,944 piculs, still a quarter of the years before 1853. The number of looms in the provinces of Zhejiang and Jiangsu decreased from 92,134 in 1852 to 26,904 in 1854. In the three former centers of the textile industry of China, Nanjing, Suzhou and Hangzhou, the numbers of looms decreases to one tenth, one quarter and one seventh respectively in the level of 1852. The quantity of silk production dropped at the same time to 1,593,138 rolls (匹) in 1880, which was lower than the latter in 1852.

Table II-30 Comparison of silk production quantities between the year 1880 and the years before the rebellion[4]

	1852			1880		
	Looms	Silk textile production (rouleaux)	Raw silk consumption (piculs)	Looms	Silk textile production (rouleaux)	Raw silk consumption (piculs)
Nanjing	50,000	2,000,000	55,687	5,000	200,000	6,188

---

① Archives Nationales de Chine (deuxième), Le bureau général de la douane de Chine. les archives de la douane ancienne de Chine. Special Series. Silk. No. 103.

② 铃木智夫.洋务运动の研究.东京:汲古书院,1992 年,第 382 页.The average of the amount of Zhejiang silk exported by Shanghai reached 30,825 piculs per year from 1856 to 1870. The author of this thesis believes that the amount of silk exported should not exceed 70% of the total amount of production , So 50,000 piculs per year is already a very reserved estimate.

③ N.Rondot. L'art de la soie: les soies. p.194.

④ 张丽:鸦片战争前的全国生丝产量和近代生丝出口增加对中国近代桑蚕业扩张的影响,第 46 页。

（续表）

	1852			1880		
Suzhou	12,000	330,552	10,600	3,000	82,638	2,944
Zhenjiang	1,250	80,300	927	1,250	80,300	927
Shengze	5,350	600,000	3,881	8,000	900,000	5,974
Danyang			200	13,750	290	
Hangzhou	20,000	359,250	12,931	3,000	71,650	2,586
Huzhou	4,080	480,000	8,620	4,000	204,000	4,310
Shaoxing	1,600	32,500	422	1,600	32,500	422
Jiaxing	225,000	1,456	6			
Ningbo	848	84,000	303	848	8,400	303
Total	92,134	4,043,002	94,827	26,904	1,593,238	23,944

The proportion of silk exported continues to increase after the 1880s, rising to about 61% of total production on the eve of the First World War[1]. Attacked by the civil war of China during 1851—1864, the domestic silk market in China failed immediately. More and more silks produced in Zhejiang and Jiangsu are now transported to Shanghai for export. The flow of Chinese silk depends more and more on the international market. If we say that the Opium War opened the door of China, we could also say that the Taiping Rebellion opened the foreign trade of Chinese silk.

In conclusion, thanks to the abundance of workforce, the high benefit of sericulture and the policies of encouragement of the government, China still retains its advantage over the amount of silk production in the world during the 19th century. However, the growth in the supply of Chinese silk to the world market is not only due to the increase in Chinese silk production but also to the price of the decrease in the consumption of silk material in China. The Chinese silk textile industry is almost completely destroyed by the

---

① Idem. p. 40.

civil wars during the Taiping Rebellion, while it is not restored until the end of the century. In this case, from the 1850s, much of Chinese silk is suddenly available for the external market, and the export rate of the industry remains very high for the rest of the century. With the large deficit of the silk material that began in the 1850s because of the silkworm disease, the silk manufacturers of France decided to increase the importation of this material from abroad. At that time, China's offer corresponded precisely to the demand of France, which became the origin of the prosperity of the silk trade between the two countries. In the next chapter, we will see the roles played by commercial intermediaries in the Franco-Chinese trade as well as the relations between these intermediaries.

Chapter III   Companies in the silk trade between France and China

After our research on the supply and demand of the silk trade between China and France, we will discuss in this chapter intermediations connecting the silk markets on both sides of the Euro-Asian continent of the 19th century. As was shown in the first chapter, the expansion of French trade in the Chinese market was greatly influenced by the existence of competition from England to the Far East. Therefore at first we will discuss the role of the English merchant and the London market for the silk trade between China and France. Moreover, as P. Verley affirmed in his book *L' Echelle du monde*, the merchants play a very important role in long-distance international trade in modern history: "the more expensive and slower the transportation of goods, the more difficult it is to circulate information, the more homogeneous the economic space is, the more important the function of those who are intermediaries between producers and consumers. Throughout modern era, merchants derive more profit from the market than manufacturers from their work. The first tends to control the latter."[1] By demonstrating the whole process of the circulation of silk from the Chinese producers to the silk manufacturers in France, we will analyze the roles of all the intermediaries in this circulation: Who operate the Franco-Chinese silk trade of the 19th century? What are their importance in the exchange? What are the relationships among different intermediaries in different stages of trade? Why such relationship or composition? At the same time, we have indicated in the following chapters that the 19th century is a century of great change in the conditions of Euro-Asian trade: changes in customs barriers, advances in transport and communication technologies, the main maritime shipping lines and the implementation of the Telegraph, etc. In this chapter we shall already observe what all these changes bring to the intermediaries of the exchange of Franco-Chinese silk and their roles for that trade.

---

[1] P.Verley. L' Echelle du monde. p.182.

I Indirect exchange by the London market and foreign domination of Chinese silk export before the 1870s

Great Britain is the most important point of distribution of raw materials and semi-finished products of Europe during the period of the Industrial Revolution. According to research by R. Findlay and K.H.O'Rourke, the proportion of re-export occupies always about 20% of Britain's total exports from the end of the 18th century to the mid-19th century, while the value of its re-export rises from 7 million pounds to 21 million pounds during this last period. At that time, raw materials from all over the world, from India to Latin America, from the United States to South Africa, often enter Europe by Great Britain[1]. Indeed, until the middle of the 19th century, the importation of Chinese silk into France also passed most often through London.

According to the data in Chapter II, even if there is already the exchange of direct trade (silk without resold by other countries) during the 17th century, regular imports of Chinese silk from China into France only begin from the year 1852, when Rémi sends 85 bales of raw silk directly from Shanghai to Lyons. Before this date, direct exchanges of this kind of raw material between these two countries are very rare: no note exists on the direct exchange of silks between France and China during 1800—1830; Only 6,700 kilograms of Chinese silks were sent directly to France from 1830 to 1836; Silk appeared only once on the exchange lists between the two countries from 1837 to 1851 (494 kilograms of raw silk in 1845). In fact, this rarity of direct exchange does not equal the non-existence of the use of Chinese silks in France. The French began to produce their silk textiles with large quantities of Chinese silks much earlier than the year 1852, because silk merchants in France used at the moment to buy Chinese silks indirectly by the London market, which is the largest port of silk distribution in Europe before the mid-19th century. London, therefore, became the most important intermediary of the silk trade between France and China at the time.

P.Cayez, in his work on the 19th century industry of Lyons, has already mentioned the re-export of silk from London to Lyons[2]. But in his research there is neither precise quantitative data, nor an explanation for the existence of trade. In this section, we will

---

① R.Findlay and K.H.O'Rourke. Power and plenty. Trade, war, and the world economy in the second millennium. New Jersey. Princeton University Press. 2007.p.327.
② P.Cayez. Crise et croissance de l'industrie lyonnaise 1850—1900. Paris. Editions du CNRS. 1980. p.31.

136

clarify that subject by observing several questions: How is the position of Chinese silk e-volving in the London market? From what moment does France begin to colossally import Chinese silk through London, and at what moment does the direct exchange of silk between France and China begin to take its place? Why is Chinese silk often arriving in France by London during this period? Which intermediaries (which companies)? In the context of multilateral trade, what does France export to England to compensate for the importation of Chinese silks by London? Why did the French silk merchants later give up the London market?

1. The dynamics of the export of Chinese silk to England

The English companies are the largest foreign importers of Chinese silk in Canton since the early 19th century. According to Table III-1-A, they control more than 90% of Chinese silks exported from China to the Western world during 1819 to 1832. Before 1834, it was the English East India Company who represent the Business interests of England in China. However, the export of silk was never its most important commercial activity in China during the first decades of the 19th century. Since the application of the *Commutation Act* in 1784, which reduced the tariff on tea imported into England, the price of tea has decreased considerably, which has greatly stimulated growth in the consumption of tea of the English. The East India Company then exported more and more of Canton's tea to England[1]. In contrast, from that date, the proportion of the silk trade became less important for the English Canton trade. During the years 1775—1785, silk made up an average of 31% of the East India Company's exchange value with China, but this proportion decreased to less than 10% from 1785 to 1795[2]. At the beginning of the 19th century, the quantities of Chinese silk import rose little despite very strong growth in the level of general exchange values between the two countries.

The turning point of the silk trade between England and China took place in 1825 when the English East India Company allow individual English merchants to engage in this trade. At the beginning this year, the silk trade begins to increase on the trade statistic between the two countries. This trend is evident even more obviously from the year 1834, when the company completely lost commercial exclusivity in China. In 1837 the total value of silk exported from the Canton to England exceeded 1,808,000 British

---

① H.B.Morse. The chronicles of the East India Company 1635—1834. Vol.1, p.44—46.

② E. H. Pritchard. The crucial years of early Anglo-Chinese relations. 1750—1800. Washington. Octagon Bookis. 1936. p.166.

pounds, or 2.5 times the highest value during the monopoly period of the company. The implementation of the commercial liberalism of England to the Far East, in other words the commitment of independent companies and individual merchants, is the departure of the prosperity of Chinese silk exports.

Table III-1-A proportions of Chinese silks exported to the United Kingdom in total quantities of Chinese silk export (piculs) [1]

Années	Royaume-Uni	Etats Unis	Pays-bas	Total	Proportion du Royaume-Uni
1819	3,618	507	0	4,125	87.71%
1820	3,625	0	0	3,625	100%
1821	6,032	0	0	6,032	100%
1822	5,178	70	0	5,248	98.67%
1823	3,211	0	0	3,211	100%
1824	3,595	95	0	3,690	97.43%
1825	6,985	545	0	7,530	92.76%
1826	4,186	260	0	4,446	94.15%
1827	3,570	267	0	3,837	93.04%
1828	7,248	328	0	7,576	95.67%
1829	5,990	347	130	6,467	92.62%
1830	6,668	285	100	7,053	94.54%
1831	60	109	0	169	35.50%
1832	221	144	0	365	60.55%

---

[1] The data from 1811 to 1830 come from Table V-1-A. 鲁傅鼎.中国贸易史.台北:文物供应社,1985 年, 第 72—73 页.The data from 1831 to 1832 come from Ministère de l' agriculture et du commerce, Document sur le commerce extérieur, Chine et Indochine, Fait commerciaux n°1, p. 60.

Table III-1-B Quantities of silks exported from China to the United Kingdom 1811—1855 (English pounds) [1]

Years	Quantities	Years	Quantities	Years	Quantities
1811	120,795	1826	554,437	1841	277,093
1812	259,858	1827	472,848	1842	180,124
1813	273,113	1828	960,000	1843	264,301
1814	409,669	1829	793,377	1844	339,793
1815	85,003	1830	883,179	1845	1,169,643
1816	87,284	1831	8,000	1846	1,834,310
1817	280,397	1832	28,000	1847	2,913,907
1818	297,086	1833	22,000	1848	1,722,800
1819	479,250	1834	583,000	1849	1,613,100
1820	480,132	1835	758,000	1850	2,214,300
1821	798,940	1836	1,282,000	1851	2,304,000
1822	685,828	1837	1,808,000	1852	2,557,100
1823	425,298	1838	720,000	1853	6,194,000
1824	476,159	1839	361,000	1854	5,148,600
1825	925,165	1840	248,000	1855	5,648,900

[1] The data from 1811 to 1830 come from Tableau V-1-a. 鲁傅鼎.中国贸易史.台北:文物供应社,1985年, 第72—73页.The data from 1831 to 1840 come from Ministère de l' agriculture et du commerce, Document sur le commerce extérieur, Chine et Indochine, Fait commerciaux n°1, p.60; The data from 1841 to 1847 come from Ministère de l' agriculture et du commerce, Document sur le commerce extérieur, Chine et Indochine, Fait commerciaux n°15, p. 3,p.13—14 ;The data from 1848 to 1855 come from Ministère de l' agriculture et du commerce, Document sur le commerce extérieur, Chine et Indochine, Fait commerciaux n°24, p.45. English livre = 0.453 kilogramme.

Graph III − 1 − C Quantities of silks exported from China to the United Kingdom 1811—1855 (English pounds)

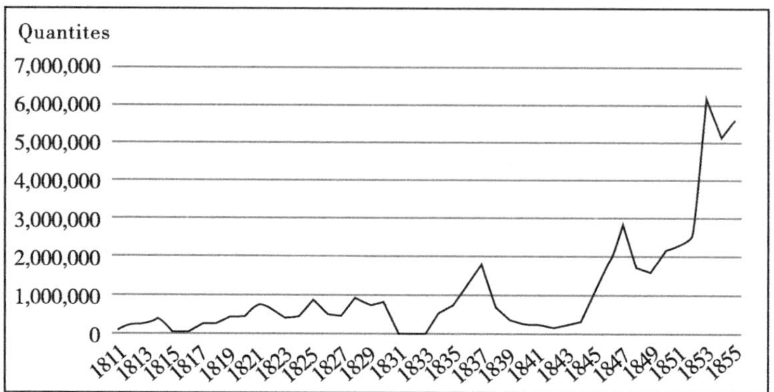

The trend of export growth of Chinese silks in the United Kingdom is temporarily interrupted by the Sino-English Opium War (1840—1842). According to the *Canton Register*[1], after the Viceroy of Guangdong and Guangxi Lin Zexu (林则徐) pronounced the prohibition of the opium trade in 1839, there were only 17 foreigners who remain in Canton, most of whom are Americans[2]. This explains the decline in the silk trade between China and the United Kingdom as shown in Graph III − 1 − C. However, the resumption of the normal commercial relationship between the two empires began very quickly after the end of the war. With the signing of the *Nanjing Treaty*, the Qing Court abolished the policy on the limitation on the export of silk in 1842. The opening of the port of Shanghai to international trade in 1843 (which is just next to the largest silk production regions in China) has also greatly stimulated the growth of China's silk exports to the United Kingdom. From 1844 to 1855, quantities exported from Chinese silks to Great Britain bounded from 339,793 pounds to 5,648,900 pounds, which is even three times higher than the summit of the Canton trade period (18,808,000 in 1837).

Moreover, thanks to the absolute advantage of long-distance maritime transport compared to other countries and the presence of its commercial companies (we will return to these points right away), the United Kingdom holds always first place among all exporters of Chinese silk to the western world. In 1846, a value of 7,946,000 francs of

---

[1] The Canton Register was an English newspaper founded by Scottish merchants James Matheson, his nephew Alexander Matheson and William Wightman Wood in Canton in 1827.

[2] G.Lanning and S.Couling, The History of Shanghai. Shanghai. Press de Kelly & Walsh. 1921. pp.166—167.

140

Chinese silk was exported to the western countries, of which 7,789,000 francs were absorbed by the United Kingdom[1]. During the 1852—1853 season, when Rémi sent 85 bales of Chinese silk from Shanghai to France, English merchants bought 31,391 bales[2], while American merchants import only 2,224 bales[3].

Table III-2 Different silk origins imported into England 1842—1856 (thousand pounds) [4]

Countries	1842	1852	1853	1854	1855	1856
Netherlands	364	271	182	156	96	92
France	1,156	172	275	148	139	158
Malta	11	70	99	139	67	62
Turkey	731	570	621	214	154	179
Egypt		911	1,863	1,540	773	2,514
India	1,360	1,335	539	697	884	610
China	180	2,148	2,838	4,577	4,437	3,724
Total	3,952	5,883	6,431	7,535	6,619	7,384

At the same time, Chinese silk plays more and more important role in the London market. Until the early 1840s, the raw silks of France and India deal with most of the imports from England. In contrast, Chinese silk takes a small proportion in the London market at that time. With the opening of China since 1842 and the fall of European sericulture in the early 1850s, Chinese silk values began to compose more than half of the imports of silk into the United Kingdom, which occupies an average of 51.77% in the total value of silks imported into England from 1852 to 1856, and that proportion is never below 50% before 1890[5].

2. Re-export of Chinese silk to France by London

In spite of a great import of Chinese silk, the silk textile industry in England can

---

[1] Ministère de l'agriculture et du commerce, Document sur le commerce extérieur, Chine et Indochine, Fait commerciaux n°14, p. 9.

[2] 1 balle = 100 kilogrammes.

[3] Ministère de l'agriculture et du commerce, Document sur le commerce extérieur, Chine et Indochine, Fait commerciaux n°22, p. 14.

[4] 北华捷报.1857 年 8 月 22 日,上海市图书馆馆藏资源.

[5] Consulter le Table II-4.

only absorb a small part of it. In other words, most of the Chinese silk that arrived in London is for re-export to other European countries, even in the United States[1]. Let us take the example of the years 1840—1846. The United Kingdom imported a total of 4,313,015 pounds of Chinese raw silk from 1840 to 1846, but kept only 1,440,572 pounds in its territory; During the same period 32,949 pounds of milled silk are transported, of which only 15,883 pounds are bought by manufacturers of domestic silk[2]. That is to say, about two-thirds of the raw silk and one-half of the milled silk imported to the United Kingdom is for re-export to other countries instead of industrial production.

The little absorption of the English silk textile industry is decided by its production capacity, whose expansion is strictly limited by the silk textile industry in France. In fact, although the silk textile industry in England, concentrating in several cities such as Spitalfields, Lancashire, Manchester and London, developed very rapidly during the first half of the 19th century[3]—the number of looms used in the manufacture of silk fabrics rose from 5,500 in 1823 to 12,000 in 1828, and to 18,000 in 1834[4]—they situate still in an inferior position in competition with that of France, whose number of looms already reached 30,000 in 1825 and 40,000 in 1834[5].

With the dominance of French silk on the European and American markets during most of the 19th century, it is very difficult for English silk to enter foreign markets, which decides that it is no more possible for the English silk textile industry to constitute to increase after the middle of the 19th century. After the abolition of the prohibition on imports of French silk into the United Kingdom and the penetration of French silk into the United Kingdom, it lost its last market—the domestic market. Most of the English silks were ruined by their Lyonss competitors. The number of silk workers in England, therefore, dropped from 130,000 in 1851 to 30,000 in 1907[6]. With a rather modest production capacity, England, as the world's largest silk market in the mid-19th centu-

---

① Prior to the completion of the American railway works from west to east, Asian goods are often transported to the United States by the Atlantic route.

② Ministère de l'agriculture et du commerce, Document sur le commerce extérieur, Chine et Indochine, Fait commerciaux n°15, p. 3. and p.13—14 .

③ S.H.R.Jones. Technology transaction costs and the transition to the factory production in the British silk industry. Journal of economic history. 1987. No°47. p.85.

④ A.D Négociant. Membre de la Chambre de commerce de Lyon. Un mot sur les fabriques étrangères de soierie. A propos de l'exposition de leurs produits faite par la chambre de commerce de Lyon. Lyon. Librairie de Mme. Duval et M. Bohaire. 1834. pp.54—55.

⑤ E.Hamaide. La relation entre Lyon et Chine au XIX siècle. p.9.

⑥ L.Gueneau. Lyon et le commerce de la soie. Thèse soutenu devant. la Faculté de droit de l'Université de Lyon. Lyon. Imprimerie L.Bascou. 1923. p. 54.

ry, is actually the largest distribution center for these raw materials to other Western countries.

French silk merchants buy regularly the silks from the London market. Before the pebrine, they get used to selling French silks with superior quality to the market to England, and then import silks with lower quality with lower price, including Chinese silks. With the growth of the supply of Chinese silk in London after the opening of China in 1842, more and more Chinese silks are brought to France by London. According to the data in Table Ⅲ-3, there is a very strong growth in terms of the absolute quantities of Chinese silks re-exported from the United Kingdom to France after 1843. However, it should be noted that before the explosion of the pebrine, the part re-exported to France takes only a very small proportion in all the Chinese silks brought to the London market: less than 4% during the years 1843—1853. Even during the first two years of the epidemic of silkworm (1854—1855), there was only a small rise: 5.10% in 1854 and 6.18% in 1855. Chinese silks do not really flourish in France by the London after the complete fall of French and Europe sericulture. In 1858 and 1859, more than half of the Chinese silks on the London market were re-exported to France. Absolute quantities rose from 158,240 kilograms to 3,800,000 kilograms from 1855 to 1859, an increase of 24 times during four years. At that time, apart from the Chinese silks kept by the local silk manufacturers of the United Kingdom (about 1/3 of the total), we could conclude that almost all the Chinese silks re-exported from London were destined to France.

Table III-3 Proportions of quantities of Chinese silk re-exported from the United Kingdom to France in quantities of all Chinese silks imported into the United Kingdom 1843—1859. (kilograms) [1]

Years	Total to United Kingdom	Re-export to France	Percentage
1843	119,178	3,020	2.53%
1844	153,926	4,065	2.64%
1845	529,848	10,290	1.94%
1846	830,942	23,546	2.83%

[1] Data for the total Chinese silks imported into England 1843—1855 come from table Ⅴ-1-B. Livre anglaise =0.453 kilogram ; Data on Chinese silks re-exported from the United Kingdom to France 1843—1855 come from Lamb S. La soie, c'es l'or. Lyon. Bureaux du courrier de Lyon. 1856. pp.71—72. Data for 1858—1859 come from de RONDOT Natalis.Conseil supérieur de l'agriculture, des manufactures et du commerce. Rapport sur l'industrie des soies et des soieries. Paris. Imprimerie impériale. 1861. p.18.

（续表）

Years	Total to United Kingdom	Re-export to France	Percentage
1847	1,320,000	29,996	2.27%
1848	780,428	29,789	3.82%
1849	730,734	28,814	3.84%
1850	1,003,078	29,275	2.92%
1851	1,043,712	32,187	3.08%
1852	1,158,366	44,550	3.85%
1853	2,805,882	68,900	2.46%
1854	2,332,316	118,840	5.10%
1855	2,558,951	158,240	6.18%
1858	2,400,000	1,330,000	55.41%
1859	7,300,000	3,800,000	52.05%

Manufacturers of silk in France continued to depend on the London market during the 1860s. According to estimates by the French Trade and Agriculture Ministry, there are about 45 million francs of Chinese silk exported by London in France in 1858[1]. In 1865, France imported a sum of 140 million francs from the raw silk of England, among them 75 million came from China[2]. The market for the re-export of silk in London maintains still its prosperity even during the first years after the opening of the Suez Canal. In the year 1871, London received 2,500,000 kilograms of Chinese, Japanese and Bengal silks, worth 135 million francs, 90 million francs of which was re-exported to France, and 45 million francs for domestic silk manufacturers and other western countries. Among these silks that come from different countries, at least 55% are Chinese silks[3].

Compared to the quantity of Chinese silk bought by London, the Chinese silk imported directly to France is much more modest during this period. In 1858, the French received 1,330,000 kilograms of Chinese silk from London, but imported directly from China only 17,000 kilograms. 75 million francs of Chinese silk was sent from England to

---

① Ministère de l'agriculture et du commerce, Document sur le commerce extérieur, Chine et Indochine, Fait commerciaux n°27, p. 4.

② Ministère de l'agriculture et du commerce, Document sur le commerce extérieur, Chine et Indochine, Fait commerciaux n°40, p. 30.

③ P. Ernest. Chambre de commerce de Lyon. Question du droit d'entrée sur les soies, Rapport par les délégués. Lyon. Imprimerie de Barret. 1871. p.12.

France in 1865, while only 18,376,000 francs of silk was imported from China to France by direct trade during this year (special trade)[1]. In fact, the direct trade in silk between France and China gradually assumed a superior position only after the beginning of the 1870s. The English re-exported almost 50 million francs of Chinese silks in France in the year 1871. During the same year 80 million of Asian silk francs come from Asia directly to Marseille, of which at least 4/5 come from China. So one might conclude that, during the years 1854 to 1870, the London market was the most important intermediary of the silk trade between France and China.

3. Why import from London?

Why did the French choose to import Chinese silk indirectly through the London market instead of importing them directly into France before the 1870s? In the reports of the French trade commissioners in China to the Commerce and Agriculture Ministry of before the 1870s, they offered their views on the reasons for the prosperity of the London silks market and the inferiorities of direct trade of silk between France and China before the 1870s.

(1) The first element that has been taken into account when they analyze the superior position of commerce from England to the Far East is the advantage of navigation. A French trade commissioner in Shanghai wrote in his report on 28 February, 1865:

"The trade relation of China are much more frequent with England than with France. We always find a ship departing for one of the English ports, but departures for our ports are extremely rare... The transport of silks, partly to the account of the various houses engaged in this branch of commerce, are never sufficiently large to be able to freely fly a ship. As for steam vessels going to England, they are also the most numerous."[2]

We will emphasize in Chapter IV that the cost of shipping English ships is already much lower and that of the French ships for the trip to China before the creation of the new line of Messagerie Maritime Company for China and the opening of the Canal of Suez. The delegate pointed out that, apart from the cost of transport, the greater number of vessels was also an advantage of England in the transport of Chinese silk. It shows that each ship often loads only a small amount of silks when shipped to Europe from China

---

[1] Refer to Table II-7 in Chapter II.

[2] Ministère de l'agriculture et du commerce, Document sur le commerce extérieur, Chine et Indochine, Fait commerciaux n°38, p. 48.

(because of the very high value of silk, buyers do not want to send all their silk in on ship to avoid safety problems), so it takes a lot of ships if you plan to carry a large quantity of silks. The boats that sail between China and England are more numerous than those between China and France, so more Chinese silks are transported to Europe by London market.

Indeed, according to statistics which were shown in Chapter IV, before the 1870s (even afterwards), the performances of French ships are still much more modest compared to those of England. There are 237.6 average French commercial ships sailing between France and China each year from 1866 to 1870, while the average number of English ships enter to or come from China is 7,341.8[1]. The inferiority of long distance sea shipping is indeed a reason for the frequency of French silk traders at the London market.

(2) "But the cause of the indirect expedition to France is," the delegate continues, "the importance of the English companies in Shanghai. Most of the great companies of London are represented there with their immense capital, and they can undertake operations of very large scale, contenting themselves with the profits produced by the high interest which their money receives."[2] Here, the delegate mentioned the problem of the installation of company in China. He argues that this is the main cause for the prosperity of the London silk market and the inferiority of direct Franco-Chinese silk trade.

In reality, this delegate is not the only person who has addressed this problem. In a letter from the Commerce, Agriculture and Public Works Ministry to the Chambers of Commerce in France in September 1864, there was more discussion about the superiority of the English and American companies and the inferiority of the French companies in China. The Minister takes the same point of view as the previous delegate and tell us the situation of the scarcity of French factories in China at the moment. In his opinion, this was a greater obstacle to the direct trade of silks of France with China. At the same time, it indicates:

"Gentlemen, the question of the real and permanent causes of our inferiority in trade with China, are those which my department cannot lose sight of, and which ought not to fall asleep from the attention of the interested in solving it. Allow me, therefore, to add some considerations to those which were the subject of my previous communication.

---

① The two averages can be obtained from Table III-12.

② Ministère de l'agriculture et du commerce, Document sur le commerce extérieur, Chine et Indochine, Fait commerciaux n°38, p. 49.

"It has often been said, and with good reason, that the luxury of installation and the extent of the means of action deployed by the great English and American companies, which in some measure monopolize China's trade, a vain ostentation than a skillful tactic to dismiss the competitors. Indeed, in the eyes of the native population as well as of the foreign colony, in any Chinese city open to external relations, commercial credit is established according to the extent of the expenditure. Successful conditions of success have so far discouraged those of our nationals who have attempted to establish trading posts, or to engage in the traffic of goods in this country, that there are hardly a hundred French merchants scattered there at all ports. About 80 of them live in Shanghai and Ning-Po; Canton, Tien-Tsin, and Tche-Fou each have one or two; There does not seem to be any at Amoy, Fou-Tchou, Kien-Kiang, Tchin-Kiang, and Formosa. In Han-Kao, our contingent is also very small.

"This being the situation, gentlemen, my department has wondered how it could be improved. It is easy to understand that a manufacturer preferably buys his silks in London, as long as the interview in Shang-Hai of an agent who would send directly to them would entail an expense higher than commission, transport and other expenses, caused by the English market. But where industrial efforts would be powerless, the association, conceived and practiced on a broad basis, would have a certain chance of triumphing.[1]

According to the Minister, the inferiority of the French counterparts in China is primarily due to the competition (even monopolies) of the English and American big companies, which discourages enormously French companies or French merchants to install a companies in China. There is indeed English and American companies that control the trade (including the silk trade) between China and Europe during the 19th century, especially before the 1870s, which have an absolute advantage in terms of quantity. In 1832, among the 22 foreign companies and 165 foreigners settling in Canton, there are 10 English companies in Canton with the commercial licenses by the East India Company and 88 people from England (comparing to 7 American companies and 20 people from the United States, 0 French comparing and 1 person from France). 55 foreign companies and 307 foreign merchants situated in Canton in 1838 (5 years after the fall of the Company's monopoly), of which 31 are English companies and 158 merchants come from England (comparing to 9 American companies and 44 Americans, 0 Houses

---

[1] Ministère de l'agriculture et du commerce, Document sur le commerce extérieur, Chine et Indochine, Fait commerciaux n°35, p.73.

French company and 1 French) ①.

After the Opium War, the British immediately expanded their business to the other four open ports, especially in Shanghai. In the statistic by a French delegate in 1845, 108 foreign companies had installed in all the five ports open to foreign trade, 68 companies were registered by the English merchants, and a single French company had installed in Canton at that time.② China's foreign trade center moved from Canton to Shanghai after the 1850s. There were already 27 English companies, but only 2 French companies in 1852. Until the end of 1859, there were 45 companies English, 14 Parsi companies, 6 American companies, but only 3 French companies in Shanghai③.

Among all the English and American houses, a small number of large companies master the majority of China's foreign trade, the most powerful being the Jardin Matheson and Co. (English, 怡和洋行), Dent and Co. (宝顺洋行) and the Russell and Co. (American, 旗昌洋行). According to the description of a French delegate, they are "the first foreign companies in China: Jardine Matheson and Co., Dent and Co., and Russell and Co. Their activities concern especially opium, teas, cottons and silks④. Indeed, these three houses have accumulated large amounts of capital through the opium trade, and then have gained more profits by investing all the accumulated capital in the tea and silk trades. Let us take the example of foreign trade in Shanghai in the year 1851. According to the *North China Herald*, the total import values in Shanghai amounted to 16,310,000 piasters in this year, and that of opium imports about 12,000,000 piasters. Among the 227 foreign ships entering the port of Shanghai in 1851, 58 ships transport the opium, in which 43 opium ships belong to the three companies above, accounting for 74% of the total⑤. In term of export, in 175 ships exporting tea and silk from China, 50 ships served for the three great companies, which make up 29% of the total number of vessels.

---

① H.B.Morse. The chronicles of the East India Company 1635—1834. Vol.1, p.82.

② Ministère de l'agriculture et du commerce, Document sur le commerce extérieur, Chine et Indochine, Fait commerciaux n°10, pp. 413—421.

③ 上海对外经济贸易易志.上海:上海社会科学院出版社,2000 年,第 53—56 页.

④ Ministère de l'agriculture et du commerce, Document sur le commerce extérieur, Chine et Indochine, Fait commerciaux n°10 p. 410.

⑤ 北华捷报.1852 年 7 月 3 日,上海市图书馆馆藏资源.

Table III-4-A The entry Ships and the import values in Shanghai under three large houses in 1851 (piaster)

Companies	Opium		Other articles		total	
	Ships	Values	Ships	Values	Ships	Values
Jardine Matheson and Co.	18	3,724,200	4	164,400	22	3,888,600
Dent and Co.	17	3,517,700	4	164,400	21	3,681,700
Russell and Co.	8	1,655,200	12	534,300	21	2,180,500
Total of the three companies	43	8,806,700	21	863,100	64	9,759,800
Total of all companies à Shanghai	58	12,000,000	105	4,318,000	163	16,301,800
Proportion of the three companies maisons	74%	74%		20%	39.26%	59.87%

Table III-4-B Ships exporting silver, tea and silk in Shanghai in 1851

Companies	Ships transporting silver	Ships transporting tea and silk	Total
Jardine Matheson and Co.	6	12	18
Dent and Co.	6	12	18
Russell and Co.	3	26	29
Total of three companies	15	50	65
Total of all companies à Shanghai	19	175	194
Proportion of the three companies maisons	78.95%	28.57%	33.50%

Beside the three large houses, the British or American small companies specialize mainly in exporting tea and silk from China or importing foreign textile products (often cotton and woolen products) to China. Although the turnover of each cottage is much less than that of large companies, as their number is larger, they export together a considerable amount of silk during this period.

Table III – 5 Entry and departure ships in Shanghai and their major article in 1851[①]

Companies	Nationality	Entry ships	Natures des articles imported à Shanghai				Departure ships	Natures des rmrchandises exportées de Shanghai			
			opium	textile products	others	Empty		silver	tea and silk	others	empty
Jardine Metheson and Co.	English	25	18	2	2	3	28	6	9	3	10
Dent and Co.	English	25	17	4	0	4	26	6	10	2	8
Russell and Co.	American	34	8	2	11	13	36	3	14	12	7
Lindsay and Co.	English	16	15	4	5	2	20	1	15	1	3
Augustine Heard and Co.	American	12	3	2	2	6	27	2	17	4	4
J. Mackrill Smith	English	17	1	2	8	5	0	0	0	0	0
D. Sassoon Sons and Co.	English	2	2	0	0	0	2	0	0	0	2
Pestonjee Framjee											
Carm and Co.	Paris	4	3	0	0	1	2	1	0	1	0
Mac. Vicar and Co.	English	12	0	7	3	2	11	0	7	1	0
Blenkin Rawson and Co.	English	8	0	1	4	3	8	0	6	1	3
Bull. Nye and Co.	American	8	0	3	2	3	7	0	4	3	1
Gbb Living ston and Co.	English	7	0	4	2	1	7	0	7	0	9
Hargreave and Co.	English	7	0	4	1	2	9	0	9	0	0
Thos. Repley and Co.	English	4	0	3	0	1	4	0	4	0	0
Syken Schwabe and Co.	English	4	0	2	2	0	7	0	4	3	0
Turner and Co.	English	4	0	2	1	1	4	0	4	0	0
Wolcott Bate and Co.	American	9	0	2	4	3	10	0	6	3	1
Gilman Bowrmn and Co.	English	3	0	0	3	0	3	0	0	2	1
Holliday Wise and Co.	English	2	0	0	1	1	2	0	1	0	1
Mackenzie and Co.	English	2	0	1	1	0	3	2	1	0	0
Reiss and Co.	English	2	0	1	0	1	3	0	3	0	0
Rathbone Worthington and Co.	English	1	0	1	0	0	2	0	0	2	0
Dirom Gray and Co.	English	1	0	0	1	0	2	0	2	0	0

① Tables III–5 are composed according to reports of movements of foreign navigations in Shanghai published by 北华捷报.1851—1852,上海图书馆馆藏资源.

（续表）

Companies	Nationality	Entry ships	Natures des articles imported à Shanghai				Departure ships	Natures des rmrchandises exportées de Shanghai			
			opium	textile products	others	Empty		silver	tea and silk	others	empty
Peninsular and Oriental Steam											
Navigation and Co.	English	1	1	0	0	0	2	0	0	2	0
W.M.Davison	English	1	0	0	1	0	1	0	0	1	0
Watson and Co.	English	1	0	0	0	1	1	0	1	0	0
Cowasjee Pallanjee and Co.	Paris	1	0	0	1	0	1	0	1	0	
d'autres companies		15	0	0	5	10	10	0	0	6	3
Total		227	58	47	58	64	238	19	128	46	54

In what ways do these English and American companies monopolize the foreign trade of China?

Firstly, we have already stated that there is a great quantity of English vessels which navigate between China and England in order to ensure trade between the two countries. What should be added is that all large companies own their own ships, even armed vessels[1]. Having no need to depend on shipping companies, they can carry their goods or receive messages from London more economically and quickly with their ships[2].

According to A.B.Lubbock's description in *The China Clippers*, large English and American commercial companies often equip "Clippers"[3]—the fastest boat in the world on the eve of the Steam Ships—to send the opium from India to China[4], and take tea and silk from China. Each large company has at least 6 or 7 Clippers that sail between China and India. In addition, to promote the exchange of goods between ports on the coast and between ports inside of China along the Yangzi River, some companies have established shipping companies and warehouses in China[5]. These institutions are helping them to monopolize navigation in China.

Secondly, another advantage of the English or American companies in China (es-

---

① A. B. Lubbock. The China Clippers. Glasgow. Brown, son & Ferguson. 1914. pp.59—60.

② I.Friel. Maritime History of Britain and Ireland. London. The British Museum Press. 2003. p.243.

③ A clipper is a sailing boat made to convey as quickly as possible perishable goods thanks to relatively thin dimensions and a large car. Established on the East Coast of the United States, clippers were at their peak in the mid-19th century on the tea and cotton trade routes of the United Kingdom and the United States.

④ A. B. Lubbock. The China Clippers. p.4.

⑤ E. J. Eitel. History of Hong-Kong. Montana. Kessinger Publishing. 2008. p.276.

pecially the large companies among them) is that they accumulate a large amount of capital, which will help them to expand their business in China.

According to the data in Table III-4, we could discover that, for a single year, 19 silver vessels were taken from China by all these companies. An American historian estimates that the Jardine Matheson and Co. earned more than 3,000,000 pounds of profit during the years 1827—1847 through the opium trade, and the profits of the other two large companies (Dent and Co. and Russell and Co.) during that time must not be lower[1]. Moreover, according to the Chinese historian NIE Baozhang, because of the insufficiency of the currencies (money) circulating in the Chinese market[2], the value of money becomes increasingly high during the first half of the 19th century, so there was a strong decline in the prices of Chinese tea and silk at the time. At the same time, the price of opium becomes higher and higher with the increase of its importation.

In order to facilitate the exchange process and to speed up the turnover of capital, the large English and American houses that control a large quantity of opium can directly obtain silks and tea by paying for opium after estimating the values of the articles according to their prices[3]. As a result, profits earned by British and American houses and their opium are immediately transferred to capital to export a large quantity of tea and silk, which will bring them more profits. This virtuous circle makes them more and more powerful on the Chinese market.

Thirdly, large English and American firms are squeezing out their competitors by controlling the finance, currency and insurance markets. At first, they lend a large amount of money to Chinese companies (their buyers or suppliers), even to Chinese local governments[4]. These loans not only bring large sums of interest, but also the fidelity of Chinese companies and the confidence of the Chinese government[5]. At the same

---

① R. M. Martin. China ; political, commercial, and social ; an official report. Charleston. BiblioBazzar. 2001. Vol 2. p. 258.

② There are still discussions about the causes for the insufficiency of money in China during the first half of the 19th century. The conventional view is that it is the importation of large quantities of opium from South Asia into China that leads to the flow of Chinese money abroad and the insufficiency of the money in China at the time. This opinion is called into question by many researchers. In particular, LIN Man-Houng, in his 2006 book, states that instead of the importation of opium, the essential elements for the deficiency of Chinese silver at the time was the Revolution Latin America and the decline in the export of Chinese products, such as tea and silk, to the world market.For the details, LIN Man-Houng. China Upside Down : Currency, Society and Indeologie, 1808-1856, Cambridge. MA and London. Harvard University Asia Center. 2006.

③ 聂宝璋:十九世纪中叶在华洋行实力的扩张与暴力掠夺.近代史研究.1981 年第 2 期,第 118—119 页.

④ 徐义生.中国近代外债史统计资料.中华书局,1962 年,第 4—5 页.

⑤ 汪敬虞:十九世纪外国在华银行实力的扩张及对中国通商口岸金融市场的控制.历史研究.1963 年第 5 期,第 123 页.

time, they monopolize the exchange market between taëls and foreign currencies by their enormous capital. The exchange of trade treaties is an indispensable link in international trade. Before the year 1833, the English East India Company and the American companies monopolized the foreign exchange business between China and England[1]. After the fall of the East India Company, the large English and American companies continue to play its role in China on the foreign exchange market. The first English banks entered China at the end of the 1840s and during the 1850s[2], but the domination of the great English companies in the foreign exchange market continued even after the appearance of the first bank.

An American merchant tells that: "Each company is at the same time its own banks. In reality, it is the old big companies that monopolize banking business."[3] On August 7, 1852, the *North China Herald* published an article in which it noted that "the Oriental Bank Corporation is not considered a real bank in Shanghai because it does not assume the traditional task of a bank, and it does not operate the traditional business of a bank. It is precisely a foreign exchange agency for international treaties, but the foreign exchange business should be profited only by merchants, not by bankers"[4]. Moreover, as we shall show in Chapter IV, English houses also master most of the insurance business in China. In 1844, there were already 25 maritime insurance agencies in China. All these 25 agencies are counters belonging to English companies, among which 11 belong to two large English houses: Jardine Matheson and Co. and Dent and Co. These two houses often oust their rivals by not offering them the marine insurance service[5]. The first US insurance agency, China Mutual Ins and Co., was created only in 1856[6], and the first insurance agency in France did not operate in China until 1863.

(3) Apart from the rivalry of the great English and American companies, the Minister mentioned another element which greatly prevented the installation of French com-

---

① M.Greenberg. British Trade and the Opening of China 1800—42. Cambridge. Cambridge University Press. 1951. p. 164.

② The Oriental Bank Corporation fonde une agence à Canton en 1845 et une autre agence à Shanghai en 1847; The Commercial Bank of India fonde ses agences à Canton en 1851 et à Shanghai en 1854; Agra and United Service Bank fonde ses agence à Canton en 1855 et à Shanghai et Hongkong en 1858 ; Chartered Mercantile Banque of India, London and China fonde ses agences à Shanghai en 1854 et à Hongkong en 1857 ; Chartered Bank of India, Australia and China fonde une agence à Shanghai en 1858.

③ F. H.H.King. Money and Monetary Policy in China 1845—1895. Harvard University Press. 1965. p. 98.

④ 北华捷报.1842 年 8 月 7 日,上海市图书馆馆藏资源.

⑤ J.King Fairbank. Trade and Diplomacy on the China Coast. Stanford. Stanford University Press. 1953. p. 238.

⑥ 北华捷报.1842 年 1 月 5 日,上海市图书馆馆藏资源.

panies in China: the high cost installation. The minister did not indicate the actual a-
mount to create and exploit a company in Shanghai. However, we could estimate that
spending for a company in China must be quite huge, especially for those do not possess
a lot of capital or turnovers. At that time, the salary of a single sales representative Henri Meynard reached 8,000 francs per year (excluding maintenance expenses)[1]. For all
the charges to install a company in China, apart from wages representatives, we must
add rents, taxes, transportation costs, registration capital and working capital, etc. In
addition, a foreign house in Shanghai will need a large amount of working capital to operate its business before the implementation of the telegraph mandate, which we will
specify in the next section. According to the data in Table III−7 in the next section, the
"annual turnover" of small French houses in Shanghai is only 200,000—250,000
francs a year. In other words, it is very difficult to assume the cost of installation in China and earn profit for these little French houses (that is a major cause for the rapid ruins
and French houses in Shanghai, we will return after). The French Consul in Shanghai
confirmed this fact in a letter from Shanghai 20 September 1864:

"We understands that a manufacturer prefers to buy in London the silks at the moment, than maintenance in Shanghai an agent who would send them to them directly,
which would entail an equal expense, and probably more expensive after we pay the
commission, transport and other expenses, than the purchase of these silks on the English market."[2]

4. The end of the re-export of Chinese silk from London to France

We already know from the text of Chapter II what has happened later. The prosperity of the London silk market continued until the 1870s. The quantity of direct import of
Chinese silk into France exceeded that in England in 1875 with the opening of the Canal
of Suez, of the reduction of the transport cost of French ships. After that, less and less
Chinese silk flock to Europe by passing the London market. And then, by replacing
England, France becomes the largest silk market in Europe. In other words, the French
no longer need the London market as an intermediary to import Chinese silks.

---

[1]　J.Fredet. Quand la Chine s'ouvrait... Charles de Montiny consul de France. Revue de l'histoire des colonies françaises. 1953. p.282.

[2]　Archives du Ministères des Affaires Etrangères. Shanghai 307CCC 5. p.74. Lettre du consul français à
Shanghai du 20 septembre 1864.

Graph III-6 Comparison of the quantities of Chinese silk exports to France and England 1845—1913(picul) [1]

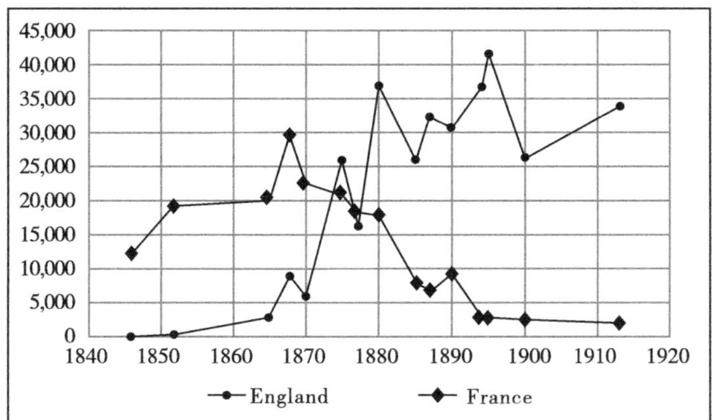

But why they are beginning to develop the direct silk trade with China after the 1850s, not before that date? The answer for this question is actually related to, apart the increase of the silk imports in France because of the silkworm disease, the evolution of the trade cost with China. Let us consider a question: if the French import Chinese silk indirectly through London, how much extra cost (comparing to the cost of buying directly from Chinese market) should be paid at the time?

A report from another trade commissioner in China, Isidore Hedde, offered us the means of calculating the total additional costs to import Chinese silk into France by London[2]: In 1845, the raw silks of Canton in first quality cost about 300 dollars a picul, which represents, per kilogram, a value of 27 francs 50 cents on the market of China. If we send a kilogram of this silk to London, we need:

---

① 上海对外经济贸易志.第 567 页.The account of silks exported to France in 1852 come from Ch.-B. Maybon, J.Fredet, Histoire de la concession française de Changhai, Paris. Librairie Plon. 1929. p. 215.The account for the quantity of silks exported to England in 1852 comes from Table III-1-B. The others come from the archieves 中国历史第二档案馆,中国海关总署办公厅.中国旧海关史料.02 卷第 584—585 页(1865),03 卷第 526—527 页(1868),04 卷 第 324—325 页(1870),06 卷第 9 页(1875),07 卷第 199 页(1877),08 卷第 665 页(1880),11 卷第 240 页(1885),13 卷第 258 页(1887),16 卷第 288 页(1890),22 卷第 328 页(1894),23 卷第 314 页(1895),31 卷第 399 页(1900),62 卷第 255 页(1913)。Archives nationales de Chine(deuxièmes), le bureau général de la douane de Chine. les archives des douanes anciennes de Chine, Beijing. Rapport commercial de Shanghai Vol 2. pp. 584—585(1865) ; Vol 3.p. 526(1868) ; vol 4.pp. 324—325(1870) ; Vol 6. p. 9(1875) ; Vol 7. p. 199(1877) ; Vol 8. p. 665(1880) ; Vol 11. p. 240(1885) ; Vol 13. p. 258(1887) ; Vol 16. p. 288(1890) ; Vol 22.p. 328(1894) ; Vol 23.p.324(1895) ; Vol. 31. p.399(1900) ; Vol 62. p.225(1913).

② Ministère de l'agriculture et du commerce, Document sur le commerce extérieur, Chine et Indochine, Fait commerciaux n°12. p. 91.

Customs Duty .... 4.5%   1.25 francs per kilo

Insurance 3.5%

Purchasing Commission 2%

Freight ....0.5%   125 francs per tonne per English vessel

Interest of 5 months ....2.5%   4.5 months is the average of the crossing

From Canton to France

Various expenses in London......5.5%

In other words, according to Isidore Hedde, a total of at least 18.5% (or about 5 francs per kilogram) is added to the price in Canton when this kind of Chinese silk arrives in London. If we re-export these silks from London to France, you must add an additional 6.5% of the original price.

Commission 3%

Interest of 3 months to 4% per year 1%

Condition 2%

Carriage ....⎤
Packaging ....⎬0.5%
Castons Duty................................⎦

We will have to add the 13.5% discount or term. So all the extra costs to import Chinese silks by London are about 38.5% of the price at that time. As indicated in Chapter II, most of the silk materials used by manufacturers in Lyons originate from the Mediterranean region before the European pebrine. The additional cost of 38.5% is quite high in relation to direct trade, but bearable for French merchants[1], because it is not worth taking the very high cost of setting up its own trading posts in China if they don't need to import a quiet large quantity of silk or other goods from distant countries like China. From the beginning of the 1860s, more and more Chinese silks were placed in French factories, which meant that more and more extra charges had to be paid to English brokers in London. From this date it is more rational for French silk merchants to set up their own trading posts or to find their own commissionaires in Canton and Shanghai, which may represent the interest of the French weaving industry.

---

[1]   We have shown in Chapter I that the value of exports from China to France is very modest before the 1850s. Moreover, there is also the problem of the inadequacy of Chinese exports to the needs of the French market .

The Commerce Minister encourages passionately his compatriots to create their silk agents in China: "This expense, which one company cannot bear, would be reduced to the sponsors of a vast counter to a very small extent. To applicate this idea, it would be sufficient for our silk importers to agree on the choice of a small number of agents who, instead of representing a particular buyer, would concentrate all the orders of the factory and act upon it. France, ultimately consuming and implementing much more silk than England, would arrive, by centralizing its operations on the square of Shang-Hai, to take the first place in the export to exercise on the courses of the raw material, influence, and ascendancy, which naturally belong to the greatest outlet of a product"[1]. This is why, with the increase in the use of Chinese silk in Lyons, more and more Chinese silk is imported directly to France. The intermediary role of the London market for the silk trade between France and China thus came to an end after the 1870s.

II The roles of French companies and foreign companies in the direct trade of Franco-Chinese silk

We have shown in the last section that almost all exchanges of Franco-Chinese silk take place through the London market during the first half of the 19th century. However, from the 1850s, more and more Chinese silks were sent directly from China to France without going through London. Until the end of the 1870s, Shanghai, Canton—Marseille, replacing Shanghai, Canton—London—Le Havre, gradually became the main transport route for silk from China to France. By showing the evolution of French silk houses throughout the 19th century in China, we will discuss in this section, on the one hand, the influence of the growth of direct trade of silk between China and France on the installation and development of French houses in China. On the other hand, we will discuss the role foreign companies play in the direct trade of silk between France and China. Are French companies in China the main intermediaries in the silk trade between France and China? Or are there other intermediaries, for example, English, German and Swiss companies? Which of them play a more important role?

1. French representatives in canton before the 1850s

We have already reported in Chapter I that after the return of the consul De

---

[1] Ministère de l'agriculture et du commerce, Document sur le commerce extérieur, Chine et Indochine, Fait commerciaux n°35 p. 73—74.

Guignes to France on 4 August 1801, there was no French representative who stays in Canton protecting the commercial interest of France in China. Before the departure of the consul to his native country, he entrusted his responsibility and the French factory to a Swiss merchant, Charles de Constant. But four years later (1804), the Swiss sublet the French factory to an Englishman. From this date, the tricolor flag no longer floated in front of the French factory in Canton[1], and it did not appear again until the year 1832, when Benoît Gernaert rebuilt the consulate in the French factory in Canton.

The truth of all these stories is reconfirmed by William C. Hunter, an American merchant who had been in Canton from 1825 to 1844. This last witness mentioned in his memoirs describing his stay in Canton that "we can see from afar that the flags of England, the Netherlands and Spain are raised in front of their factories in 1825. The Spanish pavilion actually represents the company of Philippine. After an intermittent interval of thirty years, the French flag was once again raised on 13 December 1832. But it represented only the French consulate at Canton, for the commerce of France in Canton was less than nothing."[2] Hunter does not exaggerate. There were no notes of the French trade movement in Canton from 1801 to 1832. Only two merchants, Edward Bovet and Charles Bovet who speak French lived in Canton in 1826. But they are the two watchmakers of Swiss origin[3]. Comparing the results of two censuses of foreign adults to Canton in 1832 and 1837 published by the Chinese Repository[4], we discovered that there is only one Frenchman who lives in Canton in 1832 and in 1837. The census report also shows us that the other foreigners who live in the French factories are merchants from England, the India and the United States. According to a statistic of an English historian, at the end of the monopoly of the English East India Company[5], the number of foreign houses in Canton increased from 66 in 1833 to 150 in 1837, but none of them belongs to the French merchants. In other words, from the beginning of the reopening of the French consulate in Canton to the end of the Opium War, there was no French companies that represent the interests of France in China.

---

① The word "factory" comes from the English word "factory". During the period of the foreign trade of Canton, dwellings and commercial movements of foreign traders are limited to a small area in the city of Canton. In this region, foreign administrative representatives or traders from each country are promised to rent a building like their dwelling or office. This building is called 'factory'. It should be noted that the factory does not mean 'factory' here.

② H.C. William. The Fankwae at Canton Before Treaty Days, 1825—1844. London: Kegan. Paul, Trench& Co. 1882. p. 35.

③ 林日杖.鸦片战争前后外国在华洋行经济活动初探.福建师范大学硕士学位论文,2001 年,第 15 页.

④ Chinese Repository (《中国丛报》, 又称《澳门月报》) was a monthly magazine created by English merchants in Canton in 1832.

⑤ Chinese Repository. Janvier 1837. p.23.

This situation does not improve much at the beginning of the opening of the five ports to the international trade of China. In the general list of trading houses established in Chinese ports in 1845 published by the French Ministry of Commerce and Agriculture, only one French company was found in Canton, Durran and Co., whose main exercise is the importation of wines and brandy from France into China[1]. If one adds the company that Rémi created in 1843 that sells clocks and wines to Canton[2], there are only two French houses in China at the beginning of the opening of China. In this situation, French delegates regretted that "in China so few French companies have been established, that our ports have neither agency nor factory; This is the reason why our trade has until recently only had vague and even contradictory data on the elements of import, on the tastes of indigenous consumption, and was scarcely fixed on business centers and centers of action. It is not enough for some ship-owners to be informed by their monthly correspondence on the facts relating to their speculation; it is important that there is a common and permanent source of information, together with agencies where consignments can be made in complete safety".[3]

The performance of French companies is so discreet at the moment that French manufacturers and merchants in France are obliged to buy Chinese goods from foreign companies based in China. "The first foreign commercial companies in China are those of Messrs. Jardine, Matheson and Co., Dent and Co. and Russell and Co. ... It will therefore be wise, prudent and, as it were, indispensable that the French merchants who will seriously decide to open relations with China will have in this country have a good agent chosen from among the companies which have long been established there, in order to be well informed before sending them (by means of a monthly correspondence) on the state of commerce and the price of goods. But we think that we should be careful not to choose this agent among the first-class companies, and especially among those who deal largely with the opium trade, an important and exclusive trade which absorbs all the care of those who do it. The choice of such an agent must be made among the companies whose domestic products are not such as to compete directly with our own, such as, for example, the Dutch, German, Portuguese, and even Belgian companies,

---

① Ministère de l'agriculture et du commerce, Document sur le commerce extérieur, Chine et Indochine, Fait commerciaux n°10. p. 417.

② Ch.-B. Maybon, J.Fredet, Histoire de la concession française de Shanghai, Paris. Librairie Plon. 1929. p 34.

③ Ministère de l'agriculture et du commerce, Document sur le commerce extérieur, Chine et Indochine, Fait commerciaux n°12. p. 424.

and among them are distinguished in Macao and Canton, the Reynvaan and Co. (Dutch), since time in connection with France; Tielman and Co. (Belgian), Païva and Co. (Portuguese), both also in connection with France."[1]

2. Installations of French houses in Shanghai since 1848

Arone and Rémi are the first two French traders who do business in Shanghai[2]. Arone rents a piece of land in the English concession and creates a company there in May 1848: Bac Arone and Co. (公生号), which is the first French company in Shanghai. But this company does not export silk. By specializing on the trade in ammunition, it was ruined three years later (1851).[3] Dominique Rémi, who had been doing the clock business in Canton since 1843, arrived in Shanghai with his two clerks in June 1848, and then reinstated his store in the French concession in Shanghai in 1849[4]. At the beginning, clock and wine are the only exchange goods in his company. In 1852 Rémi sent 85 bullets of silk from Shanghai to France, which was the first attempt to export silks directly from Shanghai to Lyons. After this first attempt, he transferred the focus of his business on the Chinese silks export. With the help of his nephew Edouard François Schmidt, Rémi expanded the size of his company and renamed it as Remi Schmidt and Co. (利名洋行) from 1 January 1855[5]. The annual exchange value of this company reached 12,000,000 francs in 1862, being the second highest of all French companies in Shanghai at that time, just behind that (20,000,000 francs) of the Comptoir d'Escompte de Paris in Shanghai. Influenced by the financial crisis of Europe in the middle of 1860s[6], Rémi Schmidt and Co. was forced to join the Dent and Co. (宝顺洋行 English) in 1865, modifying again its name to Rémi de Montigny[7] and Co. The following year, this company became a Dent and Co. agency[8]. Since then, the name of the company of Rémi disappeared in the list of French companies in Shanghai.

---

[1] Ministère de l'agriculture et du commerce, Document sur le commerce extérieur, Chine et Indochine, Fait commerciaux n°10. p. 410—411.

[2] The French concession in Shanghai does not yet exist at that time.

[3] G.Brossollet. Les Français de Shanghai. 1849—1949. Editions Belin. 1999. p. 29.

[4] 王垂芳.洋商史:上海 1843—1856.上海:上海社会科学院出版社,2007 年,第 131 页.

[5] 上海社会科学院.上海对外经济贸易志.第 567 页.

[6] A financial crisis is already happening before the Great Depression of 1873-1896. Some major banking institutions had already become bankrupt in the mid-1860s, such as the Pereire Brothers' Credit in France in 1867, while a first black Friday, May 11, 1866, rocked the London Stock Exchange.

[7] Archives of Foreign Affairs. Shanghai 1864—1866, 307CCC 5. March 20, 1864 letter from the Minister of Foreign Affairs to the Minister of Trade and Agriculture.

[8] 曹胜梅:晚清时期法商在沪经营活动述略 1847—1910,载于上海市档案馆编.上海档案史研究·第一辑.上海三联书店,2006 年,第 123 页.

After the fall of the cocoon crop since 1854, some French merchants were sent from France to China to develop the silk trade with the latter country. Eugene Buissonnet arrived in Shanghai in April 1854 as a sales representative for Chartron-Brisson and Co. "Despite his young age, he enjoys a reputation in the community for a man who wants to link business."[1] Having frequently gone back between France and China for the silk trade in the 1850s, he finally established his own house Buissonnet and Co. (比索内洋行) in Shanghai in the year 1860, for export of Chinese silk in France. The exchange value of this new company has reached 9,000,000 francs since its opening. Because of his commercial successes and his contributions when he assumed administrative responsibilities in the French concession[2], Benoît Adan, the French consul in Shanghai, asked the French government for an honorable title for Buissonnet[3]. In 1870, Buissonnet was obliged to return to France at the summit of his career in Shanghai because of the problem of his health, while his company is closed after his departure[4].

Henri Meynard is another well-known French silk merchant in Shanghai. He came to buy the cocoons in Shanghai from a French company (which was created by Henri Maynard, his cousin Marius Maynard, and the Fleurier Bovet brothers according to an agreement signed on November 15, 1855) in 1856 with a salary of 8,000 francs per year[5]. Its own company in Shanghai, the Meynard Cousins and Co. opened in 1859. Having registered as a simple company importing "wines and articles of Paris", it actually dealt mainly with the export of cocoons and silks from Shanghai to France[6]. Henri Meynard is also a member of the municipal council of the French concession of Shanghai during the years 1862—1865. Because of the conflict between the municipal council of the French concession and the French consul in Shanghai[7], his administrative career, as well as his trade in Shanghai, began to decline from the year 1865. In 1870 he finally

---

① Archives of Foreign Affairs. Shanghai 1851—1856, 307CCC 2. 15 juillet 1855. Foreign houses in Shanghai in 1855.

② Between 1854 and 1862, Buissonnet appointed the assessor of the tribunal of the French concession in Shanghai, the president of the Municipal Council of the French Concession in Shanghai and the head of the French army of the French concession during the rebellion of Taiping.

③ Archives des affaires étrangères. Shanghai 1861—1864, 307CCC 4. Le 2 mars 1864 lettre du consul français au Ministre du commerce et de l'agriculture.

④ Ch.-B. Maybon, J.Fredet, Histoire de la concession française de Shanghai. p. 313.

⑤ J.Fredet. Quand la Chine s'ouvrait⋯Charles de Montiny consul de France. Revue de l'histoire de colonies française. 1953. p.282.

⑥ E. Hamaide. La relation entre Lyon et Chine au XIX siècle. 2.6. Vers une filière Sino-Lyonnaise de la soie

⑦ The French consul of Shanghai Bremer de Montmorand accuses the members of the municipal councils of the French concession of Shanghai under a charge of the abuse of its authorities, and then holds the members of the council as well as fines them.

abandoned his business in Shanghai and returned to France[1].

Two other French merchants, Henry Chabert and J. Durren arrived in Shanghai to import the silks in France in 1855, but they did not establish their commercial companies in Shanghai. Henry Chabert is the representative of the Eymond and Co. of Bordeaux and returned definitively to France in 1865. J.Durren is the trade delegate sent by silk manufacturers of Lyons, who had stayed only for two years in Shanghai[2].

Three more French silk companies opened in Shanghai in the early 1860s. They were Fajard and Co. (法雅行) created by E. Fajard in 1860, Maniquet and Co. (马凯行) established by Jean Maniquet in 1861, Streicher and Co. (斯特雷行) instituted by Streicher in 1862[3]. At the end of 1863, there were 11 French companies which were installed in Shanghai, 6 of which specialized on the export of Chinese silk in France. According to the statistics in Table III-7, the annual turnover of French companies exporting silk materials (27,950,000 francs) takes an absolute advantage over those of other French companies that do not export silk (400,000 francs) at that time (if not counting the Comptoir d'escompte and la Messagerie maritime). The first group occupies about 98.59% of the total turnover among all the French commercial houses in Shanghai. That is to say, the export of Chinese silks is the most important commercial activity for the French houses in Shanghai at the time. Moreover, there is a geographical concentration of silk companies from France to Shanghai at that time. According to the sources, there are no company that exports silk at other Chinese open ports until the 1870s. Even in Canton, China's second largest port for silk exports, the appearance of the first French company that exports silks, Lacroix cousins and Co., delayed to the year 1876[4].

<hr>

[1]　Brossollet Guy. Annuaire des Français à Shanghai (1842—1955). Editions Rive Droite. 2002. p.52.

[2]　曹胜梅:晚清时期法商在沪经营活动述略 1847—1910,第 124 页。

[3]　Idem.

[4]　Archives du Ministères des affaires étrangères. Canton 3. 1866—1877 67CCC3, 10 mai 1878. lettre du consul français à Canton à Ministère des affaires étrangère. Création d'une nouvelle maison à Canton. pp. 342—344.

Table III-7 French companies in Shanghai in 1863[1]

Names	Dates of creation	Annual Buiness Volume (Francs)	Existence time (years)	Business Sphere
D.Rémi	1849	12,000,000	18	Clocks, Wines, Silks
Vaucher fr6res et Co.	1857	200,000	15	Parisian articles, silks
Legrand Fr6res and Co.	1857	200,000		Parisian articles
Maynard cousins and Co.	1859	2,500,000	11	Wines, articles parisian articles, silks
Buissonnet and Co.	1860	9,000,000	10	Silks
Fajard and Co.	1860	2,500,000		Silks
Comptoir d'escompte de Paris	1860	20,000,000	37	Banc
Sahbelle and Co.	1860	200,000		Wines
Maniquet and Co.	1861	1,500,000	3	Silks
Streicher and Co.	1862	250,000	2	Silks
Messagerie maritime and Co.	1863	80,000,000	99	post, navigation, inssurance

An interesting phenomenon is that almost all the first French houses created before the year 1865 closed or declared bankruptcy before or in the early 1870s. After the clo-

---

[1] Les informations dans ce tableau proviennent des contenus dans Ch.-B. Maybon, J.Fredet, Histoire de la concession française de Shanghai; G. Brossollet. Annuaire des Français à Shanghai(1842—1955);上海社会科学院.上海对外经济贸易志.曹胜梅:晚清时期法商在沪经营活动述略 1847—1910.

sure of the Vaucher brothers and Co. in 1873[1], the old French silk companies completely disappeared in Shanghai. Their closures are no doubt linked to rivalries between the great English and American companies, the European financial crisis in the mid-1860s, and various personal causes, but two more profound elements must not be overlooked. Firstly, the international trade at that time is the "resale" trade; Secondly, the slow communication between Asia and Europe. Silk exchange is one of the commercial movements with the greatest risk because of its great values and its seasonality. These two last elements increase the risk for these companies[2].

On the one hand, although some of the owners of these French silk companies had been the representatives of the companies in France, but the houses they created in Shanghai were independent companies (no relationship with the former companies that hired them) instead of the branch of their former employers. These companies are not necessarily able to find customers in France. Even they have stable buyers in France, they should pay for silks they buy in advance, and then their customers (if any) in Europe will pay them "by drafts at six months of sight"[3]. This mode of international trade is the "resale" trade, which not only adds to the precariousness of customers but also extends the period of the capital cycle. Comparatively, English and American companies (especially large companies among them, such as Jardine Matheson and Co. and Dent et Co.) also operate as independent houses before the 1870s (even after), but their capital is more abundant and their main commercial exercise is often the importation of opium in China, which helps them to lower the commercial risk[4].

On the other hand, the subjugation of the transmission of messages between Asia and Europe further increases the chance of the failure of the disposal of silk materials in Europe. Before the 1870s, communication between China and Europe was effected by postal ships. Even after the opening of the Suez Canal, the fastest postal ships still takes

---

[1]　The name of Vaucher brothers and Co. appeared in the list of French houses in Shanghai in 1872 on the letter of Minister of Foreign Affairs to Minister of Commerce (National Archives of France, F12.7058, September 29, 1872.), but disappeared In the list of 1874 (National Archives of France, F12.7058, December 31, 1874). So it is estimated that this house must close in 1873.

[2]　The price and quantity of silk depend on quality and quantity of silk production, which are very varied according to different seasons.

[3]　N.Rodot. Chambre de commerce de Lyon. Commerce de la France avec la Chine. Délibération prise sur le rapport de M. Rondot Séance du 12 janvier 1860.

[4]　熊月之.上海通史·晚清经济.上海:上海人民出版社,1999 年,第 209 页.

6 weeks from Europe to China①. This decides that it is not possible for European companies in Shanghai to know exactly the demand of the European market when new Chinese silks are put on sale. In this case, these silk companies in Shanghai are obliged to first buy new silks (because the amount of silks in a season is limited) without exact information from the European market, and then look for customers for these materials. If the quantity of silks requested by Europe is much lower than expected, a home in Shanghai will possibly be bankrupt.

3. Modification of the Euro-Asian trade mode and the evolution of French companies in China after 1870

One of the most important events in the history of trade between Europe and the Far East took place in the early 1870s: the implementation of telecommunications between these two regions.

In the spring of 1871, the China Submarine Telegraph Company in London extended English marine cables to Shanghai. The telecommunication between London and Shanghai was opened on April 17, 1871, while that between London and Hong Kong was implemented two months later (July 2, 1871)②. The telegraph line between China and Russia by Vladivostok is also connected on January 1, 1872, which made the Euro-Asian continental link by telegraph③.

As many historians have already concluded, the telegraphic connection leads to a strengthening of the level of integration of international markets④. The upgrading of computer transmission also brings markets closer to both sides of the Euro-Asian continent. Since then, it took only one day for the transmission of a message between Europe and

---

① Some large foreign companies in China often send a fast boat to Singapore so that they can compete first to know the situation of the market of Europe. Jardine Matheson and Co. has set up an observation post (渣甸瞭望台) at the top of Dongjiao Mountain in Hong Kong to get information from London earlier. "When the observer observes mats of ships from London or the Indies appearing on the vast sea, he immediately tells the company to send a fast boat to bring back messages." For more details on the transmission of messages between Europe and China, 冯邦彦. 香港英资财团.香港:三联书店,1996 年,第 17—20 页.

② A.T.Rixon. Telecommunications of China with Foreign Countries. The Public Opinion Quarterly. Vol.2. No° 3. 1983. p.478.

③ D.R.Headrick. The tentacles of Progress: Technology Transfer in the Age of Imperialism, 1850–1940. Oxford. Oxford University Press. 1988. p.107.

④ Many historians claim that the telegraph connection increased the level of price convergence at the markets of London and New York.K.D.Garbade and W.L.Silber. Technology, Communication and the Performance of Financial Markets: 1840—1965 The Journal of Fiance. Vol 33. No° 3. R.C.Michie. London and New York Stock Exchanges 1850—1914. London. Allen and Unwin. 1987 affirment que la connexion télégraphique a augmenter le niveau de convergence du prix au marchés de Londres et de New-York.

China, which has needed several weeks, even several months. This allows all merchants in Shanghai to know the newest information about the European market[1]. If London's demands exceeded supplies today, the extra part will be met immediately[2]. As for the silk trade, silk exporters in China require only a telegraphic message to know the quantities and quality of silks requested by the buyers in Europe, and then buy and send exactly the silks according to the command. The linkage of the telegraph decreased the blindness of the merchants for the distant market, and thus reduced the risk of the silk trade between the eastern and western worlds.

At the same time, the telegraph money transfer gradually replaces the postal money transfer in international trade, which greatly reduces the duration of trafficking. Before the 1870s, exporters in Shanghai had to pay in advance for goods, and then buyers in Europe would make payments with postal drafts for several months. After the implementation of telecommunication, exporters in China can immediately receive telegraphic drafts when sending goods to Europe[3]. After selling these bills in the foreign exchange market, they will immediately get circulation capital for the next order. The commercial risk is again much more reduced.

According to the research of historians, especially those of Wang Jingyu and Wang Xiang, the development of telecommunications leads to an evolution of the commercial mode between Europe and China. By replacing the "resale" trade, the "order" trade became the main trade mode for China's export to Europe after the 1870s[4]. Thanks to the introduction of telecommunication, buyers in Europe need no longer to collect large quantities of goods on deposit because of insufficient supply of raw materials. If they need it, it is only necessary to contact a commercial company (often their agencies or partners) in China and send their orders by telegraph. Their needs will be met right away satisfied by the companies at the open ports of China. For commercial companies at Chinese ports, there is no longer a need to blindly buy raw materials and make advance payments. What they need to do is to take orders from the companies in Europe, to buy

---

① C.Hoag. The Atlantic Telegraph Cable and Capital Market Information Flows. The Journal of Economic History. Vol 66. No°2. 2006. p.342.

② Daily News(UK). 16 October 1888.p. 367.

③ T.R.Banister. A History of the External Trade of China 1834—1881. Shanghai. Maritime Customs Decennial Reports 1922—1931. Vol. I. pp.77—78.

④ 汪敬虞: 外国资本在近代中国的金融活动, 第 108 页; 王翔: 中日丝绸业近代化比较研究, 第 426—428 页.According to their research, there is also a change in the mode of trade in the import of Europe into China. After the 1870s, consignment trade became the main format for exporting European articles to China. We will discuss here only the change of the mode of trade on the export of China in Europe which concerns the subject of this thesis.

exactly certain quantities or qualities of the goods requested in the orders, to pay for these goods with currencies sent by companies in Europe and to send goods to Europe. Profits earned by exporters at Chinese ports are no longer exchange profits, but commission costs.

Under this kind of "order" trade mode, on the one hand, more and more European companies put their commercial agencies in China, because communication between headquarters and agencies can be ensured by the telegraph; On the other hand, more and more independent foreign companies in China are gradually becoming commissioners of buyers in Europe.

What influence has such a change in the commercial mode led to the development of French houses, especially to the development of French silk houses in China after the 1870s?

The total number of foreign firms in China began to rise more rapidly after the 1870s, and remarkable growth appeared at the beginning of the 20th century. The statistics in Tables III−8 show that the total number of foreign firms in China increased from 343 in 1872 to 3,239 in 1911, an increase of almost 10 times. Two explanations for this development: on the one hand, as mentioned, more European companies set up their agencies in China after the implementation of the telegraph. On the other hand, as we have shown above, during the period of the "order" trade, commercial companies in China no longer need to pay in advance for the goods they are going to export to Europe. European buyers pay them by telegraph money order, and pay houses to their suppliers as a result. This translates into a huge reduction in working capital and capital requirements for the installation of foreign homes in China. As a result, more and more independent foreign "small companies" appeared at China's commercial ports. With such impulses, the number of French companies increased very rapidly after the 1870s. It rose from 17 to 37 between 1872 and 1898, and then saw a very strong growth during the following decades. On the eve of the Great War, the number of French companies in China reached 110. The commercial exercises of these new French companies are very diverse: banks, insurance companies, shipping companies, mining companies, importers of French articles (wines, articles from Paris, jewelery stores, watchmaking, etc.), coal houses, restaurants, hotels, hairdressers and certainly silk exporters[1].

---

(1) Archives du Ministère des affaires étrangères. 148CPCOM678. Chine. Relation commerciale avec la France 1900—1901. 29 décembre 1900. Rapport du commerce français en Chine.

Table III-8-A Number of companies and persons in China from various countries 1872—1898[①]

Years	France		England		United States		All foreign companies	
	Number of companies	Number of persons	Number of companies	Number of persons	Number of companies	Number of persons	Number of compaines	Number of persons
1872	17	244	221	1,780	42	538	343	3,673
1873	9	338	215	1,530	52	518	345	3,457
1874	7	307	215	1,537	50	530	340	3,489
1875	6	211	211	1,611	46	541	343	3,579
1876	10	298	226	1,616	45	536	358	3,607
1877	8	176	218	1,851	37	383	349	3,817
1878	9	224	220	1,958	35	420	351	3,814
1879	20	228	299	2,070	31	469	451	3,995
1880	16	164	236	2,085	31	476	385	4,051
1881	8	274	289	2,292	21	406	422	4,792
1882	12	335	298	2,402	24	410	440	4,894
1883	12	332	220	2,463	18	423	354	5,297
1884	14	424	229	2,704	21	621	380	6,364
1885	23	443	233	2,534	27	761	396	6,698
1886	24	471	256	3,438	29	741	421	7,695
1887	18	515	252	3,604	28	855	420	7,905
1888	19	467	297	3,682	29	1,020	521	8,269
1889	20	551	290	3,276	27	1,061	474	7,905
1890	19	589	327	3,317	32	1,153	522	8,107
1891	24	681	345	3,746	27	1,209	547	9,067
1892	29	862	363	3,919	31	1,312	579	9,945

① 姚贤镐.中国对外贸易史资料 1840—1895.第 1000—1003 页.

168

（续表）

Years	France		England		United States		All foreign companies	
	Number of companies	Number of persons	Number of companies	Number of persons	Number of companies	Number of persons	Number of compaines	Number of persons
1893	33	786	354	4,163	30	1,336	580	9,891
1894	32	807	350	3,989	31	1,294	552	9,350
1895	31	875	361	4,084	31	1,325	603	10,091
1896	29	933	363	4,362	40	1,439	672	10,855
1897	29	698	374	4,929	32	1,564	636	11,667
1898	37	920	398	5,148	43	2,056	773	13,421
1899	76	1,183	401	5,562	70	2,335	933	17,193
1900	82	1,054	424	5,471	81	1,908	1,006	16,881
1901	64	1,361	427	5,410	99	2,292	1,102	19,119
1902	71	1,263	426	5,482	108	2,461	1,189	18,962
1903	71	1,213	420	5,662	114	2,542	1,292	20,404
1904	67	1,734	436	5,981	106	3,220	1,602	27,227
1905	77	2,143	434	8,493	105	3,380	1,693	38,001
1906	94	2,189	492	9,256	112	3,447	1,837	38,587
1907	99	2,201	490	9,205	115	2,862	2,595	69,852
1908	88	2,029	487	9,043	109	3,545	2,407	77,960
1909	84	1,818	502	9,499	113	3,168	2,801	88,310
1910	110	1,925	601	10,140	100	3,176	3,239	141,868
1911	112	1,925	606	10,256	111	3,470	2,863	153,522
1912	107	3,133	592	8,690	133	3,869	2,328	144,754
1913	106	2,292	590	8,966	131	5,340	3,805	163,827
1914	113	1,864	534	8,914	136	4,365	3,421	164,807

Table III-8-B The various companies and persons of foreign nationalities represented in China in 1910[1]

Nationalities	Commercial companies	Number of Persons	Nationalities	Commercial companies	Number of Persons
Japan	1,601	65,434	Austrian	26	227
British	601	10,140	Italy	22	274
Russia	298	49,395	Holland	18	150
Germany	238	4,106	Belgium	13	225
Frence	110	1,925	Danmark	8	260
America	100	3,176	Norway	8	188
Spain	84	400	Hungary	3	28
Portugesa	57	3,337	Sweden	1	166
Kerea	46	2,256	Countries without traity	141	

4. The dominance of other foreign companies in the silk trade between China and France

However, the development of French companies occupying the silk trade is much more discreet compared to the growth of all French companies in China. Among the foreign companies that export silk to Shanghai, there are only four French in 1872. They are: Vaucher brothers and Co., the only silk house created since the 1850s that is not yet closed; Ulysses Pila and Co., which is an agency the Ulysses Pila and Co. of Marseille installed in Shanghai in 1869; Nachtrieb Leroy and Co., an agency of Chartron Monnier and Co. in Lyons created by Adolphe Edouard Nachtrieb in Shanghai in 1868; Lacroix Cousins and Co., an agency of another company in Lyons opened in the late 1860s[2]. In the list of 1874, there are only three French companies left because the Vaucher brothers and Co. closed in 1873[3]. Two years later (1876), the Nachtreb Leroy

---

① Archives du Ministère des affaires étrangères. 148CPCOM678. Chine. 1897—1914. 28 août 1911. The different foreign nationalities represented in China 1911.

② Archives nationales de France. F 12.7058. 29, septembre 1872. Lettre de Ministre des affaires étrangères à Ministre du commerce. Liste des maisons de soies étrangères à Shanghai.

③ Archives nationales de France. F 12.7058. 31. décembre 1874. Liste des principales maisons commerciales à Shanghai.

and Co. is also disappeared in the list because of the return to France of A.E.Nacht-
rieb[1]. The number of French companies that exports silks from Shanghai retrun to four
in 1880[2], but this figure falls again to two in 1887 (these two companies are agency of
the Ulysse Pila and Co. in Shanghai and agency of Conzon and Giraud and Co. in Shanghai) [3]. In 1900, there are 24 French companies settling in Shanghai, among which 7
companies deal with the export business of silk. They are: Ulysse Pila and Co., Conzon
and Giraud and Co., Brunet and Co., Racine Ackermann and Co., Olivier and Co.,
Tillot and Co., Chauvin, Chevalier and Co. Among these 7 companies, the Ulysse Pila
and Co. and the Conzon and Giraud and Co. have already appeared in the list of French
houses of 1887, which are the agencies in Shanghai of two French companies. The other
five French houses in Shanghai are also agencies of companies with seats in Paris or Lyons[4].

In Canton, the situation of the French silk companics is no better than in Shanghai.
After the first silk commercial company, the Lacroix Cousins and Co. was established in
Canton in 1876[5], several French companies exporting silks appear successively at this
important port. Until the opening of a new silk house, E. Pasquet and Co., in 1892,
there were only five French companies in Canton, in which four exported silks. These
four companies are: the Lacroix Cousins and Co. agency in Canton; the agency of the
Ulysse Pila and Co. in Canton, the agency of Cozon and Giraud and Co. in Canton; the
new silk company created by MM. Pasquet and Tamet, who had been the silk inspectors
at the large American company, Russell et Cie[6]. In 1902, on the list of foreign companies that export silks to Canton, we found three French in it: E. Pasquet and Co., Boyer, Mazet, Guillie and Co., and Varenne and Co.[7]. Ten years later, Boyer Mazet,
Guillie and Co., Gérin Rykébus and Co., Albert and Wullschleger and Co., the General

---

① Archives nationales de France. F 12.7058. 12. avril 1877. Liste des maisons étrangère à Shanghai

② Archives nationales de France. F 12.7058. 8 mai 1880. Rapport du consul français à Shanghai au Ministère
des affaires étrangères.

③ Archives nationales de France. F 12.7058. 12, octobre 1887. Liste des maisons commerciales françaises à
Shanghai.

④ Archives du Ministères des affaires étrangères.148CPCOM563 Chine, relation commerciale avec la France
1900—1901 29 décembre 1900. Rapport du commerce de France en Chine. pp. 65—66.

⑤ Archives du Ministères des affaires étrangères. Canton 3. 1866—1877 67CCC3, 10 mai 1878. lettre du consul français à Canton à Ministère des affaires étrangère. Création d'une nouvelle maison à Canton. pp.342—344.

⑥ Archives du Ministères des affaires étrangères. Canton 5 1889 -1900 67CCC5. 20 août 1892. une nouvelle
maison française à Canton.

⑦ Archives nationales de France. F 12.7056. Canton. Rapport commercial de Canton en 1902.

Silks and Co. are the companies that appear on the list[1].

French companies which did silk trade are very rare at other ports open to international trade during the 19th century. In the province of Sichuan, where China's third largest silk-producing region is located, the first company of French silks, the Company of Sin India, was established there only in 1911. In the same year, an old French company, Compagnie française de l'Orient, also decided to take the silk trade and abandoned its old business[2]. Shandong is the province that exports the most wild silk to foreign trade since the late 19th century. However, the appearance of the first French company exporting silks in this province was delayed until 1922, when the French Olive tree and Cie decided to create an agency at the port of Tchefou (the largest port in Shandong)[3]. According to sources, the French never extend their counters to the other ports of China.

By consulting at the evolution of French silk companies in China after the 1870s, we might find that they have two very obvious characteristics. In the first place, after the 1870s, almost all French silk houses in Shanghai or Canton were the agencies placed by companies in France, which corresponded precisely to the influence of the change in the model of international trade on the form foreign firms in China. In a second place, the totality of the number of French silk companies is constantly very discreet from the beginning of the 1870s to the eve of the Great War. Moreover, among these very few houses, the rate of bankruptcy is quite high. Very few of these houses are still open ten years after they are created.

The low presence of the French silk houses before the 1870s is understandable because of the prosperity of the London market, the competition of the great English houses, and the very high commercial risk at the time. But why did the number of French silk houses not increase even with the expansion of the Lyons market and the development of the direct silk trade between France and China after the 1870s? We found some tracks in the letters of the French Consul in Shanghai and the Foreign Affairs Minister.

On November 29, 1898, the French Consul in Shanghai filed a report with the Minister of Foreign Affairs, bearing the contents below:

"What concerns the export trade of China to France, the situation is the same as

---

① Archives nationales de France. AN F12. Canton 1907—1914. 31 mars 1912. Les exportations des soies à Canton pendant l'année 1911—1912.

② Outside the two French houses in the text, there is another French house that exports pork silk (猪鬃) to Chongqing in 1911. Archives du Ministère des affaires étrangères. 148CPCOM566 Chine. relation commerciale avec la France 1910—1911. 2 Juillet 1911. Maisons françaises à Tchong-king.

③ 宋玉娥:外国洋行与烟台的殖民地化.世界历史.1987 年第 6 期,第 112—113 页.

for the representation of our industrial establishments in the Far East, that is to say, the interests of the great French companies. Buyer of the silks are also entrusted, for the most part, to intermediaries of foreign nationality."[1]

Realized the problem, the Commerce, Industry, Post and Telegraph Ministry believe that the cooperation of the merchants of Lyons with the foreign companies in China has already prevented the commercial interest of the French companies in the Far East. These collaborations "make French commerce undergo the tendency of certain great industrialists and important establishments in the metropolis to neglect the assistance of our compatriots installed abroad and who naturally appear qualified to act as intermediaries for them"[2]. Immediately, the latter department exerted pressure at the Chamber of Commerce of Lyons, suggesting the merchants of Lyons to collaborate with their compatriots in Shanghai:

"The diplomatic and consular agents of France frequently point out in their reports that large industrial establishments and important trading houses in the metropolis entrusted their interests abroad to foreigners even when they could turn to French companies offering, at least equal guarantees. My attention has been particularly drawn to the Shanghai marketplace where, I am assured, there is a large number of French engineers and commissioners with all the guarantees of capacity and good repute.

I do not misunderstand, Mr. President, that multiple considerations and particular circumstances may oblige the French companies to choose their representatives from the merchants of other nationalities established on the spot; But I consider, with the Foreign Affairs Minister, that our merchants should be informed of the prejudice to French commerce by the tendency to neglect the assistance of our fellow-countrymen installed abroad and who are naturally qualified to serve as intermediaries.

I shall be obliged, Mr. President, to inform interested companies in our constituency of the observations of our consuls on this subject, and I hope that their patriotism will suggest to them the means of reconciling their particular interests with the general interests of the country and the French business."[3]

Is the few presence of French companies in Shanghai actually due, as the Consul

---

[1] Archives du Ministère des affaires étrangères. 148CPCOM562 Chine relation commerciale avec la France 1898—1899. 29 novembre 1898. Représentation du commerce français en Chine. pp.122—123.

[2] Archives du Ministère des affaires étrangères. 148CPCOM562 Chine relation commerciale avec la France 1898—1899. 30 décembre 1898. Représentation du commerce français en Chine. p.138.

[3] Archives du Ministère des affaires étrangères. 148CPCOM562 Chine relation commerciale avec la France 1898—1899. 27 décembre 1898. Représentation du commerce français en Chine. pp.140.

and the Minister wrote, to competition from foreign companies and the commercial collaboration of the Lyonss silk merchants with the foreign houses in Shanghai?

In reality, although the destination of Chinese exported silk was gradually moved from London to Lyons after the 1870s, it was still other foreign firms who controlled the silk trade between China and France (English, German and Swiss). They always send a considerable quantity of Chinese silk from China to France.

The English began to send the silks of China directly to France during the 1850s. In the work of S.Lamb published in 1856, it indicates that "the English Peninsular and Oriental Company imported to Marseilles two or three hundred bullets directly of Shanghai. This year, this monthly importation is from 4 to 500 bales ... All the silks that enter Marseille are sent there by English companies who buy the silk for the French merchants. The latter, one or two of them in Marseilles, three or four in Lyonss, each have a representative in Shanghai, who works at the English companies, as a particular account of the French company[1]. According to the sentences above, we can know that the commercial relationship between French merchants and English companies in Shanghai is assured by French representatives sent to the English companies in Shanghai or Canton. In 1865, of the 43,000 bales exported from China, 7,300 bales of silk are transported directly from Shanghai to France, of which only 2,500 bales are sent by the French houses. All the rest is shipped virtually by English companies[2].

The implementation of telegraphy between Europe and China not only strengthened the link between the French agencies and their headquarters in Europe, but also pushed collaborations between English traders in China and silk merchants in France. The only change is that the monopoly of the big English companies is broken because they no longer have the advantage over market information and the capital required to engage in the silk trade has been greatly diminished. Many small English houses in China became the suppliers of the merchants in France. At the same time, several German houses also participate in the competition. All this leads to an increase in the number of Chinese silk exporters and a dispersion in the quantities of Chinese silk exported, which at the same time results in increased commercial competition on the Chinese silk export market. Let us take the example of the export of Chinese silks in July 1872.

---

[1]　S.Lamb. La soie, c'est de l'or. Lyon. Bureaux du courrier de Lyon. 1856. pp.69—71.

[2]　Ministère de l'agriculture et du commerce, Document sur le commerce extérieur, Chine et Indochine, Fait commerciaux n°40. p.5—6. Rapport de M.P.Gicauel.

Table III-9 List of exporters of Chinese silk from1872/07/01 to 1872/07/26[1]

Companies	Nationalities	Bales
Adamson, Bell & Co	Britain	124
Balfour. F. H	Britain	126
Barnet Geo & Co	Britain	203
Blain & Co	Britain	
Birley, Worthington & Co	Britain	174
Birt & Co	Britain	
Borntraeger & Co	Britain	
Bourjau, Hubener & Co	Germany	264
Bovet, Brothers & Co	Britain	46
Bower, Hanbury & Co	Britain	968
Bradwell Brothers & Co	Britain	
Brand, Brothers & Co	Britain	
Bull, Purdon & Co	Britain	95
Butterfield and Swire	Britain	620
Carter & Co	Britain	17
Chapman, King& Co	Britain	70
Dent & Co	Britain	30
Dickinson & Co	Britain	50
Essex & Co	Britain	756
Fogg H & Co	Britain	19
Findlay Wade & Co	Britain	
Framje Hormusjee & Co	Britain	
Gamwell, R F	Britain	
Gibb, Livingston & Co	Britain	384
Gilman & Co	Britain	
Heard, Augustine & Co	United States	201
Helbling & Co	Britain	80
Holiday Wise & Co	Britain	30

[1] Archives nationales de France. F 12.7058. 29, septembre 1872. Lettre de Ministre des affaires étrangères à Ministre du commerce. Liste des maisons de soies étrangères à Shanghai.

（续表）

Companies	Nationalities	Bales
Hogg, Brothers	Britain	
Jardine, Matheson & Co	Britain	497
Jarvie, John & Co	Britain	309
Lacroix Cousins & Co	France	872
Lindsay, Head & Co	Britain	17
Meartens, A H	Britain	636
Milsom and Tod	Britain	
Nachtrieb, Leroy & Co	France	336
Pila & Co	France	701
Pustau, Wm & Co	Britain	
Reiss & Co	Britain	1,329
Robison, JS	Britain	
Russell & Co	United Sates	576
Sassoon, David, Sons & Co	Britain	674
Scheibler, Matthaei & Co	Britain	123
Shaw, Brothers & Co	Britain	320
Siemssen & Co	Germany	143
Skeggs, C J & Co	Britain	30
Smith, Archer & Co	United Sates	136
Taylor & Bennett	Britain	10
Tlge Nölting & Co	Germany	48
Textor & Co	Britain	1,221
Thorne, Brothers & Co	Britain	
Vaucher frères & Co	France	53
Westall, Brand & Co	Britain	374
Wright, Burkill & Co	Britain	549
Vogel Hagedorn & Co	Britain	45
Chinois		141
Divers		5,618
Total		19,198

This long list of houses exporting Chinese silk in July 1872 consists of 45 English companies, 4 French houses, 3 German companies and 3 American companies. The three largest foreign firms in China, Jardine Matheson and Co. (English), Dent et Cie (English) and Russell and Co. (American) send only 1,103 bales of Chinese silk, or one nineteenth of the total. Reiss and Co. (English), the Textor and Co. (English), and the Bower, Hanbury & Co. (English) are the three houses that dispatch most silks (3,518 bales) during the month of July in 1872. This figure only makes up 18.32% of the total export quantity, far from the monopoly level. The dispersity of the silk in each house are very remarkable in the list. Some companies export only ten bales of silks a-broad, which is obviously the result of the order trade. The four French companies bought 1,962 bales of Chinese silk, even less than the quantity of the year 1865. The export of the rest silk to France should be operated by the English and German companies.

There are many other statistics that prove that foreign companies continue to play an important role in the silk trade between France and China. For example, during the 1876—1877 trade year, Shanghai exported 73,000 bales of silk, of which 33,000 were transported to France and 31,000 to England. The share sent by foreign firms in Shanghai to all exports destined for France can be estimated at 21,000 bales, most of which are operated by English houses[1]. In Canton, 4,683 bullets of silks were sent from June 1, 1888 to May 31, 1889 for France, in which only 1,456 bales were operated by the French companies. The rest are sent to France by three German companies (Gunbold Konberg and Co., Carlowitz and Co., as well as Siemssen and Co.) and three English houses (Dent and Co., Reiss and Co. and Rowe and Co.). The advantage of foreign houses persists until the 20th century. During the 1902—1903 season 45,594 silk bales were exported from Canton, including 30,000 bales for Lyons, 4,000 bales for Milan and 1,000 bales for London. At the moment, the silk trade between China and Europe was carried out by 12 foreign companies, among which 6 were English firms (Dent and Co., T.E.Griffith and Co., Jardine Matheson and Co., Jewett and Bent and Co., Reiss and Co. and Rowe and Co.) [2], 3 companies are under the French nationality (Boyer, Mazet, Guillie and Co., E. Pasquet and Co. and Varenne and Co.), and 3 companies are the German firms (Arwhold Karbey and Co., Carbowitz and Co. as well as Siemssen

---

[1]　Archives nationales de France. F 12.7058. 20 août 1877. Lettre du Ministre des affaires étrangères au Minis-tre du commerce.

[2]　Archives nationales de France. F 12.7056. Rapport du commerce et la navigation de Canton 1888–1889.

and Co.) ①. 31,368 bales of spun silk, waste silk and cocoons are transported to Europe during the season 1911—1912, in which 23,325 bales are transported by the English, German and Swiss houses②.

Apart of becoming commissioners of French merchants in Lyons or Paris, some foreign (especially English) companies in Shanghai began to set up their agencies directly in Lyons or Paris to export silks there from the 1870s. A well-known case in the Chinese commerce history which occurs in 1873 concerns the faults of two large foreign banks in China (le comptoir d'escompte de Paris et Hongkong et Shanghai Banc of China) which should not refuse to discount a telegraph treatments for 25 silk balls between the Milson and Berry and Co. (English) in Lyons, and the Milson and Tod & Co.(English) in Shanghai③. The two firms, the Milson and Berry and Co. in Lyons, and the Milson and Tod and Co. in Shanghai, are two brothers companies who deal with the silk trade between Shanghai and Lyons. The French law of 1880 stipulates that English companies may enjoy the same rights as the French companies in France, which further encourages the installations of the English firms in Frances④. In the letter from the French consul in Canton to the French Foreign Affairs Minister, we find: "They have a favorable chance to becoming representatives of a great number of our French companies, and are consequently called upon to make serious Foreign companies that have agencies in Lyons and supply the market of this city at the same time as that of London and New York."⑤

In conclusion, before the 1870s, London was the largest silk distribution center in Europe. At that time, several large English and American companies mastered the Chinese silk expeditions to Europe. Europe-continental countries, like France, often bought silks from the distant market by London. With the import growth of the quantities of Asian silks after the explosion of the pebrine, merchants could no longer bear the additional costs of importing silks by London. The creation of the Far East line of Messagerie Maritime of France and the opening of the Suez Canal have greatly diminished the advantage of the maritime transport of England (we shall discuss precisely in the next chapter). As a result, more and more Chinese silks are sent directly to France instead of by the Lon-

---

① Archives nationales de France. F 12.7056. Rapport commercial de Canton 1902.

② Archives nationales de France. F 12.7223. 31 mars 1912. Les exportations des soies de Canton pendant l'année 1911—1912.

③ 雪珥.1873:帝国商人反击战.国家历史.2008年第24期,第29—30页.

④ Archives nationales de France. F 12.6499. Report: licenses required by commercial travelers in France. 1897.

⑤ Archives nationales de France. F 12.7056. 20 août 1892. Une nouvelle maison est instituée à Canton pour l'achat des soies.

178

don market. However, the implementation of Euro-Asian telecommunications has increased competition in the Chinese silk export market, and the majority of direct trade between China and France is still in the hands of foreign firms. Due to competition from these foreign firms, French companies can only send less than one third of the silks exported to France each year. So we could affirm that, after the decade 1870s, the English, French and German companies share the exchange of silk between China and France together.

However, we should also indicate that Chinese silks often have to undergo a very complicated circulation process before their export: there exit also a large number of intermediaries between the place of production of silks and foreign companies in China, which we will present in the next sections.

Ⅲ Chinese intermediaries

Chinese merchants are very important intermediaries connecting foreign silk companies at Chinese opening ports and the producers in China's production areas. Before export, Chinese silk often passes through a very complex circulation process inside China: it is exchanged in the hands of local silk companies, of silk shops at the opening ports, of the Tongshi (通事) and the silk compradors (丝楼买办), etc. These Chinese intermediaries control almost all the supply of silks to foreign houses during the 19th century. In this section, we will observe the process of the movement of Chinese silk in China before export, the roles of Chinese intermediaries in such process, the internal relations between all these intermediaries (means of communication, as well as the relationship between Chinese intermediaries with foreign companies).

1. The monopoly on the export of Chinese silk by "Cohong" merchants before 1842

Prior to the Opium War (1840—1842), foreign merchants could trade only with merchants from Cohong (公行) in Canton, which enjoyed monopoly in China's foreign trade. All the Chinese silks destined to be exchanged are obliged to be sent to the port of Canton, and to be sold by the merchants of Cohong to foreign merchants. Inside China, major suppliers of silk to the Cohongs are Cantonese merchants (粤商), who buy the products from inside of China and then sell them to Cohong for export. They send to Cohong both the silks of Guangdong (广东丝 whose quantities of production are very discreet) and that the silks of Zhejiang (浙江丝). According to the notes of the *New textual criticisms of the Qing dynasty* (《清朝续文献通考》) of Liu Jintang (刘锦藻), the silks of Jili (辑里丝) [1] appeared already at the European market in 1825. "The silk of Jili is so tenuous, so striking, and so tenacious, which is admired by foreigners… This kind of silk export about 50,000—60,000 bales a year."[2] At that time, more than 50 silk companies were established in the Nanxun commune (南浔) for the purchase of Jili silk, around which is located the largest silk production area of Zhejiang Province. The majority of the fifty companies belong to the two groups: Nanjing merchants (京庄) and Canton merchants (广庄). The process of silk traffic inside China at the moment is that: Zhejiang local merchants first buy all the small quantities of local peasant silks, and then sell them to the companies of these two groups; The first group are official representatives who make purchases for government textile workshops installed in Nanjing; The last are representatives of Cantonese merchants who transported the silks from Zhejiang to Canton for export[3]. *The Rules of Imperial Decrees of Qianlong* (《乾隆上谕条例》) states that "Cantonese merchants buy a large quantity of silk each year, often worth more than one million taëls. At least this value should be no less than 80,000 taëls".[4]

Local merchants of Zhejiang began to send their silks directly to Cohong at Canton in the early 19th century, as Cantonese merchants often lower the purchase price to the silk producing regions for more profits, which lead to the dissatisfaction of local merchants. After the British East India Company came to develop the trade relationship with China, there were local merchants from Zhejiang coming to Canton by boat to trade with the English merchants by Cohong. All these merchants have accumulated great riches at that time[5]. These Zhejiang merchants who carry merchandise or set up their stores in Canton are named as "Zou Guang Zhe Shang" (走广浙商, peddlers from Zhejiang to Canton). Zhang Xinxian (张新贤) [6], creator of the first silk shop in Shanghai, Mei

---

[1] The silk of Jili (辑里丝) is also called the silk of Qili (七里丝). The distance from the original place of production of this silk is 7 Chinese miles (七里, equal 3.5 kilometers) from the Nanxun commune (in Zhejiang province), so it is called silk Qili or Jili. All silks produced at the Nanxun commune are named after Jili's silks later. This kind of silk is very well known to the European market after the opening of China in 1842 thanks to its better quality.

[2] 刘锦藻.续文献通考.上海:商务印书馆,1936 年,卷 379.实业二.

[3] 许发祥.近代民族资本浔商衰落原因新探.中共中央党校硕士学位论文,2009 年,第 8—9 页.

[4] 史料旬刊.第 35 期,北京:故宫博物院文献馆,1932 年,第 33 页.

[5] 刘大钧.吴兴农村经济.上海:上海文瑞印书馆,1939 年,第 259 页.

[6] Demande de marchand Zhang Xinxian pour la création de la Compagnie de Dunli spécialisant le commerce avec les anglais(商人张新贤为禀请开设敦利号以与英商贸易事). Fonds de la Bibliothèque Britannique, O R 7418. A

Rongji（梅鸿吉）①, a well-known Jili silk quality improvement were all peddlers from Zhejiang to Canton at that time.

2. Appearance of silk shops in Shanghai after the opening of China

The Nanjing Treaty canceled the trade monopoly of Cohong in China. The opening of the Shanghai port alters the circulation route of most silks inside of China before being exported. It is no longer necessary to transport the silks from Zhejiang to Canton for export. Large foreign firms in Guangzhou set up their new agencies in Shanghai respectively, while small foreign companies moved directly to Shanghai, abandoning their businesses in Guangzhou. Shanghai, bypassing Canton, gradually becomes the largest silk export port in China. In such a situation, many former Zhejiang local merchants are beginning to try to establish direct commercial relations with foreign firms in Shanghai by creating their own silk shops（丝栈）in Shanghai ②. The merchants of Zhejiang immediately replace the Cantonese merchants as the largest commercial group that supplies the silks to foreign companies.

The first silk shop in Shanghai is a company belonging to the Dunli Company（敦利外贸商号）, which is the first Chinese firm specializing in foreign trade in Shanghai. This company was created jointly by a Zhejiang merchant（Zhang Xinxian）with two other Cantonese merchants（陈春圃, 卞博山）on October 23, 1843（Chinese calendar）, which often transported the silks of Zhjiang to Canton before the year 1842. ③

At the end of 1843, another merchant from Zhejiang, Shen Hao（沈浩）registered another silk shop, the Tong YiSilk Store（通亿丝栈）in Shanghai with capital of 10,000 taëls, which is the second silk shop in Shanghai④. According to *the commercial notes of the Chinese companies in Shanghai from March to August of the year* 1844, there are already 46 Chinese companies installed in Shanghai, among which 16 specialize or

---

① 周庆云.南浔志.卷二十一.人物四·梅宝楚传.第 16 页, 1922 年. Fonds de la bibliothèque de l' Université de Waseda.

② It should be noted that the word "store"（栈）is used instead of "house"（行）to describe Chinese silk companies in Shanghai, because these silk companies operate rather as warehouses instead of companies. We will discuss the details later.

③ 苏松太道谕准商人开设敦利号承办中外贸易事. le 23 octobre, 23ème année de Daoguang（1843）, fond de la Bibliothèque Britannique, O R 7418. B. Sinologist J.King believes that the first Chinese house in Shanghai was the Esang Company（or Esang Hong）, which was created by a comprador, A lum（阿林）, with the help of the English at the beginning of 1844 It seems that this view does not represent the historical reality because the Dunli company was opened in Shanghai at the end of 1843.

④ 上海对外经济贸易志.第 132 页.

sell silks[1].

Table III-10 Chinese silk shops in Shanghai in 1844

Names	Natures of export articles	Silk exchange quantities	Names	Natures of export articles	Silk exchange quantities
本号 Official Company	tea, silk from Zhejiang	687 bales	华记 Huaji and CO.	silk from Zhejiang Musk	14 bales
敦利 Dunli an CO.	tea, silk from Zhejiang	67 bales	位记 Weiji and CO.	silk from Zhejiang phster	
通亿 Tongyi and CO.	tea	29 bales	怡利 Yili and CO.	silk from Zhejiang	80 bales
广利 Guangli and CO.	silk from Zhejiang	48 bales	名利 Mingli and CO.	silk from Zhejiang cotton txtiles	
怡生 Yisheng and CO.	silk from Zhejiang	551 bales	长益 Changyi and CO.	porcelain, Bronze, Rhubarb, silk from Zhejiang	20 bales
公正 Gongzheng et CO.	tea, Silk from Zhejiang cotton textiles	6 bales	义记 Yiji and CO.	silk from Zhejiang	87 bales
和记 Heji and CO.	silk from Zhejiang		隆记 Longji and CO.	silk from Zhejiang	28 bales
仁记 Renji and CO.	silk from Zhejiang plaster		和山 Heshan and CO.	tea, silk from Zhejiang	57 bales

Notes: (1) The Official Company was a commercial company created by the Shanghai City Council which dealt with communications between the government and other companies.

(2) At the same time, all these companies buy foreign merchandises from foreign companies. The natures and quantities of goods purchased by these companies were not formulated.

---

[1]　道光二十四年二月至七月敦利等各商号进出口货物品种数量等录. Fond de la bibliothèque Britannique. O R 7400. 道光二十四年二月至七月敦利等各商号进出口货物品种数量等录.

182

Almost all of these silk shops are established by the Zhejiang silk merchants, who have at the same time one or more silk agencies in the production areas. According to another official document whose subject is *the quantity of received and sent silks by silk stores in Shanghai in* 1862, the number of silks shops in Shanghai increased to 24 in that year, in which the shops held by Zhejiang merchants always take the majority[1]. An investigative historian Ge Yuanxi（葛元熙）who lives at the end of the Qing Dynasty shows that the number of silk shops in Shanghai rises to 75 in 1876, in which 62 are registered by merchants of Huzhou（湖州）[2]. Huzhou is only one of the silk producing areas in Zhejiang province, so the proportion of silk stores in Shanghai registered by Zhejiang merchants should be even higher. With the development of silk industry mechanism in the Yangzi region in the late 19th century, more and more commissioners between mechanical reeling factories and foreign firms appeared in Shanghai. The shops created by these commnissionners are called "silk counters（丝号）" (because those silks counters does not have deposit as the silk shop), which served for intermediate between the sides. According to another survey Ge Yuanxi, the number of silk counters and silk shops reached 91 counters in Shanghai in the early 20th century, 70% owned by Huzhou merchants[3]. In contrast, merchants in Sichuan and Shandong didn't create their own silk shops at Shanghai until the eve of the First World War[4].

These silk shops in Shanghai bring a great wealth to the silk merchants of Zhejiang during the second half of the 19th century. The biggest merchants in Nanxun are named as 4 elephants, 8 oxens and 72 dogs, according to the sums of their fortunes. The merchants who possess more than a million taëls are described as the elephants, more than 500,000 taëls as the oxen, and more than 100,000 taëls as the dogs. Almost all these wealthy merchants have realized their original fortunes through the silk trade, although they are also investing capital in other affairs.

---

[1] 太平天国历史档案馆.吴煦档案选编.第 6 册,南京:江苏人民出版社,1983 年,第 507 页, 上海各栈丝经到数及销售数.

[2] Huzhou（湖州）is only a city of Zhejiang province Nanxun（南浔）is a municipality of Huzhou.

[3] 葛元熙.沪游杂记.上海:上海古籍出版社,1989 年,第 80—81 页.

[4] 上海对外经济贸易志.第 132 页.

Table III-11 The richest merchants in Nanxun during the 19th century[1]

Names	Commerical Mouvements
Liu Guanjing 刘贯经	Silk peddlers before the opening of Shanghai. During the Taiping Rebellion, create successively the Liu Hengshun silk company（刘恒顺丝行）, Liu Zhengmao warp company（刘正茂经行）and Liu Guanjing silk shop（刘贯经丝栈）. Instituting several Mounties and Banks later.
Gu Chunchi 顾春池	Creator of the Gu Fengsheng silk company（顾丰盛丝行）. Establish the municipal store and the Shiliupu wharf（十六铺码头）in Shanghai. Some of his descendants become compradors of foreign companies and create mechanical filture with foreign companies.
Zhang Zhuzhai 张竹斋	Patron of Nanxun's delicatessens. Create the Zhang Henghe silk company（张恒和丝行）. Also engage in the trade of salt and institute several mounts later.
Pang Yungao 庞芸皋	Apprentice in the company of Chen Yuchang. Create his own silk company, the Pang Yitai company（庞怡太丝行）during the 1850s. And then invest its wealth in rice, charcuterie, wineries, martyrs, banks, mechanical filature, etc.
Qiu Xiancha 邱仙槎	Creators of the silk company of Qiu Qichang（邱启昌丝经行）. Owner of several mounts.
Mei Yuecha 梅月槎	Creator of the Mei Hengyu silk company（梅恒裕丝行）, owns several mountains of giants at the same time. Install the Heng Yu mechanical filature（恒裕丝厂）later.
Xing Ziyuan 邢子园	Inherit the silk company of Xing Zhengmao（邢正茂丝行）from his grandfather. Owner of several mounts of piety.
Shao Yisen 邵易森	Creator of the Shao Senda silk company（邵森大丝行）. Owner of several mounts of piety.
Zhu Landi 朱兰弟	Institute the Zhu Hongmao warp company（朱宏茂经行）after the Taiping Rebellion.
Zhou Weiliu 周味六	Creator of the Zhou Shentai warp company（周申太经行）. Owner of several mounts of piety.
Zhang Peikun 张培坤	Creator of the Zhang Yuantai silk company（张源太丝行）.

① 周庆云.南浔志.卷二十.人物三.卷二十一.人物四.1922 年,早稻田大学图书馆藏书。南浔镇志编委会.南浔镇志.上海:上海科学文献出版社,1995 年.

Names	Commerical Mouvements
Jin Qinyuan 金沁园	Creator of the Jin Chengde warp company（金承德丝行）

The total fortunes of the 12 merchants above reached 60—80 million taëls of silver during the 1870s, of which Liu alone owns 20 million, and Zhang's family owns 12 million[1]. This is a fairly impressive figure, since the annual revenue of the entire Qing Empire has only 70 million taëls at that time.

At the same time, the silk shops in Shanghai play an essential role in the exchange between Chinese merchants and foreign companies. In order to elucidate the network of silk trade within China, we need to observe three relationships around the silk shops in Shanghai: the relation of the silk shops at Shanghai with the silk companies in the production areas (or the relationship of silk counterts with mechanical filature after the mechanical era); The relationship at interiors of the silk shops (or silk counters); The relationship of silk shops (or silk counters) with foreign houses in Shanghai.

3. The relationship of silk shops in Shanghai with silk houses to production areas

Before discussing the relationship between the silk shops at Shanghai and the silk companies in the production regions (as well as the relationship between the Shanghai silk counter and the mechanical filature), we will study the circulation of silks in the regions of production. Before the introduction of mechanical reeling, the unit of silk production in China is the peasant family. Having finished the work of the filature, the peasants will transport through the canals their prepared silks to the local silk companies located in the Xiang（乡）[2]. The amateur of boat who carries the silks often also serves as the intermediary between the peasants and the silk companies at Xiang. They present a silk company which offered a higher price to the peasants for earning a little remuneration apart from the cost of transport.[3] Having received a certain quantity of silk, the companies in the Xiangs will sell them to the towns（镇）, where there are many larger

---

① 陈永浩,陶水木.中国近代最大的丝商群体.杭州:浙江人民出版社,2001 年,第 1 页.

② Xiang（乡）, an administrative unit higher than the "village"（村）but lower than the "Bourg"（镇）in China. The administrative scale in China is（from low to high）: village（村）, Xiang（乡）, Bourge（镇）, District（县）, City（市）, province（省）.

③ 兴亚院华中联络部.中支那重要国防资源生丝调查报告.台北:台湾大学图书馆,1978,第 27 页.

silk companies. The latter companies will classify the silks received according to differentiations at the level of nature and quality, and then transport them to the silk shops in Shanghai[1]. Thanks to the export growth of the Chinese warps (mainly the organs from Jili of Huzhou) on the international market, more and more warps companies are established at the towns in the silk producing regions since 1870s, which led to a small evolution of the mode of circulation above: having bought the silks, some of the silk companies in the towns will sell their silks to the organs companies instead of directly to the silk shops in Shanghai. Warps companies will distribute the raw silks to skilled craftsmen for re-winding and milling (through which raw silk will become the organs), and then transport the warp to the silk shops in Shanghai[2]. Another change occurs in the process of silk circulation in production regions after the introduction of mechanical filature in China. With the increasing demand for cocoons from mechanical filature, a large number of cocoon companies were settled in the communes of Zhejiang and Jiangsu at the end of the 19th century. These last companies buy cocoons from the peasant, and then sell them to the mechanical filautre at production areas or ports. Peasants no longer need to do the reeling by themselves, and therefore sell less and less silk to the silk companies next to their homes. With the decrease in manual silk produced by the peasants, there is less and less silk companies in production areas at the beginning of the 20th century[3].

Silk shops in Shanghai are not buyer of the silk, but commissionaires between foreign companies and silk companies (warp houses) in the towns located in the production areas. Silk merchants from production areas will be shelter in a silk shop in Shanghai and shred their silks at the store depot. The silk shop will sell these silks to foreign companies by Tongshi (通事, we will present it later). If the silk shop succeeds in selling these products, silk dealers coming from provinces will have to pay a commission of 2%—5% of the total exchange value to the silk shop (food, accommodation and storage included)[4].

Also, the silk counters are the commissionaires between mechanical filature and foreign companies. More evidence is needed, what is in documents and books on these aspects. Then they have to explain better. They also hire the Tongshi to make contact with foreign companies, but the only difference is that they do not have deposits for con-

---

① G.Federico. An Economic History of the Silk Industry, 1830—1930. Cambridge: Cambridge University Press, 1997. p.164.

② 徐新吾.中国近代缫丝工业史.第 277—278 页.

③ 孙晓莹.晚清生丝业国际竞争力研究——兼与同期日本比较.清华大学硕士论文,2010 年,第 40 页.

④ 上海对外经济贸易志.第 132 页.

186

signment like the silk shops. After the success of a transaction, they also withdraw a 2%—5% commission as compensation[1].

4. The relationship within the group of silk shops in Shanghai

Let's continue to analyze the relationship inside the Chinese silk stores in Shanghai. Many scholars have already contributed to the research on relations within the groups of Chinese merchants, especially on the social and economic organizations of merchants in the Chinese colonies in south-east Asia in the 19th and 20th centuries[2]. Here we will see how relations among Chinese merchants were in the Chinese metropolitan territory.

It is not difficult to imagine that each silk shop in Shanghai is a rival to others: they make every effort to gain the confidence of foreign companies to sell more silk, or to find suppliers who offer them silks with the best price and the best quality. However, it should be noted that Chinese silk merchants in Shanghai form an alliance to protect themselves against the government for their common interest in order to monopolize the supply of silks to foreign companies in Shanghai and to fight against the domination of foreign firms by price and quality of silks. According to our research, there are two kinds of alliances between silk traders during the second half of the 19th century.

The first kind is the Merchant Union. With the growth of the export of silk and tea from Shanghai, silk merchants and tea merchants set up a Shanghai Silk and Tea Chamber of Commerce(上海丝茶业会馆)in 1854. But this Chamber were soon divided into the different Chambers of Commerce because of the differences of the tea shops and silk shop. In 1860, a Chamber of Commerce specializing on the silk business of Jili (辑里丝丝业会馆) was opened on Shanxi Street (山西路) in Shanghai, which became the most important union of silk merchants in Shanghai at this moment. However, it is not an organization that represents the interest of all silk merchants in Shanghai, as this chamber of commerce consists mainly of Zhejiang silk dealers in the silk business of Jili, "other kinds of merchants specializing in cocoons, yellow silk, wild silk possess their own Merchant Unions".[3] Moreover, because of the fall of manual silk, its influence becomes weaker and weaker. Thanks to the development of mechanical filature, the turn-

---

① 李明珠.中国近代蚕丝业及外销.第 169 页.

② For exemple, Ju-K'ang T'ien. The Chinese of Sarawak. A Study of Social Structure. London School of Economics Monographs on Social Anthropology. No°12. London. Lund Hmphries. 1953;J.T.Omohundro. Chinese Merchant Families in Iloilo: Commerce and Kin in a Central Philippine City. Quezon City. Ateneo de Manila Press. 1981. A.R.Wilson. Ambition and Identity: Chinese Merchant Elites in Colonial Manila 1800—1916. Honolulu. University of Hawai'i Press. 2004.

③ 上海市档案馆.上海丝业会馆填报调查表,1950 年 8 月 22 日.档号 B168-1-798.

over of cocoon companies and silk filatures became more and more important at the end of the 19th century. In this context, the General Chamber of cocoons and silk（上海丝茧业总公所）was established in Shanghai in August 1910. The latter Chamber of Commerce consisted of cocoons merchants, the silk producer and the contractors of mechanical filatures from the three provinces: Zhejiang（浙江）, Jiangsu（江苏）and Anhui（安徽）, so it is a relatively representative merchant organization[1].

In spite of the different members and forms, almost all silk merchant organizations in Shanghai have three common functions: first, to determine the price of silk according to the prices of the international market and of the domestic market; Second, to maintain a good reputation for members registered at this Chamber of Commerce; Thirdly, to impose the Likin[2] for the government. With these three functions, these Merchant Unions or Chambers of Commerce will help their members maintain very good relations with the government[3], their suppliers and their customers.

The second kind of alliances are based on the ties of blood and family. In other words, large silk traders are formed and maintained their alliances through marriages between their families. Consider the example of the Nanxun merchant group（南浔）, in which a very typical marriage network was established.

Graph III-12 Marriage networks of Nanxun major merchants

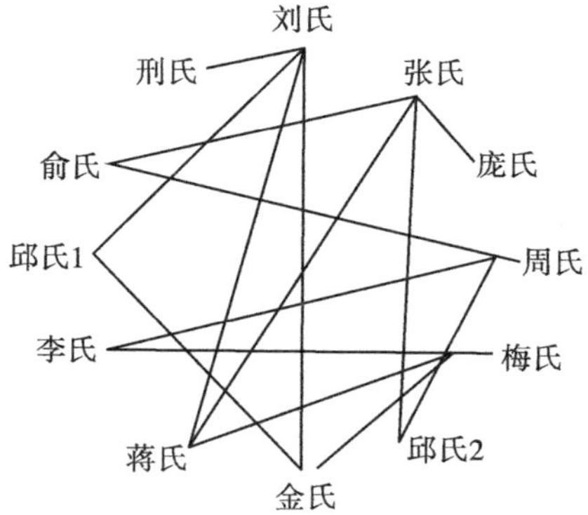

Notes: 刘氏, Family of Liu Guanjing(刘贯经); 张氏, Family of Zhang Zhuzhai(张竹斋); 庞氏, Family of Pang Yungao(庞云皋); 周氏, Family of Zhou Weiliu(周味六); 梅氏, Family of Mei Yuecha

---

① Archives municipales de Shanghai. S37-1-9, les régles de la Chambre générale de commerce des filatures et des cocons de Shanghai. septembre 1915.

② 上海市档案馆.上海丝厂茧业总公所章程,1915 年 9 月.档号 S37-1-9。

③ Shih Min-hsiung. The Silk Industry in Ch'ing China, Center for Chinese Studies, Ann Arbor. The University of Michigan Press 1976. p.77.

（梅月槎）;金氏,Family of Jin Qinyuan（金沁园）;蒋氏,Family of Jiang Xishen（蒋锡绅）;邢氏,
Family of Xing Ziyuan（邢子园）;邱氏 1,Family of Qiu Xiancha（邱仙槎）;李氏,Family of Li Weikui
（李惟奎）;俞氏,Family of Yu Tongxuan（俞桐轩）;邱氏 2,Family of Qiu Yimao（邱奕茂）

The majority of the families formulated in the above graphic have already appeared
in Table III-11 which showed the richest families of Nanxun. In this graph, it can be
seen that large families of origin in Nanxun town have formed a family network that is
much broader and more powerful than each individual merchant.

Through this alliance of families, Nanxun silk traders are able to share informations
from the market (international or domestic), helping to evade risks and borrow the capital of other traders when they need them. All these activities are very essential for the
success of the Zhejiang silk traders at the Shanghai market. Moreover, in order to maintain a good relationship with the government, the latter group even extends their marriage network to local and central government officials. For example, Liu Guanjing's
daughter marries XU Huaxiang（徐华祥）, whose father is the first-class mandarin XU
You（徐邮）, while one of Liu Guanjing's grandchildren marries the daughters of Sheng
Xuanhuai（盛宣怀）, which was the Minister of Transport and Post of the Qing Empire.
Also, one of Zhang Zhuzhai's grandchildren（张竹斋）who called Zhang Jingjiang（张
静江）marries Yao Hui（姚慧）, who is the daughter of the member of the Academy of
the Qing Empire[1]. With such a combination of marriage, the silk merchants will benefit
the shelter of the government and will possess a higher social status.

5. The relationship of silk shops in Shanghai with foreign houses

Let us now discuss the third relationship: the relationship between the Chinese silk
store and the foreign house. We have already known that Chinese silk shops were intermediaries between foreign firms and silk suppliers to production areas. However, we
have to answer why foreign companies do not buy silks directly from Chinese houses in
production areas in Zhejiang or Jiangsu? In fact, many large foreign firms in Shanghai
actually buy silks directly from production areas during the first 30 years after Shanghai
opens, because silks in production areas will be cheaper (in addition there is a reduction in domestic duties for foreign traders from the signing of *Treaty of Tianjin* to 1858),
and that the supply of silk is sure. When an English merchant recall his experiences in

---

① 潘中祥.近代江南市镇权力中心的演变——以湖州南浔为例.上海师范大学硕士学位论文,2011 年,
第 43—44 页.

China during the 1850s, he says: "We often send Chinese (compradors) inside China to buy tea and silk by giving them a large amount of money, which has already become a habit in Shanghai and Fouzhou (福州). The Canton trade also works like this in a small degree."[1] A Shanghai customs officer noted in 1867 that "foreign traders wait no longer for the Chinese soil product at the (Shanghai) market. On the contrary, their compradors often go down to the provinces with large sums of money. They pay in advance to the local companies, and then sign a contract of exchange with them".[2]

However, by the end of the 1860s, foreign firms gradually abandoned silk purchases directly to production areas.On the contrary, most of them chose to buy them at silk shops or silk counters in Shanghai. As a result, these silk shops or silk counters suppliers of foreign firms. At the same time, each foreign company has one or more silk shops or silk counters as stable suppliers.

Table III-13 Major foreign firms exporting silks from Shanghai and their suppliers in the early 20th century[3].

Companies	Mechanical Silk	Manuel Silk	Sichuan Silk	Shandong Silk
Jardin Matheson and Co. (English 怡和洋行)	Counter of Ding Yu(鼎余丝号) Counter of XU Feng (绪丰丝号) Counter of Ding Feng (鼎丰丝号)	Counter of Zheng Tai(正太丝号)	Silk Shop of Tong Kang Tai (同康泰丝栈)	Silk Shop of He Ju(合聚栈) Silk Shop of Yi Feng(益丰栈)

<hr>

① H.M.Scarth. Twelve Years in China. The people, the Rebels, and the Mandarins. By a British Resident (J. Scarth). With illustrations. London. British Library. 2011. pp.110—111.

② Archives Nationales de Chine (Deuxième), le bureau général de la douane de Chine : les archives de la douane ancienne de Chine, Vol 3. 1867—1868. p.156.

③ 上海社会科学院经济研究所.上海对外贸易 1840—1949. 上海:上海社会科学院出版社,1989 年,第 276 页.

Companies	Mechanical Silk	Manuel Silk	Sichuan Silk	Shandong Silk
Mitsui and Co. （Japanese 三井洋行）	Counter of Lu Run（陆润记）	Silk Shop of Zhen Chang（震昌丝栈） Counter of Zhengtai（正太丝号） Silk Shop of Yi Cheng（怡成丝栈）	Silk Shop of Tong Kang Tai（同康泰丝栈） Silk Shop of Tai Kang Xiang（太康详丝栈） Silk Shop of Rui Sheng Xiang（瑞生祥丝栈） Silk Shop of Yuan Xiang（宝源祥丝栈）	Silk Shop of Xiang Tong（恒祥同） Silk Shop of Heng Cheng Gong（恒成公） Silk Shop of Yi Feng Chang（益丰长）
Madier, Ribet and Co.（French 信孚洋行）	Counter of Xu Feng（绪丰丝号）	Silk Shop of Zhen Chang（震昌丝栈） Silk Shop of Zhengt Tai（正太丝号）	Silk Shop of Tong Kang Tai（同康泰丝栈）	Silk Shop of Heng Xiang Tong（恒祥同） Silk Shop of Yi Feng Chang（益丰长）
Rayner Heusser and Co.（Suisse 连纳洋行）	Counter of Zhen Yu Xiang（振裕祥）	Silk Shop of Zhen Chang（震昌丝栈） Silk Shop of Zhengt Tai（正太丝号）	Silk Shop of Tong Kang Tai（同康泰丝栈）	Silk Shop of Heng Xiang Tong（恒祥同） Silk Shop of Yi Feng Chang（益丰长）

Several reasons for such an evolution: first, because of the implementation of the new method for the acquittal of Likin (the acquittal before the sale). From the year 1864, foreign traders no longer enjoy the privilege of reducing China's domestic duties in Zhejiang and Jiangsu. From that moment, the profits of silk transmissions by themselves have greatly diminished. It will therefore be more convenient to import the silk from the silk shop nearby. Then, with the growing number of Chinese silks shops and Chinese silk counters in Shanghai, they formed a coalition of interests, gradually monopolizing

191

the supply of silk. In this case, it is no longer easy to find suppliers in production areas for foreign firms. The third element is the most essential. After the 1870s, most foreign companies in Shanghai gradually became commissioners of buyers in Europe. Under the latter form, they buy the silks according to orders from European buyers, as well as their profits come from commission fees which is fixed on a certain proportion of the values of the exported silks. For them, it is no longer necessary to buy a large quantity of silks in stock in advance, nor to send their compradors to the regions of production to find the best price. Silk dealers in Europe, furthermore, often ask them to send the ordered silks as soon as possible, so the purchase of silks inside Shanghai becomes the best choice for foreign companies.

Two modes exist in the transaction between the silk shops and the foreign companies. The first mode is the forward transaction. This way of transaction is often used in the first three decades after the opening of Shanghai (1843—1870). In this case, foreign firms have to pay to Chinese silk shops ahead for fear of the lack of supply of silk in the market, and Chinese ships are forced to send the silks to their customers termly[1]. The second mode is the spot transaction, which is used more frequently after the 1870s. The details of the latest mode are: the Chinese silk shops at Shanghai deliver silks to foreign companies, who will control the quality then discuss the price. Having decided to buy these silks, the foreign companies will note the details of this transaction in an document without paying anything. Then their ships for Europe will be loaded directly to the depots of the Chinese silk shops. Payment for the transaction often delays after foreign firms in Shanghai get the mandate of European buyers[2].

Spotting is also the most common mode of transaction between silk counters and foreign companies (except that silk counters normally do not have a deposit in Shanghai). But, from time to time, foreign companies lend a certain amount of capital in advance to silk filatures, with which the latter will buy cocoons. The cause for these loans is that mechanical silk is still a relatively demanded commodity before World War I in the Yangzi area. Foreign companies seek to guarantee the supply of mechanical silk by borrowing a little money to the silk filatures. The silk filatures, on the other hand, will the capital borrowed return to them by their silk products, which may be cheaper than those on the

---

① 聂宝章.中国买办资产阶级的发生.北京:中国社会科学院出版社,1978 年,第 139 页.

② 中国民主建国会上海市委员会,上海市工商业联合会.旧上海的外商与买办.上海文史资料.第 56 辑.上海:上海人民出版社,1986 年,第 18—19 页.

192

market①.

Chinese and foreign companies have respective intermediaries to establish a direct business relationship with each other. In the meantime, Chinese ships often hire Tongshis (通事) to communicate with foreign companies. Tongshi is not a new profession after the opening of Shanghai. This profession existed already before the Opium War in Canton, but with very different missions. During the period of commerce in Canton, they are the official representatives appointed by the government, who are in charge of communication with foreign factories. For example, they transmitted correspondence between the local government, the Cohongs and foreign factories (or ships); They communicated between the customs office and the foreign factories (or ships) for customs duties; Even they accompanied foreign merchants when they took a walk in the town of Canton②. After the abolition of the Cohong system, the missions of the Tongshis are quite different. Speaking a little English③, they become commissionaires sent to foreign houses from Chinese houses for commercial negotiations, including discussion of the price and confirmation of the quantity of exchange, etc. After an agreement is concluded, the Tongshis even have the right to sign contracts with foreign houses in the name of his boss④. They play a very important role in exchanges between Chinese houses and foreign houses. Almost all silk shops (or silk counters) own one or more Tongshis at that time. The chairman of the Shanghai Chamber of Commerce in Shanghai said: "In reality, signing a contract with these commissionaires (Tongshis) has become a habit in Shanghai."⑤

Although the Tongshis are nominally employees of Chinese companies, Chinese companies only offer them food and transportation expenses. The Tongshis' income comes mainly from commission fees in trade. However, Tongshis can accumulate a lot of money by commissions. Some Tongshis have even created their own silk shop. The boss of Yi

---

① 上海社会科学院经济研究所.上海对外贸易 1840—1949.上海:上海社会科学院出版社,1989 年,第 277 页. North China Daily. 25 septembre. 1852. Fond de la bibliothèque de Shanghai.

② C.W.Hunter. The Fankwae at Canton before Treaty Days, 1825—1844. London: Kegan. Paul, Trench& Co. 1882. p. 35.

③ In fact, most of Tongshis speak only "pidgin," said Yangjingbang English (洋泾浜英语). They can pronounce and know the main words about trade. These are people who come from Canton who monopolize Tongshis posts in Shanghai at the beginning of the opening of the port, but more and more Tongshis from Zhejiang appear in Shanghai with the later silk trade development. For the details of the evolution of the Thongshis.姚公鹤.上海闲话.上海:上海古籍出版社,1989 年,第 104—105 页.

④ 上海社会科学院经济研究所.上海对外贸易 1840—1949.上海:上海社会科学院出版社,1989 年,第 152—153 页.

⑤ 北华捷报.1852 年 7 月 3 日,上海市图书馆馆藏资源.

Cheng's silk shop（怡成丝栈）was a Tongshis from Da Cheng's silk shops（大成丝栈）①.

On the other hand, foreign firms often hire Chinese compradors to make connections with Chinese silk houses. The word "comprador" comes from Portuguese "comprar", which means "purchasers of supplies". The Chinese translation of this word is "买办", which already existed during the Ming dynasty（明朝，1368—1644），which indicated the providers of the necessities of court life②. Foreign factories in Canton had already begun employing compradors before the year 1842. However, at a time when the Cohong monopolized China's foreign trade, their missions had nothing to do with commercial operations between the Chinese and the foreigners. At that time, their responsibilities were mainly to buy supplies for foreign merchants in foreign factories（or ships），to vouch for other Chinese employees③, and to take care of the goods（money and important files）for their foreign employers, etc④. After 1842, the recruitment of "compradors" became even more important（even a necessity）for foreign companies who would like develop their business in China, because although the abolition of a monopoly of Cohong gave them commercial freedom, that also make them meet many problems.

First, the problem of language. "The intermediary, the comprador, in particular, is necessary first of all to the difficulties of language."⑤ During the period of Canton trade, the Tongshis handled the business of communication between foreign merchants, the Cohongs, the Chinese local government and the Chinese Customs office. Speaking very few Chinese, foreign merchants will need the interpreters and translators to exploit their businesses in China after the cancellations of the Cohongs and the official Tongshis.

Second, the currencyis quiet disorder at the time in China. The Chinese monetary unit is the "taël" in agent during the Qing dynasty. But there are several different kinds of taëls at the same time throughout the empire, among which four kinds are most commonly used: the treasury taël（库平两），the customs taël（海关两），the canton taël

---

① 吴桂龙.论上海开埠初期的通事和买办.史林.1996 年第 4 期,第 73 页.

② In the Official History of the Ming Dynasty, we could see the sentences：大学士彭时亦言:"光禄寺委用小人买办,假公营私,民利尽为所夺。请照宣德、正统间例,斟酌供用,禁止买办。"（明史·卷八十二·食货六.北京:中华书局 1974 年版,第 1990 页）

③ 中国第一历史档案馆:宫中砵批奏折,乾隆二十四年十月二十五日,两广总督李侍尧奏。After this year, the hiring of the Chinese is allowed, but still limited: each foreign factory（or ships）can hire at least two Swiss, four water carriers; Each foreign trader is permitted to hire only a holder of goods.梁廷枏:《粤海关志》,卷 29,夷商四。

④ 张晓棠:清朝对外贸易法治研究,中国政法大学博士论文,2007 年 9 月,第 71—72 页.

⑤ Archives des affaires étrangères. 148CPCOM563. Chine relation commerciale avec la France 1900—1901. 4, janvier 1900. Lettre de Ministre du commerce au Ministre des affaires étrangères. p. 2.

（广平两）and the channel taël（漕平两）. Nevertheless, all these units of taëls are just the standards of calculation, and hardly exist in reality. The money in the circulation are very different by different provinces. Moreover, with the development of commercial communication between China and abroad, foreign piasters（Spanish piaster, Mexican piaster Mexico, American piaster and other piasters）are used frequently in the exchanges to Chinese ports. But each type of piaster contains different percentages of silver, which further reinforces the complexity of the currencies circulated in China[1]. So foreign companies in China have to hire the compradors, who are very familiar with the Chinese monetary system in calculating or changing Chinese or foreign currencies.

Third, although the *Nanjing Treaty* opened five Chinese ports to international trade after 1842, foreign merchants did not have the right to penetrate into China before the *Treaty of Tianjin*（1858）was signed. Limited to ports, they will therefore need to send Chinese compradors to make sales and purchases in the Chinese provinces.

Inheriting all the former functions before 1842, the compradors are entrusted several new functions during the commercial period of Shanghai. They are interpreters and translators for foreign companies during transactions; They charged not only the preservation of wealth, but also accounting of their foreign employers; They raise funds that their foreign bosses need by borrowing from Chinese banks（钱庄）[2] etc. Apart from all the functions above, there are also the particular missions for the compradors who work in foreign firms exporting silks[3]. First, their mandatory responsibility is to contact the silk suppliers for foreign companies. For this purpose, they have to establish a stable relationship with the silk shops in Shanghai where the silk prices are not very high; sometimes they have to exit China and sign a contract with the companies in the production regions. In addition, they perform other fonctions during a transaction, including price debate, contract signing or payment to suppliers, etc[4].

Then, from time to time, they have to pay in advance for purchased silks when the capital of their bosses is not sufficient. According to memories of the compradors who work in the Madier, Ribet and Cie（French）, the bosses（H. Madier and J. Madier）of this French Company are two vagabonds at the beginning of their disembarkation in

---

① For the details of the types and the evolution of the currencies circulated in the Qing Empire, 彭信威.中国货币史.上海:上海人民出版社,1958 年,第 537—556 页.and MORSE. Hosea. Ballou. Currency in China. Shanghai, Kelly & Walsh. 1906.

② 郝延平.十九世纪买办——中西间桥梁.上海:上海社会科学院出版社,1988 年 9 月,第 77—88 页.

③ The compradors take care of silk business for foreign houses who are named as "silk compradors（丝楼买办）" at that time.

④ 黄逸峰、江铎.旧中国的买办阶级.上海:上海人民出版社,1982 年,第 44—45 页.

Shanghai. The disbursements of their compradors play a very important role in starting their careers in Shanghai as a silk exporter[1]. Moreover, their foreign owners ask them to guarantee for the price and quality of the silks supplied by Chinese houses (shops or counters), and they also play a role as guarantors of Chinese silk suppliers[2]. This role became more and more important after the 1870s when there was an increasing number of frauds in the silk trade[3]. Finally, many compradors manage at the same time mechanical filature belonging to foreign companies[4]. For example, the nephew of Gu Chunchi (顾春池), Gu Mianfu (顾勉夫) is a comprador in the Russell and American and Co., which manages the silk filature for this Company[5]. The filature created by Arnhold Karberg and Co. are also its compradors (Li Songjun 李松筠 and Wu Shaoqing 吴少卿)[6].

In summary, the effects of the compradors relate to each stage of silk transaction in Shanghai. A French consul in Shanghai gave these words when he mentioned 3 compradors in Shanghai: "Chinese compradors are very important as intermediaries with Chinese suppliers for French companies … No transaction takes place without the comprador intervening. It is he who attracts producers, presents their products to the boss, discusses prices. The role of the European patron of companies is limited to treating the affair with his comprador on the one hand; leaving from his or her compradors he knows practically no Chinese merchant."[7]

Having noticed the modes of transaction and the means of communication between Chinese stores and foreign houses, we have one last question: are there Chinese stores that directly export silks to Europe without intermediaries of foreign companies? In other words, are foreign firms indispensable for the export of Chinese silk abroad during the 19th century? The reality is that there is no Chinese silk arriving in Europe without passing by foreign marchants before the First World War. Three Chinese, Li Weibi (李惟

---

① 中国民主建国会上海市委员会、上海市工商业联合会.旧上海的外商与买办.上海文史资料.第 56 辑, 第 17—18 页.

② 肖楚熊.行商制度到买办制度变迁研究.广州大学硕士毕业论文,2009 年,第 25—26 页.

③ We will address this problem in the next chapter.

④ L.S.Bell. From Comprador to County Magnate: Bourgeois Practice in the Wuxi County Silk Industry. Selected in Joseph W. Esherick and Mary Backus Rankin. Chinese Local Elites and Patterns of Dominance. California. University of California Press. 1900. pp. 123—124.

⑤ 陈永浩,陶水木.中国近代最大的丝商群体.第 5 页.

⑥ 聂好春.买办与近代中国经济发展研究 1840—1927.华中师范大学博士论文,2007 年,第 60 页.

⑦ Archives des affaires étrangères. 148CPCOM565. Chine relation commerciale avec la France 1907—1909. 21, avril 190à. Les organisations commerciales à Shanghai. p. 15.

弼）, Lu Huanwen （卢焕文） and Yu Fengshao （俞凤韶） [1] made an initial inquiries on the silk market of France during the first decade of the 20th century[2].

A report on these early surveys was published in 1909, entitled *Enquêtes du marché de soies en France*, which is the first report on the situation of the Chinese silk market in Europe[3]. The first Chinese house that exports silk directly to France is Hua Tong and Co. （华通公司）, which established itself in Shanghai in 1918 and engaged in the export business of silk from 1920[4]. Several Chinese houses specializing in the export of silks overseas settle in China's ports during the 1920s and then some of them ruined during the 1930s. In official statistics of the Chinese Industry Ministry, there are totally 43 companies （foreign and Chinese） who export silk to Western countries （including Japan） in 1936 in Shanghai, in which only 3 belong to Chinese merchants and 40 belong to foreign merchants. The value of silks exported by the last three Chinese houses made up about 25% of the total value of silk exports in 1936[5].

The silk trade is not the only area in Chinese foreign trade controlled by foreign firms. In fact, during the 19th century, almost all transactions between the two countries were effected through foreign firms. The case of direct trade between Chinese merchants and commercial companies in France is very rare. The only notes on the exchange between the last two groups during this period were the direct importation of medicines from France to pharmacies created by the Chinese[6]. The appearance of Chinese houses specializing in direct trade with importers or exporters in Europe delays until the early 20th century.

The Feng Li and Co. （列丰行） of Shanghai, created by He Jifan （何积藩） in 1906 which was comprador to the several foreign companies, is the first Chinese companies that sell foreign goods commissioned in China directly by exporters in Europe. The first Chinese companies created in France to directly sell Chinese items to customers is the Yun Tong and Co. （运通行） in Shanghai, which is the supplier of the Antiquities Store of Yun Tong instituted in Paris by the Chinese Plenipotentiary Minister in France

---

① All three are employees of the Yu Tong and Cie （运通公司） Chinese in Paris, which is an antique shop created in 1901 by Zhang Jingjiang （张静江）, the Chinese plenipotentiary in France.

② 《申报》,1910 年 7 月 14 日,上海图书馆馆藏资源。

③ 周德华:蚕丝改良先驱——俞凤韶.江苏丝绸.2006 年第 5 期,第 51 页.

④ 李案、缪钟绣:二十年来之蚕丝业.国际贸易导报.1931 年第二卷第一号.

⑤ 李泽晋.全国进出口商行要览.实业部国际贸易局,1937 年,第 29 页,中国国家图书馆馆藏资源.

⑥ 上海对外经济贸易志.上海:上海社会科学院出版社,2000 年,第 158 页.

in 1901[1]. The number of Chinese companies with a direct commercial relationship with companies in Europe or the United States does not exceed five in China on the eve of the First World War. No companies among them deals with the trade of silk[2].

The reasons for the bad performance of Chinese merchants in trade between China and other countries were differences in different area of practice. However, all Chinese traders who seek to develop direct trade with western merchants during the 19th century will meet two problems. First, it is difficult to find partners (exporter or importer) in western countries. This difficulty stems partly from the monopoly of commercial information from foreign firms in China, a phenomenon that was evident before the implementation of the telegraph between Europe and East Asia in 1871. All postal vessels belong to the foreign postal companies.Some large western companies possess even their own message vessels. On the other hand, very few Chinese merchants master foreign languages for most of the 19th century. Even if there are Chinese people who can talk about it a little, they will work in foreign companies a comprador. This fact will also prevent them from communicating directly with Europe or the United States. Secondly, there is still the problem of foreign exchange settlement for Chinese houses. During the 19th century, foreign exchange offices in China are almost all in foreign companies or foreign banks, which do not change foreign currency for Chinese traders. Even after the establishment of the first Chinese banks on the eve of the First World War, Chinese merchants must deposit a large sum as guarantee funds[3]. But this is undoubtedly very difficult for most Chinese companies whose capital and turnover are very modest. Apart from the problems above, the Chinese silk houses are obliged to face a special obstacle to break the control of foreign houses in foreign trade.[4] In fact, if the Chinese want to export silk directly to western countries during this time, a great barrier for them is that: it is the foreign houses that master the right to control the quality of silk. We will clarify in Chapter V, without any public institution to control the quality of silk in China during the 19th century, silk dealers in Europe only buy silks with quality authentication signed by controllers in foreign homes.

---

① 上海社会科学院经济研究所.上海对外贸易 1840—1949.上海:上海社会学院出版社,1989 年,第 224 页.

② The first Chinese house that exports silk directly to France is Hua Tong and Co. (华通公司), which was established in Shanghai in 1918 and engaged in the export of silk from 1920.李案,缪钟绣:二十年来之蚕丝业.国际贸易导报.1931 年第二卷第一号.

③ 中国民主建国会上海市委员会、上海市工商业联合会:旧上海的外商与买办.上海文史资料.第 56 辑,上海:上海人民出版社,1986 年,第 27—28 页.

④ Details on the quality control of Chinese silks exported in Chapter V will be discussed.

198

In contrast, the authentication of quality signed by the Chinese controllers is hardly recognized during this time[1]. As a result, all Chinese traders must commission foreign companies to sell their silks in Europe in order to obtain their quality authentications. Even if there are Chinese houses that want to engage in the silk trade with the European countries, they will find neither customer in Europe nor suppliers in China. The monopoly of the right of quality control is another means of the monopoly of the export of silks for foreign companies. It is a very essential reason for the absence of Chinese companies in the silk exchanges between China and France during the 19th century.

Figure III-14 Processes of silk trade between China and France

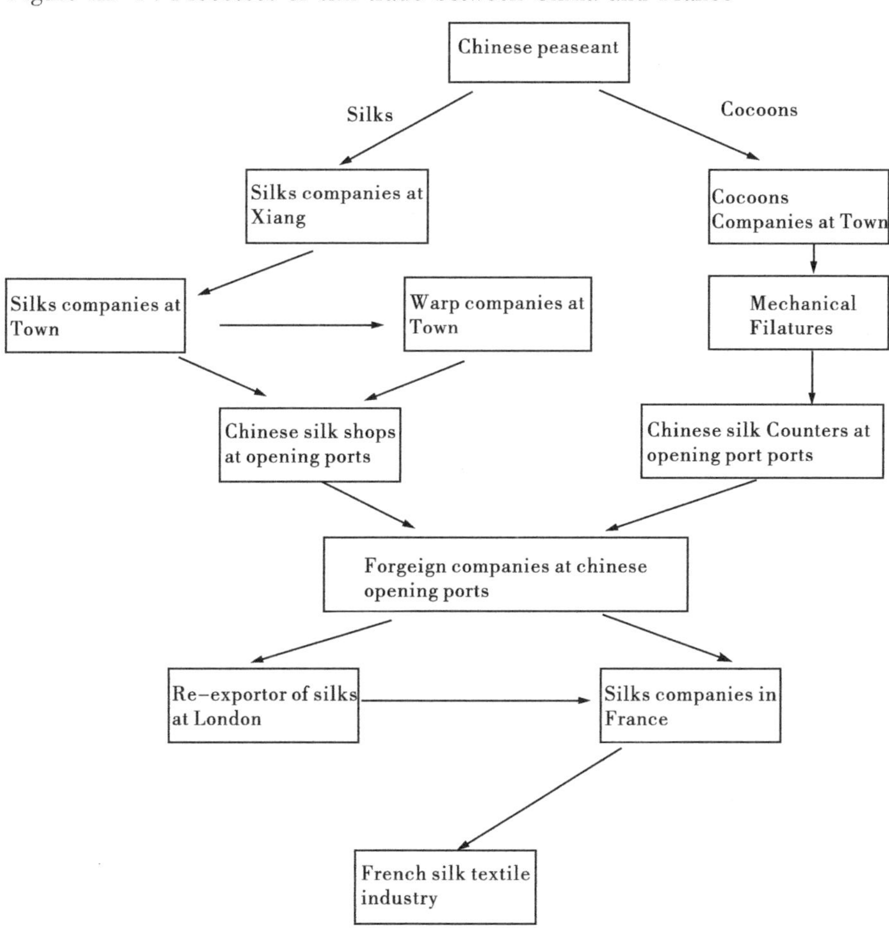

---

① 中国民主建国会上海市委员会、上海市工商业联合会：旧上海的外商与买办.上海文史资料.第56辑,第28页.

To sum up all the exchange networks in commerce, we can staked out a map describing how a Chinese silk bales comes from China to the hands of a miller or weaver in France. On the one hand, foreign companies that monopolize international trade (English, French, German, Swiss) are the essential link among all intermediaries in the silk trade process between China and France. All Chinese companies are obliged to export their silks to Europe by the latter group. On the other hand, foreign companies were hardly able to penetrate into China during the 19th century, especially after 1870s. They can't obtain the material from Chinese silks unless by establishing a stable commercial relationship with silk shops, silk counters and silk filatures, which are the necessary intermediaries for the circulation of silks inside China. The composition of intermediaries in the silk trade between France and China is complex, because of the competition and collaboration of all these intermediaries. However, it is precisely these intermediaries who compete and collaborate who carry out the development of this very important trade for China and France during the 19th century.

Chapter IV   Impact of the customs policy evolution and improvement of the transport condition

In the previous chapter, we studied the intermediary networks of the silk trade between France and China. In this new chapter, we will continue to analyze the possibility of long-distance trade, concerning the roles of two factors in the growth of the silk trade between France and China: evolutions in foreign trade policy, improvement of transport condition.

In the first section we will discuss the evolution of the entry duties of silk in France during the 19th century and its impact on the silk import to France. The second section demonstrated the changes in China's customs policy before and after the Opium War, especially the evolution of the customs tariff on silk exported, as well as its effects on the exchange of silk with France. The improvement of the transport condition is considered by K.H.O'Rourke and J.G.Williamson and other economic historians as one of the most essential impulses for the integration of the Euro-American economy. In order to ascertain whether this element is so important in the evolution of Euro-Asian trade, the third section of this chapter will analyze the influences of the implementation of the Messengerie Maritime in the Far East and the opening of the Suez Canal on the silk trade between China and France. At the same time, we will discuss another important problem, the impact of changes in trade policy and the decrease of transport costs on the prices convergence in the various Euro-Asian markets, at the end of the third section.

Ⅰ Evolution of the silk customs tariff in France and its commercial and economic influences

For a long time, the doctrine of P.Bairoch represented conventional opinion on the periodization and economic influence of French foreign trade policy. According to his research, the period of French liberalism didn't begin until the signing of the Gobden-Chevalier Treaty with England in 1860, and it was completed after the implementation of the "Méline tariff" in 1892. France, as a typical continental Europe country, pursued a policy of foreign trade much more protectionist than that of England from the years 1840 to the end of the 19th century.[1] However, foreign trade and economy expansions of France were generally more rapid during the protectionist periods than during the liberal period, so the fall of customs barriers played a negative role for the foreign trade and the economy growth of France[2].

Is P. Bairoch correct?

These opinions are often questioned by the research of other economic historians, among which the most representative is J.V. Nye's thesis, "War, Win, and Taxes: The Political Economy of Anglo-French Trade 1689—1900"[3]. In examining the evolutions of the average customs tariff in France and in England, J.V.Nye discovers that the former had been lower than the last one from the beginning of the 19th century to the end of the 1870s. According to the author, the policy of the Customs of France was freer than that of England during most of the nineteenth century, instead of the contrary conclusion of P. Bairroch. The theory of J.V.Nye is not perfect, but it has begun the wider debates on the trade policies of protectionism and liberalism in Europe. This debate of P. Bairoch and J.V.Nye is pursued by J.P.Dormois and P.Verley in France[4], which seeks to clarify questions such as: are the countries on the continent of Europe so protectionist that P.Bairoch has described? How to measure the level of protection of a country's customs tariff? How do we measure the impact of the tariff on growth? This same debate also takes place outside France on the role of protectionism, notably among K.H.O'Rourke,

---

① P.Bairoch. Mythes et paradoxes de l'histoire économique. Paris. La Découverte. 1994. pp.38—39.

② P.Bairoch. Commerce extérieur et développement économique de l'Europe au XIXe siècle. Paris. Éditions Mouton. 1976. p .162.

③ J.V.Nye. War, Wine and Taxes: The Political Economy of Anglo-French Trade, 1689—1900. Princeton and Oxford. Princeton University Press. 2007.

④ J-P.Dormois. "The I' impact of late-nineteenth-century tariffs on the productivity of European industries (1870-1930) ". In J-P. Dormois, P. Lains, eds. Classical Trade Protectionism, 1815—1914. London and New York Routledge. 2006.

A. Estevadeordal, ATJunguito, DAIrwin, F. Capie, A. Vamvakidis, J. Foreman-Peck, B. Dedinger around these problems.

Consulting the fomer research, in this section, we will try to answer questions about the evolution and impacts of the silk entrance tariff in France: how the tariff for silk France evolves during the 19th century? Does its evolution resemble what P. Bairoch described on the evolution of the general tariff in France? Is the entry duties for silk from France protectionist? What are the impacts of the tariff on the growth of silk imports and the growth of the silk economy? Most of the customs tariff data that we will cite come from the archives. In order to accomplish the absence and the accuracy of the archives of certain periods, we shall also consult the official reports and books at the time and now, including the speeches of N. Rondot before the Agriculture, Manufactures and Trade Council[1], Histoire économique de la soie of A. Beauquis[2], An Economic History of the Silk Industry by G. Federico[3] and, Contracutal relation , Tariffs and customs in the Lyons silk industry in the Nineteenth century of P. vernus[4], etc.

1. The reduction of the customs tariff on silk materials in France from 1814 to 1862

The fall of the First Empire in France was accompanied by a very short period of liberalization of the customs system from April 1814, but it lasted only for several months. The law of December 17, 1814 signed by King Louis XVIII symbolizes the restoration of protectionism in France. This legislation permits the King to take measures to prohibit the import or export of foreign goods[5]. Some types of French agricultural or industrial products are prohibited from circulating on the international market immediately, and others are imposed very high tariffs. The policy of protectionism was reinforced several times in 1816 and 1817. In 1819, the agricultural customs policy of the "movable scale of cereals" which was abolished in 1814 is reintroduced in France. Throughout the 1820s, the atmosphere of protectionism was perceived: The King promulgated sever-

① N. Rondot. Conseil supérieur de l'agriculture, des manufactures et du commerce. Rapport sur l'industrie des soies et des soieries. p. 11.

② A. Beauquis. Histoire économique de la soie. Grenoble. Grands établissements de l'imprimerie générale. 1910.

③ G. Federico. An Economic History of the silk Industry, 1830−1930. Cambridge. Cambridge University press. 2003.

④ P. Vernus. Contractual relaions, tariffs and customs in the Lyon silk industrie in the Nineteenth Century. In Alessandro Stanziani. Labour, Coercion, and Economic Growth in Eurasia. 17th—20th Centuries. Studies in Global Social History. Leyde. Brill. 2013.

⑤ M. Cliquenois. Droit public économique. Paris. Éditions Ellipses. Coll. Université-Droit. 2001. p.8.

al laws in 1820, 1822 and 1826 to strengthen the protectionist customs system on both industrial and agricultural products[1].

Under such circumstances the silk, tariffs were raised after the First Empire. During the period of the First Empire, Piedmont and Liguria[2] were part of France, allowing the Lyonsnese manufacturers to receive free duty silk from Italy, the majority of the silks they needed. But this situation changed completely after 1814. According to the order of Louis XVIII of 1814, 50 centimes must to be paid for import one kilogram of raw silk and 2 francs 4 centimes for one kilogram of molded silks[3]. The latter tariffs then increase, by an agreement dating from 1816, to 1 franc 2 centimes per kilogram for raw silk and 2 francs 4 centimes per kilogram for the thrown silk. These duties, with a series of bad harvests of cocoons which occurred during the years 1815, 1816, and 1817, throw the Lyonss producers into a real distress: the raw material becomes rarer, and consequently more costly; the warps rose from 60−64 francs per kilogram in 1814 to 88—120 francs per kilogram in 1816. The Restoration, by this distress, agreed to lower the entry duties of raw silks to 0 Francs 13 centimes per kilogram in 1816 and reduce the tariff of thrown silks to 0 francs 51 centimes per kilograms in 1817[4]. Yet this concession is granted for only 3 years. After its expiry in the year 1820, duties on the import of silks return to the rates of 1816.

According to the theory of the welfare of international trade, each country engaging the exchange with other countries is obliged to face a dilemma when it institutes the customs tariff: if one raises the right of entry of the raw materials, industries will be dissatisfied; If a customs policy is introduced in the opposite direction, the interest of the producers of the materials (often the peasants) will be deteriorated. During the first half of the 19th century, the French government have met exactly such a dilemma[5]. On the one hand, French sericulture production increased very rapidly during the first half of the 19th century. Let us recall the data demonstrated in the preceding chapter, the production of silk in France jumped from 308,157 kilograms in 1815 to 659,398 kilograms in

---

[1] P.Bairoch. Commerce extérieur et développement économique de l'Europe au XIX siècle. p. 7.

[2] Deux régions produisent abandons de matières soyeuses qui se situent au nord de l'Italie.

[3] N.Rondot. Conseil supérieur de l'agriculture, des manufactures et du commerce. Rapport sur l'industrie des soies et des soieries. p. 10.

[4] A.Beauquis. Histoire économique de la soie. Grenoble. Grands établissements de l'imprimerie générale. 1910.p.273.

[5] N.G.Mankiw. Principales of Economics. Nashville. South-Western College Pub.2011.pp.182—184.

1830[1]. It is necessary, therefore, to raise its right of entry so that this sericulture growth can continue. On the other hand, despite a very strong growth, the quantity of French sericulture is still not capable to satisfy the demand of the silk textile industry. Only 6.89% of the silk used by the French textile industry came from abroad in 1815, and this proportion rose to 32.5% during 1831—1840.[2]

In order to acquire enough raw materials, silk manufacturers ask the government to allow all foreign rawsilks to enter in France in free duty after 1820. They argue that national sericulture, despite the great and rapid progress which it has made since 1820, cannot follow Lyons in its development, and that it cannot furnish the silk necessary for weaving, neither in term of quality nor as quantity. Yet this demand, vigorously opposed by the sericulturists of the South, by the representatives of the great industries of the Metallurgy, Cotton, and the farmers (all protectionists), is always rejected by the government of the Restoration, and the duties on silks continue to be imposed according to the tariffs of 1816. Lyons does not accept san protesting this defeat; and it nevertheless continues the struggle for the conquests of the free duty of its raw materials, of which it consumes every year a greater quantity[3]. After a struggle of ten years, it finally wins its first victories at the beginning of the Monarchy of July (1830—1848).

At the level of the general regime, the Monarchy of July inherits the law of December 17, 1814, which entrusts the right of modification of the customs tariffs to the King. Nevertheless, Louis Philippe, unlike Louis XVIII, began to weaken the customs policy of protectionism. Overall some prohibitions are replaced by very high duties as well as certain customs duties are reduced by a series of laws from 1833 to 1836. Although the administration of Louis Philippe raises the tariffs of some goods by the laws of 1841 and 1845, especially in the heavy industrial and equipment industries, tariffs on some agricultural products and raw materials began to decline considerably from that time[4].

As for the customs policy on silk, in the decree of June 29, 1833, the government of Louis Philippe reduced customs tariffs on some agricultural products (Rhubarb, cocoa, etc.), and at the same time put silk in a list of articles whose "rights shall also be provisionally reduced". The reduction of the tariffs for the entry customs duties on silks was definitively effected by the law of July 2, 1836. The duty on raw silk decreased to 5

---

① Pour l'amélioration et la propagation de l'industrie de la soie en France. Annale de la société séricicole. N° 1.p. 47.

② G.Federico. An Economic History of the silk Industry, 1830—1930. pp.214—215.

③ A.Beauquis. Histoire économique de la soie. p.273.

④ G.Federico. An Economic History of the silk Industry, 1830–1930. pp.214—215.

centimes per kilogram, and the duty on silk was reduced to 10 centimes. This law stipulates simultaneously that the export duties on the two silky products above fall respectively to 3 francs and 2 francs per kilogram[1].

Obviously, according to the law of 2 July 1836 mentioned above, the administration
of Louis Philippe chose to support its textile industry by decreasing the right of entry on
raw silk to 5 cents per kilogram. The consequence of this decision is that, on the one
hand, the Lyons manufacturers can easily import Italian silk or Chinese silk re-exported
from England with 5 cents per kilogram of admission. On the other hand, the French
sericulturists and the filatures can only work as suppliers of the French textile industry
because it is very difficult to export their silk products with a relatively high export duty.
Such a commercial policy is certainly appreciated by the manufacturers of the silks of
Lyonss, and it is considered by them as a measure of foresight. In 1861 N. Rondot remarked in a speech before the Higher Council of Manufacturing and Commerce that: "If
the entry customs duties which applied to foreign silks had not been reduced by four
fifths, there were twenty four years, our silk industry, during the successive harvests of
seven years, would have diminished at least half, while it has doubled."[2]

Because of the fine harvest of cocoons in the late 1840s and early 1850s, the new
government of the Second Empire began to balance the interests of silk producers and
silk manufacturers. Firstly, it abolished the exit customs duty for all unbleached silk in
1852[3]. As a result of this measure, the quantity of French sericulture production
reached its historical peak in 1853: a quantity of 26 million kilograms[4]. Secondly, in
1853, a petition of the French silk manufacturers was also granted by Napoleon III, who
declared the suppression of the prohibition (the order of this prohibition was promulgated on 8th February 1826) silk crepe of Chinese origin[5] (which had often been transferred to France for dyeing and re-exporting by smuggling). However, manufacturers of
the silks of France are still not satisfied. The cause is that, first of all, the duty is still
very high on crepes of Chinese origin by England: 34 francs per kilogram per French

<hr />

[1]　Archives Nationales de France. F12. 2552. 29 juin 1833 et de 1836. Le tarif de douane de 1833 et de 1836.

[2]　N.Rondot. Conseil supérieur de l'agriculture, des manufactures et du commerce. Rapport sur l'industrie
des soies et des soieries. p. 11.

[3]　Idem. p.10.

[4]　L.Pasteur. Étude sur la maladie des vers à soie: notes et documents. p. 38.

[5]　Archives Nationales de France. F12 6894. 7 mars 1853. Suppression de l'interdiction de l'Angleterre des
crêpes d'origine chinoise. p. 325—339.

vessel and 37.4 francs per kilogram per foreign ship[1]; Moreover, the tariff for the entry of silk always remains at 5 centimes per kilogram, which is unacceptable to the silk manufacturers of France.

The growth of French sericulture was completed by the silkworm disease that exploded in 1854. This disaster not only ruined French sericulture immediately, but also is threatening the prosperity of the French silk textile industry because of a much greater deficit of raw materials. In this very urgent situation, the government of Napoleon III must make a choice even more difficult than that had been made by Louis Philippe. On the one hand, foreign silks must be allowed to enter with an entrance duties even lower than 5 centimes so that the need for this raw material is filled; On the other hand, we must also keep the possibility of restoration for sericulture, which was very prosperous and very fragile at that time. Finally, a compromise measure was taken by the administration: successively, it allowed duty-free entry of other materials used by the textile industry of France silk except raw silk. Napoleon III promulgated a decree in 1855 which declared that crepes of Chinese origin for dyeing would be imported duty-free under the condition of re-export in six months after dyeing.

This decree continued in 1857[2]. In 1859, the entry duty to the unbleached spun yarn (known as foil) decreased to 1.25 francs per kilogram per French ship and 1.35 francs per kilogram per foreign ship, and that of the wadding shade or azure reduced to 3.25 francs per kilogram per French ship and 3.55 francs per foreign ship[3]. A Convention of 16 November 1860 between France and Great Britain lowered the duty at 10 percent of the value on silk or mixed silk floss[4], which are materials necessary for the manufacture of certain mixed textiles.

Despite all these efforts of the government, silk manufacturers in France still do not get what they want since the 1820s: duty free for all foreign raw silks. They complain that the right of entry of 5 centimes on foreign raw silk is still not eliminated, and the government is still biased towards the silk producers. Speeches by the Delegate of the Chamber of Commerce of Lyons, N. Rondot, represented the voices of the heart of the silk manu-

---

[1]　Archives Nationales de France. F12 6894. Tableau comparatif des prix de crêpe de Chine et de crêpe de Lyon. p. 10.

[2]　Archives Nationales de France. F12 6894. Admission temporaire de crêpe de Chine. p. 287—315.

[3]　Archives Nationales de France. F12 6894. 22 mai 1859; projet de modification au tarif des douanes. la bourre et autre déchot de soie filés dit fleuret.

[4]　Archives Nationales de France. F12 6894. 15 septembre 1866. Direction générale de douane, tarif conventionnel avec le Grand Bretagne. p.179.

facturers. In a conference of January 12, 1860 at the Chamber of Commerce of Lyons, he said that:

"The present trade of France with India, China, and Australia is considerable; it exceeds four hundred millions. It is stopped in its development by the customs duties on the raw materials."[1]

In his other report on the Silk and Silk Industry for the Higher Council of Agriculture, Manufactures, and Trade in 1861, he also observed that:

"French filature is powerless to provide for consumption, it is a fact; The French manufacturers are obliged to apply to the foreign filature, because they cannot procure in France the sorts and quantities of yarn they require: there is considerable interest in ensuring the supply of our factories.

"We shall add that the import has been decreasing since 1857 and to 388,000 kilograms in 1858; The decrease is 15% in two years. Finally, several spinners have reached such perfection that their products are preferred to those of England and Switzerland, and that their considerable production is never enough to satisfy demands."[2]

Lyons exert constantly pressure on the government. At the end of 1862, the Empire government was obliged to remove the last protection from French sericulture in order to satisfy the demand of the silk manufacturers of France. On December 24, Napoleon III promulgated a decree, which has definitively abolished the import duty of raw and thrown silk[3].

The elimination of the entry silk duty facilitates again the penetration of foreign silks into France. On the one hand, a large quantity of foreign silks, notably Chinese silks, flock to the Lyons market. With Chinese materials which are very abundant and very cheap, the prosperity of the French silk industry is possible to continue. On the other hand, having lost the last protection of customs duties, more and more peasants stop planting mulberry trees or studying silkworms. The number of sericulturists lost from 297,130 in 1868 to 200,538 in 1872, and then to 180,506 the following year[4]. The silk filature are in bankruptcy because of very low profit. The quantity of silk production fell to the bottom of the valley during the 1860s. This situation hardly changed after the

---

① N.Rondot.. Chambre de commerce de Lyon. Commerce de la France avec la Chine. p.22—23.

② N.Rondot. Conseil supérieur de l'agriculture, des manufactures et du commerce. Rapport sur l'industrie des soies et des soieries. pp. 12—13.

③ Archives Nationales de France. F12 6894. 24 décembre 1862. Décret de Napoléon III pour affranchir l'importation de soie grège. p. 493.

④ E.Hamaide. La relation entre Lyon et Chine au XIXe siècle.7.1.

invention of Louis Pasteur's medical prevention method in 1869. After a small recovery, the quantity of silk production in France stabilized around 600,000 kilograms after the 1870s[1].Replacing native silks, the Chinese silks become the raw materials most used by the French silk textiles manufacturers. Its dominance in the Lyons market lasted until the First World War[2].

Let us return to two questions at the introduction to this section. How did the entry price of silk from France evolve during the 19th century? Does his evolution resemble what P.Bairoch described on the evolution of the general tariff in France? Having reviewed the evolution of customs tariffs on silk materials in France, it is already possible for us to confirm the answer for this question. It is true that the signing of the *Franco-British Trade Treaty* of 1860 (*Cobden-Chevalier Treaty*) is a very important historical milestone for the transformation of protectionism into free trade for France, even for all of Europe. According to this Treaty, England must allow a large number of French products to enter England in free of duty; Customs duties on wines and silks, the two principal commodities exported from France to England, are reduced by more than 80%; At the same time, France must abolish all prohibitions and replace them with customs duties which must not exceed 30% of the trade values (25% from 1 October 1864) ; Most tariffs on raw materials and foodstuffs are also abolished between the two countries; As a result of this Franco-English Treaty, France signed a series of treaties with other European countries, and these treaties greatly reduced the entry duties for materials which French industry needed (for example, treaty 1862 between France and Prussia brings about a 25% reduction on the customs duty for raw iron)[3].

However, the process of reducing the customs tariff for silk materials proves to us that, for some goods, the tariff reduction has already begun well before the *Cobden-Chevalier Treaty*. The customs tariff on raw silk fell to 5 cents per kilogram in 1836, and the import prohibition or tariffs on other silk materials were annulled or reduced respectively. The course of replacement of protectionism by the free trade since the beginning of the 19th century is, as the case of silk, slow and gradual, instead of a historical mutation. The Franco-English treaty in 1860 is, therefore, only an important event in a given course, instead of a point of departure. The thesis of P.Bairoch on the historical role of the treaty in 1860 therefore does not correspond to the evolution of tariffs of France, at

---

① Lshii Kanji. L'histoire de la sériciculture du Japon. Tokyo. Éditions de l'Université de Tokyo. 1972. p. 21
② G. Federico. An Economic History of the silk Industry, 1830—1930.pp.214—215.
③ P.Bairoch. Commerce extérieur et développement économique de l'Europe au XIX siècle. Paris. Mouton. EHESS. 1976. p. 11.

least not to that of every natures of goods from the beginning of the 19th century to the 1860s.

2. The restoration of customs duties on silk from France from 1872

Conventionally, the restoration of protectionism in Europe at the end of the 19th century was symbolized by the resumption of protectionist customs duties to Germany in July 1879. Although this symbolic role of Germany of Europe's restoration to protectionism is often disputed by many historians[1], even if the criterion for measuring protectionism and the level of protectionism in certain countries is often discussed[2], it must be recognized that, from the 1870s, the main western countries of the world (England, the United States, Russia, France and Italy, etc.) are beginning to raise their tariffs more or less one after the other.

According to P.Bairoch's research, France only returns to protectionism with the tariff known as the Méline of 1892. This last reform of the French customs system means an average growth of 40% in customs tariffs of all goods imported from or exported to France[3]. We see that P. Bairoch considers again the transformation of free trade to protectionism in France as a historical mutation that takes place in 1892, like the change happening before and after 1860. So, is this description of P.Bairoch on the change of the customs policy of France during the last decades of the 19th century is correct? Again, we will check it by studying the evolution of France's customs tariffs on silk materials.

Indeed, the French government has already attempted to restore customs duties on silk materials from the very beginning of the founding of the Third Republic. On May 11, 1871, a letter from the Finance Ministry invited the President of the Chamber of Commerce of Lyons to visit the Consultative Committee of Arts and Manufactures to study

---

[1] The question about Germany's role in restoring protectionism in the European is still a open debate. Many other historians argue that German tariffs are not higher than other European countries even after 1879. For the detail, consult B. Dedinger. "From virtual free-trade to virtual protectionism. Did protectionism have any part in Germany's rise to commercial power? 1850—1913". In J-P. Dormois, P. Lains, eds. Classical Trade Protectionism, 1815—1914. London and New York. Routledge. 2006. pp.219—241. A.T.Junguito. "Assessing the protectionist intensity of tariffs in nineteenth century European trade policy." In J-P. Dormois, P. Lains, eds. Classical Trade Protectionism, 1815—1914. London and New York Routledge. 2006. pp.99—120.

[2] We will address this point later.

[3] P.Bairoch. Commerce extérieur et développement économique de l'Europe au XIX siècle. Paris. Mouton. EHESS. 1976. p. 12.

a converting a 20% customs duty of the silks[1]. This last proposal of the government astonished the manufacturers of the silks of France, and immediately provoked their protests. Ernest Pariset claims in a meeting of the Chamber of Commerce of Lyons, which represented the opinions of most of the members at that time:

"London receives directly 2,500,000 kilograms of Chinese, Japanese and Bengal silks, transiting through Egypt, and representing a value of 135 million francs. It exports to France for 90 million francs, of which 75 million in raw silks destined for the French, Swiss and Italian silk textile industries.

"At Marseilles, from the extreme Asia, there are grazes estimated at about 80 millions of francs, and the Mediterranean countries send him greaves for 60 million francs, not to mention the cocoons, estimated at 17 million. If a part of the Asiatic silks goes to England, the grenades of Brousse, Syria, Adrianople, Messina, Naples, and Spain remain in the hands of the French filatures, just as the cocoons feed the French filatures.

"Italy, whose harvest is estimated at 170 million francs, is sent by Mont Cenis and Switzerland to France for 110 million silk or silk fillings.

"Let the French crop, valued at 90 million francs, be added to these quantities, and it will be found that the raw material circulating in France represents a capital of about 440 million francs.

"Making an entry duty on the raw material will not remove all the silks that do not address themselves immediately to consumption? Will it not restrict the spirit of enterprise so favorable to industry, harm the French filatures, by not putting at their disposal a great choice of raw silk and their impossible the struggle with the English mill, remove finally Lyons from the silk commerce, which would soon be headed for Milan, where Switzerland and Germany were already to be supplied?"[2]

Although the manufacturers at Lyons want to keep the free duty on silk entering in France, they finally make a concession to the government. According to the speech of Ernest Pariset, the Chamber of Commerce of Lyons offered a tariff which it could accept to the Ministry of Finance:

"The Chamber of Commerce of Lyons accepts, as less injurious to the interests of industry, and, moreover, as providing the treasury with a more certain income, 0 francs

---

[1]　E.Pariset. Chambre de commerce de Lyon, Question du droit d'entrée. Dans la séance du 15 juin 1871. Fonds de la Bibliothèque nationale de France. p.1.

[2]　E.Pariset. Chambre de commerce de Lyon, Question du droit d'entrée. Dans la séance du 15 juin 1871. Fonds de la Bibliothèque nationale de France. p.14—15.

10 cents per kilo for silk filling; 0 francs 20 cents per kilo for carded wrappers; 0 francs 50 cents per kilo for spun yarns; 1 francs 25 centimes per kilo for the raw silks; 2 francs 50 cents per kilo for worked silks."[1]

Because of the struggle of Lyons against the primordial proposal, the Ministry arrived at an accommodation with the manufacturers of the French silks. A tariff of 2.5% on all Asian silk species has been applied since 1872[2]. Following the implementation of this new silk tariff, French silk companies in Shanghai, whose interests have already been violated by the internal rights of China, immediately express their dissatisfied feeling to the French Consul in Shanghai. Having received the Shanghai Consul's letter, the French Foreign Affairs Minister conveyed the opinion of the silk companies in Shanghai to the Finance Minister, and simultaneously recounts the harmfulness of the restoration of the customs duty on raw silk:

"Monsieur and dear colleague, the manager of the Consulate General of France in Shanghai has just reported to me the effect produced in this city by the news that a 2.5% customs duty has been established on the silks on their entry into our territory.

"According to M. de Chappedelaine, we are afraid that this measure will result in stopping the trend of trade, which has been marked for some time, to import silk directly from Shanghai to France, and to prevent Lyons from becoming the great market of these raw materials, by diverting them to Switzerland, or by making them resume the road to London, which was beginning to be abandoned."[3]

But all these counsels and protests have changed nothing. The Ministry of Finance did not change its decision. Later, after Germany adopted more protectionist tariffs in 1879, the Third Republic government implemented at the same time an "imperial preference" system with its colonies during the 1880s[4]. This measure may be beneficial to some French industrial branches, but a catastrophe for the silk industry. On the one hand, the French colonies produce scarcely any silk material, but the largest regions of silk production are segregated outside this system of "imperial preference", which will undoubtedly add the cost of production and weakening the competitiveness of French silk textiles: Asian silks, which make up about 50%—60% of the consumption of French

---

[1]　Idem. p.20.

[2]　Archives Nationales de France. F12 7058. 29 septembre 1872. Lettre de Ministre des affaires étrangères au Ministre du commerce.

[3]　Idem.

[4]　L'économie mondiale, Statistique historique. Paris. OCDE. Organisation de coopération de développement économique. 2003. p. 64.

silk manufacturers, had already imposed a 2.5% customs duty to enter France since 1872; Italian raw silk, which composes another 20%—30% of French consumption, is also levied a customs duty of 1 franc per kilogram from 1888[1].

On the other hand, outlets for French silks will be limited. As main consumers of French silk are the other European and American countries, those countries will also close their doors to French silk textiles by raising their customs duties as a retaliation. At the end of the 19th century, customs tariffs on silks from England, Russia and the United States were 75%, 225% and 300%—400% respectively[2].

Thus, when the Ministry of Finance re-examined the problem of raising customs duties in March 1891, a very fierce debate took place in the Chamber of Deputies. The Customs Commission proposes a general tariff of 6 francs for raw and worked silks, but some of the deputies (notably deputies from silk producing regions) refuse to accept this proposal. The tension in the room of deputies is very evident in the speech below given by opponents of Lyons:

"Lyons, faithful to his principles of commercial liberty, and showing the good effect of liberty over his affairs, protests against all duties. It is certainly fortunate for France that the Lyonsnais have dethroned London for silk in favor of Lyons. Such victories are rare.

Although, in three years, since the establishment in 1888 of a right on Italian silks, Lyons has seen its import of Italian silks reduced by 350,000 kilograms of raw silk and 450,000 kilograms of thrown silk (report by Mr. Grand George at the Customs Valuation Commission), Lyons still receives and sells 6,500,000 kilograms of silks out of 12,500,000 offered for consumption by all the producing countries. In these 6,500,000 kilograms, half of the total production, 4,100,000 remain in the hands of the French factories, that is to say a third of the total production ... This is the power of Lyons, a precious power for French interest ...

With a duty on the greaves, however weak manufacturers might be said, we lost our reputation of producing under conditions as favorable as our rivals;

In short, as our colleague, M. Neyrand, deputy of the Loire, competent and impartial, says in a note full of common sense and remarkably clear, it would be wise to

---

① L.Gueneau. Lyon et le commerce de la soie. Thèse soutenue devant la Faculté de droit de l'Université de Lyon. Lyon. Imprimerie L. Bascou. 1923. p.120.

② G.Federico. A Economic History of The Silk Industry. 1830—1930. Cambridge. Cambridge University Press. 1997. pp.175—176.

impose the woven fabrics by leaving the entrance free."[1]

The project of an enormous levy on customs duties of the Ministry of Finance in 1891 is again wrecked by the opposition of the representatives of the silk manufacturers of Lyons. In the new law of January 11, 1892, entry fees on raw silk and cocoons are a-bolished again. However, these tariffs of 1892 are not the unilateral success of Lyons, but a compensate for the loss of the sericulturist in the new customs regime.

Table IV-1 Entry tariffs on silk in France in 1892[2]

Silk Natures	Unit	General Tariff
RawSilk		free
Worked silk	1 kilo	3 francs
Yarn of wadding silk	100 kilos 35 francs	(less than 80,500 meters)
50 francs	(more than 80,5000 meters)	
Yarn of twitches silk	100 kilos 40 francs 100 kilos 66 francs	(less than 80,500 meters) (more than 80,500 meters)
Yarn of dyed silk	Same duties	75 francs
Embroidery sewing silk	100 kg unbleached:	400 francs
A passementery, haberdashery	100 kilos dyed	600 francs
and others		
Yarn of wool	waste yarn 100 kilos	single 35 francs
(Of silk floss)	100 kilos	twisted 40 francs

The government promulgated a law on January 13, 1892 (only two days after the new customs tariff law), which offered an allowance to sericulturists. Under this Act, the allowance is 50 cents per kilogram of fresh cocoons collected[3]. Although this allowance has had little beneficial influence on the economic development of sericulture (as demonstrated in the previous chapter, its production, after rising to more than 11 million kilograms in 1894, to an average of 6.5—7.5 million kilograms in the following years),

---

[1]　Archives Nationales de France. F12 6854. Chambre des députés cinquième législature session de 1891. n° 1354. le 21 mars 1891.

[2]　Archives Nationales de France. F12 6854. La séance du 12 novembre 1891. Rapport de la commission de douanes de fils de soie, fils de soie artificielle au sénat.

[3]　A.Beauquis. Histoire économique de la soie. Grenoble. Grands établissements de l' imprimerie générale. 1910.pp.51—52.

214

it is renewed twice again in 1898 and 1909, while under the last two schemes the allowance paid to each farmer is increased to 60 centimes per kilogram of fresh cocoons. As compromise results, both new regimes established in 1892, the new silk customs tariffs and the sericulture allowance, remained valid until the First World War.

The evolution of customs tariffs on silk materials in the last decades of the 19th century has shown us that the restoration of the customs system of protectionism in France, at least for a part of goods, is not a simple reversal that P. Bairoch described, but a more complicated transformation. First of all, the import duties on certain goods, as on silk materials, have already began to rise during the 1870s. In other words, protectionism is returning to France in fact much earlier than the date believed. Second, the foundation of protectionist rights is not the result of a single effort, nor an irreversible tendency. In the case of raw silk, the customs tariff established in 1872 was finally abolished in 1892, and this duty-free tariff continued until the Great War.

Moreover, if we observe the evolution of customs tariffs on raw silk throughout the 19th century, we will discover that it is different from the conventional formula high (Period of protectionism during 1814—1860)—low (period of free trade during 1860—1892)—high (period of protectionism during 1892 – 1913), but manifests itself as a more capricious curve: it changes from 0.5 to 1.02 francs from 1814 to 1816, to 0.13 francs in 1817, to 1.02 francs in 1820, to 0.05 francs in 1836 and to 0 from 1862 to 1. 25 francs in 1872 and again to 0 from 1892, which includes three vertices and three regressions.

Graph IV – 2 Evolution of the customs tariff for the entry of raw silk in France 1814—1912[1]

---

[1]　The datas during 1814—1815 come from N. Rondot. Conseil supérieur de l'agriculture, des manufactures et du commerce. Rapport sur l'industrie des soies et des soieries. p. 10. The datas during 1815—1832 come from A. Beauquis. Histoire économique de la soie. Grenoble. Grands établissements de l'imprimerie générale. 1910. p.273. The datas during 1833—1861 come from Archives Nationales de France. F12. 2552. 29 juin 1833 et de 1836. Le tarif de douane de 1833 et de 1836. The datas during 1862—1871 come from Archives Nationales de France. F12 6894. 24 décembre 1862. Décret de Napoléon III pour affranchir l'importation de soie grège. p. 493. The datas during 1872—1892 come from Archives Nationale de France. F12 7058. 29 septembre 1872. Lettre de Ministre des affaires étrangères au Ministre du Commerce. It should be noted that the customs duty Chinese silk is collected by 2.5% of the value at that time. During this year, the average price of Chinese raw silk is 50 francs per kilo, so the customs tariff on Chinese raw silk is about 1.25 francs per kilo. The datas during 1892—1914 come from Archives Nationales de France. F12 6854. Chambre des députés cinquième législature session de 1891. n° 1354. Le 21 mars 1891.

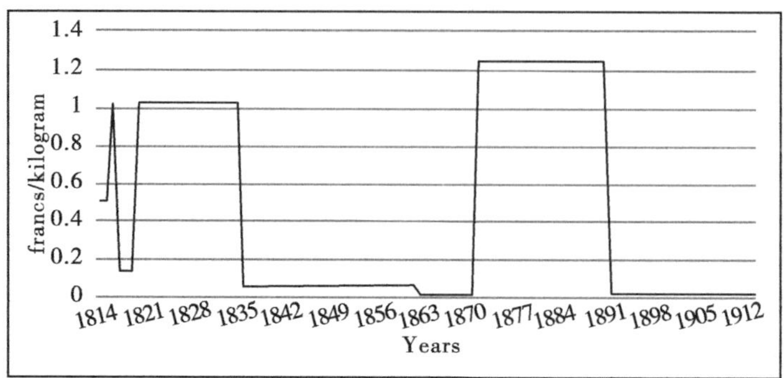

3. Measure the level of protection of the customs tariff for raw silk

At the end of this section, we will touch two questions concerning fundamental debates on the research of protectionism in the 19th century: first, do the duties on raw silk in France, despite all the conflicts between different groups for their own interests, were "protectionist" during the 19th century? Secondly, what are the relations between the customs tariff on raw silk and the growth of the silk textile industry in France? The first question concerns the question of "how to measure protection", and the second question highlights "the impact of such customs tariffs".

Indeed, the questions about "how to measure the policy of protectionism" have already been enormously discussed by recent historians. J.V.Nye's research, which challenged the conventional conclusions that England is the freest country in international trade in the 19th century and that France is relatively protectionist, provoked a great debate on the question of how to measure protection. Its argument is based on two methods for measuring the level of openness of the two countries: the average tariffs of the two countries (proportion of customs income in the total value of imports) and the evidence of tariff levels in certain sections of merchandise. After the comparison, J.V.Nye found that England's average tariff was higher than that of France until the late 1870s[1]. J.V. Nye's conclusion provoked not only much discussion of the levels of protection of England and France during the 19th century[2], but also many debates around the question of how to measure the level of protectionism. Researchers have criticized the fact that the

---

① J.V.Nye. "The myth of free-trade Britain and fortress France : Tariffs and trade in the Nineteenth Century". The journal of Economic History. Vol. 51. No°1. 1991. p. 23—46; J.V.Nye. War, Wine and Taxes : The Political Economy of Anglo-French Trade, 1689-1900. Princeton and Oxford. Princeton University Press. 2007; etc.

② Par exemple, le point de vue de J.V.Nye et son moyen de calcul ont été strictement critiqués par D.A.Irwin. Pour les détails, consulter D.A.Irwin. "Free trade and protection in nineteenth-century Britain and France revisited : A comment on Nye ." Journal of Economic History. Vol. 53. No°1. 1993. pp. 146—152.

216

average tariff does not perfectly reflect a country's level of openness or level of protection because that changes in exchange rates according to different tariffs and demand elasticities cannot occur on the average price that J.V.Nye uses. For example, in the extreme case, if a tariff of a commodity is so high that the importation of such goods is excluded, the share of this commodity falls to zero, and the tariff of such commodity will no longer contribute to the index of the average tariff. In order to overcome the imperfection of the medium above, historians and economists have proposed many other means of calculation. K.H.O'Rourke, in his article "Measuring protection: A cautionary tale" in 1997, tried to measure protection by TRI (Trade Restrictiveness Index). He concluded that France was a more liberal country for trade in goods with the highest elasticity (especially for luxury goods and exotic products), while England was relatively a more liberal country for trade with the lower elasticity (especially for manufactured products)[1].

In a publication of the same year, A.Estevadeordal used another model—trade intensity ratio—to measure the protection of the main 18 developed countries at the beginning of the 20th century. According to his calculation, France is one of the most protectionist countries among them at that time, and England is one of the freest countries. Another researcher, A.T.Junguito, stressed that the influence of tariffs on "tax products" must be considered when estimating the level of protection of a country's customs policy[2]. By removing the part of the tax products in the average tariff, the author concluded that France was no more liberal than England than before the mid-1840s, and more protectionist after the promulgation of "the corn laws" than England[3].

We shall measure, in this thesis, the level of protection of France on the merchandise we are interested in—raw silk. As our goal is to measure the level of protection on a single commodity (instead of the general level of protection of a country), we would no longer need to consider the variation in the proportion of such goods in the total value of the import with the floating price. Since this most important disadvantage of the way in which the average tariff calculation (which J.V.Nye and A.T.Junguito have used) no longer exists in the case of measuring protection a single kind of goods, we will describe here the level of protection of raw silk entry customs duty of France by this way.

---

① K.H.O'Rourke. "Measuring protection. À cautionary tale". Journal of Development Economics. No° 53. 1997. pp. 169—183.

② Tax products mean products without domestic substitutions (tobacco, sugars, etc.). The government imposes tariffs on such products only for financial revenue instead of for the protection of domestic products.

③ A.T.Junguito. "Assessing the protectionist intensity of tariffs in nineteenth century European trade policy." In J-P. Dormois, P. Lains, eds. Classical Trade Protectionism, 1815—1914. London and New York Routledge. 2006. pp.99—120.

Graph IV-3 Comparison of average customs tariffs to entry to France on the raw silk on all goods and on the all goods except tax products[1]

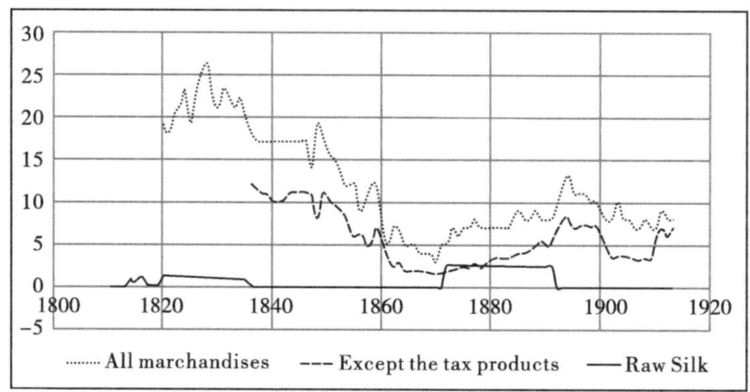

The highest series in Graph IV-3 represents the average customs tariff of all goods entered into France, as shown by J.V.Nye in his thesis. France imposes relatively high import duties on exotic products and colonies (tea, sugar, coffee, etc., known as tax products) during the 19th century, so this series is higher than the series in the middle, which represents the average customs tariff for goods entered into France except for tax products. The series in the middle is considered by A.T.Junguito to be more suitable to represent the level of protection of France because, by removing the effect of tax products, the average price of manufactures, raw materials, on which the import duties are really for the purpose of protecting domestic products.

The lowest series in the graph represents the customs tariff (in percentage) on raw silk during all periods of the 19th century. Obviously, the latter is levied at a much lower tariff than the average tariff level for most of the 19th century periods (except in the years 1872, 1873, 1874, 1876, 1878). This means that the level of protection of customs duties on raw silk is much lower compared to most goods imported into France. Moreover, the long crisis of sericulture during the second half of the century proves that its

---

[1] The datas of average tariff on all commodities come from J.V.Nye. "The myth of free-trade Britain and fortress France : Tariffs and trade in the Nineteenth Century". The journal of Economic History. Vol. 51. No°1. 1991. p. 26.The datas of average tariff on all commodities except the tax products come from d'A.T.Junguito. "Assessing the protectionist intensity of tariffs in nineteenth century European trade policy." In J-P. Dormois, P. Lains, eds. Classical Trade Protectionism, 1815—1914. London and New York Routledge. 2006. p.103—104.The datas of average tariff on raw silk come fromthe datas of the first two subsections. The customs duty on silk entering France during 1814—1861 is perceived by volume (weight) instead of by value. Therefore, the percentage of customs duty for raw silk on the total value of imports of this product shown in this graph is obtained by dividing the actual duty of one kilo of silk by the average price of one kilogram of silk.

effects of protection are so modest. So the answer to the first question will be: customs tariffs on raw silk are not, or are not sufficiently protectionist during the 19th century.

4. Impact of customs tariffs on the silk trade and the silk economy of France

Research on "the impact of tariffs on growth" is also quite abundant. At the level of international trade theory, free trade theorists argue that the effect of the tariff on the national economy is negative. Their models show that, by adding a customs duty to the price of a commodity, the situation of consumers has deteriorated: they have a much small quantity of goods at a higher price, while that of producers is improved: they sell a larger quantity of goods at a higher unit price. However, by comparing the decrease in the consumer surplus with the additional profits of the producers, there is a net loss for the national economy as a whole, as well as a loss of welfare[1]. On the other hand, protectionist theorists point out that the customs tariff is necessary for "young nations" to protect "its industries in childhood"[2]. According to them, the first producers of a "young nation" operate at higher costs than foreign competitors already in production, due to economies, scale, learning effects, and so on. It is therefore essential to protect the beginnings of an industry so that it can exist.

Among the empirical research on this problem, the most famous should be the investigating of P.Bairoch on the link between tariffs and growth in the last decades of the 19th century. In his books, he compared the growth rate during periods of free trade and protectionism in France and Europe. His conclusion was that the economies of France and Europe developed faster during the period of protectionism and free trade has slowed economic growth[3]. Although the opinion of P. Bairoch is debatable, it is still considered an important reference for economists and historians on the subject. First, some historians completely deny the point of P.Bairoch. F.Capie in his book *Tariffs and Growth*:

---

[1]　C.Kindleberger et P. Lindert. Économie internationale. Economica. Paris. 1981. p.170.

[2]　This point of view was first expressed by F. List in his National System of Political Economy of 1841, and then largely hesitated by the following protectionist theorists. Indeed, since the 1980s, many theorists, for example J. Culbertson and P. Krugman, have begun to explore in their research the role of protectionism in the new international trade environment since the end of the Second World War World with new analytical instruments, and they obtained the similar conclusion with the traditional theory of protectionism. For more informations, consult J.Culbertson. "The Folly of Free Trade". Harvard Business Review. Septembre-octobre. 1986; P.Krugman. "Introduction: New Thinking about Trade Policy." in P.Krugman. Strategic Trade Policy and the New International Economics. Cambridge. The MIT Press. 1986

[3]　P.Bairoch. " free trade and european economic development in the 19th century". European Economic review. Vol 3. No°3. 1972. pp. 211—245; P.Bairoch. Commerce extérieur et développement économique de l'Europe au XIXe siècle. Paris. Mouton. 1976 ; P. Bairoch. Mythe et paradoxes de l'histoire économique. Paris. La découverte. 1994.

some illustration from the World Economy published in 1994, determines that there is no evidence that proves that the rates accelerate economic growth in Europe in the late 19th century[1]. The thesis of is maintained by D.A.Irwin in his article "Interpreting the tariff-growth correlation of the late nineteenth century".[2]

He argue that, first, many countries, such as the growth of some countries, such as the United States, Canada and Argentina, have no ties with tariffs; Secondly, a large number of countries raise tariffs only to increase tax revenue instead of protecting local industries. Then, many researchers accept in part the conclusion of P.Bairoch. These researchers refuse to acknowledge that protection has accelerated economic growth and it was free trade that slowed it down during the 19th century, but they argue that, according to their calculations, there is a "correlation" between tariffs and growth. The most typical researches with this conclusion are those of A. Vamvakidis and K. H. O'Rourke. The first found that the Spearman[3] Correlation between average tariffs and growth, using data from 11 countries, was positive[4]; The latter used the same calculation method, but the different data (Maddison's GDP data), and its result also supported that of A.Vamvakidis[5].

Finally, there are other historians or economists who argue that the relationship between tariffs and growth was a negative correlation. For example, J,P.Dormois, in studying the correlation between the level of "protection intensity" and labor productivity of Germany, Italy and France during 1871—1930, asserted that "protection create not the growth. On the contrary, it destroys it"[6]; J.Foreman-Peck sought to estimate an eclectic model of per capita production, and concluded that average tariffs were negatively related to per capita production for residents[7]. In another empirical investigation, Dedi-

---

① F.Capie. Tariffs and Growth: Some Illustrations from the World Economy Trade. Manchester. Manchester University Press. 1994. pp.1—24.

② D.A.Irwin. "Interpreting the tariff-growth correlation of the late nineteenth century". In J—P. Dormois, P. Lains, eds. Classical Trade Protectionism, 1815—1914. London and New York Routledge. 2006. pp.153—158.

③ The Spearman correlation (named after Charles Spearman) is studied when two statistical variables seem correlated without the relationship between the two variables being of the affine type. It consists in finding a correlation coefficient, not between the values taken by the two variables, but between the ranks of these values. It allows to locate monotone correlations. It should also be noted that Spearman's correlation uses ranks rather than exact values. This correlation is used when the distributions of the variables are asymmetric.

④ A. Vamvakidis. "How robust is the growth-openness connections ? Historicall evidence," Journal of Economic Growth. Vol. 7. No°1. 2002. pp. 57—80.

⑤ K.H.O'Rourke. Tariffs and growth in the late nineteenth century. Economic Journal. No°110. 2000. pp. 456—483.

⑥ J—P.Dormois. "The I' impact of late-nineteenth-century tariffs on the productivity of European industries (1870—1930)". In J—P. Dormois, P. Lains, eds. Classical Trade Protectionism, 1815—1914. London and New York Routledge. 2006. pp.160—192.

⑦ J.Foreman-Peck. "A model of later-19th-century European economic development".Revista de Historia Economica. Vol.8. No°3. 1995. pp.441—471.

nger argued that Germany's industry, which is conventionally considered to be most benefiting from protectionism, would develop even faster if free trade policy were pursued after the 1880s[1].

In the case that we are studying, the positive correlation between the nonprotectionist customs tariff and the growth of silk imports in France is quite remarkable. The very low customs duty gave more and more foreign silks the possibility of entering France. Under such a condition of free trade, the quantity of imports of raw silk into France rose from 22,975 kilograms in the year 1815 to 198,636 kilograms in 1832[2], and to 1,095,000 kilograms in 1850, 6,000,000 kilograms in 1892 [3] and 8,195,300 kilograms in 1910, an increase of 367 times during the 19th century. Lyons became one of the most dynamic silk markets in the world during the 19th century[4]. In 1865, the quantity of silk exchange at the Lyonss market reached 2,900,000 kilograms, already exceeding 2,850,000 at the London market. In 1895, 6,250,000 kilograms of silk are sold by the market of Lyonss, much more than the 3,300,000 kilograms on by the New York market.

However, compared with the answer to the question of "the impact of the tariff" on the trade, the answer to the question of "the impact of the tariff" on the economy growth is much less obvious. On the one hand, the application of tariffs (of protection or of free trade, any) will undoubtedly improve the situation of a part of the production sections of a country; On the other hand, many other sections of production will be damaged at the same time, even ruined by exactly the same customs tariffs. Similarly, the customs policy of liberalism over silk that the government has pursued for a century positively impels the growth of the silk economy of France[5]. In the case of our research, very low tariffs on the entry of raw silk into France, as described above, led to the depression of French sericulture throughout the second half of the 19th century; Simultaneously, the same customs policy assured and increased the supply of raw materials, lowered the cost of production and finally extended the prosperity of the silk textile industry of France until the end of the 19th century. So, with such complexity, how do we estimate the impact of

---

[1]　B. Dedinger. "From virtual free-trade to virtual protectionism: or, did protectionism have any part in Germany's rise to commercial power 1850—1913". In J-P. Dormois, P. Lains, eds. Classical Trade Protectionism, 1815—1914. London and New York Routledge. 2006. pp.219—241.

[2]　Archives Nationales de France. F12. 2552. Commerce spécial de soie, résumé de 1815 à 1832.

[3]　N. Rondot. L'industrie de la soie en France. Lyon. Imprimerie Mougin-Rusand. 1894. pp. 14—15.

[4]　顾国达,滨崎实,宇山满.近代(1842—1945 年)世界生丝市场的结构.浙江丝绸工学院学报.第 10 卷,第 3 期,1993 年,第 105 页.

[5]　Here, the economy of silk means the totality of the activities of the production of raw silk and silks. It includes both the production of raw materials and manufactured production.

tariffs on the entire silk economy? Was the liberalism on the entry of foreign silks to France really suited to the economic growth of France?

Table IV−4 Quantities of sericulture production, silk textile production and trade of raw silk in 1853 and in 1900 (kilograms) [1]

	1853	1900
Raw silk production in France	2,529,182	650,000
Chinese raw silk import in France	5,950	3,343,275
Oher countries' raw silk import in France	1,083,935	7,267,989
Silk textile production in France	2,500,000	5,759,750

Let us compare the growth of the textile industry in France and the loss of French sericulture under such customs policy. As has been analyzed, France has pursued a relatively free policy on the import of raw silk during the 19th century. With very no-protective customs tariffs, the production of raw silk in France never returns to the level before the explosion of the silkworm epidemic, and only a fourth of the quantity from 1853 to the end of the 19th century. In contrast, imports of raw silk and silk production experienced respectively the significant growths during the same period. The data in Table IV−4 show us that although part of the silk economy of France—French sericulture—is damaged by low tariffs on imports of raw silk, the loss of this section of production is already well compensated, and then enormously exceeded, by the other part of the economy—the textile industry of France.

The summit of the production of raw silk took place in 1853, when 2,529,182 kilograms of raw silk were produced in all France with a value of about 288 million francs. This peak value is even lower than that of the French silk textile production during the valley period—291 million francs per year on average during the decade 1877—1886.

[1]　The datas on the quantities of the sericulture production in France come from L.Pasteur. Étude sur la maladie des vers à soie : notes et documents. p. 38. and 石井寛治.日本蚕业史分析.第 21 页.The datas on the Chinese raw silk quantities imported to France come from e Bulletin des soies et des soieries de Lyon-Revue Hebdomadaire Lyonnaise. Lyon. Administration. 1886—1910. n° 403—n°1390. and Ch.-B. Maybon, Jean Fredet, Histoire de la concession française de Shanghai, Paris. Librairie Plon. 1929. p. 215.Thedatas on the foreign raw silk quantities imported to France are obtained by dividing the quantities of imports of Chinese silk into France by the proportion of Chinese silk in the total imports of raw silk in France offered by FEDERICO Giovanni. An Economic History of the silk Industry, 1830−1930. Cambridge. Cambridge University Press. 1997. pp.214—215.The datas on the quantities of production of the silk fabrics in France come from R.Lee. France and exploitation of China 1855—1901. P.23. et de E.Hamaide. La relation entre Lyon et Chine au XIX siècle. p.9.

Except for this decade, the production value of the silk textile industry varied always between 400 million and 650 million per year during the second half of the 19th century, much higher than that of sericulture production in France. Moreover, it must be considered that almost all the French raw silk production is destined for the local market and that it is very difficult for this French raw material to enter into international competition. On the contrary, 70%—80% of the French silks textile are for the international market. In other words, the loss of sericulture for France is well compensated, and even largely surpassed by the growth of the silk textile industry during the 19th century. The whole silk economy of France shows a spectacular progress under the policy of liberalism on the entry of foreign silks.

II Evolution of the Chinese silk export customs duty and its commercial influence

The evolution of China's foreign trade policy before and after the Opium War has already been cited, presented, or discussed by many researchers. For example, in the article The Old Canton System of Foreign Trade by R. Edwards, the author presented precisely the foreign policy of the Qing Empire to find the origin of the policy of closure of the People's Republic Of China during the 1970s[1]; P.Bairoch, in order to approve of the catastrophe which liberalism had brought to the Third World, spoke of the evolutions of "protectionism" to "liberalism" of China during the 18th and 19th centuries in his book "mythes et paradoxe de l'histoire économique"[2]; in the book "Comparative History between China's Economic Policies and that of Japan" published by GAO Shujuan and FENG Bin, "The Canton system" and the new Chinese Customs regime are concerned in research on the comparison between the modern economies of China and Japan,[3]; In order to underline the essential role of certain ports for foreign trade and the economy of East Asia and South-East Asia[4], F. Gipouloux discussed the effects of the forced opening of ports to treaties on Chinese foreign trade in his book "la méditerranée asiatique";[5] The authors D. Chilosi and G.Federico also mentioned the limitation and opening up of China's

[1]　R.Edwards. "The Old Canton System of Foreign Trade." in V.H.Li. Law and Politics in China's Foreign Trade. Seattle and London. University of Washington Press. pp. 360—378.

[2]　P.Bairoch. Mythes et paradoxe de l'histoire économique. Paris. Éditions La Découverte. 1994. pp. 50—51

[3]　高淑娟,冯斌.中日对外经济政策比较史纲.北京:清华大学出版社,2003 年.

[4]　F.Gipouloux. La Méditerranée asiatique. Paris. Éditions CNRS. 2007. pp. 173—185.

[5]　F.Gipouloux. La Méditerranée asiatique. Paris. Éditions CNRS. 2007. pp. 173—185.

foreign trade in order to verify the effect of the trade barrier on the integration of the East-West market[1], etc.

In most historical research on this subject, China is conventionally determined as a closed or half-closed country before the Opium War, and as an increasingly open country after this war. Thus, the foreign exchange of China is often considered to be hampered by the "closure regime" before 1842, and to be much more dynamic thanks to the opening of China through the opium war. However, it should be noted that the validity of the two conventional conclusions still remains to be proved: first, if one measures by the customs tariff, China is truly more open after 1842 than before that date? Second, is the growth in exports of Chinese silk after the Opium War is truly linked to changes in the tariff? Is it also linked to other elements in the changes in the customs regime? In this section we will answer this question by studying the evolution of the tariff on silk exported from China and its relation to the growth of the silk trade before and after the Opium War. In observing this development, we will confirm the role of evolution of the Chinese silk customs regime in the growth of the silk trade between France and China.

At the same time, the research in this section will help clarify certain questions in the fields of global history and colonial history. First, what role did the government play in the Chinese economic dynamics and the closure of China before 1842? When contemporary historians try to explain the divergence between China and Europe in the 19th century (not only historians who emphasize the in-house specificity of Europe—religion, institution, technology, capital etc—represented by M.Weber[2], F.Braudel[3], I.Wallerstein[4], P.Brien[5], E.L.Jones,[6] but also historians who emphasize the differences in ex-

① D.Chilosi and G.Federico. "Asian Globalisations: Market Integration, trade and economic growth". 1800—1938. Economic History Working Papers. No°123. 2013. p.21.

② M.Weber. l'Ethique protestante et l'esprit du capitalisme. Paris.Gallimard. 2003.

③ F.Braudel. Civilisation matérielle, économie et capitalisme, XVe–XVIIIe siècle. Paris. Armand Colin.1979. 3 vol.

④ I. Wallerstein. The modern world-System. Vol. I. Capitalist Agriculture and the origins of the European World-Economy in the Sixteenth Century. New York and Londre. Academic Press. 1974. I. Wallerstein. The modern world-System.Vol. II. Mercantilism and the Consolidation of the European World-Economy. 1600—1750. New York. Academic Press. 1980. I. Wallerstein. The modern world-System.Vol. III. The Second Great Expansion of the Capitalist World-Economy. 1730—1840's. San Diego. Academic Press. 1989. I. Wallerstein. The modern world-System.Vol. IV. Centrist Liberalism Trumphant. 1789—1914. Oakland .University of California Press. 2011.

⑤ P.O'Brien. "European Economic Development. The Contribution of the Periphiry." Economic History Review. No°35. 1982. pp.1—32.

⑥ E.L.Jones. The European Miracle: Environements, Economies and Geopolitics in the History of Europe and Asia. Cambridge: Cambridge University Press. 1981.E.L.Jones.Growth Recurring: Economic Change in World History. New York. Oxford University Press. 1988.

ternal—colony between Europe and China like K. Pomeranz[1] and B. Wong[2], etc.),
they all agree that the Chinese government has a negative role to play against China's e-
conomic dynamics before the 19th century. They assume that the political system of
China's strong centralism is the opposite of China's economic development and China's
integration into the world. We will again check in this section the role of the Chinese
government in the evolution of the silk customs policy before the Opium War.

Secondly, what role do the countries of Europe, especially England, play in the o-
pening of 19th century China? Are their economic expansions in China based on free
trade supported by free-exchange theorists (A.Smith, Ricardians H.O.S)? Or is China
opened by political, diplomatic, even military pressures like what historians, D. Twitch-
ett, J.K.Fairbank[3], M.Greenberg[4], J.Lovell[5], Huang Yiping (黄逸平), Zhang Fuji
张复纪), Zhou Chonglin (周重林) and Tai Junlin (太俊林) described? We will answer this question by showing the efforts of the English for the opening of China from the
18th century to the mid-19th century[6].

1. Old Chinese tariff regime before 1842 and the export quota of Chinese silk

In order to eliminate rebellions in coastal areas, the Qing Empire (清帝国 1664—
1912) pursued a policy of "maritime interdiction" (海禁) at the beginning of its rule.
At that time, the Qing court prohibited all Chinese communications with foreigners on
the seaway, both in politics and trade[7]. This policy, which began in 1655 by the emperor of Shunzhi (顺治帝), was completed thirty years later (1685) by his son, the
emperor of Kangxi (康熙帝)[8]. It is from this date that the Qing Empire officially began to establish a foreign trade relationship, creating four customs to the Southeast China
shipping line: Jiangsu Customs in Songjiang (松江, 江海关), customs of Zhejiang to
Ningbo (宁波, 浙海关), customs of Fujian to Xiamen (厦门, 闽海关) and customs

---

① K.Pomeranz. The Great Divergence: China, Europe and the Making of the Modern World Economy. Princeton. Princeton University Press. 2000. p. 328—330.

② R.B.Wong. China transformed: Historical Change and the Limits of European Experience. Ithaca. Cornell
University Press. 1997.

③ D.Twitchett and J.K.Fairbank. The Cambridge History of China. Cambridge and New York. Cambridge University Press. 1978.

④ M.Greenberg. British Trade and the Opening of China 1800—1942. Cambridge University Press. 1951.

⑤ J.Lovell. The opium war: drug, dreams and the making of China. Basingstoke and Oxford. Picador. 2011.

⑥ 周重林、太俊林.茶叶战争.武汉:华中科技大学出版社,2012 年.)

⑦ 汪敬虞:论清代前期的禁海闭关.中国社会经济史研究.1983 年第 2 期,第 23—24 页.

⑧ 邓亦兵.清代前期关税制度研究.北京:燕山出版社,2008 年.

from Guangzhou to Canton (广州，粤海关) ①. However, this trade policy lasts less than a century. For fear of invasion of foreigners, the emperor of Qianlong (乾隆帝) once again closes the customs of Jiangsu, Zhejiang and Fujian from the year 1757②. As a result, Canton now becomes the only open Chinese port open to foreign trade.

Under the "one-port foreign trade regime" ("一口通商"), the Qianlong government has hesitated the tariff regime applied since the reign of Kangxi, whose composition is quite complicated. According to *The history of the Customs of Canton*, under the customs regime of Canton, goods were imposed by four kinds of duties at that time③:

(1) The permanent duty (正饷), which is an ordinary right imposed all the time on all kinds of merchandise. Tariffs of this kind are available on *Customs regulations* (《海关税则》) published by the Finance Ministry of the Empire, so these tariffs are relatively stable and light. The means of collecting this duty are different according to different kinds of goods imported or exported, which is by price, or by piece, or by volume (weight). The customs office must deposit the revenue of this duty to the national treasure (The Finance Ministry of the Qing Court).

(2) Additional taxes, which mainly include three kinds of taxes. First, the foreign-money exchange duty (加耗). This means the cost of converting the Spanish piasters to the Chinese taëls. The legal tariff for this tax is 1.6 Qian (钱) per taël④, but you actually pay 3 Qian to the customs office. Second, the picul duty (担费). According to the customs regulations, it is necessary to pay 0.38 Qian of additional tax for each picul of article. But we normally pay 1.5 Qian per picul for import and 2 Qian per picul for export. Third, the export price tax (出口货物从价税). Foreign merchant must legally pay a duty of 6% of the estimated prices for all their exported goods. The legal part of these three types of taxes will also be subject to national finances. The customs office will keep the excess part.

(3) The boat tax (船钞). The first two kinds of duties on it are taxed on exchange goods, but this right is imposed on vessels carrying goods. The boat tax is levied according to the size of the ship, whose tariffs are also written in the customs regulations. For example, a ship, any goods it carries, with length of 25 meters and width 8 meters must

---

① There are different points of view between historians on the location of the Fujian Customs. Here we adopt the opinoin of 夏秀瑞，孙玉琴.中国对外贸易史.第一册,北京:对外经济贸易大学出版社,2001 年,第 360 页.

② 中国第一历史档案馆.清实录·高宗纯皇帝实录.北京:中华书局,2008 年,乾隆二十二年十一月至二十四年 7 月.

③ 梁廷枏.粤海关志.广州:广州人民出版社,2002 年 2 月,第 419 页.

④ Qian, the weight unit of China. 1 Qian = 0.1 taël.

226

pay 1,400 taëls for boat tax; A ship with a length of 23 meters and a width of 7 meters must pay 1,100 taëls for this tax, etc. The destination of the boat tax will be national finances.

(4) Miscellaneous expenses. This mainly includes Gui Li (归礼), Hang Yong (行用), Si Li (私例). "Gui Li" means benefits to customs personnel. Foreign merchants have to pay this kind of fees to all personnel in customs (high level as general supervisor at low level as navigators). The amount of this fee is often very high: 1,950 taëls per ships on average. "Hang Yong" is a fee for paying expense of the operation of the Cohongs (公行), which monopolized China's foreign trade at that time. It normally accounts for 3%—6% of the total value of goods imported or exported. "Si Li" are rebates that are offered to the Cohong merchants in every business. As this is a kind of discount, you do not have a fixed rate.

In this customs regime, actual duties levied on goods entered or exited by Canton customs are often more expensive than statutory tariffs. The "miscellaneous" tariffs are not fixed in customs regulations, which gives customs and Cohongs the possibility of raising costs by abusing their powers. Even when foreign traders pay the additional taxes (second kind above), whose tariffs are noticed in the customs regulations, it is also necessary to pay excesses between the legal tariffs and the actual tariffs[1].

Customs duties on raw silk—the commodity studied in this thesis—follow precisely such principal taxation. On the eve of the Opium War, the price of "permanent law" silk from Zhejiang (second class) attaches to 5.4 taëls per hundred catties in customs regulations[2]. By adding the additional taxes, boat tax, and other legal expenses, 15.276 taëls are to be paid per hundred catties. But, in reality, a total of 23.733 taëls must be paid for every hundred cattle of Zhejiang silks at the customs office. For a hundred catties of the silk of Canton (first class), it's only necessary to pay 1 taël as the permanent duty[3]. But one must pay 8.765 taëls if one plus all the legal fees. With the profits to the customs officers and the Cohong, 10.57 taëls per hundred catties[4] must be paid. It is evident that the real tariffs are higher than the legal tariffs, and much higher than the permanent tariff.

Moreover, from the beginning of the period of Canton trade, the export of Chinese

---

① 陈争平.不平等条约下近代关税制度的形成及对中国经济的影响·近代中国.上海:上海社会科学院出版社,2005 年,199 页.

② H.B.Morse. The International Relations of the Chinese Empire. p.348.

③ 梁廷枏.粤海关志.第 1/4 页.

④ H.B.Morse. The International Relations of the Chinese Empire. p.348.

silk began to follow a policy of limiting the quantity exported. The implementation of this limitation stems from an increase in price of silk materials to the domestic market of China. Because of the expansion of the silk textile industry in the Jiangnan region during the first half of the 18th century, there was a tremendous rise in the price of silk materials in China at the time. Zhejiang silk costs only 130 taëls per picul at the beginning of the 18th century, but the price rises to more than 300 taëls per picul in the middle of the century[1]. Some mandarins in the central government believe that it was the growth of silk exports that led to the silk deficit in the domestic market and hence to the rise in the price of Chinese silk. Therefore, they propose to the Ministry of Finance (户部) to prohibit the export of silk so that the price of silk goes down:

"In recent years, traffickers export a large quantity of silk for profit, which leads to the high price of silk to the domestic market. So I would ask you to order Customs to prohibit the export of this commodity. If there are derogations, we have to accuse according to the article on the export of rice."[2]

On August 17, 1759, the Ministry of Finance of the Empire approved this proposal, and submitted it to the Emperor. Finally, Emperor Qianlong promulgated a decree prohibiting the export of silk at the end of 1759:

"Read and approved the twenty-fourth year of Qianlong: silk materials to the provinces of Jiangsu and Zhejiang are becoming increasingly expensive because of the export of silk from the sea route. From now on vice-kings and governors in the coastal provinces of the mandarins must order mandarins to prohibit the export of silk. If there are traders (Chinese) derogating from this order, those exporting more than 100 Jins (斤)[3] will be forced into exile, those who export less than 100 Jins will be prisoners for three years, and those who under 10 Jins will be detained for one month … "[4]

However, the exported part makes up only a small proportion of the total production of Chinese silk (we have already shown in Chapter II). So the policy prohibition of export does not succeed in lowering the price of silk to the domestic market. Moreover, the ban on the trade of silk, which was one of the most exported commodities exported from China, greatly reduced the revenue of local government finances, the turnover of merchants, and at the same time prevented the interest of the Chinese mandarins in the local government of the southwest who can no longer benefit from foreign trade. So this

---

① 刘永连：论近代粤丝出口的市场规律和特征.暨南学报.2004 年第 6 期,第 42 页.
② 清实录.高宗实录.北京:中华书局,2008 年,卷五百九十一.
③ Jin(斤), the unity of the weight of China. A Jin equals 0.5 kilogram.
④ 清朝文献统考.杭州:浙江古籍出版社,2001 年,卷 33,第 15 页.

policy is questioned by many Chinese mandarins after its application. In 1764 their representatives, the viceroy of Fujian and Zhejiang and the governor of Fujian together propose to the emperor that:

"After the prohibition of silk, we estimated that the price of silk would gradually diminish. But in reality, this price does not fall from the twenty-fourth year of Qianlong (1759) until now. On the other hand, this policy of prohibition leads to the oppositions of foreign merchants who constantly pray us to resume the foreign trade of silk and leads to the deficit of money used as the main currency in our country ... so we ask you to promulgate another decree to allow the export of silk."[1]

Having reflected on this proposal, the emperor of Qianlong decided to replace the policy of prohibition by the policy of limitation in 1764. According to the new decree, the raw silk of Zhejiang (first class) will always be completely prohibited to export; The export of silk (or warp) from Zhejiang (second class) shall not exceed 500 kilograms per ship, while exporting Guandong silk (or wild silk and silk yarn) shall not exceed 500 kg per vessel[2]. From then on, China established a regime of restrictions on foreign trade, consisting mainly of the complexity of customs duties, the quota on certain goods (especially on silk, rice, iron, sulfur, etc.), the monopoly of Cohong in the foreign exchange and of a single port open to foreign trade.

Thus, even if the exchange of China with foreign countries is not completely prohibited, it must be admitted that its foreign trade regime is rather closed and conservative before the Opium War. First, as has been shown, customs duties imposed in realities are higher than those legitimately required to be deposited, which means that the real protection in China is stronger than the official regulations (Customs regulations). Moreover, in the case of customs duties on exported silks, most (about 2/3—4/5) of the duties levied on silk are destined for state finance. In other words, the purpose of the Customs regime is rather from support central government revenue than finance and local development. Recently, the quota of goods and Conhong's monopoly also prevents the scale of China's economic communication with other countries. So we can confirm that China is indeed a half-closed country before the 1840s.

However, it is also unreasonable to simplify the relationship between the Chinese government and the economic dynamics of China at the time. Some historians claim that the Chinese government with a system of strong centralism plays a negative role (at least

---

① 皇朝经典类纂.台北:文海出版社,卷一百一十八,2854 页.
② 清朝文献统考.杭州:浙江古籍出版社,2001 年,卷 33,第 16 页.

does not play a positive role) in economic development. But in reality, the mandarins in government are not so compact on the policy to adopt, while there is often tension between the interest of the central government and that of local government. Concerning the foreign trade policy on silk (as shown above), the central government proposes to ban the trade of silk with foreign countries completely because of the economic security of the state, and local governments are calling for restarting the Chinese silk trade with foreigners for local finance and local economic development. The final decree of the emperor is a compromise between the two groups of Mandarin. Not all Chinese mandarins insist on adopting policies against China's economic development and external communication, and that different voices from different groups of Mandarins all play important roles in the process of the policies making of the Chinese state at the time.

2. Protest of foreigners

The opening of China clarifies the issue of the role of European countries in the process of integrating eastern countries into the world. As has been shown in the introduction to this section, some economists and historians assert that the economic expansion of the countries of Europe, especially that of England, is based on free trade. But what happens during the opening of China proves that their commercial success is actually based on political, diplomatic, even military pressure.

The regime of trade policy leads to the dissatisfaction of countries of exchange with China, especially that of England. Beginning in the 1750s, the latter country, as the largest trading partner with China at that time, repeatedly asked the Qing court for a more open policy to international trade, by the government and from East India Company, even by the individual merchants.

A very well-known protest event, known as the "Event of P. Flint" (洪仁辉事件), happens just a year after the Qing court closes ports of Ningbo, Songjiang and Xiamen (in 1758). P.Flint is the Trade Commissioner of the East India Company of England. Charged with the Company's mission to open a trading post at the port of Ningbo, he arrived for the first time at this port in 1755. During 1855—1856, he imported a lot of goods from Ningbo port to England, and gained a lot of profit for the Company. In 1757, the Vice-King of Guangdong and Fujian warned him not to go to the port of Ningbo because this port is already closed to foreign traders according to the new decree of the Chinese emperor. Believing he has a right to trade with China, P. Flint did not consider the Chinese Mandarin's warning and sailed to Ningbo in 1758. After arriving in

230

Ningbo, he was expelled from the port of Ningbo by the local government, while goods already embarked on his ship are detained at the same time. Then he does not return to the port of Canton as what the Ningbo mandarins have proposed, but continues to sail to the north, to the capital of the Chinese Empire to ask the Qing court to open the port of Ningbo. In the same year, he arrives in Tianjin（天津）, the port that is right next to Beijing and is never open overseas. The Governor of Tianjin promised to submit the petition of Fr. Flint to the Emperor, and proposed to him to return to Canton, awaiting the reply. P. Flint followed the advice of the governor of Tianjin and returned to Canton, but was arrested by the Canton government immediately after his arrival because of his penetration into Tianjin. Being detained for three years on the island of Macon（澳门）, P. Flint is finally expelled from China and is never allowed to return to China[1]. P.Flint's protest did not change the foreign trade policy of the Qing court. On the other hand, since this event, the Chinese government is more suspicious of foreign merchants: in 1760, the Qing court issued a new ordinance to control the activities of foreign merchants, including articles to limit the place of residence of foreigners, the contract of foreigners with the Chinese and the navigation of foreign ships on the Chinese sea, etc[2].

Despite this failure, the British did not abandon their attempt to expand the door of trade with China. In the letter of November 30, 1787 to Lieutenant C.Cathcart, the first official ambassador sent by the United Kingdom to China, the English Government emphasizes that:

"For a long time, English merchants are forced to trade with China by sacrificing their interests. The last regulation of the Chinese government stipulates that Canton is the only port that one has the right to install commercial houses, which has already imposed restrictions on the trade of the East India Company with China. Free trade at the Canton market was already destroyed by the union of Chinese merchants（Cohong）. Moreover, English traders do not have equal status before the Chinese court.

You should announce to the Chinese emperor: First, the Sino-English trade is in the interests of both countries ... Secondly, we ask for a safe place to deposit our goods ... Thirdly, it should be noted that the request of England is clearly for trade instead of for territorial ambition. We will not install our defense, but only ask the Chinese government to defend our traders and our delegates ...

---

① 中国第一历史档案馆.明清宫藏中西商贸档案 02.北京：中国档案出版社,2010 年 6 月,第 766 页,英商洪仁粹控告粤海关监督李永标案.

② 张研.清代经济简史.新北：云龙出版社,2002 年,第 435 页.

If the Chinese emperor promises to leave England in a place, it is necessary to pay attention to the position of the place, which must be suitable to the demand of English ships for safety and convenience, so that England can sell its goods and buy tea and raw materials—located about 27—30 degrees north latitude ...

If the local application is denied, you should strive to gain more privileges at the Canton market and try to change the regulations that weigh the interests of English merchants ...

You should note that the Chinese government will be able to impose a condition on you: England will no longer deal with opium trade, which is prohibited by Chinese law ... If the government officially asks you, or seeks to add an article in the future treaty, that we will no longer carry opium in China, you would be obliged to accept it. Do not sacrifice our fundamental interest in the free trade of this commodity nature ..."[1]

We find that the purposes of the Government of England at that time are to request a new place open to English commerce outside of Canton and to change foreign trade regulations of China. Until then, the way that England is very peaceful, especially through diplomatic negotiation. In order for merchants to obtain equal commercial rights in China, the British government even granted permission to stop exporting opium to China, which was the most exported commodity in China by that time.

Lieutenant C.Cathcart was unable to complete his mission because he died of illness on the way from England to China. So the presentation of the first letter of credence from the English King to the Chinese emperor delays to 1793, when the second English ambassador—V.Macartney, Baron of Lissanonron—arrives in Beijing. In this letter of credence, England added several additional demands: first, England has the right to install the embassy in the capital of China (Beijing); Secondly, China is asked to open Ningbo, Zhushan (珠山) and Tianjin to British trade, and promise to let English merchants set up trading posts in China capital; Thirdly, China is requested to exempt or reduce the customs duty to English traders; English missionaries will be allowed to propagate the Christian religion in China, etc[2].

England has already asked to modify the former customs regime in this first letter of credence. However, according to the response of the Chinese emperor to V.Macartney in the same year, all the demands that England put down are completely rejected by the Qing court. Regarding the tariff regime, the Chinese emperor replied: "There are cus-

---

① H.B.Morse. The Chronicles of the East India Company Trading to China. 1635—1834. Vol. 2 pp.160—165.
② 梁廷枏.粤海关志.广州:广州人民出版社,2002 年 2 月,第 5—12 页.

toms regulations in Canton on the customs duties that traders have to pay. All foreign countries are equal before these regulations. We cannot diminish your duties because of your trade advantage with China compared to other countries."[1]

In 1816, England's third ambassador—William Pett Lord Amherst—was sent by Prince Regent George (ie King George IV later) to China. Before his departure, he received a letter from Lord V.Castelereagh, Minister of Foreign Affairs. In the letter, Lord V. Casteleragh again asked Lord Amherst to negotiate with the Chinese Court of Business of the commercial privileges of England in China. However, this time, the letter of credence of England could not reach the Chinese emperor's hand, because Lord Amherst refused to appear before the Chinese emperor with prostration[2]. This is the last attempt by the English government to change China's foreign trade regime before the Opium War.

After the loss of the official contact of England with the central government of China in 1816, private traders continue to try to improve their condition of trade by filing petitions to the local mandarins of Canton. In 1832 two English merchants, H.H.Lindsay and C. Gutslaff, told the local government in Canton that English merchants were often extorted by the customs and that often they had to pay a lot of money apart from conventional duties, which harmed the commercial interests of the two countries. But his petition is neglected by the Canton government without answer. In 1836, thirty-eight principal foreign merchants resident in Canton sent a petition to the governor of Canton to cancel the silk export restriction. "Obliged on the one hand to embark only a small quantity on each vessel, on the other to pay double dues on the silks, regardless of the high price of this article, the petitioners will not be able to satisfy such a requirement."[3] In the letter of reply, the governor of Canton asserts that the permission to export silk in 1764 has already been a favor to foreigners, and we must not ask for more. After the failure of all these negotiations for more than half a century, the English decided to achieve their goals in a way of violence—by the Opium War in 1840.

3. China's tariff regime and the tariff on silk exported after 1842

China began to lose its customs sovereignty after the opium war with England. First, the tenth article of the *Treaty of Nanjing* between China and England (August 4, 1842) stipulates that "For all the duties which English merchants should pay, the Chi-

---

[1] Idem. p. 12.
[2] H.B.Morse. The chronicles of the East India Company Trading to China. 1635—1834. Vol. 2 pp.278—284.
[3] Archives Nationales de France. F12. 6498. le 8 septembre.1836. Le commerce des soies en Chine.

nese Government must formulate fixed tariffs by observing justice（英商应纳进口出口货税、饷费，均宜秉公议定则例）"①. In other words, tariffs for all duties levied by English merchants should be formulated in a fixed customs regulation, and these duties should be fair and rational. Then, two years later, China signed the Treaty of Wanghia on 3 July 1844 with the United States and the *Treaty of Whampoa*（《黄埔条约》) on 14 August 1844 with France.

It is written in this first treaty that "if China wishes to change the customs tariffs, the consent of the American consuls must be obtained（中国日后欲将税例更变，须与合众国领事等官议允）", ② and the last formula that "China can modify the tariffs of customs only after the permission of France（应与佛兰西会同议允后，方可酌改）"③. Since these two treaties, China is obliged to formulate its customs tariffs by negotiating with foreign countries, which symbolizes the loss of the sovereignty of formulation of the customs duties of China.

Having obtained the Hongkong concession, opened four additional trade ports and abolished the Gonghong monopoly of China's foreign trade by the *Nanjing Treaty* of 1842, finally succeeded in resolving the problems relating to quotas and customs duties in foreign trade of China by *The Annexes to the Nanjing Treaty*（《中英五口通商章程》), signed in 1843. Under the new treaty, China is obliged to stipulate a new Customs of commerce with England, from which there are several important changes: first, quotas on certain goods in foreign trade of China have been canceled; Secondly, the customs tariff is fixed at an average rate of 5% of the value of the goods; Third, additional taxes are abolished; Fourth, the boat tax will be paid per tonne instead of the size of vessel—the tariffs for each ton shall be 0.5 tons for vessels over 150 tons and 0.1 tons per ton for vessels less than 150 tons, which are much lower compared to that imposed by the old standard; Fifth, for "miscellaneous expenses", English merchants will only need to pay the pilotage fee④.

Under this new customs regime, the limitations on China's foreign trade have been canceled, the composition of customs duties is simplified, and tariffs are reduced. At the level of import tariffs, the average rate of 5% makes China now become one of the most

---

① 中国第一历史档案馆.明清宫藏中西商贸档案 06.北京:中国档案出版社,2010 年 6 月,第 722 页,中英南京条约稿本.

② 中国第一历史档案馆.明清宫藏中西商贸档案 07.北京:中国档案出版社,2010 年 6 月,第 3783 页,中英南京条约稿本.

③ 中国第一历史档案馆.明清宫藏中西商贸档案 07.北京:中国档案出版社,2010 年 6 月,第 3882 页,中英南京条约稿本.

④ 王铁崖.中外旧约章汇编.上海:三联书店,1957 年,第一册,第 35 页.

free-trade countries in the world at the time (according to how to measure protection of J.V.Nye). According to the data in Table IV-5, during the years 1864—1879 (the period of the average customs tariff valley in Europe), China's customs tariff is almost at the same level as England, France and Germany, whose average tariffs are the lowest among large European countries. After the 1880s, when customs tariffs for most European countries rose, China continued to maintain the average level of 5%. The latter average rate is even lower than that of England, considered to be the most free-trader in Europe at the time. So in the long-term, China's average import tariff remains at a very modest level compared to European countries.

Table IV - 5 Comparison of average tariffs (import) between China, England, France, Germany, Italy, Spain and the United States (percentage)[1].

	China	England	Fance	Germany	Italy	Spain	United States
1864	5.22	11	5	5	5	11.25	14
1869	5.17	9	4	7	7.25	10	35
1874	5.93	8	6	3.5	7.5	10.8	43
1879	5.89	7	7	6	9.25	14.2	31
1884	6.01	6.8	8	9	13.75	13.75	30
1889	5.29	6.5	8	9	17.5	12	29
1894	4.04	6	13	10	18.5	21	25

---

[1] The average tariff of China come from 仲伟民.茶叶、鸦片贸易对19世纪中国经济的影响.社会经济史研究.1994 年底 1 期,第 133 页.)The average tariff of England and France come from J.V.Nye. "The myth of free-trade Britain and fortress France : Tariffs and trade in the Nineteenth Century". The journal of Economic History. Vol. 51. No°1. 1991. p. 26.The average tariff of Italy and spain come from Junguito. "Assessing the protectionist intensity of tariffs in nineteenth century European trade policy." In J-P. Dormois, P. Lains, eds. Classical Trade Protectionism, 1815—1914. London and New York Routledge. 2006. p.110.The average tariff of the United States come fromB.Dedinger. "From virtual free-trade to virtual protectionism: or, did protectionism have any part in Germany's rise to commercial power 1850—1913". In J-P. Dormois, P. Lains, eds. Classical Trade Protectionism, 1815—1914. London and New York Routledge. 2006. p.231.

Graph IV-6 Comparison of China's average customs export and import rates 1864—1894[1]

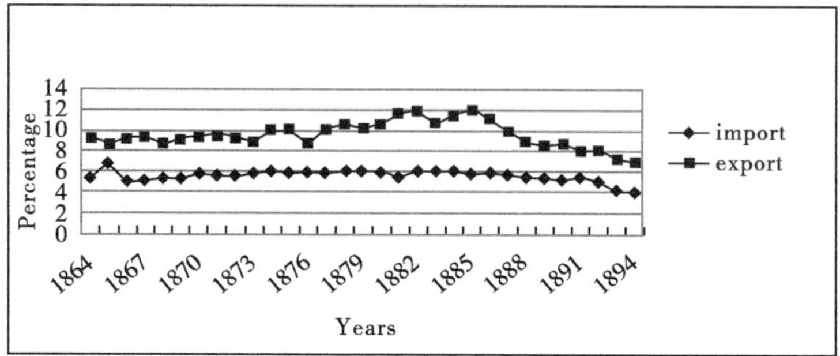

At the level of export duties, China continues to maintain an average tariff of 8%—12% on most goods exported under the new tariff regime. Export duties were also important financial resources for European countries during the 17th and 18th centuries. However, having experienced the negative effect of export duties on the competitiveness of domestic products on the external market, the latter countries gradually phased out most export duties on items exported during the 19th century. In China almost all species of local products for export must be taxed by the state before 1840[2], and this principle is hesitated by the new regime after the Opium War. In order to appease civil rebellions, reimburse compensation for external wars and finance the military and industrial modernization, the Chinese government is obliged to maintain export tariffs during the second half of the 19th century. However, export tariffs in the new regime are not quite the same as those in the old regime. Many new features have been included in the new export tariff system, which is reflected perfectly in the evolution of the export tariffs for silk materials.

---

① 仲伟民:茶叶、鸦片贸易对19世纪中国经济的影响.社会经济史研究.1994年底1期,第133页.
② 梁廷枏.粤海关志.广州:广州人民出版社,2002,第150—260页,"税则一至六".

Table IV-7 Change in customs tariffs for China silks in 1843 (taëls / cent catties)[1]

Nature	Old tariff of perrmnent duty	Old tariff of legal duty	Old tariff du real duty	Tariff en 1843	Price en 1843	proportion of customes duty in le price 1843
Silk of Zhejiang	5.4	15.276	23.733	10	350	3%
Silk of Canton	1	8.576	10.5702	10	200	5.00%
Wild silk	1.8	4.0866	4.1436	2.5	75	3.30%
Warps	5.4	12.7271	12.7841	10	400	3.30%
Wire of silk	1.8	8.1068	8.1638	10	400	2.50%
Ribbon of silk	0.75	8.6202	8.6776	10	400	2.50%

First, quotas on the export of many species of goods have been canceled in the new regime. According to the decree of 1764, raw silk of Zhejiang (first class) was completely prohibited to export, export of silk (or organsin) Zhejiang (second class) should not exceed 500 kilograms by ship, and the export of silk from Guandong (or wild silk and silk yarn) must also not exceed 500 kilograms per vessel in the former customs regime. This limitation with quotas on other goods was finally canceled by the annexes of the *Nanjing Treaty*, and replaced by new customs tariffs.

Second, export tariffs in the new regime are much more uniform and standardized compared to those of the old regime. We have already mentioned in the previous text that there are major discrepancies between the permanent duty, the legal duty and the real

---

① The datas of ancien tariff of permanent duty come from 梁廷枬.粤海关志.广州：广州人民出版社 2002 年 2 月，第 5   12 页. The datas of ancien legal tariff come from 姚贤镐：中国近代对外贸易史资料 1840—1895，第 1 卷，第 390 页.The datas in 1843 come frome 中国第二历史档案馆，中国海关.中外条约.帝国海关统计部，1917 年，第一卷.

duty in the old regime, which added the complexity of taxation. This corresponds perfectly to the case of tariffs on silk materials. 5.4 taëls silk must be paid as the permanent duty for per hundred catties of Zhejiang, 15.276 taëls as the legal duty according to the customs regulations of the old regime, but in reality it is necessary to pay 23.773 taëls in passing customs. The same phenomenon exists universally during the imposition on the other natures of silk materials. On the contrary, in the new regime of customs duties, first, there are no longer any duties (permanent, legal and real) on the same kind of goods, and the duty on each kind of silk is unique. In addition, 10 taëls per 100 catties are imposed on almost all kinds of silk materials (except on wild silk which is much cheaper than others). These two changes have dramatically simplified the method in which fees are levied.

Third, export tariffs on certain goods in the new regime have decreased considerably. According to the data in the table below, the new tariff on silk from Zhejiang decreased considerably (from 23.733 taëls to 10 taëls) compared with the old regime. As for the other natures of silk materials, changes between the old and the new tariffs are not very evident: the tariff on silk from Canton falls from 10.5702 taëls to 10 taëls, that on wild silk falls from 4.1436 taëls to 2.5 Taëls, the organsin descends from 12.784 taëls to 10 taëls, and the tariffs of the threads and ribbons are somewhat higher than those of the old regime. However, the absolute export volume of raw silk from Zhejiang, Cantonese silk, wild silk and warp is considerably higher than that of silk and silk ribbon (see data in Section 4 of Chapter II). So, generally speaking, customs duties on all the silk materials have been greatly reduced in the new regime.

The annexes to the *Nanjing Treaty* of 1843 built the fundamental principles of the new system of customs duties after the Opium War. Despite some modifications, the great principles of the silk tariffs of 1843 were always respected during the rest of the 19th century. As a result, new export tariffs for silk materials established from that date remain very stable after 1843, except that several adjustments are made during the following periods:

(1) In 1844, France obtained the same privileges as those of the English by the *Treaty of Whampoa*. The tariffs of 1843 are generally hesitated by those stipulated by this new treaty: they generally fix on ten taëls per hundred catties. Nevertheless, it should be noted that there are two small changes in this new treaty. First, the natures of the silks are more precise. Some natures of silk, yellow silk of Sée-tchuen, silk doupion, silk waste, sewing silk of Canton appeared independently in the list instead of being in-

cluded in other natures of silk, etc. Certain tariffs, such as doupion silk, silk waste and sewing silk from Canton, are again reduced (the table below is a part of the table attached as a result of the *Treaty of Whampoa*).

Table IV-8 Compensation between the export silks customs tariffs of China in the *Annexes of the Nanjing Treaty* and in the *Whampoa Treaty* (taëls / hundred catties)[1]

Natures o f silks	Tariff of Annexes *of Treaty of Nanjing*	Tariff of Whampoa *Treaty*	Difference
Raw silk and thrown silk	10	10	0
Sichuan Yellow silk	10	7	3
Doupions silk	10	5	5
Wild Yellow silk	2.5	2.5	0
Waste silk	2.5	1	1.5
Sewing silk of Canton	10	4.3	5.7
Sewing silk of other provinces	10	10	0
Wire of silk	10	10	0
All kinds of warps	10	10	0
Ribbons	10	10	0
All kinds of silk textiles	12	12	0
Sichaun silk textiles	12	4.5	7.5
Shandong silk textiles	12	4.5	7.5
Caps of silk	no data	0.9	0
Mixed textiles of silk and cotton	3	5.5	2.5

(2) In the customs regulations in 1843, customs tariffs are calculated by the unit of measure. Due to this standard of "quantity" calculation, customs tariffs remain the same despite a general trend of falling prices that appeared in the Chinese Empire during the 1850s. Then of the negotiation for the *Tianjin Treaty* (《天津条约》). In 1858, the English and French representatives asked the Chinese government to recalculate customs tariffs according to new commodity prices, so that the principle of "the average of the

---

[1] Archives Nationales de France. F12. 6498. 15 mars 1845. Traité 1844 et les tarifs de douane.

5% tariff" can be respected[1]. Under pressure from both westerns countries, the Chinese government has agreed to renew its customs tariffs in the *Tianjin Treaty*[2], and customs tariffs for most of the articles still fall. However, according to the new tariffs attached to the *Tianjin Treaty*, there is little change in customs duties for silk this time[3]. The only change is that the Chinese Government has annulled the prohibition on the export of cocoons in the latter treaty and imposes an export duty of 3 taëls per hundred catties.

Table IV-9 Customs duties of silks in customs regulations in 1858 (taëls/ hundred catties) [4]

Natures of silks	Tarifs de douane en 1858	Prix en moyen en 1858	Proportions
Silk of Zhejiang	10	278	3.60%
All kind of warps	10	278	3.60%
Waste silk	1	28	3.60%
Wild silk	2.5	70	3.60%
Concoons	3	116	2.60%
Sewing silk of Canton	4.3	120	3.60%
Sewing silk of other provinces	10	278	3.60%
Sichuan wild yellow silk	7	125	5.60%
Doupions silk	5	125	4.00%
All kind of frames	10	278	3.60%
Ribbons	10	278	3.60%
All kinds of silk textiles	12	335	3.60%
Caps of silk	0.9	24.5	3.70%
Mixed textiles of silk and cotton	5.5	150	3.70%

[1] F. WRIGHT Stanley. China's Strugglevfor Tariff Autonomy 1843—1938. Michigan. Kelly and Walsh Limited. 1938. p. 53.

[2] Archives Nationales de France. F12. 6498. Traité 1858 avec la Chine.

[3] Pour les détails, consulter Archives nationales de Chine (deuxièmes). China Maritime Customes. Treaties, Conventions, etc. Between China and Foreign States. Statistical Department of the Inspectorale General of Customs. 1917 Vol I. p.435—443.

[4] Archives nationales de Chine (deuxièmes). China Maritime Customes. Treaties, Conventions, etc. Between China and Foreign States. Statistical Department of the Inspectorale General of Customs. 1917 Vol I. p.442.

（3）According to the 27th article of the Sino-English Tianjin Treaty signed in 1858, both countries are able to adjust new customs duties in 10 years after it is signed[1]. Thus, from January 2, 1868, China and England return to the negotiating table for the interests of the respective governments: China seeks to increase its financial income by raising tariffs on major commodities in its trade, and England intends to obtain the right of exploitation of Chinese mineral springs and the right of dwelling inside China. After a long negotiation for 22 months, the Chinese Foreign Affairs Ministry（总理衙门）finally signed a revision of the *Tianjin Treaty*（《中英新修条约》）with the British representative Alcock Rutherford（British ambassador in China）between England and China on October 24, 1869[2]. By this last revision, China increased the export duty on opium from 30 taëls to 50 taëls per hundred catties, and doubled the customs tariffs on silk rape of all kinds at the cost of opening two more commercial ports, the right of mining at three Chinese places and the right of lodging at hotels in unopened ports[3].

Obviously, Alcock Rutherford expanded the new privileges of England in China by sacrificing the interests of the merchants of opium and silk. This also immediately brought the protest of the silk merchants of Lyons. In their protest they show, first of all, that the English have attained their object by sacrificing the interest of France: "If the English ambassador has consented to this enormous aggravation, it is because, on the one hand, silks in England follow a decreasing march; Its silk textile industry, since the suppression of the import duties on silks (French), cannot compete with our own; It is, on the other hand, that Sir Alcok obtained, in compensation, considerable facilities and advantages for the outlet of the cotton goods."[4]

Then they point out the damage which the new tariffs will bring to the Franco-Chinese trade: "It is sufficient to recall that the consumption of Chinese silks, which in 1855 was barely 250,000 kilograms, rose in 1859 to Lyonss only, Nearly 1,000,000 kilogram[5]... We see that these silks have paid in China, in terms of exits and circulation, from 750 to 800,000 francs; It would be, if the duty were doubled, a new tax of

① 王铁崖.中外旧约章汇编.北京:三联书店,1982 年,第一册,第 99 页.

② For more informations 费驰,刘晓东.(1868—1869 年) 中英新修条约·谈判评述.吉林大学社会科学学报.2001 年,第 2 期,第 123—128 页.

③ Archives Nationales de France. F 12.6498. 24 Octobre 1869. Convention supplémentaire au Traité de commerce et de navigation de juin 1858 entre la Grande-Bretagne et la Chine.

④ Archives Nationales de France. F 12.6498. 30 mars 1870. Lettre du président de l'Union des marchands de soie de Lyon aux membres de la Chambre de commerce de Lyon.

⑤ Idem.

750,000 francs a month, levied on our industry."[1] In the end they demanded that the Representative of France in China should receive the necessary instructions for him to oppose the raising of the silk rights and to refuse the concessions which the Chinese Government had obtained from the British Envoy.[2] "And expresses their wish" that the duties stipulated in the Treaty of Tien-Tsin be maintained with the effective guarantee of being no longer burdened with arbitrary taxes of transit or granting so often imposed by the mandarins[3]. The President of the Chamber of Commerce sends this petition to the Minister of Commerce, who transmits these observations to the Foreign Affairs Minister[4]. Due to pressures from the French government[5], and at the same time from the English opium merchants, the Government of England declared July 25, 1870, to refuse the new revision signed by Alcock Rutherford with the Chinese Government. As a result, the Sino-English bargain in the late 1860s did not change the customs tariffs of the silks of 1858[6].

(4) The last adjustment (This is the last change in the tariff of exported Chinese silk until 1914). The price of silks exported from China is related to the signatures of the commercial agreements after the Franco-Chinese war between 1883—1885. After the war of 1870, the foreign trade policy of the Third Republic gradually returned to protectionism. Opposed to a restoration of economic growth, the new government at the same time seeks to activate trade between Indochina and south-east China. Following the conquest of the Indochina of France, a new *Commercial Convention between France and China* (《越南边界通商章程》) was signed on April 25, 1886, in order to regulate the conditions under which the Commerce by land between Tonkin and the southern provinces of the Qing Empire. According to this Convention the customs tariffs of articles exported from China to Tonkin by the land frontier will generally be reduced by one-third in comparison with that of Treaty 1858. The tariffs for silk customs shall also be reduced to 2/3 than before if transported by the land border between China and Tonkin[7].

---

① Archives Nationales de France. F 12.6498. 22 féviers 1870. Lettre de la chambre du commerce de Lyon au Ministre du commerce.

② Idem.

③ Archives Nationales de France. F 12.6498. 30 mars 1870. Lettre du président de l'Union des marchands de soie de Lyon aux membres de la Chambre de commerce de Lyon.

④ Archives Nationales de France. F 12.6498. 5 mai 1870. Lettre du Ministre du commerce au président de la Chambre de commerce de Lyon.

⑤ S.F.Wrignt. China's Strauggle for the tariff autornomy 1843－1938. Shanghai. Kelly&Walsh. 1938. p.235.

⑥ H.B.Morse. l'histoire des relations de l'Empire chinois avec les étrangers. Vol II. p. 238.

⑦ 王铁崖.中外旧约章汇编.北京:三联书店,1982 年,第一册,第 220—227 页.

Table IV - 10 Silk tariff of silks in the new Franco-Chinese convention of 1886 (taëls) [1]

Natures	Customs Tariff in 1858	Tariff by the boader of Tonkin after 1886
Silk of Zhejiang	10	6.6
All kind of warps	10	6.6
Waste silk	1	0.7
Wild silk	2.5	1.7
Concoons	3	2
Sewing silk of Canton	4.3	2.8
Sewing silk of other provinces	0	6.6
Sichuan wild yellow silk	7	4.6
Doupions silk	5	3.3
All kind of weft	10	6.6
Ribbons	10	6.6
All kinds of silk textiles	12	8
Caps of silk	0.9	0.6
Mixed textiles of silk and cotton	5.5	3.6

However, this tariff reduction applies only to trade through the southwestern border of China. In other commercial seaports, customs tariffs on silk do not change. Moreover, the silk trade between Indochina and the border of south-east China is still not very dynamic. If we recall the contents of Chapter II: on the statistics of the Long-Tcheou Customs, silk appears in the list of articles only after the year 1900: the quantity of exports is only 119 piculs[2], In Sse-mao, the trade in silk is also not very important. Only one picul was exported in 1899[3] and 12 piculs in 1901[4]. Three French companies moved to Mongtze in 1903. One serves as the agency of the Compagnie Lyonsnaise d'Indochine,

---

[1]　Archives nationales de Chine (deuxièmes). China Maritime Customes. Treaties, Conventions, etc. Between China and Foreign States. Statistical Department of the Inspectorale General of Customs. 1917 Vol 1. p.442.

[2]　Archives Nationales de France. F12. 7057. 12 janvier 1901. Rapport de commerce de Long-Tcheou en 1900.

[3]　Archives Nationales de France. F12. 7057. 20 avril 1899. Rapport du commerce de Ssê-mao en 1898.

[4]　Archives Nationales de France. F12. 7057. 27 avril 1903. Rapport du commerce de Ssê-mao en 1901 et 1902.

but it does not occupy the silk trade, while the other two are for the railway construction[1]. On the seaway, Haiphong's importance in the silk trade in Southeast Asia is very modest compared with that of Hong Kong, and very few French ships arrive in Haiphong after the French occupation. Thus, the new privilege of France over the customs tariff after the war of Indochina does not favor the trade of silks between France and China.

We can answer the first question to the introduction of this section: with the abolition of the export quota, the standardization of duties and the reduction of tariffs, The scale of the export of silks, is actually more open under the customs regime of 1843 than under the trade regime of Canton. Moreover, this system of opening established in 1843 evolved very little during the rest of the century. In other words, silk is exported from China in a more free-trade customs regime after the 1840s. So we have the second question to answer. What is the relationship between the new customs regime and the growth of the silk trade between France and China?

4. Impacts of the evolution of the tariff regime on the silk trade between France and China of the 19th century

As was mentioned in the introduction to this section, the conventional opinion of the impact of the evolution of the customs regime before and after the opium war on China's foreign trade is that: The former customs regime has drastically curbed China's foreign trade before the opium war, and China's foreign trade is much more dynamic under the new regime.

Generally, this conclusion is rather reasonable, which can be proved by the evolution of the value of China's foreign trade in long-term. According to the data in Graph IV-11-A, the total annual foreign exchange value of China increases much more slowly during the Canton trade period (1757—1842) than under the new customs regime. From the year 1757 to the beginning of the 19th century, this value rises from 23 million taëls to 73 million taëls, and then stagnates between 65—75 million taëls until the day before the war of opium. In other words, during the 85 years of the Canton trade system, China's foreign trade increased by just over 3 times, or 50 million taëls at the absolute value level. During the period of the new customs regime, the foreign exchange of China reached 168 million taëls on the eve of the Sino-Japanese War of 1894, and then a very strong growth occurred from 1894 to 1913 with the opening of the "interior" of China.

---

[1] Archives Nationales de France. F12. 7057. 29 octobre 1903. Maisons de commerce français établi à Mongtze.

Since the implementation of the new customs regime on the eve of the First World War
(about 70 years), China's foreign trade is multiplying by 10, and a growth of 650 million taëls is realized at absolute value. Obviously, this growth rate has far exceeded that
of foreign trade under the old customs regime.

Graph IV-11-A Evolution in the total value of China's foreign trade 1758—1912
(average values over 10 years) [1]

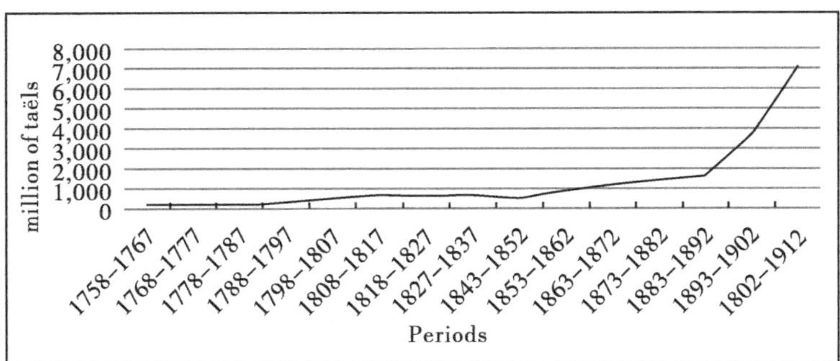

Graph IV-11-B Evolutions of import/export values of China 1817-1914[2]

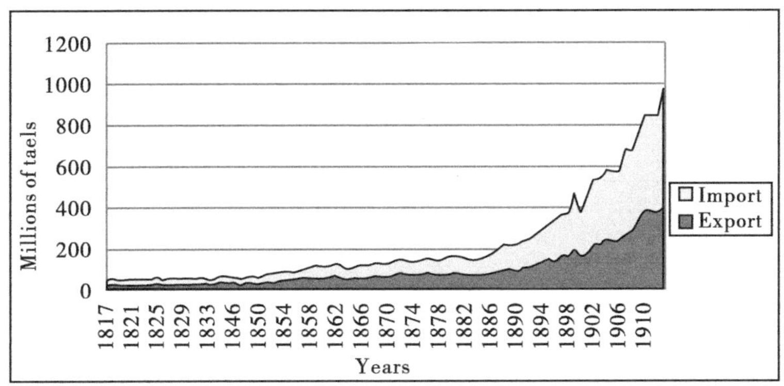

This conclusion is also valid for the relationship between the change China exports

---

① The datas during 1758—1837 come from 黄启陈.清代前期广东的对外贸易,中国经济史研究,1988 年
第 4 期,第 78 页.The datas during 1843—1858 come from 孙玉琴.中国对外贸易史.第 2 册,北京:对外经济贸易
大学出版社,2004 年,第 332 页.The datas during 1859—1912 come from 中国第二历史档案馆,中国海关总署办
公厅:中国旧海关史料,第 1—60 卷.

② The datas during 1817—1833 come from 姚贤镐.中国近代对外贸易史资料 1840—1895.第 254—257
页.The datas during 1843—1858 come from 孙玉琴.中国对外贸易史.第 2 册,北京:对外经济贸易大学出版社,
2004 年,第 332 页.The datas during 1859—1912 come froms 中国第二历史档案馆,中国海关总署办公厅:中国
旧海关史料,第 1—60 卷.

in customs regimes and the value of 19th century. According to Graph IV-11-B, Chinese exports increased very slowly from the beginning of the century to the 1840s, and growth began to accelerate only after the implementation of the new customs regime. From 1817 to 1843, China's exports increased from 19 million taëls to 25 million taëls, an increase of 6 million for 26 years. From 1843 to 1913, China's export value rose from 25 million taëls to 404 million taëls, an increase of 12 times and an absolute increase of 379 million taëls, which proves that Chinese exports are much more dynamic under the new customs regime.

So, is this conclusion still indisputable for our history —— the impacts of the evolution of China's tariff regime on the exchange of silk between France and China? Is the export of Chinese silk to France constrained by the policy of the export quota before 1842, and grows more rapidly after the simplification and reduction of the export duties of 1843?

Table IV-12 Evolution of exports of Chinese silk to France (1844—1914, kilograms)

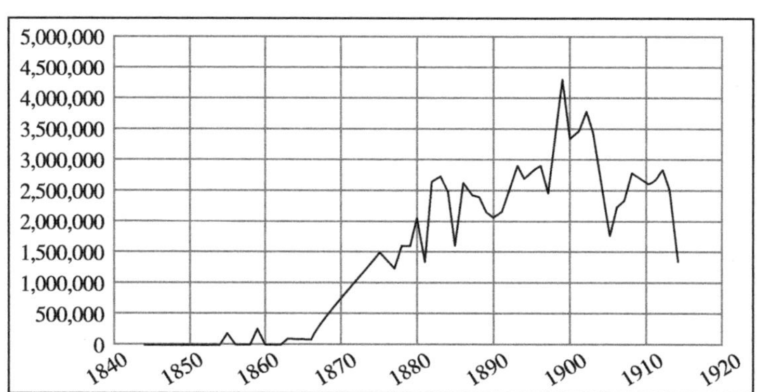

The case of the impact of the change of the customs regime on the exchange of silk between the two countries is more complicated than the case of general trade. Let us review the evolution of the direct export of Chinese silk to France from the first half of the 19th century (see table above). We have already pointed out in Chapter II that, because of the sufficiency of supply of silk materials in the Mediterranean region, France imports very little silk from the Far East during the first half of the 19th century. So, at that time, the exchange of silk between France and China was little, whose quantity is far from reaching the quota of the Chinese government. This state only changed after the

1850s (10 years after the implementation of the new customs regime in China), where the ravages of European sericulture pebrines took place. In other words, the exchange of silk between France and China is indeed very insignificant during the period of the commerce of Canton, but this is not because of the ancient customs regime of China; The export of Chinese silk to France is also growing more rapidly during the new customs regime, but the main cause is not the implementation of the new regime.

However, it should not be asserted that the export growth of Chinese silk in France has no relation to the new regime of duties. First, the abolition of the quota on the export of Chinese silks since 1843 gives the possibility of exporting Chinese silk in large quantities, which has probably eliminated a significant obstacle for the increase of the silk trade between France and China later. We shall show in the next section that the numbers of French ships leaving China are only 50—100 per year during the years 1860—1890, but the annual quantities of imports of Chinese silk into France already reach 2,000,000,000—4,000,000 kilograms. If the quota of the Chinese Government on the export of silk—maximum 500 kilograms per ship—is not yet canceled, it is impossible for France to import as much silk as it needs: 2,000,000—4,000,000 kilograms of silk to France would require 4,000—8,000 ships a year, which would have greatly exceeded the capacity of sailing from France to the Far East of the time.

Second, the reduction in customs tariffs on raw silk in the new customs regime increased the export price of Chinese silks, which ensured the competitiveness of Chinese silk on the French market during the second half of the 19th century. Under the old regime, customs tariffs on raw silks are about 5%—6.5% (according to different species) of their pre-export prices[1]. This proportion decreased to 2%—4% after the 1840s[2], and continued until the First World War. In other words, the customs tariff on silk has decreased under the new customs regime to about half of that of the old regime, or 10 taëls per picul or 2 francs per kilogram. If the difference of 2 francs per kilogram is not so essential for the outlet of Chinese silks which possess a relatively large price advantage on the French market during the years 1850—1860, this difference will be very important for the successive growth of the export of Chinese silks to France after the 1870s, the advantage of the price of which is increasingly modest. We will show in the next section that, from the 1870s, the price difference of Chinese silk with that of other countries becomes smaller and sometimes only a few cents. With regard to the competition of

---

[1]　Cette proportion est calculée selon les données du tableau III-7.
[2]　Cette proportion est calculée selon les données du tableau III-7 et tableau III-9.

silk from other countries, especially Japanese silks, the reduction of the customs duties of 2 francs per kilogram since the 1840s became very important for the extension of the status of Chinese silk in the French market after the 1870s.

In conclusion, even if the new silk customs regime implemented from 1843 is not the main cause for the beginning of the growth of the silk trade between France and China since 1850, it will be a fundamental condition for increased trade during the following decades. Thanks to the abolition of the quota, the exchange of silks between the two countries is possible to become more and more prosperous during the years 1850—1860; while this prosperity may continue after the 1870s due to the fall in the exit rate. The new customs regime of China, with relatively low entry tariffs on the silk side of France, have greatly reduced the barriers against the movement of silks between the two countries, and have created the necessary condition for the increase of the silk exchange quantity between the two countries.

We have confirmed the important role of one of the two most important elements in the integration of the global market underlined by K.H.O'Rourke and JGWilliamson—the customs barriers—in the growth of the exchange of silk between France and China during the 19th century. We will discuss the role of the other element—the improvement of the communication and transport of the 19th century—in the following section.

III Improvements in transport between France and China and the silk prices convergence on the international market

The 19th century saw a genuine revolution in maritime transport. On the one hand, the Industrial Revolution relies on steam to operate steamboats, which begins with techniqueal innovations that continued throughout the 19th century: in 1819, the first trans-atlantic crossing by a boat with a steam engine is provided; The propeller replaces the paddlewheels from 1837; Iron substituted for wood for the construction of the hull in the middle of the 19th century; The technique of double propellers begins to be vulgarized in the construction of boats during the second half of the century, etc. All innovations have greatly reduced the cost of transport and at the same time have considerably reduced transport time: transport costs on international routes were divided by four between 1820 and 1850 and the journey from London to New York decreased from 30 days to 9 days during 1840 and 1890. On the other hand, many canals (the Suez Canal, the new Kiel Canal, the Erie Canal, etc.) are built to connect rivers, lakes, the seas and the oceans, which further reduced shipping costs and the transport distance.

Over the past two decades, the economic effects of the Maritime Transport Revolution have become increasingly important to the researches of the economic historians. In 1995, Fr. Krugman published an article on the question "why world trade has increased", and asserts that theoretically, the growth of world trade is necessarily linked to techniqueal innovations in transport[1]. His conclusion was later challenged by S.L. Baier and J.H.Bergstand in 2001.According to their calculation, the contribution of reducing transport costs to economic growth is very limited[2].

K.H.O'Rourke and J. Wlliamson investigate the relationship between lower transport costs and price evolutions in different Atlantic markets, and determine the correlation between price convergence and lower transport costs; In another book that K. H. O'Rourke collaborated with R.Findlay published in 2007, the authors discover that the reduction in transport costs not only leads to growth in the volume of international trade but also to the variation in the nature of the goods transported[3]; In 2010, D.S.Jacks and Krishna Pendadur published an article to discuss the problem of the correlation between trade growth and transport costs. They compared the data from different periods, and conclude that the cost of transportation plays an important role for the growth of international trade during certain periods instead of a constant factor. In a recent publication in 2013[4], D.Chilosi and G.Federico have reworked the problem of factors of international market integration. Observing the course of integrating Asian markets with the rest of the world for a fairly long period (1800—1938), the authors found that the fall in cost played a very important part in this course during 1870—1838 instead of all eras[5].

The influence of maritime activities on the economic development of China is also a subject much discussed by historians. For example, the two books "Nanhai I and the Maritime Silk Road"[6] and "The Seaside World: Studies on the History of Trade in

---

① P.Krugman. "Growing World Trade: Causes and consequences". Brookings Papers on Economic Activity. 1995. No°1. 327—377.

② S.L.Baier and J.H.Bergstrand. "The Growth of World Trade: Tariffs, Transport Costs, and Income Similarity". Journal of International Economics. Vol 53. No°1. 2001. pp.1—27.

③ K. H. O' Rourke and J. Williamson. Globalization and History. Cambrige and London. The MIT Press.1999.

④ D.S.Jacks and Krishna Pendadur. The review of Economics and Statistics. Vol 92. No°4. 2010. pp. 745—755.

⑤ D.Chilosi and G. Federico. "Asian Globalizations : Market Integration, trade and economic growth". 1800—1938. Economic History Working Papers. No°123. 2013.

⑥ 李庆新.南海一号与海上丝绸之路.北京:五洲传播出版社,2010 年.

South China Sea and Sino-Foreign Relations of China"[1] by Li Qingxin, "Chinese Circulations: Capital, Commodities and Networks in Southeast Asia" [2] of E.Tagliacozzo and the work "The Maritime Culture of the South China Sea" of Situ Shangji[3] have all addressed the relationship between maritime activities in Nanhai and the development of the Chinese economy.

In this section, we will analyze the relationship of the Transport Revolution with the integration of the Euro-Asian economy by observing the case of the silk trade between France and China. We will first discuss the meanings of the commissioning of the Compagnie des Messageries Maritimes and the opening of the Suez Canal for the growth of the silk trade between China and France, and then analyze the Factors (including the condition of transport) that leaded to price convergence, an important symbol of economic integration, in the Eurasian silk markets and their importance.

1. The inferiority of French navigation with China in comparison with England before the 1860s

"The absolutely direct operations of France in China and of China in France are the exception, and have really only a secondary interest in the present state of trade... Armchair is surprised that this choice is exceptionally for a French ship, when there are only three or four on which our flag is floating in the four hundred vessels which sail every year from Shanghai. It is not to the China Sea, for example, that our ports arm their best clippers, and when they are found in the Wushung or Tchou-kiang, their return is seldom direct. I am not saying anything different about the price of freight. So that, to speak only of the silks of China, they come to us quite differently from French vessels in righteousness; This is the most ordinary and favorable case, by the streamers of the Compagnie Péninsulaire et Orientale[4], in Marseilles, via over land, or by the same streamers, but to Southampton, from Southampton to London, and London to Lyons; or by English sailing ship or by other sailing vessels, to London."[5]

These last remarks by Natalis Rondot have been conveyed to the information that

---

① 李庆新.濒海之地:南海贸易与中外关系史研究.北京:中华书局,2010 年.

② E.Tagliacozzo. Wen-China. Chinese Circulations: Capital, Commodities and Networks in Southeast Asia. Duke University Press. 2011.

③ 司徒尚纪.中国南海海洋文化.广州:中山大学出版社,2009 年.

④ The Oriental Peninsular Company was created in 1837. It is one of the largest English steamers companies of at that time.

⑤ N.Rondot. Chambre de commerce de Lyon. Commerce de la France avec la Chine. p.22—23.

navigation between China and France is still in a state of underdevelopment from the 18th century until the beginning of the 1860s, which is at the same time confirmed by the maritime statistics.

Graph IV-13 Comparison of ship numbers in English-Chinese and French-Chinese trade

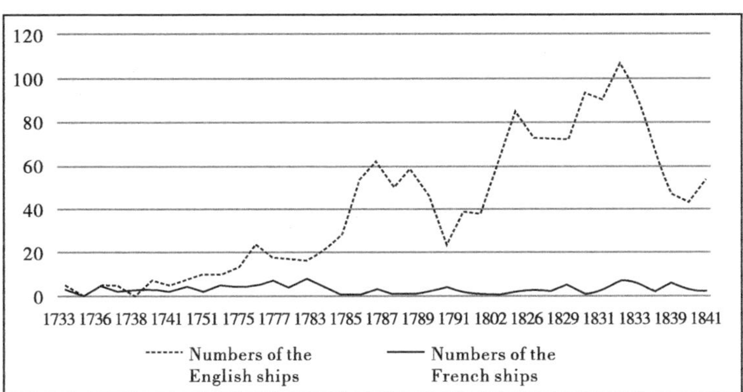

Let us remind the comparison made at the beginning of Chapter I: the numbers of the French vessels are at an absolute lower position than those of England on the China Sea before the 1840s (it manifests more clearly in the Graphic above). Moreover, the a- mount of exchange and direct navigation between China and France might even be more modest than the figures mentioned above, since, firstly, French ships arriving in China are often "small boats", Tons are between 300 and 400 tons, some even less than 300[1]. These "small boats" not only limit the quantities of exchange, but also add freight and are more subject to the risks of maritime accidents. Secondly, by observing the origins and destinations in the table above, we found that the French ships moved to Manila before arriving in China, and that some ships were even originating in Manila. In fact, French ships often stop in the middle of the journey to China. Their freight stations may be Manila, Singapore, the countries of India, etc. During their stopovers, they re- fuel, but also sell most of the goods brought. The Corvette Captain commanding "the Heroin" wrote trade experience in Asia in his report in 1843: "Our ships all go to Ma-

---

[1] It is easy to find other notes on the tonnage of French ships, which also note that they are often less than 400 tons. For example, from July 1, 1842 to June 1, 1843, the total tonnage of the French vessel (entry and exit) is 3428 tons, less than 350 tons on average for each ship. Consult Ministère de l'agriculture et du commerce, Document sur le commerce extérieur, Chine et Indochine, Fait commerciaux n°9, pp. 33—36.

nila and often to Batavia before arriving in Macau; It is easy for them to disembark three-fifths of their cargoes from France, to replace them with rice, which is cheap at Manila, and is almost always easily defeated at Canton."[1] Some notes on compositions of the exchange values of French ships to Asia in the mid-18th century confirm the Captain's estimate. "The Augustus" departed for China on November 18, 1751. Having sold 511,299 pounds of merchandise at Pondicherry, there remained only 420 pounds of cargo when he arrived at Canton. The "Puysieux", which left on October 21, 1752, carries three cargoes: "108,337 livres for Île-de-France, the second, worth 66,437 livres for Bourbon Island, and the third for China, this one with a sum of 188,402 pounds ".[2]

Table IV-14 French navigation in China during the year 1844

Ships	arrivés	From	deperture	to	tonnage
Lèocadie			Janvier 20	Manille and Bordeaux	298
Sospel	Feruery 8	Manille	4 mai	Bordeaux	246.07
Méloé	May 14	Manille and Marquises islands	26 mai	Singapore	378
Orient	June 25	Manille	1er juillet	Bordeaux	321
Icolas	November17	Le Havre		Manille	377.64
Panurge	November 20	Le Havre by Manille	28 décembre	Manille	389.12
Entry Tonnage: 1181.83			Departure Tonnage: 1692.19		

The opening of China to France after 1844 hardly improved the inferiority of shipping from France to China. Although, the movements of navigation between China and

---

[1] Ministère de l'agriculture et du commerce, Document sur le commerce extérieur, Chine et Indochine, Fait commerciaux n°5, p.17

[2] J.Meyer. La France et l'Asie : essai de statistiques - 1730 - 1785 : état de la question. In: Histoire, économie et société. 1982, 1e année, n°2. p,306,.

252

France have made some progress during the first two decades of the opening of China to France: both the numbers of navigation and the total transport tonnage between the two countries increased almost tenfold from 1845 to 1863, but it should be noted that during this period the capacity to navigate vessels under the French flag was still very low compared to that of other countries, especially compared to that of England. This is manifested by the fact that, on the one hand, the absolute quantities of goods which French ships carry are relatively small. For example, there were 21,094 tons of merchandise transferred by 53 French vessels between China and France in 1863; But during this year 379 British flag vessels sail between China and Great Britain carrying 213,114 tons of goods[1]. On the other hand, direct navigation between France and China is often dominated by foreign ships. Let us cite that in 1860, the total tonnage of direct navigation between China and France was 77,563, but the French ships occupied only 35,810, or only 46% of the total[2].

Table IV-15 Movement of direct navigation between France and China by the French ships 1845—1863[3]

Years	Entry		Departure		Total	
	Shes	tonnage	Shes	tonnage	Shes	tonnage
1845	4	872	4	1,249	8	2,121
1846	4	1,280	4	1,280	8	2,560
1847	6	2,015	14	4,560	20	6,575
1848	10	3,625	2	604	12	4,229
1849	3	863	2	756	5	1,609
1850	2	819			2	819
1851	5	1,444			5	1,444
1852	3	912	3	785	6	1,697
1853	5	1,825	32	10,156	37	11,981

---

① Ministère de l'agriculture et du commerce, Document sur le commerce extérieur, Chine et Indochine, Fait commerciaux n°37, p.7

② Ministère de l'agriculture et du commerce, Document sur le commerce extérieur, Chine et Indochine, Fait commerciaux n°20, p.7

③ Ministère de l'agriculture et du commerce, Document sur le commerce extérieur, Chine et Indochine, Fait commerciaux n°11, p.14, fait 14 . p.11. fait 16. p. 12. fait 23, p. 10. fait 24.p.37. fait 26, 19, fait 27. p.15. fait 31. p. 12. Fait 33. p. 20. Fait 36. p. 72.

（续表）

Years	Entry		Departure		Total	
	Shes	tonnage	Shes	tonnage	Shes	tonnage
1854	5	2,205	17	5,600	22	7,805
1855					37	13,655
1856	10	4,105	17	7,679	37	11,784
1857	3	1,326	1	702	4	2,006
1858	9	3,842	8	4,406	17	8,248
1859	4	1,690	50	25,749	54	27,439
1860	7	2,772	62	33,038	69	35,810
1861	5	1,953	25	12,093	30	14,046
1862	1	170	28	16,650	29	17,120
1863	5	1,819	48	19,275	53	21,094

This unfavorable performance of French ships in the navigation movements on the China Sea is by no means coincidental. A very important element for this is the inferior speed of French ships, driven by the underdevelopment of the French ships at the level of the energetic system in comparison with those of England at the time. Before the 1860s, almost all French ships sailing on the China Sea were still sailing boats, but England had already commissioned steamships at the time. The first disadvantage of these sailing boats is a long travel time in a long distance journey. Limited by the force of the wind and the ocean current, the speed of sailing is much lower than that of ships. During the 1850s, the maximum speed of large sailing ships did not exceed 7.5 nautical miles per hour, but that of steamships could reach 12 nautical miles per hour at that time.

In addition, to reload supplies, sailing boats need to stop in more stops during the journey, which will extend the sailing time of sailing boats. A report by the French Trade and Agriculture Ministry notes that "The steady state of our sailing in these Far Eastern countries is that no boat comes from France without stopping in all intermediate ports, which makes the journey time so considerable that merchants generally refrain from using a French ship".[1]They stop in either Manila, Vampoo or Singapore, and they

---

[1] Ministère de l'agriculture et du commerce, Document sur le commerce extérieur, Chine et Indochine, Fait commerciaux n°37, p.8.

park in those bunks until they are loaded. [1] "With less speed and more stopovers, as a result, a steamer only needs 50 to 60 days to travel from Shanghai to France, but it takes 4 to 5 months for a sailing boat for the same trip in the middle of the 19th century."[2]

The second disadvantage of sailing ships is higher freight. The freight of a French sailing ship which sails between France and China costs much more than that of England. According to reports from the French delegates in China, the freight of a French ship has an average of 200 francs per ton from Bordeaux to Shanghai in 1845, while the average freight of the British and American ships is only 3 livres 1/2 sterling à 4 livres (87 francs 50 centimes to 100 francs) for the same journey[3]; In 1854, we must pay 4 livres sterling (115 francs) to a English ship or 16 piaster (88—96 francs) to an American ship if we transport one ton of goods is to be transported, but the freight of the French vessel increases to 220 francs a ton at that time[4]. Many French delegates at the time attributed to the increase of the freight of the French ships to the high remuneration of the French shipowners. For example, when a French delegate in China, J-G. Houssaye, referred to the question "for the same purpose and the same kind of goods, why such a huge difference?" He replied: "The wages of our sailors, the salaries of our captains, are not as high as those of our neighbors; Supplies are cheaper in our ports than in their own; but our fearful shipowners want to earn one hundred percent; it matters to them the question of general interests, so that they realize promptly gigantic profits."[5]

However, the high remuneration of the shipowners is not the only element leading to the high freight of the French vessels to the Far East. The main cause for the high freight of French ships comes back to the problem of the small size of French ships to China. According to the data in Table IV−11, sailing vessels under the French flag sail on the China Sea are between 300 and 400 tons. But ships from England are often much larger, often exceeding 1,000 tons per ship. Already, with small sailing boats, more supplies at ports of call will undoubtedly increase the cost of transporting French ships. At the same time, the particular means of imposing the "ship duty" in China adds fur-

---

[1]   Archives Nationales de France. F12. 6498. Réflexions sur notre commerce avec la Chine. p. 9.

[2]   N.Rondot. Chambre de commerce de Lyon. Commerce de la France avec la Chine. p.16.

[3]   Ministère de l'agriculture et du commerce, Document sur le commerce extérieur, Chine et Indochine, Fait commerciaux n°10, p.500.

[4]   Ministère de l'agriculture et du commerce, Document sur le commerce extérieur, Chine et Indochine, Fait commerciaux n°22, p.15

[5]   Ministère de l'agriculture et du commerce, Document sur le commerce extérieur, Chine et Indochine, Fait commerciaux n°22, p.15.

ther to the cost of small vessels, because when a vessel enters a Chinese port, "these duties were as high for a vessel of 400 tons as for that of 1,400."[1] As a result, the cost of transporting each ton of cargo is much higher in French vessels than in England at that time.

2. Commissioning of the Maritime Messenger Company in the Far East and the end of the monopoly of England on Euro-Asian maritime transport

The inferiority of the navigation between France and China severely restricts the commercial growth of the two countries. Above all, in order to ensure the production of silks, it is necessary for French manufacturers to import Chinese silk after the explosion of the pebrine in France in 1854, but the absence of a suitable means of transport really hinders the import of Chinese silk in France. On the one hand, as has been shown a-bove, the freight of the French vessels is too high, while their journey times are too long. On the other hand, although the freight of the English vapors is cheaper and their durations are shorter, the transport capacity of the Anglo-Oriental Company of England (which is the only steam service of China in Europe during the 1850s) is often insufficient for French silk traders. The cause is that "silk is a light commodity, that the barrel of congestion does not weigh more than three hundred kilograms, and that a steamer cannot be given a whole load of silks, because the risks would be too high to be covered by the insurance companies... Therefore only two thousand to two thousand five hundred bales are loaded by steamship".

Moreover, this English company often favors English cargo owners, which leads to the fact that "this insufficiency is more marked for the French". As a result, the import of silks from the London market became the only means of purchasing Chinese silks for French silk manufacturers, although very high customs duties had to be paid in England during the age of protectionism (we have already specified the composition of the price of Chinese silk re-exported from England to France in Chapter III). With the hope of direct trade with China, the Lyonsnais sigh that "Lyons, which is the first silk market, is not the largest warehouse of this rich material!" The creation of a regular shipping line between France and China, logically, became a most urgent matter for the silk industry in France.

The Chamber of Commerce of Lyons transmits its deliberations, which contains all the difficulties concerning the transport of silk material, to the Agriculture and Trade

---

[1] Archives Nationales de France. F12. 6498. Réflexions sur notre commerce avec la Chine. p. 10.

Minister, and the Government replies that it will "establish a direct service of Transport by steamboats between France, India and China by all the means in its power".[1]

On January 1, 1863, the Compagnie des Messageries Impériales[2] opened a direct line between Hong Kong and Marseilles, which is the symbol of the creation of the regular shipping line between France and China[3]. A subsidiary line from Hong Kong and Shanghai is implemented at the same time to ensure navigation between Shanghai and Marseilles by forwarding. But there is only one steamer, the "Hydaspes" of 584 tons which deserts this auxiliary line, which is obviously insufficient for the demand of the French merchants. Two larger passenger ships, such as the "Bourdonnais" and the "Dupleix" of about 900 tons, participate in this maritime line later, but the insufficiency does not diminish. A direct line was then created between Shanghai and Marseille in 1865[4], which was provided by enormous ships like the "Yarra" and the "Salazie" with over four thousand tons of gross tonnage. Shanghai became, from that moment, one of the most important terminals of the main line of Marseille in the Far East. Ships from the Shanghai to Marseille line also deserted in Hong Kong, so this line is also called Shanghai—Hong Kong—Marseille, which will become the most important transport line for Chinese silk from China to France throughout the rest of the 19th century[5].

Table IV-16 Maritime silk freight and insurance of the port of Shanghai to Marseille and to London in the year 1875 (bales)[6]

Destination	French Vapour Ships		English Vapour Ships	
	Freight (taëls)	Insurance	Freight (taëls)	Insurance
Marseille	3.11	1.50%	3.11	1%—1.5%
Londres	3.11	1.50%	3.11	1%—1.5%

All ships serving the eastern line are now large steamships, which means less freight and higher speed. The average cost of transport from Marseille to Shanghai is immediately reduced to 70 francs per ton, which is almost the best price for transport be-

---

① N.Rondot. Chambre de commerce de Lyon. Commerce de la France avec la Chine. p.14—17

② Cette compagnie est renommée comme. la Compagnie des messageries maritime. depuis 1871.

③ 严中平.中国近代经济史 1840—1914.第 309 页.

④ Archives Nationales de France. F12. 7508. Rapports consulaires antérieurs Chine 1809—1906(3).

⑤ La Compagnie des messageries maritimes also set up its agencies in Tianjin in 1865 and in Chefou in 1888, but these lines in the north of China are always less dynamic.

⑥ Archives Nationales de France. F12. 7508. Rapports consulaires antérieurs Chine 1809—1906(3).

tween the two ports[1]. Above all, freight from vessels under the French flag carrying silk gradually falls to the same level as those in England. The travel time between the two ports also reduces to 50—60 days. In order to further reduce the navigation time of this line, the Company abolishes the stopovers of Manila and Penang at the suggestion of the Government, which reduces 8.376 nautical miles on the way from Shanghai to France[2].

After the opening of the Suez Canal, the journey time is shortened to 40 days[3]. This duration is about the same as that of the English vapors. The Messagerie Maritime Company's navigation service is monthly at the beginning. With the growth of the exchange between France and China, the Company added a bi-monthly line[4]. Ships from the monthly service are passenger ships departing from Marseille to Yokohama (by Hong Kong and Shanghai); the ships in the bi-weekly line are cargo ships departing from Antwerp, serving Dalian, Tsingtau, Hankow, Shanghai... These two lines guarantee the capacity of the transport and the regularity of traffic between China and France. The Company often renews ships serving this line to combat the rivalry of other foreign shipping companies[5]. It is the first company that uses dual propeller steam on the China Sea, raising the speed of navigation to 16 miles.[6]. With these vapors, it takes only about 30 days for the journey from Marseille to Shanghai.

At the same time, the Compagnie des Messageries Maritime established the first French insurance agency in China. As a result of the predominance of the sea ports, maritime insurance has a preponderant role. These insurance cover various dangers: damage, loss, theft of the goods, etc. In addition, due to the increasing role of banks in international trade, shipping insurance is not only a precaution, but in most cases is an obligation, because banks service of the drafts to the European companies require the insurance certificate to avoid any difficulty in case of shipwreck. In 1844 (just after the Opium War), there are already 25 establishments offering maritime insurance services to Chinese ports, but they all belong to English companies. Two bigger English companies, the Jardine Matheson et Cie and the Dent et Cie have 11 insurance from the 25 estab-

---

① Archives Nationales de France. F12. 7508. Rapports consulaires antérieurs Chine 1809—1906(3).

② 姚贤镐.中国近代对外贸易史资料 1840—1949.第 309—310 页.

③ Archives Nationales de France. F12. 7224. 12 avril 1907. Durée des traversées de Marseille à Shanghai.

④ 外商在华行业之统计.(中).申报.1926 年 11 月 29 日.

⑤ Archives Nationales de France. F12.7224. Shanghai. 1907—1908. 14 mai 1912. Rapport sur la situation commerciale et industrielle de Chanhai en 1911.

⑥ M.F.Berneron-Couvenhes. Les Messageries Maritimes. L'essor d'une grande compagnie. Paris. Presses de l'Université Paris-Sorbonne. 2007. p.190.

lishments[1]. In other words, the maritime insurance service at Chinese ports is completely monopolized by the British at the beginning of the opening of China. There is no French insurance company or company in China on the eve of the creation of the Marine Messenger Company[2]. French ships are obliged to buy their insurance from foreign insurance agencies, but the latter often offer advantages to English nationality traders. This often leads to an inferiority of the French companies when they compete with the Englishness. On several occasions, the Merchant Union is trying to organize mutual assurances, but this project has not succeeded because there are not enough merchants[3]. To solve this difficulty for the Lyons merchants and stimulate its new business in the Far East, the Compagnie des Messageries Impériales decides to also offer the marine insurance service to the cargo owners since 1863 as a coordinated service of the navigation service[4]. As a result, direct shipments between France and China are becoming more frequent, and more and more French companies prefer to send their goods with French ships[5].

The creation of the eastern line the Compagnie des Messageries Maritimes completed the monopoly of English ships on the navigation of silks between Europe and the Eastern world. To conclude the performance of the direct exchange of silk between France and China in 1863 (the first year of the creation of the eastern line of the Imperial Messenger Company), a report by the Ministry of Trade and Agriculture writes that "The direct expeditions to France of the silks from the Far East have hitherto been little commensurate with the needs of our consumption. It should be noted, however, that these shipments have doubled since 1859. The establishment of French lines which now links from Marseilles to China will favor this good trend and will hopefully lead to trade

---

① 林日杖.鸦片战争前后外国在华洋行经济活动初探.福建师范大学硕士学位论文,2001 年,第 49 页.

② Ministère de l'agriculture et du commerce, Document sur le commerce extérieur, Chine et Indochine, Fait commerciaux n°10, p.401.

③ L.Gueneau. Lyon et le commerce de la soie. p. 185.

④ Institut d'économie de l'Académie des Sciences Sociales de Shanghai. Le commerce extérieur de Shanghai 1840—1989. p. 86.

⑤ According to Lyon et le commerce de la soie of L. Gueneau, there are two means of payment for goods imported on the international market: F.O.B or C. A.F. The initials F.O.B correspond to the English expression: free on board. The foreign value simply delivers on board the ship. Freight, insurance and all other incidental expenses are at large from the buyer. The expression C.I.F (cost, insurance, freight), or C.A.F means cost, insurance, freight. The foreign seller accepts a package price, which includes all three elements. This last method removes, for the buyer, any unexpected and any additional steps. However, a campaign has been developed in France in favor of the F.O.B system, so that the buyer can choose French vessels, in the interest of their maritime and their exchange. In the Far East, Lyonnais silk merchants use only the C.A.F system.

of silks, the rational displacement demanded by this vital branch of our industry."①

Table IV-17 Exports of raw and thrown silk from China and Japan (bales) ②

Years	England	France	Total
1859—1860	63,706	5,431	69,137
1860—1861	80,295	8,439	88,754
1861—1862	67,653	5,669	73,332
1862—1863	72,844	10,420	83,264

In 1868, another major British shipping company, Ociean Steampship Company, entered into competition with the Maritime Messenger Company and the Péninsulaire and Orientale Company③. In order to avoid rivalry and gain more profit, these three major shipping companies in China (the three above included) signed an agreement with each other and established a "Navigation Alliance" in 1879④. According to the rate of freight of all the companies in this alliance will be formulated in such a standard, while the three companies will have to share quantities of the goods carried in the Alliance⑤. To fight the companies outside, the Alliance takes a measure called "dilatory dividend". That is to say, all owners who transport their cargoes with alliance ships may obtain a rebate equal to 10% of the freight already paid, on condition that they must use Alliance ships to transport their goods in the next 6 months⑥. The purpose of this measure is to maintain the "loyalty" of the cargo owners, and to make them always use the ships of the alliance. The owners will logically receive such a condition, because they will enjoy transporting the best price offered by the Alliance. The transport of goods between Europe and the Far East is now largely controlled by the Alliance, which is in reality a new monopoly organization. Because of the competition of the alliance, smaller shipping companies are in ruins one after the other. An English trade commissioner reminds us that:

---

① Ministère de l'agriculture et du commerce, Document sur le commerce extérieur, Chine et Indochine, Fait commerciaux n°37, p.28.

② Idem.

③ 严中平.中国近代经济史 1840—1914.第 1206 页.

④ F.E.Hyde, J.R.Harris. BLUE FUNEL : a history of Alfret Holt and Company of Liverpool From 1865 to 1914. Liverpool. Liverpool University Press. 1957. p. 56.

⑤ A.J.H.Latham. The international economy and the underdeveloped world, 1865—1914. London. Croom Helm Ltd. 1978. p.23.

⑥ F.E.Hyde, J.R.Harris. BLUE FUNEL : a history of Alfret Holt and Company of Liverpool From 1865 to 1914. Liverpool. Liverpool University Press. 1957. p. 56.

"The navigation on the China Sea is entirely controlled by the alliance. Last year, a very beautiful ship called the Philipe was forced to leave Hankou and then Shanghai without any merchandise. No ship out alliance does come to Shanghai or Hankou to carry goods."[1]

Thanks to the support of the Navigation Alliance, the Messengerie Maritime gradually monopolized transport between China and France. In the 8,453,837 kilograms of silk transported from Canton to France in 1911, 7,421,164 kilograms are transported by the Maritime Messenger Company, 984,984 balls by the Peninsular and Oriental Company (English), 25,000 by Hamburg A. Erika Line (German) and 23,400 by the Nippon Yuaen Kaisha (Japanese). The proportion of the Marine Courier Company is 87.78%[2].

Nevertheless, it should also be noted that, by ensuring the direct transport of silks between China and France, the monopoly of the Messageries Maritimes Company also leads to the decline of the total number of French navigations. That is to say, when more and more English, American, German and Japanese shipping lines were created at the end of the 19th century[3], despite the competition of the alliance, there exist only one long-distance shipping company under the French flag in China. A French consul recalls that, in 1892, "only a French ship that does not belong to it (la Compagnie des messageries maritimes). It is a steamer carryint to Tiensin the building materials from French industrialists who have undertaken the public work for the Chinese government."[4]

Until the end of the 19th century, French ships in China outside the Maritime Messengers Company were still mainly sailing ships, which occupied only short-haul transport between Chinese ports[5]. The creation of the second company la Compagnie des messageries maritimes of the French steams delayed to 1903, but its vapors deserted only in the River of Yangzi[6]. In 1907, the Compagnie française des Indes et de l'Extrême-Orient created une Compagnie des messageries Cantonaise at Canton, whose

---

① 聂宝璋.中国近代航运史资料.上册,第 699 页.

② Archives du Ministère des Affaires étrangères. 148CPCOM567 Chine relation commerciale avec la France 1912—1915. pp. 9—10.

③ Il existe beaucoup de conflits à l'intérieur de l'alliance après sa création, l'Alliance ne fonctionne donc pas stablement comme prévu. Pour se dégager la restriction de l'alliance, les commerçants commencent aussi à utiliser les navires dehors l'Alliance qui sont moins chère, ce.

④ Archives Nationales de France. F12. 7058 Rapports consulaires antérieurs Chine. 1809—1906(3). 18 janvier 1893. Navigation des ports ouverts de Chine 1892.

⑤ Archives du Ministère des Affaires étrangères. Pékin 242CCC 4 1869—1877. p. 314.

⑥ Archives du Ministère des Affaires étrangères. Pékin 242CCC 4 1869—1877. pp. 107—112.

steamers only sail between Hong Kong and Canton. The movements of French navigation in China, therefore, are still much less dynamic than that of England, even less dynamic than that of Germany.

Table IV-18 Navigation movements of the French, English, German and Japanese pavilions in China, 1866—1913 (the entry and exit)[1]

	French		English		German		American		Japanese	
	Shes	Tonnages	Shes	Tonnages	Ships	Tonnages	Shes	Tonnages	Shes	Tonnages
1866	234	108,918	8,276	3,921,851	2,248	620,322	3,602	1,957,687	4	1,996
1867	217	112,587	7,964	3,711,080	2,232	611,841	2,926	1,673,754	1	809
1868	249	139,165	7,165	3,332,092	1,772	467,087	3,623	2,237,327	12	4,168
1869	218	109,173	6,727	3,052,320	2,387	666,266	4,165	2,746,515	2	476
1870	194	79,824	6,577	3,125,590	1,304	370,607	4,547	3,004,746	…	
1871	277	135,829	7,160	3,330,881	1,480	428,747	4,600	3,187,643	…	
1872	223	164,346	8,360	3,954,130	1,976	607,948	5,174	3,471,293	14	5,108
1873	189	151,233	6,935	3,645,557	1,702	492,033	5,001	3,483,203	3	734
1874	145	137,253	7,382	4,738,793	1,638	530,377	4,279	3,184,360	2	480
1875	239	165,551	8,277	5,167,435	1,577	561,577	3,836	2,777,367	92	96,533
1876	228	170,749	8,604	5,181,643	1,587	661,668	3,547	2,410,421	125	117,134
1877	167	163,389	9,042	6,497,352	1,376	496,908	1,446	556,112	106	115,263
1878	174	160,073	9,973	7,439,373	1,983	743,457	1,018	341,942	126	123,887
1879	164	154,993	10,609	8,126,004	1,907	721,046	931	270,632	157	138,208
1880	128	150,207	12,397	9,606,156	1,501	632,044	1,070	287,396	201	167,902
1881	103	135,734	13,416	10,332,248	1,632	728,207	870	224,730	227	185,892
1882	192	172,381	14,337	10,814,779	1,864	882,856	762	167,801	250	194,584
1883	177	181,056	14,205	11,003,269	1,610	774,017	593	150,703	256	194,861
1884	48	93,963	14,141	12,132,949	1,758	939,763	2,381	2,140,741	296	215,105
1885	46	73,355	13,522	11,842,255	2,230	1,217,685	2,524	2,261,750	286	211,585
1886	123	158,400	16,193	14,006,720	2,702	1,499,296	413	143,799	380	270,002
1887	121	180,890	15,917	14,171,810	2,749	1,480,083	255	66,593	409	306,169

① 中国第二历史档案馆,中国海关总署办公厅.中国旧海关史料.北京:京华出版社,2001 年,第 3—63 卷.

（续表）

	French		English		German		American		Japanese	
	Shes	Tonnages	Shes	Tonnages	Ships	Tonnages	Shes	Tonnages	Shes	Tonnages
1888	176	268,644	15,115	14,069,260	2,762	1,570,035	234	84,455	326	281,900
1889	179	269,002	15,763	14,903,750	2,656	1,582,648	178	75,977	528	411,667
1890	174	239,700	16,897	16,087,895	2,140	1,343,964	155	82,946	629	505,181
1891	172	264,660	17,718	17,438,995	2,520	1,911,897	133	67,093	76	98,221
1892	144	252,920	18,973	19,316,815	2,016	1,466,133	111	61,328	84	111,570
1893	167	259,687	19,365	19,203,978	2,142	1,508,015	63	78,175	101	132,613
1894	293	348,291	20,527	20,496,347	2,429	1,983,605	107	129,127	92	138,472
1895	266	341,345	19,579	20,525,798	2,684	2,422,185	92	86,127	90	130,218
1896	427	434,413	19,711	21,847,082	2,000	1,945,019	143	165,578	546	565,992
1897	464	423,112	21,140	21,891,043	1,838	1,638,094	333	269,780	653	660,707
1898	477	420,078	22,609	21,265,966	1,831	1,685,098	743	239,152	2,263	1,569,134
1899	822	613,191	25,350	23,338,230	2,078	1,854,246	716	310,107	3,712	2,839,741
1900	978	664,987	22,818	23,052,459	3,527	4,032,147	1,311	474,479	4,917	3,871,559
1901	1,208	733,041	23,012	26,151,332	6,641	7,542,829	1,241	898,063	6,115	5,518,376
1902	1,511	833,759	24,758	26,950,202	6,046	7,220,146	1,295	493,831	6,898	7,350,513
1903	2,569	1,178,200	25,297	28,122,987	6,424	7,310,427	1,736	559,686	7,554	7,965,358
1904	2,647	1,264,320	31,298	32,933,873	6,841	7,602,304	2,716	924,809	5,755	4,290,350
1905	6,184	1,699,121	30,442	35,095,659	7,337	8,187,871	689	1,293,416	25,850	6,238,918
1906	5,514	3,125,749	28,192	33,450,560	6,315	7,477,518	582	1,351,200	25,108	11,376,430
1907	5,072	4,712,188	27,495	33,316,618	5,864	6,639,767	549	1,045,899	29,296	15,598,213
1908	3,901	5,071,689	28,445	34,405,761	5,496	6,585,671	653	998,775	30,708	18,035,138
1909	5,141	4,919,889	27,699	34,026,704	5,854	7,243,742	815	806,523	30,808	18,949,404
1910	3,766	4,923,492	28,000	34,253,439	5,361	7,060,521	1,286	725,279	31,187	18,903,146
1911	2,602	3,154,157	28,885	34,712,440	4,848	6,849,069	1,373	712,161	21,259	19,172,727
1912	1,836	1,634,468	31,909	38,106,732	4,778	6,171,684	1,622	715,001	20,091	19,913,385
1913	1,020	1,232,763	32,186	38,120,300	5,382	6,320,466	2,458	898,750	22,716	23,422,487

3. The opening of the Suez Canal and the advantage of France on the import of Chinese silk

The Suez Canal was implemented at the beginning of 1870, and the first building via the Canal arrived in China on March 19[1]. Obviously, this event is very significant for the improvement of transport between Europe and the Far East: on the one hand, the absolute length of the Suez Canal line between the Far East and the Far East, Europe is reduced to about 2/3 of that of the line of Good Hope[2]. On the other hand, without sufficient coaling stations around the continent of Africa, it was not possible for small steamers to travel to Asian countries by the line of Good Hope. The opening of the Suez Canal gives all steamers the possibility of obtaining coal by Gibraltar, Malta and Port Sait, which accelerates the popularization of the steam energy of west-eastern navigation[3]. As a result, sailing boats are replaced very quickly by steamboats in the line between the Far East and Europe, and the journey time to 30—40 days between the two continents[4].

The opening of the Suez Canal was also significant for the international trade of silk during the last decades of the 19th century. It puts an end to the inferior position of France over the importation of Asian silks in relation to England. It has already been known that London was the largest warehouse of the silks of Europe, by means of its predominance of maritime navigation between Europe and China. The silk manufacturers in the continental countries, especially France, had to import Chinese silk through London by paying a very high tariff. The creation of the direct shipping line between Marseilles and China has destroyed England's shipping monopoly on the eastern maritime line, but it should be noted that the quantities of direct importation of Chinese silks into France are still much lower than those in England after the opening of the eastern line of the French Company. If the commissioning of the companion of the Messageries Maritimes was an important condition for the direct trade of silks between France and China, it was the opening of the Canal of Suez in 1870 which definitely efface the inferiority of Marseille.

Before the Canal opened, ships bound for France (even some French ships) got used to stopping first in London, then continued to sail for Havre. Because of the implementation of the Suez Canal after the year 1870, the distance from Shanghai to Marseille becomes shorter than that of Shanghai to London. As a result, most ships for London are

---

① North China Herald. A Retrospect of Political and Commercial Affairs in China. 1868—1872. p;127. Fonds de la Bibliothèque municipale de Shanghai.

② C.Sichko. The Influence of the Suez Canal on Steam Navigation. Thèse soutenue à l' University of Colorado Boulder. 2011.p.488.

③ M.E.Fletcher. "The Suez Canal and World Shipping. 1869-1914." Journal of Economic History. 1958. No° 18. p.560.

④ 王翔.中日丝绸业近代化比较研究.第 68 页。

264

obliged to cross the Mediterranean, and sometimes even escalate to Marseille or Bordeaux. From now on, Chinese silk transported to Europe no longer needs to go through London. On the contrary, they are sent directly to Marseille, which is closer to the sellers (Shanghai) and buyers (Lyons). Let us revise the data we have demonstrated in the Chapter II. Five years after the opening of the Canal (1875), the import of Chinese silks from France exceeded that of England. Lyons is then the largest market and the largest silk warehouse in the world, until the beginning of the 20th century.

Table Ⅳ-19 (Table Ⅱ-10) Export of Chinese silks from Shanghai to France and to England, 1873—1876 (bales) ①

Année	Angleterre	France
1873	25,304	9,683
1874	26,337	22,497
1875	16,206	22,627
1876	31,000	33,000

The conclusion of K.H.O'Rourke and J. G. Williamson on the positive role of the improvement of the means of transport for the growth of international trade is again proved by the case of the silk trade between France and China. The commissioning of the Messageries Maritimes has expanded the direct import of Chinese silk into France, while the opening of the Suez Canal definitely offers France the advantage over the silk trade with China. We can conclude that the two elements highlighted by K.H.O'Rourke and J. G.Williamson, the reduction of customs barriers and the improvement of the transport condition are as significant for the growth of the Eurasian silk trade as that of the Atlantic trade.

However, there is still one question: between the two elements, customs tariff and the improvement of the transport condition, which is even more important for the growth of international trade? K.H.O'Rourke and J.G.Williamson did not answer this question when discussing Atlantic trade. As for Asian trade, they wrote that "perhaps the biggest tremor of globalization in Asia does not concern anything at all about the transport revolution, but is mainly due to the opening to the West by force".②

① Archives Nationales de France. F12. 7058. 31, janvier 1876, lettre du Ministère des Affaires Etrangère au Ministère du Commerce. Exportation des soies chinoises.
② K.H.O'Rourke et J.G.Williamson. Globalization and History. p.54.

It is true that both elements are indispensable for this growth: the silk trade between the two countries is not possible to increase so much without the cancellation of China's export quota, nor is it possible to have such a spectacular performance without the advantage of the transport of France compared to England, as K. H. O'Rourke and J. G. Williamson said. Nevertheless, it should be noted that the effect of the improvement of the transport condition on the growth of this exchange is much more direct and effective than the reduction of the customs barriers. If we revisit the graphic of the evolution of the exchange of silk between France and China, we will discover that the curve of the quantity of exchange is much more sensitive to the element of the cost of transport after the 1860s than the cancellation of the silk export quota in China after the 1840s or the very low level of the tariff on silk in France. Thus, for the growth of Eurasian trade, the role of improving the transport condition is more essential than that of tariffs.

Table Ⅳ-20(Table Ⅱ-13) Evolution of exports of Chinese silk to France (1844—1914, kilograms)

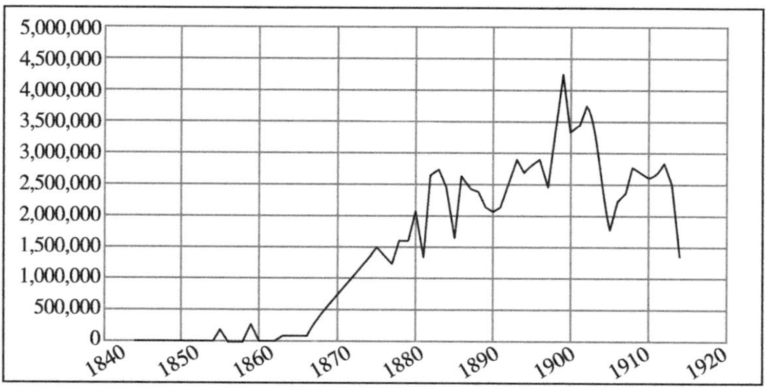

4. Convergence of silk prices on the international market

Research on the influence of customs barriers and transport costs on price evolutions in international trade is represented by the work of K. H. O'Rourke and J. G. Williamson. In their book *Globalization and History*, the two authors compared the prices of many kinds of goods (both agricultural and non-agricultural, including wheat, barley, rye, oats, meat, coffee, wool, textile cotton, copper, tin, coal, etc.) on markets on both coasts of the Atlantic Ocean (especially those of England and the United States) during 1870—1913. By observing the data, they found that price differentials for these commodities in the markets on both Atlantic coasts were greatly reduced due to lower customs tariffs and lower freight costs. Finally, they concluded that a trend of commodity price convergence was evident in the ports of both Atlantic coasts due to changes in the customs tariff and the cost of transportation. K.H.O'Rourke and J.G.Williamson believed that this conclusion is still valid beyond Atlantic trade, especially in Eurasian trade. But they have not verified it.

The gap in the work of K.H.O'Rourke and J.G.Williamson is in some way filled by recent research by D.Chilosi and G.Federico, published in 2013 under the title "Asian globalization: market integration trade and economic growth (1800—1938)"[1]. In comparison with the researches of K.H.O'Rourke and J.G.Williamson, those of D.Chilosi and G.Federico not only expanded the research objects of Atlantic commerce (markets of England and of the United States) to Western-Eastern trade (Markets of England, of the United States, of India, of Indonesia, of China, and of Japan), but also extended the period of research from 1870—1913 to 1800—1938. Moreover, they not only demonstrated the phenomenon of price convergence in western trade, but also analyzed the coefficient of the main elements (customs tariff, transport revolution, etc.) with the convergence of prices. As for the goods to be compared, D.Chilosi and G.Federico emphasized that the goods studied must be of the same quality and should be representative for the trade flow at that time. This is important for comparing commodity prices in international trade, but neglected by K.H.O'Rourke and J.G.Williamson. Considering all the elements above, D.Chilosi and G.Federico concludes that there is as much convergence of price during the period of the "first globalization (1800—1870) as during the period of the second globalization (1870—1938)". Convergence during the first period is mainly due to the change in trade policy (from monopoly of trade to liberal trade in Asian countries), and that in the second epoch is determined by the fall in the cost of transport after 1870.

Despite all these contributions, the researches of D.Chilosi and G.Federico are not perfect neither. The conclusion above is rather valid for the trade of India with England and that of Indonesia with the Netherlands, because it relies mainly on the exchange data of the four countries. There is much less data on western trade with the Far East, which relates only to exchanges of two commodities: that of tea between Canton and England, and that of China's silk and Japan with Europe and the United States. Above all, for the silk trade between the Far East and the West, the authors adopted only the

---

[1] D.Chilosi et G.Federico. "Asian Globalisations : Market Integration, trade and economic growth". 1800—1938. Economic History Working Papers. No° 123. 2013.

data during 1876—1914. So the result they obtained, which shows that the price gap between Lyons and Shanghai only decreases 2.07% during that period, cannot accurately reflect the truth of the convergence of price in the trade of the Far-East with the West before and after the transport revolution.

In order to correct the disadvantage of the research of D. Chilosi and G. Federico, we shall observe the evolution of silk prices on the markets of China and those of France and Italy for a longer period, from 1857 to 1914. We chose the mid-1850s as our starting date, because that date is the beginning of the flow of the great qualities of Asian silk in the market of continental Europe, so the price of silks in continental Europe begins to perhaps be under the influence of Asian silks. To unify the quality of the silks we are going to compare, we will adopt only the prices of the best quality silks in each market. In addition, it should be noted that the price of silk changes every week, so it is very varied even inside a single year. To make a long-term comparison, the prices of silks used are average prices for each year.

Graph IV-21 Changes in silk prices of four countries in domestic markets (francs / kilograms) [1]

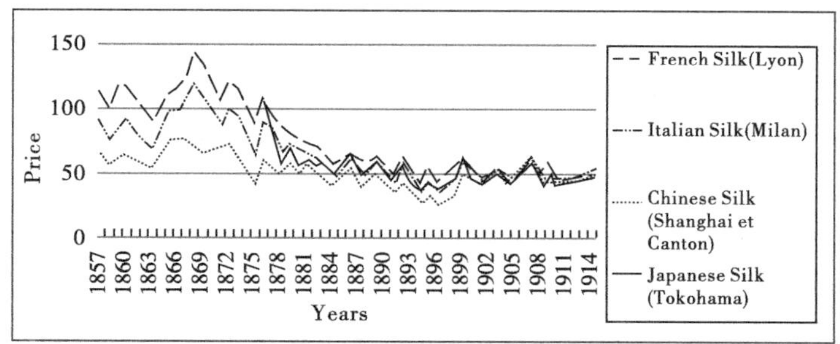

[1] The datas during 1857—1882 come from Bulletin des soies et des soieries de Lyon-Revue Hebdomadaire Lyonnaise. Lyon. Administration.6, Janvier 1883.The datas during 1883—1887 come from Bulletin des soies et des soieries de Lyon-Revue Hebdomadaire Lyonnaise. Lyon. Administration. 7, Janvier 1888. The datas during 1888—1899 come from Bulletin des soies et des soieries de Lyon-Revue Hebdomadaire Lyonnaise. Lyon. Administration. 5, Janvier 1901. The datas during 1900—1904 come from Bulletin des soies et des soieries de Lyon-Revue Hebdomadaire Lyonnaise. Lyon. Administration. 4, Mars 1905. The datas during t 1905—1908 come from Bulletin des soies et des soieries de Lyon-Revue Hebdomadaire Lyonnaise. Lyon. Administration. 1er, Mai 1909. The datas during 1909—1912 come from Bulletin des soies et des soieries de Lyon-Revue Hebdomadaire Lyonnaise. Lyon. Administration. 5, Avril 1913. The datas during 1913—1914 come from Bulletin des soies et des soieries de Lyon-Revue Hebdomadaire Lyonnaise. Lyon. Administration. 10, Juin 1916. The price of French silk is that of the raw silk of France of the first order; The price of Italian silk is that of the raw silk of Italy and Piedmont of the first order; The price of Chinese silk is that of silk of Tsatlés (辑里丝) during 1857—1877, that of machanical silk of Canton during 1878—1899, and that of mechanical silk of Shanghai during 1900—1914, which Represent the best qualities of silk during the different periods; The price of Japanese silk is that of mechanical silk from Japan.

According to the data in Graph IV-21, prices for French silk, Italian silk and Chinese silk evolved almost parallel before 1865. During this period, French silk of thefirst order at the Lyons market is still 40—50 francs more expensive than Tsatlés per kilo, the best Chinese silk at the Shanghai market. There is also a 20—30 franc shift between one kilo of Italian silk and one kilo of Chinese silk during this period. This shows that changes in China's trade policy since 1840 have little lasting influence on the price of silk in China and abroad. In other words, the trade policy element contributes very little to the convergence of silk prices in the deferent international markets of the second half of the 19th century.

French silk merchants began to resist Chinese silk because of the deterioration in the quality of Chinese silk from the late 1860s, which led to a fall in the price of Chinese silk at the Shanghai and Canton market (we will specify this event in another chapter). Because of this crisis in the quality of Chinese silk[1], deference between Chinese silk and European silk has even widened for a short time after the improvement of transport conditions between the Far East and Europe. The price gap is 70 francs between Chinese silk and French silk and 50 francs between Chinese silk and Italian silk around 1870. The difference in the price of Chinese silk with European silks reached its peaks in the second half of the 19th century.

However, it is also from that time that European silk prices begin to converge with that of Chinese silk. The price shift first returned to pre-crisis levels during 1871—1875: between 70 and 50 francs between Chinese silk and French silk, while between 50 and 30 francs between Chinese silk and Italian silk. From 1876 to 1880 the difference between the price of Chinese silk and that of French silk decreased from 50 francs to 20 francs and that of Italian silk decreased from 30 francs to 10 francs, a decrease of 3/5 and 2/3 for 5 years. The decade after the opening of the Suez Canal thus becomes a beginning period of the convergence of silk prices to the eastern and western markets. This fact again confirms the importance of the element of the fall in transport costs for the convergence of prices to the international markets of the 19th century.

Silk prices in the eastern and western markets continued to converge gradually during the last two decades of the 19th century. According to the graph, from 1900 onwards there is hardly any difference in price at different silk markets on both sides of the Eura-

---

[1] Les marchands de soie de France résistent la soie chinoise à cause de la détérioration de la qualité des soies chinoises à partir de la fin des années 1860, ce qui conduit à la baisse du prix des soies chinoises au marché de Shanghai et au marché international. Nous allons préciser cet événement dans un autre chapitre.

sian continent. From 1900 to 1914, silk price curves at the Lyons, Milan and Shanghai markets were almost combined. In other words, the convergence of silk prices to the international market was already completed at the end of the 19th century.

The convergence of 1880—1900 is certainly linked to the lasting effect of the Transport Revolution. As has been shown, the replacement of sailing ships by steam ships in the far ocean transport is a fairly lasting historical process. Until the year 1880, a half of the volume of the transport of England and France is still provided by the sailing ships[1]. In addition, a considerable proportion of steamships in the far ocean transport are still those of the old model before the 1880s[2]. Many new techniques, for example, double propellers, are used in large vessels during that period. The popularization of steam ships and the application of new techniques in Eurasian sea transport successively lowered the cost of transport during the last two decades of the 19th century, leading to the sustainable convergence of commodity prices between different markets.

However, the improvement of the transport condition is not the only essential element that leads to this convergence of prices at the end of the 19th century. Another important element, but neglected by K.H.O'Rourke, J.G.Williamson, D.Chilosi and G.Federico, is the convergence of the qualities of commodities due to industrialization in the world scale. There is not yet comparable criterion between European silks and French silks during the 19th century. So even we have adopted the best silks in the markets of France, Italy and China as our objects to compare, there is still the difference between these three types of silk at the quality level. However, what can be compared is that the silk of Tsatlés, the best Chinese silk before the implementation of mechanical reeling in China, is a nature of manual silk. It is not as homogeneous as mechanical silks and less compatible with mechanical looms in Europe, so its quality is considered worse than European mechanical silks (we will specify the differences between manual silk and mechanical silk in the next chapter). As a result, its price is still much lower than the European mechanical silks, and there is little convergence of silk prices to the Chinese and European markets until 1870. Because of deterioration in the quality of Tsatlés, the discrepancy between the prices of Chinese silk and European silks widened around 1870.

With the popularization of mechanical reeling in Guangdong Province after the 1870s (we will clarify the mechanization of the silk industry in China in the next chap-

---

①　T.May. An Economic and social History of Britain, 1760—1970, London. Longman. 1987. p.109.

②　W.R.Laird. "The Scope of Renaissance Mechanic.".Osiris. Chicago. University of Chicago Press. Vol.2. p.60.

ter), mechanical silk at the Canton market replaces Tsatlés as the best of Chinese silk. With the proximity of quality, the prices of European silks gradually brought closer to that of Chinese silk after the 1870s. However, Guangdong reeling machines are not yet the same as those of Europe. They are semi-mechanical and semi-manual, and Cantonese silk does not have the same quality as the best European silks either. So there is always a discrepancy between the prices of European silks and Chinese silk before the 1890s.

Extension of mechanical filature is slower in the Yangzi region than in Guangdong Province. Until the year 1895, there are only 12 mechanical filatures in Shanghai, and no mechanical filature in the provinces of Zhejaing and Jiangsu. However, the first mechanical filature in Shanghai used the filature machine Italian model, which are imported from Europe to China. So the mechanical silk of Shanghai, which has the same quality as that of Europe, immediately becomes the best Chinese silk after its manufacture. At the end of the 19th century and the beginning of the 20th century, more and more mechanical reeling factories were installed in the Yangzi region to supply silk to Europe. The flow of cheap Chinese silk, but with the same quality on the European market, brings down European silk prices definitely to the same level of Chinese silk, which terminate the convergence of silk prices between Europe and China.

The effect of the convergence of qualities on the convergence of silk prices in different Eurasian markets can also be proved by the case of Japanese silk. We will clarify in the next chapter that the silk production with the western filature machine already takes a considerable proportion in the production of silk in Japan since the 1880s. The convergence of the price of Japanese silk with that of European silks, as shown in Chart IV−15, was already completed after the 1880s. Obviously, the convergence of prices between Japanese silk and European silk has an indisputable link with the convergence of their qualities.

In conclusion, the decline in the tariff, which is an important factor leading to the convergence of grain prices in the Atlantic economy, is not as important for the convergence of silk prices in the Eurasian economy. On the other hand, the other element emphasized by K.H. O'Rourke and J. G. Williamson, the fall in transport costs, was indeed a key factor in the convergence of prices in the Eurasian economy during the second half of the 19th century. This suits the conclusion of the article by D. Chilosi and G. Federico. But it is not the only essential element for the convergence of prices in the Eurasian economy. Another element neglected by previous historians, the convergence of product quality among different countries with industrialization on a global scale, is another important impetus for the convergence of prices to Eurasian markets, which has been proved by our research on the price case of different silks to the Eurasian economy. In the next chapter, we will clarify the latter essential element which can greatly influence the convergence of Chinese silk prices with those of other countries: the history of the mechanization of the silk industry in China and its relationship with export of Chinese silk.

Chapter V　Industrial impact of the silk trade between France and China in the 19th century

In the previous chapter, we discussed the effects of customs tariffs and the reduction of transport costs on the growth of the silk trade between France and China during the 19th century. In this chapter, we will discuss another element that may have influences on the evolution of the silk trade between the two countries: industrialization in France and China.

In fact, the relationship between industrialization and commercial growth is a very classical issue already discussed by many historians and economists. In the article "le commerce international et genèse de la révolution industrielle anglaise", P. Bairoch examined the contribution of foreign trade to the start of industrialization in the case of Great Britain by five criteria[1], and concluded that foreign trade had played only a marginal role in the beginnings of English industrialization. His point of view is only partially accepted by R. Findlay and K.H.O'Rourke in their more recent *Power and Plenty*[2]. The two authors affirm that foreign trade was not at the origin of the English Industrial Revolution, but that it would be one of the factors of the expansion of industrialization in England. In the book *Histoire économique de la France du XVIII siècle à nos jours*[3], J-C. Asselain analyzes the industrializing effect of foreign trade on the French case, and finds that large trade has exerted an "industrializing effect" not negligible.

In terms of commercial impact on the industrialization of the Asian countries, conventional opinion (for example, affirmed by P.Bairoch in his book *Mythes et paradoxes de l'histoire économique*) is that the exchange with western countries leads to a deindus-

---

[1]　P.Bairoch. Commerce international et genèse de la révolution industrielle anglaise. Anales, Economies, Société, Civilisations, n°2, mars-avril 1973, p.541—571.

[2]　R.Findlay.K.H.O'Rourke Kevin. Power and plenty. Trade, war, and the world economy in the second millennium. New Jersey. Princeton University Press. 2007.

[3]　J-C. Asselain. Histoire économique de la France du XVIIIe siècle à nos jours. Edition du Seuil. 1984.

trialization to the Asian countries after the era of the Industrial Revolution[1]. This point of view has been questioned by other historians. In an article published in 1990, Sanjay Subrahmanyam argues that the decline of the cotton textile industry in India has already begun before the influx of English industrial products[2]. G.Riello emphasizes at the end of his book *Cotton: The Fabric that Made the Modern World* that the commercial relationship finally leads to a convergence of industrial development between the West and the East[3]. Mau Chuan-Hui has shown in his thesis and his research that the Franco-Chinese communication of knowledges and the mechanization of the silk textile industry in Europe have leaded to the progress of techniques of the silk industry in China[4].

In this chapter, we will choose a new angle between the industrialization of the two countries to analyze the relationship between industrialization and foreign trade in the 19th century: has western industrialization a positive or a negative impact on the industrialization of China? How do the reactions of China to industrialization occidental influence the evolution of trade between the two countries? On the contrary, does the dynamics of the silk trade between the two countries also have an effect on the reactions of the industrialization of two countries?

The first part of the chapter will present the traditional techniques of silk production in China. Before the 1850s, all Chinese silks exported to Europe were manufactured by such techniques. The second section focuses on the tension between the old techniques in Chinese silk production and the mechanization of the silk industry in France. The industrial revolution took place firstly in western countries and the mechanization of the silk industry in France accelerated after the 1870s. The silk materials offered by China no longer satisfied the needs of mechanical production in France. There is increasing criticism of the deterioration in the quality of Chinese silk by merchants and manufacturers in Lyonss. The third section will build China's response: in order to satisfy foreign

---

① P.Bairoch. Mythes et paradoxes de l'histoire économique. p.79.

② Sanjay Subrahmanyam. Rural Industry and Commercial Agriculture in the Late Seventeenth-Century South-Eastern India. Past & Present. No°126. 1990. 107—108.

③ G.Riello. Cotton: The Fabric that Made the Modern World. New York. Cambridge University Press. pp. 292—294.

④ Mau Chuan-Hui. L'industrie de la soie en France et en Chine de la fin du XVIIIe au début du XXe siècle: échanges technologiques, stylistiques et commerciaux. Paris. EHESS. 2002. 2 Vol. Mau Chuan-Hui. L'introduction en Chine des sciences et des techniques européennes concernant l'industrie de la soie après la guèrre de l'Opium. Etudes chinoises. Vol. XX. No°1-2. Les techniques séricicoles chinoises dans le développement de la sériciculture française de la fin du XVIIIe siècle au début du XIXe siècle. Cahier d'Histoire et de Philosophie des Sciences. No° 52. Lyon. ENS Editions. 2004. 毛传慧. 清末民初的蚕桑改良——传统与现代之间. 中国近现代行业文化研究——技艺和专业知识的传承与功能. 北京：国家图书馆出版社，2010 年.

market demand, silk production in China has begun its modernization path since the 1860s, while modernization of sericulture and China's qualitative control system start later as well. The relationship between the growth of the silk trade between France and China and the reactions of the industrializations of the two countries will be clearly demonstrated by the contents and the links between these three sections.

I Traditional silk production techniques and the qualitative criterion of the silk industry of China on the eve of the era of mechanization

To clarify what change the mechanization brings to the silk industry in China and why mechanization, we must know its original state before mechanization. Old production and the former qualitative criterion of industry, therefore, become the first elements that will be addressed in the first section of this chapter.[1]

Before we get into the details, we have to already define our research frontier, because "the silk industry in China" is a term that includes fairly abundant content. Techniqueally, the silk industry consists of three major production departments: sericulture, silk filature and of silk textile, while each department could still split up into several different sections of production. Sericulture is a sort of agricultural activity in China during the 19th century, which consists of the planting of mulberry trees and the education of silkworms. The final products of sericulture are cocoons, which are primary materials of the filature industry. Silk filature a process of making yarn and silk bundles, which consists of two stages: pulling and unwinding. Before the first half of the 19th century, these two production activities were also completed among peasants in China (In other words, silk filature has not yet become an independent industrial branch before the introduction of mechanical filature in China). On the other hand, the silk textile industry that produces silk fabrics is already beginning to emerge from agricultural production since the Chinese ancient era. Until the 19th century, much of the silk textile production activities in China were operated by artisans in the city instead of by peasants in the companion.

---

[1] "Tiaditional industry" represents the olk silk production activities with traditional trades that were used in China very commonly until the end of the 19th century, in contrast to "mechanical production" prosperous after the industrial Revolution.

1. The geographic distributions and technique of the planting of mulberry trees in China before the 1840s

The mulberry trees are not a captious plant nature. They can adapt to almost every kind of earth and any kind of climate[1].This is why, until the middle of the 19th century, this kind of tree is already planting in almost all the regions of China (from extrem south like the province of Guangdong, extreme north like the province of Liaoning). In addition, it is believed that, except in depressions, this plant can grow to all places in the countryside[2].

Despite the high adaptability of mulberry trees, the majority of Chinese sericulture production was concentrated in several provinces during the 19th century: Yangzi region (Zhejiang and Jiangsu provinces), Guangdong region, and Sichuan Region (According to the data in Chapter II, these three regions produced 80%—90% cocoons from all over China). This is due, first, to their different qualities of the leaves and trunks of the different species of mulberry which adapt better to the different climates or lands of the regions. Very different vegetation conditions determine the natures of the Chinese mulberry trees are also varied. According to three classification standards, a Chinese agronomist, WEI Jie (卫 杰), listed the main 18 natures of Chinese mulberry trees of the 19th century in his book collection of essays on sericulture:

According to their geographical origins, mulberry trees are divided into:
Huzhou Mulberry (湖桑), Sichuan Mulberry (川桑), Shandong Mulberry (鲁桑), Jing Mulberry (荆桑);
According to the species:
Theson mulberry (子桑), the female mulberry (女桑), the flower mulberry (花桑), the mulberry tree(椹桑), the Cap-Jasmine mulberry (栀桑), the fire mulberry (火桑), the Yesheng mulberry (业生桑), the sunshine mulberry (富阳桑), the soil mulberry (地桑), the mountain mulberry (山桑);
According to the plantingmethods, we have:
The moved mulberry tree (移桑), the grafted mulberry tree (接桑), the pressed mulberry tree (压桑) and the twisted mulberry tree (蟠桑).[3]

---

[1]　L.Duran. Raw silk: a practical hand-book for the buyer. New York. Silk Publishing Company. 1921. pp. 13—14.

[2]　黄世本.桑蚕简明辑说.北京:北京出版社,1998 年,第 5 页.

[3]　卫杰.蚕桑萃编.1899,第一卷,第 14 页,中国国家图书馆馆藏资源.

However, there are only a few species of mulberry—Shandong Mulberry, Jing Mulberry, Huzhou Mulberry and Fire Mulberry—which produce leaves with better qualities and easier to survive. These last mulberry areas better adapt the environment of the last three regions than in the other Chinese regions. The Shandong mulberry (鲁桑) (also called the domestic mulberry 家桑), whose good qualities leaves are thicker and larger, is originally from Shandong Province. However, it grows better in the Yangzi area, so it is planted ample in the Yangzi area. In the Yangzi region, a large quantity of Jing mulberry trees (荆桑) are also planted which have stronger trunks and are easier to survive[1]. Huzhou Mulberry (湖桑) is a graft species between the Shandong Mulberry and the Jing Mulberry. The branch of the Shandong mulberry was entred to the trunk of the Jing mulberry tree so that the advantage of the first (the larger and bigger leaves) and

the advantage of the latter (the stronger trunk) can be combined. In the western Zhejiang region, especially in Huzhou[2], this mode of grafting is most frequently used, so this kind of graft is named as Huzhou mulberry. The foliage of the fire mulberry tree is earlier than other natures of mulberry trees during the growing season, so peasants in the Yangzi region often plant a small amount of this kind of mulberry to feed silkworm babies. In the prov-

Pick mulberry leaves

ince of Guangdong[3], the majority (around 80%) of mulberry trees in the latter region are made up of Jing mulberry trees[4]. But we will also find many mulberry trees growing in this region. In Sichuan province, most peasants prefer to plant the Shandong mulberry trees. However, several other species, such as grass mulberry (草桑) and rock mulberry (磐桑), which have a specificity of resistance to moisture, are cultivated there as well[5].

Economic factors are also important for the concentration of sericulture in the three regions. In Chapter II (Section III), we have discussed three economic factors for

---

① 李明珠.中国近代蚕丝业及外销.上海:上海社会科学院出版社,1996,第 12 页.

② 张行孚.蚕事要略.台北:艺文出版社,1996 年,第 8 页.

③ 尹良莹.中国蚕业史.南京:国立中央大学蚕业学会,1947 年,第 205 页.

④ 叶超:广东珠江三角洲蚕丝业调查.中国蚕丝.第 2 卷第 5 期,1936 年,第 108—121 页.

⑤ 尹良莹.四川蚕业改进史.上海:商务印书馆,1947 年,第 27—28 页.

growth in the quantity of sericultural production in China in the 19th century: expansion of workforce, high sericulture in contrast to other agricultural activities and the extension of working hours. In fact, these factors also serve to explain the development of sericulture in the three regions at the time. However, it should be noted that the explosion of workforce is the most essential among the three factors, because it is the tension between population growth and the small expansion of the cultivated area that leads farmers to extend their labour force and engage in agricultural activities with more benefits. In fact, the demographic influence on modern economic developments in China has already attracted much attention of the fomer researchers.

P. Huang, in a series of his works and articles published in Chinese and English[1], explains the stagnation of traditional Chinese agriculture by introducing the term "involution"[2]. P. Huang says that the strong growth of rural population in China since the 17th century led to great pressure on the survival of the Chinese peasants because of the limit of expandabilité acreage, so the Chinese peasants are forced to operate other agricultural activities requiring more labor than growing grain (planting cotton, mulberry, tobacco, etc.). This last change (involution) leads to an expansion of the Chinese agricultural economy at the level of quantity but a decrease of the marginal profit per working day per farmer, thus it finally prevents the modernization of traditional Chinese agriculture. Although P. Huang's conclusion has been questioned by a large number of researchers (eg, Ramon, determines that P. Huang exaggerated the negative effects of Chinese population growth on the modernization of Chinese agriculture[3], R. B. Wong notes that it is difficult to distinguish between original and demographic pressure and the source of earnings[4].), his opinion on the positive correlation between population growth and the increase in ancillary agricultural activities of high labor intensity has been widely

------

[1] P.Huang. The peasant Economy and Social Change in North China. Stanford. Stanford University Press. 1988.P.Huang. The Peasant Family and Rural Development in the Yangzi Delta, 1350−1988. Stanford. Stanford University Press. 1990. 黄宗智.中国农村的过密化与现代化:规范认识危机及出路,上海:上海可会科学出版社,1992 年.黄宗智.中国经济史中的悖论与当前规范认识的危机.史学理论研究.1993 年第 1 期,第 42—60 页.

[2] In the research on the plantation of rice on the island of Java, C. Geertz, who used the word involution for the first time to describe the decline in marginal profit with the superabundance of working force. Consult C.Geertz. Agricultural Involution: The Processes of Ecological Change in Indonesia. Berkeley and Los Angeles. University of California Press. 1963.

[3] M.Ramon. "How Did the Modern Chinese Economy Develop? ——A Review Article." Journal of Asia Studies. Vol.50. No° 3. 1991. pp. 604—628.

[4] R.B.Wong. "Chinese Economic History and Development: A Note on the Myers-Huang Exchange. Journal of Asia Studies. Vol.51. No° 3. 1991. pp. 600—611.

278

accepted by most historians[1].

Indeed, Yangzi, Guangdong and Sichuan are three of the regions most affected by demographic pressure in China from the late 15th century to the early 19th century. From 1393 to 1816, the population of Yangzi Delta multiplied by 3, but its cultivated area hardly increased. The area of land per capita falls from 3.5 mu to 1.2 mu, a decrease of two-thirds for several centuries[2]. The population density of the province of Guangdong multiplied by 6 from 14th century to 1820, and the cultivated area by capita decreased to 1.6 mu. In Sichuan, although the absolute figure of the cultivated area by capita, 3.8 Mu, is much higher than that of Yangzi and Guangdong, it is important to note that population growth (720%) is 4.2 times faster than expansion of cultivated area (170%) from the beginning of the 18th century to the beginning of the 19th century, which means a decrease of three fourths of the area cultivated by capita during a century. Faced with such a tension between population growth and the stability of cultivated areas, farmers in the three regions are obliged to engage in agricultural activities requiring a high level of labor with the high benefit as sericulture.

Although the planting of mulberry trees shows a very strong regional concentration, until the middle of the 19th century, the levels of specialization of mulberry cultivation are still not very high in China. Even in the main sericicultural areas, pieces of land specializing in the planting of mulberry trees are still very rare. In the Yangzi River Delta, rice cultivation is still dominant until the middle of the Ming dynasty (16th century). Because of China's demographic evolution (as shown above), more and more farmers are beginning to cultivate or plant other agricultural products since the 17th century[3]. However, the planting of mulberry trees is only one of the choices among many activities of high benefit to the peasants.

In the area of Tai Lake (太湖) in the northwest of the Yangzi region, many farmers grow rape and straw matting alongside their rice fields; Cotton, soybean and indigo are grown in the northeast zone at the seashore as additional agricultural activities; In the south-east of the Yangzi Delta, tea and bamboo are planted; Even in southwestern

---

[1] This has been discussed and already proved by the researches of Chinese historians.Consult 从翰香.论明代江南地区的人口密度及其对经济发展的影响.中国史研究.1984 年第 3 期）李伯重.桑争稻田与明清江南农业生产集约程度的提高.中国农史.1885 年第 1 期.马学强.试论明清江南社会经济内变迁与劳动力转移.史林.1993 年第 1 期.

[2] 王笛：清代四川省人口、耕地及粮食问题,四川大学学报,1989 年第 3 期,第 102 页,1989 年第 4 期,第 81 页.

[3] 张家炎:明清长江三角洲地区与两湖平原经济结构演变探异.中国农史.1996 年第 3 期,第 99 页.

Zhejiang where sericulture is the most important axillary activity of the peasants, most mulberry trees are planted in dispersal at the interstices of the fields[1].

A sericulture manual published in the middle of the 19th century describes that "at each home or at each village there is always the interstices inside the walls or between the different pieces of fields where mulberry trees are planted".[2] The British botanist Robert Fortune's travel notes on villages near Hangzhou in the same period (the 1850s) confirm again this mode of planting mulberry trees: "Mulberry trees are planted in small pieces of land on Hill, while rice is grown in lower depressions"[3]. Large areas of mulberry fields didn't make its appearance untill the 1860s, with the increased need of the external market. On official or unofficial economic reports, there are many notes on purchases of large quantities of mulberry nurseries planted in large areas of fields. For example, the Annals of Wuxi and Jingui describes that Yan Ziqin (严紫卿, Gansu Provincial Justice) "bought three thousand mulberry tree nurseries and had them planted in thirty Mu of fields in 1871[4]; In 1872, Hua Yilun (华翼纶) planted mulberry trees in 15 Mu de Champs, etc."[5]

However, even in the second half of the 19th century, mulberry fields are only found in the southwestern area in the Yangzi region. In 1902, a Japanese teacher at the Wuhan Agricultural School said in his report on Chinese sericulture that "except in some villages in Huzhou and Jiaxing (嘉兴), fields that specialize on mulberry planting are very rare in the region of Yangzi."[6]In other words, apart from Huzhou and Jiaxing, the plantation of mulberry trees still remains the state of dispersal in most of the Yangzi region at the moment.

The level of concentration of mulberry in Sichuan province is even much lower than that of the Yangzi region. According to official statistics from the Sichuan Agricultural Bureau, until the end of the 19th century, rice carries more than half of cultivated area of Sichuan, while the soybean crops, wheat, potatoes, cereals are the most common ag-

---

① 陈忠平:论明清江南经济的多样化发展.中国农史.1989 年第 3 期,第 34 页.

② 沈练,仲昂庭.广蚕桑说辑补·第二卷.北京:中国书店,2007,第 48 页.The author of the general sericulture(《广蚕桑说》) is SHEN Lian (沈练), but died in 1855, before the publication of this work. The first edition of this book is published by the son of SHEN Lian in 1863. At the beginning of the reign of Guangxu (1875—1908), ZHONG Angting (仲昂庭) republished this work with certain additional contents with a new name sericicultures general additional. This is the edition we are consulting.

③ R.Fortune. Two visits to the Tea Countries of China. London. J.Murry; 1853 Vol I. p.274.

④ 无锡金匮县志.无锡市图书馆馆藏资源.

⑤ 严金清:严廉访遗稿年谱.北京图书馆馆藏珍本年谱丛刊.第 174 册,第 461 页.

⑥ 峰村喜藏.清国蚕丝业大观.东京:朝日新闻出版社,1902,第 73 页.

ricultural activities[1]. The planting area of the mulberry trees, which is only an agricultural activity that is often during the holidays or during the off-season, accounts for less than 0.36% of the total cultivated area of this province. The peasants plant mulberry trees there only beside the streets, beside the fields or beside their dwellings to insure the need for the production of silk in themselves[2]. Even in the prefectures where the silk industry is more productive, for example Tongchuan (潼川) and Santai (三台), there is not any specified mulberry field. In other regions of Sichuan, "we often can not see the mulberry tree for a hundred kilometers".[3]

The level of specialization of the mulberry plantation in Guangdong is higher than that in Yangzi and Sichuan during the first half of the 19th century, thanks to a special mode of agriculture—the "field-basin" (基塘农业), which means that the agriculture of fishing and farming, is developed in a pond and planting trees on the silt around the pond. This mode of agriculture, combining plantation and fish farming with the same e-cosystem, has already existed in certain regions of Guangdong province since the Ming dynasty (明代, 1368—1644)[4], as the cultivation of rice is no longer able to absorb the superabundance of labor with the demographic growth since the time[5].

However, due to the good flow of Cantonese tropical fruits to the North China market, fruit trees (Litchi, orange, clementine etc) were planted instead of mulberry trees in fields around the basin at the time[6]. The *New History of Guangdong* (《广东新语》), the historical work published at the time describes that "many peasants plant Litchi exclusively in their fields, and there are some hundred thousand trees (Litchi) in one village. Other peasants plant orange and clementine … All the boats coming from the north are to take the Litchis".[7]

The increase in the planting of mulberry trees began in the mid-18th century. As a result of the Zhejiang silk export limit and the Canton port's foreign trade monopoly (see Section 2, Chapter III), Cantonese silk is very demanded in the foreign market after the 1760s. As a result, more and more fields of fruit trees and rice fields are being modified to mulberry fields. The *Longshan Xiang records* (《龙山乡志》)[8] notes that

① 四川劝业道.四川第四次劝业统计表.1910 年,四川省图书馆馆藏资源.

② 姜庆湘,李守尧:四川蚕丝业,成都:四川省银行经济研究处,1946,第 22 页.

③ 陈宛溪.劝桑说.手抄本,三台县图书馆藏书.

④ 顺德区档案馆:万历.顺德县志.卷 10.杂志.第 9.

⑤ 叶显恩:明清珠江三角洲的人口问题.清史研究集.第 6 辑,光明日报出版社,1988 年,第 324—325 页.

⑥ 吴建新:明清以来广东的生态农业类型.中国农史.2005 年第 3 期,第 86 页.

⑦ 屈大均.广东新语.卷 2,地语.

⑧ 民国.龙山乡志.1913；卷 1,第 44 页,广州中山图书馆馆藏.

"almost all peasants in this Xiang (in Shunde 顺德) have been modifying their fields in mulberry gardens since the mid-19th century", and this phenomenon is gradually spreading other areas of Guangdong①.

Techniqueally, Chinese peasants already have mature methods to plant mulberry trees during the 19th century. In 1880, a customs commissioner of Zhenjiang (镇江关), F. Kleinwchter filed a report on the sericulture surveys in the Yangzi region, in which he specifically wrote the method of planting mulberry trees in that province at that time②. The good seeds of Jing mulberry are selected by putting all the seeds in water. Use only those that do not float on the water during sowing. These good seeds are usually planted in land during the month of June, on which the ashes of the wood or grass are covered simultaneously, as well as some clay to protect them. Watering and fumbling nurseries constantly grafts Shandong mulberry branches normally in April or May of next year when the diameter of the trunk of Jing mulberry tree reaches three centimeters. In December of the third year, grafted mulberry trees will be transplanted to the lands of the sericulturists. Two or three years later, sericulturists will be able to gather mulberry leaves grown to feed the silkworms. After transplanting, fertilization, pruning and sprouting, the insecticide work are very important for mulberry tree vegetation. The choices of fertilizer are very varied, but the one most preferred by the peasants is the vase, not only because this fertilizer includes abundant nutrients, but also because it is easy to get to the Yangzi region where rivers are very compact.

This opinion is proved at the same time by the phrases in an old agricultural work supplements of the manual of agriculture: "The misfortune of a family is due to lack of concert; The color of the mulberry trees is due to the lack of vase."③ In order to harvest more leaves, pruning of mulberry trees is mandatory. In the Yangzi region, round mulberry trees are often cut to limit the height of the tree. According to Huang Shiben's (黄世本) *Sericulture Summary* (《桑蚕简明辑说》), this is not only for densify leaves, but also for pick leaves without scale. It is also necessary to decompress the soil for mulberry trees during their vegetation④. Robert Fortune had the same experience when he observed sericulture in China: "It is found that the Chinese often pay much attention to

---

① 民国.顺德县志.卷 1, 台北:成文出版社,1966,第 19 页.

② F. Kleinwachter. Rapport des enquêtes sur la sériciculture de la douane de Zhenjiang en 1880. La soie de Jiangsu. 2001. No°3. pp.41—43.

③ In Chiese, 家不兴,少心齐;桑不兴,少河泥。Consult 张履祥.补农书.北京:中华书局,1958,第 1 卷,第 13 页.

④ 黄世本.蚕桑简明辑说.北京:北京出版社,1998,第 8 页.

unpack land after pruning, which leads to the excellent state of the mulberry trees."[1]

Finally, from the fear of the ravages of insects, the trunks and branches of the mulberry trees are watered with boiling water mixed with the leaves of the tobacco. After that, the seeds of insects will be killed immediately. Planting methods in the Yangzi region are more advanced than in other Chinese silk-planting regions. Many of these methods, such as grafting and pruning, are not yet fully implemented in other areas in the early 20th century.[2]

The production quantities of the leaves are different in different Chinese sericicultural regions during the 19th century. An average of 812 kilograms of mulberry leaves per Mu can be harvested (亩, 1 Mu ≈0.0667 hectare) per year in the Yangzi area[3]; The average production in the Guangdong region is 1,800 kilograms per Mu per year[4]; The harvest of mulberry leaves is only 300 kilograms per Mu per year in the Sichuan region[5]. In fact, the differences in the latter three quantities are not only due to the shift in the technique of planting mulberry trees in different regions but also because of the other elements. For example, the leaves can not be harvested twice in Yangzi or Sichuan during the year (once in spring and once in summer), but mulberry leaves grow throughout the year in Guangdong (six times a year) due to the warmer climate. That is why the amount of production in Guangdong is higher than the other regions. Another reason is that there is very abundant mud fertilizer in Yangzi and Guangdong, but this kind of fertilizer is more difficult to be found in Sichuan. The production volume of Sichuan is therefore lower than the other two regions. Moreover, the differences between different mulberry trees also influence the amount of leaf production. In Jiaxing (嘉兴, Zhejiang Sericulture Region), only 400—1400 kilograms of leaves per Mu per year are obtained in the specified gardens, but 2,500—3,700 kilograms of leaves per Mu per year if mulberry plants in dispersion[6].

<hr>

[1]　R.Fortune. Three Years Wanderings in the Northern Provinces of China. Including a visit to the Tea, Silk and Cotton Countries. London. J. Murray. 1847. p. 359.

[2]　叶超.广东珠江三角洲蚕丝业调查,第 108—121 页.尹良莹.《四川蚕业改进史》,第 27—28 页.

[3]　李明珠.中国近代蚕丝业及外销.第 15—16 页.

[4]　陈慈玉.近代中国机械缫丝工业(1860—1945).台北:"中央研究院"近代史研究所专刊,1989 年,第 160 页.

[5]　尹良莹.中国蚕业史.第 205 页.

[6]　陈恒力,王达.补农书研究.北京:中华书局,1958 年,第 36—39 页.

2. The education of silkworms and the production of cocoons during the 19th century

The Chinese have published a number of works memorizing traditional silk-education experiences at the end of the Qing Dynasty (1644—1911 清朝). The most important ones include the *Compendium of Medical Materia* (《本草纲目》1578) of Li Shizhen (李时珍), the *Exploitation of Natural Works* (《天工开物》1637) by Song Yingxing (宋应星), the *Agricultural Encyclopedia* (《农政全书》1639) by Xu Guangqi (徐光启), *Supplements the Agriculture Manual* (《补农书》) of Zhang Lvxiang (张履祥), *Summary of Major Chinese Drafts on Sericulture* (《蚕桑辑要》1896) of Shen Bingcheng (沈秉成), *Theories of sericulture* (《桑蚕说》1896) of Zhao Jingru (赵敬如), the *Collection of Tests of Sericulture* (《桑蚕萃编》1899) by Wei Jie (卫杰), etc. By order of the French royal government, sinologist J.Stanislas gave a summary of the traditional Chinese silk-rearing practices in 1837, which has made known most Chinese sericulture made in France for the first time[1]. According to his book, as well as the reports sent by French delegates of the silk industry, the Ministry of Agriculture and Commerce of France published a summary on the education of silkworms in China in its Annals in 1847[2]. According to Kleinwchter's observations in 1880, the majority of the principles and methods mentioned in the works above are amply respected and used in the activities of the educations of the silkworms of peasants in the Yangzi region in 1880. All the books above will help us to find the processes of silkworm education in China on the eve of modernization.

The number of seasons of silkworm education depends on the number of mulberry leaves harvested during the year. In the Yangzi region, silkworm education activities occur only twice a year among peasants (once in spring and once in summer) because there are only two seasons of mulberry leaves during the year. Moreover, most farmers in this area often abandon the silkworms of the summer season during the 19th century because the summer crop of mulberry leaves is much less than that of spring, and other agricultural work occupies all their time in this season (often for the sowing of rice) [3]. ZHANG Lvxiang also said that the education of silkworms in summer is one thing to "lose a large profit to try to save a small one" in his work *Supplements of the Manual of*

---

[1]　J.Stanislas. Résumé de principales traites chinoise sur la culture des mûriers et l'éducation des vers à soie. Paris. Imprimerie royale. 1837. p.1.

[2]　Ministère de l'agriculture et du commerce, Document sur le commerce extérieur, Chine et Indochine, Faits commerciaux n°12, p. 95.

[3]　上海万国生丝检验所:华中蚕丝业调查(1).丝绸.1999年第10期,第44页。

Agriculture[1]. The period of silkworm education in Sichuan province is the same as in the Jiangnan region[2]. That of Guangdong is much longer (5—6 times per year) than the other two regions because of the abundant foods for silkworms in this province[3].

The spaces of the worms in these last three regions are also different. The worms at Yanngzi produce white silk, which is cleaner and more brilliant; Guangdong belong to the tropical spaces, which produce the more supple white silk; The majority of the silks produced by worms in Sichuan have a yellow color, being thicker but with a higher tenacity[4].

It is necessary to spend more than 40 days for each silkworm education cycle in the Yangzi region during the 19th century. The whole period is composed of: 6—7 days for hatching, 28—29 days for breeding, 5 days for the cocoon formation process, 10 days for the cocoon, and another three days for butterflies lay eggs[5]. This cycle is shorter in southern China, where only 16—17 days of hatching is needed on the eve of cocoon formation (10 days shorter than in the middle of China[6]). However, the processes during the course of the silkworm education are as complicated in Guangdong as in Yangzi, in order that the silkworms can grow rapidly and healthily. They are:

(1) Hatching seeds

According to the *Supplementary Theory of Sericulture*, "when the size of the mulberry leaves is like a round copper coin, the seeds of the silkworms could be incubated".[7] At that moment the peasants had to come out their seed papers, they put them in a warm place and then wait for the seeds to hatch. To best incubate them, most peasants put seed papers inside their bed covers during their sleep so that the seeds can get extra heats exhaled by their bodies. Under such condition, seeds will become silkworm babies in 6—7 days[8].

(2) Heating basket

When the worms are hatched, they are placed on bamboo shelves where they are

---

① 张履祥.补农书.第 1 卷,第 20 页.

② 尹良莹.四川蚕业改进史.第 6 页.

③ 霍华德·伯斯韦.华南丝绸业调查.香港:商务印书馆,1925 年,第 66 页.

④ These are the general cases. In reality, there are many species of silkworms in each different region in China that produce different types of silk. For more informations, consult 陈慈玉.近代中国机械缫丝工业(1860—1945).第 58、157 页.尹良莹.四川蚕业改进史.第 67 页.

⑤ 上海万国生丝检验所:华中蚕丝业调查(1),第 45 页.

⑥ 中国经济杂志.第 5 卷第 2 期,1929 年 8 月,第 123 页.

⑦ The diameter of Chinese copper currency is almost two centimeters.

⑧ 黄世本.蚕桑简明辑说.第 22 页.

given to eat mulberry leaves cut menu. This indicates the beginning of the breeding of silkworms. During the whole breeding period, several principles must be respected: they are held warmly in the room while noise must be avoided around them. Also, do not give them water or even put them in a moist environment.

(3) Collecting leaves

Scissors should always be used to pick mulberry leaves. It is also advisable to pick the highest and most tender leaves of the mulberry tree, because they areworms' favorite[1].

(4) Four molts of silkworms, called "four sleeps" (四眠) in Chinese

The worms must eat the leaves in the interval of "each sleep". During the first two molts, the leaves will be cut to very thin pieces before they are added to racks. Normally 5—6 times of worms are given daily. After the third sleep, the worms take their meals stronger and they can eat the larger pieces of leaves. At the moment, it is added 6—7 times during the day and 2 times during the evening. As a result of the fourth molt (also called the great sleep 大眠), worms consume much more leaves than before. The frequency of adding the leaves rises to 10 times a day and it is no longer necessary to cut them[2]. At each sleep, it is necessary to disintegrate, that means to clean the worms and to frequently change the wafer. Moreover, when the worms grow, it is obligatory to use a greater number of baskets in order to give the worms the space necessary for their development[3]. Silkworms consume a considerable amount of silk before cocooning. According to the statistics of the Kleinwchter report, 20 piculs (or about 1,200 kilograms) of mulberry leaves are needed to raise 1 taël 3 qian (about 49.14 grams) of the worm babies. With those leaves, the top class silkworms will produce only 160—200 taël[4] of cocoons at the end[5].

---

① Ministère de l'agriculture et du commerce, Document sur le commerce extérieur, Chine et Indochine, Faits commerciaux n°12, p. 96.

② 沈练,仲昂庭.广蚕桑说辑补·第二卷.第 7—15 页.

③ 宋应星.天工开物.上海:上海人民出版社,1976 年,第 38 页.

④ The "Taels" here is an old unit of weight instead of silver unit, , 1 taël = 10 Qian ≈ 31.25 gram.

⑤ F. Kleinwachter. Rapport des enquêtes sur la sériciculture de la douane de Zhenjiang en 1880. p.43.

Education of silkworms in the family

（5）Formation of cocoons

It is necessary to choose carefully the mature worms among all the worms in the hurdles when the opportunity appear. "The opportunity" of this process is very important for this activity: if the selected worm is still too young, it will not produce enough silk for a complete cocoon; If the selected worm is too old, it may have already begun to cocoon in the wicker, which will prevent it from producing a good quality cocoon in the end[1]. After selecting the mature worms, they should be moved on a small stoneworm where the mature worms will quietly cocoon（called climbing 上蔟 in Chinese）[2]. We row with a few mulberry leaves on the busket crate so that the worms can eat if they are still hungry. While waiting for the complete cocoons, it is necessary to maintain in the chamber a gentle tempereture so that the worms can actively cocoon. When the cocoons are made（normally in 5 days）, they are removed and stored in the racks in a cool room[3]. At that moment, all these complete cocoons are already ready for the next step: filature.

（6）Butterfly Coupling

Before the filature, the best cocoons are taken out to prepare the seeds of next year.

① F. Kleinwachter. Rapport des enquêtes sur la sériciculture de la douane de Zhenjiang en 1880. p.41.

② 徐光启 农政全书.北京.中华书局,1956年,第31卷,第10页.

③ Ministère de l'agriculture et du commerce, Document sur le commerce extérieur, Chine et Indochine, Faits commerciaux n°12, p. 97.

To have good seeds, it is necessary to carefully remove the friezes which envelop the outer cocoons. Ten days later, the butterflies will come out of their hulls, the two sex will approach each other and we will get seed[1].

(7) Conservation of seeds

The fresh seeds are put on paper, dried by hanging them in the room (until they become black), a little lime-water on the papers, and keeps them in a cold room. When the next hatching season is over, the stored seed papers are removed and washed thoroughly with salt water or cold tea water (to kill weaker seeds). Then all these papers will be kept until hatching[2].

It should be noted that there are already seed markets for silkworms in China since ancient times. Nevertheless, until the eve of modern seed laboratories in the late 19th century, most farmers prefer to use seeds of worms made in their own home. The main reason for this is that farmers do not have confidence in the quality of the seeds circulated on the market, which are made by other farmers[3]. The cocoon markets only emerged after the prosperity of the mechanical filature factorie in China (this will be discussed in the third section). Before that, having produced the cocoons, Chinese peasants often keep them for filautre silk in their own house.

3. Silk filature on the eve of the Chinese industrial revolution

Mechanical filature began in China (more precisely, in the region of Yangzi) since the 1860s, and then gradually spread in other Chinese regions. Before that (even a long period after), we spin the silk with the traditional crafts (varied according to different regions).

Before the beginning of the traditional filature, there are still two preparatory works to be done.

The first is the sorting of the cocoons. After setting aside those destined for the seed, one must also separate good cocoons from bad; if there are two or more chrysalises in a cocoons, they shall be set apart. Only those that are tighter and smaller with a chrysalis will be selected for filature[4]. Nevertheless, the cocoons eliminated will not be wasted. Usually, the silk wadding is made with this kind of raw material, which is a

---

① Idem. p.96.
② 黄世本.蚕桑简明辑说.第 20—21 页.
③ 紫藤章.清国蚕丝业一斑.东京:农商务省生丝检查所,1911,第 57—60 页.
④ 张行孚.蚕事要略.第 14 页.

very good packing for blankets and cold-resistant garments[1].

The second is to destroy the chrysalis. The silkworm has changed into a chrysalis in the cocoon, and will come out in a new form—the butterfly. In order to escape from its home, the butterfly does not limit itself to making an opening by carefully removing the threads which form the tissue. On the contrary, it tears them and the cocoon can no longer be spun. The chrysalis needs about 10 days to finish this last metamorphosis, that is to say, the cocoon will be torn in 10 days after its formation. Thus, if it is impossible to spin the entire crop of cocoons for such a short period, the chrysalis must be perished in the cocoon so that the cocoons can be spun. The Chinese often employ four methods to achieve this goal in the first half of the 19th century.

In the Guangdong region, heat is used in the sun, or laminated by alternating layers with salt and water lily leaves in large jars, which are carefully sealed. The advantage of these latter two methods is that the quality of the cocoon is not sabotaged during the process of perishing the chrysalis, but the risk is that the dead of all the pupae are not assured. In Yangzi, there are two other methods to perish the chrysalis[2]. The chrysalises are put to death by placing the cocoons in a hot oven. This method also has great disadvantages. If the heat is not strong enough, the chrysalises of the cocoons placed in the middle of the baskets do not die. If the heat is too strong, the strand of the silk is altered. In both cases, the quantity and quality of the cocoons are detrimental, so the peasants in Yangzi prefer the other method to perish the chrysalis by employing the vapor of boiling water. A furnace is prepared on which is placed a boiler traversed by an iron cross, on which is placed a sieve full of cocoons. It is covered by a wooden lid padded on the edges so that no part of the vapor escapes. It must take care not to place the sieve until the water which is contained in the boiler, and which is only two-thirds of the vessel, is at its highest degree of boiling. It is left there for 8 to 10 minutes, and this time sufficient to destroy all the pupae. By employing this means, there is nothing to fear that the strand of the cocoon will be altered for being left too long exposed to the action of the vapor. Yet it results from the use of this means that the steam which rises from the boiler after passing through the cocoons condenses to the lid which covers the sieve, and then falls into drops, stain the cocoons, which prejudices the shade of silk[3].

----

① 汪曰桢.湖蚕述.北京:中华书局,1965 年,第 70—71 页.

② Ministère de l'agriculture et du commerce, Document sur le commerce extérieur, Chine et Indochine, Faits commerciaux n°12, p. 97.

③ L. De Teste. Du commerce des soies et soieries en France. Considéré dans ses rapports avec celui des autres états. Avignon. Lithographe de la ville. 1830. pp.43—45.

Each method manifests its own imperfection, hence in regions where the hands of works are more abundant, especially in the region of Yangzi, the process of perishing the chrysalis is often skipped[1]. In other words, the peasants immediately begin the work of the filature after sorting the cocoons without perishing the pupae. In this case, they must finish reeling all the cocoons in 10 days.

The processes of silk filature were similar in different countries at the first half the 19th century: de-cocooning the cocoon in hot water by dissolving the gummy coating which surrounds the wire in order to obtain a beam which will be the thread of the raw silk. However, in every country, even in every region of the same country, the people have its own ways and means of reeling cocoons[2]. In China, the classical asplet is constructed directly above a large basin in which the cocoons are boiled. A long wooden board on the basin supports two pillars to which are attached two small cylindrical rollers whose diameter is 6.6 centimeters and 16.5 centimeters in length. A bamboo tube hangs underneath each cylindrical roller to form the encroachment. The cocoons are placed in the warm water which is normally boiled by the fire below the basin, and then the beam of cocoon are pulled to the end (this process is called silk pull). After these bundles pass through the bamboo tubes, they are wrapped around the cylindrical rollers where they are transmitted to a wider spool or reel with a diameter of 14.85 centimeters and a length of 52.8 centimeters. Around this last reel or reeling wheel there are four pillars, of which the two front pillars is lower than the two pillars behind. A hook is installed on each front pillar to separate the bundles and then transmits them to the reel supported by the two pillars behind. In the reel or reeling wheel, the bundles are unwound to the shape of the strand (this process is called reeling of the silk). The strands produced by the reel are divided into fine silk (joined by 5 bundles) and large silk (joined by 12 or more bundles). The most valuable fabrics are manufactured with the former, and the ordinary fabrics with the latter. There is also a small stove behind the hose reel on which the silk is dried to prevent them from sticking[3]. Until then, silk is ready for the market.

The energy of the whole instrument comes from a transmission mechanism connected to the reel or reeling wheel. When the wheel is rotated, the whole instrument will turn with the same speed. In China, there are different kinds of transmission mechanisms that provide energy for the reel at the moment in different regions: it is preferred

①　A.J.Sargent. Anglo-Chinese commerce & Diplomacy. Oxford. The Clarendon Press. 1907. pp.217—218.
②　A. De Laberge. Les industries de la soie en France. Revue des Deux Mondes. Tome 101. 1890. p.6
③　李拔.蚕桑说.皇朝经世文编.卷三十七.农政.第55页.

to roll the reel with the foot pedal in the Yangzi region, but the crank is often attached to the spool wheel in the regions of Guangdong and Sichuan[1] (The foot pedal reel was popularized in the region of Guangdong only after the 1870s[2], the Sichuan area only after the 1890s[3]). The first one is more advanced than the second, because it has released both hands of unwinder, which allows him to carefully pull the beam in the basin. Also, the sizes of the foot pedal dispensers in the Yangzi area are different. For those who are smaller, a worker is enough to feed his stove, to maintain his basin, to beat his cocoons and to turn the asple. For those who are bigger, it takes 2 to 4 people to finish all this work[4].

The petal reel on foot

The crank reel

The emergence of the cocoon markets in Yangzi and Guangdong was delayed until the 1870s (the problem of the cocoon market was discussed in the third section). Without the supply of raw materials, it is impossible for the existence of the handicraft filature workshop or mechanical filature factories specializing in silk reeling in Yangzi and Guangdong[5]. This means that before the 1870s, the procedures for the education of silkworms and filature were practiced completely in a family of peasants by the family unit. This organization of silk production only evolved after the creation of mechanical filature

---

① 李明珠.中国近代蚕丝业及外销.第 15—16 页.
② 民国.顺德县志.第 1 卷,第 25 页.
③ 张肖梅.四川经济参考资料.上海.中国国民经济研究所,1939 年,第 23 页.
④ 徐光启.农政全书.第 15 页.
⑤ 张学君,张莉红.四川近代工业史.成都:四川人民出版社,1990 年,第 120 页.

and cocoon companies, which will be specified in the third section of this chapter.

4. Traditional criterion of silk quality

Table V–1 Classification of the quality silks circulated on the Canton market in 1845[1]

<table>
<tr><td></td><td></td><td></td><td>Dollars/picul[4]</td></tr>
<tr><td rowspan="3">Tsat–li</td><td>no° 1</td><td></td><td>500</td></tr>
<tr><td>2</td><td></td><td>490</td></tr>
<tr><td>3</td><td></td><td>480</td></tr>
<tr><td rowspan="3">Taysaam</td><td>no° 1</td><td></td><td>490</td></tr>
<tr><td>2</td><td></td><td>480</td></tr>
<tr><td>3</td><td></td><td>470</td></tr>
<tr><td rowspan="3">Taysaam</td><td>no° 1</td><td></td><td>420</td></tr>
<tr><td>2</td><td></td><td>410</td></tr>
<tr><td>3</td><td></td><td>400</td></tr>
<tr><td rowspan="3">See–tchuen</td><td>no° 1</td><td></td><td>410</td></tr>
<tr><td>2</td><td></td><td>400</td></tr>
<tr><td>3</td><td></td><td>390</td></tr>
<tr><td rowspan="3">Canton supérieur</td><td>no° 1</td><td>Long–kong</td><td>350</td></tr>
<tr><td>2</td><td>Long–shann</td><td>340</td></tr>
<tr><td>3</td><td>Lak–lao</td><td>330</td></tr>
<tr><td rowspan="6">Canton inférieur</td><td>no° 4</td><td>kom–tchou</td><td>300</td></tr>
<tr><td>5</td><td>Wong–linn</td><td>280</td></tr>
<tr><td>6</td><td>Hang–tann</td><td>250</td></tr>
<tr><td>7</td><td>Siou–tann</td><td>250</td></tr>
<tr><td>8</td><td>Hwei–tchok</td><td>230</td></tr>
<tr><td>9</td><td>Kaou–kong</td><td>180</td></tr>
</table>

There is already a system to distinguish different qualities of silks on the Chinese domestic market in the first half of the 19th century. At this period, this system also serves to identify the quality of silks in the export market. In this system, the main criterion for classifying the different qualities of the silks are their places of production. Inside the silks produced in the same place, they are subdivided into several orders ac-

---

[1] Ministère de l'agriculture et du commerce, Document sur le commerce extérieur, Chine et Indochine, Faits commerciaux n°12, p. 102.

cording to their specificity (elasticity, toughness, color, brilliance, finesse, etc.). In a report by Isidore Hedde (delegate of the French silk industry in China) to the Ministry of Trade and Agriculture, a list was found which noticed the classification of silk qualities circulated on the market of Canton in 1845:

According to the prices marked to the left of the list, the best Chinese silks at that time are Tsat-li, Yune-fa and Tayssam, all from the Yangzi region. The quality of the silks of Sichuan is worse than the silks of Yangzi, but better than the silks of Canton. The silk prices of Canton are the lowest, and their qualities are the worst. In addition, each kind of silk is divided into several numbers to distinguish the different qualities of the silks from the same place. It's listed below thhe descriptions of the characteristics of the main natures of the Chinese silks.

(1) The tsat li, in Mandarin Chinese qi-li (七里丝，辑里丝). The qi-li is a white, silver-spiced grape with seven cocoons, which has earned its name[1]. It is very remarkable for its metallic appearance and its whiteness. It turns very well on reeling and makes little waste: its fleets divide perfectly. Its principal uses in China are for the beautiful scarves of great beauty, for the fine silk twists and floats of Ningpo, as well as for the beautiful fabrics of crepe plain, on which rest the elegant embroideries of the great shawls[2].

They are also the most requested silk by western merchants. In Isidore Hedde's report, he admires that it "is very rare and sought after … It is a silk produced by more sophisticated processes than those used in Kwuang-tong province... It is considered superior to all the silks we receive from the Levant, for its brilliance and quality in employment. It is cleaner, less fluffy, and loses less decay than all ordinary silks, even those of France".[3]

(2) The yune-fa, in Chinese madarin yun-hua (云华丝). This raw silk is as remarkable as the previous one in its whiteness, fineness and sharpness. It is also crossed, but the nature of the silk is worse, the strand is more irregular, the reeling is harder; It therefore gives more waste. Its fleets are often capped, that is to say, they are of a strand larger at the extremity than at the beginning; Reeling and use, it is much more brittle than the previous ones[4]. Isidore Hedde indicates that "this silk is still little

---

① 嵇发根.湖丝——辑里湖丝源流考.农业考古.2003 年第 3 期,第 184—192 页.

② 浙江省档案馆.同治.湖州付志.同治十三年,卷三十一 ,第 22—23 页.

③ Ministère de l'agriculture et du commerce, Document sur le commerce extérieur, Chine et Indochine, Faits commerciaux n°12, p. 93.

④ 罗愫修.乾隆.乌程县志.卷十三.物产.上海:上海古籍出版社,1995 年,第 136 页.

known in France, perhaps the best qualities have not been used. It is asserted that in China it is destined for the most elevated uses, and its finesse makes it even prefered, for certain uses, than the tsi-li".[1]

(3) The taysanm, in Chinese Mandarin da-can (大蚕), that is to say, large verses, because it is produced by the large worms of Zhejiang. This raw silk is good for all articles that require large materials[2]. "She is better known in France than the yun-fa, and she rides it in threads and hair which are of excellent use."[3]

(4) The silks of Sse-tchuen(四川丝). The silks of Sse-tchuen often have a yellow color, so they are also called yellow silks. These last silks are famous for having more tenacity and to be specifically less heavy than other white silks. Nevertheless, according to Isidore Hedde, "they are not known in Europe."[4]

(5) The silks of Canton. All Canton silks with higher quality (No. 1, 2,3) are produced in the Shunde (顺德) district bearing the names of the bourge Shunde. These silks are finer than those of Yangzi and Sichuan, but less regular and corkier. The other silks with lower quality are the productions of other villages of Shunde district, which possesses various colors and quality even worse than the first three numbers[5]. Isidore Hedde's comments on the silks produced in Canton are: "They have the defect of not being crossed and being erased on the asple, which causes a lot of waste and makes the reel difficult, especially comparing to the silks of the Levant, such as the Mestoup, Brousses, and others, whose filature have greatly improved in recent years. We must reduce the price of silks of Canton, or rather to keep them away from our markets."[6]

We find that, with such a criterion, the qualities of silks are distinguished according to their places of production, and each nature of silk produced at certain places possesses its own characteristics. "The principal index by which the greige silks are distinguished is a cartouche in Chinese characters which always accompanies each of these kinds and indicates the places of manufacture, quality (number), quantities, dates of

---

① Ministère de l'agriculture et du commerce, Document sur le commerce extérieur, Chine et Indochine, Faits commerciaux n°12, p. 94.

② 汪曰桢.(咸丰)南浔镇志.卷二十四.物产.上海:上海科学技术文献出版社,1995年,第5页.

③ Ministère de l'agriculture et du commerce, Document sur le commerce extérieur, Chine et Indochine, Faits commerciaux n°12, p. 94.

④ Ministère de l'agriculture et du commerce, Document sur le commerce extérieur, Chine et Indochine, Faits commerciaux n°12, p. 95.

⑤ 刘克祥.桑蚕丝绸史话.北京:社会科学文献出版社,2011年,第183页.

⑥ Ministère de l'agriculture et du commerce, Document sur le commerce extérieur, Chine et Indochine, Faits commerciaux n°12, p. 91—92.

dispatch, the names of the consignor and the consignee."[1] In other words, the most evident characteristic of the old Chinese silks quality criterion is its low level of standardization.

We have already mentioned that silk production rose from 123,930 picules in 1840 to about 150,000 in 1870. According to the data in Chapter II, half of these silks produced in Chinais destined for the foreign market during the 1870s, in which approximately 50% (one quarter of all) arrive directly or indirectly in France. Quantitatively, the production of Chinese silk satisfies perfectly the demand of the French market. But qualitatively? With such production procedure and under such a quality criterion, does the quality of Chinese silks satisfy the need of the French manufacturers? The answer is no. We will see in the text below that Chinese silks (all class) have a very bad reputation on the international market, including the French market from the 1870s. So what are the main qualitative problems of Chinese silks? If there are qualitative problems, why is the quality of Chinese silks less criticized before 1870 and more criticized afterwards? We will answer these questions in the next section.

II The mechanization of the silk industry in France and the "insufficient" quality of Chinese silks

We have discovered in our sources that a large number of official warning letters were sent to Chinese merchants by French silk buyers since the 1870s, in which the French buyers strictly reproach the bad qualities of Chinese silks exported to France. This remarked that, as early as the 1870s, the specificity of Chinese silk was less and less adapted to the demand for silk quality on the French market. Why these official warnings addressed directly to the Chinese merchants appear from the 1870s, no sooner?[2] Why do Chinese silks no longer adapt to the demand of Western buyers after the 1870s? Is there a link between the mechanization of the silk textile industry in France and the insufficient quality of silk in China? If so, what is the link between the two? In this section we will answer all these questions about the deterioration of the quality of Chinese silks circulating on the international market.

---

[1]   Ministère de l'agriculture et du commerce, Document sur le commerce extérieur, Chine et Indochine, Faits commerciaux n°12, p.94.

[2]   Certainly, there are also criticisms of the poor quality of Chinese silks before the 1870s, but they often appear in the reports of trade commissioners or in the reports of French consuls sent to the official or non-official organization in France. Warnings sent directly to Chinese merchants are very rare before the year 1870.

1. Claims of the silk merchants of Lyons

In the general assembly of February 6, 1872, the Union of Silk Merchants of Lyons, preoccupied with the deterioration of the quality of Chinese silks from the harvest of 1871, appointed a Commission composed of Chamonard, Arlès-Dufour, Chartron , Milsom and Lacroix[1], to study the causes. Let us read part of their report with the title Deterioration of the silks of China of the season of 1871, which was presented to the Union of the Silk Merchants of Lyons in the session of April 2, 1872[2]:

"Untill the month of August, 1871, the market of Lyonss had been since long-term devoid of Chinese silk of fine quality; and there was received with satisfaction those of the new crop, the quality of which was expected to be very good. The sorting left a little to be desired, probably because of the eagerness of the Chinese merchants to expedite the first reeling silks on the Shanghai market; the Union hoped, from the letters and circulars of the explorers, that the followings would be better prepared.

"Unfortunately it was not as that; On the contrary, the successive arrivals were formed of silks less and less good, as nature, and more and more badly reeled.

"Thus, after the receipt of the first trunks, the great mass of silks, especially of the heaped up, was found mixed, in a greater or less proportion, according to the batches, but sometimes very strong, of fleets very irregular and coarse; Other fluffy to excess, corky, and even doupionnés; Still others, of bad color, and some, at last, so badly reeling, that they were almost indistinguishable.

"All these defects arise, and from the want of care in silk-reeling, and from the exceptional abundance of the second crop, the quality of which is always inferior to that of the first; we can even assume that the worst fleets come from districts that usually do not export their products.

"Independently of the complaints which have given rise to these defects, of which it will perhaps be difficult to prevent the continuation, there have been others, no less founded and no less general, on the little care taken by the Chinese merchants, to the assortment and packaging of silks; Which has rendered even more serious is the consequences of the negligence of the filature factories of silk. Thus, the packages are formed of silks of different merits; Many are covered with fleets of good quality and bad quality, contain within them other fleets, such as those which have just been written, and it is

---

[1] Some members of this commission, for example, Arlès-Dufour and Lacroix, are at the same time the silk merchatns who have set up commercial companies in China. See the previous.

[2] Archives Nationales de France. F12. 7058. Union des marchands de soie de Lyon. 2, avril 1872.

not possible, to account for it, without completely defeating the packets. In some lots, these mixtures constitute a real fraud, and this results in numerous difficulties between sellers and consumers.

"These facts are all the more serious, as they have occurred not only on silks of common quality, but also on those which until then had been classed perfectly by their chops, and very much appreciated by consumers. These classified silks have deteriorated progressively throughout the companion, so much so that in many cases, a tsatlée n° 3 of the end of the season, is worth only the n° 4 of the same chop.

"It is no longer important to take serious account of the fatal results of such a state of affairs; the trade, confiding in the merit of classified silks, had taken advantage of the facilities afforded by the opening of the telegraph. To make considerable business to deliver, the silks of chops must be well known and appreciated; but by the fact of the alteration of the quality of the silks delivered and shipped under the cover of these chops, a great disappointment has resulted from these cases. Also, trust in most chops is much completely lost today, and consumers no longer want to buy, as other times, on the simple designation of chops; They want not only to see the merchandise, but still visit the inside of the packages, even make them try, and send them to the factories to the process; The resulting loss of time slows down and significantly hampers our business.

"In addition, as the chop is no longer a guarantee of quality, speculation will inevitably depart from a trade so dangerous, while consumption, disgusted by poor quality of the great mass of Chinese silk, and will eventually abandon them, as it had for some years almost abandoned the silks of Japan (Mybash), which determined a decrease of 20%/25% of their value.

"This apprehension is not exaggerated, and is all the more justified, since, as a result of the progressive improvement of the results of the sericultural crops in Europe, our native silks become more abundant and cheaper comparing to those of China (last year, the silks of good Italian filature did not return to flowers at more than 65/70 francs per kilogram, parity of 23/6 to 25/francs). On the other hand, Japan (Mybash) is beginning to improve, and as prices are very low (22/francs to 25/francs), the silk industry, which has long used the Italian fabrics, excluding those from China, is beginning to return, which will create two competitions for China silks instead of one.

......

"To sum up, if we do not bring a real improvement in the reeling, filature, and classification of Chinese silks next season, their future seems to be seriously threatened; It is therefore important for all parties interested in this trade to make every effort to prevent the Chinese from continuing to treat their silks as badly in 1872 as they did in 1871. Therefore, we will make all our efforts to engage the Chamber of Commerce of Shanghai, to use all its influence with the Chinese merchants, to cut off the evil at its root.

"In order to do so, it appears to us that the Chamber of Commerce of Shanghai should summon all the representatives of the great Chinese companies (Hongs), to expose to them the danger of their silk trade, as a result of negligence in reeling; The mixture of fleets below the packaging, and the degradation of the classification.

"To entreat them, in their own interest, and that of their country, to come to an agreement among themselves, in order to react this year in an energetic manner against the negligence and frauds reported during the last season.

....

"But we hope that the authority of the Shanghai Chamber of Commerce will be efficacious enough to enlighten the Chinese merchants on their true interests, and that the silks of 1872 will bring back the consumers to the bad impression left by them in 1871; the danger threatening the trade in these silks would thus be avoided."

This long report strongly reflected the situation of the deterioration in the quality of Chinese soil silks[1] exported to France in the early 1870s, and, the dissatisfaction of the silk merchants of Lyons. Later, the report was sent to the French Agriculture and Commerce Ministry[2]. Very soon, by the French Foreign Affairs Minister[3], the French Plenipotentiary Minister in China knows the problem, and transmits the report of the Lyonsnais to the Chamber of Commerce of Shanghai[4]. The Chamber of Commerce, composed of representatives of foreign firms in Shanghai, published the report on the *Shen newspaper* (May 22, 1872)[5] and the *North China Herald* (《北华捷报》, the largest English newspaper in Shanghai) on May 25, 1872[6], in order to send this information to

---

[1]   Silk produced by manual spinning is called "Sol silk (土丝)" in China, in order to differentiate itself from the silk produced by mechanical spinning "mechanical silk (厂丝)".

[2]   Archives Nationales de France. F12. 7058. Lettre de la Chambre de commerce de Lyon au Ministre de l'agriculture et de commerce. 13, avril 1872.

[3]   Archives Nationales de France. F12. 7058. Lettre du Ministre de l'agriculture et du commerce au Ministre des affaires étrangères. 20 avril 1872.

[4]   Archives Nationales de France. F12. 7058. Lettre du Ministre des affaires étrangères au Ministre de l'agriculture et du commerce. 6 septembre 1872.

[5]   申报.1872 年 5 月 22 日,上海图书馆馆藏资源.

[6]   北华捷报.1872 年 5 月 25 日,上海图书馆馆藏资源.

Chinese silk merchants. This is the first time that the merchants of Lyons have officially and seriously blamed the Shanghai merchants on the question of the deterioration of the quality of Chinese silks.

After the publication of this last report, the quality of the Chinese manual silks does not improve. Moreover, there are now more and more complaints about this problem from western silk merchants. Not only Chinese silks in the lower classes, but also those in the upper classes are often criticized. In the month of May 1873, reproaches from the Marchants Union of Lyonss appear again on the *North China Herald*: "Chinese silks are neither clean nor regular, difficult to be unwound; it will be impossible to sell the fabrics woven by the Chinese silks, because they are very corky and their colors are not uniform.[1] In December of the same year, a report of the Chamber of Commerce of Shanghai stated that: "Following a second communication from the Union of Silk Merchants of Lyons concerning the bad preparation of the silks of China, the Board of Directors renewed its recommendations to producers but failed. The silks of the last harvest have the same defects as in previous years and it is not likely that better products will be obtained as long as foreigners are willing to buy them[2]. Three months later, another warning letter from the Union of Silk Merchants of Lyons is published on the *Shen newspaper*: "If Chinese merchants can not improve the quality of exported silks and restore reputation, the French silk industry will refuse to let Chinese silks enter France."[3]

While French merchants are not the only group that object to the poor quality of Chinese silks. Silk merchants from other countries declare their criticisms almost at the same time. In January 1873, the British Consul in Shanghai sent a letter to the Mayor of Shanghai Shen Bingcheng (沈秉成) to inform the Chinese Government of the seriousness of the quality problems existing in the silks exported from China. He advised that "Chinese merchants should first underline their reputation, avoid disturbances in the production and exchange processes, and engage in fair trade with foreign merchants".[4] On August 23 of the same year, the *North China Herald* published a letter from the Union of Silk Merchants of the United States, in which the Americans also expressed dissatisfaction with the poor quality of Chinese silks[5].

What has stimulated the criticism of so many western merchants on the quality of

① 北华捷报.1873 年 5 月 5 日,上海图书馆馆藏资源.
② Archivos du Ministère des affaires étrangères(Nantes), Shanghai, cartons roses, n°5
③ 申报.1874 年 3 月 22 日,上海图书馆馆藏资源.
④ 中国第二历史档案馆,中国海关总署办公厅.中国旧海关史料,05 卷.第 55 页.
⑤ 北华捷报.1873 年 8 月 23 日,上海图书馆馆藏资源.

Chinese silks exported? In other words, what have led to the deterioration of the quality of silks exported from China? There are already some tracks in the first report that we have shown.

According to the report, the cause for deterioration in the quality of Chinese silks, also the fact that has been mentioned most often, is fraud in the trade of silk. In reality, cases of commercial fraud already emerged at the beginning of the opening of China during the 1840s in the exchange of silks. In a report published in 1845 by the Ministry of Agriculture and Trade, it is stated that "we must be careful in Europe when these goods arrive, because they are often capped, that is to say, inner parts have been covered with costeous, veined, corky, uneven, inferior silks, and finally with those which surround them externally[1]. This phenomenon is becoming more and more common from then on, and becomes an important target of criticism in the commercial relations written by foreign traders. In the Foreign Trade Report of China in 1865, a certain quantity of Chinese silk was received by torrential rains, was found to be damp, and, delivered too quickly to the steamers, arrived in Europe, with a deterioration; A little fraud on the part of the peasants, which, in order to make the balls heavier, would have wet the inside of it, might also have been added to the effects of the humidity of the weather".[2]

The Agriculture, Commerce and Public Works Ministry of France had the following notice inserted in its Annals published in 1869: "A new type of fraud practiced on silkworm seed boxes was discovered by the Agriculture Ministry, Consul-General of France at Shang-hai. Empty cartons were imported from Japan to China to be covered with Chinese silkworm seeds and sent back to Japan to receive the stamp of the Consulate of France before being sent to Europe."[3] Similar cases are already very numerous in commercial relations before the 1870s. It is true that commercial fraud is also an important cause for the problem of the quality of Chinese silks. However, commercial frauds exist already in the silk trade from the 1840s, why did the first official warnings of the Lyonsnais merchants appear only after the beginning of the 1870s?

In fact, although commercial fraud is the most mentioned cause by the Lyonsnais, they are not the most essential element for planting the deterioration of the quality of the silks of China. Another factor that has definitively led to the quality crisis of Chinese

---

[1]　Ministère de l'agriculture et du commerce, Document sur le commerce extérieur, Chine et Indochine, Faits commerciaux n°12, p. 101.

[2]　Archives Nationales de France. F12. 7057. rapports du commerce extérieur de Chine en 1865. p.82.

[3]　Ministère de l'agriculture et du commerce et des travaux publics, Document sur le commerce extérieur, Chine et Indochine, Faits commerciaux n°45, p. 93.

silks since the 1870s is hardly mentioned in the report: the acceleration of the mechanization of the silk textile industry in France since the 1870s.

2. The acceleration of the mechanization of the silk industry in France since 1870

In France, the innovations of the silk textile techniques began already during the 18th century. Silk weaving is a rather long and delicate operation before the 18th century, because each color of the pattern must be introduced not its own shuttle. At this point, several weavers have to work in one loom to ensure manufacturing. The silk loom is first simplified by Basile Bouchon, which uses a perforated tape to program a loom in 1725. Three years later, this invention was perfected by Jean-Baptiste Falcon (Bouchon's assistant) who replaced the perforated tape with a series of perforated cards allowing better control of the textile machine[1]. From 1745 to 1755, another inventor, Jacques Vaucanson, once again improved the Bouchon and Falcon professions by automating them by hydraulics and controlling them with similar cylinders[2].

But it was the invention of the semi-automatic loom by Joseph-Marie Jacquard at the beginning of the 19th century that marked the beginning of the modernization of the silk industry. Having studied mechanics in Lyons, Joseph-Marie Jacquard developed the Jacquard loom, known as the Jacquard craft, in 1801. This machine combines the techniques of the Bouchon needles, the perforated cards of Falcon and the cylinder of Vaucanson[3]. Enclosed in a trunk at the top of the loom, the Jacquard device has four main elements. A transom holds sus-

---

① J-C. Heudin. Les créateures artificielles: des automates aux mondes virtuels. Paris. Editions Odile Jacob. 2008. p.73.

② H. Jorda. Le métier, la chaîne et le Réseau : petite histoire de la vie ouvrière. Paris. l' Harmattan. 2002. p. 22.

③ B.Gille. Histoire des techniques. Paris. La Pléiade. 1978. p.718.

pended hooks removable. Under the cross-piece, horizontal needles, twisted on themselves, each form a mouth: the stems of the hooks, before being connected to the warp threads, pass through these loops. Leaning on the left like a spring, the hands are pushed to the right in front of a square moving around an axis whose ribs carry holes. Finally, a series of perforated cards attached to each other are supported and driven by the square: these perforations determine the execution of the drawing. The whole system works as follows. Rotated, the square one face is covered with a cardboard. When the holes coincide on either side, the needles sink. On the contrary, the fullness of the card pushes the needles back, and this recoil causes the corresponding hooks to fall from the mouths. From then on, it is possible to lift the cross-bar, holding only certain hooks, the same ones which will lift the warp threads. The perforations of the card thus control the pushing of the needles, the selection and the automatic lifting of these wires, between which the shuttle must pass. The weaver has one cardboard per piece and maneuvers his cross-piece of the foot. The Jacquard craft made it possible for a single worker to manipulate the loom instead of five before, which greatly elevates the weaving efficiency.[1] It therefore produces at least three to four times more than the hand loom. Moreover, it has greatly facilitated the apprenticeship of the workers, and allows the unlimited employment of women and girls, which was not without interest in the cost price of the labor force. The invention of this profession marks the beginnings of the industrial revolution in France. The contribution of Joseph-Marie Jacquard also brings back many prizes and horrors. The Jacquard craft was further improved by another Jean-Antoine Breton from Lyons, in 1806 and 1817, who dramatically lowered the cost of building the machine[2]. Then there are many other innovations in the Lyons silk factory that were born during the rest of the 19th century, even at the beginning of the 20th century[3].

However, it should be noted that the diffusion of this innovation is very slow in France, which lasted throughout the 19th century. Despite its effectiveness, the Jac-

---

[1]   Archives municipales de Lyon. II 0250 1. J.Huchard. Soierie. Etude biographique de Josèphe-Marie Charles dit Jacquard, inventeur, mécanicien en soierie, 1752—1834.

[2]   J.Huchard. Entre la légende et la réalité. Le véritable inventeur de la mécanique dite à la Jacquard. Bulletin Municipal de la ville de Lyon. No. 5520. 10 mai 1998.

[3]   Pour les détails, consulter P.Vernus. Art, luxe et industrie. Bianchini Férier, un siècle de soieries lyonnaises, 1888—1992. Grenoble. Presse universitaire de Grenoble. 2006.P. Vernus. L'innovation dans la fabrique lyonnaise de soierie au tournant du XIXe et du XXe siècle. L'exemple de Bianchini Férier. Lyon innove. Inventions et brevets dans la soierie lyonnaise au XVIIIe et XIXe siècle. Lyon. EMCE. 2009. P.Vernus.Art, luxe et industrie. Bianchini Férier, un siècle de soieries Lyonnaises. 1888—1992. Grenoble. Presses universitaires de Grenoble. 2006.

quard loom was very difficult to popularize at the beginning of his invention[1]. One important cause is that it is badly accepted by the silk workers (the Canuts) who see in him a possible cause of unemployment. Many social movements have taken place to resist the popularization of this innovation in France, the best known of which is the Révolte des canuts in 1831[2]. For this reason, in 1834, thirty-three years after the invention, there was only 2,885 Jacquard looms among 40,000 looms in France, or only 7.21% of the total[3].

Social tension is not the only reason for the slow diffusion of mechanical trades[4]. Although many historians, such as P. Verley and P. Cayez, tried to explain that French manufacturers tried to preserve their image of quality and the exceptional artistic character of their mechanical products in the face of increasing demand and the rise of foreign competition[5], it must be admitted that the quality of mechanical silks, especially in terms of artistic value, is lower than that of manual silks. According to a research by J. Rojon, before the 1860s, images of silks (especially the rich silks produced) produced in the traditional factories of Lyons are often drawn by designers who possess an exceptional talent of art and who undertake often the Royal missions. In order to save money, the mechanical factories often later use less known artists who make drawings faster, which has greatly simplified the models of silk manufacturing in Lyons. Moreover, in order to adopt the manufacture of the mechanical looms in series, the dyeing of the silks in threads is replaced by the dyeing in piece, while the number of colors is well reduced.

All this further reduces the value of the art of silk products[6].

During the first half of the 19th century, the hand silks of Lyonss were always fa-

---

① In the book Métiers Jacquard et hauts fourmeaux aux origines de l'industrie lyonnaise. Lyon. Presses Universitaires de Lyon. 1878. of P.Cayez, the author wrote that "The first half of the nineteenth century witnessed a wide diffusion of the improved Jacquard". The quantitative basis of this conclusion is the tripling of the number of mechanical trades in France (pp. 144—145). Indeed, although the number of Jacquard trades tripled during the first half of the 19th century, its proportion in all Trades in France is still very modest, which we will show right away. So it is difficult to affirm the success of popularization in the first half of the century.

② J.Perdu. La révolte des canuts: les insurrections lyonnaises, 1831—1834. Paris. Spartacus. 2010. p.2.

③ G.Chauvy. La dure condition des forçats du lux. Historia. N° 648, 2000.12. p.74.

④ J.Rojon. Les soieries lyonnaises dans la seconde moitié du XIXe siècle et au début du XXe siècle : du produits artisanal de luxe au produit industriel de (demi-) luxe. Art & Industrie. Paris. Editions Picard. 2013. pp. 123—126.

⑤ Consulter P.Cayez, Métiers Jacquard et hauts fourmeaux aux origines de l'industrie lyonnaise. p.107.P. Verley. spécialisation industrielles, structures sociales, activités financières et intégration économique internationale au XIXe siècle ; le cas de la Grande-Bretagne et de la France. Revue d'histoire du XIXe siècle. No°23, 2001. p.56.

⑥ J.Rojon. Les soieries lyonnaises dans la seconde moitié du XIXe siècle et au début du XXe siècle : du produits artisanal de luxe au produit industriel de (demi-) luxe. Art & Industrie. Paris. Editions Picard. 2013. pp. 123—126.

vored by nobles and royal courts. Each sovereign, Napoleon I, Louis XVIII, Louis Philipe, hastened often to pass generous orders to the manufacturers of Lyonss[1]. High-quality silky fabrics are also very fashionable among wealthy classes in Europe and the United States. For them, silks do not only mean clothing, but also the social marker[2]. Due to its high artistic value and its social significance, the nobility and the wealthy class prefer to buy craft products instead of mechanical crafts. They form a very solid consumer group for French handmade silks. As a result, manual silks still retain a considerable proportion in the silk market, while hand looms are not replaced by mechanical looms for a long period.

This situation evolved since the 1870s. On the one hand, because of the increased competition of cheap products in other branches of the textile industry, silk manufacturers were obliged to reduce the price of their products. A silk manufacturing crisis took place in the early 1870s, which was the result of the war and the workers' revolution of 1870—1871. During and after this crisis, the rich fabrics are neglected and the market lost by the silk in the making of the clothes is won by the woollens. According to the description of A.Beauquis, the labor inspector in Grenoble at the time, "Fashion is, moreover, very adjusted... This Fashion is adopted by all classes of society... No matter the quality of the raw material."[3] This trend can also be confirmed by statistics. The production value of silk fabrics in France dropped from 561 million francs in the early 1870s to 291 million francs in the early 1880s, but the value of wool production in France rose from 666 million francs to 780 million francs of francs[4]. Under such circumstances, the French weavers, who had appeared to lose interest in the mechanical looms, were obliged to lower the price of silk products to reoccupy the market.

On the other hand, we have pointed out in Chapter II that a sharp drop in the price of silk raw materials after the 1870s led to an expansion of the French silk market, which required the silk textile industry increase the quantity of production. In order to both reduce the cost and increase the quantity of production, French silk manufacturers began to use the new technique on a larger scale from the 1870s.

---

[1] Pour les détails, consulter M. Bouzard-Tricou. les relations Lyon-Russie, à travers les archives de soirie lyonnaise, aux XVIIIe et XIXe siècle. Cahiers d'histoire. No°3—4. 1990. p.303—319. et M. Bouzard-Tricou. Analyse et catalogue raisonné de la production des frère Grand, fabricants de soieries à Lyon. 1807—1871, d'après les archives de la maison Tassinari et Chatel. Mémoire de maitrise. Université Lumière-Lyon 2. 1986. Vol 1. pp.21—25.

[2] H.Medick. Une culture de la considération. Les vêtements et leurs couleurs à Laichingen entre 1850 et 1820. Annales HSS. No°4. 1995. pp.75—774.

[3] A.Beauquis. Histoire économique de la soie. Grenoble. Grands établissements de l'imprimerie générale. 1910. p.217.

[4] M. Levy-Leboyer et F. Bourguignon.L'économie Française au XIXe siècle. Analyse macro-économique. p. 59.

TableV-2-A Number of silk mechanical looms in France, 1801—1914

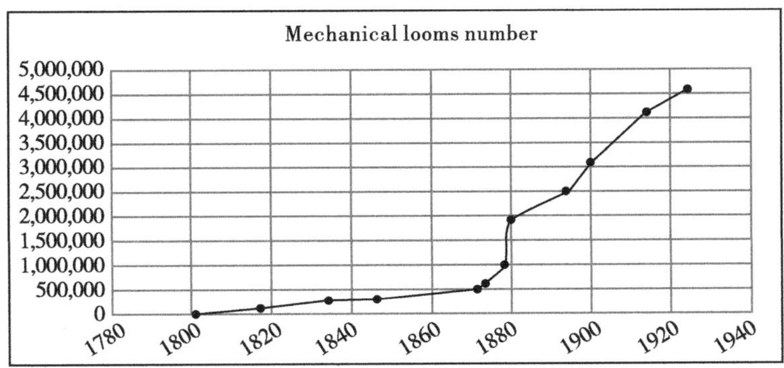

Table V-2-B Proportion of silk looms in France, 1801—1924

Years	1801	1834	1871	1900	1914	1924
Mechanical looms number	1	2,885	5,000	30,638	40,766	45,454
Manual looms number	6,999	37,115	115,000	56,043	17,270	5,413
Total	7,000	40,000	120,000	86,681	58,036	50,876
Mecanizafion rate	≈0%	7.21%	4.17%	35.61%	70.24%	89.34%

Graph V-2-C Proportion of mechanical looms of silk in France, 1801—1924

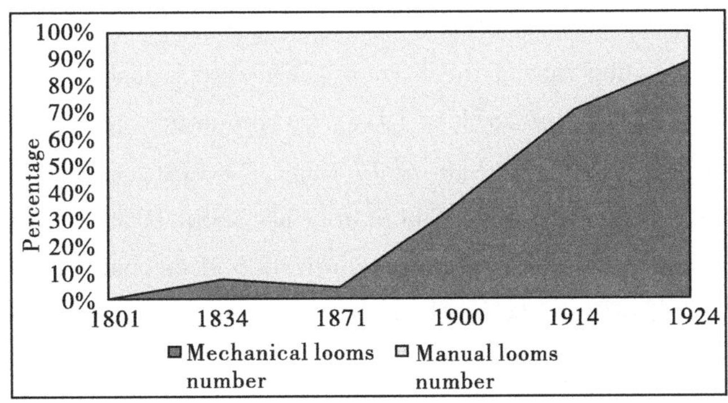

Table V-2-D Distribution of the silk looms in France in 1880—1914

Departements	1880	1894	1900	1914
Ain	378	655	1,215	1,147
Ardèche	773	1,469	1,710	2,719
Drôme	706	1,075	1,310	1,421

（续表）

Departements	1880	1894	1900	1914
Gard	0	0	0	0
Isère	11,336	12,438	15,315	18,747
Loire	2,421	3,604	4,691	8,844
Haute-Loire	0	0	0	495
Puy-de-Dôme	0	50	80	0
Rhône	1,604	3,778	4,312	5,137
Sa6ne-et-Loire	116	531	595	885
Svoie	1,046	798	810	1,031
Haute-Savoie	448	650	650	350
Total	18,828	25,008	30,688	40,766

According to the data in Table V-2-A, from 1834 to 1870, the number of mechanical looms rose from 2,885 to about 5,000, which is only a rise of 2,115. However, after this year, the looms are rapidly vulgarized into France. The number of mechanical trades in France rose from 5,000 at the beginning of the 1870s to 10,000 at the end of this decade, and then exceeded 20,000 in 1880. And then, this amount rose to 30,000 at the beginning of the 20th century and reached 40,000 before the Great War. In terms of the mechanization rate of the French silk textile industry, the growth was also only apparent after 1871. From 1871 to 1914, the proportion of mechanical looms rose from 4.17% to 70.24%, an expansion of 17 times. The process of mechanization lasts until after the Great War. Until 1924, there are only about 10% of looms in France that are not mechanical. Geographically, the popularization of mechanical looms is accompanied by a strong push of the silk textile industry in the peripheral departments around Rhone (where is the city of Lyons).

We have mentioned above that an important advantage of the mechanical trade is that it greatly facilitates the apprenticeship of the workers and considerably lowers the demand for the skill of the weavers, which will reduce the cost of labor for silk production. In the search for cheap labor, many of the Lyons factories moved their new factories to the peripheral departments. At Langjahr, owner of a silk factory written at the end of the year 1879: "What would make me decide in favor of Argentiere is that labor is excessively cheap in the country ... The day of the workers is from 1F to 1.25F while in

Vizille, Bourgoin, Voiron we pay a regular day 2.25 to our pickers and 2.5 to our weavers for a regular day."[1] From 1880 to 1914, the Isère alone accounts for almost half of the mechanical trades in the Rhône valley region. The Loire became the second major center for the mechanical production of silk, surpassing the Rhône after 1900. The diffusion of the new weaving technique is also remarkable in other departments such as Ain, Ardèche, Drôme, Saône-et-Savoie and others.

Moreover, the absolute quantity of the mechanical looms of the French silk industry is the highest in the world until the end of the 19th century (even the percentages of the mechanical trades in France are lower than those of the United States and the United States, Germany, see Table V−3). In 1871, there were 17,000 mechanical looms worldwide, of which 5,000 were used in France. The total number of mechanical trades rose to 82,600 in 1893, and France had 26,000. The other 56,600 mechanical trades are distributed as: 15,000 in the United States, 12,000 in Germany, 8,000 in Austria, 7,200 in Switzerland, 3,600 in Italy, 1,600 in Russia, and so on[2]. In 1898 there were 30,638 mechanical trades in France. This quality is superior to that of other countries. These mechanical looms, in addition to a large quantity of hand looms, ensured the place of the first silk manufacturer of the world during the 19th century[3].

TableV−3 Levels of mechanization of the silk textile industry of some industrial countries in the world in 1898 and 1910[4]

	1898				1910			
	Mechanical looms	Manual looms	Total	Mechanical rate	Mechanical looms	Manual looms	Total	Mechanical rate
France	30,638	56,043	86,681	35.61%	40,766	17,270	58,036	70.24%
United States	16,000	10,000	26,000	61.54%	78,000	3,000	81,000	96.30%
Germany	10,000	9,600	19,600	51.02%	32,000	9,000	41,000	78.05%

---

[1] P.Cayez. Crises et croissance de l'industrie lyonnaise 1850−1900. Paris. Editions CNRS. p.59.

[2] V−V. Germaine. L'industrie de la soie dans les Alpe du Nord. In. Revue de géographie alpine. pp.131—132.

[3] However, it should be noted that the advantage on the path of mechanization compared to other countries is only maintained until the end of the 19th century. At the level of the proportion of mechanical trades, France and already exceeded by some rival countries in the last years of the 19th century With the competition of the United States, the superiority of France on the absolute quantity of the mechanical trades, later, is also lost before the Great War.

[4] A. Beauquis. Histoire économiques de la soie. Grenoble. Grands établissements de l'imprimerie générale. 1910. p. 266—267.

（续表）

	1898				1910			
	Mechanical looms	Manual looms	Total	Mechanical rate	Mechanical looms	Manual looms	Total	Mechanical rate
Switzerland	11,000	23,000	34,000	32.35%	20,000	6,000	26,000	76.92%
Russia			8,000				17,000	
Italy			5,500				14,000	
England			12,500				8,000	

At the same time, there was a tendency of concentration production in the silk industry in France with the acceleration of mechanization throughout the 19th century. According to the data in Table V-4, the total number of looms (hand and machine) rose from 7,000 to 120,000 during the years 1801—1871, and then decreased to 86,681 in 1900 with the decline in the number of looms, multiplying by 12.4 times for a century. By comparison, the number of factories in France is growing very slowly. It rose from 220 of 1801 to 236 in 1900, only an increase of 7%. The average quantity of trades per factory in France, as a result, rose from 32 in 1801 to 367 in 1900 (the number of mechanical looms rose from 0 to 130 for a century), which means a very obvious concentration of production during this period. In other words, the size of the silk factory in France increased very rapidly during the 19th century, when the organization of silk textile production in France was transformed from workshops to large factories.

Table V-4 Number of looms and mechanical looms per establishment in the silk textile industry in France, 1801—1924[①]

Years	1801	1834	1871	1900
Mechanical looms number	1	2,885	5,000	30,638
Manual looms number	6,999	37,115	115,000	56,043
Total	7,000	40,000	120,000	86,681
Mechanization rate	≈0%	7.21%	4.17%	35.61%
Number of establishment	220	422	386	236

---

① P.Cayez, Métiers Jacquard et hauts fourmeaux aux origines de l'industrie lyonnaise. p.70. p.167. P.Clerget. L'industrie de la soie de France à Vallée du Rhône. Les Etudes rhodaniennes. Vol.5. N°1.1929.p.22.

（续表）

Years	1801	1834	1871	1900
Number of mechanical looms by every establishment	0	7	13	130
Number of looms by every establishment	32	95	311	367

3. Incompatibility of Chinese silk with the French mechanical textile industry

Let us return to the problem of the quality of Chinese silks. Why has the acceleration of the mechanization of the silk textile industry in France since the 1870s led to insufficient quality of Chinese silks?

（1）In another report of the Lyonsnais, the opinion is: "People have often represented China as possessing highly sophisticated industrial processes and a population of an intelligent mediocrity. On the contrary, looms and products, especially the silk fabric, are generally inferior to ours."[1] According to their opinon, the Chinese silk textile industry, which had a great reputation, is becoming very old and increasingly outmoded. In fact, it is not the quality of the Chinese who becomes worse, but the appreciation of the French on the quality of silks has changed since 1870. With the elevation of the level of the mechanism of silk textile industry in France during the 19th, the French weavers gradually change their demands on the characteristics of the silky materials they use: more regular, less corky, more tenacious, and so on. Due to the defects existing in the processes of the old silk industry as well as in the quality criterion of silk in China, these characteristics most demanded by Western buyers are just what the Chinese silks lacked. This is why the Lyons merchants complain that the underdevelopment of the old silk industry in China directly leads to the poor quality of Chinese silk. We shall show in the text below the main deficiencies in the traditional techniques of silk prodution and in the traditional silk classification system in China which lead to the incompatibility with the textile industry of La France.

In the processes of silk production, the poor quality of Chinese silkworm seeds have a bad influence on the quality of Chinese silk. Seed selection is the first step in the education of silkworms. Seeds with good quality are a most basic condition for a good harvest

---

[1] Ministère de l'agriculture et du commerce, Document sur le commerce extérieur, Chine et Indochine, Faits commerciaux n°12, p. 149.

of cocoons. During the 19th century, all Chinese seeds were made by the peasants. Although there are already some traditional methods to eliminate weaker seeds, the quality of the seeds they make is quite inferior. According to the observations of a Japanese scientist, before the 20th century, the infection rate of the silkworm epidemic are also high, on average 30%—40%[1]. With the bad seeds, the amount of cocoon production per unit in China is quite discreet: even at the beginning of the 20th century, only 35 kilograms of cocoons can be harvested on average by per 1 taël of seeds in Yangzi, even 10% less in Sichuan, and 20 kilograms to Canton[2]. These quantities of production are much less than those of Japan during the same period, where we harvest on average 63 kilograms per taël of seeds, besides that there are many useless cocoons in it.

Secondly, as mentioned in the previous section, before the introduction of the perfect technique to perish the chrysalis in 1875[3], the peasants in Yangzi prefer to reeling silk with fresh cocoons. This means that all the reeling jobs have to be finished in 10 days, otherwise the butterflies will go out and spoil the cocoons. In such a short period of time, it is difficult for them to select and classify the cocoons, which often leads to irregular silks at the level of color and fineness in the same silk bales[4]. Moreover, the hurry of the pickers during this short period often lowers the level of care of the reeling, which will also deteriorate the quality of the silk[5].

Thirdly, the traditional Chinese asplet (or reel) turns by human energy (the petal by foot or the crank), so its speed is not stable and regular. This last defect often leads to the inhomogeneity of the fineness and to the weakness of the tenacity of the silk. Moreover, at that time, the basin in which the cocoons are titrated is often heated by a traditional fire stove in China, which can not ensure the stability of the water temperature in the basin. Changing the water temperature will have a negative influence on the homogeneity of the color of the silk. As a result, the color of Chinese silk can be variable even in the same lot[6]. All these problems above will destroy the homogeneity of silk, which is an important specificity demanded by western mechanical weaving. In the modern textile industry, the word "inhomogeneity" of silk is almost synonymous with the words "poor quality".

---

① 紫藤章.清国蚕丝业一斑.第 57 页.

② 王翔.近代中国传统丝绸业转型研究.第 140—141 页.

③ In 1875, a silk merchant named XU Shou（徐寿）introduced the modern method to perish the chrysalis in China.

④ 朱新予,李锡畴.浙江丝绸史.杭州:浙江人民出版社,第 247 页.

⑤ 无锡县志.(第二册),南京:江苏人民出版社,第 945 页.

⑥ 费孝通.江村经济.北京:商务印书馆,2003,第 179—180 页.

Finally, under the old silk production condition in China, the quality of the silk depends directly on the skill of the silk-maker. "With the same amount of cocoons, a trained skidder or skilled spinner can produce more silk, the fineness is more homogeneous and the color is brighter."[1] The Taiping rebellion that ravaged the Yangzi region until the mid-1860s seriously reduced the number of skilled spinners in the region. The lack of skilled spinners should be another important techniqueal cause for the deterioration of the quality of Chinese silk from the second half of the 1860s[2].

(2) In terms of the qualitative criterion, the main problems existing in the ancient silk classification system in China are that it is impossible to judge exactly the specificity and quality of certain silk nature according to its criterion, and that the silks are not necessarily homogeneous in the same class, even in the same bale, as what a French consul at Shanghai says in his report: "Each bullet contains very different elements in terms of quality, title, color, and gummy or defective parts of it; It would be difficult to do otherwise, since each consists of the annual harvest of a large number of cultivators; In each village one or two small merchants buy in detail these crops, which they then sell to wholesale merchants, who sort out the qualities of the different silks and ball them with such an address to slip some parts of lower qualities. It takes a lot of experience to discern them."[3]

These defects decide that, first, the old criterion of the classification of Chinese silk will no longer adapt to the demand for silk production in western countries during the second half of the 19th century, when the demand of mechanical textile industry to the homogeneity of the raw materials is more and more vulgar, as we have already pointed out; If we go more deeply in this question, the old criterion of silk chops from China will no longer be able to continue to be used in international trade after the 1870s, because "business to be delivered", which prospered after the connection of the telegraphy between Europe and East Asia in 1871, demanded chops of the exchanged silks well specified.

The warnings of the western merchants during the years 1871—1873 did not immediately draw the attention of the merchants to the problems of the quality and the quality criterion of their silks, which led to the difficulty of flow and the decline in Chinese silk prices on the European market from the third quarter of 1874. According to a report from

<hr>

① 周学浚.(同治)湖州府志.卷31,台北:成文出版社,1970年,第973页.
② 铃木智夫.洋务运动の研究.东京:汲古书院,1992年,第293页.
③ Archives du Ministères des affaires étrangères. Shanghai 1856—1860. 307CCC 3. p.106.

the *Shen newspaper*, "Last year (1872), the silk brand Chuling (春翎牌) flowed very easy to 520—522 taëls by bale at the Shanghai market or 26 shillings by bale at the London market; Now its price has fallen to 400—405 taels at Shanghai and 20 shillings at London, but this kind of silk is still very difficult to sell. That is why the total quantity of silks in warehouses is only 7,500 bales at Shanghai during the last year, but it has exceeded 10,000 bullets at Shanghai for the moment. Western merchants was pleased to buying Chinese silks at Shanghai last year, but they hesitate a lot now."[1] According to Chinese Customs statistics, the languorous situation of the Chinese silk on the international market continues since that year, and their prices have scarcely exceeded 400 taëls (except 1876) untill the end of the 19th century. This is partly due to lower transport costs and increased competition in the European silk market (after the prosperous Japanese silk industry and the restoration of Italian silk), but also to the defects on the qualities of Chinese silks.

Table V-5-A The evolution of average prices of raw silk in Shanghai (customs taëls/piculs)[2]

Years	Prices	Years	Prices	Years	Prices	Years	Prices
1862	350	1870	515	1878	330	1886	300
1863	350	1871	503	1879	321	1887	320
1864	499	1872	490	1880	300	1888	306
1865	420	1873	500	1881	350	1889	315
1866	500	1874	300	1882	307	1890	340
1867	485	1875	285	1883	320	1891	281
1868	517	1876	443	1884	273	1892	306
1869	465	1877	340	1885	272	1893	315

①　申报.1873 年 7 月 5 日,上海图书馆馆藏资源.
②　王翔.近代中国传统丝绸业转型研究.第 78—79 页.

Graph V-5-B The evolution of average prices of raw silk in Shanghai (customs taëls / piculs)

The Shanghai Silk Merchant Union promulgated a project to reform the silk trade in the early 1880s, seeking for prohibiting on the phenomenon of fraud in the process of silks exchange, by packing silks strictly according to their chops[1]. Henceforth, the number of cases of fraud gradually decreased in the process of commercial circulation of silks.

However, the fraud is a general problem that existed in the 1840s. As A.Stanziani analyzes in his publications, this is a general problem related to entry into new markets, the changes of which may be linked to legal or regulatory developments.[2] In fact, the fundamental insufficiencies of Chinese silks still exist in the process of production and in the means of classifying the qualities of silks. The silk industry of China still has a long way to walk[3]. If it wants to continue to maintain its competitiveness on the world market and on the French market, it is necessary to evolve vis-à-vis an industrial revolution in the world.

---

[1]　申报.1873 年 2 月 6 日,上海图书馆馆藏资源.

[2]　For the details of A.Stanziani's discussion about the realtionship between the frauds and market economy, consult A.Stanziani. Histoire de la qualité alimentaire, 18e-20e siècles. Paris. Seuil. 2005. A.Stanziani. La fraude dans l'angro-alimentaire. Genèse Historique : La falsification du vin en France 1880-1905. Revue d'histoire moderne et contemporaine. No° 2. 2003. A.Stanziani. Information and norms in the coordination of markets. Commencial fraud in France. 1871-1905. In Analisis de Redes en Historia economica. CD-Rom. Bellaterra. Enero.2005. A.Stanziani. 《 La fraude : un équipement juridique de l'action économique. L'exemple dumarché du vin en France au XIXe siècle 》. in G. Béaur, H. Bonin et C. Lemercier. Fraude, contrefaçon et contrebande de l'antiquité à nos jours. Genève. Droz. 2006.

[3]　Dans nos sources, on ne peut guère trouver l'avertissement pareil que ceux-ci dans les années 1870 après cette réforme.

Ⅲ Reaction to the industrial revolution of the west: modernization of the silk industry in China

We have learn from the previous section that the incompatibility between the traditional crafts of the Chinese silk industry and the western silks textile industry, because of insufficient quality of Chinese silks. In this section, we will explain the reaction of silk producers in China to this incompatibility. Indeed, in order to adapt the silk industry to the quality of western silk producers (especially to the demands of France and the United States, where located the most buyers of Chinese silk), China began its modernization process: factories using mechanical reeling made their appearances in Yangzi as early as the 1860s and in Guangdong as early as the 1870s; Chinese sericulture began to evolve in the modernization after the end of the 19th century; The first modern establishment to control the quality of silk has also disappeared since the late 1870s.

By studying the process and result of the modernization of silk filature in China before the 1914, we will answer several important questions in this chapter: what is the result of the mechanization of the Chinese silk filature industry? What does modernization lead to the organization of Chinese silks production? Did the diffusion of agricultural science in China have developed Chinese sericulture? When and how China has established a quality control system for silks? What is the relationship of the modernization of the Chinese silk industry (silk filature, sericulture and quality control of silk in China) with the export of silk?

1. Modernization of the silk-reeling industry in Yangzi

An article, entitled "Mechanical Reeling" (机器缫丝说) [1], is published on the *Shen newspaper* on 5 February 1882, which leads to a debate on the need for mechanization of the reeling industry in China. From February 5, 1882 to December 2, 1882, supporters and opponents discussed the advantages and disadvantages of mechanizing the silk reeling industry in China by publishing a series of articles on the *Newspaper of*

---

[1] 机器缫丝说.申报.1882 年 2 月 5 日,上海图书馆馆藏资源.

Shen[1]. In this debate, supporters believe that the use of steam reeling is on the direction of progress, as the adoption of this new technique will improve the quality of Chinese silk and thus strengthen its competitiveness on the international market; Opponents consider that the competition of mechanical filature will lead to the unemployment of craftsmen, that the phenomenon that men and women work together will lead to the decadence of social morality, and that the non-existence of the tax on cocoons and on mechanical silk will lead to tax loss to the government, and so on. The explosion of this debate remarked that mechanization had already become an irresistible tendency for the Chinese to reflect and discuss.

When the Chinese discuss the problem of the necessity of the silkreeling mechanism, foreign silk merchants have already began to attempt to create modern reeling factories in China. The first modern silk filature are introduced by foreign silk companies in China.

The first attempt to create a mechanical reeling factory in China was carried out by Jardine Matheson and Co. of Shanghai (怡和洋行). Having discovered that the price of mechanical silk is 6 shillings higher than that of manual silk per picul on the London market, James Whittall, head of the Jardine Matheson and Co. office in Shanghai, addressed in 1859 a request to the headquarters of the company in Hong Kong for the creation of a mechanical reeling factory in Shanghai[2]. In 1861, a mechanical reeling factory belonging to that company was opened in Shanghai, the name of which is "Shanghai Silk Reeling Company (上海纺丝局)". This silk reeling factory has 100 iron hoists with steam energy manufactured in Hong Kong and employs several experienced French spinners for the training of new employees[3]. Thanks to its superior quality, the silks produced by this reeling mill are quiet demanded on the international market, so 100 reels are added to this factory in the following year (1863)[4].

The Shanghai Silk Reeling Company fell shortly since of the inadequate supply of

---

① The articles published in the *Newspaper of Shen* are：机器缫丝说.申报.1882 年 2 月 5 日,上海图书馆馆藏资源.论机器缫丝妨利后.申报.1882 年 6 月 4 日,上海图书馆馆藏资源.观缫丝局记.申报.1882 年 8 月 3 日,上海图书馆馆藏资源.缫丝三利说.申报.1882 年 8 月 9 日,上海图书馆馆藏资源.机器缫丝为害论.申报.1882 年 9 月 2 日,上海图书馆馆藏资源.闽西友论缫丝局后.申报.1882 年 10 月 20 日,上海图书馆馆藏资源.再论机器缫丝.申报.1882 年 10 月 23 日,上海图书馆馆藏资源.照译论缫丝局书.申报.1882 年 11 月 28 日,上海图书馆馆藏资源.机器缫丝有益于华民说.申报.1882 年 12 月 2 日,上海图书馆馆藏资源.

② Archives Nationale de France. F12.7058.Rapports conoulaires antérieurs Chine 1809—1906(3). 10, mars 1896. Les filatures à Shanghai. p.5.

③ 上海丝绸志.上海:上海社会科学院出版社,1998 年,第 156 页.

④ 孙晓莹.晚清生丝业国际竞争力研究——兼与同期日本比较.第 32 页.

cocoons, since at that time there is very few merchant who deals with the cocoon on the Yangzi market and provides cocoons to mechanical filature. The reason for the rarity of this kind of merchants is, first of all, that the Chinese do not have a perfect method for perishing the pupae and preserving the cocoons, which is a great obstacle to the formation of the cocoon market. As has been shown in the previous text, traditional methods of perishing chrysalises in China will damage the quality of the cocoons. In addition, the cocoons sells are not sure because customers (mechanical filature) who buy cocoons are very rare in the 1860s. In 1866, Jardine Matheson and Co. sent Huang Jipu (黄吉甫), a comprador Chinese in Jiaxing (嘉兴, a town in Zhejiang province, where is an important sericultural area of the province), who tries to create a cocoon agency equipped with cocoons ovens, in order to solve the problem of supplying cocoons. However, this agency failed to open up because of opposition from the local government of Zhejiang. Finally, this first mechanical filature in China was forced to close in the same year (1866) because of insufficient supply of raw materials[1].

Although this first attempt ended in failure, it demonstrated to the Chinese the first exemple for the organization and operation of a modern silk filature. In addition, the silk produced by the Shanghai Silk Reeling Company confirms that mechanical silks will be the future of the Shanghai silk export market. At the same time, the first attempt of the division of cocoon titration work and sericulture which enabled the breeders to be relieved of the techniqueal concerns of the titration of silk, also hampered the development of sericulture[2].

In 1875, Xu Shou (徐寿), a Chinese scientist and translator, introduced western techniques to perish the chrysalis and dry the cocoons in China[3]. The new chrysalis-like choping machine resembles any number of drawers, and is then pushed into the grooves which are to receive them. When all are filled, and everything is hermetically sealed, a cock is opened which lets out the steam which comes from a boiler whose water is boiling. Those vapor fills the whole machine, and a few minutes afterwards the cocoons are removed from which all the chrysalises are stifled. After stifling, the cocoons are carried into granaries; They are placed on clayons for drying[4]. This new machine allows the pu-

---

① 浙江通志厘金门稿·浙厘上.1919 年,第 55 页,浙江图书馆馆藏资源.

② Mau Chuan-Hui. L'introduction en Chine des sciences et des techniques européennes concernant l'industrie de la soie après la guérre de l'Opium. Etudes chinoises. Vol. XX. No°1—2. pp.210—211.

③ 北华捷报.1875 年 4 月 1 日,上海图书馆馆藏资源.

④ For more informations, consult L. De Teste. Du commerce des soies et soieries en France, considéré dans ses rapports avec celui des autres états. Avignon. Lithographe de la Ville. 1830. pp. 45—46.

pils to be choked by steam, avoiding wetting of the cocoons, which improves the quality of the dried cocoons. Thanks to this techniqueal progress, a major techniqueal obstacle has been eliminated for the supply of raw materials to the mechanical reeling industry in China, as published on the *North China Herald*: "The Chinese introduced the method of conservation of the cocoon in long-term, which will be an essential element for the success of the reeling industry in China."[1]

Mechanical reeling industry in Yangzi, correspondingly, is experiencing its first prosperous period since the late 1870s. In 1878, American Russell and Co. (旗昌洋行) established a mechanical reeling factory in Shanghai, the Kei Chong Filature Association (旗昌丝厂). This reeling factory invites a Frenchman, Paul Brunat as the techniqueian, as it is equipped by 50 reels of the European model. In 1881, the number of reels in this reeling mill increased to 200, thanks to the success of its products on the export market[2]. The Jardine Matheson and Cie engages to establish another mechanical reeling in Shanghai in 1882 with a 200 basins. In the same year (1881), the English Iveson and Co. (公平洋行) opened another reeling factory, the Iveson Reeling mill in Shanghai, which owns 104 reels of the European model. This was later imitated by English Glimour and Co. in 1891, by English Dyce and Co. in 1892, by English E. Bavier and Co. in 1893, and by German Arnhold Karberg and Co. in 1894.

In 1891, the Kei Chong Reeling mill was sold to its French techniqueian Paul Brunat because of the bankruptcy of the Russell and American Company, so it was transformed into a limited company under the name of The Shanghai Silk Filature Limited (宝昌丝厂), with a capital of 2,000 shares of 100 taëls, of which 1,619 is subscribed. Later, the business of this company is very prosperous and leased the Iveson and Co, which gives it two establishments, with 958 basins producing 1,580 piculs of silk per year and making it become the largest reeling company in China at the moment[3].

On the other hand, Chinese capital reeling companies also appeared in the Yangzi region from the 1880s. The first mechanical reeling company in Shanghai was established by Huang Zhuoqing (黄佐卿) in 1882, which is a " Zhejiang Origin[4]" comprador of

---

① 北华捷报.1875 年 4 月 1 日,上海图书馆馆藏资源.

② 今与昔.北华捷报社,第 10 页,上海图书馆馆藏资源.

③ Archives Nationale de France. F12.7058.Rapports consulaires antérieurs Chine 1809—1906(3). 10, mars 1896. Les filatures à Shanghai. p.6.孙毓棠:中日甲午战争前外国资本在中国经营的近代工业.中国近三百年社会经济史论集第 5 集.香港:崇文书店,1974 年,第 187 188 页.施敏雄.清代丝织工业的发展,台北:中国学术著作奖助委员会,1968 年,第 83—84 页.上原重美.支那蚕业大观.东京:冈田日荣堂,1929 年,第 233—241 页.藤本实也.支那蚕丝业研究.东京:东亚研究所,1943 年,第 124—125 页.

④ 农商公报.1915 年第 16 期,第 14 页.

an English company①, and "a leader of the Corporation of the silk merchants of Shang-hai②". This reeling factory is named as "Gong-he-yong" (公和永丝厂), which is e-quipped by 100 reels of the European model at the beginning of the opening. This Chinese reeling invites a foreign engineer Ang.H.Maertens to direct the techniqueal affairs③.

Ten years later (1892), with the prosperity of the business, the number of reels of this reeling factory increases to 442. At the same time, Huang creates a new reeling factory (the Xinxiang Reeling Factory, 新祥丝厂) with 416 reels in another borough of Shanghai. These two reeling factory made him become one of the biggest industrialists in China at the time. Following the opening of the Gong-he-yong Reeling Factory, several other mechanical reeling factories were successively established in Shanghai: the Kunji Silk Fialture (坤记丝厂) opened in 1884, the Yuncheng Reeling Factory (裕成丝厂) opened in 1886, the Yangchang Reeling factory(延昌丝厂) opened in 1890, the Lunhua Reeling Factory(纶华) opened in 1892, the Jinhua Reeling Factory (锦华丝厂) opened in 1892, the Xinchang Reeling Factory(信昌丝厂, bought form old filature belonging to the American Dyce and Co.) created in 1893, Zhenghe Silk Filature(正和丝厂) opened in 1894 and the Qiankang Reeling Factory (乾康丝厂) opened in 1894. Untill the end of 1894④, there are 15 mechanical reeling factories in the Yangzi region.

---

① 汪敬虞:从中国对外生丝贸易的变迁看缫丝业中资本主义的产生和发展.中国经济史研究.2001 年第 2 期,第 30 页.

② 北华捷报.1902 年 7 月 16 日,上海图书馆馆藏资源.

③ 上海研究资料.上海:上海通志馆,1936 年,第 5 页.

④ The informations about opening of the Chinese capital mechanical filatures come from: Archives Nationale de France. F12.7058.Rapports consulaires antérieurs Chine 1809–1906(3). 10, mars 1896. les filatures à Shanghai. p. 9.徐新吾.中国近代缫丝工业史.第 140–141 页.彭泽益.中国近代手工业史资料 1840—1919,第二卷.第 1430 页.铃木智夫.洋务运动の研究.第 342 页.江南事情·经济.东京:日本东亚同文会,1919 年,第 150—152 页. Nevertheless, there are divergent views on these different sources at the level of names and dates of opening of these reeling factories with Chinese capital. We believe that the notes in the letter of the French Consul in Shanghai written in 1896 (the first source cited) is more reliable, so we kept the information offered by this letter during the divergences.

Table V-6 Mechanical reeling factory in the Ynagzi Region at the end of 1894[1]

Name	Adress	Number of basins	Production (piculs)	Owner
The Shanghai silk filature limited (North Suzhou creek)	上海垃圾桥			Paul Brunat, français lveson et Cic anghise, mas
The Shanghai silk filature limited (South Suzhou creek)	上海垃圾桥	958	1580	prise en bail par Brunat
Jardine Matheson & Co Silk Filamre	新闸路	400	660	Jardine Matheson et Cie anghise
E. Bavier & Co Silk Filature	厦门路	252	420	E.Bavier, français
Gilmour & Co Silk Filature		188		Glilvour, anghis
Arnold Karberg & Co	唐家弄	344	570	Amold Karberg et Cie allermnde
公 和 永 Kung-Ho-yun Steam Silk Filamre	新闸路			黄佐卿 Huang Zuo- qing, comprador d' une maison anghise
新祥 Xin-Xiang Steam Filature	杨树浦	858	1,340	黄佐卿 Huang Zuoqing
信昌 Xin-Chang Silk Filature Limited	梵皇渡	312	520	马建忠 Ma Jianzhong
纶华 Lun-hua Silk Filature	唐家弄	388	640	叶澄衷 Ye Chengzhong
锦华 Jin-Hua Silk Filature	新闸路	208	340	陶吉斋 Tao Jizhai

[1] Archives Nationale de France. F12.7058.Rapports consulaires antéricurs Chine 1809-1906(3). 10, mars 1896. Les filatures à Shanghai. p.9.

（续表）

Name	Adress	Number of basins	Production (piculs)	Owner
坤记 Kun-ji Silk Filature		168	280	
乾康 Qian-kan Silk Filature	石子街	180	300	沈志云 Shen Zhiyun 吴少圃 Wu Shaopu, compradors de la E. Bavier et Ciep
正和 Zheng-he Silk Filature		60	75	
延昌恒 Ya-chang-heng Silk Filamre	上海垃圾桥	220	238	杨信之, Yang Xinzhi, comprador d'une maison italienne

We can see that foreign firms play a very important role in the creation of the first mechanical reeling factories in Yangzi: reeling factories with foreign capital occupy a considerable part of all reeling factories before 1894; even for some Chinese reeling factories, their owners are often the compradors who work in foreign companies at the same time. There are two causes for the latter phenomenon. First, the creation of new mechanical factories in Yangzi will require techniqueal support and capital support, and foreign firms have advantages both in techniqueal and capital. A typical example is that at the opening of the Gong-he-yong Filature, Chinese owner, Huang Zuoqing (黄佐卿), is obliged to ask the two foreign enginners for techniqueal support. Then, Ang.H.Maertens, the engineer who works in the Reeling of Jardine Matheson and the Reeling of Iveson, is sent to the Reeling of Gong-he-yong for the techniqueal direction[1]. The second cause is that foreign companies profit from extra-territoriality in China. At the same time, they can offer protection of extraterritoriality to Chinese industrialists. This is a cause even more important than the first, because before the signing of the Sino-Japanese *Shimonoseki Treaty* (《马关条约》) in 1895, it is very difficult to create a modern factory in the Yangzi regions under the "Conservative obstruction" (the details of this point will be

---

① 申报.1888 年 9 月 23 日,上海图书馆馆藏资源.

320

discussed later). This is also the reason for geographically concentrating all these reeling factories in Shanghai where it is easier to obtain the protection of foreigners.

Let us return to the debate on the western trade impact on the industrialization of Asian countries. The classic example that historians adopt to study this issue is often the evolution of the cotton industry of India under commercial influence with England. Conventional opinion (for example, affirmed by P. Bairoch in his book *Mythes et paradoxes de l'histoire économique*) is that the exchange with the western countries leads to a deindustrialisation to India following the Industrial Revolution [1]. This point of view has been examined by many historians. In an article published in 1990, S. Subrahmanyam argues that the decline of cotton textile industry India has already begun before the inflow of English industrial products[2]. G. Riello points out in his book *Cotton: The Fabric that Made the Modern World* that the commercial relationship finally leads to a convergence of industrial development between the West and the East[3]. Mau Chuan-Hui has shown in his thesis that the mechanization of the silk textile industry in Europe is advancing techniques of the silk industry in China[4]. Observing trade with western countries on the industrialization of silk reeling in China, we can already confirm that it is foreign commercial companies established in China that started or helped to begin the process of industrialization of Chinese reeling factories. This already proves the positive role of foreign trade during the creation of China's modern industry. Certainly, the surge of foreign trade to Chinese industrialization does not stop at the creation of the first factories, which we shall see later.

The sixth article of the Sino-Japanese *Shimonoseki Treaty* in 1895 opened four new ports in China[5] and stipulated that "the Japanese are allowed to establish factories and imported machinery to all opening ports". [6] Benefiting from the treatment of the more

---

[1]　P. Bairoch. Mythes et paradoxes de l'histoire économique. p.79.

[2]　S. Subrahmanyam. Rural Industry and Commercial Agriculture in the Late Seventeenth-Century South-Eastern India. Past & Present. No°126. 1990. 107—108.

[3]　G. Riello. Cotton: The Fabric that Made the Modern World. New York. Cambridge University Press. pp. 292—294.

[4]　Mau Chuan-Hui. L'industrie de la soie en France et en Chine de la fin du XVIIIe au début du XXe siècle : échanges technologiques, stylistiques et commerciaux. Paris. EHESS. 2002. 2 Vol. Mau Chuan-Hui. L'introduction en Chine des sciences et des techniques européennes concernant l'industrie de la soie après la guérre de l'Opium. Etudes chinoises. Vol. XX. No°1-2. Les techniques séricicoles chinoises dans le développement de la sériciculture française de la fin du XVIIIe siècle au début du XIXe siècle. Cahier d'Histoire et de Philosophie des Sciences. No° 52. Lyon. ENS Editions. 2004. 毛传慧. 清末民初的蚕桑改良——传统与现代之间. 中国近现代行业文化研究——技艺和专业知识的传承与功能. 北京:国家图书馆出版社,2010 年.

[5]　They are Hangzhou(杭州), Suzhou(苏州), Shashi(沙市) et Chongqing(重庆).

[6]　王铁涯. 中国旧约章汇编. 北京:三联书店,1957 年,第 618—619 页.

favored countries, the western countries obtain officially the legitimacy to establish their industries in China (there is not yet Sino-foreign treaties officially addressed the right of creation of factories of foreign countries in China). To resist the economic infiltration of foreigners and to increase his tax revenue, Emperor Guangxu (光绪帝 1871—1908) issued a decree on August 11, 1895, which encouraged Chinese capitalists to set up private Chinese factories. The change in the attitude of the Chinese authorities greatly stimulated the development of the silk-reeling industry in the Yangzi region after 1895[1]. From 1895 to 1899, forty new mechanical reeling factories were established in the region of Yangzi, with a sum of the capital of 5,263,000 Spanish piasters. Among these 40 new reeling factories, 18 are in Shanghai and 22 are dispersed in Suzhou (苏州), Wuxian (吴县), Zhenjiang (镇江) of Jiangsu Province and Hangzhou (杭州), Xiaoshan (萧山), Jiaxing Jiashan (嘉善), Shaoxing (绍兴), Fuyang (富阳), Haiyan (海盐), Pinghu (平湖), Xiashi (硖石) of Zhejiang Province[2]. During the first decade of the 20th century, 36 new reeling factories were opened in the Yangzi region with 4,476,000 Spanish piasters, 21 of which are in Shanghai and 15 are located in the other towns of Jiangsu and Zhejiang[3].

It should be noted that all the reeling factories that appeared after the year 1895 were created by the Chinese[4]. However, this does not mean that foreign firms are completely out of the silk industry in China from the moment. By contrast, they continue to engage indirectly in the production of mechanical silk by lending capital to Chinese reeling factories. According to a survey in Shanghai in 1917, all silk reeling factories in Shanghai borrowed 14.7 million taëls of capital, 6 million of which came from Qianzhuang (钱庄, traditional Chinese banks), 8.5 million from foreign companies, and 0.2 million comes from the Jiangsu bank[5]. In other words, foreign firms provide more than one-half of the working capital to Chinese filatures. This change in the role of foreign firms in the production of mechanical silk in China is due to the very high risk of this industrial branch. Since foreign firms can make a considerable profit by exporting better-quality mechanical silk, it is no longer worthwhile to continue to engage directly in the production chain. Indirect participation in production by lending money allows for-

---

① 朱寿朋.光绪朝东华录(四).北京:中华书局,1984 年,第 3637 页.

② 杜恂诚.民族资本主义与旧中国政府(1840—1937).上海:上海社会科学院出版社,1991 年,第 323—327 页.

③ 汪敬虞.中国近代工业史资料.第二辑,北京:科学出版社,1957 年,第 896—898 页.

④ 汪敬虞.中国近代经济史 1895—1927.下卷,北京:人民出版社,2012 年,第 1634 页.

⑤ 日本农商务省临时产业调查局.支那蚕丝业调查概要.1918 年,第 35—46 页.

eign firms, on the one hand, to avoid taking risks and, on the other hand, to take advantage of the profits of the production chain by the lending interest.

Geographically, Shanghai remains the fastest growing city of the mechanical reeling in the Yangzi region during this period. Until the year 1914, there were a total of 56 mechanical reeling factories in Shanghai, or 4.7 times the number of reeling factories in 1895. Simultaneously, the first reeling factories has also emerged in the provinces of Zhejiang and Jiangsu. Among all the cities of Yangzi, Wuxi (无锡, in Jiangsu Province) is another city, outside Shanghai, where the development of the reeling industry has a remarkable performance. The first reeling factory, Yuchang Reeling (裕昌丝厂, created by Zhou Shunqing 周舜卿), is not opened untill 1904 in this city[1], but this industrial branch evolved very quickly during the following years. Until the year 1910 there were already 7 reeling factories with 1,914 steamers and 623,000 piasters of capital (14% of the total investments in the Yangzi reeling industry) in Wuxi[2]. That makes it become the second big industrial city in Yangzi, just after Shanghai.

Table V-7 Evolution of mechanicalreeling factories in Shanghai, 1895—1914[3]

Years	Number of Filatures	Indice	Number des basins	Indice
1895	12	100		
1896	17	142		
1897	25	208	7,500	100
1898	24	200	7,700	103
1899	17	142	5,800	77
1900	18	150	5,900	79
1901	23	192	7,830	104
1902	21	175	7,306	97
1903	24	200	8,526	114
1904	22	183	7,826	104
1905	22	183	7,610	101

---

① 钱钟汉.周舜卿.工商经济史料丛刊.第 4 辑,北京:文史资料出版社,1984 年,第 105—107 页.

② 高景岳,严学熙.近代无锡蚕丝业资料选辑.南京:江苏人民出版社,1987 年,38—51 页.

③ Les dutus from 1895 to 1910. 上海市档案馆:上海市缫丝工业同业公会档,S37-1-96,第 90 号.中国经济月刊(英文).1925 年 3 月号,第 3—7 页.Les datas from 1911 to 1914 come from D.K Lieu. The Silk Industry of China. Kelly and Walsh edition. 1940. p.94.

（续表）

Years	Number of Filatures	Indice	Number des basins	Indice
1906	23	182	8,026	107
1907	28	233	9,686	129
1908	29	242	10,006	133
1909	35	292	11,085	148
1910	42	350	12,554	167
1911	48	400	13,738	183
1912	48	400	13,392	179
1913	49	408	13,392	179
1914	56	467	14,424	193

In terms of reeling techniques, what the first mechanical reeling factories in Yangzi are equiped are the Italian style reels, the main mechanism of which is an asplet printed by the steam energy above the basin[1]. The spinner sits down in front of the basin, pulls the bundle of cocoons with the baquettes and makes it surround the reeling wheel which turns and unwinds the bundles with silks. The water in the basin is also supplied by the steam, which keeps it in a temperature between 71℃—76℃ [2].

Thanks to the aspirated steam, the speed of rotation of the impeller is almost uniform, which can guarantee the homogeneity of the fineness as well as the tenacity of the silk; In addition, the stability of the water temperature ensures the homogeneity of the color of the silk. From the year 1888, the Yongchang Machinery Company of Shanghai（永昌机器厂）began to manufacture the steam reeling marchine, whose buyer is mainly Gong-he-yong Reeling[3]. Six years later（1894）, several companies succeeded already in making in imitation the reel of the Italian model. Untill the year 1913, all the mechanical reeling factories in Shanghai stopped importing silk reels abroad. In other words, all the reels purchased by the mechanical reeling factories in Shanghai are made

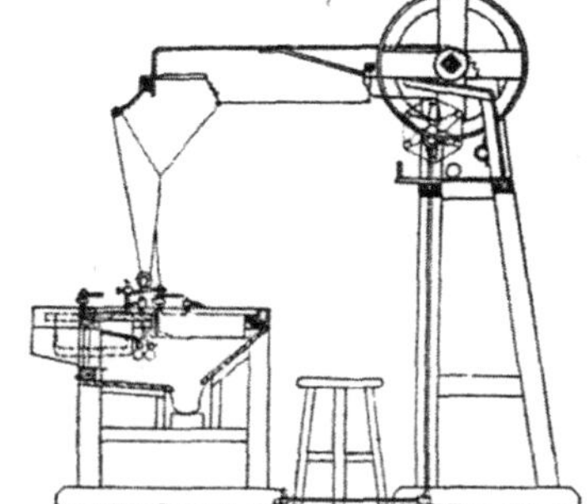

① 孙毓棠.中国近代工业史资料.第一辑,北京:科学出版社,1957年,第971页.
② 王天予.丝蚕学.北京:农业出版社,1986年,第109页.
③ 上海市工商行政管理局.上海民族机器工业.上册,上海:中华书局,1966年,第99页.

in China[1]. Italian silk reels were used in the mechanical reeling factories in Yangzi until the end of the 1920s. The techniqueal renewal did not begin until the late 1920s, when Wang Wanqing introduced the reel in Japanese style in 1929[2].

With the prosperity of the silkreeling industry, the raw materials market of this industrial branch—the cocoon market begins to form in the Yangzi region. The precise information on the date of the appearance of the first companies of the cocoons was not found. However, the date of the beginning of tax on cocoons exchanged in Zhejiang Province (noted by promulgation of the Likin Tax Regulations on the cocoons of Zhejiang in 1883) show that the emergence of large-scale cocoon exchanges should be delayed in the early 1880s. In addition, according to a report from the *Shen newspaper*, the bosses of the Gong-he-yong Reeling Factory and the Lunhua Reeling Factory have both opened several agencies to buy the cocoons in the province of Zhejiang since 1882[3], which makes us estimate that there were a proportion of cocoon companies in Yangzi which were opened and controlled directly by Shanghai reeling factories, which has solved their problem of supplying raw materials. As the cocoa trade grew, cocoa companies appeared in the late 1880s. According to a report by a Japanese delegate in 1897, at that time, the proportion of cocoon companies opened by the local owners already reaches 90% of all cocoon companies in Zhejiang and Jiangsu, while those directly belonging to the reeling factories at Shanghai account for only 10%[4].

This means that since the end of the 19th century, most of the companies of cocoons which play an intermediary role between peasants and reeling factories are already independent. Another report of a survey on the Wuxi market describes a scene on cocoon exchanges in Wuxi: "During the harvest season of the new cocoons, there always very lively price discussions in the cocoon companies. Peasants and peddlers have to dispose of their cocoons within a week for fear that butterflies will release the cocoons in 10 days, while the companies have to buy millions of cocoons during this short period so they do not have time to control precisely the cocoons' quality. Therefore it is believed that the exchange of cocoons is the stage with the most risk in the silk trade in China."[5] This confirms the relationship among peasants, cocoon companies and the silk reeling factories in the Yangzi market, and the organization of silk production in this region at

---

① 陈炽.论缫丝业.上海:鸿宝书局,1902 年,第 45 页.
② 肖爱丽.上海近代纺织技术的引进与创新.东华大学博士论义,2012 年 1 月,第 27 页.
③ 申报.1895 年 6 月 26 日,上海图书馆馆藏资源.
④ 高津仲次郎.清国蚕丝业观察报告书.农商务省农务局,1897 年,第 27 页.
⑤ 清国新开港场视察调查.京都商业会议所,1897 年第 221 页.

the end of the 19th century. Following the purchases of the cocoons from the peasants, the companies of cocoons must perish the chrysalises in several days, and then dry the cocoons and preserve them while awaiting the purchases of the mechanical reeling factories.

Figure V-8 Circulation of cocoons in the Yangzi region at the end of the 19th century

$$\text{Peasants} \xrightarrow{\text{Fresh Cocoons}} \text{Companies of cocoons} \xrightarrow{\text{Dried Cocoons}} \text{Mechanical Filatures}$$

$$\xrightarrow{\text{Mechanical silk}} \text{Foreign silk companies} \xrightarrow{\text{Mechanical silk}} \text{Internatioanl market}$$

In the Yangzi region, the cocoon market in Jiangsu Province is growing faster than that in Zhjiang. Zhejiang is the largest Chinese silkworm Province where the quantity of manual silk production is much higher than that of the Jiangsu province during the 19th century. However, the province's advantage over manual silk production is precisely its biggest obstacle to modernization in the reeling industry. The progress of the new reeling industry and the development of the cocoon market are more remarkable in Jiangsu Province, where the tradition of the old silk industry is relatively low. Wuxi (in Jiangsu Province) has become the second major center of mechanical reeling in the Yangzi River Valley. This city became, at the same time, the largest market for the distribution of cocoons in Yangzi Region at the beginning of the 20th century. Apart Wuxi, cocoon markets have already been formed in several other cities of Jiangsu.

Tables V-9-A The quantities of fresh cocoa production in each province in China[1]

Provinces	Quantites of production(piculs)	Proportions(%)
江苏 Jiangsu	350,000	10.5
浙江 Zhejiang	1,000,000	30
广东 Guangdong	1,000,000	30
四川 Sichuan	600,000	18.1
安徽 Anhui	30,000	0.9
湖北 Hebei	100,000	3
湖南 Hunan	20,000	0.6
山东 Shandong	60,000	1.8

---

① 上海万国生丝检验所.1925 年华中蚕丝业调查.丝绸.1999 年第 10 期,第 55 页.

（续表）

Provinces	Quantites of production(piculs)	Proportions(%)
河南 Henan	100,000	3
其他 Others	70,000	2.1
Total	330,000	100

Tables V-9-B The production quantities of dried cocoons and manual silkes in the provinces of Zhejiang and Jiangsu[1]

Provinces	Production regions	Quantites of production of the dried cocons(piculs)	Quantities of production of the manual silk(piculs)
江苏 Jiangsu	无锡 Wuxi	55,000	
	常州 Changzhou	30,000	
	苏州 Suzhou	15,000	3,000
	苏北 Subei	11,000	2,000
	Totality of Jiangsu	111,000	5,000
浙江 Zhejiang	嘉兴 Jiaxing	30,000	20,000
	辑里 Jili	10,000	35,000
	绍兴 Shaoxing	25,000	5,000
	Totality of Zhejiang	65,000	60,000

Tables V-9-C Origin of dried cocoons on the Shanghai market[2]

Provinces	Production Regions	Year 1908	Year 1909	Year 1910
江苏 Jiangsu	无锡 Wuxi	49,000	60,000	48,000
	常州 Changzhou	12,000	10,000	7,000
	江阴 Jiangyin	12,000	10,000	8,000
	苏州 Suzhou		3,000	2,100
	其他 Others		1,000	800
	Totality of Jiangsu	73,000	84,000	65,900

---

① 上海万国生丝检验所.1925 年华中蚕丝业调查,第 55 页.
② 紫藤章.清国蚕丝业一斑.第 57—60 页.

（续表）

Provinces	Production Regions	Year 1908	Year 1909	Year 1910
浙江 Zhejiang	嵊县 Shengxian	11,000	13,000	9,100
	萧山 Xiaoshan	2,000	7,000	5,600
	嘉兴 Jiaxing	2,000	3,000	2,400
	杭州 Hangzhou		1,000	800
	海宁 Haining	1,000	3,000	2,100
	湖州 Huzhou	3,500	7,000	5,600
	余杭 Yuhang	700	500	1,600
	塘栖 Tangqi	2,000	2,000	1,600
	其他 Others	1,000	3,000	2,300
	Totality of Zhejiang	23,000	39,000	29,000
Total		96,200	123,500	95,800

2. Modernization of the silk-reeling industry in the Guangdong region and other parts of China

The first mechanical silk reeling factory in Guangdong, named Ji-chang-long（继昌隆）, was erected by Chen Qiyuan（陈启沅）, a Cantonese merchant in Nanhai Prefecture（南海县）in 1873. This reeling factory is also the first reeling mill created by the Chinese（9 years earlier than the Gong-he-yong reeling factory in Shanghai）. According to Chen's memorials published in 1876, he "went to the ports of the countries of Southeast Asia when he was young to trade there in 1854 ..." During his stay at Annam, he conducted observations on French mechanical reeling factories and tried to know the structure of the new reel ... Having accumulated great wealth, he decided to return to his homeland and to teach the peasants the new method of reeling in the autumn of 1873.[1] Then, according to what memories of a descendants of Chen Qiyuan's collaborator says, "Chen Qiyuan brought an old steamer to the village of Jian（简村, a Nanhai district village, Chen Qiyuan's birthplace）and transformed it into a steam reeling machine. The Ji-chang-long Silk Reeling factory was installed in the village in 1873 and

---

[1] 陈启沅.广东蚕桑谱.自序,1876年,第1—3页,广州市中山图书馆馆藏资源.

328

put into operation the following year". [1]

Different from the case of the Yangzi region, where the opening of the first mechanical reeling factories concentrates in metropolises, the first mechanical reeling factory in Guangdong appears in a small village. At first, Chen had intended to open his reeling mill in Guangzhou, where it is easier to get techniqueal direction and financial support, but he finally renounces this idea [2]. The main reason is that the obstructions coming from government would be greater in the metropolis. In addition, several village advantage has drawn the attention of Chen: although the village is further away from the market of the sale, it is just next to the cocoon production area; the laborers are cheaper there than those of Canton; Chen knows more about the local elites in the village than they do in Canton, and so on. However, to the traditional Chinese society of the time, it is difficult to open a modern factory in which men and women work together, even in his native country [3]. To prepare the creation of this first reeling mill, Chen has made a lot of preparations: he finances the public works, offers food and medicines to the poor, and tries to convince the local elites to create reeling factories together with him [4]. All this gave him a good reputation, which gained confidence from the members of the village. Having spent so much money and vigor, Chen succeeded in creating the first modern reeling mill in Chinese capital in China in 1873.

This reeling factory is quiet prosperious after its opening. The Nanhai Yearbooks note that "the quality of silk produced by the Ji-chan-long reeling factories is much better than other canton silks, so this kind of silk is very demanded at the market as well as its price is higher, which brings a lot of profit to its boss". [5] Encouraged by Chen Qiyuan and excited by profits, other Cantonese merchants successively installed their mechanical reeling factories in the Zhu River Delta: in 1874, 4 new mechanical reeling factories were opened; In 1880, there are in total 10 reeling factories with 2,400 new reels which produce 950—1,000 piculs of silks per year [6]; Until the year 1881 there are

---

① 陈滚滚.陈联泰与均和安机器厂的概况.广东文史资料.第 20 辑,广州:广东人民出版社,1965 年,第 54 页.

② 汪敬虞.关于继昌隆丝厂的若干史料及值得研究的几个问题.学术研究.1962 年第 6 期。第 96 页.

③ For example, a report by *North China Herald*(《北华捷报》), June 13, 1874, states that "the Chinese believe that the spinners are going to be injured by machines, that machines are very noisy and that the chimneys of the factories are going to hurt geomancy (Feng Shui, (风水) of a village, etc."

④ 苏耀昌.华南丝区——地方历史的变迁与世界体系理论.郑州:中州古籍出版社,1987 年,第 155—156 页.

⑤ (宣统)南海县志.卷 21,列传 8,艺术,陈启沅条,南海图书馆馆藏资源.

⑥ 中国第二历史档案馆,中国海关总署办公厅.中国旧海关史料09.第 214 页.

already 14—15 mechanical reeling factories in Cuangdong Province, 11 of which are located in Nanhai District and 3—4 are in Shunde (顺德, another district of Guangdong)[1]. What is remarkable is that all these first reeling factories in Guangdong are created without the protection of foreigners (the case of Yangzi). Different of the case of Shanghai, the reeling industry in Guangdong is established by the Chinese themselves.

With the growth of the number of mechanical reeling factories in Guangdong, the contradiction between industrial production and manufacturing production is becoming more and more evident, as has often happened all of the world. What is to be noticed is that, the prosperity of the reeling industry has hardly affected the interests of the peasants who produce manual silk, since the latter group can always make a profit by supplying the cocoons to the reeling factories mechanical, or work directly in the factory like spinners. In reality, the most great resentment against mechanical reeling comes from the weavers of the traditional silks which work in textile factories, because the prosperity of the mechanical reeling now makes them lack of raw materials. On the one hand, because of the development of mechanical reeling factories, peasants in Nanhai sell their cocoons to mechanical reeling factories and thus no longer supply manual silk to manual weavers; On the other hand, the mechanical silk produced by new reeling factories is destined for the foreign market instead of the domestic market. As a result, less and less manual silk is supplied to the silk textile factories in Guangdong. The insufficiency of the supply of silk materials leads to the closure of large numbers of textile factories and to the unemployment of traditional weavers. An event of violence between weavers and reeling factories occurred in 1875[2]. The event of 1881 remarks the summet of the movements against the Macanization reeling in Guangdong Province. On October 5, 1881, after a meeting of the Corporation, more than two thousand weavers entered the factories at Nanhai, damaged reels and destroyed factory premises[3]. Industrialists in Nanhai are demanding the protection of the district government. The mayor of Nanhai Xu Gengbi (徐赓陛) suppressed the sedition[4], but decided at the same time to prohibit the reopening of mechanical reeling factories for fear of the expansion of unemployment and a sec-

---

① 王翔.近代中国传统丝绸业转型研究.第 103 页.

② 北华捷报.1875 年 10 月 19 日,1875 年 10 月 26 日,上海图书馆馆藏资源.

③ (宣统)南海县志.卷 26,杂录,机器缫丝条,南海图书馆馆藏资源.北华捷报.1875 年 10 月 19 日,1875 年 10 月 26 日,上海图书馆馆藏资源.

④ 北华捷报.1881 年 11 月 7 日,上海市图书馆馆藏资源.申报.1881 年 11 月 8 日,上海市图书馆馆藏资源.

ond sedition[1]. In this situation, the first capitalists of Nanhai are forced to move their mechanical reeling machines to Macon (澳门) [2].

The order to prohibit the creation of the factories in Nanhai was abolished in 1886[3]. With the increase in the demand for mechanical silks on the international market, the prosperity of the reeling industry reappeared in Guangdong province from the second half of the 1880s. According to a Cantonese Customs report, "in 1991 there were more than fifty Zhu River delta mechanical factories".[4] The trend of expansion of the reeling factories in Guangdong Province is maintained until the early 20th century. In 1902, "the number of mechanical reeling factories reaches 86 in the district of Shunde, and there are other reeling factories in other districts in Guangdong Province". [5] Until 1906, Total of 176 mechanical reeling factories in Guangdong province, including 124 in the Shunde District (which accounts for more than 70% of total reeling factories), 45 in the Nanhai District, Xinhui District (新会), 2 in Sanshui (三水) and 1 in Zhongshan (中山)[6]. Among the 109 reeling factories operating in Guangdong in 1910, 82 are located in Shunde (75% of the total), 21 in Nanhai, 5 in Xinhui, and 1 in Fanpan (番禺).

Thanks to the encouragement of the Republican government, the number of mechanical reeling factories in Guangdong rose from 109 in 1910 to 162 in 1912 (a growth of 49%), and the number of new reels increased from 42,100 to 65,000 during the two years (an increase of 54.39%)[7]. In 1918, there were 147 mechanical reeling factories in Guangdong, in which 114 were in Shunde (78% of the total), 30 in Nanhai, 1 in Sanshui, 1 in Xinhui and 1 in Fanpan[8]. In other words, new Cantonese reeling factories created since the 1880s still retain the same characteristics as those of the first reeling factories created in the 1870s: they are all created by Chinese manufacturers. In terms of geographical distribution, they are still in the countryside instead of concentrating in the metropolis of Canton or in the concession. In addition, during this period, there was a tendency of concentration of the Cantonese factories at Shunde, which is also the lar-

---

① 徐赓陛.不自慊斋漫存.南海书牍,卷6,1882年,第21页,收录于沈云龙.中国近代史料丛刊.第78辑第773种,台北:台湾文海出版社,1994年.
② 北华捷报.1882年4月22日,上海市图书馆馆藏资源.
③ 张之洞.张文襄公全集.奏议,卷35,台北:文海出版社,1963年,第21页.
④ 五十年各埠海关报告(1882—1931).北京:中国海关出版社,2009年,广州口,第577页.
⑤ 王翔.近代中国传统丝绸业转型研究.第111页.
⑥ (民国)顺德县志.卷1,物产,丝部,广州:中山大学出版社,1993年,第21页.
⑦ 紫藤章.清国蚕丝业一斑.第213页.
⑧ 通商汇纂.东京:外务省通商局,1906年,第38号,第12页,武汉大学图书馆馆藏资源.

gest cocoon production area in Guangdong Province. By contrast, the number of factories in the origin place of modern Chinese factories, Nanhai, is much more modest at the entering the 20th century[1].

Techniqueally, new reels that the first Cantonese Fialtures use are different from those in Yangzi. According to the memories of Chen Qiyuan, the steam engine and hose reels used in the Ji-chang-long reeling factory are drawn by himself, instead of importing from abroad[2]. According to the Design of Machines (机器大偈

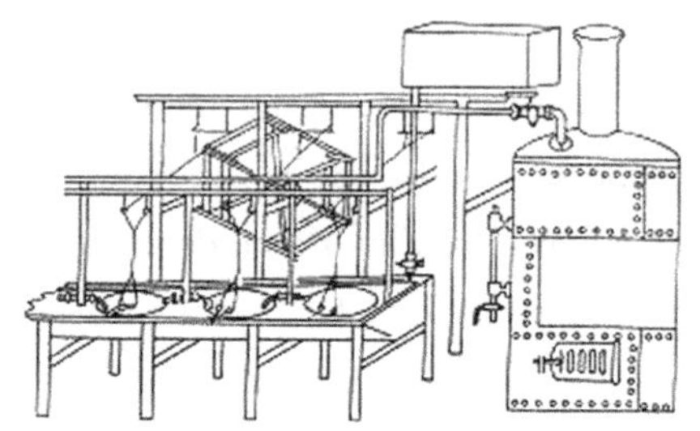

图) in his memories[3], the adaptation of a new system of coisure, the co-erection to the Chambon, and the use of steam, allows the improvement of silk pulled; A single cauldron supplies several basins, thus saving heating. Simultaneously, the atmosphere of the operating room is heated by the same generator which helps the strands to dry faster. In this installation, the movement of the asplet is no longer impressed by the spinners, which could then concentrate on the drawing of the cocoons, allowing obtain a better pulled silk thread[4].

However, the energy that rotates reels does not come from steam energy in the Ji-chang-long reeling mill. Chen Qiyuan's grandson Chen Tianjie (陈天杰) in his memoirs said that "it was the spinners who pulled the bundles of cocoons into the basin, led them to the asple and spun the asplet by pedaling an iron baquette".[5] In other words, Ji-chan-Long Reeling Factory is only a reeling machine equipped with steam engines, instead of that using steam energy. According to the report of Lv Xuehai (吕学海), subsequently reeling factories in Guangdong Province are completely constructed by imitating the Ji-chang-long model[6]. This confirms that the first mechanical reeling factories in Guangdong are not exactly "mechanical factories", but the workshops between industrialization and manufacture. In fact, the first reeling factories using steam energy did not appear in Guangdong Province until the beginning of 1890. This innovation was ac-

---

① 松下宪三郎.支那制丝业调查复命书.东京:农商务省农务局,1918年,第41页.

② 陈启沅.广东蚕桑谱.自序,第1—3页,广州市中山图书馆馆藏资源.

③ 陈启沅.广东蚕桑谱.广州市中山图书馆馆藏资源.

④ Mau Chuan-Hui. L'introduction en Chine des sciences et des techniques européennes concernant l'industrie de la soie après la guérre de l'Opium. Etudes chinoises. Vol. XX. No°1-2. p.213.

⑤ 金枝,庄为玑.近代华侨投资国内企业史资料选集(广东卷).福州:福建人民出版社,1989年,第224页.

⑥ 吕学海.顺德丝业调查报告.引自彭泽益.中国近代手工业史资料.第44页.

cepted by all the Cantonese factories only at the beginning of 20th century[1].

Cocoon markets exist also in Guangdong Province, but in different forms of these in Yangzi. According to the notes of the Shunde Yearbooks and the Nanhai Yearbooks, in the Zhu River Delta, there is no "cocoons companies" which acts as an intermediary between peasants and factories, cocoons in Yangzi. The reason for the absence of this kind of intermediary is that almost all Cantonese reeling factories settle in the countryside, where is just aside, or even within the cocoon production area. In this case, companies of cocoons, which are used to dry, store and transport cocoons, are not indispensable. On the other hand, there is regular fairs which binds cocoon sellers and cocoon buyers. These cocoon fairs are opened by local merchants, who normally have to invest 20 thousand taëls to rent land and build infrastructure. The details of the process of cocoon exchange at fairs are: peasants go to the fair to sell their cocoons; Buyers sent by reeling factories or brokers called "Shui Tou" (水头) come here simultaneously to buy peasants' cocoons; If an exchange is concluded, buyers or brokers must pay 3% of the exchange value to the organizers of this fair, and farmers must pay 1.5%; After the exchanges, buyers sent by the reeling factories will take the cocoons to their own reeling factories, while brokers will immediately seek out reeling factories which need cocoons and sell them to them; Finally, the smothering and drying of the cocoons will be done in reeling factories[2].

From the late 19th century, there are many such kind of cocoon fairs, especially in the Shunde and Nanhai districts. According to a survey by a Japanese delegate, in the Guangdong region, there are 10 cocoon fairs with a trade value of more than 1 million piasters by fair, and the number of fairs with a lesser trade value of 1 million piasters reached 19 at the beginning of the 20th century. The prosperity of these fairs provides the possibility for Cantonese mechanical factories to obtain enough raw materials, which is a very important element for the development of this industrial branch in Guangdong.

---

① J. G. Kerr. Guide to the City and Suburbs of Canton. Hong-kong. Kelly&Walsh. 1904. Excursion 5. p.14.
② （民国）顺德县志.卷3,建制,墟市,广州:中山大学出版社,1993年,第7页.（宣统）南海县志.卷4,物产,蚕部,南海图书馆馆藏资源.

Graph V-10 Circulation of cocoons in the Guangdong region at the end of the 19th century

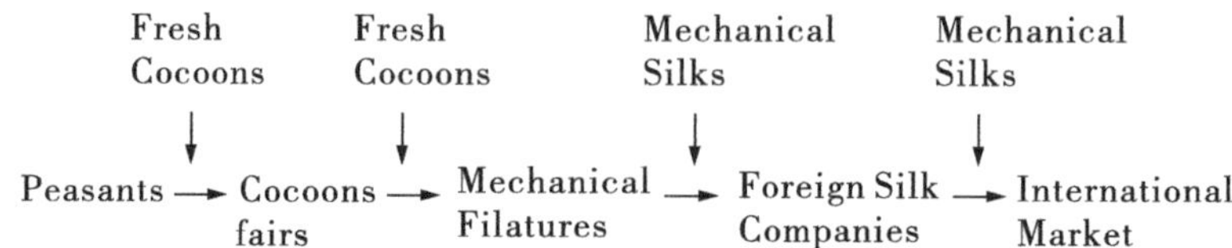

The appearance of the cocoon market is a result of the mechanization of silk reeling, which results in an important evolution of the silk production organization. Before the introduction of mechanical reeling in China, almost all silk production processes were finalized in a peasant family, and it was the peasants who had the direct commercial relationship with the silk market. With the emergence of mechanical reeling, reeling became a specialized production activity in reeling factories, and the peasants were exclusively concerned with the production of cocoons. In the silk market, producers and sellers of silk are transferred from peasants to reeling factories. The two production activities—cocoon production and silk reeling—are linked by commercial intermediaries, namely the cocoon houses in Yangzi, or the cocoon markets in Canton.

The development of the mechanical reeling industry is very modest in other Chinese regions. The first mechanical reeling factory appears very early in Shandong Province, where the production of wild silk is most abundant in China. The Crasemann & Hagen & Co. is installing a mechanical reeling factory in Zhifu (a strict of Yantai City in Shandong Province) in 1877—called Yantai Reeling Company (烟台缫丝局), equipped with reels in French model[1]. Later (1882), this last reeling factory began to absorb Chinese capital because of its debts[2], and then was sold to the Chinese government in 1885[3]. Other mechanical reeling factories only made their appearance in the early 20th century in Shandong Province. Until the year 1911, there are only three mechanical factories in Shandong, which concentrated in the port of Yantai[4]. In the middle of China,

---

① 中国第二历史档案馆,中国海关总署办公厅.中国旧海关史料14.第83页.

② 中国股票档案,第114号,烟台缫丝局股票,藏于中国国家博物馆.申报.1883年7月25日,上海市图书馆馆藏资源.

③ It was Sheng Xuanhuai (盛宣怀), a very famous pimp of "modernization movements" (洋务运动) of China, who bought the Yantai Spinning from the Chinese government. For more details,《申报》,1887年2月5日,上海图书馆馆藏资源。

④ Rapports des décennies des douanes de Chine (1882—1931). Beijing. Editions des douanes chinoises. 2009. Port de Yantai.p.229.

Hubei and Hunan's viceroy Zhang Zhidong（张之洞）[1] created the Hubei Reeling Company（湖北缫丝局）in Wuhan（武汉）in 1894. However, due to the financial problem, only a part of this reeling factory start to produce the silk since the year 1895[2]. From then on, no other mechanical reeling machines appeared in the province of Hubei until the fall of the Qing dynasty.

In Sichuan Province, modern reeling wasn't born untill the year 1905, which is marked by the equipment of 100 reels in Italian style by Chen Kaizhi（陈开沚）in his reeling factory—The Pinong Filature（裨农丝厂）to the Santan District（三台县）[3]. In 1911, Chen Kaizhi installed two other mechanical reeling machines—Bichuan Reeling Factory（敝川丝厂）in Chongqing, and Huaxin Reeling Factory in Jiading（嘉定）[4]. Zhang Senkai（张森楷）is another industrialist who make many contributions to the modernization of the silk industry in Sichuan, which successively creates two mechanical reeling factories in 1908 and 1911[5]. Despite all these efforts, the number of mechanical reeling factories in Sichuan is still very modest: only 5 until the year 1914.

There is no mechanical reeling mill in other Chinese provinces before 1914. In other words, outside the provinces of Jiangsu（Shanghai belongs to Jiangsu at that time）, Zhejiang, Guangdong, Shandong, Hubei and Sichuan, the influence of the modern reeling industry is almost zero in all other regions of China during that time.

Thus, we could conclude that the distribution of the reeling industry manifested a very strong geographical concentration before the year 1914. The modernization of the silk-reeling industry took place only in provinces before that year. In addition, among these several provinces, most of the new factories are located in the Yangzi region and the Guangdong region, which has easier access to the external market, supply of raw materials, new reeling technology and capital. Within the Yangzi region, the mechanical reeling industry is concentrated in two cities: Shanghai and Wuxi, while more than 90% of the mechanical reeling factories in Guangdong are concentrated in the two districts of Shunde and Nanhai.

---

① 五十年各埠海关报告(1882—1931).北京:中国海关出版社,2009 年,烟台口,第 229 页.

② 张之洞.张文襄公全集.奏议,卷 35,台北:文海出版社,1963 年,第 21 页.

③ 四川官报.第四册,1905 年 2 月新闻第 5 号,中国国家图书馆馆藏资源.

④ 张学军,张莉红.四川近代工业史.成都:四川人民出版社,1990 年第 120 页.

⑤ 陈慈玉.近代中国的机器缫丝工业 1860—1945.台北"中央研究院"近代史研究专刊,1989 年,第 208 页.

3. Result of the modernization of the reeling industry in China before the year 1914

The proportion of the quantity of mechanical silk in the total quantity of silks produced in a country is an important standard for assessing its level of modernization of the reeling industry. However, as we have shown in Chapter II, statistical sources on the total production quantities of all China before 1914 are very limited, which is an obstacle to calculating this proportion. So we will estimate the quantitative level of silk reeling modernization in China at the period by calculating another proportion: the proportion of the quantity of mechanical silk exported in the total quantity of China silk export.

Table V-11-A Proportions of mechanical silk in all silks exported from Guangdong, Shanghai and all of China[1]

Years	Proportions of the mechanical silks exported from Canton	Proportions of the mechanical silks exported from Shanghai	Proportions of the mechanical silks exported from China
1904	89.60%	23.60%	41.90%
1905	92.20%	27.30%	41.70%
1906	95.90%	23.20%	39.20%
1907	95.70%	24.10%	50.90%
1908	92.30%	24.10%	38.60%
1909	95.30%	27.30%	37.10%
1910	95.60%	32.00%	58.10%
1911	93.20%	34.90%	57.00%
1912	93.00%	28.00%	47.00%
1913	95.20%	32.20%	48.10%
1914	93.90%	43.30%	52.40%

[1]　The datas of year 1904 come from 中国第二历史档案馆,中国海关总署办公厅.中国旧海关史料.第39卷,211页,595页,第40卷,第60页.The datas of year 1905 come from Idem. 第41卷,227页,499页,第620页. The datas of year 1906 come from Idem. 第43卷,272页,497页,第627页.The datas of year 1907 come from Idem. 第45卷,266页,517页,第622页.The datas of year 1908 come from Idem. 第47卷,288页,555页,第713页. The datas of year 1909 come from Idem. 第49卷,340页,383页,624页.第50卷,71页.The datas of year 1910 come from Idem. 第52卷,377页,414页,662页.第53卷,138页.The datas of year 1911 come from Idem. 第55卷,306页,346页,605页.第56卷,145页.The datas of year 1912 come from Idem. 第58卷,297页,345页,625页.第59卷,132页.The datas of year 1913 come from Idem. 第61卷,503页,564页.第62卷,245页,567页.The datas of year 1914 come from Idem. 第63卷,532页,533页.第65卷,241页,547页.

Notes: (1) Mechanical silk has not been distinguished with other natures of raw silk in the statistics of the customs of Canton before the year 1904, so the table begins from the year 1904.

(2) The mechanical silk exported from Chongqing did not appear in the Chongqing Customs statistics until after 1909, so: from 1904 to 1908, the total quantity of mechanical silk from China included mechanical silks exported from Chongqing, Guangdong, Shanghai, and Yantai (烟台). From 1909 to 1914, the total quantity of mechanical silk from China includes mechanical silks exported from Guangdong, Shanghai, Yantai and Chongqing.

(3) In Chinese Customs statistics, the natures of the exported silks include: manual raw silk, manual yellow silk, manual wild silk, manual rewaxed silk, reeling mechanical silk, yellow reeling silk, wild mechanical reeling silk.

Graph V-11-B Proportions of mechanical silk in all silks exported from Guangdong, Shanghai and all of China.

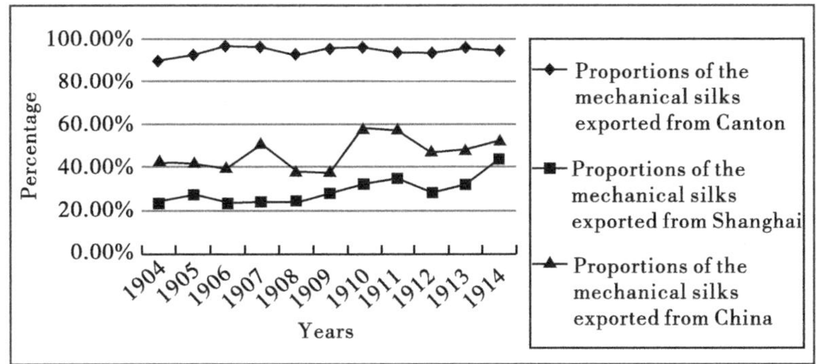

From the table above, we can see that the proportion of mechanical silk already reaches about 50% of all the silks exported from China on the eve of 1914. The progress of the mechanization of the reeling factory is very evident. In the region of Yangzi during the years 1904 to 1914, the quantity of the export of mechanical silk is almost doubled. However, the level of popularity of this industrial branch in Yangzi is much lower than that in Guangdong during that period: Mechanical silk in Guangdong is higher than 90% in all silks exported (except 1904, 89.60%), while the proportion of mechanical silk exported from Yangzi never exceeded 45% at the period (in most years it only accounts for 20%—30%). In other words, during this period, manual silk is consistently in a higher position in the silk exported from Shanghai. If we consider the quantity of manual silks absorbed by the Chinese domestic market, the proportion of mechanical silks in all silks produced in Yangzi should be much smaller than the data in the tables.

Two facts may be the explanations for the low level of mechanization of the reeling mill in the Yangzi region. The first obstruction against the progression of Yangzi's mechanical reeling industry stems from opposition from the Conservatives. The prosperity of the mechanical manufacture of silk will worsen the interests of groups whose professions concern the exchange of manual silk, and therefore necessarily provoke their opposition. In Guangdong, there are also opposition groups, but the opponents are mainly composed of textile artisans, who have fewer economic funds and less links with the government. Different from the case of Guangdong, the opponents in Yangzi are mainly composed of manual silk merchants, who control the main economic social funds and who have a more intimate relationship with the local government, so mechanical reeling machines met with much more resistance than in Guangdong. What the first reeling factory in China—Shanghai Reeling Company—underwent and was closed just because of this kind of resistance during the 1860s.

In fact, since the closure of this first silk mill in Yangzi, there is awalys the voices against the development of this new industrial branch, as there is a series of measures to limit its development. In September 1882 (just during the debate on the necessity of introducing mechanical reeling on the *Shen newspaper* in 1882 mentioned at the beginning of this section), the Governor of Jiangsu Province Wei Rongguang (卫荣光) instructs the mayor of Shanghai Shao Youlian (邵友濂) to close the American Qichang Reeling (旗昌丝厂) and the English Iveson Reeling (公平丝厂)[1]. Two months later (in November), the Mayor of Shanghai received another order from the Viceroy of Jiangzu, Jiangxi and Anhui, who said that the two reeling factories should be closed immediately. Fortunately, the two reeling factories were saved by the protests of the British and American consuls to Li Hongzhang (李鸿章, prime minister and the important leader of the modernization movement at the end of the Qing dynasty). In October 1882[2], the government of Jiangsu refused the demands of the reeling factories in Shanghai seeking to open cocoon companies there[3].

In the Zhejiang Cocoon Likin Tax Regulations of 1883, the government promulgates that cocoon companies cannot be opened in Zhejiang without the guarantee of the traditlend silk companies[4]. This gives the possibility of opening the cocoon companies to the hands of their biggest competitor—Chinese silk companies. After the Sino-Japanese War of 1894, the Chinese central government began to encourage the creation of private

---

① 奉阻缫丝.申报.1882 年 9 月 15 日,上海市图书馆馆藏资源.
② 议禁缫丝.申报.1882 年 11 月 15 日,上海市图书馆馆藏资源.
③ 禀批照录.申报.1882 年 10 月 19 日,上海市图书馆馆藏资源.
④ 浙江省茧捐章程.光绪刻本.上海市图书馆馆藏资源.

factories, but the local opponents in Yangzi still possess their means against the development of the reeling industry. According to a letter from the Viceroy of Jiangsu, Jiangxi and Anhui, the Likin on cocoons for Shanghai's mechanical reeling factories has 12 taëls per picul in Zhejiang and 9 taëls per picul in Jiangsu, 240% and 180% of that on a picul of cocoons intended for manual silk (which counts only 5 taels per picul)[1].

In 1908, Shanghai reeling factories proposed to set up a silk quality control establishment in Shanghai (to be specified later), but this plan was unsuccessful because of the opposition of the manual silk shops at Shanghai[2]. To limit the evolution of cocoon companies in 1910, the Jiangsu Provincial Government stipulated that it is forbidden to open new cocoon companies in the districts where there are already more than five such houses. In the same year, the government of Zhejiang province stipulated that only one cocoons company could be built within the 10-kilometer radius[3].

The second fact that prevents the growth of the mechanical rate of silk production in the Yangzi region is the restoration of the traditional textile factories in this region. As has been said, traditional textile factories have declined during the Taiping rebellion, but a trend of restoration appears in the three centers of the Yangzi textile factories (Nanjing, Hangzhou and Suzhou) since the year 1880. At the beginning of this decade, there are only 5,000 looms in Nanjing, 5,500 in Suzhou and 3,000 in Hangzhou[4]. Until the end of the first decade of the 20th century, these last three figures date back to 10,000, 9,000, and 4,300, while the silk fabric production amounts to 200,000 rolls, 160,000 rolls and 105,000 rolls[5] respectively. If the production of textile manufactures is reported in other cities of Yangzi, the scale of production of silk fabrics should be even greater. In their fabric manufacturing processes, almost all of these textile factories in Yangzi produced with the traditional techinics and using manual silk as their raw materials. The large-scale need for the internal market in the Yangzi region thus ensures the disposal of manual silk, which greatly prevents the development of mechanical reeling factories. The demand for manual silk did not begin to diminish until after the 1920s, when modern looms became dominant in the production of silk fabrics.

---

① 刘坤一.刘坤一遗集.第 4 卷,奏疏二十六.遵查被劾道员据实复陈折.光绪二十二年七月二十九日,北京:中华书局,1959 年,第 1543 页.

② In fact, this project did not become reality until after the year 1821. Consult Robert Yeok-Yin Eng. Economic Imperialism in China: Silk Production & Exports, 1861–1932. Institute of East Asia Studies of the University of California. pp.185—186.

③ 王翔.近代中国传统丝绸业转型研究.第 131 页.

④ 李明珠.中国近代蚕丝业及外销.第 187 页.

⑤ 杨大金.现代中国实业志.长沙:商务印书馆,1928 年,第一卷,第 146 页,第 148—149 页.

If we evaluates the level of modernization of the reeling industry in China before the year 1914 with the qualitative standard, the result is not perfect either. As shown above, steam energy was only used at the beginning of the 20th century in mechanical reeling factories in Guangdong Province. Although mechanical silk occupies an absolute quantitative superiority in the export market, its quality is always the aim of criticism of foreigners. The French consul at Canton remarks in his commercial report of 1908: "In a general way, it seems that the silk industry in the region of Canton is in decay. The European silk shoppers complain of the inferior quality of the reeling silks."[1] According to studies by a Japanese historian, the order of qualities of mechanical silks on the international market before the First World War is (from top to bottom): French mechanical silk, Italian mechanical silk, Yangzi mechanical silk, Japanese mechanical silk, Cantonese silk[2]. In other words, the quality of Cantonese mechanical silk is the worst among all the main types of mechanical silks. The price of the Cantonese silk is the lowest among all the mechanical silks because of its inferior quality.

At the market of Lyons in 1896, the mechanical silks of France and Italy are worth 38 francs per kilo, the price of Japanese silk is 35 francs per kilo, and the Cantonese silk costs only 28 francs kilo[3]. A reformer of the Guangdong silk industry writes in his investigations report: "The mechanical silk exported from Canton has a very bad reputation among foreign customers. The Textile Association of the United States has already advised us to improve its quality several times. Nevertheless, because of the political events that happen frequently, the government has not had time to deal with them; The producers in the reeling factory do not listen to these advice either; merchantrs even make frauds to earn more profits. All this leads to the failure of Cantonese silk on the international market."[4]

Although the quality of the mechanical silk produced in Yangzi is better than that in Guangdong, innovation and the introduction of new techniques in reeling factories are still delayed in Yangzi region compared with those in Italy and France, Japan during the same period. For example, the multi-crusher reeling veeling invented in Japan in 1903, but this type of machine was not introduced in China until after 1929[5].

---

① Archives Nationales de France. F12.7223. Canton 1907—1914. Rapport du consul de Canton au Ministère du commerce. 19 November 1909. p.22.

② 铃木淳.机械丝用气罐制造的发展.史学杂志.第 101 编,第 7 号,1992 年,第 43 页.

③ 石井宽治.日本蚕丝业史分析.东京:东京大学出版社,1972 年,第 35 页.

④ 刘伯渊.广东省蚕业调查报告书.广州:广东省地方农林实验场,1922 年,第 89 页.

⑤ 肖爱丽.上海近代纺织技术的引进与创新.东华大学博士论文,2012 年 1 月,第 27 页.

The inferior quality of silk produced in Chinese mechanical reeling silks comes from a management model in Chinese mechanical reeling factories—the lease model. This means that, the owner of the mechanical reeling mill does not do the production of mechanical silk by itself; by contraires, he rents out the premises and equipment of his (their) reeling factories to someone who wants to engage in the production and trade of mechanical silk; apart from the rent of the factory, the tenant pays the wages of the workers, capital for the cocoons, various expenses. He keeps all the benefits of silk manufacturing but also assumes responsibility for losses. The lease model emerged in China in the early 20th century, and became more and more common for decades to come.

According to a survey report published in 1928, only nine reeling factories do not use the lease model among the 93 reeling factories in Shanghai during 1927[1]. In fact, according to a Chinese researcher, this model is also fashionable in Wuxi and Guangdong Province at the moment[2]. Obviously, the high level of popularization of this management model is due to its advantage. On the one hand, it will reduce the risk of the plant owner, who can earn an annual rent of approximately 15% of the total capital invested in the factory premises and equipment, no matter the producer of mechanical silk gains profits or loses its capital. On the other hand, the tenant can reduce a large sum of expenses to buy the premises and equipment of the reeling factory. However, the lease model has a very bad influence on the technical progress of the silk reeling industry in China: most owners do not want to renew equipment in their factories; Tenants are only interested in the profits of the year in which they engage in production. As a result, the reeling technique in China is increasingly underdeveloped.

Despite all these problems, the growth of the reeling industry in China still has an important influence on the silk trade between China and France. Mechanical silk is becoming more and more important due to the modernization of the silk reeling industry in China for several decades. According to the information in Table V−12−A, although the total quantity of silks exported from China to France hardly increased during the pre-war years, the absolute amount of mechanical silk in the Franco-Chinese trade rose from 1,387 piculs in 1894 to 11,258 piculs in 1914, its proportion in the whole increased from 4.69% to 76.79%. If we add the Cantonese silk exported to France by Hong Kong, the growth should be even stronger. This evolution of the proportion of mechanical silk in

------

① 上海丝厂之调查.经济半月刊.第 2 卷,第 12 期,1928 年 6 月 15 日.
② 张国辉.甲午战后四十年间中国现代缫丝工业的发展和不发展,第 101—102 页.

the Franco-Chinese trade means that, despite quantitative stagnation, there has been a qualitative progression in the silk trade between China and France during the two decades before the First World War.

Table V-12-A The proportion of mechanical silk in all silks exported from China to France (piculs) [1]

Years	Mechanical Silk destined to France	All kinds of Silks destined to France	Proprotions
1894	1,387	29,592	4.69%
1895	1,894	35,021	5.41%
1896	2,277	23,433	9.72%
1897	5,093	31,953	15.94%
1898	3,904	28,491	13.70%
1899	5,560	38,854	14.31%
1900	3,386	28,734	11.78%
1901	7,309	27,154	26.92%
1902	6,383	25,953	24.59%
1903	7,258	17,404	41.70%
1904	5,765	20,147	28.61%
1905	6,442	15,533	41.47%
1906	7,958	21,250	37.45%
1907	8,281	23,790	34.81%
1908	9,519	22,681	41.97%
1909	12,348	24,234	50.95%
1910	15,292	24,779	61.71%
1911	13,448	21,140	63.61%
1912	13,930	28,248	49.31%

---

① 中国第二历史档案馆,中国海关总署办公厅.中国旧海关史料.第22卷,328页;第23卷,第314页;第24卷,第336页;第25卷,第339页;第27卷,第347页;第29卷,第393页;第31卷,第399页;第33卷,第397页;第35卷,第474页;第37卷,第528页;第39卷,595页;第41卷,第449页;第43卷,第298页;第45卷,517页;第47卷,第555页;第49卷,第35页;第52卷,第662页;第55卷,第39页;第58卷,第39页;第61卷,第93页;第64卷,第88页。

（续表）

Years	Mechanical Silk destined to France	All kinds of Silks destined to France	Proprotions
1913	17,264	27,428	64.26%
1914	11,258	14,661	76.79%

Notes: The quantities of silk re-exported by Hong Kong are not included in the data in this table.

Graph V-12-B The proportion of mechanical silk in all silks exported from China to France[1]

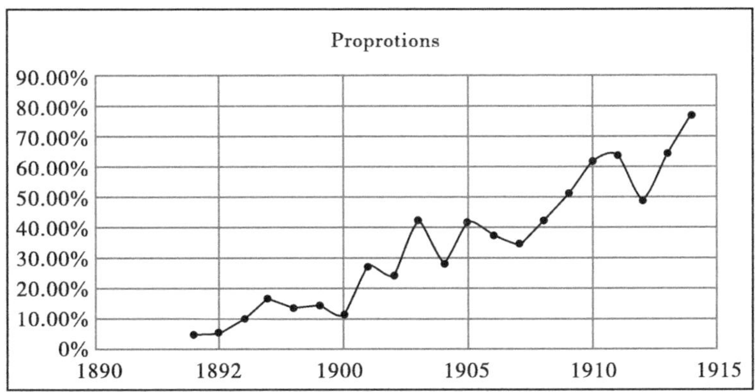

Table V-12-C The proportions of mechanical silk in silks sold from China to various countries in 1910 (piculs) [2]

Importers	Mechanical Silk	Totality of silks	Percentage
United Kingdom	5	1,036	1%
Hong kong	42,453	44,682	95%
French Indochina	0	0	0%
India	0	8,154	0%
English America	15	85	18%
United States	3,604	14,405	25%
Australia	0	0	0%
Belgimn	0	0	0%

---

① All the datas of 1904 come from the Table V-12-A.
② 中国第二历史档案馆,中国海关总署办公厅.中国旧海关史料.第 52 卷, 662 页.

（续表）

Importers	Mechanical Silk	Totality of silks	Percentage
Egypt	0	2,107	0%
France	15,292	24,779	62%
Germany	0	401	0%
Italy	2,431	9,630	25%
Japan	107	468	23%
Korea	0	1	0%
Mexico	0	89	0%
Russia	61	269	23%
Spain	0	37	0%
Switserland	0	130	0%
Turkey	0	2,480	0%
Alegeria	0	62	0%
Macao	0	375	0%
Canada	15	75	20%
China	2	1,800	0%
Total	63,969	110,184	58%

Comparatively, the mechanization of the Chinese silk reeling industry has much less influence on the silk trade between China and other countries, even on that with the United States. In fact, France is the biggest beneficiary of the modernization of the Chinese silk reeling industry. Already, according to what we have shown in the second chapter (section 1), it maintains the largest importer of Chinese silks in the world from 1875 until the explosion of the Great War of 1914, 40%—60% at the time. Comparatively, the proportion of the former great importer of England decreased from 72.6 percent to 1.3 percent between 1870 and 1910, and that of the United States increased from 11 percent in 1875 to 25 per cent during the same period. Moreover, France is the largest importer of Chinese mechanical silk before 1914. Let us take the example of 1910. At the level of absolute quantity, France imported 15,292 piculs of Chinese mechanical silks during this year, even much higher than the total imported by all the other countries. At the level of the proportion, 62% of the Chinese silks imported by France are mechanical silks, much higher than those of the United States, Italy, Japan, Russia,

England and America ranging from 1% to 25%. This distribution of Chinese silks is explained by the level of mechanization of the silk textile industry of the various importing countries. France possesses more mechanical looms, so it prefers to import from China more mechanical silks than other countries with less mechanical looms, such as England, Indochina, India, Algeria, Turkey or Egypt[1]. However, this explanation is not perfect, because the United States, whose mechanical level of the silk textile industry is higher than France imports less Chinese mechanical silk than France. Why does the United States import less Chinese silk than France? Indeed, the performance of the international exchange of industrial products is also a problem of different needs or criteria of each country. We should return to this question in subsection E.

At the same time, it should be noted that, according to the data in Table V-12-C, China hardly keeps mechanical silks that it produced. In other words, almost all Chinese mechanical silks were destined for foreigners at that time. The Chinese silk reeling industry is a production section with strong export orientation. Its prosperity comes completely from the need of the international market. The foreign trade has only offered the techniqueal and capital support to the Chinese mechanical reeling industry during the start-up period, but also offered it the market for its strengthening.

4. The beginning of the diffusion of modern science of sericulture in China

The modernization of the Chinese silk industry is manifested not only by the introduction of new machinery and reeling techniques, but also by the spread of modern sericulture science in China. Indeed, the introduction of modern science in China is already beginning in the "Modernization Movement" (洋务运动, 1861—1995). Piloted by the Chinese government from the 1860s, the Modernization Movement mainly targets military reinforcement[2] at the beginning. Thus, the schools or translation establishments established by the government are mainly concerned with the introduction of western military sciences. Liang Qichao (梁启超) [3] explained in the commentary on the reform (《变法

---

[1]　However, this explanation is not perfect, because the United States, whose mechanical level of the silk textile industry is higher than France, imports less Chinese mechanical silk than France. Indeed, the performance of international trade of industrial products is another problematic of the commodity criterion. We will return to this question in the next section.

[2]　There are already a number of official institutions specializing in the translation of foreign books in China since the 1860s, including the Beijing School of Translation (京师同文馆), Shanghai Language School (上海广方言馆), Cantonese Language School (广州广方言馆), the Southern Chinese Arsenal Translation Bureau (江南制造总局翻译馆).

[3]　Politician and Reformist in Wuxu Reform (戊戌变法) in 1898.

通议》) that this last phenomenon is due to the former thoughts of the mandarins in the modernization movement: "The advantage of western countries over China is their military industries, which is the origin of our failure in wars. If we learn their military techniques, our enemies will undoubtedly be beaten." [1]

After the 1870s, industrial modernization received more and more attention, and strengthening the economy became another goal of the movement. From the moment, more and more knowledge about the textile industry, the metallurgical industry and the natural sciences are introduced [2]. Although the dissemination of modern knowledge during this period (1872—1895) involved very little in agronomy, the introduction of this knowledge, especially that of the natural sciences, provided the scientific basis for the diffusion of sericicultural knowledge in the future.

The first person who sees the need for improvement of traditional Chinese sericulture is a forgeiner. In 1886, F. Kleinwachter, a German commissioner of the Ningbo Customs Commissioner, suggested that the local government of Zhejiang protect itself from epidemics and study silkworms by introducing western scientific methods, a great foresight are refused by Chinese mandarins [3]. Three years later (1889), pushed by the latter customs commissioner, Zhejiang Customs sent a Chinese student, Jiang Shengjin (江生金) to France to learn new sericicultural methods. Unfortunately, due to insufficient knowledge in the natural sciences, Jiang's learning outcome is not ideal. For 7 months he managed to master only the Pasteur method for the selection of healthy eggs in graining and the basic method for seed conservation, which are far from sufficient to indicate the reform of Chinese sericulture [4].

The dissemination of modern sericultural knowledge in China did not begin until the late 1890s. On the one hand, after the failure of the war with Japan in 1894—1895, some Chinese mandarins and intellectuals began to account for the—development of the political and economic systems of China in relation to those of Japan. On the other hand, after the 1890s, the silk industry, being a China's advantage economic branch, is increasingly threatened by that of Japan which has already begun to introduce modern western sericicultural knowledge. Under such circumstances, the improvement of Chi-

---

① The text in Chinese is 中国官局旧译之书,兵学几居其半。中国素未与西人相接,相接者兵已。于是震动与其屡败之烈,忧然以西人之兵法为可畏,谓彼所驾我者,兵也,吾但能师其长技,他不足敌也。故其所译专以兵为主。梁启超:变法通议.饮冰室合集.第一册,北京:中华书局,1989 年第 64 页.

② 汤菊平.洋务运动对中国近代科学技术的影响研究.上海:东华大学硕士毕业论文,2006 年.

③ In fact, F. Kleinwachter sent a letter containing 15 proposals to the Chinese government. For more informations, consult 尹良莹.中国蚕业史.第 56—59 页.

④ 周谷平.浙江近代蚕丝教育之历史研究.杭州大学学报.1997 年第 1 期,第 108 页.

nese sericulture, logically attracts more attention from reformists during the economic reform movement from the end of the 19th century to the beginning of the 20th century in China. A large number of reformers engaged in practices of Chinese sericulture modernization, as well as the Qing government and the Republican government have taken a series of mesures to improve this economic branch. Precisely, the efforts to modernize Chinese sericulture concern mainly those aspects during that period[1].

First, the translation of foreign books and the publication of agricultural journals. After the Sino-Japanese War, some Chinese refomers realized that it was necessary to introduce new foreign agricultural techniques, and they thought that "translation and publication of books and journals are the best means of introduction of new methods in Chinese agriculture".[2] In 1896, scholars who support political reform form an association for the improvement of Chinese agriculture[3], and the latter association in 1897 founded the first review of Chinese agriculture—*Journal of Agronomy* (《农学报》) in Shanghai[4]. The purpose of this review is to disseminate modern agricultural knowledge in China through the translation of the newest foreign agronomic literature. Before its publication in 1905, more than 700 articles were translated from foreign memoirs in this journal, of which serial culture took a large proportion. The dissemination of this journal is supported by the local authorities who order their reading from their subordinates and subscribe to all the traditional schools. The content of the various issues reflects the interest of the innovative elites in foreign techniques and in the global silk trade[5].

During the political reform in 1898, the Emperor of Guangxu（光绪帝）promulgated a decree: "Agriculture is the economic base of a country, so we must straighten this production department immediately ... The schools in each province must translate the foreign agronomic books to facilitate the learning of new foreign agricultural techniques."[6] Despite the failure of most projects in the reform in 1898, the policy supporting the translation of the agronomic works of the Qing court continued until the end of the dynasty. Thanks to the encouragement of the government, Chinese scholars have sparked a surge of translations of foreign agricultural articles throughout the Empire. Ini-

---

[1]　In fact, most of the measures put into practice during the Qing Dynasty's economic reform from the late 19th century to the early 20th century are inherited by the Republican government

[2]　农学报.第 1 期,第 1 页,1897 年。上海图书馆馆藏资源.

[3]　中国史学会.戊戌变法.上海:神州国光社,1953 年,第四卷,第 427—431 页.

[4]　农学报.第 1 期,第 7 页,1897 年。上海图书馆馆藏资源.

[5]　Mau Chuan-Hui. L'introduction en Chine des sciences et des techniques européennes concernant l'industrie de la soie après la guerre de l'Opium. Etudes chinoises. Vol. XX. No°1-2. p.223.

[6]　光绪朝东华录.第四册,北京:中华书局,1958 年,第 4105 页.

tially, the official translation establishments of each province began to translate foreign agricultural works. For example, the Translation Bureau of the Arsenal of South China (江南制造总局翻译馆) has translated 7 natures of foreign agricultural works during the years 1898—1902, the well-known Italian book *Storia deibachida setagovernati coinuovi Metodi nel* 1816 *nel regno Lombardo-Veneto* (《意大利蚕书》) of Danadolo is included. Moreover, many translations of sericulture books are published by non-governmental organizations. Agricultural associations and schools of agronomy in different provinces have founded a total of 11 kinds of new agricultural journals from 1897 to 1911, of which four journals specialized in sericulture. These newspapers enable the Chinese to access the newest sericicultural knowledge of the world and apply them to the agricultural activities of the peasants.

Table V-13 List of agricultural journals and magazines at the end of the Qing Dynasty[1]

Noms des Publications	Dates de fondation	Lieu de fondation	Fondateur
《农学报》 *Journal d' agronomie*	05/1897	上海 Shanghai	农学会 Association d' agronomie
《湖北农学报》*Journal d' agronomie de Hubei*	06/1897	武昌 Wuchang	湖北农业学堂 Ecole d' agriculture de Hubei
《北直农话报》*Journal d' agriculture de Hebei*	02/1905	保定 Baoding	直隶高等农业学堂 Ecole supéieure d' agriculture de Hebei
《农桑学杂志》*Revue de sériciculture*	06/1906	东京 Tokyo	益群书社 Librainie de Yiqun
《吉林农报》*Journal agricole de Jilin*	1908	吉林 Jilin	吉林省农学会 Association d' agronomie de Jilin
《蚕学报》 *Journal de sériciculture*	1908	广州 Canton	广州蚕学堂 Ecobe de séiciculture de Canton
《农工杂志》*Revue de l' agriduclture et de l' industrie*	12/1909	杭州 Hangzhou	浙江农工研究会 Association de sétudes de lagficulture et de lindsutrie

<hr>

① 史和,姚福申,叶翠娣.中国近代报刊名录.福州:福建人民出版社,1991 年.

（续表）

Noms des Publications	Dates de fondation	Lieu de fondation	Fondateur
《蚕从》*Revue de vers à soie*	12/1909	成都 Chengdu	
《湖北农报》*Journal d'agriculture de Hubei*	1910	武昌 Wuchang	湖北农务总会 Union d'agriculture de Hubei
《中国蚕丝业会报》*Journal de la corporation de l'industrie de la soie de China*	09/1909	东京 Tokyo	中国商业研究会 Association des études du commerce de China
《福建农工商官报》*Bulletin de l'agriculture de l'industrie et du commerce de Fujian*	12/1909	福州 Fuzhou	福建农工商局 Bureau de l'agriculture de l'industrie et du commerce de Fujian

Notes：*The Silk Industry Journal* and *Journal of the China Silk Industry Corporation* are founded in Tokyo from Japan, but their founders are Chinese as well as their texts are also in Chinese.

Table V-14 Summaries of the first issue of the Canton Sericulture Journal[1]

（1）Map of Nan Hai Prefecture（南海）.

（2）Classification of lands suitable for sericulture.

①Land suitable for sericulture.②The nature and constitution of sericulture-friendly lands in the southern parts of Shatou（沙头）, Nanpan（南畔）.③The nature and constitution of sericulture-friendly land at the top of Xi Qiao Mountain（西樵）.④The nature and constitution of land suitable for sericulture of Jian Cun Pao（简村堡）……

（3）Method of planting of mature trees.

①Of the different species of mice. ②Breeding of seedlings.

（4）Local processes for breeding silkworms.

①Magnaneries. ②Installations for worms. ③Cleaning. ④Hashing of leaves. ⑤How to give leaves. ⑥Déliterments. ⑦Suspensions of food. ⑧Sleep. ⑨Superchargement. ⑩Leaf supply. ⑪Lighting.

（5）Information on worm diseases.

①Worm diseases. ②Worms stiffness. ③Worms. ④Worms inconsistency. ⑤Black

---

[1] At present, the original of the Canton sericulture journal can not be found in libraries and archives in China. The contents quoted here come from Archives Nationales de France. F12. 7223 Canton. 1907-1914. lettre du Ministre des affaires étrangères au Ministre du commerce. le 10 mai 1909.

skate disease. ⑥White horn. ⑦Worms. ⑧Spots on the tail.

(6) Local reeling processes.

①Unwinding tools. ②From to employee. ③Degree of heat to boil cocoons. ④Degree of heat for reeling. ⑤Conservation of cocoons. ⑥Silk conservation. ⑦Fleet shape. ⑧Causes of ease or difficulty of reeling. ⑨Importance of waste. ⑩Purchase process of cocoons. ⑪Spinners. ⑫Price of labor. ⑬Elasticity. ⑭Resistances. ⑮Finesse. ⑯Knots. ⑰Humidity.

(7) Translation of Japanese newspapers.

①From the influence of heating on the raising of worms—extracted from the "Gazette sericicole" of Tokyo.②The ratio of the species of worms to the reeling factories—extracted from the same gazette.③The breeding of silkworms in America—extracted from the same gazette.

(8) Translation of Japanese treaties.

①Fertilizers, translated by Lin Ying-sin to Hiang-chen.②Worms and reeling factories. Translated by Wang Houen.③The newest means to remedy the diseases of worms, translated by Pan Po.④Essential Principle of Reeling, translated by Li Yuan.

(9) Dialogue.

A non-textual board showing how the silk should be unwound as recommended by the silk association of America.

(10) Wild silkworms.

Observing the summaries of Canton's sericulture journal in Table V–14, we can see the scientific nature of this review. Moreover, we found that there are two special sections on "translations of Japanese newspapers and treaties" in this journal. In fact, it is a very common phenomenon in all the new agricultural journals of the time. The sericultural books and articles from Japan occupy a considerable part in all foreign agricultural works and articles translated from abroad into Chinese at that time. According to studies by Chinese researchers, the proportion between the number of articles translated from Japan and the number of articles translated from western countries in the *Journal of Agronomy* is about 7.6 : 1[①], besides many western books are translated from the language Japanese. The preference of Chinese translators for works and articles in Japanese is due not only to the similarity of the languages of the two countries. Having seen a sudden progression of Japanese sericulture for a very short time, Chinese intellectuals want to

---

① 衣保中,郭欣旺.藤田丰八与清末中国西方农学引进.东北亚论坛.2004 年第 3 期,第 80 页.

imitate Japan's development model, which had also found itself in a passive position in the economic relationship with western countries.

In reality, these sericicultural knowledge introduced from Japan serve as important references to the Chinese to establish modern sericulture in China. For example, by consulting the translation of a Japanese article "Methods for the control of silkworm seeds" (蚕种检验法)[1] published in issue 13 of the *Journal of Agronomy*, Chinese agronomists begin to report on relationship between the poor sericultural crop and the poor quality of Chinese silkworms and the need for foundation a silkworm control system in China.

The Chinese have also attempted to modernize sericulture by establishing modern sericultural education and sending students abroad. Given the underdevelopment of manual silk production and the competitiveness of Japanese silks, Lin Qi (林启), the Mayor of Hangzhou, prayed in 1897 for the governor of Zhejiang to train new silkworms will help popularize sericulture methods in China[2]. With the support of the Provincial Governor and Lin's efforts, the construction of the first modern Chinese sericultural school—Zhejiang Sericultural School (浙江蚕学馆)—began in the middle of the same year. This school was opened in April 1898, the courses of which include physics, chemistry, biology, meteorology, pedology, the planting of mulberry trees, the physiology of silkworms, dissection of silkworms, education silkworms, macroscopic operation, seed rearing, seed control, silk control, etc[3].

The study period of the school is 2 years, and the examination system is elaborated by imitating the system practiced at the Japanese agricultural school[4]. At the beginning of the school's opening, Jiang Shengjin (who learned new sericulture techniques in France) assumed responsibility for the school's study director. After his resignation, this post is successively assured by three Japanese teachers recommended by the Japanese consul in Hangzhou[5]. Following the expiry of the contracts of the Japanese professors, the students who studied sericulture in Japan continue to teach in this school. In the first class of study, there are 25 students at school[6], mostly from literates who had

---

[1] The original text of the Japanese is published in the newspaper of the *Agricultural Union of Japan* (《日本农会报》), and this article is translated in Chinese by Tengtian Fengba (藤田风把), a Japanese agronomist.

[2] 农学报.第 21 册,第 1 页。上海图书馆馆藏资源.

[3] 农学报.第 41 册,第 3 页。上海图书馆馆藏资源.

[4] 农学报.第 10 册,第 12 页,上海图书馆馆藏资源.

[5] The three Japanese professors are HONG Muchang (轰木长) et Qiandao Deuxième(前岛次郎) et Xiyuande Premier(西原德太郎). 董伟丽.浙江蚕学馆与中国近代蚕业科技的发展.浙江大学硕士学位论文,第 14—15 页.

[6] 五十年各埠海关报告(1882—1931).北京:中国海关出版社,2009 年,第 48 页.

passed the Chinese Public Servant Exam. At the end of the study period, 16 students graduated, most of whom later served as teachers to sericultural associations in major sericultural districts in the Yangzi region[1]. The opening of the seraglio school in Hangzhou remarked the departure of modern sericultural education in China. Until the end of the Qing dynasty, the school trained about 150 qualified students[2], serving almost all of them in sericultural education and research establishments, which prepared the personal condition and techniqueal condition for sericultural modernization in China.

Apart from the Zhejiang Sericultural School, another school, the Private Girls' Sericulture School in Shanghai (上海私立女子桑蚕学堂) created by Shi Liangcai (史量才) in 1903 also has a great influence on the progression of sericultural education in China. This school offered three kinds of sericicultural training: the preparatory class for 2 years, the regular class for 3 years and the additional class for 0.5 years[3]. All girls aged 15—30 are allowed to attend school. In order to systematically indoctrinate scientists' scientific knowledge, we have used the modern school system and the modern curriculum in this school. In such a system, students will master most of the knowledge required when their studies are completed.

Table V-15 Regular classes of private school of Shanghai Girls Sericulture (hours per week)[4]

First Year	hours	Second Year	hours	Third Year	hours
Morality	2	Pathology	3	Education of silkworms	4
Chinese	12	Phntation of mulberry	3	Filature of silk	4
Mathematics	4	Physics(mine)	6	Chemistry	4
Dissection of worms Biology of worms	4	Japanese(Written comprehension)	3	Japonais(Oral comprehension) English	2
Microscope	2	Economy	3		
Physics(plants and animals)	9			Design(machine)	3
				Pedology	2

---

① 徐铮,袁宣萍.杭州丝绸史.北京:中国社会科学出版社,2011 年,第 130 页.
② Idem. p.130.
③ 朱有瓛.中国近代学制史料.第二辑·下,上海:华东师范大学出版社,1986 年,第 634 页.
④ Idem. p.635.

This girls sericulture school became a public school and moved to Suzhou（苏州）in 1913, which offered free education, food and shelter to students. Its new name is Jiangxu Provincial Girls Sericulture School（江苏省立女子蚕业学校）. Through several reforms of the Republican government, this school became one of the major educational establishments and experimental grounds after 1918. Many of this school's students became cadres during the reform of Chinese sericulture later[1].

Other schools specializing in sericultural education are successfully founded before or after the opening of the last two schools: Wuxi Sericulture Association（蚕学会）in 1899, Hangzhou Sericulture Girls Municipal School（杭州府桑蚕女子学堂）in 1907, the primary school of sericulture of Qiantiang（钱塘县蚕桑初级师范学堂）in 1908[2], etc. Moreover, sericultural departments are also founded in some schools of agriculture at that time, including the department of sericulture at the Agricultural School of Suzhou（苏州农校）opened in 1907[3], the sericultural department of the School Zhejiang Agricultural Secondary School（浙江中等农业学堂）opened in 1910[4], etc. Different from Zhejiang Graduate School and the Private Girls' Sericulture School in Shanghai, these latter sericultural schools and the last sericulture department emphasize the teaching of sericulture practices, the popularization of modern sericulture methods and the training of new sericiculturists.

A remarkable feature of these schools and sericultural departments created at the end of Qing is that their geographical distribution is limited in the region of Yangzi. The diffusion of the teaching of modern sericulture to the other Chinese regions was only realized after the foundation of the Republic of China in 1912. The Ministry of Education of the Republican Government of Beijing promulgated the Regulations of the agricultural schools on December 7, 1912[5], which divide courses in the new agricultural schools into five major disciplines: agronomy, forestry, veterinary science, sericulture and fisheries science. The courses founded in the discipline of sericulture are re-divided into the two sub-disciplines: sericulture and silk production, which include:

---

① 费孝通.江村经济:中国农民的生活.北京:商务印书馆,2001 年,第 205—209 页.

② 中国农业遗产研究室太湖地区农业史研究课题组.太湖地区农业史稿.北京:农业出版社,1990 年,第 201 页.

③ 中华职业教育社.全国职业教育概况.商务印书馆,1935 年,第 150 页.

④ For more informations of this school, consult 王庄穆.民国丝绸史.北京:中国纺织出版社,1995 年,第 105 页.

⑤ The republican government of Beijing exists from 1912 to 1927, and then it is replaced by the government of the Kuomintang.

（1）Sericulture

①Mathematics；②English；③Physics；④Chemistry；⑤Zoology；⑥Botany；⑦Theory of agronomy；⑧Theory of sericulture；⑨Economy；⑩Meteorology；⑪Pedology；⑫Fertilizers；⑬Ravage of insects；⑭Bacteriology；⑮Anatomy of silkworms；⑯Biology of silkworms；⑰Pathology of silkworms；⑱Education of silkworms；⑲Silk-making theory；⑳Planting of mulberry trees；㉑Silkworm economics；㉒Silkworms Regulations and laws of the silk industry；㉓The theory of wild silkworms；㉔Theory of artificial silk；㉕Practice of the manufacture of sericicultural instruments；㉖Practices of the sanitizing of sericulture instruments and the sericulture room；㉗Practice of the education of silkworms；㉘Experimentation of the silkworm epidemic；㉙Practices of pup choking，cocoon drying and silk manufacturing；㉚Manufacturing practices and Of seed control；㉛Practices of cocoon and silk control；㉜Experimentation of chemical analyzes；㉝Practice of planting of mulberry trees；㉞Experimentation of bacteria；㉟Anatomy practices of silkworms；㊱French（option course）.

（2）Production of silk

①Mathematics；②English；③Graphic Engineering；④Physics；⑤Chemistry；⑥Analytical Chemistry；⑦Theory of Commerce；⑧Theory of Industry；⑨Theory of the Silk Industry；⑩Economy；⑪Theory of Education in Silkworms；⑫Fabrication of silk；⑬Mechanics；⑭Weaving theory of weft；⑮Theory of weaving and dyeing；⑯Management of the factory；⑰The regulations and laws of the silk industry；⑱Method of registration；⑲Theories of the choking of chrysalises and drying cocoons；⑳Methods of cocoon and silk controls；㉑Artificial silk theory；㉒Wild silk decoupling；㉓Use of waste silk；㉔Practices of choking of chrysalises，cocoon drying and silk manufacturing；㉕Practice of graphic engineering；26. Practices of cocoon and silk testing；㉗Practice of packaging Silk；㉘Practice of analytical chemistry；㉙Internship；㉚Practice of weaving and dyeing；㉛French（option course）.[1]

The Ministry of Education issued another decree on August 4, 1913, which classifies future agricultural schools into three categories：the first-type school（甲种学校），the second-type school（乙种学校），school of girls（女子学校）. Departments of sericulture consist, without exception, of the most important parts in the three kinds of schools, the syllabic syllabuses of which are founded according to the regulations of the agricultural schools of December 7, 1912. The greatest difference between the sericicul-

---

① 中国第二历史档案馆.中华民国史档案资料汇编·第三辑北洋政府·教育.南京:凤凰出版社,1991年,第98—100页.尹良莹.中国蚕业史.南京:国立中央大学蚕业学会,1947年,第60—63页.

tural sections in these three types of school are their periods of study: 4 years for the school of the first-type, 3 years the school of the second-type and 2 years for the school of girls. Moreover, local governments also founded several "Public Schools of Sericulture"（蚕业讲习所）in some provinces. Different from the first three types of schools, this type of school focuses on the basic training of sericulture practices, because its pedagogical objective is rather peasants or sericulturists[1]. Until the year 1918, schools specializing in sericulture, agricultural schools with sericultural sections and schools of public sericulture were already distributed among the many provinces in the Republic of China.

Table V-16 Distribution of sericultural education in China in 1918[2]

Names of provinces	First-type School	Second-type School	School of girls	Public Schools of Sericulture
直隶 Zhili	1	1		
奉天 Fengtian	1	1	1	
山东 Shandong	3	47		
河南 Henan	9	40		
山西 Shanxi	2	4		
江苏 Jiangsu	1		1	1
安徽 Anhui	1	2		3
福建 Fujian	1			
浙江 Zhejiang	1	5		1
湖北 Hubei	1	8	1	
湖南 Hunan	3	5	1	1
陕西 Shanxi	1	4		1

---

① 中国第二历史档案馆.中华民国史档案资料汇编·第三辑北洋政府·教育.南京:凤凰出版社,1991年,第101—104页.尹良莹.中国蚕业史.南京:国立中央大学蚕业学会,1947年,第64—69页.

② Idem. pp.101-104. It should be noted that modern sericulture education begins in Guangdong Province later than in other Chinese sericicultural regions. It's settled in Canton only after the year 1918, when the sericulture department was founded at the University of Lingnan（岭南大学）. However, the founding of the sericultural department at Lingnan University in 1918, with the founding of the sericultural department at Nanjing University in the same years note the beginning of higher education sericulture in China. For more informations consult 黄永安.岭南大学的蚕丝改良机构与广东制丝改良失败.广州文史资料.广州:中国人民政治协商会议广州市委文史资料研究委员会,第13辑,1964年,195页.)上海万国生丝检验所.1925年华中丝业调查(3).丝绸.1999年第12期,第48—49页.

（续表）

Names of provinces	First-type School	Second-type School	School of girls	Public Schools of Sericulture
广西 Guangxi	1			
云南 Yunnan	1	32		
贵州 Guizhou	1	2		
四川 Sichuan		3		1
江西 Jiangxi			1	
Total	27	114	5	8

At the same time, the Chinese government (both central and local) send a large number of Chinese students abroad to learn and introduce the newest sericulture technique in China. In order to train teachers of Zhejiang Graduate School, the mayor of Hangzhou (Lin Qi 林启) sends two students, Ji Kan (嵇侃) and Wang Youling (汪有龄) to Japan at the end of 1897, who are the first two students studying agriculture in Japan funded by the government. In August 1899, the Foreign Affairs Ministry of the Qing Court enacted the *Rules for Students to be Educated abroad*, which stated that "qualified students should be sent to schools of agriculture, of industry and of commerce"[1], which means that the central government is also beginning to attach importance to the expedition of Chinese students abroad for learning foreign agricultural techniques. In June 1901, the Viceroy of Zhejiang and Jiangsu, Anhui and Jiangxi Liu Kunyi (刘坤一) and the viceroy of Hunan and Hubei Zhang Zhidong (张之洞) submit together a petition in which they advise the central government to give official posts to pupils who have obtained diplomas at Japanese agricultural schools according to their marks abroad[2]. With the encouragement and financial support of the government, more and more Chinese students went to Japan or western countries for agricultural and sericulture knowledge.

However, most Chinese students often choose Japan, instead of western country as their study country because of lower spending as well as more similar language and culture. According to a statistical report of the Association of Chinese Students in Japan,

---

[1] Zhu Youhuan. Les sources de l'histoire du système d'enseignement de Chine pendant l'époque moderne. p.935. 朱有瓛.中国近代学制史料.第二辑·下,第 935 页.

[2] 朱有瓛.中国近代学制史料.第二辑·下,第 940 页.

356

there are already more than 300 Chinese students studying sericulture at Japanese schools in the year 1908, which include very famous schools like the The Tokyo Imperial College, the Sapporo Agricultural School, the East Asia Sericular School, the Shinano Graduate School, the Morioka Higher School of Agriculture and Forestry, the Municipal Agricultural School of Osaka[1], etc. On the other hand, among the 180 Chinese students sent to Europe in 1910, only 15 students learned agriculture and sericulture[2].

The third measure taken by Chinese to modernize sericulture is to improve the quality of the seeds of silkworms. The Chinese economist Qian Chenxu（钱承绪）states that "the greatest inferiority of the Chinese silk industry is the devastation of the seed epidemic"[3]. Indeed, as mentioned in the second section of this chapter, the infection rate of the silkworm epidemic is quite high at the beginning of the 20th century in China, on average 30%—40%[4]. The poor quality of the seeds of silkworms in China is, therefore, a major obstacle to the growth of the quantity of the sericultural crop at that time. Improving the quality of the seeds is logically a necessary and urgent for the development of Chinese sericulture.

The first Chinese settlements that try to perfect silkworm species also appear in the Yangzi region. According to the agronomy journal published in July 1898, the Zhejiang Sericultural School has a silkworm seed laboratory, which is the first silkworm seed laboratory in China. "The seeds raised in the laboratory of the school come from Italy, France, Japan, the Chinese communes of Xinchang（新昌）, Fenghua（奉化）and Yuhang（余杭）. All species of seeds are very good, except that the infection rate of the pebrin of Yuhang seeds is very high … the laboratory produced seeds by selecting the best cocoons. It has obtained a thousand leaves of seeds, of which five hundred leaves are already ordered by sericiculturists."[5]

According to the text above, the laboratory of Zhejiang Graduate School is already beginning to select pure species of seeds without epidemic in 1898. The second Chinese seed laboratory is founded in Shanghai by Shanghai Agricultural Association at the end of the year 1898. A Japanese, Iharakaku Tarou（井原鹤太郎）is employed as the research director in this laboratory, which tries to select healthy seeds by comparing Chi-

①　清国留学生会馆编.清国留学生会馆历次报告.转引自王翔.近代中国传统丝绸业转型研究.第 184 页.

②　刘真,王焕深.留学教育——中国留学教育史料.台北:台湾国立编译馆,1980 年,第一册,第 236—237 页.

③　钱承绪.中国蚕丝业问题之总检讨,上.经济研究.第一卷第 9 期,1940 年 5 月,第 135 页.

④　紫藤章.清国蚕丝业一斑.第 57 页.

⑤　农学报.第 40 册,第 2 页,上海图书馆馆藏资源.

nese seeds and Japanese seeds[1]. Many other laboratories were established successively during the last years of the Qing dynasty in Yangzi region.

Table V-17 Silkworm seed laboratories in Yangzi region during the later years of the Qing Dynasty[2]

Names of laboratories	Adress	Fondation dates	Quantities of the papers of seeds produced per year
Laboratory of Zhejiang sericulture School	Lac de l'Ouest de Hangzhou 杭州西湖	1898	1,000
Laboratory Shanghai Agricultural Association	Shanghai et Huan'an de Jiangsu 上海和江苏淮安	1898	
Tongxiang laboratory	Tongxiang 桐乡	1900	300—500
Wuzhen laboratory	Wuzhen 乌镇	1900	100—500
Chongde laboratory	Chongde 崇德	1900	300—500
Laboratory of Hangzhou Municipal Sericulture School	Hangzhou 杭州	1907	500—700
Laboratory of Qiantang Sericulture Normal School	District de Qiantang 钱塘县	1908	500—700

However, the improving the seeds of silkworms situate still in a very primary state during the last years of the Qing Dynasty. Geographically, this attempt is spread very discreetly in other regions of the empire: serial silkworm improvement experiments are only a small part of all agricultural experiments carried out in agricultural laboratories in Zhili（直隶）, Shandong（山东）, Shanxi（山西）, Liaoning（辽宁）, Beijing（京

---

① 白鹤文、杜富全、闵宗殿.中国近代农业科技史稿.北京：中国农业科技出版社,1995 年,第 323 页.
② 张英丽.十九世纪末二十世纪初中国对日本蚕业新科技的引进和影响.古今农业.2005 年第 4 期,第 59 页.

358

师)①, and do not exist at all in other provinces. Techniqueally, the level of scientific research on the improvement of Chinese silkworm seeds is much less developed: their research is limited to purifying a certain seed space, instead of on the education of the new crossed spaces which possess greater immunity. Despite all efforts, the techniqueal underdevelopment of Chinese sericulture did not improve until the ruin of the Qing dynasty. Quantitatively, according to the surveys carried out at the time that have already been shown and discussed in Chapter II, the production of Chinese cocoons in 1915 (three years after the ruin of the Qing dynasty) 2,779,911 piculs, now almost at the same level as that of 1898 (the beginning of the spread of scientific knowledge of sericulture in China), 2,819,000 piculs. The stagnation of the production quantity of Chinese sericulture is confirmed by the studies of Nakano Akila. According to his estimate, from the beginning of the 20th century to the year 1918, it rose by 2,833,000 picules to 2,9999,811 piculs, a slight increase of 5.89%. Qualitatively, the productivity of Chinese sericulture is still low compared to other countries. At the end of the Qing dynasty, most modern sericultural knowledge is intended only for agromomists, and pupils in agricultural schools. The group that deals directly with the sericulture production—the peasants, whose rate of illiteracy in the Chinese countryside is quite high, are not able to directly access the newspapers and magazines. Although some provinces have established "Schools of Public Sericulture" (蚕业讲习所), whose purpose is to learn new knowledge and practices directly from peasants, the number (only 8 in all China until 1918) and the scale of this kind of establishment is far from the need of the distribution of knowledge to the peasants. Most farmers still use traditional methods for the planting of mulberry trees and the education of silkworms②. In addition, special establishments have not yet been established to produce and distribute the improved seeds in large quantities to farmers. So, until the 1910s, most Chinese farmers still use old seed species manufactured at home or purchased from the traditional agricultural market. In 1916 there are only 1,000 papers of new seeds distributed to peasants (by agricultural schools and agricultural laboratories) in Zhejiang province, while the distribution quantities in

---

① Among agricultural laboratories founded in China at the end of the Qing Dynasty, only these laboratories apply sericultural research. Zhili Agricultural Laboratories established in 1902, Shandong and Shanxi Agricultural Laboratories established in 1903, Liaoning and Beijing Agricultural Laboratories established in 1906. For more details, consult 石元春.二十世纪中国学术大典:农业科学.福州:福建教育出版社,2001 年,第 639 页.

② 张英丽.十九世纪末二十世纪初中国对日本蚕业新科技的引进和影响.古今农业.2005 年第 4 期,第 58 页.

other Chinese provinces are even much less[1]. The seeds left by the farmers are still original seeds with an infection rate of silkworm diseases reaching 30%—40%[2], which leads to very low productivity of Chinese sericulture. 1 taël（两）[3] of average seed produces only 2,020 taëls cocoons in Yangzi region, 1,920 taëls in Sichuan region and 1,200 liangs in Guangdong region, much lower than 3.850 taëls in Japan[4].

Table V-18 (Table II-24) Quantity of cocoon and silk production in China, 1840—1926 (picul / year)

	1840	1880	1898	1915—1917	1925	1926
	cocoons, silks	cocoons, silks	cocoons, silks	cocoons, silks	cocoons, silks	cocoons, silks
浙江 Zhejiang		825,500 63,500	1,017,000 78,231	876,766 67,444	1,000,000 76,923	1,140,000 87,692
江苏 Jiangsu		275,200 21,169	350,000 26,923	266,745 20,519	350,000 26,923	545,000 41,923
广东 Guangdong		576,100 717,000	717,000 55,154	768,300 59,100	1,000,000 76,923	1,057,400 81,338
四川 Sichuan		205,800 15,831	317,000 23,385	640,000 49,231	600,000 46,154	468,000 36,000
湖北 Hubei		70,100 6,085	7,846 100,000	100,000 7,692	100,000 7,672	122,900 9,454
山东 Shandong		24,100 1,854	45,000 3,462	70,000 5,385	60,000 4,615	110,000 8,462
安徽 Anhui		10,800 831	30,000 2,308	30,000 2,308	30,000 2,308	97,000 7,462
广西 Guangxi				12,000 923	65,520 5,040	55,600 4,277
河南 Henan		100,800 7,754	142,000 10,923	121,000 9,308	100,000 7,692	42,900 3,300
湖南 Hunan		6,500 5,00	11,250 865	16,000 1,231	20,000 1,538	...
陕西 Shanxi						6,500 500
福建 Fujian						3,900 300
其他 Others		17,100 1,315	99,000 7,615	79,500 6,115	70,000 5,385	13,000 1,000
Total	1,611,673 123,930	2,121,000 163,154	2,819,000 216,846	2,779,911 213,832	3,330,000 256,154	3,622,300 281,715

Table V-19 Evolution of the quantities of cocoon production in Chinese provinces (Piculs)[5]

---

① 王庄穆.民国丝绸史.北京:中国纺织出版社,1995 年,第 13 页.
② 紫藤章.清国蚕丝业一斑.东京:农商务省生丝检查所,1911 年,第 57—60 页.
③ 1 taël = 50 gramms.
④ 陈慈玉.近代中国的机械缫丝工业(1860—1945).台北:"中央研究院"近代史研究专刊,1989 年,第 58 期,第 179 页.
⑤ NAKANO Akila. Development of Capitalism in China. Tokyo. The Japan Council of Pacific Relations. 1931. p.95

Provinces	Beginning of the 20th century	Year 1918	Year 1929
江苏 Jiangsu	350,000	266,745	500,000
浙江 Zhejiang	1,017,000	876,766	1,140,000
安徽 Anhui	30,000	30,000	100,000
湖北 Hubei	102,000	100,000	123,000
湖南 Hunan	25,000	16,000	
四川 Sichuan	317,000	640,000	470,000
山东 Shandong	45,000	70,000	110,000
河南 Henan	142,000	57,000	
广东 Guangdong	717,000	768,300	1,000,000
广西 Guangxi	12,000	55,000	
其他 Others	72,000	95,000	
Total	2,833,000	2,999,811	3,700,000

The inadequacies of the measures implemented by the Qing government are offset by the efforts of the Government of the Republic, which inherits and continues the work of modernizing Chinese sericulture since its creation in 1912. In the first instance, farmers and sericulturists have direct access to new sericultural knowledge and mastery of new sericulture methods, a large number of "sericulture breeding areas" are created in most Chinese provinces. Until the 1930s, each "Sericulture Improvement Zone" has an "Institute of Sericulture" which directly teaches new sericicultural techniques to sericulators. For example, Jiangsu province has set up some 100 "sericulture improvement zones" in its territory, which were distributed among its 26 main sericultural prefectures in 1935[1].

Secondly, the government encourages entrepreneurs to create "Seed factories", which manufacture and sell the best seeds of silkworms to sericulture and peasants.

According to the Chinese Industry Annals statistics published in 1933, there are already 115 "seed factories" in Jiangsu Province, and the amount of production of new seeds in Yangzi region reaches 2 million seeds papers[2]. In 1933, at least 50% of peasants in Jiangsu and 30% of Zhejiang farmers adopted the new seeds produced by the

---

① 俞筠蠲.江苏蚕丝业之今昔观.蚕业杂志.1947 年 5 月,第 48 页.
② 实业部贸易局.中国实业志.南京:实业部,1933 年 江苏省,蚕桑.

"seed factories".[1] Until the year 1937, almost all peasants in Jiangsu use the new seeds, the adoption rate in Zhejiang rises to 50%[2]. With the new seeds, farmers can produce 400 taëls of cocoons per taël of seeds, or barely twice the amount of original cocoon production[3]. Across China, there was a 25%—30% increase in cocoa production in the late 1920s compared with 1915. In the long-term, the diffusion of modern sericultural science has actually promoted the development of Chinese sericulture.

5. The creation of the modern silk quality control system

We have shown in the first section of this chapter that the classical Chinese criterion (which judges the quality of silk by the place of production) is used to distinguish different silk qualities in China's export market before the middle of the 19th century. However, after the 1870s, this ancient criterion for classifying Chinese silk quality no longer adapted the evolution of the international silk market: first, with the popularization of mechanical weaving in the importing countries of the silk, the homogeneity within the same class of silky materials is increasingly in demand; Then, "the business to be delivered (the order trade)" which flourished after the connection of the telegraphy between Europe and East Asia, also demands well-defined chops from the exchanged silks. As a result, the introduction of a new silk quality control system in China is now a very urgent matter for China's silk trade with western countries.

The first attempt to introduce a new silk control system is in Canton. Because of the humid climate in Guangdong Province, it is necessary to examine the condition of silk before placing it on the market. It was the Hong Kong Chamber of Commerce that took the initiative of founding a Condition of silks in Canton in 1860. This plan wasn't realized untill the year 1879, when the foreign companies in Canton there established a "Condition of silks" under the direction of Knaff, former employee of the Silk Condition Bureau in Lyons. However, fraud in the silk trade in Canton does not diminish after the foundation of this condition. Until the year 1909, these sentences appeared again in the report by the French consul at Canton: "In a general way, it seems that the silk industry in the Canton region is decaying. The European silk merchants complain about the inferior quality of silks from reeling factories and raw silk."[4] The cause for this is that most

---

① 蒋国宏.民国前期广东蚕种改良的绩效与不足.南通大学学报.2012 年第 6 期,第 64 页.
② 谭熙鸿.十年来之蚕丝实业.中华书局,1948 年,第 7 页.
③ 王翔.近代中国传统丝绸业转型研究.第 188 页.
④ Archives Nationales de France. F12. 7223 Canton 1907—1914. Rapport du Consul de Canton à Ministère du commerce. 19 novembre 1909.

silks are not sent there to condition. For example, in 1881, only less than one third of the silk traded in the Canton export market was sent controled.

Table V-20 The silks passed to the condition from 1st January to 31st December 1882[1]

Types of silks	Number of bales conditioned	Number of bales exchanged	Proportions
Statlées(Manual silk)	1,129	4,744	23.80%
Reeled	420	655	64.12%
Re-reeled	426	1,405	30.32%
Total	1,975	6,804	29.03%

The establishment and development of a silk quality control facility in Shanghai is even more difficult than in Canton. The project of founding such an establishment in Shanghai is not proposed until the beginning of the 20th century. In 1908, Chinese Commerce and Industry Ministry suggests to establish a Silk Inspection Office in Shanghai to avoid deterioration in the quality of Chinese silk exports. But this plan is not realized.

The main reason for the difficulty of opening the conditions in China and the embarrassed situation after their opening, according to the analysis of the French Consul in Canton in a report to the Ministry of Foreign Affairs, is that "Chinese merchants didn't want to establish a control such that 'Condition', which cut short any fraud, no longer allowed them to sell their wet silks, and therefore heavier, at the same price as dry silk. They coalesced to ruin the 'Condition' and agreed among themselves not to pass any market to the conditioned weight."[2] This point of view is supported by many historians. When Robert Yeok-Ying, an American historian, explained the cause for the founding of an inspection office in Shanghai in 1908, he said that "this proposal is strongly opposed by Chinese silk merchants in Shanghai. They argue that there is no fraud among the silks exchanged in Shanghai. The new control system will make them change the packing of the silks, which will increase the price of their silks; Moreover, they will

① Idem.
② Archives Nationales de France. F12 7056. Rapports consulaires Chine 1809—1906. Rapport du commerce Canton en 1882.

lose some silk quality and a lot of time during checkout, which will reduce the competitiveness of their goods in the market".[1]

It is true that the resistance of Chinese traders is a major obstacle to the establishment and development of silk quality control establishments in China, but this is not the only obstacle. Indeed, after the prosperity of the "order trade" (since the 1870s), many large foreign firms exporting silk successively established "silk quality control offices" in their companies. According to the memory of the former compradors, this type of control office is called the "silk decouper (摇丝间)", where there are apparatuses to examine the indices of each qualitative aspect of the silks (condition, titration, color, regularity, toughness, etc.). Five small "packages" are taken from each silk bale (the weight of each small package is about 100 grams) as samples to be examined after some silk balls have arrived in foreign houses in Shanghai or Canton.

Then, techniqueians (often Chinese) of these companies will remove certain number of silk bundles in each "package" and detangle them to the silk threads. Quality inspectors (丝检员, often foreigners) of these companies will examine the quality of these yarns and estimate the grade of all silk balls according to the result of the check. After the check, these houses will send reports to their customers in Europe or the United States by joining packs of silk sample.[2] Before exporting these silks, these companies will print their name on each bullet in order to declare that these silks have already been controlled by them. These labels are written as: M.F.C (Madier Frères and Co., French inspection); J.M.C (Jardine, Matheson and Co., English inspection); S.R.C (Sulzer, Rudolph and Co., Swiss Inspection[3]), etc. During this period, there is no unified quality standard for Chinese silk exported. For buyers in Europe or the United States, quality control of silk by these foreign intermediaries in Shanghai or Canton means a guarantee of the quality of Chinese silks, so they prefer to import Chinese silks with check labels[4]. As already mentioned, as a result, Chinese sellers have no way of exporting Chinese products directly to Europe or the United States. Most of their silks are exported to Eu-

---

① R.Yeok-Ying. Eng. Economic Imperialism In China——Silk Production and Exports. 1861—1932. Berkeley. University of California. 1986. pp. 185-186.

② 申伯访问录,黄仰之访问录,三井洋行买办朱书绅访问录,正太丝号职员徐毓申访问录,信孚洋行职员吴锡麒访问录,连纳洋行职员徐继昌访问录,转引自上海社会科学院经济研究所.上海对外贸易1840—1949.上海:上海社会科学院出版社,1989 年,第 278—279 页.

③ L.Gueneau. Lyon et le commerce de la soie. Thèse soutenu devant la Faculté de droit de l'Université de Lyon. Lyon Imprimerie L/ Bascou. 1923. p.172.

④ The unique quality standard for Chinese silks wasn't established by the Government of the Republic of China untill the year1929.

rope or the United States by foreign silk traders in Shanghai. The monopoly of quality control becomes another means of controlling the export of Chinese silks to foreign firms in China. In order to prolong this kind of monopoly, foreign intermediaries constitute another group which strongly opposes the foundation of the public institution of quality control of silk in China. The fall of the 1908 project is just due to the resistance of foreign houses in Shanghai[1].

The opening of the first public silk quality establishment in Shanghai, the Shanghai International Silk Inspection Office (万国生丝检验所), delays until the year 1922. In order to import Chinese silk with good quality, and to break the monopoly on the qualitative control of foreign commercial intermediaries in Shanghai, the Union of Silk Merchants of the United States sends to Shanghai its delegates who work in the New York Silk Inspection Office in February 1920 to discuss with the main importers of the Chinese mechanicial silk in order to establish a public establishment in Shanghai. Two years later, the International Silk Inspection Bureau, organized and funded by the United States Silk Merchant Union and the Shanghai Silk Cooperation (each charged 150,000 Yuan of organization fee) established in Shanghai to ensure the quality of Chinese silk exported. It is the New York Silk Inspection Office that provides techniqueal support, so its quality certificate is recognized by all Silk Quality Inspection Offices in the United States.

The International Silk Inspection Bureau in Shanghai encountered very soon the financial problem after its founding, because most silks in Shanghai are not sent there to control quality. On the one hand, the inspection fees are paid by the silk dealers, so they do not want to have their silks checked by the control office. On the other hand, in order to maintain its monopoly on quality control of silk, foreign commercial companies in Shanghai make every effort to persuade Chinese traders not to control the quality of their silks by this public office, and even provokes a debate on a newspaper with the organizer of International Silk Inspection Bureau[2]. On October 31, 1929, the Shanghai International Silk Inspection Office was purchased by the Government of the Republic of China, becoming part of Shanghai Goods Inspection Bureau. From November 1, 1929, Shanghai Goods Inspection Office replaces Shanghai International Silk Inspection Office as the only public establishment that controls the quality of silks exported from Shanghai. Initially, the deposit of silks at this establishment to control the quality is at will. On

---

[1]　中国人民政治协商会议上海市委员会文史资料工作委员会编.上海文史资料选集.第 56 辑.旧上海的外商与买办.上海:上海人民出版社,第 23 页.

[2]　中国人民政治协商会议上海市委员会文史资料工作委员会编.上海文史资料选集.第 56 辑.旧上海的外商与买办.上海:上海人民出版社,第 23 页.

January 11, 1930, Shanghai Goods Inspection Bureau issued *Silk Inspection Regulations* (《生丝检验细则》), which stipulates that as from April 1, 1930, all silks to be exported are obliged to be sent to the Bureau for weight control, and this inspection is free of charge. However, until that moment, inspecting the quality of the silks (homogeneity, finesse, tenacity, etc.) is always at will and paying, so there are still not many silks that are placed under control of their qualities by the establishment. In order to encourage quality control, the Chinese Industry Ministry allows the Bureau to free the quality control costs of the silks to be exported in 1932. Only from that time most Chinese silks begin to control quality by a public institution. By consulting the silk classification standards in Japan and the United States, Shanghai Goods Inspection Bureau issued *Silk Classification Criteria* (《生丝检验分级标准》) in 1936, and announced that all silks exported from Shanghai are obliged to fix their prices according to the certificate of classification delivered by the Bureau after the checks of the weight and the quality of the silks. Unified and modern inspection criteria was not settled in China until that time[1].

Until now, we have demonstrated the processes and results of modernization, silk reeling, sericulture and qualitative control of silk in China, as well as their influence on the organization of silk production. With all these elements, we can return to one of the most important problems of this thesis: the relationship between the growth of foreign trade and industrialization.

As we have shown at the beginning of this chapter, the relationship between foreign trade and industrialization is a subject already treated by historiography. At the level of the western commercial impact on the industrialization of the Asian countries, conventional opinion (for example, affirmed by P. Bairoch in his book) is that the exchange with western countries leads to a deindustrialisation to the Asian countries following the era of the Industrial Revolution[2]. However, this point of view has been examined by other historians. In an article published in 1990, Sanjay Subrahmanyam argues that the decline of the cotton textile industry in India has already begun before the influx of English industrial products[3]. G. Riello emphasizes at the end of his book *Cotton: The Fabric that Made the Modern World* that the commercial relationship finally leads to a conver-

---

① 上海市地方志.专业志,上海丝绸志,第三篇解放前的丝绸工业,第一章缫丝业,第四节万国生丝检验所,上海市地方志办公室.

② P. Bairoch. Mythes et paradoxes de l'histoire économique. p.79.

③ Sanjay Subrahmanyam. Rural Industry and Commercial Agriculture in the Late Seventeenth-Century South-Eastern India. Past & Present. N°126. 1990. 107—108.

gence of industrial development between the West and the East①. Mau Chuan-Hui has shown in his thesis and his research that the Franco-Chinese communication of knowledges and the mechanization of the silk textile industry in Europe have leaded to the progress of techniques of the silk industry in China②.

The case of the industrialization of Chinese silk-reeling undoubtedly supports the opinions of Mau Chuan-Hui: of course, trade with western countries has positive impacts on the mechanization of the silk-reeling industry Chinese. Already, the industrialization of the Chinese silk-reeling factories has been orginated from the evolution of the silk quality demand of the foreigner customers, which stems from the acceleration of mechanization of the textile industry in the main countries of the world (especially that of France). If the Chinese silk industry has no connection with the foreign market, the mechanization of this industrial branch would not, or would take place much later. The requirement of customers in foreign trade is the sufficient condition for the mechanization of the silk-reeling industry. In addition, foreign trade not only provides capital and techniqueal support in the start-up stage of the silk reeling mechanization in China, but also offers it the external market for industrial production, which has offered the necessary conditions for industrialization of a less developed country. Serving at the same time as the sufficient condition and the necessary conditions, foreign trade obviously plays the most dynamic role the industrialization of the Chinese silk filatures.

There is as much debate about industrial influence of the international trade on western countries. In the book *The Industrial Revolution in the Eighteenth Century* published in 1962, P. Mantoux asserts that there is a close relationship between foreign trade and the origin of the English Revolution: "Seeds (of revolution in industry of cotton) were in fact brought to England on the ships of the East India Company, while this new industry was the child of the trade of East India."③ He indicates that the possibility of exporting cotton goods to India is the strongest impetus for the innovations and ad-

---

① G.Riello. Cotton. The Fabric that Made the Modern World. New York. Cambridge University Press. pp. 292—294.

② Mau Chuan-Hui. L'industrie de la soie en France et en Chine de la fin du XVIIIe au début du XXe siècle: échanges technologiques, stylistiques et commerciaux. Paris. EHESS. 2002. 2 Vol. Mau Chuan-Hui. L'introduction en Chine des sciences et des techniques européennes concernant l'industrie de la soie après la guerre de l'Opium. Etudes chinoises. Vol. XX. No°1—2. Les techniques séricicoles chinoises dans le développement de la sériciculture française de la fin du XVIIIe siècle au début du XIXe siècle. *Cahier d'Histoire et de Philosophie des Sciences*. No°52. Lyon. ENS Editions. 2004. 毛传慧. 清末民初的蚕桑改良——传统与现代之间,《中国近现代行业文化研究——技艺和专业知识的传承与功能》,北京:国家图书馆出版社,2010 年.

③ P.Mantoux. The Industrial Revolution in the Eighteenth Century. New York. Harper Torchbooks. 1962. p. 203.

vancement of the cotton industry of England[1]. P. Mantoux's point of view was denied by
P. Bairoch, who in his paper published in 1973 on international trade and the genesis of
the English industrial [2] revolution re-examined the contribution of foreign trade to the
start of English industrialization in 18th century from five criteria:

— One or the request directly related to the commercial activity and the navigation.

— Opening of external outlets for production.

— Investment in the industry of profits of commercial origin.

— Development of a banking infrastructure.

— Techniqueal borrowing.

According to the calculation of P.Bairoch, foreign trade contribution rates are very
low (less than 20%) for the five criteria[3]. He concludes that foreign trade played only a
marginal role in the beginnings of English industrialization.

If we examine the contribution of foreign trade to the industrialization of France by
the criteria of P. Bairoch, the conclusion will undoubtedly be that trade with China
hardly serves to accelerate French industrialization. The export of French products to
China is very modest, so Franco-Chinese trade hardly contributes to the expand of markets for French production, nor to the increase in investment in the industry of profits,
neither for the development of a banking infrastructure in France nor for the techniqueal
borrowing of French industry. It is true that the extension of the shipping line to the Far
East of Compagnie Messagerie Maritime de France has increased the demand for steam
ships, but the number of vessels in the shipping line of China remains minimal in relation to the total number of steam ships produced in France or in contrast to the number
of steam ships employed in the commerce of France with other countries.

However, if one evaluates the contribution of Franco-Chinese trade to French industrialization with another criterion—the supply of raw materials to production—the
conclusion is completely different. Indeed, J.C. Asselain indicates in his book *Histoire
économique de la France du XVIII siècle à nos jours* that an impetus of foreign trade for
industrialization omitted by P. Bairoch is the supply of raw materials. To prove his point
of view, he took the example of sugar industries, distilleries, tobacco factories and tan-
neries in Bordeaux, which needed a large quantity of raw materials from abroad. In fact,

---

[1] Idem. p.204.

[2] P.Bairoch. Commerce international et genèse de la révolution industrielle anglaise. Anales, Economies,
Société, Civilisations, n°2, mars-avril 1973, p.541—571.

[3] J-C. Asselain. Histoire économique de la France du XVIIIe siècle à nos jours. p.69.

the example of the relationship between the importation of Chinese silk into the silk industry of France will be more typical to prove the importation of raw materials for the industrialization of France.

The silk industry is one of the most important industrial sectors in France in the 19th century: silk fabric was the most exported commodity in France until the 1870s, which represent 32.7% of French export value in 1858 and 21.0% in 1873[1]. However, French sericulture still does not satisfy the demand of its textile industry since the first decades of the 19th century. After the 1850s, it was further weakened because of the diseases of silkworms. The fall of sericulture in the entire Mediterranean region after 1860 cut the last supply of silk from the nearby market. At that time, China is the only country capable to supply a great quality silk to the European market. It is the Chinese silk that saved the textile industry from the silk of France and completed its insufficiency of raw materials after the ravage of the disease of the silk worms in Europe.

Mechanization of the silk textile industry in France accelerated from 1870 to 1913, but the deficiency of raw materials became more and more serious during this period: only 10%—20% of silk consumed by the textile industry in France was produced in France. During this time, more than 50% of silk used by the textile industry in France comes from China, which ensures its growing demand on the raw material in the process of mechanization. If there is no import of Chinese silk, the French mechanical looms will miss the materials, and the mechanization of the textile industry of silk can not spread so quickly in France. R.Findlay and K. H. O'Rourke show in their book *Power and Plenty* that the import of cotton from the United States during the 19th century is an indispensable element in the industrialization of cotton in England[2]. In fact, the importation of Chinese silk is as important, even a necessary condition, for the industrialization of France as the import of cotton for the industrialization of England.

---

① M. Levy-Leboyer et F.Bourguignon. L'Economie française au XIXe siècle. p.65.

② R,Findlay et K.H.O'Rourke. Power and plenty. Trade, war and the world economy in the second millennium. p.334.

Conclusion

This book discusses the silk trade between China and France during the 19th century, with the ambition to clarify certain specific aspects of Euro-Asian trade during the globalization of the 19th century. The essential issues in this book are the role, evolution, impulses, commercial intermediations and industrial impacts of the silk trade between the two countries.

I Importance of the exchange of silk in the growth of the Franco-Chinese trade of the 19th century

What is the role of the exchange of silk in the Franco-Chinese trade of the 19th century? In fact, the exchange of silk between France and China not only plays an essential role in the Franco-Chinese trade, but also is a very important part in the multilateral exchanges of the world.

The value of exports of French products to China is still very modest during the 19th century. The main cause for the inferiority of France's trade with China before the 1840s is the long-term influence of the conflicts between France and England from the Great Revolution. After the opening of China, the monopoly of England on the trade of cotton and opium with China and the mismatch of exports from France and China to the markets of each other continues prevents the growth of Franco-Chinese trade.

By contrast, the value of exports of Chinese products to France increased very rapidly in 1844, especially after the 1860s, because of the growth of imports of Chinese silk into France. At the level of proportion, the value of the exchange of silk always composes most of the total value of the Franco-Chinese trade from the 1860s to the early 20th century. In terms of absolute quantity, the value of the silk trade between France and China is enormous compared to the value of the silk trade between China and other countries, even compared to the values of trade in the world silk market. So we can com-firm without exaggeration that silk plays an enssential role in the Franco-Chinese trade.

Moreover, from the 1860s, the exchange of silk between France and China was an important part of the world's multilateral trade at the time. France exports its silk fabrics to England to pay for imports of silk materials from China, England exports cotton goods to China to pay for silk fabrics produced in France, and China exports its silk material to France to buy the cotton fabrics from England. The economies of countries on different continents integrate into each other by international trade, and Franco-Chinese trade expanded in these multilateral exchanges.

II The growth of silk trade between France and China: result from the sustainable increase in demand in France and a strong supply capacity of China

Among the three major suppliers of raw silk in the 19th century world (Italy, China and Japan), the proportion of silk in Italy shows a declining trend in the world's major silk import markets (London, Lyons and New York) throughout the 19th century; By contrast, the silk market occupancy rate of the Chinese silk permanently increases in the markets of the three importers, and finally dominates these three markets until the end of the 19th century; Japanese silk replaces the role of Chinese silk only at the beginning of the 20th century. It is no exaggeration to say that China plays the essential role for the supply of silky material to the world market during the 19th century. Among the three major purchasers of raw silk, England plays an intermediary role between the largest buyers (France and the United States) and the largest sellers (Italy and China) of silk in the world, and its import quantity of silk has markedly declined after the 1870s; France, as the world's largest exporter of silk fabrics, also became the world's largest importer of silk from the 1850s; Its place is not surpassed by the United States until the beginning of the 20th century. Therefore, China and France is the most important exporter and the largest buyer of silk in the world during the 19th century, which formed a very important part of the silk trade of the world.

The volume of the exchange of silk between France and China was very rare before the 1850s, became regular after 1852, grew rapidly from 1860 to 1885, prospered from 1886 to 1903, and stagnated after 1904. In other words, the exchange of Franco-Chinese silk went through remarkable and lasting growth during the second half of the 19th century.

The increase of trade is often linked to a harmonious supply-demand relationship. On the side of demand in France, the general rise in purchasing power in all European countries and in the United States, the decrease in the price of silk in Europe and the spread of mixed silk during the 19th century allowed the French silk industry to expand its international market. Because of this expansion of the French silk market in Europe (especially in England) and in the United States, the production of French silk fabrics, which is concentrated in the départements of the Rhône valley, maintains a trend of successive growth until the end of the 1870s, both in terms of value and in terms of quantity. Despite the obvious decline in the value of production during the crisis of 1876—1893, due to a fall in the price of silk, the quantity of production still continues to grow. At the end of the 1890s, the value of this production rose to the level of the 1870s, and the quantity continued to increase. As a result, the silk textile industry of France needs a considerable amount of silk material for its growing tissue production.

However, French sericulture can never satisfy this demand. During the sericultural crisis in France, which began in the middle of the 19th century, the deficit between consumption and the supply of silk became more and more important. Although Louis Pasteur has found the precaution against silkworm disease and has been in operation since 1869, the quantity of French silkworm production remains still much lower than that before the explosion. The cause is that Chinese silk, which entered the French market during the ravages of the diseases of the silkworms in Europe, gradually destroyed French sericulture at a much lower price, which prolongs the sericultural crisis in France to the 20th century.

In terms of the supply capacity of China, thanks to the abundance of working force, the high benefit of sericulture and the government's encouragement policies, China still retains its advantage over the quantity of production of silk in the world during the 19th century. However, the growth in the supply of Chinese silk to the world market is not only due to the increase in Chinese silk production, but also to the price of the decrease in the consumption of silk material in China. The textile industry of Chinese silk is almost completely destroyed by the civil wars during the Taiping Rebellion, while it is not completely restored until the end of the century. In this case, from the 1850s, much more Chinese silk is suddenly available to the foreign market, and the Chinese silk keep at a very high rate of export for the rest of the century.

With the large deficit of the silk material since the 1850s, silk fabrics producers in France decided to increase imports of this material from the Far-East. At that time,

China's offer corresponded precisely to the demand of France, which is the origin of the prosperity of the silk trade between the two countries.

III A complex relationship among Chinese houses, French houses and other foreign houses

Who have practiced the silk trade between France and China? What is their relationship? Before the 1870s, London was the largest silk distribution center in Europe. At that time, several large English companies monopolized Chinese silk export and ousted their competitors by mastering a large number of vessels, a lot of capital, and the finance, currency and insurance markets. Europe-continental countries, such as France, often buy silks from the distant market by London. With the import growth of the quantities of Asian silks after the explosion of the pebrine, the French merchants no longer want to bear the additional costs of importing the Chinese silk from London.

The creation of the Far East line of Messagerie Maritime of France and the opening of the Suez Canal have greatly diminished the advantage of the maritime transport of England. As a result, more and more Chinese silks are sent directly to France instead of by the London market. However, the implementation of Euro-Asian telecommunications has increased the competition of the Chinese silk export market, and the majority of direct trade between China and France is still in the hands of other foreign companies. Due to competition from these foreign firms, French companies can only send less than one third of the silks exported to France each year. The English, French and German companies share together the direct exchange of silk between China and France.

Apart from foreign commercial companies, Chinese trading companies also play an important but different role in the Franco-Chinese silk trade.Chinese silk merchants are divided into several parts, the most important of which are silk shops in Shanghai, because they are commissionaires between foreign companies at Shanghai and silk companies in the towns which are located in the production regions. The silk shops at Shanghai form as the alliances at the same time by merchant unions and by marriage networks, in order to protect themselves against the government for their common interest, in order to monopolize together the supply of silks to the foreign companies in Shanghai, and to combat the domination of foreign firms by price and quality of silks.

On the one hand, foreign companies that monopolize international trade are the essential link among all intermediaries in the silk trade process between China and France.

All Chinese traders are obliged to export their silks to Europe by the latter group. On the other hand, foreign companies were hardly able to penetrate to the interior of China during the 19th century. They can obtain the material from Chinese silks only by keeping a stable commercial relationship with Chinese silk shops, which are the necessary intermediaries for the circulation of silks inside China. The composition of intermediaries in the silk trade between France and China is complex, resulting from the competition and collaboration of all these intermediaries. However, it is these intermediaries competing and collaborating with each other who have realized the development of this trade.

IV Impulse of the change in customs policies and the improvement of the transport condition on the trade in silk

Are the two most important elements driving the integration of the Athlantic economy underlined by KHO'Rourke and J.G.Williamson, the change in customs policies and the improvement of the transport condition, have the same roles for the growth of the Franco-Chinese silk trade ?

In order to confirm the influence of policy change on trade, we must, first of all, measure the level of protection of the silk customs policy. In order to measure the level of protection of the entry customs tariff on silk in France, we adopted the methods of calculations of J.V.Nye and A.T.Junguito. The result is that silk is imposed a much lower customs duty in France than the French average entry customs tariff level during most periods of the 19th century. In other words, the level of protection of customs duties on raw silk is much lower compared to most goods imported into France. The customs tariffs on raw silk are not, or are not sufficiently protectionist during the 19th century. The very low customs duty gave foreign silks the possibility of entering France. The positive correlation between the non-protectionist customs tariff and the growth of silk imports in France is quite remarkable. Under such a condition of free trade, there was a notable increase in the quantity of imports of raw silk into France. Lyons became one of the most dynamic silk markets in the world during the 19th century.

In China, even if the Chinese trade with foreign countries is not completely prohibited, it must be admitted that its foreign trade regime is very closed and conservative before the Opium War. Firstly, as has been shown, tariffs imposed in realities are higher than those that should legitimately be deposited, which means that the actual protection in China stronger than the official regulations (*the Customs regulations*). Moreover, in the case of customs duties on exported silks, most (about 2/3—4/5) of the duties levied on silk are destined for state finance. In other words, the purpose of the Customs regime is rather to support central government revenue than finance and local development. With the quota of silk export quantity and Conhong's monopoly, we can confirm that China is indeed a half-closed country before the 1840s.

However, it is also unreasonable to simplify the relationship between the Chinese government and the economic dynamics of China at the time. Many historians claim that the Chinese government with a system of strong centralism plays a negative role (at least does not play a positive role) in economic development. But in reality, the mandarins in government are not so compact on the foreign trade policy, while there is often tension between the interest of the central government and that of local government. Concerning the foreign trade policy on silk (as shown above), the central government proposes to ban the trade of silk with foreign countries because of the political, military and economic security of the state, while the local governments are calling for restarting the Chinese silk trade with foreigners for local finance and local economic development. The final decree of the emperor is a compromise between the two groups of Mandarin. Not all Chinese mandarins insist on adopting policies against China's economic development and external communication, and that different voices from different groups of Mandarins play the important roles in the process of the policies making of the Chinese state.

After the Opium War, many new elements and features were included in the new system of export tariffs, which is reflected also in the evolution of the silk export tariffs. First, quotas on the export of many species of goods have been canceled in the new regime. Second, export tariffs in the new regime are much more uniform and standardized compared to those of the old regime. Third, export tariffs on certain goods in the new regime have decreased considerably. It is true that the export of silk is growing more rapidly after the implementation of the new customs regime. But it is difficult to confirm that the evolution of China's customs system is the origin of the growth of Chinese silk exports to France. Because of the sufficiency of supply of silk materials in the Mediterranean region, France imports very little silk from the Far East during the first half of the 19th century. So, at that time, the exchange of silk between France and China was almost nil, whose quantity is far from reaching the quota of the Chinese government. This state only changed after the 1850s (10 years after the implementation of the new customs regime in China), where the ravages of European sericulture pebrines took place. In other words, the exchange of silk between France and China is indeed very insignificant during the period of the commerce of Canton, but this is not because of the ancient customs regime of China; The export of Chinese silk to France is also growing more rapidly during the new customs regime, but the main cause is not the implementation of the new regime.

Nor should it be asserted that the export growth of Chinese silk in France has no relation to the new regime of rights. First, the abolition of the quota on the export of Chinese silks since 1843 gives the possibility of exporting Chinese silk in large quantities, which has probably eliminated a significant obstacle for the increase of the silk trade between France and China later. Second, the reduction in customs tariffs on raw silk in the new customs regime decreased the export price of Chinese silks, which ensured the competitiveness of Chinese silk on the French market during the second half of the 19th century, especially after the 1870s. So even though the new silk customs regime implemented from 1843 is not the main cause for the beginning of the growth of the silk trade between France and China since 1850, it will be a fundamental condition for increased trade during the following decades.

The beginning of the service of the Messageries Maritimes has expanded the direct import of Chinese silk into France, while the opening of the Suez Canal definitely offers France the advantage over the silk trade with China. The conclusion of K. H. O'Rourke and J. G. Williamson on the positive role of the improvement of the means of transport for the growth of international trade is proved again by the case of the silk trade between France and China. The two elements that K. H. O'Rourke and J. G. Williamson pointed out, the reduction of customs barriers and the improvement of the transport condition, are also significant for the growth of the Eurasian silk trade.

V The silk trade and the enter-action of industrial revolutions in France and China

What is the relationship between the Franco-Chinese silk trade and their industrialization?

The industrialization of the silk reeling industry is due to the change of the demand of the silk quality of the foreign customers, resulting from the acceleration of the mechanization of the silk textile industry in the main purchaser countries (especially that of France). If the Chinese silk industry has no connection with the foreign market, the mechanization of this industrial branch would not, or would take place much later. The requirement of customers in foreign trade is the sufficient condition for the mechanization of the silk reeling industry. In addition, foreign trade not only provides capital and technical support in the take-off stage of the silk reeling mechanization in China, but also offers it the external outlet for industrial production, which is the necessary conditions for industrialization of a less developed country. Serving at the same time as the sufficient condition and the necessary conditions, foreign trade plays the most dynamic role in the process of the Chinese silk filature industrialization.

The Chinese silk import ensured the modernization of the silk textile industry in France. The silk industry is one of the most important industrial sectors of France of the 19th century. However, French sericulture is not capable to satisfy the demand of its textile industry since the first decades of the 19th century. After the 1850s, it was further weakened because of the diseases of silkworms. The fall of sericulture in the entire Mediterranean region after 1860 cut the last supply of silk from the nearby market. At that time, China is the only country capable of supplying high quality silk to the European market. It is the Chinese silk that saved the French silk textile industry and completed its insufficiency of raw materials after the ravage of the disease of the silk worms in Europe. Mechanization of the silk textile industry in France accelerated from 1870 to 1913, but the deficiency of raw materials became more and more serious during this period: only 10%—20% of silk consumed by the textile industry in France was produced in France. During this period, more than 50% of silk used by the textile industry in France comes from China, which ensures its growing demand on the raw material in the process of industrialization.

In the other direction, the modernization of Chinese silk industry contributes also to the integration of the Eurasian economy. Through the modernization of silk spinning in China, the quality of Chinese silk is similar to silk in other industrial countries of the world. The convergence of silk quality, apart from the reduction in customs tariffs and the improvement of transport which historians have emphasized, is another important factor leading to the convergence of prices, which is one of the most important symbols of Economic integration of the world.

The graph below shows the relationship between trade, industrialization, the convergence of quality and economic integration during the economic globalization of the 19th century. Trade accelerates the convergence of quality through the inter-reaction of industrialization. The convergence of quality leads to the convergence of prices and the integration of the economy, which makes the trade more dynamic. The four elements above form a closed circle with a positive influence on each other.

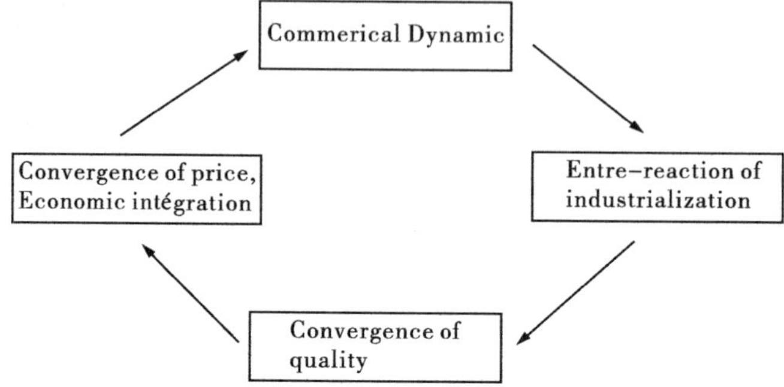

Bibliographie

I Sources in Europe and in United States

1. Archives

Archives Nationales de France(AN)

*AN F*12 2552
29 juin 1833 tarif de douane de 1833
Relevé des soies écrues expédiées de Lyon en transit 1816—1824
Les soies expédiées de Milan et Naples 1828—1832
Tableau des valeurs des soieries exporté de France aux divers pays 1821—1831
Commerce spécial des soies en 1832
Tableau de l'importation et de l'exportation des soies de 1820 à 1827

*AN F*12 6341
Lettre de Forth-Rouen au Ministre des Affaires étrangères du 4 avril 1849, AN,
F12 6341

*AN F*12 6498
3, septembre 1829, lettre du Ministre des Affaires étrangères au Ministre de l'industrie et du commerce
4, novembre 1839, lettre de Chambre de Commerceau Ministre de l'industrie et
du commerce
15 mars 1845, lettre du Ministre des Affaires étrangères au Ministre de l'industrie
et du commerce, traité 1844 et tarif de douane

20, février 1846 lettre de du Ministre des Affaires étrangères au Ministre de l'industrie et du commerce

21, juin 1833, journal de Paris

1836 le commerce des soies en Chine

1840, lettre à Messieurs les députés

1843 lettres des chambres du commerce au Ministre de l'industrie et du commerce

1939, réflexions sur notre commerce avec la Chine

1860—1882commerce chino-français et commerce chino-anglais

Traité 1858

*AN F*12 6499

22 mai 1897 rapport de Chambre de commerce de Shanghai

1897 notes sur la finance Chine, douanes maritimes, Likin etc

Circulation monétaire, M. de Brandt, ministre d'allemagne en Chine

Déret du 12 janvier 1860, droit à l'importation sur soie

29avril1894, prohibition d'importer des machines en Chine

1883Bulletin de Statistique et de Législaion comparée, M.F

Pétition par M. Richou à la Chambre des Députés

Tarif douanier Chine 1883

Traité 1858

Traité 1860

*AN F*12 6894

N° 9 18 janvier 1919, l'industrie de soie de Japon en de 1913 à 1917

N°23, 24, 25, 26, 27, 28, 29 : 8 mai 1906 Pétition des maisons d'exportation de Shanghai

N°53 : Chambre des députés cinquième législature session de 1891, n°1354, le 21 mars 1891

N°58 : la séance du 12 novembre 1891, rapport de la commission de douanes de fils de soie, fils de soie artificielle au sénat

N°70 exportation des tissus de soie de France en 1890

N° 86 87 : le 8 juin 1892 renseignment de la réduction douanier des filés soie de Chine

N°158 : 22 mai 1859 projet de modification au tarif des douanes : la bourre et autres déchet de soie filès dit fleuret

N°16723m juillet 1854, demande de l'admission de l'exceptionnelle 117 pièces de tissus de soie importées d'Angleterre d'origine chinois

N°179 : 15 septembre 1866, Direction générale de douane, tarif coventionnels avec Grand Bretagne

N°259 : juin 1858 augmentation d'exportaion de ruban de soie de France 1853—1857

N° 287,288, 289, 291, 292, 293, 294, 295, 297, 314, 315 : 1853—1857 admission temporaire de crêpe de Chine

N° 325, 327, 328, 329, 334, 335, 337, 339 : suppression de l'interdiction de l'importation de l'Angleterre d'origine chinoise le 25 févier 1853

N° 355, 356, 357, 358 destination de tissus de soie française 1839—1843

N° 493 24 décembre 1862, décret de Napoléon III pour franchir l'importation de grège de soie

*AN F*12 6951

N°68, 179, 193 : 1865—1910 admission temporaire de fils de bourre de soie et tissus de soie aux maisons des Chambre de commerce de Lyon et du dép, du Haut-Rhin

*AN F*12 7056

13 août 1904 consommation des soies en France 1868—1877

6 septembre 1894 rapport   commercial Canton 1893

10 novembre 1890 bulletin comercial Canton 1890

12 septembre 1878 exportation des soies de Canton en France janvier à juillet 1878

20 août 1892 une nouvelle maison est établi à Canton pour l'achat des soies

Rapport du commerce et la navigation Canton 1889

Rapport commercial Canton 1902

Rapport du commerce Canton 1882

Le marché des soies à Canton en 1891 et 1892

Rapport de la navigation Canton 1877

Rapport du commerce et de la navigation Canton 1891

31 octobre 1894 commerce de thé à Foutchéou

6 octobre 1903lettre de consul de Hankéou au Ministre des Affaires étrangères

L'exportation des soies à Hankéou 1885—1888

19 juillet 1879 les maisons étrangères à Hong Kong 1879

Navigation des étrangers à Shanghai 1874, 1875, en Chine 1874

*AN F*12 7057

Report on the trade of China, Hankow 1865

9 février 1892, rapport du commerce de Mongtze en 1891

15 févier 1893 rapport de commerce à Long tchéou en 1892

19 février1903, 27avril1903 les rapports du commerce Mongtze, Ssemao, TchengYue 1902

20 avril 1899, rapport du commerce de Ssê-mao pendant le quatième trimestre 1898

19 Février1903, 27avril1903 les rapports du commerce Mongtze, Ssemao, TchengYue

25 mars 1891, rapport de commerce de Pakhoi, 1890 1891 1892

25 mai 1903, rapport du commerce avec Yunhan et Guangsi 1901

26 janvier 1893, 31 mai 1895, les rapports du commerce de Mongtze 1892, 1893, 1894

29 octobre 1903 maisons d commerce françaises établies à Mongtze

30 octobre 1889 rapport de commerce Pakhoi 1883—1888

Augementation de la navigation française à Pakoi 1896—1902

Rapport de commerce de Pakhoi 1891,1892 1899

Rapport de commerce Long Tchéou 1900 et en 1901

2 février 1876, lettre de légation de France en Chine au Ministre des Affaires étrangères

11 novembre 1864 lettre du Ministre des Affaires étrangères au Ministre de l'industrie et du commerce

25 juin 1886 lettre du Ministre des Affaires étrangères au Ministre de l'industrie et du commerce

31 décembre 1868 rapport du consul anglais

Navigation des pays divers en Chine 1903

6 septembre 1866 lettre du Ministre des Affaires étrangères au Ministre de l'industrie et du commerce

1863 la première maison française établie à Shanghai

Le commerce de ré-exportation des soies japonaises de Chine en France 1865

Les marchadises d'échange entre la France et la Chine en 1865 et les navigations

Rapports on the trade of China, Shanghai 1865, soie

Shipping trade with China, divers contries 1865

*AN F*12 7058

17 novembre 1876 lettre du Ministre des Affaires étrangères au Ministre de l'industrie et du commerce

2 avril 1872, Union des marchands de soie de Lyon

La navigation de Shanghai 1875 par pays destination et provenance

12 avril 1877 liste des maisons étranères à Shanghai

Frêt et des assurances maritimes du port de Shanghai pour l'année

List of members of Shanghai general chamber of commerce 1876

List of members of Shanghai general chamber of commerce 1877

14 janvier 1884 lettre duMinistre des Affaires étrangères au Ministre de l'industrie et du commerce

Marchandises exportées des 14 ports chinois 1875

31 janvier 1876 lettre du Ministre des Affaires étrangères au Ministre de l'industrie et du commerce

20 août 1877, lettredu Ministre des Affaires étrangères au Ministre de l'industrie et du commerce

29 septembre 1872 lettre du Ministre des Affaires étrangères au Ministre de l'industrie et du commerce

Quantité d'échange des soies à Shanghai 1874—1878 par pays

29 mai 1884 lettre du Ministre des Affaires étrangères au Ministre de l'industrie et du commerce

8 mai 1880, rapport de Consul de Shanghai au Ministre des Affaires étrangères

Rapport du commerce des soies de Shanghai 1883

Commande du gouvernement chinois de 1886 à 1890

31 décembre 1874 liste des principales maisons de commerce à Shanghai

12 octobre 1887 liste des maisons de commerce française à Shanghai

1 janvier 1872 lettredu Ministre des Affaires étrangères au Ministre de l'industrie et du commerce

10 mars 1896. Rapports consulaires antérieurs Chine 1809—1906(3). Les filatures

à Shanghai

3 janvier 1906 importation des machines en Chine et en Japon

10 mars 1896 les filatures à Shanghai

11 août 1893, Northe China Daily News

14 janvier 1884, réponse aux questions sur les vers à soie chinois, M. Pila

Annual meeting and report Shanghai général chamber of Commerce 1889

18 janvier 1893, navigation des ports ouvertes de Chine 1892

La navigation française à Shanghai pendant le 4ème trimestre 1884

La navigation française à Shanghai, troisième trimestre 1883

AN F12 7223 Canton 1907—1914

3 septembre 1908 décision de la corporation des marchands de soie de Canton

8 janvier 1912, situation du commerce du Lappa 1909

10 mai 1909 lettre dedu Ministre des Affaires étrangères au Ministre de l'industrie
et du commerce

10 mars 1914 exportation cantonaises pour la France et les colonies française 1913

17 janvier 1912 exportations de Canton sur la France et des colonies de France

19 novembre 1909 consul de Cantonau Ministre de l'industrie et du commerce

29 mars 1912 commerce du district de lappa en 1910

31 mais 1912 les exportations des soies de Canton pendant l'année 1911—1912

28 avril 1913 les exportations des soies de Canton pendant l'année 1912—1913

AN F12 7223 Fouchéou 1907—1915

3 mai 1911

14 novembre 1908 commerce extérieur de Foutchéou

18 féviers 1909, marché du thé à Fou-tchéou pendant l'année 1908—1909

19 mars 1909 lettre des conseils aux exportateurs français

AN F12 7223 Hankéou 1907—1912

8 juin 1907 lettre de consul de Hankéou à M.A.E

AN F12 7224 Mong Tseu, Teng Yue, Sseu Mao Hoï hao 1907—1920

26 août 1907 rapport commercial de Mongtseu, Teng Yue, Sseu mao Hoï hao 1906

AN F12 7224 Pékin 1907—1918

6 mars 1907 rapport de légation de Chine

9 mai 1913 lettre de M.A.E à M.C

*AN F*12 7224 *Shanghai* 1907—1918

4 octobre 1908 concurrence de la marine commerciale japonaise

12 avril 1907 durée des traversées Marseille Shanghai

14 mai 1912 rapport sur la situation commerciale et industrie de Changhai en 1911

*AN F*12 7225 *Swatow* 1907—1918

Rapport commerciale de Swatow, 1906, 1907

*AN F*12 7225 *Tchéfou* 1907—1912

7 decembre 1909 rapport commercial Tchéfou 1908

12 nomvembre 1908 rapport commerciaux Tchéfou 1907

23 mars 1910 rapport commercial Tchéfou 1909

16 avril 1912 exportation des soies par le port de Tchéfou en 1910 et 1911

*AN F*12 7225 *Tchentou* 1911—1920

13 novembre 1911 Envoie d'échantillons de soie

*AN F*12 7225 *Tchongking* 1907—1917

31 décembre 1907 rapport commercial Chongking 1906

18 septembre 1909 commerce général de Tchong-king en 1908

2 juin 1910 la création d'une nouvelle maison française à Tchong-king 1910

31 mars 1910 le commerce français à Tchong-king 1909

4 octobre 1910 échantillons envoyées à chambre de commerce de Lyon

Le commerce de Tchong-king en 1914

*AN F*12 7288

N°1 Lettre de Rouher à Desgrand du 4 avril 1862, AN, F12 7288 (Dossier Maison Desgrand) et AN, F12 6767 (Dossier Cie des Messageries Impériales)

*AN F*12 7414

1 mars 1898 les français à Canton 1898

25 octobre 1893 les français à Canton 1893

*AN F*12 7595

19 novembre 1816 Considération sur le commerce de Chine ;

4 octobre 1818 Pétition par à ministre de commerce, à ministre de navire et à ministre d'interieur pour le commerce avec la Chine

M.A.E Canton 1824—1844 67*CCC* 1

N°34, 37 : 23 mai 1829 rapport de Benoît Gernaert sur le navire saisie par le police chinois

N°46 : 30 octobre 1829 lettre du Ministère des Affaires Etrangères au consul de Canton, Comte Dussumier, en mentionnant vers à soie chinois

N° 57, 58 : 20 novembre 1830, lettre de consul de Canton au Ministère des Affaires Etrangères

N°59, 60, 61, 62 : 24 novembre 1830, deux lettre entre le consul de Canton et le Ministère des Affaires Etrangères

N°65, 66 : 10 decembre 1851 lettre de consul de Canton au Ministère des Affaires Etrangères

N° 92, 95 : 26 novembre 1835, lettre de consult au Ministère des Affaires Etrangères

N°105 : Canton pas de correspondance 1838 et 1839

N°108 : 1840, lettre de chancelier J.P. Nanloffells (Hollandais) du consulat à Canton au Ministère des Affaires Etrangères

N°111,114 : 24 septembre 1840 Macao lettre de C.Alex.Challage au Ministère des Affaires Etrangères

N°118, 119 : 29 janvier 1841, lettre de C.Alex.Chanllaye au Ministère des Affaires Etrangères : résentation de Hong-Rong

N° 120 : Macao 28 février 1841 lettre de C.Alex.Challage au Ministère des Affaires Etrangères

N°185 Traité de Nanking

N°206, 207 : Macao, 23 janvier 1843, lettre de C.A.Challaye au Ministère des Affaires Etrangères sur manifest de navire du trois mat (l'Elisabeth) l'orient à Bordeaux via manille

N°210 : l'exportation de thé et de soie de Chine à l'Angleterre de 1er juillet 1842 à 1er mars 1843

N°212(a, b) Macao le 20 et le 26 mars 1843, lettre de C.A.Challaye au Ministère des Affaires Etrangères sur les natures et les valeurs des marchandises transportés par deux navire français

N°288, 293 : 20 septembre 1843, comte de Ratti Menton au Ministère des Affaires Etrangères en joignant la lettre de Vice-Roi de Canton

N°301, 317 : Le 22 et le 26 jour de la 8ème lune de 23ème année de Dao Guan, traduction de déclaration de vice-roi de doit des commerçant français à 5 port comme les anglais

N°318, 328 : le 8 octobre 1843 dernier traité en 17 articles entre la Chine et l'Angleterre

N°419, 422 : Macao, 24 mars 1844, lettre de Ch. Lefebvre de Bécout au Ministère des Affaires Etrangères sur le navire français (le Josephe) à Macao

N°434 le 12 juillet lettre de Ch. lefebvre de Bécourt à M. A. E sur trois navires franiçais visitant Chine pendant le 2ère trimestre en 1844

N°460, 461 : Macao, le 9 novembre 1844, lettre de Lefebvre de Bécourt au Ministère des Affaires Etrangères sur aucun navire français viennent en Chine pendant le 3ème trimestre 1844

M.A.E Canton 2 1845—1865 67CCC 2

N°1, 2 : 1er janvier 1845, lettre de Charles Lefevre de Bécourt au Ministère des Affaires Etrangères

N°23, 24 : 7 Avril 1845, Lettre de ch. lefevre Bécourtau Ministère des Affaires Etrangères

N°33, 34 : 3 juillet 1845 lettre de Ch. Lefevre de Bécourt au Ministère des Affaires Etrangères

N°50 : 17 octobre 1845, Ch.Lefevre de Bécourtau Ministère des Affaires Etrangères

M.A.E Canton 1866—1877 67CCC 3

N° 244, 245 31 décembre 1872 Mouvement des navires de commerce friançais pendant l'année 1872

N°371, 372 : 31 décembre 1876 mouvement de navigation française à canton pendant l'année 1876

N°380 : 9 mars 1877 lettre de Edmond de Lagrenéau Ministère des Affaires Etrangères : exportation de soie de Canton de 1873 à 1877

N°342, 344 : 10 mai 1876 lettre de Dabry de Thiersant au Ministère des Affaires

Etrangères : création d'une nouvelle maison à Canton

M.A.E. Canton 1878—1889 67*CCC* 4

N°395, 433 : 25 septembre 1889 Commerce et navigation en 1888

N°24, 26 : 31 décembre 1878 mouvement de soie dans la province de Canton en 1878

N°115 : 25 août 1884 interdiction de l'entrée de la rivière de Canton aux navires français

N°133, 137 : 2 août 1886   réclamation de paix de vice roi de deux Guang

N°310, 331 : 10 juillet 1888 Rapport sur le commerce de Canton en 1887

N° 388 enseignements sur Guanxi Tchongqing, Si kang Long théou

M.A.E Canton 1889—1900 67*CCC*5

N°63—70 : 25 novembre 1892 rapport commerciaux Commerce et navigation de Canton en 1892

N°94—101 : 28 juillet 1894 rapports commerciaux commerce et navigation de Canton en 1893

N°221—238 : 14 janvier 1897 commerce et navigations de Canton 1895

N°257—276 : 24 août 1897 commerce et navigation de Canton en 1897

N°321—338 : Rapport des commerces et des navigations de Canton

N°60, 61 : 20 août 1892 une nouvelle maison français à Canton

N°288 : 31 mai 1898 note sur le commerce de saint-rhouï

M.A.E Shanghai 1847—1851 707*CCC* 1

N°60—64 : 19 septembre 1848 lettre de Montigny au Ministère des Affaires Etrangères : commande des tissus français des catholique à Southow

N°98—101 : 16 janvier 1849 commande de catholique chinois à l'industrie française

M.A.E Shanghai 1851—1856 707*CCC* 2

N°254—259: rapport commercial de port de Shanghai première trimestre 1855

N°140 25: août 1853 etat du marché de Changhai à la dute de ce jour

N°266—276: 15 juillet 1855 les maisons étrangère à Shanghai en 1855

N°340—351: 6 févier 1856 rapport de commerce et navigation de Shanghai

M.A.E Shanghai 1856—1860 307*CCC* 3

P430 27 juin 1860 droit de sortie de soies chinoises

M.A.E Shanghai 1861—1864 307*CCC* 4

P57 6 avril 1861 la vente du navire français Madras

P59 19 avril 1861 les maisons français dans la concession française de Shanghai

P183 maisons de commerce de France à Shanghai 1861

P367 exportation des soies grèges et moulinées de Chine et du Japon en Angleterre et en France

P387—389 25 décembre 1863 la création de la compagnie des messageries maritime

P422—424 mouvement de la navigation de Bâtiments français dans le port de Shanghai

M.A.E Pékin 1858—1863 242*CCC* 1

P1 12 févier 1858 ouverture du port de Canton

AME Pékin 242*CCC* 2 1864—1866

P24 24 avril 1864 la voie de terre du commerce de soie

P85—88 28 Juin 1864, les commerces avec Chine par pays divers en 1863

P157—158 une maison du commerce des soies de France à Shanghai

P225—P231 1er août 1865 commerce français avec la Chine en 1864

P242—P243 5 septembre 1865 permis des bâtiments français venant de la Cochinchine et du japon d'entrer Chine comme canotage

M.A.E Pékin 1869—1877 242*CCC* 4

Important P314—326 2 févier 1876 le commerce de France en Chine 1875

P107—112 10 avril 1870 le rapport du commerce de Suantow 1869

P113—114 22 mai 1870 le rapport du commerce de Tche-fou 1869

P206 20 décembre1872 l'étude sur l'étucation des vers à soie de Chan-tong

P228—237 19 juillet1873 l'amélioration de régime de douane chinois

P287—288 6 janvier 1875 une maison française est arrêtée à Hangzhou pour payer encore une fois le droit de transi

P305—307 4 janvier1876 l'importation des soies en France a dépassé l'Angleterre en 1875

P371—372 16 décembre 1876 un procès entre Lacroix Cousin à Canton et une maison chinoise

AME Pékin 1878—1886 242*CCC* 5

Important P21—45 7 juin 1878 rapport sur Likin en Chine

P435—438 12 mars 1886 résumé des résultats des négociations

M.A.E Pékin 1886—1889 242*CCC* 6

P114—116 5 avril 1886 présentation des produits du Se-tchuan M. de Bezaure 1886

P159—169 convention entre la France et la Chine 1886 25 avril 1886

P258—262 24 avril 1887 projet d'ouverture de la navigation entre Tchongqing et Y Tchang

P348 20 avril 1888 projet des maisons française pour créer des filatures de soie à Shanghai

P350—351 17 mais 1888 les difficultés auxquelles des filatures rencontrent

M.A.E Pékin 1896—1898 242*CCC* 8

P156—158   P224—232 22, rapport de la chambre générale de commerce de Shanghai sur la taxe et la réponse

M.A.E Pékin 1898—1901 242*CCC* 9

P47—57 rapport commerciale de Shandong 1897

P108—109 les navigations de Canton, Swantow et Pakhoi 1897

P131—134 rapport commerciale de Se-tchuan

P146—149 rapport commercial de la soie en Chine

P270—279 statistique de la douane française sur le commerce franco-chinois 1899

M.A.E Tchong-king 1896—1907

P22 févier 1897 une commande des soies de sabans par une maison de Tchonqing

P3—9 29 juillet 1897 rapport de commerce de Tchong-qing en 1896 et 1897

P13—P29 mission Baux à Sétchuan

P41—42,47—48 commerce de Tchong-qing 1896—1897

P121 P127, 31 mars 1900 rapport du commerce de Tchongqing, 1900

M.A.E Thefou 1897—1901

P2—9 3 févier 1897 rapport commercial de Tchefou 1896

P17—18 8 mai 1897 les exportations des produits de Tchefou en 1896

P74—75 1er août 1899 les exportations de Tchefou et les pays qui l'opèrent 1898

P105—108 18 août 1900 les exportations de Tchefou 1899

Important P137—139 5 juillet 1901 les exportations de Tchefou en 1900

M.A.E 148*CPCOM*599 *Chine relation commerciale avec la France* 1896

P1—92 Mission lyonnaise en Chine 1896

P141 P147—159 exposition des échantillons français dans la boutique d'un Chinois

M.A.E 148*CPCOM*560 *Chine relation commericale avec la France* 1896—1897

P4—14 20 octobre 1986 mission de Lyon, l'exportation Tchongqing, Foutchou et
Yunnan

P32 le plan de la rivière de Tonkin à Yunnan

P121 P127 30 octobre 1896 mission lyonnaise rappot de Consul Rocher

M.A.E 148*CPCOM*561 *Chine relation commerciale avec la France* 1897

P44—P49 17 féviers 1897 délégué de la mission de Lyon arrvive à Shanghai

P57—P59 18 mai 1897 Route du Tonkin à Yunnan fou

P206—239 rapport général de la Mission yonnaise d'exploration commerciale en
Chine

M.A.E 148*CPCOM*562 *Chine relation commericale avec la France* 1898—1899

P122—123 P138—140 P201—202 11 novembre 1898, lettre duMinistre de l'industrie et du commerce au Ministre des Affaires étrangères

P78—79 26 août 1896 navigation de Lao-kay à Hanoi

P91—94 19 septembre 1898, le concurrence des maisons étrangères avec lesquelles
française en Chine

P105—106 28 septembre 1898, filature de soie à Tchenjiang

P142—143 10 janvier 1899 demande de l'ouverture de Tchentou

P172—177 pénétration de Tonkin à Sechuan

M.A.E 148*CPCOM*563 *Chine relation commerciale avec la France* 1900—1901

P60—87 29 décembre 1900 rapport du commerce français en Chine

P2—4 4 janvier 1900 lettre duMinistre de l'industrie et du commerce au Ministre des Affaires étrangères

P11—41 Mission envoyée par le crédit Lyonnais 1898—1899

P88—130 5 janvier 1901 rapport du commerce entre la France et la Chine

P138—142 28 mai 1901 le texte sur New York Times

M.A.E 148CPCOM564 Chine relation commerciale avec la France 1902—1906

P40—44 5 mai 1902 rapport de la légation français à Beijing

P45—51 P111—114 mai 1902 l'opinion de la chambre de Lyon sur le problème de Likin

P58 P64 P65 23 août 1902 lettre campagnie lyonnais de Indochine

P131—135 le commerce franco-chinois 1903

P140—141 21 mars 1905 conclusion éventuelle d'un nouveau traité de commerce

P149 24 juin 1905 le navire anglais avec les marchandises chinois

M.A.E 148CPCOM565 Chine relation commerciale avec la France 1907—1909

P1—6 24 janvier 1907 échange de la France avec l'extrême-orient en 1905

P15 21 avril 1908 note sur l'organisation commerciale à Shanghai

P47 5 Juin 1908 commerce entre Swantoz et l'Indo-chine Française

P162—186 19 mars 1909 conseils aux exportations françaises en Chine

M.A.E 148CPCOM566 Chine relation commericale avec la France 1910—1911

P17—20 26 avril 1910 le commerce entre la France et la Chine

P149—158 30 mai 1911 voyage pour examiner l'état de production de Sse tchuan

P159—170 P180—188 juin 1911 maisons française à Tchogqing

P194 12 août1911 l'envoie des échantillons des soies de Sse tchuan en France

M.A.E 148CPCOM567 Chine relation commerciale avec la France 1912—1915

P6—19 17 janvier 1912 exportation de Canton en France en 1911

P25—29 17 févier 1912 création d'une nouvelle maison française occupant le

P80—98 30 janvier 1913 exportation de Canton en France 1913

P144—167 10 mars 1914 exportation de Canton en France 1913

P172—208 24 octobre 1914 débouché pour le commerce français en Chine

P218 19 décembre 1914 commerce allemand de produit français en Chine

P226—231 4 mais 1915 intéret française à Hankou

M.A.E 148*CPCOM*568 *Chine relation commericale avec la France 1916—1917*

P42—50 9 août 1916 rapport de la chambre de commerce française de Chine

M.A. E 148*CPCOM*578 *Chine riz, thé, soie, etc. marché extérieur et intérieur 1907—1908*

P11—13 25 avril 1907 exportation des soies de Janpon et de Chine

P27—34 3 mai 1907 Nomenclature des marchandises expédiées à 1 Chentou

P122—123 25 novembre 1907 crise commercial en Chine

P246—247 9 juillet 1908 envoi d'un échantillon de soie de Tchentou en France

M.A.E 148*CPCOM*579

Chine riz, thé, soie, etc. marché extérieur et intérieur 1909—1911

P25—32 23 févier 1909 la création de CanXueBao à Canton

P132—133 28 juillet 1910 exportation des soies grèges de Canton

M.A. E 148*CPCOM*580 *Chine riz, thé, soie, etc. marché extérieur et intérieur 1912—1917*

P12—20 6 avril 1912 exportation de la soie à Tchefou en 1910

P21—25 9 avril 1912 l'influence de la révolution sur l'exportation des soieries Canton

P35—49 31 mai 1913 l'exportation des soies à Canton saison 1911—1912

M.A.E 148*CPCOM*674 *Chine correspondances commerciales diverse 1896—1918*

M.A.E 148*CPCOM*675 *Chine renseignements commerciaux des consuls 1909—1911*

M.A.E 148*CPCOM*676

Chine renseignements commerciaux des consuls 1912—1917

28 août 1913 exportations de soies campagne 1912—1913

M.A.E 148*CPCOM*677 *Chine 1897—1914*

15 novembre 1907 rapport commercial Tchongqing 1906

1 octobre 1907 commerce de Tchefou 1906—1907

Rapport sur le commerce extérieur de la Chine en 1907

Rapport commercial Tchong king 1908

18 juillet 1908 rapport commercial de Tchéfou pour 1907

Mouvement commercial et maritie de Tchéfou en 1911

30 octobre 1909 rapport commercial de Tchéfou pour 1908

M.A.E148CPCOM678 Chine 1897—1914

19 janvier 1910 rapport sur le commerce extérieur de Chine 1908

30 avril 1917 rapport commerciale de Tchongqing 1916

9 septembre 1910 statistique du commerce et de la navigation de Théfou en 1909

12 mai 1912 ropport sur la situation commerciale et industrielle de Changhai 1911

8 octobre 1915 commerce de Chine avec divers pays 1914

28 août 1911 les maisons des dervers pays en Chine

2. Publications

A. B. Lubbock. *The Opium Clippers. Glasgow.* Brown, son & Ferguson. 1933.

A. Beauquis.*Histoire économique de la soie.* Grenoble. Grands établissements de l'imprimerie générale. 1910.

A. de la Berge. *Les industries de la soie en France. Revue des Deux Mondes.* Tome 101. 1890.

A. Maddison.*L'économie chinoise perspective historique, centre de développement de l'organisation de coopération et développement économiques.* Paris. Les éditions de l'OCDE, 1998

A. Maddison.*L'économie mondiale. Statistiques Historiques.* Paris. OCDE. 2003.

A. Perquer. *La France et la Chine. Correspondant.* 25 oct. 1894.

A. Right.*Twentieth Century Impressions of Hong Kong, Shanghai and other Treaty Ports of China.* London. Lloyd's. Greater Britain publishing Company. 1908.

A.Beaux. *Etat comparatif de l'industrie de la soie en France et en Italie.* Paris. Charavay. 1886.

A.D Négociant.*Un mot sur les fabriques étrangères de Soierie, A propos de l'exposition de leurs produits faite par la chambre de commerce de Lyon.* Lyon. Librairiie de Mme.

Durval et M. Bohaire. 1834.

A.Estevadeordal. *Measuring protection in the early twentieth century. European Economic History Review.* No°1. 1997.

A.F.Lindley. *Ti Ping Tien Kwoh* : *The History of the Ti—Ping Revolution, including a Narrative of the Author's Personal Adventure.* London. Day& Son. 1866.

A.J.H.Latham et H. Kawakatsu. *Intra-Asian Trade and industrialisation*: *Essays in Memory OF Yasukichi Yasuba.* New York. Routledge. 2009.

A.J.H.Latham. *The international economy and the underdeveloped world, 1865—1914.* London. Croom Helm Ltd. 1978.

A.J.Sargent. *Anglo-Chinese commerce & Diplomacy.* Oxford. The Clarendon Press. 1907.

A.R.Wilson. *Ambition and Identity*: *Chinese Merchant Elites in Colonial Manila 1800—1916.* Honolulu. University of Hawai'i Press. 2004.

A.Regalsky. *Exportation des capitaux et groupes investisseurs*: *les investissements français en Argentine, 1880—1914.* Histoire Economie et Société. *No°4. 2001.*

A. Stanziani. Histoire de la qualité alimentaire, *18e—20e* siècles. *Paris. Seuil.* 2005.

A. Stanziani. La fraude dans l'angro-alimentaire. Genèse Historique : La falsification du vin en France *1880—1905.* Revue d'histoire moderne et contemporaine. *No°2.* 2003.

A. Stanziani. Information and norms in the coordination of markets. Commencial fraud in France, *1871—1905.* In Analisis de Redes en Historia economica. *CD—Rom. Bellaterra. Enero.* 2005.

A. Stanziani. La fraude : un équipement juridique de l'action économique. L'exemple dumarché du vin en France au XIXe siècle. in G.Béaur, H. Bonin et C.Lemercier. Fraude, contrefaçon et contrebande de l'antiquité à nos jours. *Genève. Droz.* 2006.

A.T.Rixon. Telecommunications of China with Foreign Countries. The Public Opinion Quarterly. *Vol.2. No°3.* 1983.

A. Vamvakidis. How robust is the growth-openness connections? *Historicall evidence,* Journal of Economic Growth. *Vol. 7. No°1.* 2002.

Admission du maire de Songjiang à la création de la Compagnie de Dunli spécialisant le commerce extérieur, le 23 octobre, 23ème année de Daoguang(1843), fond de la Bibliothèque Britannique, O R 7418. B. （苏松太道谕准商人开设敦利号承办中外贸易事）

Annale de la société séricicole, *No° 1. Paris. Imprimerie de Madame Huzard.* 1837.

*B.Gille.*Histoire des techniques. *Paris. La Pléiade.* 1978.

B. Ohlin. Interregional and International Trade. Cambridge. Havard University Press. 1933.

B.R.Michell.*European historical statistics.* London. Macmillan. 1975.

B.R.Mitchell, *International Historical Statistics, Europe,* 1750—2000. Press Palgrave Macmillan, 2001.

B.R.Mitchell.*International Historical Statistaics, Africa, Asia and Oceania* 1750—1988. New York. Stockton Press. 1995.

Bulletin des soies et des soieries-Revue Hebdomadaire Lyonnaise. No°1—1390. Lyon. 1877—1903.

C. Lomdard-Salmon. *Les dessins industriels philippins d'Antonio D. Malantie. Une commande de la mission de Lagrené en Chine (1843—1846). Archipel.* Vol 67. 2004.

C. Zanier Claudio, Bassino Jean-Pascal. *Echanges, appropriation et diffusion de technologies d'origine étrangère au Japon : le cas de la sériciculture et de l'industrie de la soie (1860—1900). Ebisu.* N. 31, 2003.

C.F.Remer.*Foriegn investments in China.* New York. H. Fertig. 1968.

C.Geertz.*Agricultural Involution: The Processes of Ecological Change in Indonesia.* Berkeley and Los Angeles. University of California Press. 1963.

C.Hoag. *The Atlantic Telegraph Cable and Capital Market Information Flows.* The *Journal of Economic History.* Vol 66. No°2. 2006.

C.Kindleberger et P. Lindert. *Economie international. Economica.* Paris. 1981.

C.Sichko.*The Influence of the Suez Canal on Steam Navigation.* Thèse soutenue à l' University of Colorado Boulder. 2011.

C.W. Howard and K.P.Buswell. *A Survey of the Silk Industry in South China. Hongkong.* The Commercial Press. 1925.

Ch. Cousin-Montaubanq.*L'expédition de Chine de* 1860. *Souvenir du général Cousin-Montauban.* Paris. Plon.1932.

Ch.−B. Maybon et J.Fredet.*Histoire de la concession française de Shanghai.* Paris Librairie Plon, 1929.

Ch.−P. Péguy. *L'industrie française des déchets de soie. Revue de géographie alpine.* Tome 32. No°2. pp. 1944.

Chambre de commerce de Lyon, rapport général sur l'origine, les travaux et les conclusions, mission lyonnaise d'exploration commerciale en Chine 1895—1897. présenté par M. Henri Brenier, directeur de la Mission, Fonds de la Bibliothèque natinale de France.

Chine. Annale de Géographie, 1895. pp.176—179. Fonds de la Bibliothèque Nationale de France.

Comité International de Coordination des recherches Nationales en Démographie. La population de l' Italie. Roma. Viminalgrafica. 1974.

Conseil d' administration Municipale de la Concession Française à Hangkeou. Compte-rendu de la Gestion pour l' exercice 1907. Budget 1908. Hankou. Zenhua Printing Office. 1908

D. Faure.*China and Capitalism, A History of Business Enterprise in Modern Chine.* Hongkong. Hong Kong University Press, 2006.

D. Ricardo. *On the Principles of Political Economy and Taxation.* London. John Murray. 1821.

D.A.Irwin. *Free trade and protection in nineteenth-century Britain and France revisited : A comment on Nye. Journal of Economic History.* No°1. Vol. 53. 1993.

D.Chilosi and G.Federico. *Asian Globalisations: Market Integration, trade and economic groth, 1800—1938. Economic History Working Papers.* No°123. 2013.

D.K Lieu. *The Silk Industry of China.* Shanghai. Kelly and Walsh edition. 1940.

D.Quataert. *D. The silk industry of Brussa 1880—1914.* In T.Jacques. *Islamoglu and Inan. The Otomman Empire and the world economy.* Cambridge University Press. 1987.

D.R.Headrick.*The tentacles of Progress: Technology Transfer in the Age of Imperialism, 1850—1940.* Oxford. Oxford University Press. 1988.

D.S.Jacks and K.Pendadur.*The review of Economics and Statistics.* Vol 92. No°4. 2010.

Daily News(UK). 16. octobre 1888.

*De la Politique Commercial de la France Depuis 1860: extrait du mémoire diplomatique.*Paris. Imprimerie Dubuisson et Cie. 1865.

Demande de marchand Zhang Xinxian pour la création de la Compagnie de Dunli spécialisant le commerce avec les anglais. Fond de la Bibliothèque Britannique, O R 7418. A（商人张新贤为禀请开设敦利号以与英商贸易事）

E. De Bvier.*La sériciculture. Le commerce des soies et des graines et l' industrie de lu soie au Japon.* Lyon. Pitrat aine. 1874.

E. *De Martonne E. La mission lyonnaise d'exploration en Chine. Annales de*

Géographie. Tome. 6, No°27. 1897.

E. H. Pritchard. *The crucial years of early Anglo-Chinese relations*, *1750—1800*. Washington. Octagon Bookis. 1936.

E. Hyde Francis. Harris. J. R. Blue Funnel. *A history of Alfret Holt and Company of Liverpool From* 1865 *to* 1914. Liverpool. Liverpool University Press. 1957.

E. Kahane. *Pasteur*, *pages choisies*. *Classique du peuple*. Paris. Edition Sociales. 1957.

E.Hamaide. *la relation entre Lyon et Chine au XIXe siècle*. Thèse pour obtenir le grade de docteur de l'université Lumière Lyon. 2006.

E.J. Eitel. *History of Hong-Kong*. *Montana*. Kessinger Publishing. 2008.

E.Reynier. *La soie en Vivarais*. *Etude d'histoire et de géographie économiques*. Marseille. Laffitte Reprints. 1981.

E.Reynier. *Les industries de la soie en Vivarais*. *In*: *Revue de géographie alpine*. Tome 9 No°2. pp. 173—227. 1921.

E.Tagliacozzo. *Wen-China*. *Chinese Circulations*: *Capital*, *Commodities and Networks in Southeast Asia*. Durham. Duke University Press. 2011.

Economic History Review. No°1.1997.

F. Albert-Auguste. *Histoire de la Concession Française de CHANG-HAI*. Paris. De Soye et Fils. Imprimeurs, 1889.

F. Capie, *Tariffs and Growth*: *some illustrations from the World Economy*, 1850—1940(*insights from Economic History*). Manchester. Manchester University Press. 1994.

F. Kleinwachter. Rapport des enquêtes sur la sériciculture de la douane de Zhenjiang en 1880. *La soie de Jiangsu*. No°3. 2001.

F. List. *Système national d'économie politiuqe*. Collection Tel. Paris. Gallimard. 1998.

F.Capie. *Tariffs and Growth* : *Some Illustrations from the World Economy Trade*. Manchester. Manchester University Press. 1994.

F.Crouzet. *L'économie britannique et le Blocus continental*. Paris. Presses universitaires de France. 1958.

F.Crouzet.ois. *De la supériorité de l'Angleterre sur la France*. *L'économique et l'imaginaire*, *XVIIe-XXe siècle*. Paris, Perrin. 1985.

F.J.Laffey. *French Imperialism and the Lyon Mission to China*. Thèse soutenue à l'Université de Cornell. 1966.

F.R. Mason. *The American silk industry and the tariff*. Cambridge MA. American Economic Association. 1910.

FAIRBANK John King. *Trade and Diplomacy on the China Coast. The Opening of the Treaty Ports*, *1842—1854*. Cambridge. MA. Harvard University Press. Vol 1.1953.

F.H.H.King. *Money and Monetary Policy in China 1845—1895*. Harvard University Press. 1965.

G. Durand.*Lyon et l'Extrême-Orient. Le monde des soies. Lyon et l'Extrême-Orient*, actes du colloque du 17—19 novembre 1994.

G. Valérien. *La production de la soie dans le monde. Annales de Géographie.* Tome 9. No°44. 1900.

G.Brossollet. *Annuaire des Français à Shanghai* (*1842—1955*). Editions Rive Droite. 2002.

G.Chauvy. *La dure condition des forçats du lux. Historia.* No° 648. 2000.

G.Dejoint. la politique économique du Directoire.*Revue Economique.* No°3. 1951.

G.Ellis.*Napoleon's Continental Blockade. The Case of Alsace.* Oxford. Clarendo Press. 1981.

G.Federico, *An Economic History of the Silk Industry*, 1830—1930. Cambridge: Cambridge University Press, 1997.

G.Brossollet.*Les Français de Shanghai* : 1849—1949. Editions Belin. 1999.

G.Lanning and S.Couling, *the History of Shanghai*. Shanghai. Press de Kelly & Walsh. 1921.

G.R.Hawke. *The United States Tariff and protection in the late nineteenth century. Econominc history review.* No°28.1988.

G.Riello.*Cotton: The Fabric that Made the Modern World.* New York. Cambridge University Press. 2013.

H. Cordier. *Histoire générale de la Chine et de ses relations avec les pays étrangers.* Paris. Librairie Paul Geuthner. Vol III.1920.

H. Cordier. *La Chine en France au XVIIIe siècle.* In: *Comptes-rendus des séances de l'Académie des Inscriptions et Belles-Lettres*, 52ᵉ *année.* No°9. 1908.

H. Cordier.*Les origines de Deux établissements Français dans l'extrême-orient Chang-haï-Ning-po.* Paris. Ecole des Langues orientales vivantes. 1896.

H. Le Thanh. *Les relations commerciales entre Lyon et l'IndoChine* (*1858—1920*). Dess Ride. *Rapport de recherche bibliographieque*, 2002.

H.Algoud.*La soie, art et histoire.* Paris. Payot. 1928.

H.B.Morse .*The International Relations of the Chinese Empire.* New York. Longmains, Green. 1910.

H.B.Morse.*The Gilds of China*. London. New York. Longmans, Green. 2d. 1932

H.Clouzot.*Le métier de la soie en France*. Paris. Devambez. 1910.

H.Herbette. *La soie en Indochine*. *Annales de Géographie*. Vol.41. No°230.1932.

H.J. Voth. *Time and Work in England, 1750—1830*. Oxford. Oxford University Press. 2000.

H.Jorda.*Le métier, la chaîne et le Réseau : petite histoire de la vie ouvrière*. Paris. l' Harmattan. 2002.

H.M.Scarth.*Twelve Years in China. The people, the Rebels, and the Mandarins. By a British Résident (J. Scarth). With illustrations*. London. British Library. 2011.

H.Maxwell-Lefroy.*Report on an inquiry into the silk industry in India. Vol. I. The Silk industry*. Calcutta. Superintendent of the Government Printing Office. 1916.

H.Medick. *Une culture de la considération. Les vêtements et leurs couleurs à Laichingen entre* 1850 *et* 1820. *Annales HSS*. No°4. 1995.

I.Friel. *Maritime History of Britain and Ireland*. London. The British Museum Press. 2003.

I.Hedde, E.Renard, A.Haussmann et N. Rondot. *Etude pratique du commerce d' exortation de la Chine*. Paris. Librairie du commerce chez Renard. 1848.

Imprimerie et libraire administratives de Paul Dupont. 1852—1887.

J. d'Aguilar.*Pasteur et le ver à soie*. Histoire des science. No°99. 1995.

J. Marseillee. *Empire colonial et capitalisme français. Histoire d' un divorce* Paris. Albin Michel. 2005.

J. Meyer. *La France et l'Asie : essai de statistiques −1730—1785 : état de la question. Histoire, économie et société*. No°2. 1982.

J. Sottas.*Une escadre française aux Indes en* 1690 : *l' histoire de la Compagnie Royales des Indes Orientales 1664—1719*. Paris : Librairie Plon. 1905.

J. Stanislas.*Résumé de principales traites chinoise sur la culture des mûriers et l' éducation des vers à soie*. Paris. Imprimerie royale. 1837.

J.A.Aamakwa. *The Japanese raw silk in relation to the American and French silk industries. Kwansei Gakuin University Annual Stadies*. No°34. 1985.

J.Culbertson. *The Folly of Free Trade. Harvard Business Review*. Septembre-octobre. 1986.

J.F.Klein. *Une histoire impériale connectée? Hai Phong : jalon d' une statégie lyonnaise en Asie orientale (1881—1886)*. Recherche en Sciences Sociales de l' Asie sur

Sud-Est, No°13—14. 2009.

J.Foreman-Peck. *A model of later-19th-century European economic development. Revista de Historia Economica*. Vol.8. No°3. 1995.

J.Fredet. *Charles de Montiny consul de France. Revue de l'histoire de colonies française*. Janvier 1953.

J.Goghegan. *Somme accounts of silk in India. Especially of the various attempts to encourage and extend sericulture in taht country*. Calcutta. Office of the Superintendent of Government Printing.1872.

J.H.Fabre.*Souvenirs entomologiques*. 9ème série. Paris. Delagrave. 1923.

J.K Fairbank and Kwang-Ching Liu.*The Cambridge Histoy of China. Cambridge.* Cambridge University Press. Vol 11. Late Ch'ing 1800—1911. 1980.

J.M.Legay et G. Chavancy. *La phase pastorienne de la sériciculture. La crise de la pébrine et ses conséquences. Natures Sciences Sociétés*. Vol.12. 2004. No°4.

J.Mabire.*L'Eté rouge de Pékin. La révolte des boxeurs récit.* Paris. Editions du Rocher. 2006.

J.Perdu.*La révolte des canuts : les insurrections lyonnaises, 1831—1834.* Paris. Spartacus. 2010.

J.R.Hanson.*Trande in transition. Export from the Third World. 1840—1900.* New York. Academic Press. 1980.

J.Rojon. *Les soieries lyonnaises dans la seconde moitié du XIXe siècle et au début du XXe siècle : du produit artisanal de lux au produit industriel de (demi−) luxe. Art et Industrie.* 2013.

J.T.Omohundro.*Chinese Merchant Families in Iloilo : Commerce and Kin in a Central Philippine City.* Quezon City. Ateneo de Manila Press. 1981.

J.Thobie.*Intérêt et impérialisme français dans l'empire ottoman (1895—1914).* Paris. Publications de la Sorbonne. 1977.

J.V.Nye, consulter J.V.Nye.*War, Wine and Taxes : The Political Economy of Anglo-French Trade, 1689—1900.* Princeton and Oxford. Princeton University Press. 2007.

J.V.Nye. *The myth of free-trade Britain and fortress France : Tariffs and trade in the Nineteenth Century.The journal of Economic History.* Vol. 51. No°1. 1991.

J−C Heudin. *Les créateures artificielles: des automates aux mondes virtuels.* Paris. Editions Odile Jacob. 2008.

J−C.Asselain.*Histoire économique de la France du XVIIIe siècle à nous jours.* Edition du Seuil. 1984.

J-F.Klein. *Un Lyonnais en Extrême—Orient. Lyon.* Editions Lyonnaises d'Art et d'histoire. 1994.

J-P.Daviet.*Nouvelle histoire économique de la France contemporaine.* T.1.Paris. Editions La Decouverte. 1993.

J-P. Poussou. *Le dynamisme de l'économie française sous Louis XVI. Revue économique.* Vol. 40. No°6. 1989.

J-P.Dormois and P.Lains.*Classical trade Protectionism 1815—1914.* London and New York. Routledge. 2006.

Ju-K'ang T'ien. *The Chinese of Sarawak. A Study of Social Structure. London School of Economics Monographs on Social Anthropology.* No° 12. London. Lund Hmphries. 1953.

K.H.O'Rourke and J.G. Williamson.*Globalization and History: The Evolution of a Nineteenth Century Atlantic Economy.* Cambridge: MA: MIT Presse.1999.

K.Pomeranz.*The Great Divergence : China, Europe and the Making of the Modern World Economy.*Princeton. Princeton University Press. 2000.

K.Pomeranz.*Une grande divergence: la Chine, l'Europe et la construction de l'économie mondiale.* Paris. Albin Michel. 2010.

K.D.Garbade and W.L.Silber. *Technology, Communication and the Performance of Financial Markets: 1840—1965.*

K.H.O'Rourke. *Measuring protection. A cautionary tale. Journal of Development Economics.* No°53. 1997.

K.H.O'Rourke. *Tariffs and growth in the late nineteenth century. Economic Journal.* No°110. 2000.

L. de Teste.*Commerce de soie et soierie en France. Considéré dans ses rapports avec celui des autres états.* Avignon : Imprimeurie-Librairie Mme V. Guichard Aîné, 1830.

L. Duran.*Raw silk: a practical hand-book for the buyer.* New York. Silk Publishing Company. 1921.

L. Raveneau. *La Chine économique d'après les travaux de la mission lyonnaise 1895—1897. Annales de Géographie.* Tome. 8. No°37. 1899.

L.Bergeon.*L'Industrialisation de la Fance au XIXe siècle.* Paris.Hatier. 1979.

L.de Teste.*Du commerce des soies et soieries en France, considéré dans ses rapports avec celui des autres états, Avignonn. Lithographe de la ville.* 1830.

L.Dermigny.*La Chine et l'occident : le commerce à Canton au XVIIIe siècle,*

1719—1833. Paris. S.E.V.P.E. 1964. Vol.I. p.394.

L.Gueneau.*Lyon et le commerce de la soie*. Thèse soutenu devant la Faculté de droit d l'Université de Lyon. Lyon. Imprimerie L. Bascou. 1923.

L.M.Li.*China's silk Trade Traditionnal Industry in the Modern World* 1842—1937. Cambridge. Concil on East Asian Studies. Harvard University. 1981.

L.M.LI. *Silks by sea: trade, technology and enterprise in China and Japan. Business history review*. Vol.56. No°2.1982.

L.Pasteur.*Etudes sur la maladie des vers à soie : notes e documents*. Paris. Imperimerie de Gauthier-Villars. 1879.

L.S. Bell. *From Comprador to County Magnate: Bourgeois Practice in the Wuxi County Silk Industry*. Selected in Joseph W. Esherick and Mary Backus Rankin.*Chinese Local Elites and Patterns of Dominance*. California. University of California Press. 1900.

L'économie mondiale, Statistique historique. Paris. OCDE. 2003.

La mission lyonnaise d'exploration commerciale en Chine 1895—1897. Fonds de la Bibliothèque natinale de France.

Les natures et les quantités des marchandises importées ou exportées par des maisons chinoises à Shanghai du février au juillet de la 24ème année de Daoguang (calendrier chinois). Fonds de la bibliothèque Britannique. O R 7400. （道光二十四年二月至七月敦利等各商号进出口货物品种数量等录）

Lin Man-Houng.*China Upside Down : Currency, Society and Indeologie, 1808—1856*, Cambridge. MA and London. Harvard University Asia Center. 2006.

Lyon, Alexandre Rey. *Imprimeur editeur, 1897. Fonds de la Bibliothèque natinale de France*.

M. Bouzard-Tricou.*Analyse et catalogue raisonné de la production des frère Grand, fabricants de soieries à Lyon. 1807—1871, d'après les archives de la maison Tassinari et Chatel*. Mémoire de maitrise. Université Lumière–Lyon 2. Vol 1. 1986.

M. Bouzard-Tricou. *Les relations Lyon-Russie, à travers les archives de soirie lyonnaise, aux XVIIIe et XIXe siècle. Cahiers d'histoire*. No°3—4. 1990.

M. Detrie.*France-Chine-Quand deux mondes se rencontrent*. Editions Gallimard, 2004.

M. Levy-Leboyer et F. *Bourguignon. L'Economie Française au XIX siècle, Analyse macro-économique*. Paris. Economica. 1986.

M. Lévy-Leboyer. *Un aspect de l'exportation des capitaux en Chine : les entreprises franco-belges 1896—1914, La position internationale de la France, aspects économiques et financers XIXe – XXe siècle.* Rénuni par M.Lévy–Leboyer, Paris. EHESS. 1997.

M. Meuleau.*Des Pionners en Extrême-Orient.* Paris. Fayard. 1990.

M. Zimmermann. Les Chemins de fer et le commerce extérieur de la Chine.*Annales de Géographie.* Tome 20. No°114. 1911.

M.Ame. *Etude sur les tarifs de douanes et les traités de commerce.* Vol. I. Paris. 1876.

M.Arnoud.*De la balance du commmerce et des relations commerciales extérieures de la France.* Paris. Puisson. 1791.

M.Cliquenois.*Droit public économique.* Paris. Editions Ellipses. Coll. Université – Droit. 2001.

M.E.Fletcher. *The Suez Canaal and world shipping. 1869—1914. Journal of Economic History.* N°18. 1958.

M. Greenberg.*British Trade and the Opening of China 1800—1842.* Cambridge. Cambridge University Press. 1951.

M.F.Berneron-Couvenhes.*Les Messageries Maritimes. L' essor d' une grande compagnie.* Paris. Presses de l' Université Paris-Sorbonne. 2007.

M.Levy-Leboyer. *Capital Investment and Economic Growth in France. 1820—1930.* dans *The Cambridge Economic History of Europe.* Vol. VII. Part. I Cambrige. Cambrige University Press. 1978.

M.Rainelli. *La nouvelle théorie du commerce international.* Paris. La Découverte. 2003.

M.Ramon. *How Did the Modern Chinese Economy Develop? ——A Review Article. Journal of Asia Studies.* Vol.50. No° 3. 1991.

M.Shichiro.*The History of the Silk Industry in the United States.* New York. Silk Publishing Co. 1930.

M. Zimmermann. *La production et la consommation de la soie. Annales de Géographie.* No°135. 1916.

M–A. Privat-Ravigny.*Les prémices de la mondialisation, Lyon rencontre la Chine au 19ᵉ siècle.* Lyon. EMCC. 2009.

Mau Chuan-hui. *L' introduction en Chine des techniques européennes de l'industrie de la soie. Études chinoises: bulletin de l'Association française d'études chinoises.* Vol. 20. No° 1—2.2001.

Mau Chuan-Hui. *Les techniques séricicoles chinoises dans le développement de la séricicniturefrançaise de la fin du XVIIIe siècle au début du XIXe siècle. Cahier d' Histoire et de Philosophie des Sciences.* No°52. Lyon. ENS Editions. 2004.

Ministère de l'Agriculture et du Commerce ; Faits Commarciaux. No° 1—51. Paris.

N. Bensacq-Tixier.*Histoire des diplomates et consuls français en Chine* (1840—1912). Paris. Les Indes savantes. 2008.

N. Rondot.*Le titrage de la soie*, Paris. Librairie de Gullaumin et Cie. 1859.

N. Shinonaga, *La formation de la Banque Industrielle de Chine*, *Le Mouvement social*, No°155.1991.

N.Rondot. *Chambre de commerce de Lyon. Commerce de la France avec la Chine. Délivération prise sur le rappot de M.Rondot. Séance du 12 janvier 1860.* Lyon : De Luois Perrin. 1860.

N.Rondot. *Conseil supérieur de l'agriculture, des manufactures et du commerce. Rapport sur l'industrie des soies et des soieries.* par MM. Natalis Rondot. Paris. Imprimerie mpériale. 1861.

N.Rondot. *L'art de la soie ; les soies.* Paris. Imprimeries nationales. 1885.

N.Rondot.*L'industrie de la soie en France.* Lyon. Imprimerie Mougin-Rusand.1894.

Notrice sur le conditionnement des soies par le procéde de la dessication absolue. Lyon. Imprimerie de Barret. 1842.

P.Bairoch. *Commerce extérieur et développement économique de l'Europe au XIX siècle.* Paris. Mouton. EHESS. 1976.

P.Bairoch. *Commerce international et genèse de la revolution industrielle anglaise. Anales, Economies, Société, Civilisations.* No°2, Mars—Avril. 1973.

P.Bairoch. *Free trade and European Economic Development in the 19th Century. European Economic review.* Vol. 3. No°3. 1972.

P. Bairoch. *Geographical Structure and Trade Balance of European Foreign Trade from 1800 to 1970. The Journal of European Economic History.* No°3. 1974.

P.Bairoch, *Les structures du commerce extérieur de la France 1879—1970*, *La position internationale de la France, aspects économiques et financers XIXe - XXe siècle.* Rénuni par M.Lévy-Leboyer, Paris. EHESS. 1997.

P.Bairoch. La Place de la France sur les marchés internationaux,*La position internationale de la France, aspects économiques et financers XIXe - XXe siècle.* Rénuni par M.Lévy-Leboyer, Paris. EHESS. 1997.

P. Bairoch. *Les trois révolutions agricoles du monde développé ; rendements et productivité de 1800 à 1985. Annales. Economies. Sociétés. Civilisations.* Vol. 44. No°2. 1989.

P.Bairoch. *Mythes et paradoxes de l' histoire économique.* Paris. La découverte. 1994.

P.Cayez.*Crise et croissance de l' industrie lyonnaise 1850—1900.* Paris. Editions du CNRS. 1980.

P. Cayez.*Métiers Jacquard et hauts fourneaux aux origines de l' hidustrie lyonnaise.* Lyon. Presses Universitaires de Lyon. 1978.

P.Claudel.*Correspondance consulaire de Chine (1896—1909).* Paris. Presses Universitaires de Franche-Comté. 2005.

P. Debré.*Louis Pasteur.* Paris. Editions Flammarion. 1995.

P. O' Brien and C. Keyber.*Economic Growth in Britain and France : two paths towards the 20th Century.* London. G.Allen aud Unwin. 1978.

P.Clerget. *Les industries de la soie dans la vallée du Rhône. Les Études rhodaniennes.* Vol. 5. No°1, 1929.

P.Dane and W.A.Cole. *British Economic Growth 1688—1959. Trends and Structure.* Cambridge. University Cambridge Press, 1967.

P.Ernest.*Chambre de Commerce de Lyon Question du droit d'entrée sur les soies.* Rapport par les délégués, Lyon. impr. De Barret.1871.

P.Huang.*The Peasant Economy and Social Change in North China. Stanford.* Stanford University Press. 1988.

P.Huang. *The Peasant Family and Rural Development in the Yangzi Delta,* 1350—1988. Stanford. Stanford University Press. 1990.

P.J.Cain and A.G.Hopkins. *The Political Economy of Expansion overseas, 1750—1914. E.H.R.* Second Series, Vol. XXXIII. 1980.

P.Krugmain. *Introduction : New Thinking about Trade Policy.* In P.Krugmain. *Strategic Trade Policy and the New International Economics.* Cambridge. The MIT Press. 1986.

P.Krugman. *Growing World Trade : Causes and consequences. Brookings Papers on Economic Activity.* No°1.1995.

P.Mantoux *Industrial Revolution in the Eighteenth Century.* New York. Harper Torchbooks. 1962.

P.Tain. *L' expédition de Chine .* Paris. Michel Lévis éditeurs. 1862.

P.Verley.*Nouvelle histoire économique de la France contemporaine. 2. L' industrialisation, 1830—1914.* Paris. Editions LA DECOUVERTE. 2003.

P. Verley. *Spécialisation industrielles, structures sociales, activités financières et intégration économique internationale au XIXe siècle* : *le cas de la Grande-Bretagne et de la France. Revue d' histoire du XIXe siècle.* No°23. 2001.

P.Verley.*l' Echelle du monde.* Paris. Editions Gallimard. 1997.

P. Verley.*La revolution industrielle.* Paris. Gallimard. 2005.

P.Vernus.*Art, luxe et industrie. Bianchini Férier, un siècle de soieries lyonnaises,* 1888—1992. Grenoble. Presses universitaires de Grenoble, 2006.

P.Vernus. *Contractual relaions, tariffs and customs in the Lyon silk industrie in the Nineteenth Century.* In Alessandro Stanziani. *Labour, Coercion, and Economic Growth in Eurasia. 17th-20th Centuries. Studies in Global Social History.* Leyde. Brill. 2013.

P.Vernus. *L' innovation dans la fabrique lyonnaise de soierie au tournant du XIXe et du XXe siècle. L' exemple de Bianchini Férier. Lyon innove. Inventions et brevets dans la soierie lyonnaise au XVIIIe et XIXe siècle.* Lyon. EMCE. 2009.

Pan Shu-lun(潘序伦). *The Trade of the United States with China.* New York. China Trade Bureau.1924.

R. Fortune.*Three Years Wanderings in the Northern Provinces of China. Including a visit to the Tea, Silk and Cotton Countries.* London. J. Murray. 1847.

R. Girault.*Emprunts russes et investissement français en Russie,* 1887—1914. Paris. Armand Colin. 1973.

R. Lee.*France and the exploitation of CHINA 1885—1901, A Study In Economic Imperialism.* Hong Kong. Oxford University Press. 1989.

R. Y. Eng. *Economic Imperialism in China*: *Silk Production & Exports, 1861—1932.* Oalkland. University of California Press. 1996.

R. Yeok-Ying. Eng. *Economic Imperialism In China——Silk Production and Exports, 1861—1932.* Berkeley. University of California. 1986.

R.B.Wong. *Chinese Economic History and Development*: *A Note on the Myers-Huang Exchange. Journal of Asia Studies.* Vol.51. No° 3. 1991.

R.Baldwin. *Determinants of the Commodity Structure of US Trade. Américain Economic Review.* No°61. Mars 1971.

R.C.Michie.*London and New York Stock Exchanges 1850—1914.* London. Allen and Unwin. 1987.

R.Davis. *The Industrial Revolution and British Overseas Trade.* London. Leicester University Press. 1979.

R.Edwards. *The old Canton System of Foreign Trade.* In V.H.Li. *Law and Politics in China's Foreign Trade.* Seattle and London. University of Washington Press. 1977.

R.Findlay and K. H.O'Rourke.*Power and plenty. Trade,war,and the world economy in the second millennium. New Jersey. Princeton University Press.* 2007.

R.Fortune. *Two visits to the Tea Countries of China.* London. Murry. Vol I. 1853.

R. M. Montgomery. *China; political, commercial, and social: an official report.* Charleston. BiblioBazzar. Vol 2. 2001.

R.Poidevin.*La relation économique et financière entre la France et l'Allemagne de 1898 à 1914.* Paris. Armand.Colin. 1969.

R.Roehl. *French industrialization: a reconsidération. Explorations in Economic History.* No°3. 1976.

R.Tolaini.*Le titre au XIX siècle. Progrès technique et perfectionnement des systèmes d'évaluation de la qualité dans l'industrie de la soie,* Cahiers de metrologie, 1996.

S. Min-hsiung.*The Silk Industry in Ch'ing China.* Ann Arbor. University of Michigan. 1976.

S. Subrahmanyam. *Rural Industry and Commercial Agriculture in the Late Seventeenth-Century South-Eastern India. Past&Present.* No°126. 1990.

S.F. Wrignt. *China's Strauggle for the tariff autornomy 1843—1938.* Shanghai. Kelly&Walsh. 1938.

S.H.R.Jones. *Technology transaction costs and the transition to the factory production in the British silk industry. Journal of economic history.* No°47. 1987.

S.L. Baier and J.H. Bergstrand. *The Growth of World Trade: Tariffs, Transport Costs, and Income Similarity. Journal of International Economics.* Vol 53. No°1. 2001.

S.Lamb.*La soie, c'est de l'or.* Lyon. Bureaux du courrrier de Lyon. 1856.

S.P.Ville.*Transport and the development of the European Euronomy, 1750—1918.* Houndmills Basingstoke and London. Macmillan Press. 1990.

Sugihara Kaoru.*Labour-intensive Industrialisation in Global History..* London. Routledge. 2013.

Suglihara Kaoru.*Japan, China, and the Growth of the Asian internatioanl Economy, 1850—1949.* Oxford. Oxford University Press. 2005

T.C.Tsing.*De la Production et du Commerce de la Soie en Chine.* Thèse soutenue à l'Unisversité de Lyon-Faculté de Droit. Lyon. Imprimerie BOSC Frère&RIOU. 1928.

T.May.*an Economic and social History of Britain, 1760—1970,* London. Longman. 1987.

T.R. Banister. *A History of the External Trade of China 1834—1881.* Shanghai. *Maritime Customs Decennial Reports 1922—1931.* Vol. I. 1933.

Tcheng Tse-sio.*Les relations de Lyon avec la Chine*. Thèse soutenue à l'Université de Lyon. Paris. Liberairie L. Rodstein. 1936.

The Journal of Fiance. Vol 33. No°3. 2012.

V.Kham.*Le commerce français en Indochine et en Asie orientale* (1860—1975) : *les maisons de commerce françaises et l'essor du commerce colonial*. Paris. Thèse soutenue à Université Paris 7. 2006.

V–V. Germaine. *L'industrie de la soie dans les Alpes du Nord. Revue de géographie alpine*. Tome 30. No°01. 1942.

W. Leontief. *Studies in the Structure of the American Economy. Oxford*. Oxford University Press. 1953.

W.R.Laird. *The Scope of Renaissance Mechanic. Osiris*. Chicago. University of Chicago Press. Vol.2. 1936.

W.W.Rostow.*The Stages of Economic Growth* : *A Non-Communist Manifesto*. Cambridge. Cambridge Université Press. 1960.

II Sources in China and in Japan

1. Archives

中国第一历史档案馆(北京)

中国第一历史档案馆:《明清宫藏中西商贸档案 06》,北京:中国档案出版社,2010 年
P3209 广州将军庆宝奉上谕
英吉利谎称防法兰西盗贼增兵广东
P3212—3214 两广总督李鸿宝奏折
外国妇人不得进城
P3665—3672 靖逆将军奕山奏折
侦查法兰西等国情形
P3674—3680 中英南京条约稿本

中国第一历史档案馆:《明清宫藏中西商贸档案 07》,北京:中国档案出版社,2010 年 6 月
P3783—3791 钦差大臣江南总督奢英奏折

米利坚等过通商章程业经议定

P3802—3813 钦差大臣江南总督耆英奏折

大西洋意大里亚过通商章程议定

P3873—3875 两广总督耆英奏折

法公使请减丁香及酒税并准其所谓

P3876—3889 军机大臣穆彰阿奏折

遵议酌定法国通商章程

P4104—4111 英法美各国商约条款准驳清单

P4168—4190 广东巡抚耆龄奏折

洋人在广东省城及澳门等地设馆招工拐卖人口

中国第一历史档案馆:《清宫粤港澳商贸档案全集》,北京:中国书店,2002 年

03-0524-049 奏报查明丝斤实在价值情形事 乾隆二十五年十二月十七日

03-0629-041 奏报丝斤等货出洋无夹带事 乾隆二十八年三月二十四日

03-0813-024 奏为请驰当丝之禁事 乾隆十二年五月三十日

03-0822-016 奏报春花蚕丝收成分数事 乾隆三十四年四月二十五日

03-0824-023 奏报春花蚕丝收成分数事 乾隆三十九年四月十八日

03-0828-020 奏报春花蚕丝收成分数事 乾隆四十一年四月十九日

03-1076-052 奏报查明闽省各海口并无私带丝斤等出洋事 乾隆五十八年十月十九日

03-1102-029 复奏并无出洋私贩丝巾等情形 乾隆四十二年十一月二十八日

03-1004-012 奏请本港出洋船只府照外洋夷商之例配代土丝绸缎事情 乾隆二十九年三月十七日

03-1104-014 复奏出洋丝巾驰禁事 乾隆二十九年三月初八日

03-1104-015 复奏出洋丝巾毋庸禁止事 乾隆二十九年三月初四

03-1104-015 遵旨议奏丝斤出洋情形事 乾隆二十九年三月初九

03-1104-021 奏报并无违例贩运丝斤等物出洋情形事 乾隆二十九年十一月十一日

03-1390-003 奏请严谨丝出外洋事 乾隆二十五年正月二十九日

03-1748-098 奏请驰查海运以通商贩事 嘉庆十二年八月初二日

03-1853-35 奏陈西洋岛人与中国通商贸易等事 嘉庆四年十月

03-2734-014 奏为通商全局告遵旨核实酌情保举出力各员事 道光二十三年九月二十二日

片录旨查照事致军机处咨文 光绪二十二年二月二十二日

03-7120-024 奏为在籍绅士前国子监祭酒经理苏州缫丝纺纱两厂益臻妥善事光绪二十四年闰三月二十八日

03-7122-076 奏报整顿福建船政延聘法国洋员情形及议定各洋员薪费数目事光绪二十二年九月十三日

03-7123-018 奏为福州船厂为法国东京西贡总督代制浅水小轮船情形事 光绪二十五年七月二十日

03-7224-005 奏为船政第四届派复发国肄业学生请交出使大臣管理以节靡费事 员工需额是留年三月初九日

03-7128-054 奏为江苏在籍绅士候选道周廷弼独办机器缫丝长桌有成效请破格奖励事 光绪三十年十一月初二日

04-01-01-1039-036 奏为浙省饷需奇绌请将抽捐丝商外省赈捐改作本省防饷事 光绪二十六年六月二十二日

04-01-06-0012-010 奏为办理江苏开办缫丝纺织两厂应还息借商款移作上午股份未协事 光绪朝

04-01-12-0539-109 奏为法国新任使臣李梅到京并送国书事 光绪是三年七月初十日

04-01-30-0127-006 奏为新任四川督臣琦善函开以英夷如果前来恳请定界通商原折事 道光二十七年

04-01-30-0127-019 奏为遵旨严加防范英夷进口通商密饬文武妥为办理事道光三十年五月二十八日

04-01-35-1192-017 奏请弛禁海运以通商贩事 嘉庆十二年八月初二日

04-01-36-0006-029 奏为丝价日昂请严谨出洋事 乾隆二十四年闰六月二十五日

04-01-36-0118-053 奏为候选郎中祝承租包办苏州缫丝仿纱公司并委总董助理事

中国第二历史档案馆（南京）

中国历史第二档案馆,中国海关总署办公厅:《中国旧海关史料,01 卷》,北京:京华出版社,2001 年

P81 P91 烟台生丝贸易统计

P1—81 广州上海生丝贸易统计

P101 P118 P171 P183 P296 宁波生丝贸易统计

P147,165,167 广州生丝贸易统计

P467,485 P494 P53—78 1864 上海转口丝与内产丝出口到英国与法国情况

中国历史第二档案馆,中国海关总署办公厅:《中国旧海关史料,02 卷》,北京:京华出版社,2001 年

    P53—78 1865 上海转口丝与内产丝出口到英国与法国情况

    P291 P319 1865 广东大部分生丝经由香港出口

    P449—469 1865 烟台出口丝织品

    P555—585 1866 年上海出口生丝

    P847—895 1866 年广州出口生丝

中国历史第二档案馆,中国海关总署办公厅:《中国旧海关史料,03 卷》,北京:京华出版社,2001 年

    P51—62 P225 1867 广州生丝出口

    P153—197 1867 上海向英法生丝出口量

    P424 1867 烟台出口到上海

    P526 1868 上海向英法生丝出口量

    P531 P540 1868 广州出口生丝

中国历史第二档案馆,中国海关总署办公厅:《中国旧海关史料,04 卷》,北京:京华出版社,2001 年

    P21 P45 1869 上海向英法生丝出口量

    P49 P59 1869 广州向英法生丝出口量

    P307 P325 1870 上海向英法生丝出口量

    P329 P339 1870 广州生丝出口

    P581 P600 1871 上海生丝出口

    P605 P615 1871 广州生丝出口

中国历史第二档案馆,中国海关总署办公厅:《中国旧海关史料,05 卷》,北京:京华出版社,2001 年

    P31—51 1872 上海生丝对外出口量

    P59—71 1872 广州

P223 1868—1872 烟台生丝出口量

P309 P331 1873 上海

P337 P353 1873 广州

P537 P551 1869—1873 烟台

P627 P649 1874 上海

P655 P671 1874 广州

中国历史第二档案馆,中国海关总署办公厅:《中国旧海关史料,06 卷》,北京:京华出版社,2001 年

P29 P59 1875 上海生丝出口英美量

P65—79 1875 广州

P359 P381 1876 上海生丝出口英美量

P387 P401 1876 广州生丝出口

中国历史第二档案馆,中国海关总署办公厅:《中国旧海关史料,07 卷》,北京:京华出版社,2001 年)

P75 P89 1873—1877 烟台生丝出口量

P177 P199 1877 上海生丝向英法出口生丝量

P345 P359 1877 广州出口生丝量

P469 P483 1874—1878 烟台生丝出口

P585 P611 1878 上海生丝出口

P755 P770 1878 广州生丝出口

中国历史第二档案馆,中国海关总署办公厅:《中国旧海关史料》,北京:京华出版社,2001 年)

各国航船数 1866—1913

中法贸易量 1905—1914

中国向各国出口丝量 1904—1914

中国第二历史档案馆:《中华民国史档案资料汇编·第三辑北洋政府·教育》,南京:凤凰出版社,1991 年,第 98—100 页)

上海市档案馆（上海）

上海市档案馆:从丝业会馆到缫丝业同业会——浅析近代上海缫丝也同业团体变迁,《上海会馆史研究论丛第一辑》收录,上海社会科学院出版社,2011 年
上海市档案馆:上海丝业会馆填报调查表,1950 年 8 月 22 日,档号 B168-1-798
上海市档案馆:上海丝厂茧业总公所章程,1915 年 9 月,档号 S37-1-9
上海市档案馆:上海市缫丝工业同业公会档,S37-1-96,第 90 号。

顺德县档案馆（顺德）

顺德区档案馆:万历《顺德县志》,卷 10,《杂志》第 9

浙江省档案馆（杭州）
浙江省档案馆:同治《湖州副志》,同治十三年,卷三十一

2 Publications

白鹤文、杜富全、闵宗殿:《中国近代农业科技史稿》,北京:中国农业科技出版社,1995 年
百伦:生丝检验分级标准及其研究的历史考察,《丝绸史研究》,第三卷。
本野英一:论 19 世纪 80 年代洋行买办的法律地位,《近代史研究》,1990 年第 1 期
日本农商务省临时产业调查局:《支那蚕丝业调查概要》,1918 年
兴亚院华中联络部:《中支那重要国防资源生丝调查报告》,台北:台湾大学图书馆,1978 年
三菱合资公司资料:中国对美生丝贸易的变迁,《资料汇报》,1924 年 171 号
四川劝业道:《四川第四次劝业统计表》,1910 年,四川省图书馆馆藏资源
满铁上海事务所:《江苏省无锡县农村实态调查报告书》,1941 年,上海市图书馆馆藏资源
工商部技术厅:《首都丝织业调查记》,南京:工商部,1930 年
浙江省厘金总局:《浙省新定机器缫厂茧灶缴捐章程》,上海图书馆藏
曹胜梅:晚清时期法商在沪经营活动述略（1847—1910）,载于上海市档案馆

编：《上海档案史研究·第一辑》，上海：上海三联书店，2006 年

曹树基：《中国人口史》，第五卷《清时期》，上海：复旦大学出版社，2001 年

曹雯：《清朝对外体制研究》，北京：社会科学文献出版社，2010 年

上海万国生丝检验所：《1925 年华中蚕丝业调查》，《丝绸》，1999 年第 10 期

上海市工商行政管理局：《上海民族机器工业》上册，北京：中华书局，1966 年

陈慈玉：《近代中国的机械缫丝工业（1860—1945）》，台北："中央研究院"近代史研究专刊，1989 年，第 58 期

陈东有：《走向海洋贸易带：近代世界市场互动中的中国东南商人行为》，南昌：江西高校出版社，1998 年

陈滚滚：《陈联泰与均和安机器厂的概况》，《广东文史资料》第 20 辑，广州：广东人民出版社，1965 年

陈恒力，王达：《〈补农书〉研究》，北京：中华书局，1958 年

陈娟娟，黄能馥：《丝绸史话》，北京：中华书局，1980 年

陈启沅：《广东蚕桑谱》，1876 年，广州市中山图书馆馆藏资源

陈三井：《从北圻到中国：十九世纪一个里昂商人的殖民观》，《史学集刊》，1996 年第 2 期

陈三井：《近代中法关系史论》，台北：三民书局，2004 年

陈思：民国《江阴县续志》卷十一，1921 年，江阴市史志办公室藏书

陈万明，王希贤：《中国近代生丝出口贸易兴衰探略》，《南京农业大学学报》，1985 年第 2 期

陈宛溪：《劝桑说》，手抄本，三台县图书馆藏书

陈永浩，陶水木：《中国近代最大的丝商群体》，杭州：浙江人民出版社，2001 年

陈越：《近代裁厘运动》，安徽师范大学硕士毕业论文，2007 年

陈争平：《不平等条约下近代关税制度的形成及对中国经济的影响》，《近代中国》，上海：上海社会科学院出版社，2005 年

陈炽：《论缫丝业》，上海：鸿宝书局，1902 年

陈忠平：《论明清江南经济的多样化发展》，《中国农史》，1989 年第 3 期

陈英：《近代四川蚕桑丝业的发展（1891—1930）》，四川师范大学硕士学位论文，2011 年

袁继成：《近代中国租界史稿》，北京：中国财经出版社，1988 年

《中国经济月刊》（英文），1925 年 3 月号，中国国家图书馆馆藏资源

《中国丛报》，1837 年 1 月，广东省文史馆馆藏资源

《光绪朝东华录》，第四册，北京：中华书局，1958 年

中国民主建国会上海市委员会、上海市工商业联合会:《旧上海的外商与买办》,《上海文史资料》,第 56 辑,上海:上海人民出版社,1986 年

中国人民政治协商会议广州市委员会文史资料研究委员会编:《广州文史资料·广州的洋行与租借》,广州:广东人民出版社,1992 年

中国近代经济史资料丛刊编辑委员会:《帝国主义与中国海关资料丛编之四——中国海关与中法战争》,北京:中华书局,1983 年

从翰香:《论明代江南地区的人口密度及其对经济发展的影响》,《中国史研究》,1984 年第 3 期

汤菊平:《洋务运动对中国近代科学技术的影响研究》,上海:东华大学硕士毕业论文,2006 年

上海万国生丝检验所:《华中蚕丝业调查(1)》,《丝绸》,1999 年第 10 期

蚕丝业同业组合中央会编纂:《支那蚕业大观》,东京:冈田日荣堂,1929 年

峰村喜藏:《清国蚕丝业大观》,东京:朝日新闻出版社,1902 年

戴新兰,陈庆官,夏永林:《中国生丝检验的变革》,《四川丝绸》,2004 年第 4 期

戴一峰:《论晚清的子口税与厘金》,《中国社会经济史研究》,1993 年第 4 期

邓绍辉:《晚清赋税结构的演变》,《四川师范大学学报》,1997 年第 4 期

邓亦兵:《清代前期关税制度研究》,北京:燕山出版社,2008 年

董伟丽:《浙江蚕学馆与中国近代蚕业科技的发展》,浙江大学硕士学位论文,2006 年

杜恂诚:《民族资本主义与旧中国政府(1840—1937)》,上海:上海社会科学院出版社,1991 年

中国农业遗产研究室太湖地区农业史研究课题组:《太湖地区农业史稿》,北京:农业出版社,1990 年

范虹钰,盛帮跃:近代太湖地区的蚕业教育与蚕种改良(1897—1937),《中国农史》,2012 年

范金民,金文:《江南丝绸史研究》,北京:农业出版社,1993 年

范金民:《明清江南商业的发展》,南京:南京大学出版社,1996 年

范金民:《16 至 19 世纪前期中日贸易商品结构的变化》,《安徽史学》,2012 年第 1 期

费驰,刘晓东:《1868—1869 年〈中英新修条约〉谈判评述》,《吉林大学社会科学学报》,2001 年,第 2 期

费孝通:《江村经济:中国农民的生活》,北京:商务印书馆,2001 年

冯邦彦:《香港英资财团》,香港:三联书店,1996 年

冯杨：《低关税与近代中国经济发展研究》，西南财经大学硕士毕业论文，2001年

付志宇：《近代中国税收现代化的思想史考察》，成都：西南财经大学出版社，2010年

藤本实也：《支那蚕丝业研究》，东京：东亚研究所，1943年

高海燕：《近代外国在华洋行、银行与中国钱庄》，《社会科学辑刊》，2003年第二期

高景岳，严学熙：《近代无锡蚕丝业资料选辑》，南京：江苏人民出版社，1987年

高淑娟，冯斌：《中日对外经济政策比较史纲》，北京：清华大学出版社，2003年

葛夫平：《中法关系史话》，北京：社会科学文献出版社，2011年

盖海萍：《厘金制度的兴废》，《石家庄职业技术学院学报》，2001年第1期

葛元熙：《沪游杂记》，上海：上海古籍出版社，1989年

工藤恭吉：《德川的养蚕制丝业》，水原庆二，山口启二编：《讲座日本技术的社会史》(第三卷纺织)，东京：日本评论社，1983年

顾国达：《近代中国的生丝贸易与世界生丝市场供求结构的经济分析》，日本京都工艺纤维大学博士论文，1995年

顾国达，滨崎实，宇山满：《近代1842—1945年生丝世界市场的形成过程以及供给需求情况的变化》，《浙江丝绸学院学报》，1993年第3期

顾国达，滨崎实，宇山满：《近代世界生丝市场的结构》，《浙江丝绸工学院学报》，1993年，第10卷，第3期

顾国达：《十九世纪的中美生丝贸易与美国丝绸业的发展》，《浙江学刊》，2001年第2期

顾家相：《浙江通志·厘金门稿》，1919年，上海图书馆藏

顾良辉：《清代江苏厘金制度研究》，上海师范大学硕士毕业论文，2007年

郭松民：《18、19世纪的中国农业生产和农民》，《民命所系：清代的农业和农民》，北京：中国农业出版社，2010年

古田和子：《技术转变与地区适应——近代中日缫丝业比较》，《丝绸》，1993年第1期

霍华德·伯斯韦：《华南丝绸业调查》，香港：商务印书馆，1925年，第66页

马士：《东印度公司对华贸易编年史1—3》，广州：中山大学出版社，1991年

马士：《中华帝国对外关系史1—3》，北京：商务印书馆，1963年

韩佩金：《重修奉贤县志》，卷十九，台北：成文出版社，1970年

赫树权：《外国洋行在中国》，《商业研究》，1988年12期

何本方:《清代户部诸关初探》,《南开大学学报》,1984 年第 3 期

何炳康:《1368—1953 中国人口研究》,上海古籍出版社,1989 年

《明史》,卷八十二《食货六》,北京:中华书局,1974 年

侯鹏:《浙江厘金制度的创办与衍生形态述论》,《苏州科技学院学报》,2012 年第 4 期

侯鹏:《晚清浙江丝茧厘金与地方丝茧市场》,《史林》,2009 年第 5 期

侯鹏:《清代浙江厘金研究》,上海师范大学硕士毕业论文,2008 年

胡卫军:《关于日本的茧及生丝检验变迁所带来的生丝品质变化的调查研究》,《桑蚕通报》,1986 年第 3 期

胡忠仁:《从政治学角度看历史上湖州桑蚕业的兴盛》,《古今农业》,2002 年第 3 期

华文云:《关于生丝期货交易中经常面临的问题以及生丝检验证书的可信度》,《江苏丝绸》,2003 年第 6 期

黄广廓:《子口税述论》,《郑州大学学报》,1988 年第 3 期

黄景斌:《19 世纪中西贸易的关键情节》,《光明日报》,2011 年 3 月 27 日

黄君霆:《日本养蚕业的盛衰》,《世界农业》,1984 年第 3 期

黄培炎,张琪:《五十年来中国之对外贸易统计》,《最近五十年——申报馆五十周年纪念》,上海:申报馆,1923 年

黄启陈:《清代前期广东的对外贸易》,《中国经济史研究》,1988 年第 4 期

黄世本:《蚕桑简明辑说》,北京:北京出版社,1998 年

黄为放:《丝绸文化》,长春:吉林文史出版社,2010 年

黄逸峰,江铎:《旧中国的买办阶级》,上海:上海人民出版社,1982 年

黄永安,《岭南大学的蚕丝改良机构与广东制丝改良失败》,《广州文史资料》第 13 辑,广州:中国人民政治协商会议广州市委文史资料研究委员会,1964 年

黄振南:《中法战争诸役考》,桂林:广西师范大学出版社,1998 年

荒木干雄:《近代日本养蚕农家经营的发展》,《国外农学》,1994 年第 2 期

上海社会科学院经济研究所,上海丝绸进出口公司:《近代江南丝织工业史》,上海:上海人民出版社,1991 年

上海社会科学院经济研究所:《上海对外贸易 1840—1949》,上海:上海社会科学院出版社,1989 年

嵇发根:《湖丝——辑里湖丝源流考》,《农业考古》,2003 年第 3 期

嵇发根:《丝绸之府五千年——湖州丝绸文化研究》,杭州:杭州出版社,2007 年

姜公韬：《中国通史·明清史》，北京：九州出版社，1978 年

蒋国宏：《民国前期广东蚕种改良的绩效与不足》，《南通大学学报》，第 28 卷，第 6 期，2012 年

蒋国宏：《日本近代蚕种改良及对中国影响初探》，《兰州学刊》，2011 年第 9 期

姜庆湘，李守尧：《四川蚕丝业》，成都：四川省银行经济研究处，1946

金普森，易继苍：《买办与中国近代社会阶层的变迁》，《浙江大学学报》，2002 年 5 月

《农学报》，1897 年第 1 期，上海市图书馆馆藏资源

《农学报》，1897 年第 10 期，上海市图书馆馆藏资源

《农学报》，1897 年第 21 期，上海市图书馆馆藏资源

《农学报》，1898 年第 41 期，上海市图书馆馆藏资源

《农商公报》，1915 年第 16 期，上海市图书馆馆藏资源

《申报》，1872 年 5 月 22 日，上海市图书馆馆藏资源

《申报》，1874 年 3 月 22 日，上海市图书馆馆藏资源

《申报》，1888 年 9 月 23 日，上海市图书馆馆藏资源

《申报》，1895 年 6 月 26 日，上海市图书馆馆藏资源

《申报》，1881 年 11 月 8 日，上海市图书馆馆藏资源

《申报》，1882 年 10 月 19 日，上海市图书馆馆藏资源

《申报》，1882 年 11 月 15 日，上海市图书馆馆藏资源

《申报》1882 年 9 月 15 日，上海市图书馆馆藏资源

《申报》，1926 年 11 月 29 日，上海市图书馆馆藏资源

《四川官报》第四册，1905 年 2 月新闻第 5 号，中国国家图书馆馆藏资源

康波：《法国东印度公司与中法贸易》，《学习与探索》，2009 年第 6 期

木宫泰彦：《日支交通史》下卷，上海：商务印书馆，1931 年

李明珠：《中国近代蚕丝业及外销》，徐秀丽译，上海：上海社会科学院出版社，1996 年

《上海生丝检验所积极改进蚕种》，《银行周报》，1928 年第 12 期

《明治大正国势总览》，东京：东洋经济新报社创刊三十周年纪念版第二辑，1927 年

《上海对外经济贸易志》，上海：上海社会科学院出版社，2000 年

黄启臣：《清代前期广东的对外贸易》，《中国经济史研究》，1988 年

实业部贸易局：《中国实业志》，南京：实业部，1933 年

《皇朝政典类纂》，台北：文海出版社，卷一百一十八，1982 年

《广东蚕》,《中国经济杂志》,第 5 卷第 2 期,1929 年

《中华文明史话》编委会:《丝绸史话》,北京:中国大百科全书出版社,2010 年

《北华捷报》,1882 年 4 月 22 日,上海市图书馆馆藏资源

乐嗣炳:《中国蚕丝》,上海:世界书局,1935 年

雷斌:《十九世纪末二十世纪初的中法关系研究 1894—1914》,西南交通大学硕士学位论文,2002 年

《江南事情·经济》,东京:日本东亚同文会,1919 年

《无锡金匮县志》,无锡市图书馆馆藏资源

《(民国)顺德县志》卷 1,《物产》广州:中山大学出版社,1993 年

《清朝文献统考》,杭州:浙江古籍出版社,2001 年,卷 33

李案,缪钟绣:《二十年来之蚕丝业》,《国际贸易导报》,1931 年第二卷第一号

李拔:《蚕桑说》,《皇朝经世文编》卷三十七《农政》

李伯重:《江南农业的发展 1620—1850 年》,上海:上海古籍出版社,2007 年)

李伯重:《明清江南农业资源的合理利用》,《农业考古》,1985 年第 2 期

李伯重:《桑争稻田与明清江南农业生产集约成都的提高》,《中国农史》,1885 年第 1 期

李伯重:《"终岁勤动":夸张还是现实?》,《学术月刊》,2008 年第 4 期

李灿:《近代锡沪缫丝工业比较研究》,华东师范大学硕士学位论文,2009 年 5 月

李超琼:《石船居杂著眷稿·芙蓉行记》,作于 1895 年 8 月,转引自铃木智夫:《洋务运动の研究》,东京:汲古书院,1992 年

李根蟠:《中国农业史》,台北:文津出版社,1987 年

李国荣:《清朝洋商密档》,北京:九州出版社,2010 年

李隆生:《清代的国际贸易》,台北:红蚂蚁图书有限公司,2010 年

李庆新:《南海一号与海上丝绸之路》,北京:五洲传播出版社,2010 年

李庆新:《濒海之地:南海贸易与中外关系史研究》,北京:中华书局,2010 年

李希圣:《庚子国变记》,上海:上海书店出版社,1982 年

李明珠:《中国近代蚕丝业及外销(1842—1937)》,上海:上海社会科学院出版社,1996 年

连心豪:《近代中国的走私与海关缉私》,厦门:厦门大学出版社,2011 年

梁方仲:《中国历代户口、田地、田赋统计》,北京:中华书局,2008 年

梁启超:《变法通议》,《饮冰室合集》第一册,北京:中华书局,1989 年

梁廷枏:《粤海关志》,广州:广东人民出版社,2002 年

廖声丰,顾良辉:《百年来厘金研究评述》,《中国社会经济史研究》,2012 年第 4 期

廖声丰,胡晓红:《近年来厘金制度研究综述》,《大庆师范学院学报》,2009 年第 2 期

廖宗麟:《中法战争史》,天津:天津古籍出版社,2002 年

林日杖:《鸦片战争前后外国在华洋行经济活动初探》,福建师范大学硕士学位论文,2001 年

郝延平:《十九世纪的买办——中西间桥梁》,上海:上海社会科学院出版社,1988 年

刘备军:《中国近代厘金制度研究》,北京:中国财政经济出版社,2004 年

刘伯渊:《广东省蚕业调查报告书》,广州:广东省地方农林实验场,1922 年

刘大钧:《吴兴农村经济》,上海:上海文瑞印书馆,1939 年

刘锦藻:《续文献通考》,上海:商务印书馆,1936 年,卷 379,《实业二》

刘克祥:《桑蚕丝绸史话》,北京:社会科学文献出版社,2011 年

刘坤一:《刘坤一遗集》第 4 卷,奏疏二十六,《遵查被劾道员据实复陈折》,光绪二十二年七月二十九日,北京:中华书局,1959 年

刘梅英:《厘金制度和子口税制度比较浅析》,《学术论坛》,1998 年第 4 期

刘永连:《论近代粤丝出口的市场规律和特征》,《暨南学报》,2004 年第 6 期

刘真,王焕深:《留学教育——中国留学教育史料》,台北:台湾"国立"编译馆,1980 年

《(民国)南汇县续志》,卷二十,2009 年,上海市浦东新区地方志办公室影印

宣统《南海县志》,卷 21,列传 8,艺术,陈启沅条,南海图书馆馆藏资源

宣统《南海县志》,卷 26,杂录,机器缫丝条,南海图书馆馆藏资源

《无锡县志》第二册,南京:江苏人民出版社,1995 年

《浙江通志厘金门稿·浙厘上》,1919 年,浙江图书馆馆藏资源

中国史学会:《戊戌变法》,上海:神州国光社,1953 年,第四卷

中华职业教育社:《全国职业教育概况》,商务印书馆,1935 年

石井宽治:《日本蚕丝业史分析》,东京:东京大学出版会社,1972 年

鲁傅鼎:《中国贸易史》,台北:中央文物供应社,1985 年

陆景琪:《试论清代厘金制度》,《文史哲》,1957 年第 2 期

罗婧:《世界市场与苏嘉湖桑蚕丝织工业圈》,《上海师范大学学报》,2010 年 5 月

罗愫修:《(乾隆)乌程县志》,卷十三,《物产》,上海:上海古籍出版社,1995 年

罗玉东：《中国厘金史》，上海：商务印书馆，1936 年 8 月

马学强：《论明清江南社会经济内变迁与劳动力转移》，《史林》，1993 年第 1 期

毛传慧：《清末民初的蚕桑改良——传统与现代之间》，《中国近现代行业文化研究——技艺和专业知识的传承与功能》，北京：国家图书馆出版社，2010 年

《清实录》，《高宗实录》，北京：中华书局，2008 年，卷五百九十一

莫铭：《近代浙江湖丝的对外贸易》，《古今农业》，1995 年第二期

中野明，《中国资本主义的发展》，东京：日本亚太关系委员会，1931 年

聂宝璋：《十九世纪中叶在华洋行势力的扩张与暴力掠夺》，近代史研究，1981 年第 2 期

聂宝章：《中国买办资产阶级的发生》，北京：中国社会科学院出版社，1978 年

聂宝璋：《中国近代航运史资料》，上海：上海人民出版社，1983 年 11 月

《北华捷报》，1868—1872，P.127，上海图书馆馆藏资源

《北华捷报》，1902 年 7 月 16 日，上海市图书馆馆藏资源

《北华捷报》，1875 年 10 月 19 日，上海市图书馆馆藏资源

《北华捷报》，1875 年 4 月 1 日，上海市图书馆馆藏资源

《北华捷报》，1873 年 8 月 23 日，上海市图书馆馆藏资源

《北华捷报》，1872 年 5 月 25 日，上海市图书馆馆藏资源

《北华捷报》，1876 年 10 月 26 日，上海市图书馆馆藏资源

《北华捷报》，1873 年 5 月 5 日，上海市图书馆馆藏资源

《北华捷报》，1852 年 8 月 7 日，上海图书馆馆藏资源

《北华捷报》，1881 年 11 月 7 日，上海市图书馆馆藏资源

《清国新开港场视察调查》，京都商业会议所，1897 年

黄宗智：《中国农村的过密化与现代化：规范认识危机及出路》，上海：上海社会科学出版社，1992 年

黄宗智：《中国经济史中的悖论与当前规范认识的危机》，《史学理论研究》，1993 年第 1 期

潘中祥：《近代江南市镇权力中心的演变——以湖州南浔为例》，上海师范大学硕士学位论文，2011 年

庞鸿文：《（光绪）常昭合志稿》卷四十六，1904 年，上海图书馆馆藏资源。

《论今昔》，上海：北华捷报社，上海市图书馆馆藏资源

彭信威：《中国货币史》，上海：上海人民出版社，1958 年

彭雨新：《辛亥革命前后珠江三角洲乡镇缫丝工业的发展及其典型意义》，《中国社会经济史研究》，1989 年第 1 期

彭泽益：《中国近代手工业史资料》第 1 卷，三联书店，1957 年

钱承绪：《中国蚕丝业问题之总检讨》上，《经济研究》第一卷第 9 期，1940 年 5 月

钱钟汉：《周舜卿》，《工商经济史料丛刊》第 4 辑，北京：文史资料出版社，1984 年

曲从规：《陈启沅与中国近代机器缫丝业》，《史学月刊》，1985 年第 3 期

屈大均：《广东新语》卷 2，地语，1687 年

曲星：《中法关系的缘起及历史演变》，《法国研究》，1998 年第 2 期

廖伯乐：《中国通商口岸——贸易与最早的条约港》，上海：东方出版中心，2010 年

《五十年各埠海关报告（1882—1931）》，广州口，北京：中国海关出版社，2009 年

《浙江丝绢酌定章程》，同治三年刻本，上海图书馆藏

《浙江省茧捐章程》，光绪刻本，上海图书馆藏

《驻法刘大臣为法京创设万国商会事谘商部文》，《商务官报》，1910，第 19 册

《史料旬刊》第 35 期，北京：故宫博物院文献馆，1932 年

莱特：《中国关税沿革史》，姚曾虞译，北京：三联书店，1958

山本三郎：《制丝业近代化の研究》，群马县：群马县文化事业振兴会，1975 年

山口和雄：《明治前期经济的分析》，东京：东京大学出版社会，1956 年

山肋梯二郎：《长崎的唐人贸易》，吉川弘文馆，1964 年

邵一飞：《试析自梳女习俗的起源、构成和基本特征》，《文化遗产》，2012 年第 2 期

沈练，仲昂庭：《广蚕桑说辑补·第二卷》，北京：中国书店，2007 年

沈协和，刘文达：《日本出口生丝检验标准的变革》，《丝绸》1985 年第 2 期

沈云龙：《中国近代史料丛刊》第 78 辑第 773 种，台北：台湾文海出版社，1994 年

沈祖炜，华萍：《上海与法国的贸易：过去、现在与未来》，《上海社会科学院学术季刊》，1997 年第 4 期

史和，姚福申，叶翠娣：《中国近代报刊名录》，福州：福建人民出版社，1991 年

石立民：《1885—1949 年桂越边境贸易的发展》，《东南亚纵横》，1995 年第 2 期

石元春：《二十世纪中国学术大典：农业科学》，福州：福建教育出版社，2001 年

川胜平太：《东亚经济圈的形成与发展——亚洲国家间竞争 500 年》（六），东

京：东京大学出版社，1997 年

寿充一，寿乐英：《外国银行在中国》，北京：中国文史出版社，1996 年

孙玉琴：《中国对外贸易史》，第 2 册，北京：对外经济贸易大学出版社，2004 年

孙东茂：《顺德自梳女风俗纪谈》，《民俗》，1987 年第 2 期

司春玲：《上海外滩与近代外商银行》，《高校社科动态》，2007 年第 6 期

司徒尚纪：《中国南海海洋文化》，广州：中山大学出版社，2009 年。

苑朋欣：《清末新政时期柞蚕丝业的发展及其原因》，《中国社会经济史研究》，2011 年第 1 期

宋应星：《天工开物·乃服》，上海：中华书局，1959 年

宋玉娥：《外国洋行与烟台的殖民地化》，《世界历史》，1987 年第 6 期

《上海研究资料》，上海：上海通志馆，1936 年

苏全有：《论清代中英茶叶贸易》，《聊城大学学报》，2004 年第 2 期

苏全有：《近代中国生丝出口缘何落败与日本》，《北京商学院学报》，2000 年第 6 期

苏耀昌：《华南丝区——地方历史的变迁与世界体系理论》，郑州：中州古籍出版社，1987 年

孙可为：《浙江最早的机械缫丝厂和清末绍兴蚕织业》，《丝绸》，1999 年第 4 期

孙疏堂：《中日甲午战争前外国资本在中国经营的近代工业》，《中国近三百年社会经济史论集第 5 集》，香港：崇文书店，1974 年

孙毓棠：《中国近代工业史资料》第一辑，北京：科学出版社，1957 年

孙翊刚：《中国税务史》，北京：中国税务出版社，2003 年

孙悦：《丝之江南》，上海：上海远东出版社，2010 年

孙玉琴：《中国对外贸易史》，北京：清华大学出版社，2008 年

铃木智夫：《洋务运动の研究》，东京：汲古书院，1992 年

铃木淳：《机械丝用气罐制造的发展》，《史学杂志》，第 101 编，第 7 号，1992 年

托马斯·莱昂斯：《中国海关与贸易统计》，杭州：浙江大学出版社，2009 年

高津仲次郎：《清国蚕丝业观察报告书》，东京：农商务省农务局，1897 年

谭熙鸿：《十年来之蚕丝实业》，北京：中华书局，1948 年

田永秀：《法国在华经济势力之全貌》，成都：西南交通大学出版社，2005 年

上原重美：《支那蚕业大观》，东京：冈田日荣堂，1929 年

上原重美，《支那四川省的蚕丝》东京：蚕丝业同业组合中央会，1927

上海社会科学院经济研究所：《上海对外贸易（1840—1949），上册》，上海：上海社会科学院出版社，1989 年

《顺德均安志》，中山图书馆馆藏资源

《上海丝绸志》，上海：上海社会科学院出版社，1998 年

紫藤章：《清国蚕丝业一斑 》，东京：农商务省生丝检查所，1911 年）

威廉·亨特：《广州番鬼录》，广州：广州人民出版社，2009 年

王垂芳：《洋商史：上海 1843—1956》，上海：上海社会科学院出版社，2007 年

王笛：《清代四川省人口、耕地及粮食问题》，四川大学学报，1989 年第 3—4 期

王宏斌：《太平天国时期生丝大量出口说明了什么》，《史学月刊》，1987 年第 6 期

汪敬虞：《从中国对外生丝贸易的变迁看缫丝业中资本主义的产生和发展》，《中国经济史研究》，2001 年第 2 期

汪敬虞：《十九世纪外国在华银行实力的扩张及对中国通商口岸金融市场的控制》，《历史研究》，1963 年第 5 期

汪敬虞：《中国近代经济史 1895—1927》下卷，北京：人民出版社，2012 年

汪敬虞：《论清代前期的禁海闭关》，《中国社会经济史研究》，1983 年第 2 期

汪敬虞：《关于继昌隆丝厂的若干史料及值得研究的几个问题》，《学术研究》，1962 年第 6 期

汪敬虞：《中国近代工业史资料》，第二辑，北京：科学出版社，1957 年

汪堃：《昆新两县续修合志》，卷八，1880 年，昆山市图书馆馆藏资源

王立璋：《中英商约谈判中的裁厘加税问题》，《哲学史学研究》，2012 年 1 月

汪曰桢：《（咸丰）南浔镇志》，卷二十四，《物产》，上海：上海科学技术文献出版社，1995 年

汪曰桢：《湖蚕述》，北京：中华书局，1965 年

王天予：《丝蚕学》，北京：农业出版社，1986 年

王铁崖：《中外旧约章汇编》，上海：三联书店，1957 年

王文圣：《晚清重庆海关的历史考察》，合肥：安徽大学出版社，2012 年

王翔：《近代中国传统丝绸业转型研究》，天津：南开大学出版社，2005 年

王翔：《中国丝绸史研究》，北京：团结出版社，1990 年

王翔：《中日丝绸业近代化比较研究》，石家庄：河北人民出版社，2002 年

王新生：《广东与长野器械缫丝业比较研究》，《历史研究》，1993 年第 3 期

王彦成，王亮：《清季外交史料》，南京：书目文献出版社，1987 年

王庄穆：《民国丝绸史》，北京：中国纺织出版社，1995 年

王祖畬：《（民国）太仓州志》，卷三，1918 年，中国国家图书馆馆藏资源。

卫杰：《蚕桑汇编》，北京：中华书局，1956 年 10 月

吴桂龙:《论上海开埠初期的通事和买办》,《史林》,1996 年第 4 期

吴桂龙:《论晚清上海外侨人口的变迁》,《史林》,1998 年第 4 期

吴建新:《明清民国顺德的基塘农业与经济转型》,《古今农业》,2011 年第 1 期

吴建新:《明清以来广东的生态农业类型》,《中国农史》,2005 年第 3 期

武堉干:《中国国际贸易史》,长沙:湖南教育出版社,2010 年

吴圳义:《清末上海租界社会》,台北:台湾文史哲出版社,1978 年

夏永林,陈庆官,戴新兰:《日本生丝检验的变革》,《四川丝绸》,2004 年第 4 期

鲜于浩,雷斌:《法国与丝绸之路》,《社会科学研究》,2004 年第 4 期

鲜于浩,田永秀:《近代中法关系史稿》,成都:西南交通大学出版社,2003 年

肖爱丽:《上海近代纺织技术的引进与创新》,东华大学博士论文,2012 年

熊月之:《上海通史·晚清经济》,上海:上海人民出版社,1999 年

许道夫:《中国近代农业生产及贸易统计资料》,上海:上海人民出版社,1983 年

许涤新,吴成明:《中国资本主义发展史》,北京:人民出版社,1985 年

许发祥:《近代民族资本浔商衰落的原因》,中共中央党校硕士学位论文,2009 年

徐松:《宋会要辑稿·食货第六十四》,北京:中华书局,1857 年

许檀:《明清时期区域经济的发展》,《中国经济史研究》,1999 年第 2 期

徐新吾:《中国近代缫丝工业史》,上海:上海人民出版社,1990 年

徐毅:《晚清江苏地区厘金制度的起源与推广实态考察》,《历史档案》,2006 年第 3 期

徐毅:《江苏厘金制度研究,1853—1911》,上海:上海财经大学出版社,2009 年

徐毅:《晚清上海厘金制度与地方社会》,《中国社会科学院研究生院学报》,2007 年第 6 期

徐毅:《晚清厘金制度起源路径新论》,《广西师范大学学报》,2007 年 4 月

徐义生:《中国近代外债史统计资料》,中华书局,1962 年

徐铮、袁宣萍:《杭州丝绸史》,北京:中国社会科学出版社,2011 年

雪珥:《1873:帝国商人反击战》,《国家历史》,2008 年第 24 期

孙晓莹:《晚清生丝业国际竞争力研究——兼与同期日本比较》,清华大学硕士论文,2010 年

矢木明夫:《制丝业》,地方史研究协议会编:《日本产业史大系》,东京:东京大学出版会,1961 年

山田盛太郎:《日本资本主义分析》,东京:岩波书店,昭和 41 年。

严金清:《严廉访遗稿年谱》,《北京图书馆藏珍本年谱丛刊》,第 174 册

严锴:《鸦片战争前法国对华贸易落后原因探析》,《湖北社会科学》,2012 年第 5 期

阎万英,尹英华:《中国农业发展史》,天津:天津科学技术出版社,1992 年

严中平:《中国近代经济史 1840—1894》,北京:人民出版社,1989 年

严中平:《中国近代经济史统计资料选辑》,北京:中国社会科学出版社,2012 年

杨大金:《现代中国实业志》,长沙:商务印书馆,1928 年

杨华山:《晚清厘金与中国早期现代化建设》,北京:人民出版社,2011 年

杨家骆:《太平天国文献汇编》,台北:鼎文书局,1973 年,第 6 卷

杨文华:《论中法战争以前厘金与子口税的消长与变迁》,《史学月刊》,1989 年第 1 期

杨元华:《从黄埔条约到巴拉迪尔访华——中法关系 1844—1994》,福州:福建人民出版社,1995 年

杨元华:《中法关系史》,上海:上海人民出版社,2006 年

杨源兴:《五口通商时期的丝茶出口贸易》,《学术研究》,1984 年第 3 期

杨运义:《关于生丝品质分级方法的探讨》,《江苏丝绸》,1995 年第 5 期

姚公鹤:《上海闲话》,上海:上海古籍出版社,1989 年

姚贤镐:《中国近代对外贸易史资料 1840—1895》,北京:中华书局,1962 年

叶超:《广东珠江三角洲蚕丝业调查》,《中国蚕丝》,第 2 卷第 5 期,1936 年

叶显恩:《明清珠江三角洲的人口问题》,《清史研究集》,第 6 辑,光明日报出版社,1988 年

衣保中,郭欣旺:《藤田丰八与清末中国西方农学引进》,东北亚论坛,2004 年第 3 期

易棉阳,姚会元:《1980 年以来中国近代银行史研究综述》,《近代史研究》,2005 年第 3 期

尹良莹:《四川蚕业改进史》,上海:商务印书馆,1947 年

尹良莹:《中国蚕业史》,南京:国立中央大学蚕桑学会,1931 年

永积洋子:《唐船输出入商品数量一览 1637—1833》,东京:东京创文社,1987 年

虞和平:《洋务运动时期中外贸易状况变化的几个问题》,《晚清国家与社会》,第 513—528 页,2007 年

俞筼蠋:《江苏蚕丝业之今昔观》,《蚕业杂志》,1947 年 5 月

袁继成：《近代中国租界史稿》，北京：中国财经出版社

张爱萍：《湖州地区的民间蚕神故事及蚕神信仰》，《温州师范学院学报》，2005年6月

张迪恩：《外国洋行垄断生丝输出对上海地区丝厂业的影响 1894—1937》，《中国经济史研究》，1986年第1期

张国辉：《甲午战后四十年间中国现代缫丝工业的发展和不发展》，《中国经济史研究》，1989年第1期

张宏：《关于近代厘金制度的思考》，《传承》，2008年第4期

张健参：《中国蚕业史话》，上海：上海科学技术出版社，2009年

张建华：《中法黄埔条约交涉——以拉萼尼与耆英之间的来往照会函件为中心》，《历史研究》，2001年第2期

张家炎：《明清长江三角洲地区与两湖平原经济结构演变探异》，《中国农史》，1996年第3期

张丽：《鸦片战争前的全国生丝产量和近代生丝出口增加对中国近代桑蚕业扩张的影响》，《中国农史》，2008年第4期

张立武：《厘金对晚清时期工商业及国家财政的双重影响》，东北师范大学硕士毕业论文，2004年5月

张履祥：《补农书》，北京：中华书局，1958

张茂元：《近代中国机器缫丝技术应用与社会结构变迁》，北京大学博士毕业论文，2008年6月

张天护：《清代法国对华贸易问题之研究》，《外交月报》，卷8，1936年第6期

张肖梅，《四川经济参考资料》，上海：中国国民经济研究所，1939年

张晓堂：《清朝对外贸易法治研究》，中国政法大学博士论文，2007年

张行孚：《蚕事要略》，台北：艺文出版社，1996年

张学军，张莉红：《四川近代工业史》，成都：四川人民出版社，1990年

张研：《清代经济简史》，新北：云龙出版社，2002年

张艳国，刘俊峰：《略论晚清钱庄与洋行关系的互动性》，《学术研究》，2003年第11期

张雁深：《中法外交关系史考》，长沙：长沙史哲研究社，1950年，第13页

张英丽：《十九世纪末二十世纪初中国队日本蚕业新科技的引进和影响》，《古今农业》，2005年第4期

张之洞：《张文襄公全集》，奏议，卷35，台北：文海出版社，1963年

赵尔巽：《清史稿·一五五卷》，北京：中华书局，1977

赵娟霞：《近代商业制度从公行制到买办制的演进初探》，《现代财经》，2010年第9期

赵书文，韩明希，李德辉：《简明人口学词典》，兰州：甘肃人民出版社，1997年

郑斌：《蚕桑指要》，1725年首次刊印，1900年手抄本再次发行，第1卷，上海市图书馆馆藏资源

郑起东：《晚清政府劝农桑、兴水利的重农政策》，《广西社会科学》，2006年第9期

郑绍辉：《晚清赋税结构的演变》，《四川师范大学学报》，1997年第4期

郑友揆：《中国的对外贸易和工业发展（1840—1948）——史实的综合分析》，上海：上海社会科学院出版社，1984年

仲伟民：《茶叶、鸦片贸易对19世纪中国经济的影响》，《社会经济史研究》，1994年第1期

中村质：《近世长崎贸易史の研究》，东京：吉川弘文馆，1988年

周德华：《蚕丝改良先驱——俞凤韶》，江苏丝绸，2006年第5期

周德华：《1880年镇江关桑叶丝绸调查报告》，《江苏丝绸》，2001年第3期

周谷平：《浙江近代蚕丝教育之历史研究》，《杭州大学学报》，1997年第1期

周庆云：《南浔志》卷二十一，《人物四·梅宝楚传》，第16页，1922年

周湘：《广州外洋行商人》，广州：广东人民出版社，2002年

周学浚：《（同治）湖州府志》，卷31，台北：成文出版社，1970年

朱美予：《世界蚕丝业概观》，上海：商务印书馆，1934年

朱寿朋：《光绪朝东华录》（四），北京：中华书局，1984年

朱新予，李锡畴：《浙江丝绸史》，杭州：浙江人民出版社，2008年

朱有瓛：《中国近代学制史料》，第二辑·下，上海：华东师范大学出版社，1986年

紫藤章：《清国蚕丝业一斑》，东京：农商务省生丝检查所，1911年